Methods of Meta-Analysis

Third Edition

Methods of Meta-Analysis

Third Edition

Correcting Error and Bias in Research Findings

Frank L. Schmidt

University of Iowa

John E. Hunter

Michigan State University

Los Angeles | London | New Delhi
Singapore | Washington DC

Los Angeles | London | New Delhi
Singapore | Washington DC

FOR INFORMATION:

SAGE Publications, Inc.
2455 Teller Road
Thousand Oaks, California 91320
E-mail: order@sagepub.com

SAGE Publications Ltd.
1 Oliver's Yard
55 City Road
London EC1Y 1SP
United Kingdom

SAGE Publications India Pvt. Ltd.
B 1/I 1 Mohan Cooperative Industrial Area
Mathura Road, New Delhi 110 044
India

SAGE Publications Asia-Pacific Pte. Ltd.
3 Church Street
#10-04 Samsung Hub
Singapore 049483

Acquisitions Editor: Vicki Knight
Editorial Assistant: Jessica Miller
Digital Content Editor: Katie Guarino
Production Editor: Laura Barrett
Copy Editor: Gillian Dickens
Typesetter: C&M Digitals (P) Ltd.
Proofreader: Wendy Jo Dymond
Indexer: Will Ragsdale
Cover Designer: Candice Harman
Marketing Manager: Nicole Elliott

Printed in the United States of America

Library of Congress Cataloging-in-Publication Data

Hunter, John E. (John Edward), 1939–2002.

Methods of meta-analysis : correcting error and bias in research findings / Frank L. Schmidt, University of Iowa, John E. Hunter, Michigan State University. — Third edition.

pages cm
Includes bibliographical references and index.

ISBN 978-1-4522-8689-1 (hardcover : alk. paper)

1. Social sciences—Statistical methods. 2. Meta-analysis. I. Schmidt, Frank L. II. Title.

HA29.H847 2015
300.72—dc23   2013039086

This book is printed on acid-free paper.

14 15 16 17 18 10 9 8 7 6 5 4 3 2 1

Brief Contents

Detailed Contents

List of Tables

CHAPTER 4

CHAPTER 6

CHAPTER 7

List of Figures

Preface

Meta-analysis is today even more important to the research enterprise than it was when the last edition of this book appeared in 2004 (a fact that is fully explored in Chapter 1). One reason for this is that meta-analysis is increasingly providing the foundation for evidence-based professional practice in a wide variety of fields, ranging from human resource management to medicine. In recent years, there have been important new methodological developments in meta-analysis, and these are addressed in this book. This book has been prepared to be more user-friendly than the previous editions. Many detailed derivations of equations for which proof no longer need be presented have been eliminated (with references given to sources where they can be found by those interested). In addition, a great deal of effort has been put into making the language of this book as clear as possible to all readers regardless of their statistical and psychometric backgrounds.

Certain new topics appear in multiple chapters throughout the book. For example, there is an expanded treatment of confidence intervals (CIs) in meta-analysis in Chapters 5 (for correlations) and Chapter 8 (for d values), along with discussion of the difference between the information provided by CIs and credibility intervals (CrIs). And in the example meta-analyses presented in Chapters 3, 4, 7, and 9, CIs are computed for mean observed and corrected effect sizes, along with CrIs. Discussions of the proper interpretation of the percentage or proportion of variance accounted for in meta-analysis are found in these same chapters. The key point is that the square root of the proportion of variance is the correlation between statistical and measurement artifacts and the observed correlations or d values and that this statistic is more informative than the proportion of variance accounted for.

Many improvements have been made in the package of meta-analysis programs available for applying the methods presented in this book. Some examples include the following. It is now possible to import data files from Excel. All programs now provide CIs around mean observed and corrected effect sizes, as well as CrIs. New features now make it easier to run meta-analyses when there is no range restriction. The upper limit on the number of studies in a meta-analysis has been raised to 1,000. A method of detecting and correcting publication bias (cumulative meta-analysis) has been added. A full list of program improvements can be found in the Appendix to this book. Throughout this book, the example meta-analyses presented are now calculated using the programs in this package.

It is appropriate to point out that the presentations in the book do not rigidly follow statistical conventions. For example, σ^2 might appear without the circumflex that indicates that it is not the actual population value but rather an estimate of that value (i.e., $\hat{\sigma}^2$). We use statistical symbols in this manner for convenience, and in all cases, the context and the text makes it clear which symbols stand for estimates and which stand for actual population parameters. We are aware that our usage of symbols causes some statisticians to tear their hair out.

There have been important improvements and additions in individual chapters. Here we summarize only the major changes. Corrections for measurement error are critical in meta-analysis, but there is often confusion as to the appropriate type of reliability coefficient to use. To address this, Chapter 3 now contains an expanded and more complete treatment of this question to guide users.

Chapter 4 has been greatly simplified by focusing only on the single most accurate method for artifact distribution meta-analysis, the interactive nonlinear (INTNL) method. All example meta-analyses in Chapter 4 are now calculated with the programs for this method. The long technical derivation of the multiplicative method, which has proved to be less accurate, has been dropped. Also, there is now a much clearer presentation of methods for conducting a mixed meta-analysis—one in which one artifact is corrected individually in each study while the other artifacts are corrected based on artifact distributions. This presentation is accompanied by a detailed worked numerical example.

In Chapter 5, the long technical derivation of the equations for correcting indirect range restriction has been dropped, because that material has since been published in a major journal (Hunter, Schmidt, & Le, 2006). Chapter 5 now presents an expanded discussion of the issues involved in path analyses based on meta-analytic correlation matrices, an application that has now become common in the literature. There is also an updated and expanded discussion of the problems created by use of Fisher's z in meta-analysis of correlations. In Chapter 6, only minimal changes have been necessary.

Chapter 7 now contains an improved presentation of methods for conducting meta-analysis of d values when artifacts beyond sampling error and measurement error in the dependent variable measure are corrected for. There is a clear explanation of how to convert d values to point-biserial correlations, conduct the meta-analysis in the r statistic metric, and then convert the meta-analysis results back into the d statistic metric. This approach to meta-analysis of d values has become increasingly common in the literature.

Important changes have been made in Chapter 8. The most common experimental design, the independent groups design, is covered in detail in Chapter 7. But many other experimental designs are encountered in the literature. Chapter 8 now presents the needed equations for computing the appropriate d values from these designs and the equations for the sampling error variance of the resulting d values. These methods allow d values from these experimental designs to be included in the meta-analysis along with the d values from the independent groups design. An equation is also presented for adjusting the sample sizes of the different designs, so that the d value and the adjusted N can be entered into the meta-analysis programs written for the independent groups design studies. This step ensures that the sampling error variances computed by the programs are correct.

Chapter 9 ("General Technical Issues in Meta-Analysis") contains much new material. This chapter examines in detail the issues involved in detecting and calibrating moderators in meta-analysis. This includes discussion of subgrouping of studies, hierarchical meta-analysis via subgrouping, multilevel and hierarchical linear models (HLM) for meta-analysis, mixed models in meta-analysis, and meta-regression. Statistical problems in the use of meta-regression, which are often ignored in published applications, are discussed in detail. There is an in-depth discussion of the debate over optimal study weights in meta-analysis. This chapter also presents a detailed discussion of second-order sampling error in meta-analysis and a new method for conducting second-order meta-analysis, along with two exercises applying this new method. (Other meta-analysis exercises are provided at the end of Chapters 3, 4, and 7.) In connection with confidence intervals, there is an explanation of the differences in how these are computed in the Hunter-Schmidt and the Hedges-Vevea meta-analysis methods. Finally, there is a discussion of the use of the odds ratio statistic in psychology and social science research.

Chapter 11 presents an updated discussion of different methods of meta-analysis, including one recently developed approach (SEM-based meta-analysis). There is also updated information on software available for conducting meta-analyses using different methods.

Chapter 12 includes a new discussion of how the results of meta-analyses have been and should be presented in research reports and published articles. Reporting standards in meta-analysis are important, and the evidence indicates that they need improvement.

Chapter 13 presents a greatly expanded treatment of source bias and publication bias, an area that has recently received much attention in the literature. Because of the potential effects on the accuracy of meta-analyses in the literature, the recent research and findings on research fraud and QRPs (questionable research practices), which result in biased results in

primary studies, are also explored. Next, there is a discussion and evaluation of nine different methods of detecting (and sometimes correcting)
publication and source bias. Finally, there is a discussion of software for
detecting publication bias.

The methods presented in this book differ from other approaches to
meta-analysis in a wide variety of technical ways. However, all of these
differences stem from one central difference: a difference in how the purpose of meta-analysis is defined. The avowed purpose of other methods of
meta-analysis is to describe and summarize the results reported by studies
in a given research literature (Rubin, 1990). The purpose of our methods
is very different. In our view, the purpose of meta-analysis is to estimate
what the results would have been if all the studies had been conducted
without methodological limitation or flaws. The results of perfectly conducted studies would reveal the underlying construct-level relationships—
that is, the true "state of nature." It is these relationships that we as scientists
are interested in, as Rubin (1990) and others have noted. Our methods
estimate these relationships. We are much less interested in attaining an
accurate description and summary of the results reported by necessarily
flawed primary studies. This critical distinction is developed in more
detail near the end of Chapter 1 and in Chapter 14.

Brief History of This Book

This book is labeled as the third edition. In actuality, it should be considered the fourth edition. The first edition was really the Hunter, Schmidt,
and Jackson (1982) book. This was followed by Hunter and Schmidt
(1990b) and Hunter and Schmidt (2004), and now Schmidt and Hunter
(2014). Gene V. Glass published the first journal article on meta-analysis in
1976 in an education journal (*The Educational Researcher*). In that article,
he laid out the essential rationale and defined many of the basic features of
meta-analysis as it is known today. He also coined the label *meta-analysis*.
Our work was not in educational psychology but in industrial and organizational psychology. Unaware of Glass's work, we developed our meta-
analysis methods in 1975 and applied them to empirical data sets from
personnel selection research. But instead of immediately submitting our
report for publication, we submitted it to the James McKeen Cattell
Research Design Contest sponsored by Division 14 (The Society for
Industrial and Organizational Psychology) of the American Psychological
Association. To be eligible for this award, entries must not have already
been published or accepted for publication (i.e., in press). Our development
and initial application of meta-analysis (then called "validity generalization") won the Cattell award for 1976, but the 1-year delay in publication
(Schmidt & Hunter, 1977) meant that our first meta-analysis article
appeared 1 year after Glass's. Glass's 1976 article was not only the first in

time but also the first to emphasize meta-analysis as a fully general set of methods that should be applied to the integration of research literatures in all areas. At that time, our major emphasis was on solving the problem of the apparent substantial variability of test validities in the personnel selection literature (see Chapter 4). But we were aware of the potential of our methods for application to other research literatures. So when Lee J. Cronbach suggested to us in correspondence in early 1978 that our methods could be applied to research literatures in many areas of the behavioral and social sciences, we had already begun to think about a possible book presenting our methods in that light. That book was published in 1982 (Hunter et al., 1982). (But again Glass was first; he and his coauthors published their meta-analysis book in 1981; Glass, McGaw, & Smith, 1981.) Since then, the methods initially presented in our 1982 book have been widely applied. As indicated earlier, that book was followed by three subsequent editions, including this book.

An edited book devoted entirely to the history and impact of our meta-analysis methods is available (Murphy, 2003). This book is a good source of information beyond that contained in this book. In particular, Chapter 2 of that book, by the authors of this book, presents a history of the development of these methods. A history of these methods will also be published in the journal *Research Synthesis Methods* in 2014 (Schmidt, in press). DeGeest and Schmidt (2011) present a detailed account of the impact of these methods on cumulative knowledge in the areas of industrial-organizational psychology, human resources, management, and organizational behavior.

Organization of This Book

In scientific reports, a review of earlier developments is usually presented first. In the case of this book, that would be a review of previous methods of integrating research literatures (pre–meta-analysis methods). But in the case of this topic, such a review would be difficult for readers to fully understand without first having knowledge of meta-analysis principles and methods. Therefore, we first present the methods of psychometric meta-analysis in some detail. Then later in the book (Chapter 11), we present a review and critique of other research integration methods.

In the course of conducting a meta-analysis on a particular relationship, the temporal sequence of steps is as follows: (1) search for and gather studies, (2) extract and code information from the studies, (3) apply meta-analysis methods to the information extracted, and (4) present the results in a report or article. This book discusses all four steps, but not in their natural chronological order. The reason for this is that in order to know what is required in the first two steps, you must know in detail what you are going to do in the third step. Therefore, we cover meta-analysis methods first and then return to issues of defining the study domain, locating studies, deciding what to code, and writing up the meta-analysis report. Finally, we go back one step further and present recommendations for improvements in reporting practices in primary studies that are necessary for optimal application of meta-analysis methods to those studies.

My coauthor, John (Jack) Hunter, died on June 26, 2002. His contributions to the development of the methods presented in this book were beyond enumeration. The story of his life is sketched in Schmidt (2003). To me, he was not only an inspired collaborator of 30 years but also a best friend. The great loss to psychology and the other social sciences is in addition to my personal loss. This book is dedicated to his memory. Of course, all errors and omissions in this edition (and in the 2004 book; the second edition) are mine. I would like to believe that he would approve of this third edition.

Frank L. Schmidt

Acknowledgments

Jack Hunter has now been gone 12 years, but his contributions to the psychometric meta-analysis methods live on in the third edition of this book, and I want to give them first place in any acknowledgments. I would like to thank all of my colleagues and PhD students whose persistent curiosity and questions about meta-analysis stimulated the development of many ideas in this book. I would also like to thank them for urging me to revise and update the 2004 edition of this book and for encouraging me to finish it once I had started. The wait has been long, but I hope they will be happy with the final product. Special thanks go to In-Sue Oh, Huy Le, Michael McDaniel, Deniz Ones, Hannah Rothstein, Vish Viswesvaran, and Kenneth S. Law for their insightful comments on draft chapters. I would like to thank Vicki Knight, who arranged the contract for this revision and assisted along the way, as well as our production editor, Laura Barrett, and our copy editor, Gillian Dickens, for their patience, professionalism, and support.

Thank you to all of the reviewers for their time and input: Christopher M. Berry, Texas A&M University; Terri D. Pigott, Loyola University Chicago; Steven Pulos, University of Northern Colorado; Emily E. Tanner-Smith, Vanderbilt University; and Jeffrey B. Vancouver, Ohio University.

I owe a special debt to my wife, Cindy, for her support and encouragement during the long process of preparing this new edition. Finally, we would like to thank Linda Bostian for her dedication, skill, and professionalism in preparing this manuscript, even when the work extended to weekends and afterhours.

About the Authors

Frank L. Schmidt is the Gary F. Fethke Leadership Professor Emeritus in the Department of Management and Organization in the Tippie College of Business at the University of Iowa. He received his PhD in industrial-organizational psychology from Purdue University and has been on the faculties of Michigan State and George Washington Universities. He has authored or coauthored seven books and nearly 200 articles and book chapters on measurement, statistics, research methods, individual differences, and personnel selection. He headed a research program in the U.S. Office of Personnel Management in Washington, D.C., for 11 years, during which time he published numerous research studies in personnel psychology, primarily with John Hunter. Their research on the generalizability of employment selection method validities led to the development of the meta-analysis methods presented in this book. Professor Schmidt has received the Distinguished Scientific Award for Contributions to Applied Psychology from the American Psychological Association (APA) (jointly with John Hunter) and the Distinguished Scientific Contributions Award from the Society for Industrial and Organizational Psychology (SIOP) (also jointly with John Hunter). He has also received the Ingram Olkin Award and the Frederick Mosteller Award, both for contributions to meta-analysis methodology; the Scientific Award for Applications of Psychology from the Association for Psychological Science; the Gold Medal Lifetime Achievement award from the APA Foundation; and the Distinguished Career Award for Contributions to Human Resources and the Distinguished Career Achievement Award for Contributions to Research Methods, both from the Academy of Management. He is a Fellow of the APA, the Association for Psychological Science, and SIOP and is past president of Division 5 (Measurement, Statistics, & Evaluation) of the APA.

John E. (Jack) Hunter (1939–2002) was a professor in the Department of Psychology at Michigan State University. He received his PhD in quantitative psychology from the University of Illinois. Jack coauthored four books and authored or coauthored more than 200 articles and book chapters on a wide variety of methodological topics, including confirmatory and exploratory factor analysis, measurement theory and methods, statistics, and research methods. He also published numerous research articles on such substantive topics as intelligence, attitude change, the relationship between attitudes and behavior, validity generalization, differential validity/selection fairness, and selection utility. Much of his research on attitudes was in the field of communications, and the American Communications Association named a research award in his honor. Professor Hunter received the Distinguished Scientific Award for Contributions to Applied Psychology from the American Psychological Association (APA) (jointly with Frank Schmidt) and the Distinguished Scientific Contributions Award from the Society for Industrial and Organizational Psychology (SIOP) (also jointly with Frank Schmidt). He was a Fellow of APA, Association for Psychological Science, and SIOP and was a past president of the Midwestern Society for Multivariate Experimental Psychology. For the story of Jack's life, see Schmidt (2003).

PART I

Introduction to Meta-Analysis

Integrating Research Findings Across Studies

1

Before we delve into a discussion of methods, we would like to consider a concrete example. The next section presents a set of studies to be reviewed, then a sample narrative review, followed by a critique of this review. It has been our experience that personal experience with the problems of such a review greatly enhances the learning process.

General Problem and an Example

A major task in all areas of science is the development of theory. In many cases, the theorists have available the results of a number of previous studies on the subject of interest. Their first task is to find out what empirical relationships have been revealed in these studies so they can take them into account in theory construction. In developing an understanding of these relationships, it is often helpful in reviewing the studies to make up a table summarizing the findings of these studies. Table 1.1 shows such a summary table put together by a psychologist attempting to develop a theory of the relationship between job satisfaction and organizational commitment. In addition to the observed correlations and their sample sizes, the psychologist has recorded data on (1) sex, (2) organization size, (3) job level, (4) race, (5) age, and (6) geographical location. The researcher believes variables 1, 2, 3, and 4 may affect the extent to which job satisfaction gets translated into organizational commitment. The researcher has no hypotheses about variables 5 and 6 but has recorded them because they were often available.

As an exercise in integrating findings across studies and constructing theory, we would like you to spend a few minutes examining and interpreting the data in Table 1.1. We would like you to jot down the following:

1. The tentative conclusions you reached about the relationship between job satisfaction and organizational commitment and the variables that do and do not moderate that relationship

2. An outline of your resulting theory of this relationship

A TYPICAL INTERPRETATION OF THE EXAMPLE DATA

A typical report on the findings shown in Table 1.1 would run like this: The correlation between occupational commitment and job satisfaction varies from study to study with the correlation varying between −.10 and .56. Although 19 out of 30 studies found a significant correlation, 11 of 30 studies found no relationship between commitment and satisfaction.

For male work populations, commitment and satisfaction were correlated in 8 studies and not correlated in 7 (i.e., correlated in 53% of the studies), while for women there was a correlation in 11 of 15 cases (or in 73% of the studies). Correlation was found in 83% of the large organizations but in only 50% of the small organizations. Correlation was found in 79% of the blue-collar populations but in only 50% of the white-collar populations. Correlation was found in 67% of the populations that were all white or mixed race, while correlation was found in only 50% of those work populations that were all black. Correlation was found in 83% of the cases in which the workforce was all younger than 30 or a mixture of younger and older workers, while not a single study with only older workers found a significant correlation. Finally, 65% of the studies done in the north found a correlation, while only 58% of the southern studies found a correlation. Each of the differences between work populations could be taken as the basis for a hypothesis that there is an interaction between that characteristic and organizational commitment in the determination of job satisfaction.

If the studies done on older workers are removed, then significant correlation is found for 19 of the remaining 23 studies. Within these 23 studies with younger or mixed-age work populations, all 10 correlations for large organizations were significant.

There are 13 studies of younger or mixed-age work populations in small organizations. Within this group of studies, there is a tendency for correlation between organizational commitment and job satisfaction to be more likely found among women, among blue-collar workers, in all-black work populations, and in the north.

Table 1.1 Correlations between organizational commitment and job satisfaction.

Study	N	r	Sex	Size of Organization	White vs. Blue Collar	Race	Under vs. Over 30	North Vs. South
1	20	.46*	F	S	WC	B	U	N
2	72	.32**	M	L	BC	Mixed	Mixed	N
3	29	.10	M	L	WC	W	O	N
4	30	.45**	M	L	WC	W	Mixed	N
5	71	.18	F	L	BC	W	O	N
6	62	.45**	F	S	BC	W	U	N
7	25	.56**	M	S	BC	Mixed	U	S
8	46	.41**	F	L	WC	W	Mixed	S
9	22	.55**	F	S	WC	B	U	N
10	69	.44**	F	S	BC	W	U	N
11	67	.34**	M	L	BC	W	Mixed	N
12	58	.33**	M	S	BC	W	U	N
13	23	.14	M	S	WC	B	O	S
14	20	.36	M	S	WC	W	Mixed	N
15	28	.54**	F	L	WC	W	Mixed	S
16	30	.22	M	S	BC	W	Mixed	S
17	69	.31**	F	L	BC	W	Mixed	N
18	59	.43**	F	L	BC	W	Mixed	N
19	19	.52*	M	S	BC	W	Mixed	S
20	44	−.10	M	S	WC	W	O	N
21	60	.44**	F	L	BC	Mixed	Mixed	N
22	23	.50**	F	S	WC	W	Mixed	S
23	19	−.02	M	S	WC	B	O	S
24	55	.32**	M	L	WC	W	Mixed	Unknown
25	19	.19	F	S	WC	B	O·	N
26	26	.53**	F	S	BC	B	U	S
27	58	.30*	M	L	WC	W	Mixed	S
28	25	.26	M	S	WC	W	U	S
29	28	.09	F	S	BC	W	O	N
30	26	.31	F	S	WC	Mixed	U	S

*$p < .05$.

**$p < .01$.

CONCLUSIONS OF THE REVIEW

Organizational commitment and job satisfaction are correlated in some organizational settings but not in others. In work groups in which all workers are older than 30, the correlation between commitment and satisfaction was never significant. For young or mixed-age work populations, commitment and satisfaction are always correlated in large organizations. For young or mixed-age work populations in small organizations, correlation was found in 9 of 13 studies with no organizational feature capable of perfectly accounting for those cases in which correlation was not found.

These findings are consistent with a model that assumes that organizational commitment grows over about a 10-year period to a maximum value at which it asymptotes. Among older workers, organizational commitment may be so uniformly high that there is no variation. Hence, among older workers, there can be no correlation between commitment and job satisfaction. The finding for large organizations suggests that growth of commitment is slower there, thus generating a greater variance among workers of different ages within the younger group.

CRITIQUE OF THE SAMPLE REVIEW

The preceding review was conducted using review practices that characterize many narrative review articles not only in psychology but in sociology, education, and the rest of the social sciences as well. Yet every conclusion in the review is false. The data were constructed by a Monte Carlo run in which the population correlation was always .33. After a sample size was randomly chosen from a distribution centering about 40, an observed correlation was chosen using the standard distribution for r with mean $\rho = .33$ and variance

$$\frac{(1-\rho^2)^2}{N-1}.$$

That is, the variation in results in Table 1.1 is entirely the result of sampling error. Each study is conducted on a small sample and hence generates an observed correlation that departs by some random amount from the population value of .33. The size of the departure depends on the sample size. Note that the largest and smallest values found in Table 1.1 are all from studies with very small samples. The larger sample size studies tend to show less of a random departure from .33.

The moderator effects appear to make sense, yet they are purely the results of chance (i.e., sampling error). The values for the organizational characteristics were assigned to the studies randomly.

The crucial lesson to be learned from this exercise is this: "Conflicting results in the literature" may be entirely artifactual. The data in Table 1.1

were generated by using one artifact for generating false variation across studies, sampling error. There are other artifacts that are found in most sets of studies: Studies vary in terms of the quality of measurement (reliability) of their scales; researchers make computational or computer errors; people make typographical errors in copying numbers from computer output or in copying numbers from handwritten tables onto manuscripts or in setting tables into print; researchers study variables in settings with greater or smaller ranges of individual differences (range variation); and so on. In our experience (described later), many of the interactions hypothesized to account for differences in findings in different studies are nonexistent; that is, they are apparitions composed of the ectoplasm of sampling error and other artifacts.

Problems With Statistical Significance Tests

In the data set given in Table 1.1, all study population correlations are actually equal to .33. Of the 30 correlations, 19 were found to be statistically significant. However, 11 of the 30 correlations were not significant. That is, the significance test gave the wrong answer 11 out of 30 times, an error rate of 37%. Many people express shock that the error rate can be greater than 5%. The significance test was derived in response to the problem of sampling error, and many believe that the use of significance tests guarantees an error rate of 5% or less. This belief is false. Statisticians have pointed this out for many years; the possibility of high error rates is brought out in discussions of the "power" of statistical tests. However, statistics instructors are well aware that this point is not understood by most students. The 5% error rate is guaranteed only if the null hypothesis is true. If the null hypothesis is false, then the error rate can go as high as 95%.

Let us state this in more formal language. If the null hypothesis is true for the population and our sample data lead us to reject it, then we have made a Type I error. If the null hypothesis is false for the population and our sample data lead us to accept it, then we have made a Type II error. The statistical significance test is defined in such a way that the Type I error rate is at most 5%. However, the Type II error rate is typically left free to be as high as 95%. The question is which error rate applies to a given study. The answer is that the relevant error rate can only be known if we know whether the null hypothesis is true or false for that study. If we know that the null hypothesis is true, then we know that the significance test has an error rate of 5%. Of course, if we know that the null hypothesis is true and we still do a significance test, then we should wear a dunce cap, because if we know the null hypothesis to be true, then we can obtain a 0% error rate by ignoring the data. That is, there is a fundamental circularity to the significance test. If you do not know whether the null hypothesis is true or false, then you do not know whether the relevant error rate is

Type I or Type II; that is, you do not know if your error rate is 5% or some value as high as 95%. There is only one way to guarantee a 5% error rate in all cases: Abandon the significance test and use a confidence interval.

Consider our hypothetical example from Table 1.1. However, let us simplify the example still further by assuming that the sample size is the same for all studies, say $N = 40$. The one-tailed significance test for a correlation coefficient is $\sqrt{N-1} \, r \geq 1.64$; in our case, $\sqrt{39} \, r \geq 1.64$ or $r \geq .26$. If the population correlation is .33 and the sample size is 40, the mean of the sample correlations is .33, while the standard deviation is $(1-\rho^2)/\sqrt{N-1} = (1-.33^2)/\sqrt{39} = .14$. Thus, the probability that the observed correlation will be significant is the probability that the sample correlation will be greater than .26 when the population value is .33 and a standard deviation of .14:

$$P\{r \geq .26\} = P\left\{\frac{r-.33}{.14} \geq \frac{.26-.33}{.14}\right\} = P\{z \geq -.50\} = .69.$$

That is, if all studies were done with a sample size of 40, then a population correlation of .33 would mean an error rate of 31% (i.e., $1 - .69 = .31$).

Suppose we alter the population correlation in our hypothetical example from .33 to .20. Then the probability that the observed correlation will be significant drops from .69 to

$$P\{r \geq .26\} = P\left\{z \geq \frac{.26-.20}{.15} = .39\right\} = .35.$$

That is, the error rate rises from 31% to 65%. In this realistic example, we see that the error rate can be over 50%. A two-to-one majority of the studies can find the correlation to be not significant despite the fact that the population correlation is always .20.

Error rates of 50% or higher have been shown to be the usual case in many research literatures. Thus, reviewers who count the number of significant findings are prone to incorrectly conclude that a relationship does not exist when it does. Furthermore, as Hedges and Olkin (1980) pointed out, this situation only gets worse as more studies are conducted. The reviewer will become ever more convinced that the majority of studies show no effect and that the effect thus does not exist. Statistical power has been examined in much of the research literature in psychology, starting with Cohen (1962) and extending up to the present. In most literatures, the mean statistical power is in the .40 to .60 range and is as low as .20 in some areas (Hunter, 1997; Schmidt, 1996; Schmidt & Hunter, 2003; Sedlmeier & Gigerenzer, 1989). And, surprisingly, over time there has been little or no increase in statistical power in published studies (Sedlmeier & Gigerenzer, 1989. Maxwell (2004) explores the reasons why this is the case. Other possible reasons are given in Chapter 13.

If the null hypothesis is true in a set of studies, then the base rate for significance is not 50% but 5%. If more than 1 in 20 studies finds significance, then the null hypothesis must be false in some studies. We must then avoid an error made by some reviewers who know the 5% base rate. For example, if 35% of the findings are significant, some have concluded that "Because 5% will be significant by chance, this means that the number of studies in which the null hypothesis is truly false is 35 − 5 = 30%." Our hypothetical example shows this reasoning to be false. If the population correlation is .20 in every study and the sample size is always 40, then there will be significant findings in only 35% of the studies, even though the null hypothesis is false in all cases.

The typical use of significance test results leads to gross errors in traditional review studies. Most such reviews falsely conclude that further research, focused on moderator variables, is needed to resolve the "conflicting results" in the literature. These errors in review studies can only be eliminated if errors in the interpretation of significance tests can be eliminated. Yet those of us who have been teaching power to generation after generation of graduate students have been unable to change the reasoning processes and the false belief in the 5% error rate (Sedlmeier & Gigerenzer, 1989).

This example illustrates a critical point. Traditional reliance on statistical significance tests in interpreting studies leads to false conclusions about what the study results mean; in fact, the traditional approach to data analysis makes it virtually impossible to reach correct conclusions in most research areas (Hunter, 1997; Schmidt, 1996, 2010).

A common reaction to the preceding critique of traditional reliance on significance testing goes something like this: "Your explanation is clear, but I don't understand how so many researchers (and even some methodologists) could have been so wrong so long on a matter as important as the correct way to analyze data? How could psychologists and other researchers have failed to see the pitfalls of significance testing?" Over the years, a number of methodologists have addressed this question (Carver, 1978; Cohen, 1994; Guttman, 1985; Meehl, 1978; Oakes, 1986; Rozeboom, 1960; Schmidt & Hunter, 1997). In their statistics classes, young researchers have typically been taught a lot about Type I error and very little about Type II error and statistical power. Thus, they are unaware that the error rate is very large in the typical study; they tend to believe the error rate is the alpha level used (typically .05 or .01). In addition, empirical research suggests that most researchers believe that the use of significance tests provides them with many nonexistent benefits in understanding their data. For example, most researchers believe that a statistically significant finding is a "reliable" finding in the sense that it will replicate if a new study is conducted (Carver, 1978; Oakes, 1986; Schmidt, 1996; Schmidt & Hunter, 1997). For example, they believe that if a result is significant at the .05 level, then the probability of replication in subsequent studies (if conducted) is 1.00 − .05 = .95. This belief is completely false. The probability of replication is the statistical power of the study and is almost invariably much lower than .95 (e.g., typically .50 or less). Killeen (2005a, 2005b) proposed a statistic called *P-rep* that he claimed gives the probability that a research finding would be replicated in a new study. For a few years, this statistic was widely used. However, Trafimow, MacDonald, Rice, and Carlson (2010) demonstrated mathematically that the *P-rep* statistic did not in fact provide this probability. Today *P-rep* is rarely used.

Most researchers also believe that if a result is nonsignificant, one can conclude that it is probably just due to chance, another false belief, as illustrated in our example in which all nonsignificant results were Type II errors. There are other widespread but false beliefs about the usefulness of information provided by significance tests (Carver, 1978; Oakes, 1986). Discussion of these beliefs can be found in Schmidt (1996) and Schmidt and Hunter (1997).

Another fact is relevant at this point: The physical sciences, such as physics and chemistry, do not use statistical significance testing in interpreting their data (Cohen, 1990). Instead, they use confidence intervals. It is no accident, then, that these sciences have not experienced the debilitating problems described here that are inevitable when researchers rely on significance tests. Given that the physical scientists regard reliance on significance testing as unscientific, it is ironic that so many psychologists defend the use of significance tests on grounds that such tests are the objective and scientifically correct approach to data analysis and interpretation. In fact, it has been our experience that psychologists and other behavioral scientists who attempt to defend significance testing usually equate null hypothesis statistical significance testing with scientific hypothesis testing in general. They argue that hypothesis testing is central to science and that the abandonment of significance testing would amount to an attempt to have a science without hypothesis testing. They falsely believe that significance testing and hypothesis testing in science are one and the same thing. This belief is tantamount to stating that physics, chemistry, and the other physical sciences are not legitimate sciences because they do not test their hypotheses using statistical significance testing. Another logical implication of this belief is that prior to the introduction of null hypothesis significance testing by R. A. Fisher (1932) in the 1930s, no legitimate scientific research was possible. The fact is, of course, that there are many ways to test scientific hypotheses—and that significance testing is one of the least effective methods of doing this (Schmidt & Hunter, 1997).

Is Statistical Power the Solution?

Some researchers believe that the only problem with significance testing is low power and that if this problem could be solved there would be no problems with reliance on significance testing. These individuals see the solution as larger sample sizes. They believe that the problem would be solved if every researcher, before conducting each study, would calculate the number of subjects needed for "adequate" power (usually taken as power of .80) and then would use that sample size. What this position overlooks is that this requirement would make it impossible for most studies ever to be conducted. At the start of research in a given area, the questions are often of the form "Does Treatment A have an effect?" (e.g., Does interpersonal skills training have an effect? Does cognitive behavior therapy work?). If Treatment A indeed has a substantial effect, the sample size needed for adequate power may not be prohibitively large. But as research develops, subsequent questions tend to take the form "Is the effect of Treatment A larger than the effect of Treatment B?" (e.g., Is the effect of the new method of training larger than that of the old method? Is Predictor A more valid than Predictor B?). The effect size then becomes the *difference* between the two effects. Such effect sizes will often be small, and the required sample sizes are therefore often quite large—1,000 or 2,000 or more (Schmidt & Hunter, 1978). And this is just to attain power of .80, which still allows a 20% Type II error rate when the null hypothesis is false—an error rate most would consider high. Many researchers cannot obtain that many subjects, no matter how hard they try; either it is beyond their resources or the subjects are just not available at any cost. Thus, the upshot of this position would be that many—perhaps most—studies would not be conducted at all.

People advocating the power position say this would not be a loss. They argue that a study with inadequate power cannot support a research conclusion and therefore should not be conducted. Such studies, however, contain valuable information when combined with others like them in a meta-analysis. In fact, accurate meta-analysis results can be obtained based on studies that *all* have inadequate statistical power individually, because meta-analysis can provide precise estimates of average effect size. The information in these studies is lost if these studies are never conducted.

The belief that such studies are worthless is based on two false assumptions: (1) the assumption that every individual study must be able to justify a conclusion on its own, without reference to other studies, and (2) the assumption that every study should be analyzed using significance tests. One of the contributions of meta-analysis has been to show that no single study is adequate by itself to answer a scientific question. Therefore, each study should be considered as a data point to be contributed to a later meta-analysis. In addition, individual studies should be analyzed using not significance tests but point estimates of effect sizes and confidence intervals.

How, then, *can* we solve the problem of statistical power in individual studies? Actually, this problem is a pseudoproblem. It can be "solved" by discontinuing the significance test. As Oakes (1986, p. 68) noted, statistical power is a legitimate concept only within the context of statistical significance testing. If significance testing is not used, then the concept of statistical power has no place and is not meaningful. In particular, there need be no concern with statistical power when point estimates and confidence intervals are used to analyze data in studies and meta-analysis is used to integrate findings across studies.

Our critique of the traditional practice of reliance on significance testing in analyzing data in individual studies and in interpreting research literature might suggest a false conclusion, namely, that if significance tests had never been used, the research findings would have been consistent across different studies examining a given relationship. Consider the correlation between job satisfaction and job performance in Table 1.1. Would these studies have all had the same findings if researchers had not relied on significance tests? Absolutely not: The correlations would have varied widely (as indeed they did). The major reason for such variability in correlations is simple sampling error—caused by the fact that the small samples used in individual research studies are randomly unrepresentative of the populations from which they are drawn. Most researchers severely underestimate the amount of variability in findings that is caused by sampling error.

The law of large numbers correctly states that large random samples are representative of their populations and yield parameter estimates that are close to the actual population values. Many researchers seem to believe that the same law applies to small samples. As a result, they erroneously expect statistics computed on small samples (e.g., 50 to 300) to be close approximations to the real (population) values. In one study we conducted (Schmidt, Ocasio, Hillery, & Hunter, 1985), we drew random samples (small studies) of $N = 30$ from a much larger single data set ($N = 1,455$; $r = .22$) and computed results on each $N = 30$ sample. The resulting validity estimates varied dramatically from "study" to "study," ranging from −.21 to .61, with all this variability being due solely to sampling error (Schmidt, Ocasio, et al., 1985). Yet when we showed these data to researchers, they found it hard to believe that each "study" was a random draw from the same larger study. They did not believe simple sampling error could produce that much variation. They were shocked because they did not realize how much variation simple sampling error produces in research studies.

There are two alternatives to the significance test. At the level of review studies, there is meta-analysis. At the level of single studies, there is the confidence interval.

Confidence Intervals

Consider Studies 17 and 30 from our hypothetical example in Table 1.1. Study 17, with $r = .31$ and $N = 69$, finds the correlation to be significant at the .01 level. Study 30, with $r = .31$ and $N = 26$, finds the correlation to be not significant. That is, two authors with an identical finding, $r = .31$, come to opposite conclusions. Author 17 concludes that organizational commitment is highly related to job satisfaction, while Author 30 concludes that they are unrelated. Thus, two studies with identical findings can lead to a review author claiming "conflicting results in the literature."

The conclusions are quite different if the results are interpreted with confidence intervals. Author 17 reports a finding of $r = .31$ with a 95% confidence interval of $.10 \leq \rho \leq .52$. Author 30 reports a finding of $r = .31$ with a 95% confidence interval of $-.04 \leq \rho \leq .66$. There is no conflict between these results; the two confidence intervals overlap substantially.

Consider now Studies 26 and 30 from Table 1.1. Study 26 finds $r = .53$ with $N = 26$, which is significant at the .01 level. Study 30 finds $r = .31$ with $N = 26$, which is not significant. That is, we have two studies with the same sample size but apparently widely divergent results. Using significance tests, one would conclude that there must be some moderator that accounts for the difference. This conclusion is false.

Had the two studies used confidence intervals, the conclusion would have been different. The confidence interval for Study 26 is $.25 \leq \rho \leq .81$, and the confidence interval for Study 30 is $-.04 \leq \rho \leq .66$. It is true that the confidence interval for Study 30 includes $\rho = 0$, while the confidence interval for Study 26 does not; this is the fact registered by the significance test. The crucial thing, however, is that the two confidence intervals show an overlap of $.25 \leq \rho \leq .66$. Thus, consideration of the two studies together leads to the correct conclusion that it is possible that both studies could imply the same value for the population correlation ρ. Indeed, the overlapping intervals include the correct value, $\rho = .33$.

Two studies with the same population value can have non-overlapping confidence intervals, but this is a low-probability event (about 5%). But, then, confidence intervals are not the optimal method for looking at results across studies; that distinction belongs to meta-analysis.

Confidence intervals are more informative than significance tests for two reasons. First, the interval is correctly centered on the observed value rather than on the hypothetical zero value of the null hypothesis. Second, the confidence interval gives the researcher a correct picture of the extent of uncertainty in small sample studies. It may be disconcerting to see a confidence interval as wide as $-.04 \leq \rho \leq .66$, but that is far superior to the frustration produced over the years by the false belief in "conflicting results."

Confidence intervals can be used to generate definitions for the phrase "small sample size." Suppose we want the confidence interval for the correlation coefficient to define the correlation to the first digit, that is, to have a width of $\pm.05$. Then, for small population correlations, the minimum sample size is approximately 1,538. For a sample size of 1,000 to be sufficient, the population correlation must be at least .44. Thus, under this standard of accuracy, for correlational studies, "small sample size" includes all studies with less than a thousand persons and often extends above that.

There is a similar calculation for experimental studies. If the statistic used is the d statistic (by far the most frequent choice), then small effect sizes will be specified to their first digit only if the sample size is 3,076. If the effect size is larger, then the sample size must be even greater than 3,076. For example, if the difference between the population means is .30 standard deviations, then the minimum sample size that yields accuracy to within ±.05 of .30 is 6,216. Thus, given this standard of accuracy, for experimental studies, "small sample size" begins with 3,000 and often extends well beyond that. Now think about the fact that many, perhaps most, experimental studies in behavior labs have total Ns between 20 and 50.

Since the publication of the first edition of this book in 1990, recognition of the superiority of confidence intervals and point estimates of effect sizes over significance tests has grown exponentially. The report of the task force on significance testing of the American Psychological Association (APA) (Wilkinson & The APA Task Force on Statistical Inference, 1999) stated that researchers should report effect size estimates and confidence intervals. The fifth and sixth editions of the APA *Publication Manual* stated that it is almost always necessary for primary studies to report effect size estimates and confidence intervals (American Psychological Association, 2001, 2009). Twenty-one research journals in psychology and education now require that these statistics be reported (B. Thompson, 2002). Some have argued that information on the methods needed to compute confidence intervals is not widely available. However, there are now helpful and informative statistics textbooks designed around point estimates of effect size and confidence intervals instead of significance testing (Cumming, 2012; Kline, 2004; Lockhart, 1998; Smithson, 2000). The Cumming (2012) book includes excellent online computer programs that make calculations easy and that illustrate critical statistical facts and principles. B. Thompson (2002) presents considerable information on computation of confidence intervals and cites many useful references that provide more detail (e.g., Kirk, 2001; Smithson, 2001). The August 2001 issue of *Educational and Psychological Measurement* was devoted entirely to methods of computing and interpreting confidence intervals. There are many other such publications (e.g., Borenstein, 1994).

Despite these developments, most published articles still use significance tests. How this can be is something of a mystery, given the fact that this practice has been completely discredited. Orlitzky (2011) argues that the problem is that the evidence against significance testing has not been *institutionalized*. Articles discrediting significance testing have been aimed at inducing individual researchers to change their statistical practices, not at a broader, more systematic or institutional change. But it very difficult for individual researchers to go against what has become an institutionalized practice in most journals. What is needed, he contends, is top-down disciplinary-wide changes in the research culture. This is a broad recommendation. For example, he says that urging individual journal editors to require effect sizes and confidence intervals will produce little change. There must be an enforceable agreement at the level of the entire discipline that proper data analysis procedures must be used in primary studies, along with major changes in the way research methods are taught in graduate programs. This is a long-term proposition for culture change. Fortunately, as we will see next, meta-analysis makes it possible to make progress in developing cumulative knowledge in the interim even if significance testing continues to be used in individual primary studies.

Meta-Analysis

Is there a quantitative analysis that would have shown that all the differences in Table 1.1 might stem from sampling error? Suppose we compute the variance of the correlations, weighting each by its sample size. The value we obtain is .02258 ($SD = .150$). We can also compute the variance expected solely from sampling error. The formula for the sampling error variance of each individual correlation r_i is

$$(1 - .331^2)^2/(N_i - 1),$$

where .331 is the sample size–weighted mean of the correlations in Table 1.1. If we weight each of these estimates by its sample size (as we did when we computed the observed variance), the formula for variance expected from sampling error is

$$S_e^2 = \frac{\sum_{i=1}^{i=30} \left[\frac{N_i \left(1 - .331^2\right)^2}{N_i - 1} \right]}{\sum N_i}.$$

This value is .02058 ($SD = .144$). The ratio of variance expected from sampling error to actual (observed) variance is $.02058/.02258 = .91$. Thus, sampling error alone accounts for an estimated 91% of the observed variance in the correlations. The square root of the .91 is the correlation between the sampling errors and the observed correlations. This correlation is .95 and is a more informative index than the percent of variance accounted for (Schmidt, 2010). The best conclusion is that the relationship between job satisfaction and organizational commitment is constant across sexes, races, job levels, ages, geographical locations, and size of organization. (The difference between a correlation of 1.00 and our value of .95 is due to second-order sampling error, which is discussed in Chapter 9.) The best estimate of this constant value is .331, the sample size–weighted mean of the 30 correlations. When in our oral presentations researchers analyzed the data from these 30 studies qualitatively, different people came to different conclusions. In contrast, all researchers applying the quantitative method used here would (barring computational errors) come to exactly the same conclusion.

For theoretical purposes, the value .331 is not the one we want, because it is biased downward by unreliability in both measures. The effect of measurement error is to reduce all the observed correlations, and hence the mean correlation, below the actual correlation between the two constructs. What we are interested in is the construct-level correlation, because this correlation reflects the underlying science. Suppose from information in the 30 studies we estimate the average reliability of job satisfaction measures at .70 and the average reliability of organizational commitment measures at .60. Then the estimated correlation between true scores on the measures is $.331/\sqrt{.70(.60)} = .51$. This value is the best estimate of the construct-level correlation. Schmidt, Le, and Oh (in press) have shown that true scores and construct scores typically correlate about .98, so true score correlations are good estimates of construct correlations. The necessity of correcting for measurement error is discussed by Hedges (2009b, chap. 3).

Most artifacts other than sampling error that distort study findings are systematic rather than random. They usually create a downward bias in the obtained study r or d value. For example, all variables in a study must be measured and all measures of variables contain measurement error. There are no exceptions to this rule. The effect of measurement error is to downwardly bias every correlation or d value. Measurement error can also cause *differences* between studies: If the measures used in one study have more measurement error than those used in another study, the observed rs or ds will be smaller in the first study. Thus, meta-analysis must correct both for the downward bias and for the artifactually created differences between different studies. Corrections of this sort are discussed in Chapters 2 to 7.

Traditional review procedures are inadequate to integrate conflicting findings across large numbers of studies. As Glass (1976) pointed out, the results of hundreds of studies "can no more be grasped in our traditional narrative discursive review than one can grasp the sense of 500 test scores without the aid of techniques for organizing, depicting and interpreting data" (p. 4). In such areas as the effects of class size on student learning, the relationship of IQ to creativity, and the effects of psychotherapy on patients, literally hundreds of studies can accumulate over a period of only a few years. Glass (1976) noted that such studies collectively contain much more information than can be extracted from them using narrative review methods. He pointed out that because we have not exploited these gold mines of information, "We know much less than we have proven." What is needed are methods that will integrate results from existing studies to reveal patterns of relatively invariant underlying relationships and causalities, the establishment of which will constitute general principles and cumulative knowledge.

At one time in the history of psychology and the social sciences, the pressing need was for more empirical studies examining the problem in question. In many areas of research, the need today is not additional empirical data but some means of making sense of the vast amounts of data that have been accumulated. Because of the increasing number of areas within psychology and the other social sciences in which the number of available studies is quite large and the importance to theory development and practical problem solving of integrating conflicting findings to establish general knowledge, meta-analysis has come to play an increasingly important role in research. Such methods can be built around statistical and psychometric procedures that are already familiar to us. As Glass (1976) stated,

> Most of us were trained to analyze complex relationships among variables in the primary analysis of research data. But at the higher level, where variance, nonuniformity and uncertainty are no less evident, we too often substitute literary exposition for quantitative rigor. The proper integration of research requires the same statistical methods that are applied in primary data analysis. (p. 6)

Role of Meta-Analysis in the Behavioral and Social Sciences

The small-sample studies typical of psychological research produce seemingly contradictory results, and reliance on statistical significance tests causes study results to appear even more conflicting. Meta-analysis integrates the findings across such studies to reveal the simpler patterns of relationships that underlie the research literature, thus providing a basis for theory development. Meta-analysis can correct for the distorting effects of sampling error, measurement error, and other artifacts that produce the illusion of conflicting findings.

The goal in any science is the production of cumulative knowledge. Ultimately, this means the development of theories that explain the phenomena that are the focus of the scientific area. One example would be theories that explain how personality traits develop in children and adults over time and how these traits affect their lives. Another would be theories of what factors cause job and career satisfaction and what effects job satisfaction in turn has on other aspects of one's life. Before theories can be developed, however, we need to be able to precisely calibrate the relationships between variables. For example, what is the relationship between peer socialization and level of extroversion? What is the relationship between job satisfaction and job performance?

Unless we can precisely calibrate such relationships among variables, we do not have the raw materials out of which to construct theories. There is nothing for a theory to explain. For example, if the relationship between extroversion and popularity of children varies capriciously across different

studies from a strong positive to a strong negative correlation and everything in between, we cannot begin to construct a theory of how extroversion might affect popularity. The same applies to the relationship between
job satisfaction and job performance.

The unfortunate fact is that most research literatures do show conflicting findings of this sort. Some studies find statistically significant relationships and some do not. In much of the research literature, this split is
approximately 50–50 (Cohen, 1962, 1988; Schmidt, 2010; Schmidt &
Hunter, 1997; Schmidt, Hunter, & Urry, 1976; Sedlmeier & Gigerenzer,
1989). This has been the traditional situation in most areas of the behavioral and social sciences. Hence, it has been very difficult to develop
understanding, theories, and cumulative knowledge.

Today meta-analysis is being widely applied to solve this problem. The
extent of the use of meta-analysis is mirrored in the fact that a Google
search using this term produces over 50 million hits.

THE MYTH OF THE PERFECT STUDY

Before meta-analysis, the usual way in which scientists attempted to
make sense of the research literature was by use of the narrative subjective
review. In much of the research literature, however, there were not only
conflicting findings but also large numbers of studies. This combination
made the standard narrative subjective review a nearly impossible task—
one shown by research on human information processing to be far beyond
human capabilities. How does one sit down and make sense of, say, 210
conflicting studies?

The answer as developed in many narrative reviews was what came to be
called the myth of the perfect study. Reviewers convinced themselves that
most—usually the vast majority—of the available studies were "methodologically deficient" and should not even be considered in the review. These
judgments of methodological deficiency were often based on idiosyncratic
ideas: One reviewer might regard the Peabody Personality Inventory as
"lacking in construct validity" and throw out all studies that used that
instrument. Another might regard use of that same inventory as a prereq-
uisite for methodological soundness and eliminate all studies *not* using this
inventory. Thus, any given reviewer could eliminate from consideration all
but a few studies and perhaps narrow the number of studies from 210 to,
say, 7. Conclusions would then be based on these seven studies.

It has long been the case that the most widely read literature reviews are
those appearing in textbooks. The function of textbooks, especially
advanced-level textbooks, is to summarize what is known in a given field.
No textbook, however, can cite and discuss 210 studies on a single relationship. Textbook authors would often pick out what they considered to
be the one or two "best" studies and then base textbook conclusions on

just those studies, discarding the vast bulk of the information in the research literature. Hence, the myth of the perfect study.

In fact, there are no perfect studies. All studies contain measurement error in all measures used, as discussed later. Independent of measurement error, no study's measures have perfect construct validity. Furthermore, there are typically other artifacts that distort study findings. Even if a hypothetical (and it would have to be hypothetical) study suffered from none of these distortions, it would still contain sampling error—typically a substantial amount of sampling error—because sample sizes are rarely very large. Hence, no single study or small selected subgroup of studies can provide an optimal basis for scientific conclusions about cumulative knowledge. As a result, reliance on "best studies" did not provide a solution to the problem of conflicting research findings. This procedure did not even successfully deceive researchers into believing it was a solution—because different narrative reviewers arrived at different conclusions because they selected a different subset of "best" studies. Hence, the "conflicts in the literature" became "conflicts between the reviews."

SOME RELEVANT HISTORY

By the mid-1970s, the behavioral and social sciences were in serious trouble. Large numbers of studies had accumulated on many questions that were important to theory development and/or social policy decisions. Results of different studies on the same question typically were conflicting. For example, are workers more productive when they are satisfied with their jobs? The studies did not agree. Do students learn more when class sizes are smaller? Research findings were conflicting. Does participative decision making in management increase productivity? Does job enlargement increase job satisfaction and output? Does psychotherapy really help people? The studies were in conflict. As a consequence, the public and government officials were becoming increasingly disillusioned with the behavioral and social sciences, and it was becoming more and more difficult to obtain funding for research. In an invited address to the American Psychological Association in 1970, Senator Walter Mondale expressed his frustration with this situation:

> What I have *not* learned is what we should do about these problems. I had hoped to find research to support or to conclusively oppose my belief that quality integrated education is the most promising approach. But I have found very little conclusive evidence. For every study, statistical or theoretical, that contains a proposed solution or recommendation, there is always another, equally well documented, challenging the assumptions or conclusions of the first. No one seems to agree with anyone else's approach. But more distressing I must confess, I stand with my colleagues confused and often disheartened.

Then, in 1981, the director of the Federal Office of Management and Budget, David Stockman, proposed an 80% reduction in federal funding for research in the behavioral and social sciences. This proposal was politically motivated in part, but the failure of behavioral and social science research to be cumulative created the vulnerability to political attack. This proposed cut was a trial balloon sent up to see how much political opposition it would arouse. Even when proposed cuts are much smaller than a draconian 80%, constituencies can usually be counted on to come forward and protest the proposed cuts. This usually happens, and many behavioral and social scientists expected it to happen. But it did not. The behavioral and social sciences, it turned out, had no constituency among the public; the public did not care (see "Cuts Raise New Social Science Query," 1981). Finally, out of desperation, the American Psychological Association took the lead in forming the Consortium of Social Science Associations to lobby against the proposed cuts. Although this super association had some success in getting these cuts reduced (and even, in some areas, getting increases in research funding in subsequent years), these developments should make us look carefully at how such a thing could happen.

The sequence of events that led to this state of affairs was much the same in one research area after another. First, there was initial optimism about using social science research to answer socially important questions. Do government-sponsored job-training programs work? We will do studies to find out. Does Head Start really help disadvantaged kids? The studies will tell us. Does integration increase the school achievement of black children? Research will provide the answer. Next, several studies on the question are conducted, but the results are conflicting. There is some disappointment that the question has not been answered, but policy makers—and people in general—are still optimistic. They, along with the researchers, conclude that more research is needed to identify the supposed interactions (moderators) that have caused the conflicting findings. For example, perhaps whether job training works depends on the age and education of the trainees. Maybe smaller classes in the schools are beneficial only for lower IQ children. It is hypothesized that psychotherapy works for middle-class but not working-class patients. That is, the conclusion at this point is that a search for moderator variables is needed.

In the third phase, a large number of research studies are funded and conducted to test these moderator hypotheses. When they are completed, there is now a large body of studies, but instead of being resolved, the number of conflicts increases. The moderator hypotheses from the initial studies are not borne out, and no one can make sense out of the conflicting findings. Researchers conclude that the question that was selected for study in this particular case has turned out to be hopelessly complex. They then turn to the investigation of another question, hoping that this time the question will turn out to be more tractable. Research sponsors, government officials, and the public become disenchanted and cynical.

Research funding agencies cut money for research in this area and in related areas. After this cycle has been repeated enough times, social and behavioral scientists themselves become cynical about the value of their own work, and they publish articles endorsing the belief that behavioral and social science research is incapable, *in principle,* of developing cumulative knowledge and providing general answers to socially important questions. Examples of this include Cronbach (1975), Gergen (1982), and Meehl (1978).

Clearly, at this point, there was a critical need for some means of making sense of the vast number of accumulated study findings. Starting in the late 1970s, new methods of combining findings across studies on the same subject were developed. These methods were referred to collectively as *meta-analysis,* a term coined by Glass (1976). Applications of meta-analysis to the accumulated research literature (e.g., Schmidt & Hunter, 1977) showed that research findings were not nearly as conflicting as had been thought and that useful and sound general conclusions could, in fact, be drawn from existing research. The conclusion was that cumulative theoretical knowledge is possible in the behavioral and social sciences, and socially important questions can be answered in reasonably definitive ways. As a result, the gloom and cynicism that had enveloped many in the behavioral and social sciences lifted.

In fact, meta-analysis has even produced evidence that cumulativeness of research findings in the behavioral sciences is probably as great as that in the physical sciences. We have long assumed that our research studies are less consistent than those in the physical sciences. Hedges (1987) used meta-analysis methods to examine variability of findings across studies in 13 research areas in particle physics and 13 research areas in psychology. Contrary to common belief, his findings showed that there is as much variability across studies in physics as there is in psychology. Furthermore, he found that the physical sciences used methods to combine findings across studies that were "essentially identical" to meta-analysis. The research literature in both areas—psychology and physics—yielded cumulative knowledge when meta-analysis was properly applied. Hedges's major finding is that the frequency of conflicting research findings is no greater in the behavioral and social sciences than in the physical sciences. The fact that this finding has been so surprising to many social scientists points up the fact that we have long overestimated the consistency of research findings in the physical sciences. Furthermore, in the physical sciences, no research question can be answered by a single study, and physical scientists must and do use meta-analysis to make sense of their research literature, just as we do. (And, as noted earlier, in analyzing data in individual studies, the physical sciences do not use significance tests; they use point estimates and confidence intervals.)

Other changes have also been produced by meta-analysis. The relative status of reviews has changed dramatically. Journals that traditionally published only primary studies and refused to publish reviews have now published meta-analytic reviews in large numbers for some years. In the past, research reviews were based on the narrative subjective method, and they had limited status and gained little credit for one in academic raises or promotions. The rewards went to those who conducted primary research. Not only is this no longer the case, but there also has been a more important development. Today, many discoveries and advances in cumulative knowledge are being made not by those who do primary research studies but by those who use meta-analysis to discover the latent meaning of existing research literatures. Today, behavioral or social scientists with the needed training and skills are making major original discoveries and contributions by mining the untapped veins of information in the accumulated research literatures.

The meta-analytic process of cleaning up and making sense of the research literature not only reveals the cumulative knowledge that is there but also provides clearer directions about what the remaining research needs are. That is, we also learn what kinds of primary research studies are needed next. However, some have raised the concern that meta-analysis may be killing the motivation and incentive to conduct primary research studies. Meta-analysis has clearly shown that no single primary study can ever resolve an issue or answer a question. Research findings are inherently probabilistic (Taveggia, 1974), and, therefore, the results of any single study could have occurred by chance. Only meta-analytic integration of findings across studies can control sampling error and other artifacts and provide a foundation for conclusions. And yet meta-analysis is not possible unless the needed primary studies are conducted. In new research areas, this potential problem is not of much concern. The first study conducted on a question contains 100% of the available research information. The second contains roughly 50%, and so on. Thus, the early studies in any area have a certain status. The 50th study, however, contains only about 2% of the available information, and the 100th, about 1%. Will we have difficulty motivating researchers to conduct the 50th or 100th study? If we do, we do not believe this will be due to meta-analysis. When the narrative review was the dominant method of research integration, reviewers did not base their conclusions on single studies but on multiple studies. So no researcher could reasonably hope then—as now—that his or her single study could decide an issue. In fact, meta-analysis represents an improvement for the primary researcher in one respect: All available relevant studies are included in a meta-analysis, and hence, every study has an effect. As we saw earlier, narrative reviewers often threw out most of the relevant studies and based their conclusions on a handful of their favorite studies.

Also, it should be noted that those who raise this question overlook a beneficial effect that meta-analysis has had: It prevents the diversion of valuable research resources into truly unneeded research studies. Meta-analysis applications have revealed that there are questions on which additional research would waste scientifically and socially valuable resources. For example, already as of 1980, 882 studies based on a total sample of 70,935 had been conducted relating measures of perceptual speed to the job performance of clerical workers. Based on these studies, our meta-analytic estimate of this mean correlation is .47 and its $SD_\rho = .22$; Pearlman, Schmidt, & Hunter, 1980). For other abilities, there were often 200 to 300 cumulative studies. Clearly, further research on these relationships is not the best use of available resources.

If one or more new studies appear after a meta-analysis has been completed, how should the meta-analysis be updated to include these new studies? Schmidt and Raju (2007) showed that the optimal method is to recompute the meta-analysis including those studies (i.e., use the "medical method" of updating a meta-analysis rather than a Bayesian approach).

Role of Meta-Analysis in Theory Development

As noted earlier, the major task in the behavioral and social sciences, as in other sciences, is the development of theory. A good theory is simply a good explanation of the processes that actually take place in a phenomenon. For example, what actually happens when employees develop a high level of organizational commitment? Does job satisfaction develop first and then cause the development of commitment? If so, what causes job satisfaction to develop and how does it affect commitment? How do higher levels of mental ability cause higher levels of job performance? Only by increasing job knowledge? Or also by directly improving problem solving on the job? The social scientist is essentially a detective; his or her job is to find out why and how things happen the way they do. To construct theories, however, we must first know some of the basic facts, such as the empirical relationships among variables. These relationships are the building blocks of theory. For example, if we know there is a high and consistent positive population correlation between job satisfaction and organization commitment, this will send us in particular directions in developing our theory. If the correlation between these variables is very low and consistent, theory development will branch in different directions. If the relationship is highly variable across organizations and settings, we will be encouraged to advance interactive or moderator-based theories. Meta-analysis provides these empirical building blocks for theory. Meta-analytic findings tell us what it is that needs to be explained by the theory. Meta-analysis has been criticized because it does not directly generate or develop theory (Guzzo, Jackson, & Katzell, 1986). This is akin to criticizing word processors because they do not generate books on their own. The results of meta-analysis are indispensable for theory construction, but theory construction itself is a creative process distinct from meta-analysis.

As implied in the language used in our discussion, theories are causal explanations. The goal in every science is explanation, and explanation is always causal. In the behavioral and social sciences, the methods of path analysis (see, e.g., Hunter & Gerbing, 1982) and structural equation modeling (SEM) can be used to test causal theories when the data meet the assumptions of the method. The relationships revealed by meta-analysis—the empirical building blocks for theory—can be used in path analysis and SEM to test causal theories. Experimentally determined relationships can also be entered into path analyses along with observationally based relationships. It is only necessary to transform d values to correlations (see Chapter 7). Thus, path analyses can be "mixed." Path analysis and SEM cannot demonstrate that a theory is correct but can disconfirm a theory, that is, show that it is not correct. Path analysis can therefore be a powerful tool for reducing the number of theories that could possibly be consistent with the data, sometimes to a very small number, and sometimes to only one theory (Hunter, 1988). For an example, see Hunter (1983a). Every such reduction in the number of possible theories is an advance in understanding.

Application of path analysis or SEM requires either the correlations among the theoretically relevant variables (correlation matrix) or the covariances among the variables (variance-covariance matrix). Meta-analysis can be used to create correlation matrices for the variables of interest. Because each meta-analysis can estimate a different cell in the correlation matrix, it is possible to assemble the complete correlation matrix, even though no single study has included every one of the variables of interest (see, e.g., Viswesvaran & Ones, 1995). If these correlations are appropriately corrected for the biasing effects of artifacts such as measurement error, it is then possible to apply path analysis or SEM to test causal (or explanatory) theories (Cook et al., 1992, pp. 315–316). One example of this is Schmidt, Hunter, and Outerbridge (1986). This study used meta-analysis to assemble the correlations among the variables of general mental ability, job experience, job knowledge, work sample performance, and supervisory evaluations of job performance. (These correlations were homogeneous across studies.) The path analysis results are shown in Figure 1.1. This causal model fit the data quite well. As can be seen in Figure 1.1, both job experience and general mental ability exert strong causal influence on the acquisition of job knowledge, which, in turn, is the major cause of high performance on the job sample measure. The results also indicate that supervisors based their ratings more heavily on employees' job knowledge than on actual performance capabilities. This causal model (or theory) of job performance has since been supported in other studies (Schmidt & Hunter, 1992). Today the research literature contains many studies that use meta-analysis in this manner.

Figure 1.1 Path model and path coefficients.

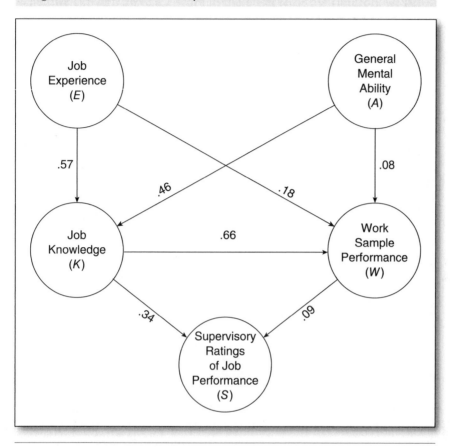

Note: Adapted from "Impact of Job Experience and Ability on Job Knowledge, Work Sample Performance, and Supervisory Ratings of Job Performance," by F. L. Schmidt, J. E. Hunter, and A. N. Outerbridge, 1986, *Journal of Applied Psychology, 71,* 432–439. Reprinted by permission of the authors.

Becker (1989; 2009, chap. 20) and Becker and Schram (1994) discussed the possibilities of using meta-analysis in this manner. Becker (1992) used this approach in examining a model of the variables affecting the achievement in science of male and female high school and college students. In that case, there were insufficient studies available to obtain meta-analytic estimates of some of the needed correlations; nevertheless, progress was made and the information needed from future research was pinpointed. Becker (1996) and Shadish (1996) provided additional discussion. Although there are technical complexities that must be dealt with in using meta-analysis in this manner (Cook et al., 1992, pp. 328–330), it is a promising approach to accelerating cumulative knowledge in the social sciences. Technical questions related to this use of meta-analysis are discussed in Chapter 5.

Meta-Analysis in Industrial-Organizational Psychology

There have been numerous applications of meta-analysis in industrial-organizational (I/O) psychology. The most extensive and detailed application of meta-analysis in I/O psychology has been the study of the generalizability of the validities of employment selection procedures (Schmidt, 1988; Schmidt & Hunter, 1981, 1998). The findings have resulted in major changes in the field of personnel selection. Validity generalization research is described in more detail in Chapter 4.

Recent meta-analyses in organizational psychology have addressed a broad range of topics across different levels of analysis. At the levels of the organization or business unit, Harter, Schmidt, and Hayes (2002); Harter, Schmidt, Asplund, and Kilham (2010); and Whitman, Van Rooy, and Viswesvaran (2010) demonstrated that unit-level job satisfaction and employee engagement has positive, generalized effects on business unit financial performance and customer satisfaction. Another meta-analysis showed, across 83 different organizations, the generalized positive effects on job performance of the Productivity Measurement and Enhancement System (ProMES; Pritchard, Harrell, DiazGranadaos, & Guzman, 2008), a performance management system designed by organizational psychologists to provide workers and employees with quick and effective feedback on their performance. Meta-analyses of team research continue to be popular, with one meta-analysis summarizing how different teamwork processes affect team effectiveness (LePine, Piccolo, Jackson, Mathieu, & Saul, 2008).

Other meta-analyses focused on individuals as the unit of analysis. One such study examined the relationship between job turnover and the five-factor model (FFM) of personality and found that Emotional Stability is a generalized negative predictor of turnover (Zimmerman, 2008). Another study attempted to untangle the ambiguous causal relationship between job attitudes and job performance (Riketta, 2008). Other studies focused on multicultural and international issues. Dean, Roth, and Bobko (2008) meta-analytically examined ethnic and gender subgroup differences in assessment center ratings to show that gender differences in ratings from these evaluations are smaller than previously thought, but that some ethnic subgroup differences are larger than previously believed. Taras, Kirkman, and Steel (2010) showed that Hofstede's (1980) cultural value dimensions had validity in predicting (in decreasing order) individual emotions, attitudes, behaviors, and job performance. Geyskens, Krishnan, Steenkamp, and Cunha (2009) presented an extensive examination of the use of meta-analysis in management-related research.

Older examples also span a variety of topics and units of analysis. C. D. Fisher and Gitelson's (1983) meta-analysis examined the negative and positive correlates of conflict and ambiguity for members' roles in teams. Meta-analyses of leadership performance were also popular. An example is a meta-analytic test of Fiedler's contingency theory of leadership, a dominant theory of leadership at the time (L. H. Peters, Harthe, & Pohlman, 1985). Other meta-analyses studied questions about attitudes and beliefs, such as the relatively low accuracy of self-ratings of ability and skill (Mabe & West, 1982) and the negative relationship between job satisfaction and absenteeism (Terborg & Lee, 1982). Other studies focused on more specific interventions and assessments, such as the small but positive effect of realistic job previews in reducing subsequent employee turnover (Premack & Wanous, 1985); the positive, generalizable validity of the LSAT for predicting performance in law school (Linn, Harnisch, & Dunbar, 1981a); and the limited abilities of financial analysts to predict stock growth (Coggin & Hunter, 1983). In short, researchers have pursued and continue to pursue meta-analytic studies across a wide variety of subjects and continue to recognize psychometric meta-analysis as an important research tool.

Additional examples of influential meta-analyses are found in the literature on managerial training. Burke and Day's (1986) meta-analysis on the effectiveness of managerial training prompted a subsequent stream of meta-analytic research on management training, including D. B. Collins and Holton (2004); Taylor, Russ-Eft, and Taylor (2009); and Powell and Yalcin (2010). The conclusions from these studies have repeatedly been that management training programs can be effective in nearly all situations at changing particular behaviors and for the acquisition of knowledge, particularly in the areas of time management and human relations skills. Other meta-analyses have assessed the results of training across a variety of organizational contexts. For example, a recent meta-analysis examined how combinations of training content, trainee attributes, and trainees' affective reactions to training influence the outcomes of a training program (Sitzmann, Brown, Casper, Ely, & Zimmerman, 2008). Other meta-analytic studies investigated the relationships among different training criteria such as behavior, learning, and performance (Alliger, Tannenbaum, Bennett, Traver, & Shotland, 1997), or how trainees use their training in applied settings and share knowledge from training with others (Arthur, Bennett, Edens, & Bell, 2003). All three meta-analyses have had powerful impacts on traditional models of learning and training in I/O psychology, resulting in updates to D. L. Kirkpatrick's (2000) widely used model of learning, a demonstration of the effectiveness of lectures as a form of training, and reconsideration of the value of affective reactions to training.

Colquitt, LePine, and Noe (2000) used meta-analysis to further expand on Alliger et al.'s (1997) work and examine how individual differences, situational factors, and job career factors influenced an individual's motivation during training and the subsequent outcomes of this motivation. Colquitt et al.'s (2000) work established the importance of motivation as a critical factor in determining the efficacy of training, how individuals

transfer learning from training to their work performance, and how effective they are in sharing training knowledge with others. In a more recent
study of the impact of motivation, Payne, Youngcourt, and Beaubien
(2007) have used meta-analytic methods to calibrate the impact of goal
orientation (a psychological variable reflecting the motivation of individuals to learn versus the motivation to perform well in front of others) on
training outcomes. These two meta-analyses have influenced how researchers conduct subsequent primary studies and created new opportunities for
researchers to examine the role of motivation in training. In short,
meta-analysis has affected research on management training, motivation
in training, and training in general by demonstrating the validity and
value of training to organizations across the board.

Meta-analysis has also been used extensively in the leadership literature, a popular topic of study in I/O psychology and organizational behavior (OB). Meta-analysis has provided some clarity on a difficult subject, as
well as changing how studies were conducted in light of the findings of the
meta-analyses. Judge, Colbert, and Ilies (2004) reported a relatively low
relationship between general cognitive ability and leadership, noting that
this relationship is weaker than expected based on earlier qualitative
reviews. Similar work was done demonstrating that leadership cannot be
explained solely as a result of personality traits in the popular FFM framework (Judge, Bono, Ilies, & Gerhardt, 2002). Several years later, this line of
research inspired a group of researchers to consider conceptual models of
positive ("bright-side") and negative ("dark-side") personality traits in
leaders linked to leadership emergence and efficacy (Judge, Piccolo &
Kosalka, 2009). Finally, multiple meta-analyses have been used to show
the validity, uniqueness, and importance of transformational (charismatic)
leadership, a specific set of leadership behaviors highly motivating to
employees and a central topic of research in the leadership literature (Bono
& Judge, 2004; Eagly, Johannsen-Schmidt, & van Engen, 2003; Eagly,
Karau, & Makhijani, 1995). Applications of meta-analysis have produced
important changes in research conclusions, fundamental changes in existing theoretical paradigms, and the development of new lines of research.

Wider Impact of Meta-Analysis on Psychology

Some have viewed meta-analysis as merely a set of improved methods for
doing literature reviews. Meta-analysis is actually more than that. By quantitatively comparing findings across diverse studies, meta-analysis can discover
new knowledge not inferable from any individual study and can sometimes
answer questions that were never addressed in any of the individual studies
contained in the meta-analysis. For example, no individual study may have
compared the effectiveness of a training program for people of higher and
lower mental ability; by comparing mean d value statistics across different

groups of studies, however, meta-analysis can reveal this difference. That is, moderator variables (interactions) never studied in any individual study can be revealed by meta-analysis, greatly facilitating the development of cumulative knowledge. M. E. Chan and Arvey (2012) provide an analysis of the positive impact of meta-analysis on the development of knowledge in psychology and the social sciences. Richard, Bond, and Stokes-Zoota (2003) review the impact of 322 meta-analyses in social psychology. And Dieckmann, Malle, and Bodner (2009) provide an assessment of the use of meta-analysis in several areas of psychological research. Carlson and Ji (2011) presented an analysis of how meta-analytic studies are used and cited in the wider psychological literature. They found that the frequency of citations to meta-analyses (vs. primary studies) has been rapidly increasing in recent years.

Even though it is much more than that, meta-analysis is indeed an improved method for synthesizing or integrating the research literature. The premier review journal in psychology is *Psychological Bulletin.* Over time since 1980, a steadily increasing percentage of the reviews published in this journal have been meta-analyses and a steadily decreasing percentage have been traditional narrative subjective reviews. It is not uncommon for narrative review manuscripts to be returned by editors to the authors with the request that meta-analysis be applied to the studies reviewed (Cooper, 2003). Most of the remaining narrative reviews published today in *Psychological Bulletin* focus on research literature that is not well enough developed to be amenable to quantitative treatment.

Although a movement toward change began about 2010, most of the meta-analyses that have appeared in *Psychological Bulletin* have employed fixed effects methods, resulting in many cases in overstatement of the precision of the meta-analysis findings (Schmidt, Oh, & Hayes, 2009). (See Chapters 5 and 8 for a discussion of fixed vs. random meta-analysis models; confidence intervals are too narrow when the fixed effect model is used.) Despite this fact, these meta-analyses produced findings and conclusions that are more accurate than those produced by the traditional narrative subjective method. Many other journals have shown the same increase over time in the number of meta-analyses published. Many of these journals had traditionally published only individual empirical studies and had rarely published reviews up until the advent of meta-analysis in the late 1970s. These journals began publishing meta-analyses because meta-analyses came to be viewed not as "mere reviews" but as a form of empirical research. As a result of this change, the quality and accuracy of conclusions from the research literature improved in a wide variety of journals and in a corresponding variety of research areas in psychology. This improvement in the quality of conclusions from the research literature has expedited theory development in many areas in psychology.

The impact of meta-analysis on psychology textbooks has been positive and dramatic. Textbooks are important because their function is to summarize the state of cumulative knowledge in a given field. Most people—students and others—acquire most of their knowledge about psychological theory and findings from their reading of textbooks. Prior to meta-analysis, textbook authors faced with hundreds of conflicting studies on a single question subjectively and arbitrarily selected a small number of their preferred studies from the literature and based the textbook conclusions on only those few studies. Today, most textbook authors base their conclusions on meta-analysis findings (Myers, 1991), making their conclusions and their textbooks much more accurate. We cannot overemphasize the importance of this development in advancing cumulative knowledge in psychology.

Because multiple studies are needed to solve the problem of sampling error, it is critical to ensure the availability of all studies on each topic. A major problem is that many good replication articles are rejected by the primary research journals. Journals currently put excessive weight on surprising and novel findings in evaluating studies and often fail to consider either sampling error or other important technical problems such as measurement error. Many journals will not even consider "mere replication studies" or "mere measurement studies." Many persistent authors eventually publish such studies in journals with lower prestige, but they must endure many letters of rejection, and publication is often delayed for a long period of time. Problems of this sort, including the general issue of publication bias, are discussed in more detail in Chapter 13.

To us, this clearly indicates that we need a new type of journal—whether hard copy or electronic—that systematically archives all studies that will be needed for later meta-analyses. The American Psychological Association's Experimental Publication System in the early 1970s was an attempt in this direction. However, at that time, the need subsequently created by meta-analysis did not yet exist; the system apparently met no real need at that time and hence was discontinued. Today, the need is so great that failure to have such a journal system in place is retarding our efforts to reach our full potential in creating cumulative knowledge in psychology and the social sciences.

In view of the large number of meta-analyses available in the psychology and social sciences literatures, some readers may wonder why the examples we use in this book to illustrate meta-analysis principles and methods do not employ data from those meta-analyses. The primary reason is that the amount of data (the number of correlations or d statistics) is usually so large as to result in cumbersome examples. For pedagogical reasons, we have generally employed examples consisting of small numbers of studies in which the data are hypothetical. As explained in the following chapters, meta-analyses based on such small numbers of studies would not ordinarily yield results that would be optimally stable. (We discuss second-order sampling error in Chapter 9.) However, such examples provide the means to simply and clearly illustrate the principles and methods of meta-analysis, and we believe this is the crucial consideration.

Impact of Meta-Analysis Outside Psychology

IMPACT IN BIOMEDICAL RESEARCH

The impact of meta-analysis may be even greater in biomedical research than in the behavioral and social sciences (Hunt, 1997, chap. 4). Hundreds of meta-analyses have been published in leading medical research journals such as the *New England Journal of Medicine* and the *Journal of the American Medical Association*. Already as of 1995, the medical literature contained between 962 and 1,411 meta-analyses, depending on the method of counting (Moher & Olkin, 1995). This number is much greater today. In medical research, the preferred study is the randomized controlled trial (RCT), in which participants are assigned randomly to receive either the treatment or a placebo, with the researchers being blind as to which treatment the participants are receiving. Despite the strengths of this research design, it is usually the case that different RCTs on the same treatment obtain conflicting results. This is partly because the effect sizes are often small and partly because (contrary perhaps to widespread perceptions) RCTs are often based on small sample sizes. In addition, the problem of information overload is even greater in medicine than in the social sciences; more than a million medical research studies are published every year. No practitioner can possibly keep up with the medical literature in his or her area.

The leader in introducing meta-analysis to medical research was Thomas Chalmers. In addition to being a researcher, Chalmers was also a practicing internal medicine physician who became frustrated with the inability of the vast, scattered, and unfocused medical research literature to provide guidance to practitioners. Starting in the mid-1970s, Chalmers developed his initial meta-analysis methods independently of those developed in the social and behavioral sciences. Despite being well conducted, his initial meta-analyses were not well accepted by medical researchers, who were critical of the concept of meta-analysis. In response, he and his associates developed "sequential meta-analysis"—a technique that reveals the date by which enough information had become available to show conclusively that a treatment was effective. Suppose, for example, that the first RCT for a particular drug had been conducted in 1975 but had a wide confidence interval, one that spans zero effect. Now, suppose three more studies had been conducted in 1976, providing a total of four studies to be meta-analyzed—and the confidence interval for the meta-analytic mean of these studies is still wide and still includes 0. Now, suppose five more RCTs had been conducted in 1977, providing nine studies for a meta-analysis up to this date. Now, if that meta-analysis yields a confidence interval that excludes 0, then we conclude that, given the use of meta-analysis, enough information was already available in 1977 to begin using this drug. On the basis of their meta-analysis findings and statistics on the disease, Chalmers and his associates then computed how many lives would have been saved to date had use of the drug begun in 1977. It turned out that, considered across different treatments, diseases, and areas of medical practice, a very large number of lives would have been saved had medical research historically relied on meta-analysis. The resulting article (Antman, Lau, Kupelnick, Mosteller, & Chalmers, 1992) is widely considered the most important and influential meta-analysis study ever published in medicine. It was even reported and discussed widely in the popular press (for example, the *New York Times* Science Section). It assured a major role for meta-analysis in medical research from that point on (Hunt, 1997, chap. 4).

Chalmers was also one of the driving forces behind the establishment of the Cochrane Collaboration, an organization that applies sequential meta-analysis in medical research in real time. This group conducts meta-analyses in a wide variety of medical research areas—and then updates each meta-analysis as new RCTs become available. That is, when a new RCT becomes available, the meta-analysis is rerun with the new RCT included. Hence, each meta-analysis is always current. The results of these updated meta-analyses are available on the Internet to researchers and medical practitioners around the world. It is likely that this effort has saved hundreds of thousands of lives by improving medical decision making. The Cochrane Collaboration website is www.cochrane.org. Another major early contributor to the development of meta-analysis methods for medical research is Richard Peto (1987). Later in the book, we discuss in detail methods of correcting for the biasing effects of measurement error, using methods from psychometric theory. Completely independently of these methods from psychometric theory, Peto developed different but equivalent methods of correcting for measurement error in medical research. For an application of these methods, see MacMahon et al. (1990). Examples of the use in medical research of the methods presented in this book include Fountoulakis, Conda, Vieta, and Schmidt (2009) and Gardner, Frantz, and Schmidt (1999). Problems related to publication bias and research fraud in the biomedical sciences are discussed in Chapter 13.

IMPACT IN OTHER DISCIPLINES

Meta-analysis has also become important in research in finance, marketing, sociology, ecology, and even wildlife management. Other areas in which meta-analysis is now being used include (Hafdahl, 2012) higher education, biological psychiatry, physical therapy, nursing practice, neuroscience, cardiology, forestry, and occupational counseling. An example of meta-analysis use in criminal justice is provided in Gendreau and Smith (2007). In fact, today it is difficult to find a research area in which meta-analysis is unknown. In the broad areas of education and social policy, the Campbell Collaboration is attempting to do for the social sciences what the Cochrane Collaboration (on which it is modeled) has done for medical practice (Rothstein, 2003; Rothstein, McDaniel, & Borenstein, 2001). Among the social sciences, perhaps the last to assign an important role to meta-analysis has been economics. However, meta-analysis has recently become important in economics, too (see, e.g., T. D. Stanley, 1998, 2001; T. D. Stanley & Jarrell, 1989, 1998). Another example in economics is the meta-analysis by Harmon, Oosterbeck, and Walker (2000); their study meta-analyzed a large number of studies on the financial returns to education and found an overall average rate of return of 6.5%. They also found that returns to education have fallen since the 1960s. There now is a doctoral program in meta-analysis in economics (www.feweb.vu.nl/re/Master-Point/). In 2008, an international conference on meta-analysis usage in economics was held in Nancy, France (Nancy-Universite, 2008). Meta-analysis is now also used in political science (see, e.g., Pinello, 1999).

Meta-Analysis and Social Policy

By providing the best available empirically based answers to socially important questions, meta-analysis can influence public policy making (Hoffert, 1997; Hunter & Schmidt, 1996). This can be true for any public policy question for which there is a relevant research literature—which today includes most policy questions. Examples range from the Head Start program to binary chemical weapons (Hunt, 1997, chap. 6). The purpose of the Campbell Collaboration, described previously, is specifically to provide policy-relevant information to policy makers in governments and other organizations by applying meta-analysis to policy-relevant research literatures on social experiments. For more than 20 years, the U.S. General Accounting Office (GAO; now renamed the General Accountability Office), a research and evaluation arm of the U.S. Congress, has used meta-analysis to provide answers to questions posed by senators and representatives. For example, Hunt (1997, chap. 6) described how a GAO meta-analysis of the effects of the Women, Infants, and Children (WIC) program, a federal nutritional program for poor pregnant women, apparently changed the mind of Senator Jesse Helms and made him a supporter of the program. The meta-analysis found evidence that the program reduced the frequency of low-birth-weight babies by about 10%.

This meta-analysis was presented to Senator Helms by Eleanor Chelimsky, for years the director of the GAO's Division of Program Evaluation and Methodology. In that position, she pioneered the use of meta-analysis at GAO. Chelimsky (1994) stated that meta-analysis has proven to be an excellent way to provide Congress with the widest variety of research results that can hold up under close scrutiny under the time pressures imposed by Congress. She stated that the GAO has found that meta-analysis reveals both what is known and what is not known in a given topic area and distinguishes between fact and opinion "without being confrontational." One application she cited as an example was a meta-analysis of studies on the merits of producing binary chemical weapons (nerve gas in which the two key ingredients are kept separate for safety until the gas is to be used). The meta-analysis did not support the production of such weapons. This was not what the Department of Defense (DOD) wanted to hear, and the DOD disputed the methodology and the results. The methodology held up under close scrutiny, however, and in the end Congress eliminated funds for these binary weapons.

By law, it is the responsibility of the GAO to provide policy-relevant research information to Congress. So the adoption of meta-analysis by the GAO is a clear example of the impact that meta-analysis can have on public policy. Although most policy decisions probably depend as much on political as on scientific considerations, it is possible for scientific considerations to have an impact with the aid of meta-analysis (Hoffert, 1997). Cordray and Morphy (2009) provide an extended discussion of the role of meta-analysis in the formulation of public policy. They emphasize the point that special care must be taken to ensure the objectivity of policy-related meta-analyses. In particular, they examine the meta-analysis conducted by the Environmental Protection Agency on the health effects of secondhand smoke as an example of a biased meta-analysis. This example is important because numerous laws were passed against environmental tobacco smoke based a faulty meta-analytic conclusion that it was harmful to health. Cordray and Morphy (2009) outline the steps necessary to ensure objectivity in meta-analyses.

Meta-Analysis and Theories of Data and Theories of Knowledge

Every method of meta-analysis is of necessity based on a theory of data. It is this theory (or understanding of data) that determines the nature of the resulting meta-analysis methods. A complete theory of data includes an understanding of sampling error, measurement error, biased sampling (range restriction and range enhancement), dichotomization and its effects, data errors, and other causal factors that distort the raw data results we see in research studies. Once a theoretical understanding of how these factors affect data is developed, it becomes possible to develop methods for correcting for their effects. The necessity of doing so is presented in detail in Schmidt, Le, and Oh (2009). In the language of psychometrics, the first process—the process by which these factors (artifacts) influence data—is modeled as the attenuation model. The second process—the process of correcting for these artifact-induced biases—is called the disattenuation model. If the theory of data on which a method of meta-analysis is based is incomplete, that method will fail to correct for some or all of these artifacts and will thus produce biased results. For example, a theory of data that fails to recognize measurement error will lead to methods of meta-analysis that do not correct for measurement error. Such methods will then perforce produce biased meta-analysis results. Most current methods of meta-analysis do not, in fact, correct for measurement error, as noted in Chapter 11. But in research methodology, the thrust is always in the direction of increased accuracy, so eventually methods for meta-analysis that do not correct for study artifacts that distort empirical findings will have to incorporate these corrections. This has already happened to some extent in that some users of these methods have "appended" these corrections to those methods (e.g., Aguinis, Sturman, & Pierce, 2008; Hall & Brannick, 2002). One's theory of data is also part of one's theory of knowledge or theory of epistemology. Epistemology is concerned with the ways in which we can attain correct knowledge. One requirement of an effective epistemology in empirical research is proper correction for the artifacts that distort the empirical data.

Sampling error and measurement error have a unique status among the statistical and measurement artifacts with which meta-analysis must deal: They are *always* present in all real data. Other artifacts, such as range restriction, artificial dichotomization of continuous variables, or data transcription errors, may be absent in a particular set of studies being subjected to meta-analysis. There is always sampling error, however, because sample sizes are never infinite. Likewise, there is always measurement error, because there are no perfectly reliable measures. In fact, as we will see in subsequent chapters, it is the requirement of dealing simultaneously with both sampling error and measurement error that makes even relatively simple meta-analyses sometimes seem complicated. We are used to dealing with these two types of errors separately. For example, when psychometric texts (e.g., Lord & Novick, 1968; Nunnally & Bernstein, 1994) discuss measurement error, they assume an infinite (or very large) sample size, so that the focus of attention can be on measurement error alone, with no need to deal simultaneously with sampling error. Similarly, when statistics texts discuss sampling error, they implicitly assume perfect reliability (the absence of measurement error), so that they and the reader can focus solely on sampling error. Both assumptions are highly unrealistic because all real data simultaneously contain both types of errors. It is admittedly more complicated to deal with both types of errors simultaneously, yet this is what meta-analysis must do to be successful (see, e.g., Cook et al., 1992, pp. 315–316, 325–328; Matt & Cook, 2009, chap. 28).

The question of what theory of data (and therefore of knowledge) underlies a method of meta-analysis is strongly related to the question of what the general purpose of meta-analysis is. Glass (1976, 1977) stated that the purpose is simply to summarize and describe the studies in the research literature. As we will see in this book, our view (the alternative view) is that the purpose is to estimate as accurately as possible the construct-level relationships in the population (i.e., to estimate population values or parameters), because these are the relationships of scientific interest. This is an entirely different task; this is the task of estimating what the findings would have been if all studies had been conducted perfectly (i.e., with no methodological limitations). Doing this requires correction for sampling error, measurement error, and other artifacts (if present) that distort study results. Simply describing the contents of studies in the literature requires no such corrections and does not allow estimation of the parameters of scientific interest.

Rubin (1990, 1992) critiqued the common, descriptive concept of the purpose of meta-analysis and proposed the alternative offered in this book and previous editions of this book. He stated that, as scientists, we are not really interested in the population of imperfect studies per se, and hence an accurate description or summary of the results of these studies is not really important. Instead, he argued that the goal of meta-analysis should be to estimate the true effects or relationships—defined as "results that would be obtained in an infinitely large, perfectly designed study or sequence of such studies." According to Rubin (1990),

> Under this view, we really do not care *scientifically* about summarizing this finite population (of observed studies). We really care about the underlying scientific process—the underlying process that is generating these outcomes that we happen to see—that we, as fallible researchers, are trying to glimpse through the opaque window of imperfect empirical studies. (p. 157)

This is an excellent summary of the purpose of meta-analysis as we see it and as embodied in the methods presented in this book.

Conclusion

Until recently, the psychological research literature was conflicting and contradictory. As the number of studies on each particular question became larger and larger, this situation became increasingly frustrating and intolerable. This situation stemmed from reliance on defective procedures for achieving cumulative knowledge: the statistical significance test in individual primary studies in combination with the narrative subjective review of the research literature. Meta-analysis principles have now correctly diagnosed this problem and have provided the solution. In area after area, meta-analytic findings have shown that there is much less conflict between different studies than had been believed; that coherent, useful, and generalizable conclusions can be drawn from the research literature; and that cumulative knowledge is possible in psychology and the social sciences. These methods have also been adopted in other areas such as medical research. A prominent medical researcher, Thomas Chalmers (as cited in Mann, 1990), has stated, "[Meta-analysis] is going to revolutionize how the sciences, especially medicine, handle data. And it is going to be the way many arguments will be ended" (p. 478). In concluding his oft-cited review of meta-analysis methods, Bangert-Drowns (1986) stated,

> Meta-analysis is not a fad. It is rooted in the fundamental values of the scientific enterprise: replicability, quantification, causal and correlational analysis. Valuable information is needlessly scattered in individual studies. The ability of social scientists to deliver generalizable answers to basic questions of policy is too serious a concern to allow us to treat research integration lightly. The potential benefits of meta-analysis method seem enormous. (p. 398)

Study Artifacts and Their Impact on Study Outcomes

2

In this chapter, we look at how research artifacts distort correlational research findings. Later, in Chapter 6, we look at how these same artifacts distort findings in experimental research. The goal of a meta-analysis of correlations is a description of the distribution of actual (i.e., construct-level) correlations between a given independent and a given dependent variable. If all studies were conducted perfectly, then the distribution of study correlations could be used directly to estimate the distribution of actual correlations. However, studies are never perfect. As a result, the relationship between study correlations and actual correlations is more complicated.

There are many dimensions along which studies fail to be perfect. Thus, there are many forms of error in study results. Each form of error has some impact on the results of a meta-analysis. Some errors can be corrected and some cannot. We refer to study imperfections as "artifacts" to remind ourselves that errors in study results produced by study imperfections are artifactual or manmade errors and not properties of nature. In later chapters, we present formulas that correct for as many artifacts as possible. Correction of artifacts requires auxiliary information such as study sample sizes, study means and standard deviations, estimates of reliability, and so on.

The complexity of formulas depends on two things: (1) the extent of variation in artifacts and (2) the extent of variation in actual correlations. Formulas for meta-analysis would be simplest if artifacts were homogeneous across studies, that is, if all studies had the same sample size, all had the same reliability for the independent and dependent variables, all had the same standard deviations, and so forth. If artifacts were homogeneous, then the primary calculations would all be simple averages and simple variances. In actuality, artifacts vary from study to study; hence, more complicated weighted averages are necessary.

If there is nonartifactual variation in actual construct-level correlations, that variation must be caused by some aspect of the studies that varies from one study to the next, that is, a "moderator" variable. If the meta-analyst anticipates variation in actual correlations, then studies will be coded for aspects that are thought to be potential moderators. For example, studies can be coded as based on white-collar or blue-collar workers. If the variation in actual correlations is large, then the key question is this: Is the moderator variable one of those we have identified as potential moderators? If we find that some coded study characteristics are large moderators, then the overall meta-analysis is not particularly important. The key meta-analyses will be those carried out on the moderator study subsets where the variation in actual correlations is smaller in magnitude (and perhaps 0).

Study Artifacts

We have identified 11 artifacts that alter the size of the study correlation in comparison to the actual correlation. These artifacts are listed in Table 2.1 along with typical substantive examples from the personnel selection research literature. The most damaging artifact in narrative reviews has been sampling error. Sampling error has been falsely interpreted as conflicting findings in almost every area of research in the social sciences. However, some of the other artifacts induce quantitative errors so large as to create qualitatively false conclusions (Hunter & Schmidt, 1987a, 1987b) or to greatly alter the practical implications of findings (Schmidt, 1992, 1996, 2010; Schmidt & Hunter, 1977, 1981). This is especially important to consider when several artifacts work in conjunction. A more technical discussion of research artifacts can be found in Schmidt, Le, and Oh (2009). With the exception of sampling error, other methods of meta-analysis ignore the biasing effects of these artifacts. Only the methods of psychometric meta-analysis presented in this book address these artifacts.

SAMPLING ERROR

Sampling error affects the correlation coefficient additively and nonsystematically. If the actual correlation is denoted ρ and the sample correlation r, then sampling error is added to the sample correlation in the formula

$$r = \rho + e \tag{2.1}$$

Table 2.1 Study artifacts that alter the value of outcome measures (with examples from personnel selection research).

1. Sampling error:
   Study validity will vary randomly from the population value because of sampling error.

2. Error of measurement in the dependent variable:
   Study validity will be systematically lower than true validity to the extent that job performance is measured with random error.

3. Error of measurement in the independent variable:
   Study validity for a test will systematically understate the validity of the ability measured because the test is not perfectly reliable.

4. Dichotomization of a continuous dependent variable:
   Turnover, the length of time that a worker stays with the organization, is often dichotomized into "more than . . ." or "less than . . ." where . . . is some arbitrarily chosen interval such as 1 year or 6 months.

5. Dichotomization of a continuous independent variable:
   Interviewers are often told to dichotomize their perceptions into "acceptable" versus "reject."

6. Range variation in the independent variable:
   Study validity will be systematically lower than true validity to the extent that hiring policy causes incumbents to have a lower variation in the predictor than is true of applicants.

7. Attrition artifacts: Range variation in the dependent variable:
   Study validity will be systematically lower than true validity to the extent that there is systematic attrition in workers on performance, as when good workers are promoted out of the population or when poor workers are fired for poor performance.

8. Deviation from perfect construct validity in the independent variable:
   Study validity will vary if the factor structure of the test differs from the appropriate structure of tests for the same trait.

9. Deviation from perfect construct validity in the dependent variable:
   Study validity will differ from true validity if the criterion (e.g., the measure of job performance) is deficient or contaminated.

10. Reporting or transcriptional error:
    Reported study validities differ from actual study validities due to a variety of reporting problems: inaccuracy in coding data, computational errors, errors in reading computer output, and typographical errors by secretaries or by printers.
    Note: These errors can be very large in magnitude.

11. Variance due to extraneous factors that affect the relationship:
    Study validity will be systematically lower than true validity if incumbents differ in experience on the job at the time they are assessed for performance.

The size of the sampling error is primarily determined by the sample size. Because the effect is unsystematic, the sampling error in a single correlation cannot be corrected. Sampling error and the corrections for it in meta-analysis are discussed in detail in Chapters 3 and 4 (for correlations) and in Chapters 6 and 7 (for d values).

ERROR OF MEASUREMENT

Simple error of measurement is the random measurement error assessed as unreliability of the measure. Error of measurement has a systematic multiplicative effect on the correlation. If we denote the actual correlation by ρ and the observed correlation by ρ_o, then

$$\rho_o = a\rho \tag{2.2}$$

where a is the square root of the reliability. Because a is a number less than 1 in magnitude, the size of the correlation is systematically reduced by error of measurement. For a fairly high reliability such as $r_{xx} = .81$ (a typical reliability of a test of general cognitive ability), the correlation is multiplied by $\sqrt{.81}$ or .90, that is, reduced by 10%. For a low reliability of .36 (the average reliability of a supervisor global rating of job performance on a one-item rating scale), the correlation is multiplied by $\sqrt{.36}$ or .60, a reduction of 40%.

There is a separate effect for error of measurement in the independent variable and error of measurement in the dependent variable. Thus, for error in both variables—the usual case—we have

$$\rho_o = ab\rho \tag{2.3}$$

where a is the square root of the reliability of the independent variable and b is the square root of the reliability of the dependent variable. For a test of general cognitive ability predicting the immediate supervisor's rating on a single global item, the correlation would be multiplied by $(.90)(.60) = .54$. That is nearly a 50% reduction.

The necessity of correcting for the biasing effects of measurement error is widely recognized (e.g., see Hedges, 2009b; Matt & Cook, 2009). Different procedures for estimating reliability capture different sources of random error of measurement. In the next chapter (Chapter 3), we discuss these procedures and point out which types of reliability are needed in particular research situations.

DICHOTOMIZATION

Despite its considerable disadvantages, dichotomization of continuous variables is quite common in the literature (MacCallum, Zhang, Preacher, & Rucker, 2002). If a continuous variable is dichotomized, then the point biserial correlation for the new dichotomized variable will be less than the correlation for the continuous variable. If the regression is bivariate normal, the effect of dichotomizing one of the variables is given by

$$\rho_0 = a\rho$$

where a depends on the extremeness of the split induced by the dichotomization. Let P be the proportion in the "high" end of the split and let $Q = 1 - P$ be the proportion in the "low" end of the split. Let c be the point in the normal distribution that divides the distribution into proportions P and Q. For example, $c = -1.28$ divides the distribution into the bottom 10% versus the top 90%. Let the normal ordinate at c be denoted $\phi(c)$. Then

$$a = \phi(c) / \sqrt{PQ} \tag{2.4}$$

The smallest reduction in the correlation occurs for a median, or 50–50, split, where $a = .80$, a 20% reduction in the correlation.

If both variables are dichotomized, there is a double reduction in the correlation. The exact formula is more complicated than just the product of an "a" for the independent variable and a "b" for the dependent variable. The exact formula is that for the tetrachoric correlation. However, Hunter and Schmidt (1990a) showed that the double product is a very close approximation under the conditions holding in most current meta-analyses. Thus, the attenuation produced by double dichotomization is given by

$$\rho_0 = ab\rho$$

If both variables are split 50–50, the correlation is attenuated by approximately

$$\rho_0 = (.80)(.80)\rho = .64\rho$$

that is, by 36%. For splits more extreme than 50–50, there is even greater attenuation. If one variable has a 90–10 split and the other variable has a 10–90 split, then the double-product estimate of attenuation is

$$\rho_o = (.59)(.59)\rho = .35\rho$$

That is, there is a 65% reduction in the correlation. If the actual correlation is greater than $\rho = .30$, then the reduction is even greater than that predicted by the double-product formula (Hunter & Schmidt, 1990a).

RANGE VARIATION IN THE INDEPENDENT VARIABLE

Because the correlation is a standardized slope, its size depends on the extent of variation in the independent variable. At one extreme, in a population in which there is perfect homogeneity (no variance) in the independent variable, the correlation with any dependent variable will be 0. At the other extreme, if we fix the amount of error about the regression line and then consider populations in which the variance of the independent variable progressively increases, the population correlations increase eventually to an upper limit of 1.00. If correlations from different studies are to be compared, then differences in the correlations due to differences in spread (variance) in the independent variable must be controlled. This is the problem of range variation in the independent variable.

The solution to range variation is to define a reference population and express all correlations in terms of that reference population. We will now discuss how this is done when range restriction (or range enhancement) is produced by direct truncation on the independent variable measure (direct range restriction). For example, suppose only the top 30% on an employment test are hired (range restriction). Or suppose a researcher includes only the top and bottom 10% of subjects on an attitude measure (range enhancement). (We discuss *indirect* range restriction later in this section and in more detail in Chapter 3.) If the regression of the dependent variable onto the independent variable is linear and homoscedastic (bivariate normality is a special case of this), and there is direct truncation on the independent variable, then there is a formula (presented in Chapter 3) that computes what the correlation in a given population would be if the standard deviation were the same as in the reference population. This same formula can be used in reverse to compute the effect of studying the correlation in a population with a standard deviation different from that of the reference population. The standard deviations can be compared by computing the ratio of standard deviations in the two groups. Let u_X be the ratio of the study population standard deviation divided by the reference group population. That is,

$u_X = SD_{study} / SD_{ref}$. Then the study population correlation is related to the reference group population by

$$\rho_o = a\rho$$

where

$$a = u_X / [(u_X^2 - 1)\rho^2 + 1]^{1/2} \qquad (2.5)$$

This expression for the multiplier contains the actual correlation ρ in the formula. In practice, it is the attenuated correlation ρ_o that is observed. A useful algebraic identity in terms of ρ_o was derived by Callender and Osburn (1980):

$$a = [u_X^2 + \rho_o^2 (1 - u_X^2)]^{1/2} \qquad (2.6)$$

The multiplier a will be greater than 1.00 if the study standard deviation is larger than the reference standard deviation. The multiplier a will be less than 1.00 if the study standard deviation is smaller than the reference standard deviation.

There are two cases in which range variation produced by direct selection appears in the empirical literature: (1) scientifically produced artificial variation and (2) variation that arises from situation constraints. Scientific variation can be produced by manipulation of the data. The most frequent of these infrequent cases are those in which the scientist creates an artificially high variation by deliberately excluding middle cases (Osburn, 1978). For example, a psychologist studying anxiety might use an anxiety inventory test to preselect as "high" or "low" those in the top 10% and bottom 10%, respectively. The correlation between anxiety and the dependent variable calculated in this selected group will be larger than the correlation in the original (reference) population. The increase in the correlation would be determined by the increase in the standard deviation of the independent variable. If the original population standard deviation were 1.00, then the standard deviation in a group composed of the top and bottom 10% would be 1.80. For this artificially inflated range variation, the multiplier would be

$$a = 1.80 / [(1.80^2 - 1)\rho^2 + 1]^{1/2}$$
$$= 1.80 / [1 + 3.24\rho^2]^{1/2}$$

For example, if the reference correlation were .30, the multiplier would be 1.58 and the study correlation would be .48, a 58% increase in the correlation. In a small-sample study, this increase in the study correlation would greatly increase the statistical power and, hence, make the significance test work much better. That is, the significance test would have higher statistical power to detect the correlation (Osburn, 1978).

In field studies, the range variation is usually range restriction. For example, suppose a football team measures the speed of applicants running the 40-yard dash. If only those in the top half were selected, then the standard deviation among those considered would be only 60% as large as the standard deviation among all applicants. The applicant correlation between speed and overall performance would be reduced by the multiplier

$$a = .60 / [(.60^2 - 1)\rho^2 + 1]^{1/2}$$
$$= .60 / [1 - .64\rho^2]^{1/2}$$

If the correlation were $\rho = .50$ for applicants, the multiplier would be .65, and the correlation among those selected would be reduced to

$$\rho_0 = a\rho = .65(.50) = .33$$

a 34% reduction in the correlation.

In addition to the direct range restriction or enhancement discussed here, range restriction can also be indirect. For example, suppose subjects who volunteer (sign up) to participate in a study are self-selected—for example, they are mostly on the high end of the extroversion distribution. Their standard deviation *(SD)* on an extroversion measure is lower than that of the general population. This is indirect range restriction. Suppose we know that people in a certain job were not hired using the test we are studying but we have no record of how they were hired. Yet we find that their *SD* on the test we are studying is smaller than the *SD* for the applicant population, indicating the presence of range restriction. Again, this is a case of indirect range restriction. In indirect range restriction, people are not selected directly based on scores on the independent variable but on other variables that are correlated with the independent variable. Occasionally, we know or can find the scores on the related variables they were selected on—but this is rare. As in the preceding examples, we typically do not know how the range restriction was produced—but we know that it occurred because the sample *SD* is smaller than the population *SD*. Most range restriction in real data is, in fact, of this sort (Hunter et al., 2006; Linn et al., 1981a; Mendoza & Mumford, 1987).

Indirect range restriction of this sort reduces correlations more than direct range restriction (Hunter et al., 2006; Mendoza & Mumford, 1987). To determine how large this reduction is, we can still use the formula for the attenuation factor "*a*," given previously, but we now have to use a different ratio of *SD*s. Instead of the ratio of observed *SD*s (called u_X), we must use the ratio of true score *SD*s (called u_T). This ratio must be computed using a special formula. This ratio is also used in the formula for correcting for indirect range restriction. Both direct and indirect range restriction and their associated formulas are discussed in Chapters 3 and 4. Mendoza and Mumford (1987) were the first to derive formulas for correcting for this (ubiquitous) form of indirect range restriction. Developments relating these corrections to meta-analysis were presented by Hunter et al. (2006). The availability of these formulas greatly increases the accuracy of meta-analyses involving range restriction. The necessity of correcting for the biases created by range variation is widely recognized (e.g., see Matt & Cook, 2009).

The correction for indirect range restriction presented in Hunter et al. (2006) is based on the assumption that any range restriction that exists on the dependent variable (y) is fully mediated (i.e., caused by) range restriction on the independent variable (x). This means that range restriction on the third variable (called s) is not a direct cause of range restriction on y; the third variable directly causes range restriction only on x. As noted by Hunter et al. (2006), in most contexts, this assumption is likely to hold (or hold to a close enough approximation). But in cases in which this assumption is substantially violated, the Hunter et al. (2006) correction is less accurate (Le & Schmidt, 2006). A method of correcting for indirect range restriction has recently been developed, based on earlier work by Bryant and Gokhale (1972), that does not require this assumption (Le, Schmidt, & Oh, 2013). However, this method requires the user to know the range restriction ratio (u) for the dependent variable (y), which is not required by the Hunter et al. method. In personnel selection, the y measure is job performance, and its SD in the applicant population (i.e., its unrestricted SD) is virtually impossible to estimate. So this method of correction cannot be used in studies in which the dependent variable is job performance or other behaviors on the job. More generally, it cannot be used with dependent variable measures for which data do not exist on a broader population that allows computation of an unrestricted SD. This includes many types of behavioral measures used in psychological research. But in studies focused on the relation between psychological or organizational constructs (e.g., between job satisfaction and organizational commitment), it may be possible to estimate the needed u ratio based on some broader population SD (e.g., from national norms or workforce norms). In such cases, the Le et al. (2013) method can be used, and if the fundamental assumption underlying the Hunter et al. (2006) method is violated in such data, the Le et al. method will produce more accurate results than will the Hunter et al. method.

RANGE VARIATION IN THE DEPENDENT VARIABLE

Range variation on the dependent variable is usually produced by attrition artifacts. For example, in personnel selection, the study correlation is computed on current workers (i.e., incumbents) because data on job performance are available only on those hired. However, workers with poor performance are often fired or quit voluntarily. Those who participate in the study will be only those still on the job. This population will differ from applicants because of that attrition. Attrition also occurs in longitudinal studies, whether correlational or experimental. In experimental studies, such attrition reduces the standard deviation, which distorts the d value statistic.

There is one special case of attrition artifacts that can be eliminated with statistical formulas: the case in which there is no range restriction on the independent variable. If there is selection on the dependent variable, this will cause induced selection on any independent variable correlated with it. Assume that there is no selection other than this form of induced selection. In such a case, attrition artifacts can be treated statistically as range variation on the dependent variable. Statistically, the independent and dependent variables are symmetrically related to the correlation coefficient. The special case of attrition artifacts described previously exactly reverses this symmetry. Thus, the formulas are the same, except that the standard deviation ratio u is defined by the dependent variable rather than by the independent variable (i.e., it becomes u_Y instead of u_X). In such a case, range restriction on the dependent variable may be either direct or indirect. If it is direct, the correction formulas for direct range restriction should be used. If indirect, the correction formulas for indirect range restriction should be used. However, as noted earlier, it is often not possible to estimate u_Y because the unrestricted SD_Y is not known.

In personnel selection, most studies are affected by both range restriction on the independent variable and by attrition artifacts on the dependent variable (in addition to terminating poor performers, employers also promote good performers). However, at present, there are no exact statistical methods for simultaneously correcting for both range restriction and attrition artifacts, even in the case of direct range restriction. The underlying mathematical problem is that selection on one variable changes the regression for the other variable in a complex way so that the regression is no longer linear and homoscedastic. For example, when there is selection on the predictor, the (reverse) regression of the predictor onto job performance is no longer linear and homoscedastic.

However, Alexander, Carson, Alliger, and Carr (1987) proposed an approximation method for making such a "double" correction for range restriction. These authors noted that after one has selected directly on the independent variable, the regression of the independent variable onto the dependent variable (the "reverse regression") is no longer linear and homoscedastic. Thus, the slope of that regression line will not remain the same when direct restriction is introduced on the dependent variable. They conjectured, however, that it might not change much. The same is true for homoscedasticity: The conditional variance will not remain exactly the same after the second truncation, but perhaps it does not change by much. If both changes are small, then the assumption of no change would yield an approximation equation for correction of range restriction, which might be accurate enough for practical purposes. They derived their equation for a special case of double range restriction: double truncation. That is, they assumed that the range restriction is direct on both variables and is caused by a double threshold: Any data point is lost if the independent variable is less than an x cutoff value or if the dependent variable is less than a y cutoff value. Thus, in the study population—what they call the "doubly truncated population"—the only people remaining are those for whom both variables are above the respective thresholds. In the case of personnel selection, this would correspond to a situation in which hiring was done using only the test and using it with a fixed threshold and where termination from the job was based on a specific fixed performance-level threshold. There is probably no actual selection situation that fits the double-truncation model, but it is a good mathematical beginning point. Alexander et al. (1987) tested their correction approximation for various double-truncation combinations. They varied each cutoff value independently from −2.0 standard deviations below the mean (which eliminates only the bottom 2.5% of cases) to + 2.0 standard deviations (where 97.5% of cases are eliminated). They varied the untruncated population correlation from −.90 to +.90. The accuracy of this method is quite good: 84% of their estimated values are within 3% of the correct value. The worst fit is for the population correlation of .50. For that value, the corrected correlations are as much as 6% too high in 8.6% of the combinations. The combinations where the fit is poorer are the combinations where there is high selection on both variables and where the two cutoff scores are about equal. This would be predicted by the fact that the formula works perfectly for direct range restriction on one variable only. The cases showing the greatest inaccuracy may not be very realistic. If the cutoff is 1.0 standard deviation above the mean for both variables, then the truncated population usually represents little more than 3% of the untruncated population. Elimination of 97% of the original population would probably rarely occur in real data.

The findings for absolute accuracy are even more promising. Alexander et al. (1987) found that 90% of corrected correlations differ by no more than .02 from the actual correlation. In fact, if the corrected correlation is rounded to two places, the estimated corrected correlation is within .02 in 94% of cases. In no case was their formula off by more than .03. The poorest fit is for a population correlation of .60, where 17% of cases were off by .03. The cases of poor absolute fit were essentially the same as the cases with poor percentage fit: the cases of equally severe selection on both variables. The method of Alexander et al. is certainly accurate enough for practical purposes. The obvious next question is, Does the formula remain accurate for the more common and therefore more realistic case of indirect selection? Our calculations indicate that the formula is even more accurate in that case. The contribution of Alexander et al. appears to be a major breakthrough in this area.

IMPERFECT CONSTRUCT VALIDITY IN THE INDEPENDENT VARIABLE

This section is considerably longer than the other sections on study artifacts. In our judgment, however, this is unavoidable because it is essential to develop an understanding of how study outcomes are distorted by departures from perfect construct validity. This section and the following section are of necessity based on path analysis. We have tried to make the discussion as simple as possible, and we believe most readers will be able to follow it.

The independent variable used in a given study may suffer from either of two kinds of error of measurement: random error or systematic error. The effect of random error was discussed under the label "error of measurement." The extent to which a measure is free of random error is measured by the coefficient of reliability of that measure. This section treats systematic error under the label "imperfect construct validity." The phrase "construct invalidity" would also be correct grammatically, but there are many who would react to the word *invalidity* in an absolute sense. That is, some would react to the word *invalidity* as if it meant "completely invalid" and would disregard the study. Actually, it is infrequent that a study independent variable is so construct invalid that the study should be disregarded. Instead, imperfect construct validity may be dealt with adequately in any of three ways: (1) by using a statistical correction formula, (2) by treating variations in measurement strategy as a potential moderator variable, or (3) (for minor departures from perfect validity) by ignoring the imperfection. If the imperfection is ignored, then the study correlation is attenuated by an amount proportional to the quantitative departure from perfect construct validity. If there is variation across studies in the extent of construct validity and it is ignored, that variation contributes to uncontrolled artifact variation in the residual variance computed as the final step in meta-analysis. That is, ignored variation in construct validity would have the same appearance as a real moderator variable.

Construct validity is a quantitative question, not a qualitative distinction such as "valid" or "invalid"; it is a matter of degree. In most cases, construct validity can be quantified as a correlation coefficient, namely, the correlation between the variable intended and the variable as measured. We will define the construct validity of the independent variable measure as the correlation between the intended independent variable and the actual independent variable used in the study when both variables are measured without random error (measurement error). This definition is used to distinguish between the effects of random and systematic error.

The error in the actual study used will be assessed by a correlation called the "operational quality" of the measure. The operational quality is determined in part by the extent of construct validity and in part by the reliability of the study variable.

The effect of systematic error on the correlation between independent and dependent variables depends not only on the extent of construct validity of the study independent variable but also on the qualitative structure of the causal relationships among the three variables: the intended or desired independent variable, the study independent variable, and the dependent variable. In certain cases, the effect of systematic error is simple: The correlation between the independent and dependent variable is multiplied by the construct validity of the study independent variable. However, there are cases where this simple relationship does not hold. In such cases, the meta-analyst may not be able to use the study.

Consider an example in which we want to examine the relationship between general cognitive ability and performance in recreational activities. Because performance in recreational activities depends on learning, we hypothesize that people with high cognitive ability will perform better than average. We find a survey study of a large bowling league in which one of the variables is the bowling performance average. The study has no measure of general cognitive ability, but it does have a measure of amount of education. Suppose we use the education variable as an imperfect indicator for cognitive ability. In the language of econometrics, we use education as a "proxy variable" for ability. How good a proxy is amount of education for cognitive ability? One answer would be the correlation between education and ability. However, there are two other considerations that enter into this decision. First, there is the question of which correlation to use: the correlation between ability and actual education or the correlation between ability and the study measure of education. This is the issue of distinguishing between construct validity and reliability. Second, there is the issue of the relationship between the proxy variable and the dependent variable. For certain kinds of relationships, the effect of using a proxy variable is easily quantified and can be computed from the coefficient of construct validity. For other relationships, the effect may be much more complicated. In such complicated cases, use of the proxy variable may be problematic.

To show the distinction between systematic and random error of measurement, suppose the study does not have a perfect measure of education. Although we would like a measure of the exact amount of education, the study recorded only the measure

$X = 0$ if the person did not finish high school,

$X = 1$ if the person finished high school but not college,

$X = 2$ if the person finished college.

Figure 2.1   Path model showing the causal nature of imperfect construct validity in using education as a proxy variable for general cognitive ability.

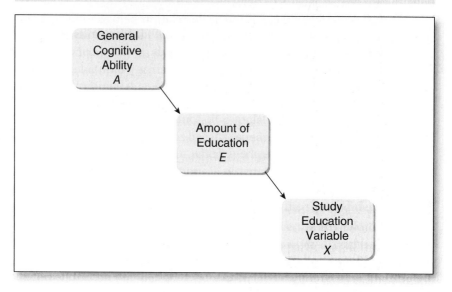

There are, then, two kinds of error in the study variable. There is the systematic error produced by using education instead of ability, and there is the random error produced by using an imperfect measure of education. This situation is illustrated in the path diagram in Figure 2.1.

In Figure 2.1, general cognitive ability is the independent variable that we wanted to measure. Thus, the ability variable in the path diagram is implicitly assumed to be perfectly measured. Figure 2.1 shows an arrow from general cognitive ability to amount of education where amount of education is assumed to be perfectly measured. This represents the assumption that ability is one of the causal determinants of amount of education. If ability were the sole cause of differences in the amount of education, then ability and education would be perfectly correlated and there would be no problem in using education as a proxy for ability. In fact, the correlation between ability and education is only about .50, and there is thus a considerable discrepancy between the two measures. The size of the correlation between ability and education determines the size of the path coefficient from ability to education and, hence, measures the extent of systematic error in substituting education for ability. The correlation between ability and education where both are perfectly measured is the construct validity of education as a measure of ability. The construct validity of education as a measure of ability is the first path coefficient in Figure 2.1.

Figure 2.1 also shows an arrow from amount of education to the study education variable X. Qualitatively, this arrow represents the introduction of random error into the measure of education. Quantitatively, the path coefficient measures the amount of random error. The path coefficient for this arrow is the correlation between actual amount of education and the study education measure. This correlation is less than 1.00 to the extent that the study measurement procedure introduces random error into the estimate of education. The square of the correlation between actual and estimated education is the reliability of the study measure of education.

The total discrepancy between the intended independent variable of ability and the study measure of education is measured by the correlation between the two. According to path analysis, the correlation between ability and the study measure of education is the product of the two path coefficients. That is,

$$r_{AX} = r_{AE}\, r_{EX}. \tag{2.7}$$

Let us define the phrase "the operational quality of the proxy variable" to be the correlation between the intended variable and the study proxy variable. Then we have shown that the operational quality is the product of two numbers: the construct validity of the proxy variable, r_{AE}, and the square root of the reliability of the proxy variable, $r_{EX} = \sqrt{r_{XX}}$.

The key semantic issue in the definition of the phrase "construct validity" is to choose between two correlations: the correlation between the intended variable and the proxy variable as perfectly measured, or the correlation between the intended variable and the study variable as measured with random error. The substantial and conceptual meaning of the phrase "construct validity" is represented by the correlation between intended and proxy variables measured without random error. Thus, we label that correlation as "construct validity." On the other hand, the total impact of substitution depends also on the amount of random error in the study variable, and, hence, we need a name for that correlation as well. The name used here is "operational quality." We can thus say that the operational quality of the study proxy variable depends on the construct validity of the proxy variable and the reliability of the study measure. In a simple case such as that of Figure 2.1, the operational quality is the product of the construct validity and the square root of the reliability of the proxy measure.

We can now consider the main question: What is the effect of systematic error in the measure of cognitive ability on the observed correlation between ability and performance? This is answered by comparing two population correlations: the desired correlation between cognitive ability and performance versus the correlation between the study measure of education and performance. To answer this question, we must know the causal relationship among education, ability, and performance. Consider the causal model shown in Figure 2.2.

Figure 2.2 shows an arrow from cognitive ability to bowling performance. This arrow represents the hypothesized effect of differences in learning ability on differences in performance. Figure 2.2 shows no causal

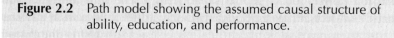

Figure 2.2 Path model showing the assumed causal structure of ability, education, and performance.

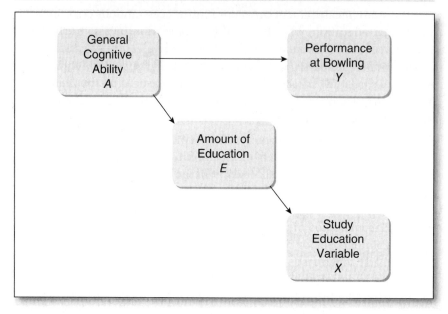

arrow from education to performance. This corresponds to the assumption that the material learned in mastery of bowling does not depend on the specific material learned in school. Thus, among people matched on cognitive ability, there would be no correlation between amount of education and performance at bowling. According to this path model, ability is a common causal antecedent to both performance and education. Therefore, the correlation between the study education variable X and the performance measure Y is the product

$$r_{XY} = r_{AE} r_{EX} r_{AY} \qquad (2.8)$$

Thus, the desired population correlation r_{AY} is multiplied by two other correlations: the construct validity of education as a measure of ability, r_{AE}, and the square root of the reliability of the study education measure, r_{EX}. Denote the product of these two correlations by a. That is, define a by

$$a = r_{AE} r_{EX} \qquad (2.9)$$

Then a is the operational quality of the study independent variable as a measure of cognitive ability. The desired population correlation r_{AY} is related to the study population r_{XY} by

$$r_{XY} = a r_{AY} \qquad (2.10)$$

Because *a* is a fraction, this is an attenuation formula. The observed correlation is attenuated by the factor *a*. That is, the lower the operational quality of the study independent variable, the greater the attenuation of the study correlation between independent and dependent variables.

The total attenuation of the effect size is given by the net attenuation factor, which is the operational quality of the study independent variable. However, this net attenuation factor is itself the product of two other attenuation factors. One factor is the square root of the study variable reliability. This is the familiar attenuation factor for random error of measurement. The second factor is the construct validity of the study variable as a measure of the intended independent variable. Thus, one factor measures the effect of random error while the second factor measures the effect of systematic error.

The previous example shows that under certain conditions, the effect of systematic error on the study effect size is to multiply the desired population effect size by the operational quality of the study proxy variable. A second example will show that this simple formula does not always work. Finally, we will present a third example, which shows a different causal structure for which the same simple attenuation formula can be used.

Consider now a meta-analysis on the relationship between general cognitive ability and income. Suppose the study has no measure of ability but has the same imperfect measure of amount of education as considered in the first example. The causal structure for these variables will differ from

Figure 2.3   Path model showing the assumed causal structure of ability, income, and education.

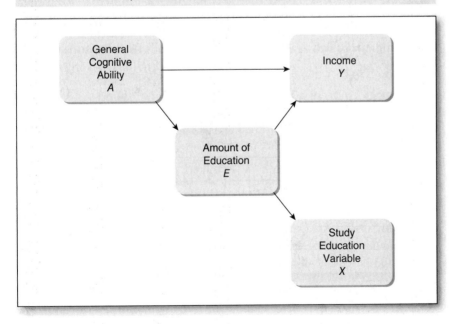

the causal structure in Figure 2.2. The assumed causal model for ability, education, and income is shown in Figure 2.3.

Figure 2.3 shows an arrow from general cognitive ability to income. This corresponds to the fact that once people are working at the same job, differences in cognitive ability are a prime determinant of job performance and, hence, of how high the person rises in the job and of income level. However, Figure 2.3 also shows an arrow from amount of education to income. The amount of education determines what job the person starts in and, hence, sets limits on how high the person will rise. This arrow from education to income distinguishes the structure of the causal models in Figures 2.2 and 2.3. The path coefficients for the arrows to the dependent variable are no longer simple correlations but are beta weights, the multiple regression weights for cognitive ability, b_{AY}, and education, b_{EY}, in jointly predicting income. The study effect size correlation r_{XY} is given by path analysis to be

$$
\begin{aligned}
r_{XY} &= r_{EX}(b_{EY} + r_{AE}b_{AY}) \\
&= r_{AE}r_{EX}b_{AY} + r_{EX}b_{EY}
\end{aligned}
\tag{2.11}
$$

By contrast, the simple education formula would have been

$$
r_{XY} = r_{AE}\, r_{EX}\, r_{AY}
\tag{2.12}
$$

In both models, the effect of random error of measurement is the same. In both models, it is true that

$$
r_{XY} = r_{EX}\, r_{EY}
\tag{2.13}
$$

The difference between the models lies in the structure of the correlation between education and income. If education has a causal impact on income, as in Figure 2.3, then the correlation between education and income is

$$
r_{EY} = r_{AE}\, b_{AY} + b_{EY}
\tag{2.14}
$$

whereas in the simpler model, the correlation would have been

$$
r_{EY} = r_{AE}\, r_{AY}
\tag{2.15}
$$

The larger the causal impact of education on income, the greater the difference between the models. The most extreme case would be one in which the assumption (known to be false) is made that there is no direct causal impact of ability at all. That is, assume that the beta weight for ability is 0; that is, $b_{AY} = 0$. Then, for the complex model,

$$
r_{EY} = r_{AY} / r_{AE}
\tag{2.16}
$$

instead of

$$r_{EY} = r_{AY} r_{AE} \qquad (2.17)$$

That is, in this extreme case, the effect of substitution would be to divide the effect size correlation by the construct validity rather than to multiply the effect size correlation by the construct validity!

The key to the product rule in the previous examples is the assumption that the only causal connection between the dependent variable and the proxy variable is the intended independent variable. In the first example, the intended independent variable (ability) is causally prior to the proxy variable, and the proxy variable has no link to the dependent variable. It is also possible to have the proxy variable be causally prior to the intended variable. However, the product rule will fail if there is any path from the proxy variable to the dependent variable that does not go through the intended variable.

Consider a third example. Suppose we hypothesize that teachers with a strong knowledge of their subject matter will do a better job of teaching due

Figure 2.4 Path model showing the assumed causal structure of teacher's specialized knowledge, teacher's overall GPA, teacher's grade point average in selected education courses, and student performance.

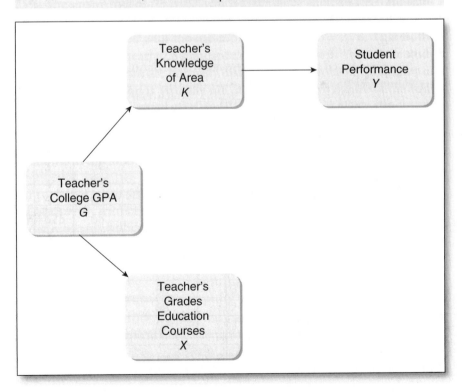

in part to having more time saved by eliminating look-up tasks, having more cognitive options for presentation, and so on. A large metropolitan high school system has national test scores for students that can be averaged for each class. Thus, we have a dependent variable for student performance. However, it is impractical to construct knowledge tests for all the teaching areas. Assume that the amount learned in a specialty is primarily a function of how well the teacher learns and how much the teacher studies in general. Learning in general would be measured by college grade point average (GPA). So, instead of a specialized knowledge test, we use the teacher's college grade point average as a proxy variable for knowledge of area. The total grade point average is not available, but a code for grades in key education courses is stored in the computer. The design for this construct validity problem is shown as a path diagram in Figure 2.4.

Figure 2.4 shows an arrow from the teacher's GPA to the teacher's knowledge of area. Thus, the proxy variable is causally prior to the intended independent variable. There is no other path from GPA to the dependent variable. The path coefficient from GPA to knowledge is the construct validity of GPA as a measure of specialized knowledge. This path coefficient measures the extent of systematic error in the GPA measure. There is an arrow from overall GPA to GPA in the key education courses. The size of this path coefficient measures the extent of random error in the study variable. The correlation between the study grade point variable X and the performance measure Y is the product

$$r_{XY} = r_{KG}\, r_{GX}\, r_{KY} \tag{2.18}$$

Thus, the desired population correlation r_{KY} is multiplied by two other population correlations: the construct validity of GPA as a measure of knowledge (r_{KG}) and the square root of the reliability of the study GPA measure (r_{GX}). Denote the product of these two correlations by a. That is, define a by

$$a = r_{KG}\, r_{GX} \tag{2.19}$$

Then a is the operational quality of the study independent variable as a measure of specialized knowledge. The desired population correlation r_{KY} is related to the study population r_{XY} by

$$r_{XY} = a r_{KY} \tag{2.20}$$

Because a is a fraction, this is an attenuation formula. The observed correlation is attenuated by the factor a. That is, the lower the operational quality of the study independent variable, the greater the attenuation of the study correlation between the independent and dependent variable.

We can now summarize the two most common cases in which construct validity of the independent variable can be quantified and where systematic error of measurement is easily corrected. The imperfect construct validity will be correctable if the imperfect measure or proxy variable stands in one of two causal relationships to the intended independent variable and the dependent variable. Consider the path diagrams in Figure 2.5. Figure 2.5a shows the imperfect variable as causally dependent on the intended independent variable and as having no other connection to the dependent variable. Figure 2.5b shows the imperfect variable as causally antecedent to the intended independent variable and as having no other connection to the dependent variable. The key to both path diagrams is the assumption that there is no extraneous causal path from the imperfect variable to the dependent variable that does not go through the intended independent variable.

Figure 2.5a shows the case in which the intended independent variable is antecedent to the study independent variable. This case can be described by saying that the study variable is influenced by "extraneous factors."

This is the most common case for a proxy variable. For example, many employers use educational credentials as a proxy variable for general cognitive ability (Gottfredson, 1985). Although cognitive ability is an important determinant of amount of education, education is influenced by many other variables (such as family wealth) as well. The path diagram in Figure 2.5a assumes that these other influences are not correlated with the dependent variable (say, job performance) and, hence, are "extraneous factors" from the point of view of using the study variable as a proxy variable.

Figure 2.5b shows the case in which the study variable is causally antecedent to the intended variable. For example, the intended variable in a study of political values might be "political sophistication." The study variable might be general cognitive ability. Although cognitive ability is an important determinant of sophistication, it does not measure other causal determinants of political sophistication such as political socialization by politically active parents.

In either Figure 2.5a or 2.5b, the correlation between the observed study independent variable X'' and the dependent variable Y can be written as a triple product:

$$r_{X''Y} = r_{X''X'} r_{X'X} r_{XY} \qquad (2.21)$$

In the notation of the article by Gottfredson (1985), this triple product would be

$$r_o = abr \qquad (2.22)$$

where

$a = r_{X''X'} =$ the square root of the reliability of X'' and

$b = r_{X'X} =$ the construct validity of X'.

Figure 2.5   Path models for cases in which the effect of imperfect construct
validity is to attenuate the desired effect size correlation by
multiplying the effect size by the construct validity of the proxy
variable ($r_{xx'}$ in both cases).

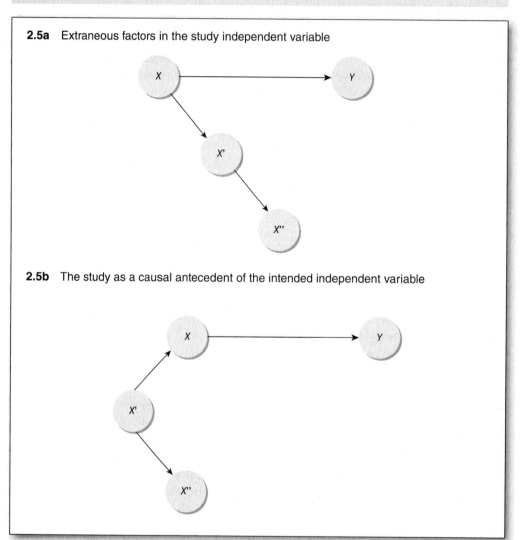

2.5a   Extraneous factors in the study independent variable

2.5b   The study as a causal antecedent of the intended independent variable

If X' were a perfect measure of X, then the value of b would be 1.00 and
the triple product would reduce to the equation for random error of measurement. If the measure is imperfect, then b will be less than 1.00, and the
triple product will represent a reduction beyond that caused by error of
measurement. That is, ab will be less than a to the extent that X' is not
perfectly construct valid.

Note that, in this path diagram, X is assumed to be perfectly measured.
Thus, path coefficient b is the correlation between X' and X corrected for
attenuation due to random error of measurement. Note that parameter a

is the usual square root of the reliability of X'' that would be used to correct $r_{X''Y}$ for attenuation due to error in X''. The presence of the third factor b represents the difference between a model of imperfect construct validity and a model of random error of measurement.

As an example, suppose education is used as a proxy for general cognitive ability and assume that the "extraneous" factors in education are unrelated to the dependent variable. Assume that the correlation between ability and education is .50 and that the reliability of the study education measure is .90. The multipliers would be given by $a = \sqrt{.90} = .95$ and $b = .50$. The study correlation would be related to the actual correlation by

$$r_o = abr = (.95)(.50)r = .48r.$$

In this example, there would be little error if random error were ignored (a 5% error) but a large error if imperfect construct validity were ignored.

IMPERFECT CONSTRUCT VALIDITY IN THE DEPENDENT VARIABLE

There can also be deviations from perfect construct validity in the dependent variable. Some deviations can be corrected, but some cannot.

Figure 2.6 shows one case in which the effect of imperfect construct validity can be quantified. Figure 2.6a shows the abstract case in which the study variable is causally taken from personnel selection research.

Consider the example in Figure 2.6b: the use of supervisor ratings to measure job performance in a personnel selection validation study. The

Figure 2.6 Correctable imperfect construct validity in the dependent variable.

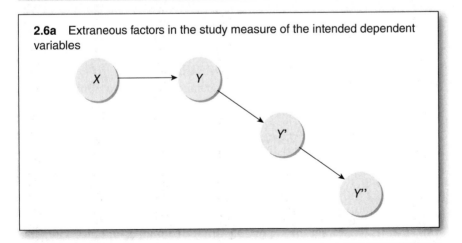

2.6a Extraneous factors in the study measure of the intended dependent variables

(Continued)

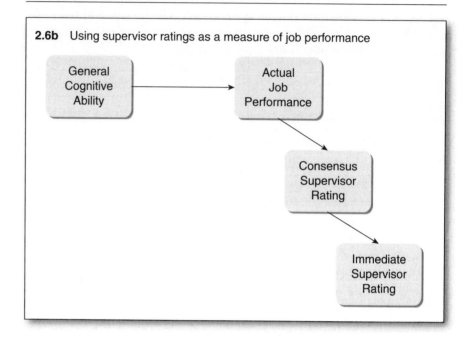

2.6b Using supervisor ratings as a measure of job performance

ideal measure would be an objective measure of job performance such as a construct-valid, perfectly reliable, work sample test. Instead, the study uses supervisor perception (ratings) as the measure. The ideal rating would be a consensus judgment across a population of supervisors. Instead, the observed study variable is the rating of the immediate supervisor. Thus, the idiosyncrasy of that supervisor's perceptions is a part of the error of measurement in the observed ratings. Extraneous factors that may influence human judgment include friendship, physical appearance, moral and/or lifestyle conventionality, and more.

The triple-product rule for this quantifiable form of imperfect construct validity is given by the following path analysis:

$$\rho_{xy''} = \rho_{xy}\rho_{yy'}\rho_{y'y''} \tag{2.23}$$

That is,

$$\rho_o = ab\rho$$

where

ρ_o = the observed correlation,

$a = r_{y'y''}$ = the square root of the reliability of y'',

$b = r_{yy'}$ = the construct validity of y', and

ρ = the true score correlation between ability and actual job performance.

In the case of the example in Figure 2.6b, cumulative empirical data from a meta-analysis indicate that the correlation between actual job performance and consensus ratings is only .52 (Hunter, 1986). The reliability of the immediate supervisor rating depends on the quality of the rating instrument. For a summating rating, the reliability would average .47 (Rothstein, 1990); for a single global rating, the reliability would average .36 (Hunter & Hirsh, 1987; King, Hunter, & Schmidt, 1980). The reduction in validity from using a single global rating measure would be given from $a = \sqrt{.36} = .60$ and $b = .52$; that is,

$$\rho_o = ab\rho = (.60)(.52)\rho = .31\rho$$

a reduction of 69% in the observed correlation.

In this example, the new factors in the dependent variable were not only extraneous to the intended dependent variable but also uncorrelated with the independent variable. However, in some cases, the extraneous variable is related to both the dependent *and* the independent variables. Such cases are more complex, and it is not always possible to correct for the effect of the extraneous variable on the construct validity of the dependent variable. These cases are beyond the scope of this book.

COMPUTATIONAL AND OTHER ERRORS IN THE DATA

The most difficult artifact in meta-analysis is data errors. Bad data can arise from any step in the scientific process. The raw data may be incorrectly recorded or incorrectly entered into the computer. The computer may correlate the wrong variable because the format was incorrectly specified or because a transformation formula was incorrectly written. The sign of the correlation may be wrong because the analyst reverse-scored the variable, but the person who read the output did not know that, or because the reader thought the variable had been reverse-scored when it had not. When computer output is put into tables, the correlation can be incorrectly copied; the sign may be lost or digits may be reversed; or, when the table is published, the typesetter may miscopy the correlation.

These types of errors are much more frequent than we would like to believe (Tukey, 1960; Wolins, 1962). Tukey maintained that all real data sets contain errors. Gulliksen (1986) made the following statement:

> I believe that it is essential to check the data for errors before running my computations. I always wrote an error-checking program and ran the data through it before computing. I find it very interesting that in every set of data I have run, either for myself or someone else, there have always been errors, necessitating going back to the questionnaires and repunching some cards, or perhaps discarding some subjects. (p. 4)

Furthermore, some errors are likely to result in outliers, and outliers have a dramatic inflationary effect on the variance. In a normal distribution, for example, the *SD* is 65%, determined by the highest and lowest 5% of data values (Tukey, 1960). Data errors of various kinds probably account for a substantial portion of the observed variance in correlations and *d* values in many research literatures.

The upshot of this is that virtually every meta-analysis with a large number of correlations and some meta-analyses with a small number of studies will contain some data errors. If the bad data could be located, they could be thrown out. However, the only bad data that can be identified are correlations that are so far out of the distribution that they are clearly outliers. Outlier analysis works best when study samples are at least moderate in size. If sample sizes are small, it is difficult to distinguish true outliers from extremely large sampling errors. (Outlier analysis is discussed in Chapter 5.)

Thus, even if the present list of artifacts were complete (it is not) and even if all known artifacts were controlled (rarely possible), there would still be variation in study outcomes due to data errors. In actual meta-analyses, there is always attenuation and false variation due to unknown and uncontrolled artifacts in addition to bad data. These considerations led Schmidt and Hunter (1977) to propose their "75% rule," which asserted as a rule of thumb that if in any data set known and correctable artifacts account for 75% of the variance in study correlations, it is likely that the remaining 25% is due to uncontrolled artifacts. It is unwise to assume that all unexplained variance is due to real moderator variables, because it is never possible to correct for all artifacts that cause variation across studies (see, e.g., Schmidt et al., 1993).

EXTRANEOUS FACTORS INTRODUCED BY THE STUDY PROCEDURE

The measurement process or observation procedure of the study might cause variation on the dependent variable due to a variable that would not have existed (or that would have been constant) had the study been done perfectly. As an example, consider the effect of job experience in a concurrent validity study of job performance. In personnel selection, applicants can be considered as a cohort. When applicants are compared, they are implicitly being compared as if they were to start work simultaneously. In a concurrent validity study, performance is measured on all current workers, workers with different amounts of experience on the job. This means that workers will differ in performance in part because they differ in job experience (Schmidt, Hunter, & Outerbridge, 1986). This would not be true of applicants hired at the same time. Thus, the differences in experience constitute an extraneous variable created by the study observation procedure.

The abstract path diagram for this process is shown in Figure 2.7a, while Figure 2.7b shows the case for job experience. If there had been no extraneous variable introduced into the situation, the observed correlation would be equivalent to the partial correlation between the independent variable and the dependent variable with the extraneous variable held constant. Because the extraneous variable is not correlated with the independent variable, the formula for the partial correlation is

$$\rho_{xy \times z} = \rho_{xy} / \sqrt{1 - \rho_{zy}^2} \qquad (2.24)$$

This can be regarded as a correction for attenuation due to experience. If we reverse the equation, we obtain the attenuation formula. Let a be the reciprocal of the denominator of the equation for the partial correlation; that is,

$$a = 1 / \sqrt{1 - \rho_{zy}^2} \qquad (2.25)$$

Figure 2.7 Path diagrams for an extraneous variable produced by the study procedure.

2.7a Path diagram for an extraneous variable Z introduced by study procedure

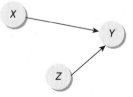

2.7b Experience differences as an extraneous variable produced by concurrent validation procedure

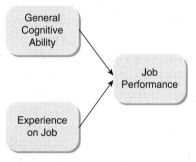

Then

$$\rho_o = a\rho \tag{2.26}$$

The reader may ask why we do not just compute the partial correlation in each individual study. In fact, that would solve the problem. That is, if experience were recorded in the study and the partial correlation were used as the study correlation, then there would be no need for further statistical correction. This would also eliminate the increase in sampling error produced by statistical correction. This correction is similar to that for dichotomization. If the right correlation were given in the original research report (or if the additional correlations necessary to compute it were given), then there would be no need to use after-the-fact statistical correction. This is typically not the case, however, and so correction is needed.

BIAS IN THE SAMPLE CORRELATION

From time to time, statistically sophisticated observers have noted that the sample correlation is not an "unbiased" estimate of the population correlation, where the word *unbiased* is used in the strict sense of mathematical statistics. From this, they have often then leaped to two false conclusions: (1) that the bias is large enough to be visible and (2) that use of the Fisher z transformation eliminates the bias (see, e.g., James, Demaree, & Mulaik, 1986). However, Hunter, Schmidt, and Coggin (1996) showed that, for sample sizes greater than 20, the bias in the correlation coefficient is less than rounding error. Even in meta-analysis, the bias for smaller sample size domains (i.e., $N < 20$) would be trivial in comparison to distortions due to sampling error. They also showed that the positive bias in the Fisher z transformation is always larger than the negative bias in r (especially if the population correlations vary across studies). Thus, it is always less accurate to use the Fisher z transformation. As we will see in Chapter 5, use of the Fisher z transformation can cause serious inaccuracies in random effects meta-analysis models—the meta-analysis model of choice for almost all real data (Hunter & Schmidt, 2000; Schmidt & Hunter, 2003; Schmidt, Oh, & Hayes, 2009). Furthermore, it would be a very rare case in which it would be worthwhile to correct the bias in the correlation coefficient at all. However, so the reader can make his or her own decision, we include the attenuation formula and correction here.

The average sample correlation is slightly smaller than the population correlation. Assume that the population correlation has already been attenuated by all other artifacts. Then the bias in the sample correlation is given to a close approximation (Hotelling, 1953) by

$$E(r) = \rho - \rho(1-\rho^2)/(2N-2) \tag{2.27}$$

In our present multiplier notation, we would write

$$\rho_o = a\rho$$

where the attenuation multiplier is

$$a = 1 - (1 - \rho^2)/(2N - 2) \qquad (2.28)$$

and ρ_o is the expected sample correlation.

The bias is greatest and, therefore, the bias multiplier is smallest if $\rho = .50$, so that

$$a = 1 - .375/(N - 1) \qquad (2.29)$$

In personnel selection research, the median sample size is 68 and the multiplier is, therefore, $1 - .006 = .994$, which differs only trivially from 1.00. Because the typical attenuated correlation is less than .25 in value, the bias in the typical personnel selection research study would be less than the difference between the average sample correlation of .2486 and the population correlation of .25, a difference less than rounding error.

Only in meta-analyses with an average sample size of 10 or less would the bias be visible at the second digit. If correction is desired, then the preceding attenuation formula can be used with the average study correlation as the estimate of ρ. That is, $\hat{\rho} = r/a$, where r is the observed correlation. However, this correction is included in the Hunter-Schmidt meta-analysis programs described in the Appendix to this book. For population correlations less than .50, the attenuation factor is closely approximated by the linear multiplier $(2N - 2)/(2N - 1)$, and the correction for bias is affected by multiplying the observed correlation by $(2N - 1)/(2N - 2)$. This approximation is convenient for use by those who don't use the Hunter-Schmidt meta-analysis programs.

Sampling Error, Statistical Power, and the Interpretation of Research Findings

AN ILLUSTRATION OF STATISTICAL POWER

Traditional methods of interpreting research literatures lead to disastrous errors (Schmidt, 1992, 1996; Schmidt & Hunter, 1997; Schmidt, Ocasio, et al., 1985). For example, consider research on the validity of nontest procedures for predicting job performance as measured by supervisory ratings. Hunter and Hunter (1984) found that the average observed correlation for reference checks was .20, and for interests, it was .08. Consider a predictor of job performance that has a mean observed validity of .10. Suppose this is the population correlation and it is constant across all settings. The attenuated population value of .10 may seem small, but after correction for downward biases due to artifacts, it might correspond to an operational validity of .20 and, hence, might have practical value (Schmidt, Hunter, McKenzie, & Muldrow, 1979). If 19 studies were conducted and arranged by order of observed validity, the results would be as shown in Table 2.2. Table 2.2 presents findings for studies based on three sample sizes: (1) the classic recommended minimum of $N = 30$; (2) the median N of 68 found by Lent, Auerbach, and Levin (1971b) for studies published in the Validity Information Exchange in *Personnel Psychology*; and (3) $N = 400$, a sample size considered by many psychologists to be "large."

Clearly, the correlations in Table 2.2 vary over a wide range. Bearing in mind that the actual value of the correlation is always .10, we will now examine two traditional interpretations of these "findings": (1) that of the naive reviewer who takes observed correlations at face value and does not use significance tests and (2) that of the "more sophisticated" reviewer who applies significance tests.

If the studies are each based on 30 people, the naive reviewer reaches the following conclusions:

1. Six of the 19 studies (or 32%) find negative validities. That is, 32% of the studies show that job performance is predicted in reverse rank order of actual job performance.

2. Using a liberal standard of .20 for "moderate" correlations, in only 32% of the settings does the validity reach even a moderate level.

3. Overall conclusion: In most cases, the procedure is not related to job performance.

If the naive reviewer is faced with 19 studies, each based on $N = 68$, he or she concludes as follows:

1. Four of the 19 studies (or 21%) find negative validity.

2. In only 21% of the settings (4 of 19) does the validity reach the moderate level of .20.

3. Overall conclusion: In most cases, the procedure is not related to job performance.

Naive reviewers do not even begin to reach correct judgments unless the typical study has a sample size of 400 or more. Even at $N = 400$, there is enough sampling error to produce validity coefficients that differ in magnitude by a factor of .18/.02, or 9 to 1.

If each study is based on $N = 400$, the naive reviewer arrives at the following conclusions:

1. No studies find negative validity.

2. No studies report validity even as high as the "moderate" .20 level.

3. Overall conclusion: The selection method predicts performance poorly in all settings and almost not at all in many settings.

It has been a traditional belief that the use of significance tests enhances the accuracy of study interpretations (Hunter, 1997; Schmidt, 1996; Schmidt & Hunter, 1997). So let us examine the interpretations of a reviewer who applies significance tests to the studies in Table 2.2. If the studies are each based on $N = 30$, the reviewer reaches the following conclusions:

1. Only 2 of the 19 studies (11%) find significant validity.

2. The procedure is not valid almost 90% of the time; that is, it is "generally invalid."

Table 2.2   Nineteen studies.

	N = 30	N = 68	N = 400
Study 1	.40**	.30**	.18**
Study 2	.34*	.25*	.16**
Study 3	.29	.23*	.15**
Study 4	.25	.20*	.14**
Study 5	.22	.18	.13**
Study 6	.20	.16	.13**
Study 7	.17	.15	.12**
Study 8	.15	.13	.11**
Study 9	.12	.12	.11**
Study 10	.10	.10	.10**
Study 11	.08	.08	.08*
Study 12	.05	.07	.09*
Study 13	.03	.05	.08*
Study 14	−.00	.04	.08
Study 15	−.02	.02	.07
Study 16	−.05	−.00	.06
Study 17	−.09	−.03	.05
Study 18	−.14	−.05	.04
Study 19	−.20	−.10	.02

*Significant by one-tailed test. **Significant by two-tailed test.

When each study is based on $N = 68$, the reviewer concludes as follows:

1. Only 4 of the 19 studies (21%) find significant validity.

2. Thus, in the overwhelming majority of cases, the procedure is invalid.

The reviewer's conclusions from the $N = 400$ studies are as follows:

1. Only 13 of the 19 studies (68%) find significant validity.

2. Thus, in 32% of the settings, the procedure does not work.

3. Conclusion: The method predicts job performance in some settings but not in others. Further research is needed to determine why it works in some settings but not in others.

These conclusions based on significance tests are *not* more accurate that those of the naive reviewer. With small sample sizes ($N < 400$), the conclusions are no more accurate using the significance test, and, even with a sample size of 400, reviewers relying on traditional interpretations of significance tests do not reach correct conclusions from cumulative research. The reason the significance tests lead to errors of interpretation is that they have a very high error rate. An error is the failure to detect the constant underlying correlation of .10 in a study. The percentage of time that the statistical test will make this error in our example is

	$N = 30$	$N = 68$	$N = 400$
Two-tailed test	92%	88%	48%
One-tailed test	86%	80%	36%

These error rates are very high. The percentage of the studies in which the significance test does *not* make this error is called its statistical power. Statistical power is 100% minus the error rate. For example, when one-tailed tests are used in our 19 studies, and $N = 68$ in each study, the error rate is 80%. The statistical power is $100\% - 80\% = 20\%$. That is, the significance test is correct only 20% of the time. The next section examines statistical power in more detail.

A MORE DETAILED EXAMINATION OF STATISTICAL POWER

The problems created by low statistical power in individual studies are central to the need for meta-analysis. This section explores the question of statistical power in more detail.

Suppose the population correlation between supervisory consideration and job satisfaction is .25 in all settings. This is the correlation prior to corrections for unreliability (measurement error). Now, suppose studies are conducted in a large number of settings, each with $N = 83$. For simplicity, assume that the same instruments are used in all studies to measure these two variables, so reliabilities are constant across studies. Assume also that the subjects in each study are a random sample from the population of all possible employees, and range variation and the other artifacts discussed previously do not vary across studies. Then the average observed correlation across all these studies will be .25, the true value. However, there will be substantial variability due to sampling error; the SD of the correlations will be

$$SD_r = \sqrt{\frac{(1-.25^2)^2}{83-1}} = .103$$

This distribution of correlations is shown on the right in Figure 2.8a. The other distribution in Figure 2.8a is the one that would have resulted if the true population correlation had been $\rho = 0$, instead of $\rho = .25$. This null distribution is the basis of the statistical significance test. Its mean is 0. The SD of the null distribution is not the same as the SD of the real distribution, because the true value of ρ is 0,

$$SD_{NULL} = \sqrt{\frac{(1-0^2)^2}{83-1}} = .110$$

The .05 significance value for a one-tailed test is the point in the null distribution where only 5% of the correlations would be larger than that value. The 5% significance level is thus 1.645 SDs above the mean of the null distribution, that is, above 0. Therefore, to be significant, a study r must be at least as large as $1.645(.110) = .18$. If the true ρ really were 0, only 5% of study correlations would be as large as .18 or larger. That is, the Type I error rate would be 5%. Because $\rho = .25$, and not 0, however, there can be no Type I errors, only Type II errors. What percentage of the study rs will be .18 or larger? If we convert .18 to a z score in the r distribution, we get

$$z = \frac{.18-.25}{.103} = -.68$$

The percentage of values in a normal distribution that is above .68 standard deviations below the mean is .75, as can be determined from any normal curve table. Therefore, the statistical power is .75; 75% of all these studies will obtain a statistically significant correlation. In Figure 2.8a, this represents the area to the right of .18 in the observed r distribution. That area contains 75% of the observed r s. For the remaining 25% of the studies, the traditional conclusion would be that the correlation, being nonsignificant, is 0. This represents the area to the left of .18 in the observed r distribution. That area contains 25% of the observed rs. This conclusion is false; the correlation is always .25, and it has only that one value. Thus, the probability of Type II error (concluding there is no relationship when there is) is .25.

The studies in this example have higher statistical power than many real studies. This is because the true correlation (.25) is larger than is often the case for real-world population correlations. Also, the sample size ($N = 83$) is larger here than is often the case in real studies, further increasing statistical power. For example, the mean validity coefficient for a typical employment test measuring verbal or quantitative aptitude is about .20 before correction for range restriction and criterion unreliability, and sample sizes in the literature are often smaller than 83.

Figure 2.8b illustrates a case that is more representative of many real studies. In Figure 2.8b, the true value of the correlation (the population correlation) is .20, and each study is based on a sample size of $N = 40$. The standard deviation of the observed correlations across many such studies is

$$SD_r = \sqrt{\frac{(1-.20^2)^2}{40-1}} = .154$$

The SD in the null distribution is

$$SD_{\text{NULL}} = \sqrt{\frac{(1-0^2)^2}{40-1}} = .160$$

To be significant at the .05 level (again, using a one-tailed test), a correlation must be above the zero mean of the null distribution by $1.645(.160) = .26$. All correlations that are .26 or larger will be significant; the rest will be nonsignificant. Thus, to be significant, the correlation must be larger than its true value! The actual value of the correlation is always .20; observed values are larger (or smaller) than the true value of .20 only because of random sampling error. To get a significant correlation, we must be lucky enough to have a positive random sampling error. Any study in which r is equal to its real value of .20—that is, any study that is perfectly accurate in estimating r—will lead to the false conclusion that the correlation is 0! What percentage of the correlations will be significant? When we convert .26 to a z score in the observed r distribution, we get

$$z = \frac{.26 - .20}{.154} = .39$$

The percentage of values in a normal distribution that is above a z score of .39 is 35%. In Figure 2.8b, this 35% is the area above the value

Figure 2.8   Statistical power: Two examples.

2.8a   Statistical power greater than .50

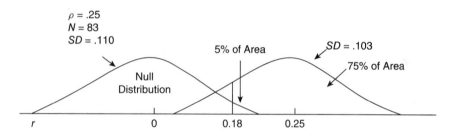

One tailed test, $\alpha = .05$: 1.645(.110) = .18 = Required r.

$$Z = \frac{.18 - .25}{.103} = -.68$$

P (Type II Error) = .25; Statistical Power = .75

2.8b   Statistical power less than .50

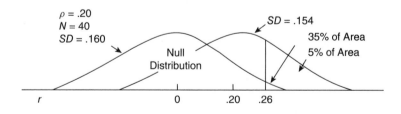

One tailed test, $\alpha = .05$: 1.645(.160) = .26 = Required r.

$$Z = \frac{.26 - .20}{.154} = .39$$

P (Type II Error) = .65; Statistical Power = .35

of .26 in the observed r distribution. So only 35% of all these studies will get a significant r, even though the true value of r is always .20; it is never 0. Statistical power is only .35. The majority of studies—65%—will falsely indicate that $\rho = 0$; 65% of all studies will reach a false conclusion.

A vote-counting procedure has often been used in the past (see Chapter 11) in which the majority outcome is used to decide whether a relationship exists. If a majority of the studies show a nonsignificant finding, as here, the conclusion is that no relationship exists. This conclusion is clearly false here, showing that the vote-counting method is defective. Even more surprising, however, is the fact that the larger the number of studies that are conducted, the greater is the certainty of reaching the false conclusion that there is no relationship (i.e., that $\rho = 0$)! If only a few studies are conducted, then just by chance a majority might get significant correlations, and the vote-counting method might not result in an erroneous conclusion. For example, if only five studies are done, then by chance three might get significant correlations. If a large number of studies are conducted, however, we are certain to zero in on approximately 35% significant and 65% nonsignificant. This creates the paradox of the vote-counting method: If statistical power is less than .50, and if the population correlation is not 0, then the more research studies there are, the more likely the reviewer is to reach the false conclusion that $\rho = 0$ (Hedges & Olkin, 1980).

These examples illustrate statistical power for correlational studies, but they are equally realistic for experimental studies. In experimental studies, the basic statistic is not the correlation coefficient but the standardized difference between the means of two groups, the experimental and control groups. This is the difference between the two means in standard deviation units and is called the d value statistic (see Chapters 6, 7, and 8). The d statistic is roughly twice as large as the correlation. Thus, the example in Figure 2.8a corresponds to an experimental study in which $d = .51$; this is a difference of one half a standard deviation, a fairly substantial difference. It corresponds to the difference between the 50th and 69th percentiles in a normal distribution. The corresponding sample sizes for Figure 2.8a would be $N = 42$ in the experimental group and $N = 41$ in the control group (or vice versa). These numbers are also relatively large; many experimental studies have far less in each group.

The example in Figure 2.8b translates into a more realistic analogue for many experimental studies. Figure 2.8b corresponds to experimental studies in which there are 20 subjects each in the experimental and control groups. Many studies, especially laboratory studies in social psychology, organizational behavior, marketing, and human decision making, have 20 or fewer (sometimes only 5 or 10) in each group. The ρ of .20 corresponds to a *d* value of .40, a value as large as or larger than many observed in real studies. In fact, a review of experimental studies in social psychology found that the average *d* value was .42 (Richard et al., 2003).

Thus, these two examples illustrating the low statistical power of small-sample studies and the errors in conclusions that result from traditional use of significance tests in such studies generalize also to experimental studies. Because the properties of the *d* statistic are somewhat different, the exact figures given here for statistical power will not hold; statistical power is actually somewhat lower in the experimental studies. However, the figures are close enough to illustrate the point.

How would meta-analysis handle the studies shown in Figures 2.8a and 2.8b? First, meta-analysis calls for computing the mean *r* in each set of studies. For the studies in Figure 2.8a, the mean *r* would be found to be .25, the correct value. For Figure 2.8b, the computed mean would be .20, again the correct value. These $\bar{r}$s would then be used to compute the amount of variance expected from sampling error. For the studies in Figure 2.8a, this would be

$$S_e^2 = \frac{(1-\bar{r}^2)^2}{N-1}$$

and

$$S_e^2 = \frac{(1-.25^2)^2}{83-1} = .0107$$

This value would then be subtracted from the amount of variance in the observed correlations to see whether any variance over and above sampling variance was left. The observed variance is $(.10344)^2 = .0107$. Thus, the amount of real variance in the correlations across these studies is $S_\rho^2 = .0107 - .0107 = 0$. The meta-analytic conclusion is that there is only one value of $\rho(\rho = .25)$ and all the apparent variability in *r*s across studies is sampling error. Thus, meta-analysis leads to the correct conclusion, while the traditional approach leads to the conclusion that $\rho = 0$ in 25% of the studies and varied all the way from .18 to approximately .46 in the other 75% of the studies.

Likewise, for the studies in Figure 2.8b, the expected sampling error is

$$S_e^2 = \frac{(1-.20^2)^2}{40-1} = .0236$$

The variance actually observed is $(.1537)^2 = .0236 = S_r^2$. Again, $S_r^2 - S_e^2 = 0$, and the meta-analytic conclusion is that there is only one value of ρ in all the studies—$\rho = .20$—and all the variability in rs across different studies is just sampling error. Again, meta-analysis leads to the correct conclusion, while the traditional use of statistical significance tests leads to false conclusions. The principle here is identical for the d statistics. Only the specific formulas are different (see Chapter 7).

The examples in Figures 2.8a and 2.8b are hypothetical, but they are not unrealistic. In fact, the point here is that real data often behave in the same way. For example, consider the real data in Table 2.3. These data are validity coefficients obtained in a study of nine different job families in Sears, Roebuck and Company (Hill, 1980). For any of these seven tests, validity coefficients are significant for some job families but not for others. For example, the arithmetic test has significant validity coefficients for job families 1, 2, 5, 8, and 9; the validity is not significant for job families 3, 4, 6, and 7. One interpretation of these findings—the traditional one—is that the arithmetic test should be used to hire people in job families 1, 2, 5, 8, and 9, because it is valid for these job families but not for the others. This conclusion is erroneous. Application of the meta-analysis methods that we present in this book shows that for the tests in Table 2.3, all the variation in validities across job families is due to sampling error. The nonsignificant validities are due only to low statistical power.

Another example in which sampling error accounts for all the variation in study outcomes in real data is given in Schmidt, Ocasio, et al. (1985). In that extensive study, observed correlation coefficients varied across different studies all the way from −.21 to .61, a range of .83 correlation points. Yet the true value of ρ was constant in every study at .22. (In fact, each study was a random sample from a single very large study.) Sampling error in small-sample studies creates tremendous variability in study outcomes. Researchers have for decades underestimated how much variability is produced by sampling error.

Of course, sampling error does not explain all the variation in all sets of studies. In most cases, other artifacts also operate to cause variance in study outcomes, as discussed earlier in this chapter. And, in some cases, even the combination of sampling error and other artifacts (such as measurement error and range restriction differences between studies) cannot explain all the variance. However, these artifacts virtually always account for important amounts of variance in study outcomes.

Table 2.3 Validity coefficients from the Sears study.

Job Family	N	Sears Test of Mental Alertness			Sears Clerical Battery			
		Linguistic	Quantitative	Total Score	Filing	Checking	Arithmetic	Grammar
1. Office Support Material Handlers	86	.33*	.20*	.32*	.30*	.27*	.32*	.25*
2. Data Processing Clerical	80	.43*	.51*	.53*	.30*	.39*	.42*	.47*
3. Clerical-Secretarial (Lower Level)	65	.24*	.03	.20	.20	.22	.13	.26*
4. Clerical-Secretarial (Higher Level)	186	.12*	.18*	.17*	.07	.21*	.20	.31*
5. Secretarial (Top Level)	146	.19*	.21*	.22*	.16*	.15*	.22*	.09
6. Clerical With Supervisory Duties	30	.24	.14	.23	.24	.24	.31	.17
7. Word Processing	63	.03	.26*	.13	.39*	.33*	.14	.22*
8. Supervisors	185	.28*	.10	.25*	.25*	.11	.19*	.20*
9. Technical, Operative, Professional	54	.24*	.35*	.33*	.30*	.22*	.31*	.42*

*p < .05.

When and How to Cumulate

In general, a meta-analytic cumulation of results across studies is conceptually a simple process:

1. Calculate the desired descriptive statistic for each study available and average that statistic across studies.

2. Calculate the variance of the statistic across studies.

3. Correct the variance by subtracting the amount due to sampling error.

4. Correct the mean and variance for study artifacts other than sampling error.

5. Compare the corrected standard deviation to the mean to assess the size of the potential variation in results across studies in qualitative terms. If the mean is more than two standard deviations larger than 0, then it is reasonable to conclude that the relationship considered is always positive.

In practice, cumulation usually involves a variety of technical complexities that we will examine in later chapters.

Cumulation of results can be used whenever there are at least two studies with data bearing on the same relationship. For example, if your study at Crooked Corn Flakes contains a correlation between job status and job satisfaction, then you might want to compare that correlation with the correlation found in your earlier study at Tuffy Bolts. However, to correct for sampling error with two correlations, it is possible to use a strategy different from the corrected variance procedures presented in Chapters 3 and 4. One can simply compute confidence intervals around each correlation, as discussed in Chapter 1. If the two confidence intervals overlap, then the difference between the two correlations may be due solely to sampling error (cf. Schmidt, 1992, 1996), and the average is the best estimate of their common value.

Undercorrection for Artifacts in the Corrected Standard Deviation (SD_ρ)

The corrected standard deviation of results across studies should always be regarded as an overestimate of the true standard deviation. Procedures developed to date correct for only some of the artifacts that produce spurious variation across studies. There are other artifacts that have similar effects. The largest of these is computational or reporting errors. If you have 30 correlations ranging from .00 to .60 and one correlation of −.45 (a case we encountered in one of our studies), then it is virtually certain that the outlier resulted from some faulty computational or reporting procedure, for example, failing to reverse the sign of a variable that is reverse scored, or using the wrong format in a computer run, or a typographical error, and so on. Other artifacts that create spurious variation across studies include differences in the reliability of measurement, differences in the construct validity of measurement (such as criterion contamination or criterion deficiency in personnel selection studies), differences in the variances of measured variables in different studies (such as differences in restriction in range in personnel selection studies), and differences in the amount or strength of the treatment (in experimental studies). Indeed, the relevant question in many settings is this: Is all the variation across studies artifactual? In the personnel selection area, this has been the conclusion in a number of areas, such as single-group validity, differential validity by race or ethnic group, specificity of ability test validity across setting or time, and amount of halo in ratings made using different methods (cf. Schmidt & Hunter, 1981; Schmidt, Hunter, Pearlman, & Hirsh, 1985; Schmidt et al., 1993). However, it is very important to *test* the hypothesis that all variation is artifactual—and not just *assume* a priori that this is the case, as fixed effects meta-analysis models do. The models and procedures presented in this book are all random effects models, and they test this hypothesis empirically. The distinction between fixed effects and random effects meta-analysis models is presented in Chapters 5 and 8.

Some artifacts can be quantified and corrected for. Corrections for differences in reliability and restriction in range were first made by Schmidt and Hunter (1977) and Schmidt, Hunter, Pearlman, and Shane (1979); these are described in Chapters 3 and 4. Differences in the construct validity of measures can be corrected using similar techniques if there is an integrated study available that provides a path analysis relating the alternate measures to each other (see the discussion earlier in this chapter). Quantitative differences in treatment effects (such as magnitude of incentive) can be coded and corrected after the initial cumulation establishes the relationship (if any) between that aspect of the treatment and the study outcome (see Chapters 6 and 7).

However, these corrections depend on additional information that is frequently not available. For example, reliabilities and standard deviations are often not included in correlational studies. They are not even considered in most experimental studies. And, alas, computational and reporting errors will never be fully quantified and eliminated.

If there is large, real variation in results across studies, then any conclusion based solely on the summary result entails a certain amount of error. This is the familiar problem of ignoring interactions or moderator effects. However, errors of even greater magnitude can be made if variation caused by artifacts is attributed to nonexistent methodological and substantive moderators. For example, before the era of meta-analysis, one well-known psychologist became so discouraged by the variation in results in several research areas that he concluded it was unlikely that any finding in psychology would ever hold from one generation to the next, because each cohort would always differ on some social dimension that would alter research outcomes (Cronbach, 1975). Such a position reflects the reification of sampling error variance and other artifactual variance (Schmidt, 1992, 1996; Schmidt & Hunter, 2003). Such reification leads not only to epistemological disillusionment but also to immense wasted effort in endlessly replicating studies when enough data already exist to answer the question (Schmidt, 1996).

If there is a large corrected standard deviation, it may be possible to explain the variation across studies by breaking the studies into groups on the basis of relevant differences between them. This breakdown can be an explicit subdivision of studies into categories, or it can be an implicit breakdown using regression methods to predict study outcomes from study characteristics. Both of these will be considered in detail in Chapters 3, 4, 7, and 9. However, we show in the next section that such a breakdown should be attempted only if there is a substantial corrected variance. Otherwise, the search for moderators can introduce serious errors into the interpretation of the studies by virtue of capitalization on sampling errors.

Coding Study Characteristics and Capitalization on Sampling Error in Moderator Analysis

As is apparent in the literature today, meta-analysis is often thought of as a three-step process: (1) cumulation of descriptive statistics (effect sizes; correlations or d values) across studies; (2) the coding of study characteristics (perhaps as many as 40 or more), such as date of study, number of threats to internal validity, and so forth; and (3) regression of study effect sizes onto the coded study characteristics. This process can lead to serious errors in conclusions about moderators. In our research, in which we have made corrections for sampling error and other artifacts, we have often found little appreciable variation across studies remaining after these corrections (e.g., see Schmidt et al., 1993). That is, it is our experience that there is often little real variation in study results after sampling error and other artifacts are removed (despite the fact that it is never possible to correct for *all* artifacts causing variation across studies). In such cases, all or most observed correlations of study effect sizes with study characteristics are the result of capitalization on sampling error due to the small number of studies.

If there is little variation other than sampling error, then the dependent variable (study outcome: the r or d statistic) has low reliability. For example, if 90% of between-study variance in correlations is due to artifacts, then the reliability of the study outcome variable is only .10, and therefore the *maximum possible* real correlation between any study characteristic and study outcome is the square root of .10, which is .31. Therefore, large observed correlations between study characteristics and study outcomes could occur only because of sampling error. Correlating study characteristics with study outcome statistics (rs or d values) leads to massive capitalization on chance when the correlations that are large enough to be statistically significant are identified ex post facto. Sampling errors are very large because the *sample size* for this analysis is not the number of

Table 2.4   Expected values of the multiple R of study characteristics with study outcomes when all study characteristics correlate zero with study outcomes and with each other.

Number of Study Characteristics in Regression Equation	Total Number of Study Characteristics	Number of Studies							
		20	40	60	80	100	200	400	800
2	6	.49	.34	.28	.24	.21	.15	.11	.07
3		.51	.36	.29	.25	.22	.16	.11	.08
4		.53	.37	.30	.26	.23	.16	.12	.08
2	8	.53	.37	.30	.26	.23	.17	.12	.08
3		.57	.40	.33	.28	.25	.18	.13	.09
4		.61	.42	.35	.30	.27	.19	.13	.09
2	10	.57	.40	.32	.28	.25	.18	.12	.09
3		.62	.43	.35	.31	.27	.19	.13	.10
4		.66	.46	.38	.33	.29	.21	.14	.10
2	13	.61	.43	.35	.30	.27	.19	.13	.09
3		.67	.47	.38	.33	.29	.21	.14	.10
4		.72	.50	.41	.36	.32	.22	.16	.11
2	16	.64	.45	.36	.32	.28	.20	.14	.10
3		.71	.49	.40	.35	.31	.22	.16	.11
4		.77	.54	.44	.38	.34	.24	.17	.12
2	20	.68	.48	.37	.34	.30	.21	.15	.11
3		.76	.53	.43	.37	.33	.23	.16	.12
4		.83	.58	.47	.41	.36	.26	.18	.13
2	25	.70	.49	.40	.35	.31	.22	.15	.11
3		.79	.55	.45	.39	.34	.24	.17	.12
4		.86	.60	.49	.43	.38	.27	.19	.13
2	30	.73	.51	.41	.36	.32	.22	.16	.11
3		.82	.57	.46	.40	.36	.25	.18	.13
4		.90	.63	.51	.44	.39	.28	.20	.14
2	35	.75	.52	.42	.37	.33	.23	.16	.11
3		.84	.59	.48	.42	.37	.26	.18	.13
4		.93	.65	.53	.46	.41	.29	.20	.14
2	40	.76	.53	.43	.38	.33	.24	.17	.12
3		.87	.61	.50	.43	.38	.27	.19	.13
4		.97	.68	.55	.48	.42	.30	.21	.15
2	50	.80	.55	.45	.39	.35	.24	.17	.12
3		.90	.63	.51	.44	.39	.28	.20	.14
4		1.00	.70	.57	.49	.44	.31	.22	.15

Note: Actual multiple $R = 0$ in all cases in this table.

persons in the studies but the *number of studies*. For example, the multiple regression of study outcome onto 40 study characteristics (typical of current meta-analyses) with only 50 studies as observations (typical of current meta-analyses) would lead by capitalization on sampling error to a multiple correlation near 1.00. Indeed, some studies have more study characteristics than studies, a situation in which the multiple correlation is always 1.00 by fiat. The authors of many meta-analyses that employ this approach focus as much on the resulting estimates of the regression weights as on the multiple correlation. But these regression weights are also often the result of capitalization on sampling error. Those that are statistically significant often (perhaps usually) are Type I errors. This is a serious problem in meta-regression and is discussed in more detail in Chapter 9.

Many meta-analyses are conducted in the following manner. The researchers first examine their 40 study characteristics to find the 5 that are most highly correlated with study outcomes. Then they use multiple regression with those 5, using a shrinkage formula (if one is used at all) for 5 predictors. Picking the best 5 out of 40, however, is approximately the same as doing a step-up regression from 40 predictors, and hence, one should use 40 in the shrinkage formula rather than 5 (Cattin, 1980). In many cases, the proper shrinkage correction would show the actual multiple correlation to be near 0.

Table 2.4 illustrates how severe the problem of capitalization on chance is when only those study characteristics that correlate highest with study outcomes are retained and entered into the regression analysis. Table 2.4 depicts a situation in which every study characteristic correlates 0 with study outcomes and all study characteristics correlate 0 with each other. Thus, the true value of all multiple correlations in Table 2.4 is 0; all multiple correlations in the table are produced solely by capitalization on sampling error. Consider a typical example. Suppose the number of study characteristics coded is 20 and the 4 that correlate highest with study correlations are retained and used in the regression analysis. If the number of studies is 100, then the expected multiple R is .36, a value that is highly "statistically significant" ($p = .0002$). If there are 60 studies, then the spurious multiple R will, on average, be .47. If there are only 40 studies, it will be .58. Remember that in every cell in Table 2.4, the true multiple R is 0. The values in Table 2.4 are *mean* values; they are not the largest values. Approximately half the time, the observed multiple Rs will be *larger* than the values in Table 2.4. The situation in which 4 study characteristics out of 20 are retained is representative of some actual meta-analyses. However, larger numbers of study characteristics are often coded; for example, it is not unusual for 40 to 50 characteristics to be coded. If 40 are coded and 4 are retained, the spurious multiple R can be expected to be .68 with 40 studies, .55 with 60 studies, and .48 with 80 studies. The reason the multiple R is spuriously large is that the retained study characteristic correlations are biased upward from their true value of 0 by capitalization on (chance) sampling error. For example, if there are 60 studies and 40 study characteristics are coded but only the top 4 are retained, then the correlation for the retained 4 will average .23. These retained characteristics then yield a bogus multiple R of .55.

Thus, it is apparent that the problem of capitalization on chance in conventional moderator analysis in meta-analysis is extremely severe. Many moderators identified in published meta-analyses using regression and correlation methods are almost certainly not real. Those that were identified purely empirically, and not predicted a priori by a theory or hypothesis, are particularly likely to be illusions created by capitalization on sampling error.

On the other hand, those moderators that *are* real are unlikely to be detected because of low statistical power. The discussions of statistical power earlier in this chapter apply to correlations between study characteristics and study outcomes just as well as to other correlations. The sample size—the number of studies—is usually small (e.g., 40–100), and the study characteristic correlations are likely to be small because much of the variance of observed study outcome statistics (rs and d values) is sampling error variance and other artifactual variance. Thus, statistical power to detect real moderators will typically be quite low. Hence, the real moderators are unlikely to be detected, and, at the same time, there is a high probability that capitalization on sampling error will lead to the "detection" of nonexistent moderators. This is indeed an unhappy situation.

To take all variation across studies at face value is to pretend that sampling error does not exist. Because most studies are done with small samples (e.g., less than 500 subjects), the sampling error is quite large in comparison to observed outcome values. Thus, to ignore sampling error is to guarantee major statistical errors at some point in the analysis. The classical reviewer's error is to report the range of outcome values; the range is determined by the two most extreme sampling errors in the set of studies. The error in many current meta-analyses is capitalization on chance and low statistical power in relating variation across studies in r or d values to coded study characteristics. What we have sketched here is a brief overview of this problem, presented at the beginning of this book to alert readers early to the seriousness of the problem. In Chapter 9, we discuss additional technical considerations involved in this approach to the detection of moderators.

We do not claim to have the answer to the problems of capitalization on chance and low statistical power in moderator analysis. In fact, there is no solution to this problem within statistics. It is well known within statistics that the statistical test does not solve the problem; the Type I error versus Type II error trade-off is unavoidable. Thus, if issues are to be resolved solely on statistical grounds, then the answer to subtle questions can only be to gather more data, often vast amounts of data. A more workable alternative is to develop theories that allow new data to be drawn indirectly into the argument. These new data may then permit an objective resolution of the issue on theoretical grounds (see Chapter 11).

A Look Ahead in the Book

The two most common research designs for empirical studies are the correlational study and the two-group intervention study (i.e., an experimental study with independent treatment and control groups). Strength of relationship in correlational designs is usually measured by the correlation coefficient. We present methods for cumulating the correlation coefficient in Chapters 3 and 4. Some have argued that the slope or covariance should be cumulated, rather than the correlation. However, slopes and covariances are comparable across studies only if exactly the same instruments are used to measure the independent and dependent variables in each study. It is a rare set of studies in which this is true. Thus, only in rare cases can the slope or covariance be cumulated because it is in the same metric in all studies. Furthermore, the strength of relationship represented by a slope or covariance can only be known when these numbers are compared to the standard deviations, that is, only when the correlation coefficient is computed. We examine the cumulation of slopes and intercepts in detail in Chapter 5.

The statistic most commonly reported in experimental studies of treatment effects is the t test statistic. However, t is not a good measure of strength of effect because it is multiplied by the square root of the sample size and, hence, does not have the same metric across studies. When sample size is removed from the t statistic, the resulting formula is the effect size statistic d. We will consider the effect size statistic d in Chapters 6 to 8. We also consider its correlational analogue, the point biserial correlation. It is often better to convert d values to point biserial correlations, conduct the meta-analysis on these correlations, and then transform the final result back to the d value statistic. Some would argue for use of proportion of variance instead of r or d, but proportion of variance accounted for (or explained) has many defects. For example, it does not preserve the sign or direction of the treatment effect. Also, as a consequence of the loss of sign, the squared effect measure mean is biased. Proportion of variance indexes are discussed and critiqued further in Chapter 5.

Chapters 3 to 5 on the correlation coefficient and 6 to 8 on d values assume that each entry is based on a statistically independent sample. However, it is frequently possible to obtain more than one relevant estimate of a correlation or effect size from the same study. How, then, should multiple estimates of a relationship from within the same study contribute to a cumulation across studies? This question is taken up in Chapter 10.

Publication bias and related problems are important because they can distort the results of meta-analyses. This issue is discussed in detail in Chapter 13. A further look ahead in the book is presented in the Preface.

PART II

Meta-Analysis
of Correlations

Meta-Analysis of Correlations Corrected Individually for Artifacts

3

Introduction and Overview

In Chapter 2, we examined 11 study design artifacts that can affect the size of the correlation coefficient. At the level of meta-analysis, it is possible to correct for all but one of those artifacts: reporting or transcriptional error. Except for outlier analysis, we know of no way to correct for data errors. Outlier analysis can detect some but not all bad data and is often problematic in meta-analysis (as discussed in Chapter 5). Sampling error can be corrected for, but the accuracy of the correction depends on the total sample size that the meta-analysis is based on. Our discussion of meta-analysis in this chapter and in Chapter 4 implicitly assumes that the meta-analysis is based on a large number of studies. If the number of studies is small, then the formulas presented here still apply, but there will be nontrivial sampling error in the final meta-analysis results. This is the problem of "second-order" sampling error, which is discussed in Chapter 9.

The 10 potentially correctable study design artifacts are listed in Table 3.1. To correct for the effect of an artifact, we must have information about the size and nature of the artifact. Ideally, this information would be given for each study (i.e., each correlation) individually for each artifact. In that case, each correlation can be corrected individually, and the meta-analysis can be conducted on the corrected correlations. This type of meta-analysis is the subject of this chapter.

Some advocate an approach different from that of correcting each correlation in the meta-analysis for artifacts. In this alternative approach, the reliabilities, range restriction values, and other artifacts in each study are coded and tested as potential moderator variables in meta-regression (Borenstein, Hedges, Higgins, & Rothstein, 2009, chap. 38). A significant meta-regression coefficient indicates the importance of that artifact. A major problem with this approach is low statistical power (Hedges & Pigott, 2004); as a consequence, the results frequently indicate that the artifacts are not important when in fact they are. Another problem is that this approach does not produce an estimate of the mean corrected correlation and its *SD*. The methods presented in this chapter do not have these problems. The limitations and problems of meta-regression are discussed in Chapter 9.

Artifact information is often available only on a sporadic basis and is sometimes not available at all. However, the nature of artifacts is such that, in most research domains, the artifact values will be independent across studies. For example, there is no reason to suppose that reliability of measurement will be either higher or lower if the sample size is large or small. If the artifacts are independent of each other and independent of the size of the true population correlation, then it is possible to base meta-analysis on artifact distributions. That is, given the independence assumption, it is possible to correct for artifacts at the level of meta-analysis even though we cannot correct individual correlations. This type of meta-analysis is the subject of Chapter 4. Finally, if no information is available on an artifact, then the meta-analysis cannot correct for that artifact. Note that this does not mean that the artifact does not exist or that it has no impact. It merely means that the meta-analysis does not correct for that artifact. If no correction is made for an artifact, then the estimated mean and standard deviation of true effect size correlations are not corrected for the effect of that artifact. The estimates will be inaccurate to the extent that uncorrected artifacts have a substantial impact in that research domain.

Although there are 10 potentially correctable artifacts, they will not all be discussed at the same level of detail. First, sampling error is both non-systematic and of devastating effect in narrative reviews of the literature. Thus, sampling error will be discussed first and in considerable detail. The systematic artifacts will then be considered one by one. Here, too, there will be differences in the length of the presentation. This does not mean that some are less important than others. Rather, it is a matter of mathematical redundancy. Most of the artifacts have the effect of attenuating the true correlation by a multiplicative fraction, and hence, these artifacts all have a very similar mathematical structure. Once we look at error of measurement and range variation in detail, the others are mathematically similar and, hence, can be treated more briefly. However, it is important to remember that an artifact that may have little or no effect in one research domain may have a large effect in another. For example, there are research domains where the dependent variable has never been dichotomized; hence, there need be no correction for that artifact at all.

Table 3.1 Study artifacts that alter the value of outcome measures (with examples from personnel selection research).

1. Sampling error:

   Study validity will vary randomly from the population value because of sampling error.

2. Error of measurement in the dependent variable:

   Study validity will be systematically lower than true validity to the extent that job performance is measured with random error.

3. Error of measurement in the independent variable:

   Study validity for a test will systematically understate the validity of the ability measured because the test is not perfectly reliable.

4. Dichotomization of a continuous dependent variable:

   Turnover, the length of time that a worker stays with the organization, is often dichotomized into "more than . . . " or "less than . . . " where . . . is some arbitrarily chosen interval such as 1 year or 6 months.

5. Dichotomization of a continuous independent variable:

   Interviewers are often told to dichotomize their perceptions into "acceptable" versus "reject."

6. Range variation in the independent variable:

   Study validity will be systematically lower than true validity to the extent that hiring policy causes incumbents to have a lower variation in the predictor than is true of applicants.

7. Attrition artifacts: Range variation in the dependent variable:

   Study validity will be systematically lower than true validity to the extent that there is systematic attrition in workers on performance, as when good workers are promoted out of the population or when poor workers are fired for poor performance.

8. Deviation from perfect construct validity in the independent variable:

   Study validity will vary if the factor structure of the test differs from the appropriate structure of tests for the same trait.

9. Deviation from perfect construct validity in the dependent variable:

   Study validity will differ from true validity if the criterion (e.g., the measure of job performance) is deficient or contaminated.

10. Reporting or transcriptional error:

    Reported study validities differ from actual study validities due to a variety of reporting problems: inaccuracy in coding data, computational errors, errors in reading computer output, or typographical errors by secretaries or by printers.

    Note: These errors can be very large in magnitude.

11. Variance due to extraneous factors that affect the relationship:

    Study validity will be systematically lower than true validity if incumbents differ in experience on the job at the time they are assessed for performance.

In research on employee turnover, however, almost every study dichoto-mizes the dependent variable, and the dichotomization is based on administrative conventions that often lead to very extreme splits. Thus, none of the artifacts in Table 3.1 can be routinely ignored, no matter how short our treatment of that artifact may be and regardless of whether it can be corrected or not.

Consider the effect of sampling error on the study correlation. At the level of the single study, sampling error is a random event. If the observed correlation is .30, then the unknown population correlation could be higher than .30 or lower than .30, and there is no way that we can know the sampling error or correct for it. However, at the level of meta-analy-sis, sampling error can be estimated and corrected for. Consider first the operation of averaging correlations across studies. When we average correlations, we also average the sampling errors. Thus, the sampling error in the average correlation is the average of the sampling errors in the individual correlations. For example, if we average across 30 studies with a total sample size of 2,000, then sampling error in the average cor-relation is about the same as if we had computed a correlation on a sam-ple of 2,000. That is, if the total sample size is large, then there is very little sampling error in the average correlation. The variance of correla-tions across studies is another story. The variance of correlations is the average *squared* deviation of the study correlation from its mean. Squar-ing the deviation eliminates the sign of the sampling error and, hence, eliminates the tendency for errors to cancel themselves out in summa-tion. Instead, sampling error causes the variance across studies to be systematically larger than the variance of population correlations that we would like to know. However, the effect of sampling error on the vari-ance is to add a known constant to the variance, which is the sampling error variance. This constant can be subtracted from the observed vari-ance. The difference is then an estimate of the desired variance of popu-lation correlations.

To eliminate the effect of sampling error from a meta-analysis, we must derive the distribution of population correlations from the distri-bution of observed correlations. That is, we would like to replace the mean and standard deviation of the observed sample correlations by the mean and standard deviation of the population correlations. Because sampling error cancels out in the average correlation across studies, our best estimate of the mean population correlation is simply the mean of the sample correlations. However, sampling error adds to the variance of correlations across studies. Thus, we must correct the observed variance by subtracting the sampling error variance. The dif-ference is then an estimate of the variance of population correlations across studies.

Once we have corrected the variance across studies for the effect of sampling error, it is possible to see if there is any real variance in results across studies. If there is a large amount of variance across studies, then it is possible to look for moderator variables to explain this variance. To test our hypothesized moderator variable, we break the set of studies into subsets using the moderator variable. For example, we might split the studies into those done on large corporations and those done on small businesses. We then do separate meta-analyses within each subset of studies. If we find large differences between subsets, then the hypothesized variable is indeed a moderator variable. The meta-analysis within subsets also tells us how much of the residual variance within subsets is due to sampling error and how much is real. That is, the meta-analysis tells us whether we need look for a second moderator variable.

Although it is pedagogically useful for us to present the search for moderator variables immediately after presenting the method for eliminating the effects of sampling error, that search is actually premature. Sampling error is only one source of artifactual variation across studies. We should eliminate other sources of variance before we look for moderator variables. Another important source of correctable variation across studies in most domains is variation in error of measurement across studies. That is, a variable such as job satisfaction can be measured in many ways. Thus, different studies will often use different measures of the independent variable or different measures of the dependent variable. Alternate measures will differ in the extent to which they are affected by error of measurement. Differences in amount of measurement error produce differences in the size of the correlations. Differences in correlations across studies due to differences in error of measurement often look like differences due to a moderator variable. Thus, we obtain a true picture of the stability of results across studies only if we eliminate the effects of measurement error. The same is true of other study design artifacts. However, measurement error is always present in every study, while other artifacts, such as dichotomization or range restriction, are sometimes present and sometimes not present.

Correctable artifacts other than sampling error are systematic rather than unsystematic in their impact on study correlations. Let us discuss error of measurement as one example of a correctable systematic artifact. At the level of the individual person, error of measurement is a random event. If Bill's observed score is 75, then his true score could be either greater than 75 or less than 75, and there is no way of knowing which. However, when we correlate scores across persons, the random effects of error of measurement produce a systematic effect on the correlation coefficient. Error of measurement in either variable causes the correlation to be lower than it would have been with perfect measurement. We present a formula for "attenuation" that expresses the exact extent to which the correlation is lowered by any given amount of error of measurement. This same formula can be algebraically reversed to provide a formula for "correction for attenuation." That is, if we know the amount of error of measurement in each variable, then we can correct the observed correlation to provide an estimate of what the correlation would have been had the variables been perfectly measured.

The amount of error of measurement in a variable is measured by a number called the reliability of the variable. The reliability is a number between 0 and 1 that measures the percentage of the observed variance that is true score variance. That is, if the reliability of the independent variable is .80, then 80% of the variance in the scores is due to the true score variation, and, by subtraction, 20% of the variance is due to variation in errors of measurement. To correct for the effect of error of measurement on the correlation, we need to know the amount of error of measurement in both variables. That is, to correct the correlation for attenuation, we need to know the reliability of both variables.

Error of measurement can be eliminated from a meta-analysis in either of two ways: at the level of single studies or at the level of averages across studies. If the reliability of each variable is known in each study, then the correlation for each study can be separately corrected for attenuation. We can then do a meta-analysis on the corrected correlations. This type of meta-analysis is the subject of this chapter. However, many studies do not report the reliability of their instruments. Thus, reliability information is often only sporadically available. Under such conditions, we can still estimate the distribution of the reliability of both the independent and the dependent variables. Given the distribution of observed correlations, the distribution of the reliability of the independent variables, and the distribution of the reliability of the dependent variable, it is possible to use special formulas to correct the meta-analysis to eliminate the effects of error of measurement. Meta-analysis based on such artifact distributions is the subject of the next chapter.

If each individual correlation is corrected for attenuation, then the meta-analysis formulas will differ slightly from the formulas for meta-analysis on uncorrected correlations. The average corrected correlation estimates the average population correlation between true scores. This, in turn, estimates the correlation between the actual constructs (Schmidt, Le, & Oh, 2013). The observed variance of the corrected correlations can be corrected for sampling error simply by subtracting a constant—the sampling error variance. However, the sampling error in a corrected correlation is larger than the sampling error in an uncorrected correlation. Therefore, a different formula must be used to compute the sampling error variance for corrected correlations.

The other correctable artifact most studied in psychometric theory (and in personnel selection research) is range restriction (although our formulas also handle the case of range enhancement or range variation). In many contexts, the standard deviation of the independent variable is approximately the same across studies (i.e., is the same to within sampling error—which will produce *some* variation in standard deviations). In such cases, the meta-analysis need not correct for range variation. However, if the standard deviation of the independent variable differs radically from study to study, then there will be corresponding differences in the correlation from study to study. These differences across studies will look like differences produced by a moderator variable. Thus, if there are big differences in the standard deviation of the independent variable across studies, then a true picture of the stability of results will appear only if the effects of range variation are eliminated. To do this, we compute the value that the correlation would have had had the study been done on a population with some reference level of variance on the independent variable.

Range deviation can be corrected at the level of the single study. If we know the standard deviation of the independent variable in the study, and if we know the standard deviation in the reference population, then there are range correction formulas that will produce an estimate of what the correlation would have been had the standard deviation of the study population been equal to the standard deviation of the reference population. As noted in the previous chapter, these correction procedures are different for direct and indirect range variation. If we correct a correlation for range departure, then the corrected correlation will have a different amount of sampling error than an uncorrected correlation. Therefore, a meta-analysis on corrected correlations must use a different formula for the sampling error variance.

In an ideal research review, we would have complete information about artifacts on each study. For each study, we would know the extent of range departure and the reliabilities of both variables. We could then correct each correlation for both range departure and error of measurement. We would then do a meta-analysis of the fully corrected correlations.

Discussion of other correctable artifacts will be taken up when the needed mathematical tools have been presented. Skipping these artifacts at this time is by no means intended to imply that they are less important. For example, in turnover studies, dichotomization has an even larger attenuating effect on study correlations than does error of measurement.

The remainder of this chapter is presented in four main sections. First, we give a complete treatment of meta-analysis with correction for sampling error only. Second, we present a detailed treatment of error of measurement and range departure, both in terms of the corrections for single studies and in terms of the effect of the correction on sampling error. Third, we describe a more abbreviated treatment of each of the other correctable artifacts. Fourth, we present meta-analysis for the case of individually corrected correlations, that is, meta-analysis as it is done when full information is available on the artifact values in each study. Examples of published studies of this sort include Carlson, Scullen, Schmidt, Rothstein, and Erwin (1999); Judge, Thorensen, Bono, and Patton (2001); and Rothstein, Schmidt, Erwin, Owens, and Sparks (1990).

At present, we know of no research domain where the information has been available to correct for every one of the correctable artifacts listed in Table 3.1. Some meta-analysis methods (e.g., Glass et al., 1981) do not even correct for sampling error; they take each study outcome at face value; other methods address sampling error but do not correct for measurement error or range variation. (See the discussion in Chapter 11.) In personnel selection research, correction is typically made only for sampling error, error of measurement, and range restriction. Most current personnel selection meta-analyses in the literature have made no correction for dichotomization or imperfect construct validity. Furthermore, there will probably be more correctable artifacts defined and quantified over the coming years. And even if all correctable artifacts were corrected, there is still reporting error and other data errors.

It is important to keep in mind that even a fully corrected meta-analysis will not correct for all artifacts. Even after correction, the remaining variation across studies should be viewed with skepticism (see Chapters 2 and 5). Small residual variance is probably due to uncorrected artifacts rather than to a real moderator variable.

Bare-Bones Meta-Analysis: Correcting for Sampling Error Only

We will now present a detailed discussion of sampling error. To keep the presentation simple, we will ignore other artifacts. The resulting presentation is thus written as if the study population correlations were free of other artifacts. In later sections, we will discuss the relationship between sampling error and other artifacts. This section also presents the mathematics of a meta-analysis in which sampling error is the only artifact corrected. Alas, there are those who do not believe that other artifacts exist. There are also those who believe that if there are artifacts in the original studies, then those same artifacts *should be* reflected in the meta-analysis. They believe that the purpose of meta-analysis is only to describe observed results and that meta-analysis should not correct for known problems in research design (see Chapter 11). However, most scientists believe that the goal of cumulative research is to produce better answers than can be obtained in isolated studies (Rubin, 1990). From that point of view, the purpose of meta-analysis is to estimate the relationships that would have been observed if studies had been conducted perfectly (Rubin, 1990), that is, to estimate construct-level relationships (see Chapters 1, 11, and 14). Given this purpose for meta-analysis, a meta-analysis that does not correct for as many artifacts as possible is an unfinished meta-analysis. We hold that view. If a meta-analysis corrects only for sampling error, then it is the mathematical equivalent of the ostrich with its head in the sand: It is a pretense that if we ignore other artifacts, then their effects on study outcomes will go away.

ESTIMATION OF SAMPLING ERROR

The best estimate of the mean correlation is not the simple mean across studies but a weighted average in which each correlation is weighted by the number of persons (or other subjects) in that study. Thus, the estimate of the population correlation is

$$\bar{r} = \frac{\sum [N_i r_i]}{\sum N_i} \qquad (3.1)$$

where r_i is the correlation in study i and N_i is the number of persons in study i. The corresponding variance across studies is not the usual sample variance but the frequency-weighted average squared error

$$s_r^2 = \frac{\sum [N_i (r_i - \bar{r})^2]}{\sum N} \qquad (3.2)$$

Two questions are often asked about this procedure. First, is the weighted average always better than the simple average? Hunter and Schmidt (1987a) presented a detailed discussion of this. Their analysis showed that it is a very rare case in which an unweighted analysis would be better, contrary to the position taken by Bonett (2008, 2009). (See the discussion of study weighting in Chapter 9.) Second, why do we not transform the correlations to Fisher z form for the cumulative analysis? The answer is that the Fisher z transformation produces an estimate of the mean correlation that is upwardly biased and less accurate than an analysis using untransformed correlations (see the discussions in Chapters 2 and 5; also, Hall & Brannick, 2002; Hunter et al., 1996; Schmidt, Oh, & Hayes, 2009; Schulze, 2004, 2007).

The frequency-weighted average gives greater weight to large studies than to small studies. If there is no variance in population correlations across studies, then the weighting always improves accuracy. If the variance of population correlations is small, then the weighted average is also always better. If the variance of population correlations across studies is large, then as long as sample size is not correlated with the size of the population correlation, the weighted average will again be superior. That leaves one case in which the weighted average could prove troublesome. For example, in one meta-analysis, we found 13 studies on the validity of bio-data in predicting job success. One of these studies was done by an insurance consortium with a sample size of 15,000. The other 12 studies were done with sample sizes of 500 or less. The weighted average will give the single insurance study over 30 times the weight given to any other study. Suppose that the insurance study were deviant in some way. The meta-analysis might then be almost entirely defined by one deviant study. In a situation such as this, we recommend two analyses: a first analysis with the large-sample study included and a second analysis with the large-sample study left out. We have not yet had to figure out what to do should the two analyses show a major discrepancy. (In our case, they did not.) (See the related discussion of fixed vs. random effects meta-analysis models in Chapters 5 and 8 and the discussion of methods of weighting studies in random vs. fixed models of meta-analysis in Chapter 9.)

It is well known that the variance of any variable can be computed using either N or $N - 1$ in the denominator. The formulation in Equation (3.2) corresponds to use of N in the denominator. The advantage of using N in the denominator is that it leads to a more accurate estimate of the variance in the sense of statistical efficiency. When N is used, the mean square error is lower, an important consideration in meta-analysis. This means that the average squared departure of the estimate from the population value is smaller. The square root of this value is the root mean square error, the measure of the accuracy of an estimation procedure. Use of $N - 1$ instead of N leads to a slight reduction in bias but at the expense of a reduction in overall accuracy.

CORRECTING THE VARIANCE FOR SAMPLING ERROR AND A WORKED EXAMPLE

Consider the variation in correlations across similar studies on a research question. The observed variance S_r^2 is a confounding of two things: variation in population correlations (if there is any) and variation in sample correlations produced by sampling error. Thus, an estimate of the variance in population correlations can be obtained only by correcting the observed variance S_r^2 for sampling error. The following mathematics shows that sampling error across studies behaves like error of measurement across persons and that the resulting formulas are comparable to standard formulas in classical measurement theory (reliability theory).

We begin with a treatment of sampling error in an isolated study. In an isolated study, the correlation is based on a sample: a specific sample of the population of people who might have been in that place at that time, a sample of the random processes in each person's head that generate error of measurement in test responses or supervisor ratings and so on, and a sample of time variation in person and situational parameters. This is represented in statistics by noting that the observed correlation is a sample from the distribution of correlation values that would be observed if the study were replicated many times except for the random factors. These replications are hypothetical in the sense that a real study usually contains only one such sample. However, the replications are not hypothetical in that they do represent real variation. There have been thousands of actual experiments testing the theory of statistical sampling error, and all have verified that theory. Sampling error in an isolated study is unobservable but present nonetheless.

For any study, then, there is a real population correlation ρ (which is usually unknown) that can be compared to the study correlation r. The difference between them is the sampling error, which we will denote by e. That is, we define sampling error e by the formula

$$e = r - \rho$$

or

$$r = \rho + e$$

The distribution of observed correlations for the (usually hypothetical) replications of the study is always centered about the population correlation ρ, although the sampling error varies randomly. If we ignore the small bias in the correlation coefficient (or if we correct for it as discussed later), then the average sampling error will be 0 and the standard deviation of the sampling error will depend on the sample size. The sampling error in a particular correlation can never be changed (and, in particular, is not changed when a statistical significance test is run). On the other hand, if replications of the study could be done, then sampling error could thus be reduced. Because the average error is 0, the replicated correlations can be averaged, and the average correlation is closer to the population correlation than the individual correlations. The sampling error in the average correlation is the average of the individual sampling errors and is thus much closer to 0 than the typical single sampling error. The average correlation has smaller sampling error in much the same way as a correlation based on a larger sample size. Thus, replicating studies can potentially solve the problem of sampling error.

Whereas replication is not possible in most individual studies, replication does take place across different studies. Consider the ideal special case: a meta-analysis for a research domain in which there is no variation in the population correlations across studies and in which all studies are done with the same sample size. This case is mathematically identical to the hypothetical replications that form the basis of the statistics of isolated correlations. In particular, the average correlation across studies would have greatly reduced sampling error. In the case in which the population correlation varies from one study to another, the replication is more complicated, but the principle is the same. Replication of sampling error across studies enables us to use averaging to reduce the impact of sampling error. If the number of studies is large, the impact of sampling error can be virtually eliminated.

How big is the typical sampling error? Because sampling error has a mean of 0, the mean sampling error does not measure the size of the sampling error. That is, because a negative error of $-.10$ is just as bad as a positive error of $+.10$, it is the absolute value of the error that counts. To assess the size of errors without the algebraic sign, the common statistical practice is to square the errors. The average squared error is the variance, and the square root of that is the standard deviation of the errors. It is the standard deviation of sampling errors that is the best representation of the size of errors. Consider, then, the isolated study. In the common case in which the underlying distribution is the bivariate normal distribution, the standard deviation of the sampling errors is given by

$$\sigma_e = (1 - \rho^2) / \sqrt{(N-1)}$$

where N is the sample size. Technically, our use of this formula throughout this book is tantamount to the assumption that all studies are done in contexts where the independent and dependent variables have a bivariate normal distribution, but the statistics literature has found this formula to be fairly robust in the face of departures from normality. However, under conditions of range restriction, this formula underestimates sampling error variance to some extent. That is, actual sampling variance is greater than the value predicted by the formula, leading to undercorrections for sampling error variance. Using computer simulation, Millsap (1989) showed this for direct range restriction, and Aguinis and Whitehead (1997) showed it for indirect range restriction. This means that corrections for sampling error variance are undercorrections, leading to overestimates of SD_ρ, particularly in validity generalization studies. This could create the appearance of a moderator where none exists. However, in research areas where there is no range restriction, this problem does not occur.

The effect of averaging across replications is dramatic in terms of sampling error variance. If the sample size in each replication is N and the number of studies is K, then the sampling error variance in the average of K correlations is the variance of the average error e; that is,

$$\text{Var}(\overline{e}) = \text{Var}(e)/K \tag{3.3}$$

In other words, the effect of averaging across K studies is to divide the sampling error variance by K. Because the total sample size in K studies is K times the sample size in a single study, this means that to increase the sample size by a factor of K is to reduce the sampling error variance by a factor of K. This is exactly the same rule as that for increasing the sample size of a single study. Thus, replication can reduce sampling error in the same way as using larger samples.

In practice, the effect of increasing sample size is not quite as impressive as the previous formula would suggest. Unfortunately, it is not the variance but the standard deviation (standard error) that counts. The standard deviation of the average error is divided only by the square root of the number of studies. Thus, to cut the standard error in half, we must average four studies rather than two studies. This is important in judging the number of missing studies in a meta-analysis when that number is small. For example, if an investigator randomly misses 10 out of 100 potential studies, the sampling error variance is increased by 10%, but the sampling error standard error is increased by only 5%. Thus, missing a few studies randomly usually does not reduce the accuracy of a meta-analysis by nearly as much as might be supposed.

We come now to the meta-analysis of correlations taken from different studies. The power of meta-analysis to reduce the problem of sampling error lies in the fact that sampling errors are replicated across studies. The ultimate statistical error in meta-analysis will depend on two factors: the size of the average sample size for the individual studies and the number of studies in the meta-analysis. For the mean correlation, it is the total sample size that determines the error in the meta-analysis. For the estimate of the variance of correlations, the computations are more complicated, but the principle is similar.

Let the subscript i denote the study number. Then the error variable e_i represents the sampling error in the sample correlation in study i; that is, we define e_i by

$$r_i = \rho_i + e_i$$

Then the mean of the error within hypothetical replications is 0. The average error across studies is

$$E(e_i) = 0$$

The variance across hypothetical replications of any one study is denoted by

$$\sigma_{e_i}^2 = \frac{(1-\rho_i^2)^2}{N_i - 1} \tag{3.4}$$

In going across studies, this hypothetical and unobserved variation becomes real and potentially observable variation. This is similar to the case of observing a sample of people or scores from a distribution of people or scores. It differs from the usual case in statistics because the sampling error variance differs from one study to the next. Nonetheless, the critical fact is that the variance of sampling error becomes visible across studies. The formula

$$r_i = \rho_i + e_i$$

is analogous to the true score, error score formula from measurement error theory:

$$X_p = T_p + e_p$$

where X_p and T_p are the observed and true scores for person p. In particular, sampling error (signed sampling error, not sampling error variance) is unrelated to population values across studies (cf. Hedges, 1989; Schmidt, Hunter, & Raju, 1988). Thus, if we calculate a variance across studies, then the variance of sample correlations is the sum of the variance in population correlations and the variance due to sampling error; that is,

$$\sigma_r^2 = \sigma_\rho^2 + \sigma_e^2$$

The implication of this formula is that the variance of observed correlations is larger than the variance of population correlations, often much larger. The reason it is larger is because squared sampling errors are always positive and do not cancel out when averaged. Thus, the average squared deviation of observed correlations is systematically larger than the average squared deviation of population correlations because sampling error makes a systematically positive contribution to the squared deviation.

The formula $\sigma_r^2 = \sigma_\rho^2 + \sigma_e^2$ has three variances. If any two of the variances are known, the third can be computed. In particular, if the sampling error variance σ_e^2 were known, then the desired variance of population correlations would be (Cook et al., 1992)

$$\sigma_\rho^2 = \sigma_r^2 - \sigma_e^2$$

Of these three variances, only the variance of observed correlations is estimated using a conventional variance calculation, that is, average squared deviation of given numbers. If we knew the value of the sampling error variance, then it would not matter that we could not compute it as a conventional variance. The fact is that the sampling error variance need not be given as an empirical number; it is given by a statistical formula. The sampling error variance across studies is just the average of the sampling error variances within studies. If study correlations are weighted by sample size N_i, then the error variance across studies is

$$\sigma_e^2 = Ave\sigma_{e_i}^2 = \frac{\sum[N_i\sigma_{e_i}^2]}{\sum N_i} = \frac{\sum[N_i[(1-\rho_i^2)^2]/[N_i-1]]}{\sum N_i} \qquad (3.5)$$

This formula is used in our Windows-based meta-analysis computer program package. (See the Appendix for a description and availability.) However, Law, Schmidt, and Hunter (1994b) and Hunter and Schmidt (1994) showed via computer simulation that this formula is more accurate if ρ_i is estimated by $\bar{r}$. That is, in computing the sampling error variance for each individual study, $\bar{r}$ is used in place of r_i. This modification is used in our computer programs. (See Chapter 5 for further discussion of this.)

Approximation formulas are available for use in hand calculations of meta-analysis. In Equation (3.5), the fraction $N_i / (N_i - 1)$ is close to unity. If we take this fraction as unity, and we use the approximation that average $(\rho^2) \cong (average \ \rho)^2$, then we have the almost perfect approximation

$$\sigma_e^2 = \frac{(1-\bar{r}^2)^2 K}{T} \tag{3.6}$$

where K is the number of studies and $T = \sum N_i$ is the total sample size. The corresponding estimate of the variance of population correlations is thus

$$\text{est } \sigma_\rho^2 = \sigma_r^2 - \sigma_e^2 = \sigma_r^2 - \frac{(1-\bar{r}^2)^2 K}{T}$$

There is an even better estimate of the sampling error variance. Consider the special case in which all studies have the same sample size N. The ratio $N_i/(N_i - 1)$ is then simply the constant $N/(N-1)$, which factors out of the summation. We then have

$$\sigma_e^2 = Ave(1-\rho_i^2)^2 / (N-1)$$

If we estimate ρ_i by the average correlation across studies (Hunter & Schmidt, 1994; Law et al., 1994b), we have the approximation

$$\sigma_e^2 = (1-\bar{r}^2)^2 / (N-1) \tag{3.7}$$

This formula is exactly analogous to the formula for sampling error in the single study

$$\sigma_e^2 = (1-\rho^2)^2 / (N-1)$$

Consider again the typical case where sample size varies from one study to the next. Let the average sample size be denoted by $\bar{N}$; that is,

$$\bar{N} = T / K$$

Our first approximation could be written as

$$\sigma_e^2 = (1-\bar{r}^2)^2 / N$$

while the second improved approximation is

$$\sigma_e^2 = (1-\bar{r}^2)^2 / (\bar{N}-1)$$

The second approximation is accurate both when the population correlations are all the same (Hunter & Schmidt, 1994)—when it is optimal—and also when there is variation in population correlations analysis (Law et al., 1994b). The corresponding estimate of the variance of population correlations is

$$\sigma_\rho^2 = \sigma_r^2 - \sigma_e^2 = \sigma_r^2 - (1 - \bar{r}^2)^2 / (\bar{N} - 1)$$

This equation allows an empirical test of the hypothesis that $\sigma_\rho^2 = 0$.

An Example: Socioeconomic Status and Police Performance

Bouchard (1776, 1860, 1914, 1941) postulated that differences in upbringing would produce differences in response to power over other people. His theory was that because lower-class parents obtain obedience by beating their children to a pulp while middle-class parents threaten them with loss of love, lower-class children would grow into adults who are more likely themselves to use physical force to gain compliance. He tested his theory by looking at the relationship between socioeconomic status of origin of police officers and brutality in police departments. His independent measure was socioeconomic status measured in terms of six classes, ranging from 1 = upper, upper class to 6 = lower, lower class. His brutality measure was the number of complaints divided by the number of years employed. Only patrol officers were considered in the correlations, which are shown in Table 3.2. The meta-analysis of these data is as follows:

$$\bar{r} = \frac{100(.34) + 100(.16) + 50(.12) + 50(.38)}{100 + 100 + 50 + 50} = \frac{75.00}{300} = .25$$

$$\sigma_r^2 = \frac{100(.34 - .25)^2 + 100(.16 - .25)^2 + 50(.12 - .25)^2 + 50(.38 - .25)^2}{100 + 100 + 50 + 50}$$
$$= \frac{3.31}{300} = .011033$$

The average sample size is

$$\bar{N} = T / K = 300 / 4 = 75$$

Thus, the sampling error variance is estimated to be

$$\sigma_e^2 = (1 - \bar{r}^2)^2 / (N - 1) = (1 - .25^2)^2 / 74 = .011877$$

The estimate of the variance of population correlations is thus

$$\sigma_\rho^2 = \sigma_r^2 - \sigma_e^2 = \sigma_r^2 - (1 - \bar{r}^2)^2 / (\bar{N} - 1)$$
$$= .011033 - .011877 = -.000844.$$

Because the estimated variance is negative, the estimated standard deviation is 0; that is,

$$\sigma_\rho = 0$$

Some readers have been bothered by this example. They ask, "How can a variance be negative, even if only −.0008?" The answer is that the estimated variance of population correlations is not computed as a conventional variance, that is, the average squared deviation of given numbers. Rather, it is computed as the difference between the given variance of observed correlations and the statistically given sampling error variance. Although there is little error in the statistically given sampling error variance, the variance of observed correlations is a sample estimate. Unless the number of studies is infinite, there will be some sampling error in that empirical estimate. If the population difference is 0, then error will cause the estimated difference to be positive or negative with probability one half. Thus, in our case, sampling error caused the variance of observed correlations to differ slightly from the expected value, and that error caused the estimating difference to be negative. There is no logical contradiction here. In analysis of variance and in Cronbach's generalizability theory, estimation of components of variance using expected mean square formulas also produces negative observed estimates for similar reasons. Such estimates are always taken as 0. W. A. Thompson (1962) provides a detailed discussion of negative variance estimates in statistics. This question is addressed further in Chapter 9, in the discussion of second-order sampling error and second-order meta-analysis.

Consider the empirical meaning of our results. Bouchard claimed that his results varied dramatically from city to city. His explanation was that Washington, D.C., and Richmond are southern cities, and southern hospitality is so strong that it reduces the incidence of brutality in the lower classes and, hence, reduces the correlation in those cities. However, our analysis shows that all the variation in his results is due to sampling error and that the correlation is always .25.

Table 3.2 Correlations between socioeconomic status and police brutality (United States).

Location	Date	Sample Size	Correlation
Philadelphia	1776	100	.34*
Richmond, VA	1861	100	.16
Washington, D.C.	1914	50	.12
Pearl Harbor	1941	50	.38*

*Significant at the .05 level.

The fact that all the variance of the observed rs is explained by sampling error does not mean that the mean r (.25) is estimated without error. What is the confidence interval (CI) for the mean r of .25? The SD of the observed rs is .10501. This is the square root of the observed variance, which is .011033; $k = 4 =$ the number of studies. The SE of mean r is $SD_r / \sqrt{k} = .10501/2 = .05252$. The lower bound of the CI is then .25 − (1.96) (.05252) = .14. The upper bound of the CI is .25 + (1.96)(.05252) = .35. So we have the following CI:

$$.14 < .25 < .35$$

Confidence intervals and procedures for computing them are discussed in more detail in Chapter 5. The reader will also find a discussion of the difference between confidence intervals and credibility intervals there. The computer programs described in the Appendix provide both types of intervals as part of their output.

MODERATOR VARIABLES ANALYZED BY GROUPING THE DATA AND A WORKED EXAMPLE

A moderator variable is a variable that causes differences in the correlation between two other variables. For example, in the police brutality study discussed previously, Bouchard postulated that geographic region (North vs. South) would be a moderator variable for the relationship between socioeconomic status and brutality. If there is true variation in results across studies, then there must be such a moderator variable (or possibly more than one) to account for such variance. On the other hand, if the analysis shows that the variation in results is due to sampling error, then any apparent moderating effect is due to capitalization on sampling error. This was the case in Bouchard's work.

If the corrected standard deviation suggests substantial variation in population correlations across studies, then a moderator variable derived from a theory or hypothesis can be used to group the observed correlations into subsets. Within each subset, we can calculate a mean, a variance, and a variance corrected for sampling error. A moderator variable will reveal itself in two ways: (1) the average correlation will vary from subset to subset, and (2) the corrected variance will *average* lower in the subsets than for the data as a whole. These two facts are mathematically dependent. By a theorem in analysis of variance, we know that the total variance is the mean of the subset variances plus the variance of the subset means. Thus, the mean uncorrected within-subset variance must decrease to exactly the extent that the subset means differ from one another. This means that if the average correlation varies across subsets, then the average standard deviation of the subsets *must* be less than the standard deviation in the combined data set.

An Example: Police Brutality in Transylvania

In order to justify a European sabbatical, Hackman (1978) argued that Bouchard's work on police brutality needed a cross-cultural replication. So he gathered data in four cities in Transylvania, carefully replicating Bouchard's measurement on socioeconomic status and brutality. His data are given along with Bouchard's in Table 3.3.

Analysis of the Whole Set

$$\bar{r} = \frac{100(.34) + \ldots + 100(.19) + \ldots + 50(.23)}{100 + \cdots + 100 + \cdots + 50} = \frac{105.00}{600} = .175$$

$$\sigma_r^2 = \frac{100(.34 - .175)^2 + \ldots + 50(.23 - .175)^2}{100 + \ldots + 50} = \frac{9.995}{600} = .016658$$

$$N = T / K = 600 / 8 = 75$$

$$\sigma_e^2 = \frac{(1 - .175^2)^2}{74} = .012698$$

$$\sigma_\rho^2 = .016658 - .012698 = .00396$$

$$\sigma_\rho = .063$$

The percent variance accounted for by sampling error is $.012698/.016658 = 75\%$. The square root of .75 is .87, which is the correlation between the sampling errors and the observed r values. The corrected standard deviation of .063 can be compared with the mean of .175 $.175/.063 = 2.78$. That is, the mean correlation is nearly 2.8 standard deviations above 0. Thus, if the study population correlations are normally distributed, the probability of a zero or below-zero correlation is virtually nil. So the qualitative nature of the relationship is clear: The population correlation is positive in all studies.

However, the variation is not trivial in amount relative to the mean. This suggests a search for moderator variables. The moderator analysis is as shown in the following table.

United States	Transylvania
$\bar{r} = .25$	$\bar{r} = .10$
$\sigma_r^2 = .011033$	$\sigma_r^2 = .011033$
$\sigma_e^2 = .011877$	$\sigma_e^2 = .013245$
$\sigma_\rho^2 = -.000844$	$\sigma_\rho^2 = -.002212$
$\sigma_\rho = 0$	$\sigma_\rho = 0$

In both groups, the proportion of variance accounted for by sampling error is 1.00. The square root of 1.00 is 1.00, which is the correlation in each group between sampling errors and the observed r values. Analysis of the subsets shows a substantial difference in mean correlations, $\bar{r} = .25$ in the United States and $\bar{r} = .10$ in Transylvania. The corrected standard deviations reveal that there is no variation in results within the two countries.

In this case, there was only one moderator. When there are multiple moderators, the moderators may be correlated, and hence, they will be confounded if examined sequentially one at a time. In these cases, it is important to conduct moderator analyses hierarchically to avoid such confounding (see Chapter 9).

Hackman explained the difference between the two countries by noting that vampires in the United States live quiet, contented lives working for the Red Cross, while vampires in Transylvania must still get their blood by tracking down and killing live victims. Vampires in Transylvania resent their low station in life and focus their efforts on people of high status, whom they envy. Middle-class policemen who work at night are particularly vulnerable. Thus, there is less variance in social class among the policemen in Transylvania, and this restriction in range reduces the correlation. According to this hypothesis, correcting for range restriction would make the two mean correlations equal (at .25). Later in this chapter, we will examine range corrections that can be used to test this hypothesis.

Table 3.3 Correlations between socioeconomic status and police brutality (United States and Transylvania)

Investigator	Location	Sample Size	Correlation
Bouchard	Philadelphia	100	.34*
Bouchard	Richmond, VA	100	.16
Bouchard	Washington, D.C.	50	.12
Bouchard	Pearl Harbor	50	.38*
Hackman	Brasov	100	.19
Hackman	Targul-Ocna	100	.01
Hackman	Hunedoara	50	−.03
Hackman	Lupeni	50	.23

*Significant at the .05 level.

After a heated exchange at the Academy of Management convention, Bouchard bared his fangs and showed Hackman that American vampires can still be a pain in the neck. Bouchard then noted that the difference in the results reflected the fact that his studies were done at times when the country was going to war. This increase in aggressive excitement increased the general level and the variance of brutality and, thus, increased its reliability of measurement and, hence, the level of correlation. According to this hypothesis, correcting for measurement error in the brutality measure would reveal that the two mean correlations are really equal at the level of true scores. This hypothesis can be tested using the corrections for measurement error discussed later in this chapter. This example of bare-bones meta-analysis illustrates why it is an incomplete form of meta-analysis. If there is no consideration of measurement error or range variation, conclusions are of necessity uncertain.

CORRECTING FEATURE CORRELATIONS FOR SAMPLING ERROR AND A WORKED EXAMPLE

Suppose some study feature is coded as a quantitative variable y. Then that feature can be correlated with the outcome statistic across studies. For example, if correlations between dependency and school achievement varied as a function of the age of the child, then we might code average age in study i as y_i. We could then correlate age of children with size of correlation across studies. An example of this method is given by Schwab, Olian-Gottlieb, and Heneman (1979). However, such a correlation across studies is a confounding of the correlation for population values with y and the noncorrelation of the sampling error with y. This is directly analogous to the role of error of measurement in attenuating correlations based on imperfectly measured variables (Cook et al., 1992, chap. 8, pp. 325–326). Thus, the observed correlation across studies will be smaller than would be the case had there been no sampling error in the correlations.

To avoid confusion between the basic statistic r, which is the correlation over persons within a study, and correlations between r and study features over studies, the correlations over studies will be denoted by "Cor." For example, the correlation between the correlation r and the study feature y across studies will be denoted $\text{Cor}(r, y)$. This is the observed correlation across studies, but the desired correlation across studies is that for population correlations, ρ_i. The desired correlation across studies is $\text{Cor}(\rho, y)$. Starting from the formula $r_i = \rho_i + e_i$, we calculate a covariance over studies and use the principle of additivity of covariances to produce

$$\sigma_{ry} = \sigma_{\rho y} + \sigma_{ey} = \sigma_{\rho y} + 0 = \sigma_{\rho y}$$

If this covariance across studies is divided by standard deviations across studies, then we have

$$Cor(r, y) = \frac{\sigma_{ry}}{\sigma_r \sigma_y} = \frac{\sigma_{\rho y}}{\sigma_r \sigma_y}$$

$$= \frac{\sigma_{\rho y}}{\sigma_\rho \sigma_y} \frac{\sigma_\rho}{\sigma_r}$$

$$= Cor(\rho, y) \frac{\sigma_\rho}{\sigma_r}$$

However, the covariance of r_i with ρ_i is

$$\sigma_{r\rho} = \sigma_{\rho\rho} + \sigma_{e\rho} = \sigma_{\rho\rho} + 0 = \sigma_\rho^2$$

Hence, the correlation across studies is

$$Cor(r, \rho) = \frac{\sigma_{r\rho}}{\sigma_r \sigma_\rho} = \frac{\sigma_\rho^2}{\sigma_r \sigma_\rho} = \frac{\sigma_\rho}{\sigma_r} \tag{3.8}$$

Thus, the observed correlation across studies is the product of two other correlations, the desired correlation and reliability-like correlation:

$$Cor(r, y) = Cor(\rho, y)\, Cor(r, \rho)$$

The desired correlation is then the ratio

$$Cor(\rho, y) = \frac{Cor(r, y)}{Cor(r, \rho)} \tag{3.9}$$

which is precisely the formula for correction for attenuation due to error of measurement if there is measurement error in one variable only. What is the correlation between r and ρ over studies? We have the variance of r as estimated by S_r^2. We need only the variance of ρ, which was estimated in the previous section of this chapter. Thus, the "reliability" needed for use in the attenuation formula is given by

$$\text{Reliability of } r = \{Cor(r, \rho)\}^2$$

$$= \frac{\sigma_\rho^2}{\sigma_r^2} = \frac{\sigma_r^2 - (1 - \bar{r}^2)^2 / (\bar{N} - 1)}{\sigma_r^2} \tag{3.10}$$

Hence,

$$Cor(\rho, y) = \frac{Cor(r, y)}{\{[\sigma_r^2 - (1 - \bar{r}^2)^2 / (\bar{N} - 1)] / [\sigma_r^2]\}^{1/2}} \tag{3.11}$$

An Example: The Tibetan Employment Service

Officials in the Tibetan Employment Service have been using a cognitive ability test for some years to steer people into various jobs. Although they have relied on content validity for such assignments, they have also been gathering criterion-related validity data to test their content validity system. In their content validity system, test development analysts rate each occupation for the extent to which it requires high cognitive ability, with ratings from 1 = low to 3 = high. They have concurrent validity studies on six occupations chosen to stratify the full range of the content validity continuum. These data are shown in Table 3.4. The analysis is as follows:

$$\bar{r} = .30$$

$$\sigma_r^2 = .048333$$

$$\bar{N} = T / K = 600 / 6 = 100$$

$$\sigma_e^2 = .008365$$

$$\sigma_\rho^2 = .048333 - .008365 = .039968$$

$$\sigma_\rho = .20$$

$$\text{Rel}(r) = \frac{\sigma_\rho^2}{\sigma_r^2} = \frac{.0400}{.0483} = .83$$

The percentage of variance due to sampling error is only 17%. The square root of .17 is .41, which is the correlation between sampling errors and the observed r values. This is a relatively low value. We leave it to the interested reader to compute the CI around the mean observed r of .30. (Refer to the example in Table 3.2 for guidance in computing this CI.)

Let y_i be the cognitive rating of the i th occupation. Then

$$\text{Cor}(r, y) = .72$$

$$\text{Cor}(\rho, y) = \frac{.72}{\sqrt{.83}} = .79$$

The study found very large variation in validity, even after correction for sampling error. The correlation was .72 between rating and observed correlation and rose to .79 after correction for sampling error. In this case, only 17% of the variance of the correlations was due to artifacts, so the reliability of the study correlations was .83 (i.e., 1 −.17). Ordinarily, reliability would be much lower and, hence, the correction would be much larger. For example, if 70% of the variance were due to artifacts, then the reliability would be only 1 −.70 = .30. The correction factor would be $1/(.30)^{1/2} = 1.83$.

Table 3.4 Tibetan employment service test validities.

Occupation	Cognitive Rating	Validity (Correlation)	Sample Size
Monastery Abbot	3	.45*	100
Magistrate	3	.55*	100
Holy Man	2	.05	100
Farmer	2	.55*	100
Bandit	1	.10	100
Yak Chip Collector	1	.10	100

*Significant at the .05 level.

In this example, we have corrected only for unreliability in the dependent variable (the validity correlations). However, as in all studies, the independent variable also contains measurement error, and so we should also correct for unreliability in the ratings of the cognitive requirements of the jobs, as pointed out by Orwin and Cordray (1985). Suppose in this particular case, the reliability of these ratings was found to be .75. Then the true score correlation between ratings and test validity would be

$$\text{Cor}(\rho, y_t) = \frac{.72}{\sqrt{.83(.75)}} = .91$$

So it is apparent that in a real analysis of this sort, it is critical to correct for measurement error *in both measures* (Cook et al., 1992, chap. 7; MacMahon et al., 1990; Orwin & Cordray, 1985). Otherwise, construct-level relationships will be underestimated.

Recall the discussion in Chapter 2 on the dangers of capitalization on sampling error in relating study characteristics to study effect sizes. This danger does not occur in this example because only one moderator is examined and that moderator was hypothesized in advance. However, this would be a danger if multiple study characteristics were examined and they were not hypothesized in advance. Note that the .91 is the standardized regression weight for predicting standard score *r* values (*r*s in *z* score form) from the standardized cognitive requirements rating. Hence, this is an example of meta-regression. Meta-regression (usually in unstandardized metric) is widely used in meta-analysis today. The strengths and weaknesses of meta-regression are discussed in detail in Chapter 9.

Artifacts Other Than Sampling Error

ERROR OF MEASUREMENT AND CORRECTION FOR ATTENUATION

Variables in science are never perfectly measured. Indeed, sometimes the measurement is very crude. Since the late 1890s, we have known that the error of measurement attenuates the correlation coefficient. That is, error of measurement systematically lowers the correlation between *measures* in comparison to the correlation between the variables themselves. This systematic error is then exaggerated by the unsystematic distortions of sampling error. In this section, we review the theory of error of measurement and derive the classic formula for correction for attenuation. Measurement error has a special status among systematic artifacts: It is the only systematic artifact that is always present in every study in every meta-analysis.

We will then look at the impact of error of measurement on sampling error and confidence intervals. In particular, we will derive the confidence interval for individual corrected correlations. From this base, we will later consider the impact of error of measurement as it varies in amount from one study to another.

Let us denote by T the true score that would have been observed on the independent variable had we been able to measure it perfectly. We then have

$$x = T + E_1$$

where E_1 is the error of measurement in the independent variable. Let us denote by U the true score that would have been observed on the dependent variable had we been able to measure it perfectly. We then have

$$y = U + E_2$$

where E_2 is the error of measurement in the dependent variable. Let us use the traditional notation by denoting the reliabilities by r_{xx} and r_{yy}, respectively. We then have

$$r_{xx} = \rho_{xT}^2$$
$$r_{yy} = \rho_{yU}^2$$

The desired correlation is the population correlation between perfectly measured variables, that is, ρ_{TU}, but the observed correlation is the sample correlation between observed scores r_{xy}. There are two steps in relating the one to the other: the systematic attenuation of the population correlation by error of measurement and the unsystematic variation produced by sampling error.

The systematic attenuation can be computed by considering the causal pathways from x to T to U to y. According to the rules of path analysis, ρ_{xy} is the product of the three paths from x to y; that is,

$$\rho_{xy} = \rho_{xT}\rho_{TU}\rho_{Uy} = \rho_{xT}\rho_{yU}\rho_{TU}$$
$$= \sqrt{r_{xx}}\sqrt{r_{yy}}\rho_{TU}$$

At the level of population correlations, this leads to the classic formula for correction for attenuation:

$$\rho_{TU} = \frac{\rho_{xy}}{\sqrt{r_{xx}}\sqrt{r_{yy}}} \tag{3.12}$$

At the level of observed correlations, we have

$$r_{xy} = \rho_{xy} + e$$

where e is the sampling error in r_{xy} as before. Thus,

$$\sigma_r^2 = \sigma_\rho^2 + \sigma_e^2$$

where the sampling error variance is given by the formulas of earlier sections.

If we correct the observed correlation using the population correlation formula, then we have

$$r_c = \frac{r_{xy}}{\sqrt{r_{xx}}\sqrt{r_{yy}}} = \frac{\sqrt{r_{xx}}\sqrt{r_{yy}}\rho_{TU} + e}{\sqrt{r_{xx}}\sqrt{r_{yy}}}$$

$$= \rho_{TU} + \frac{e}{\sqrt{r_{xx}}\sqrt{r_{yy}}} \tag{3.13}$$

We can write a new equation for the corrected correlation

$$r_c = \rho_c + e_c \tag{3.14}$$

where e_c is the sampling error in the corrected correlation r_c and where the population value $\rho_c = \rho_{TU}$. The error variance for the corrected correlation can then be computed from the error variance for uncorrected correlation and the reliabilities of the two variables (Hedges, 1995):

$$e_c = \frac{e}{\sqrt{r_{xx}}\sqrt{r_{yy}}}$$

$$\sigma^2_{e_c} = \frac{\sigma^2_e}{r_{xx}r_{yy}} \qquad\qquad (3.15)$$

Thus, if we correct the observed correlation for attenuation, we increase the sampling error correspondingly. In particular, to form the confidence interval for a corrected correlation, we apply the correction formula to the two endpoints of the confidence interval for the uncorrected correlation. That is, in the case of correction for attenuation, just as we divide the point estimate of the correlation by the product of the square roots of the reliabilities, so, too, we divide each endpoint of the confidence interval by the same product.

An Example of Correction for Attenuation

Suppose that if organizational commitment and job satisfaction were perfectly measured, the correlation between true scores would be $\rho_{TU} = .60$ Suppose instead that we measure organizational commitment with reliability $r_{xx} = .45$ and that we measure job satisfaction with reliability $r_{yy} = .55$. Then the population correlation between observed scores would be

$$\rho_{xy} = \sqrt{r_{xx}}\sqrt{r_{yy}}\rho_{TU} = \sqrt{.45}\sqrt{.55}\rho_{TU}$$
$$= .50(.60) = .30$$

That is, the effect of error of measurement in this example is to reduce the correlation between true scores by 50%—from a true score population correlation of .60 to a study population correlation of .30 between observed scores. If we apply the correction formula, we have

$$\rho_{TU} = \frac{\rho_{xy}}{\sqrt{r_{xx}}\sqrt{r_{yy}}} = \frac{.30}{\sqrt{.45}\sqrt{.55}} = \frac{.30}{.50} = .60$$

That is, correction for attenuation works perfectly for population correlations; it is perfectly accurate when sample size is infinite.

Consider the impact of sampling error. If the sample size for the study is $N = 100$, then the standard error of the observed correlation (from $\rho_{xy} = .30$) is $(1 - .30^2)/\sqrt{99} = .091$. Thus, it would not be uncommon to observe a correlation of .20 in the actual study. If we compare the observed correlation of .20 with the desired correlation of .60, then we see that there is a massive error. However, this error can be broken into two components: the systematic error of attenuation and the unsystematic error due to sampling error. The systematic error reduced the correlation from .60 to .30. The unsystematic error is the difference between an observed r of .20 and the population attenuated correlation of .30.

Let us correct for attenuation and look at the error in the corrected correlation:

$$r_c = \frac{r_{xy}}{\sqrt{r_{xx}}\sqrt{r_{yy}}} = \frac{.20}{\sqrt{.45}\sqrt{.55}} = \frac{.20}{.50} = .40$$

The sampling error in the corrected correlation is the difference between the estimated .40 and the actual .60. Thus, we have

$$r = \rho_{xy} + e = \rho_{xy} - .1 = .30 - .10 = .20$$
$$r_c = \rho_c + e_c = \rho_c - .2 = .60 - .20 = .40$$

Therefore, as we doubled the observed attenuated correlation to estimate the unattenuated correlation, we doubled the sampling error as well. On the other hand, we reduced the systematic error from .30 to 0. We can combine both types of error and look at total error. Total error has been reduced by 50%:

$$\text{Total error for } r = .60 - .20 = .40$$
$$\text{Total error for } r_c = .60 - .40 = .20$$

The standard error for the observed correlation would be calculated as

$$\frac{1 - .20^2}{\sqrt{99}} = .096$$

The 95% confidence interval for the observed correlation is given by $r \pm 1.96\sigma_e = .20 \pm 1.96(.096)$ or $.01 \le \rho \le .39$, which includes the actual value of $\rho_{xy} = .30$. We then correct each endpoint of the confidence interval to obtain

Lower Endpoint	*Upper Endpoint*
$r_1 = .01$	$r_1 = .39$
$r_{1c} = \dfrac{.01}{\sqrt{.45}\sqrt{.55}}$	$r_{2c} = \dfrac{.39}{\sqrt{.45}\sqrt{.55}}$
$= \dfrac{.01}{.50} = .02$	$= \dfrac{.39}{.50} = .78$

Let us compare the confidence intervals of corrected and uncorrected correlations:

$$.01 \le \hat{\rho}_{xy} \le .39$$
$$.02 \le \hat{\rho}_{TU} \le .78$$

We see that the center of the confidence interval changes from the uncorrected correlation of .20 to the corrected correlation .40. At the same time, the width of the confidence interval doubles, reflecting the increased sampling error in the corrected correlation.

This point can be made dramatically with confidence intervals. If measurement of both variables were perfectly reliable, then the population correlation would be .60, and the standard error would be $(1-.60^2)/\sqrt{99} = .064$. This is much smaller than the standard error for a correlation of .30, which is .091. Thus, if we can reduce error of measurement substantively, then we can obtain larger observed correlations *and smaller confidence intervals*. Substantive elimination of error of measurement is vastly superior to elimination by statistical formula after the fact.

We could have obtained the same confidence interval in a different way. Suppose we erected the confidence interval around the corrected correlation using the sampling error formula for e_c. The center of the confidence interval is then $r_c = .40$. The sampling error variance is then given by

$$\sigma^2_{e_c} = \frac{\sigma^2_e}{r_{xx}r_{yy}} = \frac{\sigma^2_e}{(.45)(.55)} = \frac{(1-2^2)^2/99}{.2475} = .0376$$

That is, the sampling error standard deviation for the corrected correlation is $\sigma_{e_c} = (.0376)^{1/2} = .19$. The confidence interval is then given by $.40 \pm 1.96\sigma_{e_c}$ or $.02 \le \rho_{TU} \le .78$. This is the same confidence interval obtained earlier using the other method.

Statistical Versus Substantive Correction

If we use statistical formulas to correct for attenuation, we obtain larger corrected correlations with a wider confidence interval. There are two conclusions that might be drawn from this fact. (1) *False conclusion:* Because correcting for attenuation increases the amount of sampling error, maybe we should not correct for attenuation. *Key fact:* If we do not correct for attenuation, then we do not eliminate the *systematic* error. In our example, the error in the uncorrected correlation was $.60 - .20 = .40$. Thus, the error in the corrected correlation was only half as large as the error in the uncorrected correlation. (2) *True conclusion:* We could greatly improve our statistical accuracy if we could reduce the error of measurement substantively, that is, by using more reliable measurement procedures in the first place.

USING THE APPROPRIATE RELIABILITY COEFFICIENT

Different methods of estimating reliability capture or reflect different sources of measurement error. Most methods of estimating reliability capture some but not all types of measurement error. In making corrections for measurement error, the researcher should make every effort to use the appropriate type of reliability coefficient. Estimation of the appropriate reliability coefficient requires the identification of the kinds of measurement error that exist in the specific research domain and requires the gathering of data that allows each kind of measurement error to be reflected in the reliability coefficient. In most current meta-analyses, the unit of analysis is the person (or rat or pigeon or . . .), and the variable measured is some behavior of the person. For this case, there is an extensive theory of reliability developed by psychometricans, and there has been extensive testing of that theory (see, e.g., Cronbach, 1947; J. C. Stanley, 1971; Thorndike, 1951). This is the case discussed in this book. However, meta-analyses are being conducted in other areas. For example, Rodgers and Hunter (1986) conducted a meta-analysis in which the measures were business unit productivity measures. Another example of this is Harter et al. (2002). In both meta-analyses, the unit of measurement was not the individual employee but the business unit (e.g., individual companies, individual stores, or individual bank branches), and in both meta-analyses, special reliability estimation procedures had to be used. However, such cases are the exception. Suppose the unit of analysis in the study is persons, the usual case. The measure is usually obtained in one of three ways: (a) the behavior is directly recorded (as in test scores or closed-ended questionnaire answers, here called "response data"), (b) the behavior is assessed by an observer (here called a "judgment or rating"), or (c) the behavior is observed and recorded by an observer (here called "coded response data"). The reliability considerations are different for each of these cases.

In the measurement of a given construct, the assumption is that the construct being measured is the primary cause determining that behavior, response, or rating. Error of measurement is present to the extent that the behavior or response is also determined by other causes, causes extraneous to the construct. At least three kinds of measurement error have been identified by psychometric theory: random response error, specific error, and transient error (cf. Le, Schmidt, Harter, & Lauver, 2010; Le, Schmidt, & Putka, 2009; Schmidt & Hunter, 1996, 1999b; Schmidt, Le, & Ilies, 2003; J. C. Stanley, 1971; Thorndike, 1949, 1951).

Random Response Measurement Error

Random response error is usually the most serious source of measurement error. Except for highly practiced responses, such as giving one's name, most human acts have a sizable random element. Random response error can be thought of as noise in the human nervous system (Le et al., 2009; Schmidt & Hunter, 1999b; Thorndike, 1949, 1951). Random response error can occur, for example, as result of misreading the wording of an item (e.g., missing the critical word *not*). Random response errors are uncorrelated across items or responses.

Specific Factor Measurement Error

A person's response can also be affected by something peculiar about the measurement situation, for example, an idiosyncratic response to a specific word used in an opinion item. The influence of such stimulus-specific agents is called specific error or specific factor error. Specific factor error is associated with individual items in a measure. (It is actually the person-by-item interaction.) Each different item for measuring a construct has specific factor measurement error unique to that item. Likewise, each different *scale or test* has specific factor measurement error that is unique to that scale or test (Le et al., 2009, 2010). Specific factor errors are unique in that they are uncorrelated not only with each other but also with the construct being measured. As such, they must be considered errors of measurement and cannot be considered part of the construct being measured. Specific factor measurement error is the explanation for the fact that, even after correcting for random response error, no two items or scales measuring the same thing on the same occasion are correlated 1.00. Without specific factor measurement error, this correlation would be 1.00.

Transient Measurement Error

A person's response can also be affected by an influence that varies randomly over time, such as mood or illness. For example, a bad cold at the time of measurement could cause a lower score on a job satisfaction measure. Being in an unusually good mood on the day of measurement could create a transient measurement error in the opposite direction. Neither of these effects can be considered part of the actual construct and so must be regarded as measurement errors. In this example, the actual construct of job satisfaction is the typical or average level of satisfaction with one's job. The influence of such time-varying factors is called transient measurement error. Each of these three forms of error of measurement enters differently into the designs traditionally used to measure reliability (Le et al., 2009, 2010; Schmidt et al., 2003; J. C. Stanley, 1971; Thorndike, 1951).

METHODS OF ESTIMATING RELIABILITY COEFFICIENTS

Coefficient Alpha Reliability

A method of estimating reliability captures or reflects a particular type of measurement error only if that type of measurement error lowers the reliability estimate. The most commonly used estimate of reliability is Cronbach's alpha coefficient (Cronbach, 1947) for continuous items or its equivalent, the KR-20 reliability estimate for dichotomous items. Cronbach (1947) referred to this type of reliability as the coefficient of equivalence, because it estimates the correlation between two randomly parallel measures *administered at the same point in time*. This estimation procedure makes measurement error visible by obtaining multiple responses in a given measurement session—eliciting behaviors to various situations or stimuli (e.g., items) that are equivalent in that they are all caused mainly by the construct to be measured. The independent responses allow for independent sampling of the random response errors and independent sampling of the specific factor errors in individual items. Reliability estimated by this method detects and measures the extent of random response error and specific factor error. However, if there is transient error, this design will not detect it; thus, the reliability coefficient will be too large by the amount of transient error. Hence, it will undercorrect for measurement error when used in the correction formulas. This form of reliability is often referred to as "internal consistency reliability," but this usage is erroneous, because coefficient alpha and KR-20 can be very large even when the internal consistency of the items (i.e., the average item intercorrelation) is very low. This occurs when the number of items is large.

Test-Retest Reliability

Another common reliability estimation procedure is the test-retest design. A behavior is measured with the same scale or test at two points in time that are far enough apart so that the transient error factor is not repeated but close enough in time so that there is no real change in the construct to be measured. The two measures will allow for new (independent) sampling from the random response error distribution and new (independent) sampling from the transient error distribution. However, if there is specific error, this design will not detect it; thus, the reliability coefficient will be too large by the relative amount of specific error. Specific factor measurement error is not detected because the same specific errors occur at Time 1 and Time 2 due to use of the same scale (same set of items) at both times. Thus, specific factor errors are correlated over time. This form of reliability is called test-retest reliability, although better language would substitute the phrase "reliability estimate" for the word *reliability*. Cronbach (1947) referred to this type of reliability estimate as the coefficient of stability (CS).

Delayed Parallel Forms Reliability

If all three kinds of measurement error are present, then the correct reliability will be obtained only by an estimation procedure in which both the determinants of specific error and the temporal determinants of transient error are resampled. This is the "delayed parallel forms" design. Cronbach (1947) referred to this type of reliability estimate as the coefficient of equivalence and stability (CES). Given two forms of the measure and two occasions, it is possible to separately estimate the extent of each of the three kinds of error (cf. Cronbach, 1947; Le et al., 2009, 2010; Schmidt et al., 2003; J. C. Stanley, 1971; Thorndike, 1949, 1951). If all three kinds of error are present, then the delayed parallel forms reliability (CES) will be smaller than either the parallel forms reliability estimate (coefficient alpha or KR-20) or the test-retest reliability estimate. Using the wrong reliability estimate causes an underestimate of the impact of error of measurement. Thus, correction using the wrong reliability means that some source of error is not calibrated and, as a result, the correlation is not corrected for attenuation due to that type of measurement error. That is, correction using the wrong reliability means that the corrected correlation will correspondingly underestimate the actual correlation between constructs. This will, of course, cause a downward bias in estimates of mean correlations in the meta-analysis. If a primary researcher or a meta-analyst is forced to use CE or CS estimates of reliability because CES estimates are not available, the study or meta-analysis should point out that full correction for measurement error was not possible and that the results reported are therefore conservative (i.e., have a downward bias). The report should also point out that such an incomplete correction for measurement error yields results that are much more accurate than failure to make any correction at all for measurement error.

Underestimation of correlations between constructs caused by use of the wrong reliability estimates is a cause of the problem of construct proliferation in many areas of behavioral science. Often the erroneous conclusion that results is that the two constructs are "correlated but not identical." For example, this was the conclusion reached in the literature for the constructs of job satisfaction and organizational commitment. But Le et al. (2010) showed that when this correlation is properly corrected for the downwardly biasing effects of measurement error, it is .92, suggesting that these two constructs are empirically indistinguishable by respondents and are probably only one construct. There may be many other such erroneous conclusions in the literature, all contributing to the problem of construct proliferation. The question of construct redundancy is further explored in Schmidt, Le, and Oh (2013).

Judgments by Raters

If a construct such as job performance is assessed by an observer such as the person's immediate supervisor, there are two sources of error in the measurement: random response error in the judgment and idiosyncrasy in rater perception (called "halo"; cf. Hoyt, 2000; Schmidt, Viswesvaran, & Ones, 2000; Viswesvaran, Ones, & Schmidt, 1996; Viswesvaran, Schmidt, & Ones, 2005). A judgment by a single rater is a response and is therefore subject to random response error and to transient error. These two sources are the only sources of measurement error captured by reliability methods based on only one rater. Specifically, the correlation between ratings of individuals by the same rater made at two different times (i.e., intrarater reliability) is reduced by these two types of measurement error and thus captures their effects. Hence, it has the same properties as a test-retest reliability estimate.

But in every research area involving people perception, human perception of other people has shown considerable idiosyncrasy of perceptions and judgments. In most areas, there are large differences in the perceptions of different raters. This idiosyncratic bias associated with each rater (halo) is not part of the construct being assessed and is therefore measurement error (Hoyt, 2000; Viswesvaran et al., 1996, 2005). This form of measurement error functions as specific factor error associated with each rater. It is also referred to as halo error. Thus, the proper reliability estimate must take differences in perception into account as well as randomness in the judgment made by each judge. The appropriate estimation of reliability for judgments is the correlation between judgments made independently by different raters. This reliability estimate is called interrater reliability. The correlation between judges will be reduced appropriately by random response error in the judgments and by differences between raters in perception (halo error). Transient error is also controlled, because transient errors of different raters are not correlated. Specific factor measurement error is controlled by use of multiple items in the rating scale. If two judgments (say, "quality of work" and "quantity of work") are each made by two raters, then it is possible to separately estimate the effect of random response error, item-specific error (specific to these two rating scale items), and idiosyncrasy error (also called "halo"; Viswesvaran et al., 1996, 2005). Specific methods for doing this are presented in Le et al. (2009) and Schmidt et al. (2000). Since the cause of the transient error is typically independent in the two judges, this reliability coefficient will also be appropriately lowered by transient error, although transient error will not be distinguishable from idiosyncrasy (halo) error. Interrater reliability is the CES (delayed parallel forms reliability) for ratings. Studies of this sort have found average interrater reliabilities of about .50 for supervisory ratings of job performance (cf. Rothstein, 1990; Schmidt et al., 2000; Viswesvaran et al., 1996). Intrarater reliability, estimated by correlating ratings made by the same rater at two different times, is much higher (around .85; Viswesvaran et al., 1996) but is a gross overestimate of actual reliability. Hence, use of intrarater reliability instead of interrater reliability leads to serious undercorrection for the bases created by measurement error.

Coded Response Data

Some constructs are too complicated to be directly rated. Thus, the data used are a coding by an observer of the behavior. For example, one might code the degree of need for achievement expressed in a story told by the subject in response to a picture shown to the subject. Differences between the codings by different observers are called "coding error." A critical error often made in this context is to consider as error only the discrepancy between coders. While coding error is one important source of error in the measurement, there is also random response error, specific factor error, and transient error in the behavior coded. For example, suppose that coders were so well trained that they agreed to a correlation of .95 in their assessments of the amount of achievement motivation contained in the stories. However, suppose that from one week to the next, there is a correlation of only .40 between the achievement imagery in successive stories told by the same people. The "reliability" of .95 would not reflect this instability (random response error and transient error) in inventing stories and would, thus, greatly overestimate the actual reliability in question. This error is actually common in the literature in studies based on coded response data.

In the case of coded response data, it is critical that the reliability estimates be based on two separate administrations of the measure. That is, the first coder should code responses obtained at Time 1 and the second coder should code responses from the same individuals obtained at Time 2. The correlation between these two codings provides the only accurate estimate of the reliability of coded response data. If both coders code responses obtained on a single occasion, the resulting correlation grossly overestimates reliability, resulting in a large downward bias in meta-analysis estimates. For a more complete treatment of measurement error in coded response data, see Schmidt and Hunter (1996, 1999b).

Implications of Measurement Error for Meta-Analysis

What are the implications of these facts about measurement errors and reliability estimates for meta-analysis? Unlike other systematic artifacts, measurement error is always present. Accurate corrections for measurement error are critical to accurate meta-analysis results (Cook et al., 1992, pp. 315–316; Hedges, 2009b; Matt & Cook, 2009). Some advocate an approach different from that of correcting each correlation in the meta-analysis for measurement error. In this alternative approach, the reliabilities in each study are coded and tested as a potential moderator variable in meta-regression (Borenstein et al., 2009, chap. 38). A statistically significant relationship indicates that measurement error affects the observed correlations. One problem with this approach is that we know a priori that measurement error *must* affect the observed correlations. In this connection, a major problem with this approach is low statistical power (Hedges & Pigott, 2004); the results frequently falsely indicate that reliability (measurement error) does not affect the observed correlations. Another problem is that this approach does not produce an estimate of the mean corrected correlation and its *SD*. The limitations and problems of meta-regression are discussed in Chapter 9.

The use of inappropriate reliability estimates to make corrections for measurement error in meta-analysis leads to reduced accuracy of results. For example, recent research indicates that there is transient measurement error in commonly used psychological measures (e.g., personality and ability measures) (Schmidt et al., 2003). This means that the common practice of using coefficient alpha and KR-20 reliability estimates to correct for measurement error in meta-analysis typically leads to undercorrections and, hence, produces a downward bias in estimates of mean correlations, because coefficient alpha and KR-20 reliabilities do not detect or remove the effects of transient error. Likewise, use of test-retest reliability estimates also leads to undercorrections, because of failure to control for specific factor measurement errors. Whether one is correcting each coefficient individually (as described in this chapter) or using distributions of reliability coefficients (as described in Chapter 4), all relevant sources of measurement error should be considered and, to the extent possible given available data, reliability estimates that capture all these sources of measurement error should be used (Schmidt et al., 2003). As discussed earlier in this section, this is particularly critical when the goal is to determine whether two ostensibly different constructs are really the same construct, because the problem of construct proliferation is very serious today in psychology and all the social sciences.

Unfortunately, most available estimates of reliability are alpha coefficients or KR-20 estimates (i.e., estimates of the CE) and so do not take transient error into account. Estimates of the CES coefficient are rare in the literature and not very common even in test manuals. Estimates of the amount of transient error in a variety of scales are around 4% to 5% (see, e.g., Schmidt et al., 2003). (These values are larger for trait measures of affectivity.) Hence, CE estimates can be adjusted or corrected for transient error by subtracting .04 or .05 from these reliability estimates, as suggested in Schmidt et al. (2003). Such adjustment figures, however, are not (yet) available for all types of scales. Therefore, it is important to bear in mind that in research, as in other areas, "the perfect is the enemy of the good." It would be a false argument to state that unless ideal estimates of reliability can be used, no correction for measurement error should be made. As noted earlier, use of coefficient alpha estimates (CE estimates) when CES estimates (delayed parallel forms estimates) are more appropriate still leads to final results that are much more accurate than does failure to make any correction for the biasing effects of measurement error. However, in such a case, the researcher should point out that only an incomplete correction for measurement error was possible and the resulting corrected values therefore contain a downward bias.

Another important implication is that when ratings are used, use of intrarater reliabilities will lead to very severe undercorrections for measurement error. To avoid this, interrater reliabilities should always be used, and (except in very special cases) intrarater reliabilities should not be used. Also, in artifact distribution meta-analysis (discussed in Chapter 4), one should never use a *mixture* of intra- and interrater reliabilities in the reliability artifact distribution. Fortunately, interrater estimates (unlike CES estimates for tests and scales) are widely available (cf. Rothstein, 1990; Viswesvaran et al., 1996).

The use of inappropriate reliability estimates has been a problem in some applications of meta-analysis. It is important to remember that different types of reliability estimates are not all equally appropriate.

RESTRICTION OR ENHANCEMENT OF RANGE

If studies differ greatly in the range of values present on the independent variable, then the correlation will differ correspondingly. Correlations are directly comparable across studies only if they are computed on samples from populations with the same standard deviation on the independent variable. Range correction formulas are available that take a correlation computed on a population with a given standard deviation and produce an estimate of what the correlation would have been had the standard deviation been different. That is, range correction formulas estimate the effect of changing the study population standard deviation from one value to another. To eliminate range variation from a meta-analysis, we can use range correction formulas to project all correlations to the same reference standard deviation.

As noted in Chapter 2, range restriction (or range enhancement) can be either direct or indirect—and range correction procedures are different for the two cases. Direct range restriction occurs when there is direct truncation on the independent variable. For example, if only those in the top 50% of test scores are hired, and no one with a lower test score is hired, we have direct range restriction. Likewise, it is direct range *enhancement* if an experimenter selects as subjects only those in the top 10% and the bottom 10% of scores on, say, a measure of conscientiousness to participate in a study. The statistic we need to know to correct for direct range restriction is the ratio of the observed *SD* in the restricted sample to the observed *SD* in the unrestricted sample; that is, s_x / S_x. This ratio is referred to as u_x; that is, $u_X = s_x / S_x$. If we know this ratio, we can use the Thorndike Case II (Thorndike, 1949) direct range restriction formula to correct for range restriction. By using the reciprocal of this statistic, that is, S_x / s_x, we can use this same formula to correct for direct range enhancement. This ratio is referred to as U_x; that is, $U_x = S_x/s_x$.

Indirect range restriction occurs when people are selected on a third variable that correlates with the independent variable. For example, if we are evaluating the validity of a new engineering aptitude test for admissions into an engineering college and all our engineering students were originally admitted based on a college entrance examination, then there will be indirect range restriction on the engineering aptitude test, because the two tests will be positively correlated. If selection into the college is based *only* on the entrance examination (direct range restriction on that exam, with no other information being used), and if we know the restricted and unrestricted *SD* on that examination and the correlation between the two exams in the selected group, there is a formula for correcting for this sort of indirect range restriction (called the Thorndike Case III indirect range restriction correction formula; Thorndike, 1949). However, this situation is very rare, because selection on the third variable (here the college entrance exam) is rarely direct (because other variables are also used in selection) and because, even if it is direct, we rarely have the needed statistics on the third variable. Thus, this correction formula can rarely be applied. For this reason, we do not develop applications of this formula.

The type of indirect range restriction that is most common is the situation in which people have been selected on an unknown (unrecorded) combination of variables and that combination (or composite) of variables is correlated with the independent variable, producing indirect range restriction on the independent variable (Linn, Harnisch, & Dunbar, 1981b). A common example is the case in which people have been hired based on some unknown combination of, say, an interview, an application blank, and a background check, and we find that the *SD* on the test we are studying is considerably smaller in this selected (incumbent) group than the *SD* in an application population (the unrestricted *SD*), indicating there is indirect range restriction on our independent variable. That is, we find u_x is less than 1.00. Linn et al. (1981b) showed that students admitted to law schools were an example of this sort of indirect range restriction. Another example is the case in which people who volunteer to participate in a study have a lower *SD* on extroversion scores (the independent variable); that is, u_x is again less than 1.00. Here, indirect range restriction is produced by some unknown combination of self-selection variables. Most range restriction in real data is, in fact, caused by this sort of indirect range restriction (Hunter et al., 2006; Linn et al., 1981b; Mendoza & Mumford, 1987; Thorndike, 1949). As in the case of direct selection, we can also have indirect range *enhancement*. For example, the *SD* on extroversion of those volunteering for the study might be *larger* than the *SD* of extroversion in the reference population. However, in the case of indirect selection, range enhancement appears to be relatively rare.

The key statistic we must know to correct for indirect range restriction of this sort is not u_X but u_T, where u_T is the ratio of *true score SDs*. That is, $u_T = s_T/S_T$. As we will see, there are special formulas for computing u_T from u_X and other information. If we have indirect range enhancement (instead of range restriction), the statistic we need is $U_T = S_T/s_T$. The correction for indirect range restriction is made using the same correction formula used to correct for direct range restriction but with u_T used in that formula in place of u_X. Likewise, to correct for range enhancement, U_T is substituted in that formula for U_X. The availability of these corrections greatly increases the accuracy of meta-analyses involving range restriction corrections. Later in this chapter, we present more detailed information on indirect range restriction. A full development can be found in Hunter et al. (2006). Le and Schmidt (2006) showed via computer simulation that this procedure is quite accurate and more accurate than the Case II formula for direct range restriction when the range restriction is in fact indirect. Using computer simulation, Li, Chan, and Cui (2010) compared the accuracy of this method and the Thorndike Case III procedure (which requires much more information and therefore usually cannot be used) and found them to be about equally accurate.

The correction for indirect range restriction presented in Hunter et al. (2006) is based on the assumption that any range restriction that exists on the dependent variable (y) is fully mediated (i.e., caused by) range restriction on the independent variable (x). This means that range restriction on the third variable (called s) is not a direct cause of range restriction on y; the third variable directly causes range restriction only on x. As noted by Hunter et al. (2006), in most contexts, this assumption is likely to hold (or hold to a close enough approximation). But in cases in which this assumption is substantially violated, the Hunter et al. (2006) correction is less accurate (Le & Schmidt, 2006). A method of correcting for indirect range restriction has recently been developed, based on earlier work by Bryant and Gokhale (1972), that does not require this assumption (Le et al., 2013). However, this method requires the user to know the range restriction ratio (u) for the dependent variable (y), which is not required by the Hunter et al. method. In personnel selection, the y measure is job performance, and its SD in the applicant population (i.e., its unrestricted SD) is virtually impossible to estimate. So this method of correction cannot be used in studies in which the dependent variable is job performance or other behaviors on the job. More generally, it cannot be used with dependent variable measures for which data do not exist on a broader population that allows computation of an unrestricted SD. This includes many types of behavioral measures used in psychological research. But in studies focused on the relation between psychological or organizational constructs (e.g., between job satisfaction and organizational commitment), it may be possible to estimate the needed u ratio for the dependent variable based on some broader population SD (e.g., from national norms or workforce norms). In such cases, the Le et al. (2013) method can be used, and if the fundamental assumption underlying the Hunter et al. (2006) method is seriously violated in that data set, the Le et al. (2013) method will produce more accurate results than the Hunter et al. method. In the example meta-analyses in this book that correct for indirect range restriction, we apply the Hunter et al. (2006) method, because this method is applicable in more situations and because it is rare for its fundamental assumption to be seriously violated.

For each study, we need to know the standard deviation of the independent variable s_x. Range departure is then measured by relating that standard deviation to the reference standard deviation S_x. The comparison used is the ratio of the standard deviation in the study group to the reference standard deviation that is, $u_X = s_x / S_x$. The ratio u_X is less than 1 if the study has restriction in range (the usual case) and greater than 1 if the study has enhancement of range. The correlation in the study will be greater than or less than the reference correlation depending on whether the ratio u_X is greater than or less than 1, respectively. In direct range restriction, the correction for range restriction depends on the value of u_X. In indirect range restriction, the correction depends on u_T, which is a function of u_X and r_{xx_a}, the reliability of the independent variable in the unrestricted population. These corrections depend on two assumptions. First, the relationship in question must be linear (or at least approximately so). Second, the variance of the independent variable must be equal (or at least approximately so) at each level of the dependent variable. This latter condition is known as homoscedasticity (Gross & McGanney, 1987). One additional assumption is required for the correction for indirect range restriction: the assumption that range restriction on the dependent variable occurs only through range restriction on the independent variable. This assumption is typically reasonable (Hunter et al., 2006).

As noted previously, the major computational difference between direct and indirect range restriction is that in direct range restriction, we use u_X in making range corrections, and in indirect range restriction, we use u_T. The correction formula is otherwise identical. There are also some differences, described later in this chapter, in the order in which corrections for measurement error are made. The extra steps involved in computing u_T make the mathematics of correcting for indirect range restriction somewhat more complicated than is the case for direct range restriction and, therefore, make the presentation somewhat more mathematically complicated and lengthy. However, once u_T is computed and substituted for u_X, the correction equation is the same. The computation of sampling error variance and confidence intervals for range-corrected correlations is also identical in form. Therefore, to simplify our presentation, we present most of the following discussion in terms of direct range restriction corrections and forgo the presentations for indirect range restriction corrections at this point. (We will return to the topic of indirect range restriction later in this chapter.) Before proceeding, we present the necessary formulas for computing u_T:

$$u_T = s_T/S_T$$

$$u_T = \left[\frac{u_X^2 - (1 - r_{XX_a})}{r_{XX_a}} \right]^{1/2} \tag{3.16}$$

where r_{XX_a} is the reliability of the independent variable in the unrestricted group. If only the reliability in the *restricted* group (r_{XX_i}) is known, r_{XX_a} can be computed as follows:

$$r_{XX_a} = 1 - \frac{s_{X_i}^2 (1 - r_{XX_i})}{s_{X_a}^2} \tag{3.17a}$$

$$r_{XX_a} = 1 - u_X^2 (1 - r_{XX_i}) \tag{3.17b}$$

This equation can be reversed to give r_{XX_i} for any value of r_{XX_a}:

$$r_{XX_i} = 1 - U_X^2 (1 - r_{XX_a}) \tag{3.17c}$$

where $U_X = 1/u_X$.

In this section, we use the direct range restriction model to explore range departure in the context of a single study in which population correlations are known. In the following section, we consider the effect of correcting a sample correlation for range departure. We will find that the sampling error of the corrected correlation differs from that of the uncorrected correlation, and we will show how to adjust the confidence interval correspondingly. After this treatment of range correction in single studies, we consider the effect of range correction in meta-analysis. At that point, we treat both indirect and direct range restriction.

We cannot always study the population that we wish to use as a reference point. Sometimes we study a population in which our independent variable varies less than in the reference population (restriction in range), and sometimes we study a population in which it varies more widely than in the reference population (enhancement of range). In either case, the same relationship between the variables produces a different correlation coefficient. In the case of enhancement of range, the study population correlation is systematically larger than the reference population correlation. This problem is compounded by sampling error and by error of measurement.

Consider personnel selection research. The reference population is the applicant population, but the study is done with people who have already been hired (because we can get job performance scores only for those on the job). If the people hired were a random sample of the applicants, then the only problems would be sampling error and measurement error. Suppose, however, the test we are studying has been used to select those who are hired. For example, suppose those hired are above the mean on the test; that is, we have direct range restriction. Then the range of test scores among the job incumbents is greatly reduced in comparison to the applicant population. We would thus expect a considerable reduction in the size of the population correlation in the incumbent population compared to the applicant population. If test scores are normally distributed in the applicant population, then the standard deviation for people in the top half of the distribution is only 60% as large as the standard deviation for the entire population. Thus, if the standard deviation were 20 in the applicant population, it would be only .60(20) = 12 in the incumbent population of those hired. The degree of restriction in range would thus be $u_X = 12/20 = .60$.

The formula for the correlation produced by direct selection on the independent variable is called the formula for direct restriction in range, although it works for enhancement, too, as we shall see. Let ρ_1 be the reference population correlation and let ρ_2 be the study population correlation. Then

$$\rho_2 = \frac{u_X \rho_1}{\sqrt{(u_X^2 - 1)\rho_1^2 + 1}} \qquad (3.18)$$

where

$$u_x = \frac{\sigma_{x_2}}{\sigma_{x_1}}$$

is the ratio of standard deviations in the two populations. In the case of direct restriction in range, we have $u_x < 1$ and, hence, $\rho_1 > \rho_2$. In the case of direct range enhancement, we have $u_x > 1$ and, hence, $\rho_2 > \rho_1$.

In the case of our personnel selection example, we have $u_X = .60$ and, hence,

$$\rho_2 = \frac{.60\rho_1}{\sqrt{(.60^2 - 1)\rho_1^2 + 1}} = \frac{.60\rho_1}{\sqrt{1 - .64\rho_1^2}}$$

For example, if the correlation between test and job performance in the applicant population were .50, then the correlation in the study population would be

$$\rho_2 = \frac{.60(.50)}{\sqrt{(1 - .64(.50)^2}} = \frac{.60(.50)}{.92} = .33$$

That is, if the study were done on only the top half of the distribution on the independent variable, then the population correlation would be reduced from .50 to .33. If undetected and not corrected, this difference between .50 and .33 would have profound implications for the interpretation of empirical studies.

Suppose, however, we have the data, that is, $\rho_2 = .33$ and $u_X = .60$, and we wish to correct for restriction in range. We could reverse the roles of the two populations. That is, we could regard the applicant population as an enhancement of the incumbent population. We could then use the same formula as before with the ρs reversed; that is,

$$\rho_1 = \frac{U_X \rho_2}{\sqrt{(U_X^2 - 1)\rho_2^2 + 1}} \tag{3.19}$$

where

$$U_X = \frac{\sigma_{x_1}}{\sigma_{x_2}} = \frac{1}{u_X}$$

is the ratio of standard deviations in the opposite order. This formula is called the correction for restriction in range, although it also works for correction for enhancement. In the personnel example, we plug in $\rho_2 = .33$ and $U_X = 1/u_X = 1/.60 = 1.67$ to obtain

$$\rho_1 = \frac{1.67(.33)}{\sqrt{(1.67^2 - 1)(.33)^2 + 1}} = \frac{1.67(.33)}{1.09} = .50$$

Thus, at the level of population correlations (i.e., when N is infinite), we can use the formula for restriction in range to move back and forth between populations of different variance with perfect accuracy. If range restriction were indirect, substituting u_T and U_T for u_X and U_X, respectively, would allow us to do this same thing.

The situation is more complicated if there is sampling error. If we apply the formula for correction for restriction in range to a sample correlation, then we get only an approximate estimate of the reference group population correlation. Moreover, the corrected correlation will have a larger amount of sampling error. This situation is analogous to that in correction for attenuation due to measurement error. There is a trade-off. To eliminate the systematic error (downward bias) associated with restriction in range, we must accept the increase in sampling error produced by the statistical correction. If we could correct substantively—that is, if the study could be done on a sample from the reference population—then there would be no increase in sampling error, because there would be no correction. In fact, in the case of restriction in range, a study done on the applicant population sample (if it could be done) would have a larger correlation and, hence, less sampling error and a smaller confidence interval.

The confidence interval for the corrected correlation is easy to obtain. The correction formula can be regarded as a mathematical transformation. This transformation is monotone (but not linear) and, hence, it transforms confidence intervals. Thus, the confidence interval is obtained by correcting the endpoints of the confidence interval using the same formula that is used to correct the correlation. That is, the same range correction formula that is applied to the correlation is applied to the endpoints of the confidence interval.

Consider the personnel example with direct range restriction in which the population correlations are .50 for the applicant population and .33 for the study population. If the sample size is 100, then the standard error for a correlation of $\rho = .33$ is $\sigma_c = (1 - .33^2)/\sqrt{99} = .09$. If the sample correlation came out low, it might be something such as .28, which is low by .05. Corrected for restriction in range of $U_X = 1.67$, we have

$$r_c = \frac{1.67(.28)}{\sqrt{(1.67^2 - 1)(.28^2) + 1}} = \frac{.47}{1.07} = .44$$

The standard error of the observed r of .28 is .093. The 95% confidence interval on the observed r of .28 is

Lower Endpoint	Upper Endpoint
$r_1 = .10$	$r_2 = .46$
$r_{c_1} = \dfrac{1.67(.10)}{\sqrt{(1.67^2 - 1).10^2 + 1}}$	$r_{c_2} = \dfrac{1.67(.46)}{\sqrt{(1.67^2 - 1).46^2 + 1}}$
$= .16$	$= .65$

Thus, the confidence interval for the corrected correlation is $.16 \leq \rho_c \leq .65$, which includes the actual value of $\rho_c = .50$. This confidence interval is much wider than the confidence interval for the uncorrected correlation and wider yet than the confidence interval that would have been found had the study been done in the reference population sample.

In this example, the range restriction is direct. We remind the reader that if the range restriction were indirect, one would use u_T in place of u_X. Otherwise, the procedures would be identical.

Range Correction and Sampling Error

There is no difficulty in obtaining a confidence interval for a corrected correlation using the range correction formula; we simply correct the two endpoints of the confidence interval for the uncorrected correlation. However, it is not so easy to compute the standard error of the corrected correlation. Correction for attenuation due to measurement error is a linear operation; the uncorrected correlation is just multiplied by a constant. Thus, the standard error is multiplied by the same constant (and the sampling error variance is multiplied by the square of that constant). However, the range correction formula is not linear, and there is no exact formula for the resulting standard error. (The nature of the nonlinearity is that, for the same value of u_X, the correction increases smaller correlations by a greater percentage increase than it increases larger correlations.) The extent of nonlinearity depends on the size of the numbers involved; that is, the extent to which U_X is different from 1 and the extent to which the uncorrected correlation has a square much greater than 0. If the nonlinearity is not too great, then we can approximate the sampling error by pretending that we have just multiplied the uncorrected correlation by the constant

$$\alpha = \frac{r_c}{r}$$

The sampling error would then be approximately

$$\sigma^2_{e_c} = \alpha^2 \sigma^2_e \qquad (3.20)$$

To see the extent of this approximation, let us consider our personnel research example. We center our confidence interval for the corrected correlation about the corrected correlation itself, that is, around $r_c = .44$. The error standard deviation for the uncorrected correlation is $(1-.28^2)/\sqrt{99} = .093$, and the ratio of corrected to uncorrected correlations is $.44/.28 = 1.57$. Hence, the estimated standard error for the corrected correlation is $(1.57)(.093) = .146$. The corresponding confidence interval is $.15 \leq \rho_c \leq .73$. This implied confidence interval differs only slightly from the confidence interval obtained by correcting the endpoints; that is, $.16 \leq \rho_c \leq .65$.

There is a more accurate estimate of the standard error that can be obtained using Taylor's series, as suggested by Raju and Brand (2003) and Raju, Burke, and Normand (1983). For large sample size, the sampling error in the corrected correlation induced by the sampling error in the uncorrected correlation is proportional to the derivative of the correction function. Whereas the correlation is multiplied by the constant α, the standard error is multiplied by the number $a\alpha$, where

$$a = 1/[U_X^2 - 1)r^2 + 1] \qquad (3.21)$$

The variance would be multiplied by $a^2\alpha^2$. In the personnel selection example, we have $\alpha = 1.57$ and

$$a = 1/[(1.67^2 - 1)(.28)^2 + 1] = 1/1.0352 = .8770$$

Thus, the standard error is multiplied by $.8770(1.57) = 1.38$ instead of 1.57. The standard error of the corrected correlation is therefore estimated as $(.8770)(1.57)(.093) = .130$. The confidence interval found using the improved estimate of the standard error is

$$.19 < \rho < .69$$

This is in comparison to the correct interval obtained by correcting the confidence interval endpoints, which was

$$.16 < \rho < .65$$

This improved estimate of the standard deviation is barely worth the trouble for hand calculations, although it is easy to introduce into computer programs, and we have done so. The Windows-based meta-analysis program VG6 (see the Appendix for a description) includes this refinement. Again, we note that if the range restriction were indirect, U_T would be used in the preceding formula for a in place of U_X. (Bobko & Reick, 1980, also presented an equation for the standard error of a correlation corrected for range restriction; their formula appears different on the surface but produces the same results as our procedure. The same is true for the formulas presented by Cureton, 1936; Kelly, 1947; and Raju & Brand, 2003. Mendoza, Stafford, & Stauffer, 2000, presented a method of estimating the confidence interval for a corrected correlation without estimating its *SE*. See also Forsyth & Feldt, 1969.)

An Example: Confidence Intervals. Consider a personnel selection validation study with direct range restriction and using job performance ratings by a single supervisor. Given an observed correlation of .30 with a sample size of 100, the confidence interval for the uncorrected validity coefficient is $P[.12 \leq \rho \leq .48] = .95$. From King et al. (1980), we know that the reliability of the supervisor ratings in the applicant pool is at most .60. If the selection ratio is 50%, then the formulas in Schmidt et al. (1976) show that the ratio of the standard deviation of the applicant group to that of the incumbent population (U_X) is 1.67. The point correction of the observed validity coefficient is therefore

$$r_1 = \frac{1.67r}{\sqrt{(1.67^2 - 1)r^2 + 1}} = .46$$

$$r_2 = \frac{r_1}{\sqrt{.60}} = .60$$

The confidence interval for the corrected validity is obtained by applying the same corrections to the endpoints of the confidence interval for the uncorrected validity:

Lower Endpoint

$$r_1 = \frac{1.67(.12)}{\sqrt{(1.67^2 - 1).12^2 + 1}}$$

$$= .20$$

$$r_2 = \frac{.20}{\sqrt{.60}} = .26$$

Upper Endpoint

$$r_1 = \frac{1.67(.48)}{\sqrt{(1.67^2 - 1).48^2 + 1}}$$

$$= .67$$

$$r_2 = \frac{.67}{\sqrt{.60}} = .86$$

Hence, the confidence interval for the corrected validity is

$$P\{.26 \leq \rho \leq .86\} = .95$$

DICHOTOMIZATION OF INDEPENDENT AND DEPENDENT VARIABLE MEASURES

The mathematics of dichotomization is very similar to that of correction for attenuation and will thus be developed succinctly. Some aspects of dichotomization were discussed in Chapter 2; a more detailed treatment is presented in Hunter and Schmidt (1990a) and MacCallum et al. (2002). The key fact is that the impact of dichotomizing a continuous variable is to multiply the population correlation by an attenuating factor that is less than 1.00. This systematic attenuation can be corrected by dividing the attenuated correlation by the same factor. That is, if we know the factor by which the study correlation was attenuated, then we can restore the study correlation to its original value by dividing by that same attenuation factor. If we divide a variable by a constant, then the mean and the standard deviation are divided by that same constant. Thus, the corrected correlation coefficient has a mean that is divided by the attenuation factor and a sampling error that is divided by the attenuation factor. Thus, the sampling error in the corrected correlation is larger than the sampling error in the uncorrected correlation. However, there is no other way to eliminate the systematic error (downward bias) introduced by the dichotomization.

Consider an example. Suppose the independent variable is split at the median. Then the attenuation factor is .80, and thus, the population correlation is reduced by 20%. If ρ is the true population correlation and ρ_o is the attenuated population correlation, then

$$\rho_o = .80\rho$$

This equation is algebraically reversible. To undo multiplication by .80, we divide by .80:

$$\rho_o/.80 = (.80\rho)/.80 = \rho$$

That is,

$$\rho = \rho_o/.80$$

is the formula for correction for dichotomization. The formula works perfectly for population correlations and works to eliminate the systematic error in the sample correlation.

The study sample correlation r_o is related to the study population correlation in the usual manner:

$$r_o = \rho_o + e_o$$

where e_o is the usual sampling error. If we correct the point biserial correlation to eliminate the attenuation due to dichotomization, then the corrected correlation r_c is given by

$$\begin{aligned}
r_c = r_o/.80 = (\rho_o + e_o)/.80 &= \rho_o/.80 + e_o/.80 \\
&= (.80\rho)/.80 + e_o/.80 \\
&= \rho + e_o/.80
\end{aligned}$$

Let us denote by e_c the sampling error in the corrected correlation. We then have

$$r_c = \rho + e_c$$

Thus, the population correlation corresponding to the corrected sample correlation is the desired true correlation; that is, the systematic part of the sample correlation is restored to its pre-dichotomization value ρ. However, the sampling error e_c is not the usual sampling error associated with a population correlation of ρ. Rather, e_c is the sampling error associated with a corrected correlation. Had there been no dichotomization to begin with, the standard deviation of the sampling error (the standard error) would have been

$$\sigma_e = (1 - \rho^2)/\sqrt{(N-1)}$$

Instead, the standard deviation of the sampling error in the corrected correlation σ_{e_C} must be computed from the sampling error of the uncorrected correlation σ_{eo}. The sampling error standard deviation of the uncorrected correlation is

$$\sigma_{eo} = (1-\rho_o^2)/\sqrt{(N-1)}$$
$$= [1-(.80\rho)^2]/\sqrt{(N-1)}$$
$$= [1-.64\rho^2]/\sqrt{(N-1)}$$

The sampling error standard deviation of the corrected correlation is

$$\sigma_{e_C} = \sigma_{eo}/.80 = 1.25\sigma_{eo}$$

Consider an example. Suppose the population correlation for the original continuous variables is $\rho = .50$. The population correlation with the independent variable split at the median is

$$\rho_o = .80\rho = .80(.50) = .40$$

If the sample size is $N = 100$, then the sampling error standard deviation for non-dichotomized variables is

$$\sigma_e = (1-.50^2)/\sqrt{99} = .0754$$

The sampling error standard deviation of the uncorrected correlation is

$$\sigma_{eo} = (1-.40^2)/\sqrt{99} = .0844$$

The sampling error standard deviation of the corrected correlation is

$$\sigma_{e_C} = \sigma_{eo}/.80 = .0844/.80 = .1055.$$

Whereas 95% of sample correlations for non-dichotomized variables will be spread over

$$.35 < r < .65$$

the corrected correlations spread over the range

$$.29 < r_c < .71$$

For a more extreme split, the cost of correction will be higher. For a 90–10 split, the attenuation factor is .59, and the contrasting probability intervals are much more different from each other:

$$.35 < r < .65 \text{ if no dichotomization}$$
$$.20 < r_c < .80 \text{ if one variable is split } 90-10$$

The situation is even more extreme if both variables are dichotomized. Consider a case from personnel selection. Hunter and Hunter (1984) found an average correlation of .26 between (continuous) reference recommendations and job performance ratings. Suppose (hypothetically) that there were no errors of measurement in the study and that, for purposes of communicating to the employer, the company psychologist decided to dichotomize the two variables. He dichotomizes the reference variable into "generally positive" versus "generally negative." He finds that 90% of past employers give positive ratings while 10% give negative ratings. He splits the supervisor performance ratings at the median to produce "above average" versus "below average." The effect of the double dichotomization (Hunter & Schmidt, 1990a) is to attenuate the correlation of .26 to

$$\rho_o = (.59)(.80)\rho = .472\rho = (.472)(.26) = .12$$

The corrected correlation is thus

$$r_C = r_o \, / \, .472 = 2.12 r_o$$

That is, the observed correlation must be more than doubled to correct the attenuation produced by the dichotomization. The sampling error is correspondingly increased. For a sample size of $N = 100$, the 95% confidence intervals in sample correlations are $.08 < r < .44$ if the variables are not dichotomized and $-.15 < r_C < .67$ for a 10–90 split and a 50–50 split.

Furthermore, it is not likely that the reference evaluations in a local validation study will have reliability as high as that in the Hunter and Hunter (1984) data. The reference check studies reviewed by Hunter and Hunter checked across three or more past employers and used professionally developed scales to assess employer ratings. The correlation of .26 is corrected for the attenuation due to error of measurement in the performance ratings only. Suppose the validation study asks for references from just one past employer and uses performance ratings by the immediate supervisor. If good rating scales are used in both cases, the reliability of each variable would be expected to be at most .60. Because both reliabilities are equal, the square roots are also equal at .77. The attenuation factor for error of measurement is thus

$$\rho_o = a_1 a_2 \, \rho = (.77)(.77)\rho = .60\rho = (.60)(.26) = .156$$

This correlation is then attenuated by double dichotomization

$$\rho_{oo} = a_3 a_4 \rho_o = (.59)(.80)\rho_o = .472\rho_o = .472(.156) = .074$$

The net attenuation for both error of measurement and dichotomization is

$$\rho_{oo} = (.60)(.472)\rho = .2832\rho$$

This value of .2832 is thus the attenuation factor for the correction of the sample correlation. That is, the corrected correlation r will be

$$r_C = r_{oo}/.2832 = 3.53\ r_{oo}$$

That is, one must more than triple the observed sample correlation to correct for the attenuation produced by both error of measurement and double dichotomization. The sampling error is similarly increased. For a sample size of $N = 100$, the 95% probability intervals are

$.08 < r < .44$ if perfect measurement and no dichotomization

and

$-.43 < r_C < .95$ if the correlation is corrected for measurement error and dichotomization in both variables.

Hence, it is clear that the combination of dichotomization and measurement error can greatly reduce the amount of information conveyed by a sample (study) correlation.

IMPERFECT CONSTRUCT VALIDITY IN INDEPENDENT AND DEPENDENT VARIABLE MEASURES

We define the construct validity of a measure as its true score correlation with the actual construct or trait it is supposed to measure. The case of construct validity is similar to the case of error of measurement if the path analysis permits a simple multiplicative attenuation (see Chapter 2 for the required conditions). If error of measurement is treated separately, then the impact of imperfect construct validity is to multiply the true population correlation by an attenuation factor equal to the construct validity of the variable. If there is imperfect construct validity in both variables, and if both proxy variables satisfy the path analysis requirements, then the effect is a double attenuation, that is, multiplication by the product of the two construct validities. Because the attenuation effect is systematic, it can be algebraically reversed. To reverse the effect of multiplying the correlation by a constant, we divide the correlation by the same constant. Thus, to restore the correlation to what it would have been had the variables been measured with perfect construct validity, we divide the study correlation by the product of the two construct validities. Note that, for perfect construct validity, we divide by 1.00, which leaves the correlation unchanged. So perfect construct validity is a special case of imperfect construct validity. These concepts are described in more detail in Schmidt et al. (2013).

For example, let the construct validity of the independent variable be a_1 and let the construct validity of the dependent variable be a_2. The impact of imperfect construct validity is to multiply the true correlation by the product $a_1 a_2$. That is,

$$\rho_o = a_1 a_2 \rho$$

The correction formula divides by the same attenuation factors

$$\rho_o / a_1 a_2 = (a_1 a_2 \rho) / a_1 a_2 = \rho$$

The corrected sample correlation is thus

$$r_C = r_o / a_1 a_2 = (1/a_1 a_2) r_o$$

which multiplies the standard error by the same factor $(1/a_1 a_2)$.

The attenuating effect of imperfect construct validity combines with the attenuating effect of other artifacts. Consider another example:

$a_1 = .90 =$ the square root of the reliability of X, $r_{XX} = .81$;

$a_2 = .90 =$ the square root of the reliability of Y, $r_{YY} = .81$;

$a_3 = .90 =$ the construct validity of X;

$a_4 = .90 =$ the construct validity of Y;

$a_5 = .80 =$ the attenuation factor for splitting X at the median; and

$a_6 = .80 =$ the attenuation factor for splitting Y at the median.

The total impact of the six study imperfections is

$$\rho_o = (.9)(.9)(.9)(.9)(.8)(.8)\rho = .42\rho$$

Thus, even minor imperfections add up. Had the true correlation been .50, the study population correlation would be

$$\rho_o = .42\rho = .42(.50) = .21$$

a reduction of over one half. The formula for the corrected correlation is

$$r_C = r_o / .42 = 2.38\, r_o$$

Thus, to restore the systematic value of the study correlation, we must more than double the correlation.

ATTRITION ARTIFACTS

As noted in Chapter 2, attrition artifacts can usually be treated as range variation on the dependent variable. If there is range variation on the dependent variable but not on the independent variable, then the mathematical treatment is identical to the treatment of range variation on the independent variable; we merely interchange the role of variables X and Y. To our knowledge, there are no meta-analysis methods that correct for range restriction on both the independent and the dependent variables. However, as noted in Chapter 2, the approximation methods for doing this developed by Alexander et al. (1987) are fairly accurate and could be adapted for use in meta-analysis. To date, this has not been done to our knowledge. The combined accuracy enhancements produced by use of indirect range restriction corrections (Hunter et al., 2006) and the Alexander et al. (1987) methods could be important, especially in the area of validity generalization. The more accurate validity estimates are likely to be substantially larger (Hunter et al., 2006).

EXTRANEOUS FACTORS

As discussed in Chapter 2, easily correctable extraneous factors in the research setting usually enter into the causal model for the research design in much the same form as the extraneous factors in the measurement of a proxy variable for the dependent variable. At the level of the study, it would be possible to correct the study effect correlation by partialing out the extraneous factor. If the extraneous factor was not controlled in the original analysis, then the attenuation factor is

$$a = \sqrt{(1 - \rho_{EY}^2)} \qquad (3.22)$$

where ρ_{EY} is the correlation between the extraneous factor and the dependent variable. The impact on the study effect correlation is to attenuate the population correlation by the multiplicative factor

$$\rho_o = a\rho$$

This formula can be algebraically reversed

$$\rho = \rho_o / a$$

to yield the correction formula for the sample correlation

$$r = r_o / a$$

The standard error is divided by the same factor and increases correspondingly.

The mathematics is otherwise identical to that for attenuation due to error of measurement. The impact of extraneous factors can combine with the impact of other artifacts. The compound impact is to multiply the attenuation factors for the other factors by the attenuation factor for the extraneous factor.

BIAS IN THE CORRELATION

As noted in Chapter 2, the purely statistical bias in the sample correlation as an estimate of the population correlation is normally trivial in magnitude, and it is rarely worthwhile to correct for it. This is why this bias is not listed in Table 3.1 (or in Table 2.1 in Chapter 2). However, we provide the computations to check the size of the bias in any given application. The impact of bias is systematic and can be captured to a close approximation by an attenuation multiplier. If the population correlation is less than .70 (usually the case), then the best attenuation multiplier for meta-analysis is the linear attenuation factor (Hunter et al., 1996):

$$a = 1 - 1 / (2N-1) = (2N-2) / (2N-1) \qquad (3.23)$$

This attenuation factor is most useful in meta-analysis because it is independent of the population correlation ρ. For applications with population correlations larger than .70 (a rare condition), the more accurate attenuation factor is

$$a = 1 - (1-\rho^2) / (2N-1) \qquad (3.24)$$

In thinking about the size of the population correlation, remember that it is the population value *before* any corrections for artifacts creating a downward bias. Hence, it is unlikely to be larger than .70. Note that, if the preceding nonlinear attenuator is used, then correction for bias due to an extraneous variable should always be the last artifact corrected. In the case of multiple artifacts, the ρ in the attenuation formula will be the population correlation already attenuated for all other artifacts.

The impact of bias on the population correlation is a systematic reduction,

$$\rho_o = a\rho$$

The correction formula follows from the algebraic reversal of this equation,

$$\rho = \rho_o / a$$

to yield

$$r_C = r_o/a$$

The standard error is divided by the same factor and increases correspondingly. The sampling error *variance* is divided by a^2.

Multiple Simultaneous Artifacts

Table 3.1 lists 11 artifacts, 9 of which are potentially correctable by the use of multiplicative artifact attenuation factors. The other two artifacts are sampling error, which is corrected by a different strategy, and bad data, which can be corrected only if the bad data can be identified and corrected or thrown out (see Chapter 5). This section considers the compound of all the multiplicative artifacts. It is implicitly understood that range variation on both the independent and dependent variable is not simultaneously considered (Hunter & Schmidt, 1987b). Thus, the analysis would contain at most eight multiplicative artifacts. Note again that the artifact attenuation is caused by the real imperfections of the study design. The attenuation of the true correlation will thus occur whether we can correct for it or not.

Consider again the six artifact examples from the section on construct validity. The artifact attenuation factors are

$a_1 = .90 =$ the square root of the reliability of X, $r_{XX} = .81$;

$a_2 = .90 =$ the square root of the reliability of Y, $r_{YY} = .81$;

$a_3 = .90 =$ the construct validity of X;

$a_4 = .90 =$ the construct validity of Y;

$a_5 = .80 =$ the attenuation factor for splitting X at the median; and

$a_6 = .80 =$ the attenuation factor for splitting Y at the median.

The total impact of the six study imperfections is determined by the total attenuation factor

$$A = (.9)(.9)(.9)(.9)(.8)(.8) = .42$$

If the true correlation for the study is $\rho = .50$, the attenuated study correlation is only

$$\rho_o = .42\rho = .42(.50) = .21$$

If the sample size is $N = 26$, then the linear bias attenuation factor is

$$a_7 = 1 - 1/(2N-1) = 1 - 1/25 = .96$$

The total attenuation factor for all seven artifacts is thus

$$A = .42(.96) = .40$$

and the attenuated study population correlation is

$$\rho_o = .40\rho = .40(.50) = .20$$

With a sample size of 26, the sampling error variance of the uncorrected correlation is

$$\text{Var}(e_o) = [1 - .20^2]^2 / (26 - 1) = .0368$$

The sampling error variance of the corrected correlation is

$$\text{Var}(e_C) = \text{Var}(e_o) / A^2 = .0368 / .40^2 = .2304$$

Thus, the sampling error standard deviation is $\sqrt{.2304} = .48$. The 95% probability interval for the observed *corrected* correlation (r_c) is

$$-.44 < r_C < 1.44$$

If the sample size were increased to $N = 101$, the probability interval for the corrected correlation would shrink to

$$.03 < r_C < .97$$

The preceding example is an extreme case, but not unrealistic. All artifact values were derived from the empirical literature. This example shows that there is only limited information in the best of small-sample studies. When that information is watered down with large methodological artifacts, then there may be almost no information in the study. Ideally, studies with better methodology would greatly reduce these artifacts and, hence, eliminate the need for large statistical corrections. However, most methodological artifact values are determined by the feasibility limitations of field and lab research. Thus, researchers frequently have little leeway for improvement. This means that there will nearly always be a need for statistical correction and, hence, that there will nearly always be a need to greatly reduce sampling error via use of large samples.

Meta-Analysis of Individually Corrected Correlations

The examples of the preceding sections show that individual studies usually contain only very limited information. The random effects of sampling error are unavoidable. Furthermore, the other artifacts in study designs are often caused by factors outside the control of the investigator.

Thus, the information in most studies is diluted by statistical artifacts such as those listed in Table 3.1 and perhaps still further by artifacts yet to be delineated and quantified in future research. Solid conclusions can thus only be built on cumulative research combining the information across studies. The traditional narrative review is clearly inadequate for this complex task (see Chapter 11). Thus, there is no alternative to meta-analysis. If one pretends that the only study artifact is sampling error, then the meta-analysis techniques given earlier in this chapter would be used. However, if other artifacts are acknowledged and if information about the artifacts is available, then the values estimated by meta-analysis will be much more accurate if the study artifacts are corrected.

There are three kinds of artifacts in Table 3.1. First, there are bad data: recording, computing, reporting, and transcriptional errors. If the error is so large that the resulting correlation is an outlier in the meta-analysis, then the deviant result can be detected and eliminated (see Chapter 5). Otherwise, bad data go undetected and, hence, uncorrected. Second, there is the nonsystematic and random effect of sampling error. That effect can be eliminated in meta-analysis or at least greatly reduced. Third, the table contains nine artifacts that are systematic in nature—artifacts that produce a systematic downward bias. These we call the correctable artifacts. For each correctable artifact, there is a quantitative factor that must be known in order to correct the study correlation for that artifact. Given the necessary artifact values for the research domain in question, meta-analysis can correct for that artifact.

There are three cases in meta-analysis: (1) Artifact values are given in each individual study for all artifacts, (2) artifact values are only sporadically given for any artifact in the various studies, and (3) artifact values are given for each study on some artifacts but are only available sporadically on other artifacts. The case of individually available artifact information is treated in this chapter. The case of sporadically available information is covered in Chapter 4, as is the last case of mixed artifact information (i.e., the case in which artifact information is available for each study for some but not all artifacts).

We now consider the case where artifact information is available on nearly all individual studies. The missing artifact values can be estimated by inserting the mean value across the studies where information is given. This is done automatically by our VG6 computer program, described later. At that point, each artifact value is available for each study. There are then three phases to the meta-analysis: (1) performing the computations for each of the individual studies, (2) combining the results across studies, and (3) computing the estimated mean and variance of true effect size correlations in the designated research domain.

INDIVIDUAL STUDY COMPUTATIONS

The computations for each study are the computations used in correcting the correlation for artifacts. We begin with the observed study correlation and the sample size for that study. We next collect each piece of artifact information for that study. These values are placed in a table and may be read into a computer file. This analysis can be performed by the Windows-based program VG6 (described in the Appendix). In the current version of these programs, these data files can be read in from the Excel program, making it more convenient to use the programs.

We (and the program) next do the computations to correct for artifacts. Under most conditions, the effect of each correctable artifact is to reduce the correlation by an amount that can be quantified as a multiplicative factor less than 1.00, which we call the attenuation factor. Under these conditions, the net impact of all the correctable artifacts can be computed by simply multiplying the separate artifact attenuation factors. This results in a compound artifact attenuation factor. Dividing the observed study correlation by the compound attenuation factor corrects the study correlation for the systematic reduction caused by those artifacts.

For each study, we first compute the artifact attenuation factor for each artifact. Denote the separate attenuation factors by a_1, a_2, a_3 and so forth. The compound attenuation factor for the several artifacts is the product

$$A = a_1 a_2 a_3 \ldots \tag{3.25}$$

We can now compute the corrected study correlation r_C. We denote the study observed correlation by r_o and the corrected correlation by r_C. The corrected correlation is then

$$r_C = r_o / A \tag{3.26}$$

This estimate of r_C has a slight downward (i.e., negative) bias (Bobko, 1983), but the degree of underestimation is so small as to be trivial.

For purposes of estimating sampling error, it is necessary to estimate the mean uncorrected correlation. This is the sample size weight average of the observed correlations. The sampling error variance in the corrected correlation is computed in two steps. First, the sampling error variance in the uncorrected correlation is computed. Then the sampling error variance in the corrected correlation is computed from that. The sampling error variance in the uncorrected correlation, $\text{Var}(e_o)$, is

$$\text{Var}(e_o) = [1 - \bar{r}_o^2]^2 / (N_i - 1)$$

where $\bar{r}_o$ is the mean uncorrected correlation across studies (Hunter & Schmidt, 1994; Law et al., 1994b) and N_i is the sample size for the study in question. The sampling error variance in the corrected correlation is then given by (Hedges, 1995)

$$\text{Var}(e_C) = \text{Var}(e_o) / A^2 \tag{3.27}$$

where A is the compound artifact attenuation factor for that study. For simplicity, denote the sampling error variance by ve'. That is, define ve' by

$$ve' = \mathrm{Var}(e_c)$$

The preceding computation of sampling error variance is corrected for all artifacts. However, we can refine our estimate of the contribution of the range correction to sampling error. Because the attenuation factor for range variation contains the correlation itself, the corresponding sampling error increase is only in proportion to the derivative of the attenuation instead of the attenuation factor itself. This difference is small in many cases. However, a more accurate estimate can be computed using a more complicated formula for sampling error variance. Compute a first estimate of ve using the preceding formula. Label the first estimate ve'. The improved estimate is then

$$ve = a^2\, ve'$$

where a is computed as

$$a = 1/[(U_X^2 - 1)r_0^2 + 1]$$

in the case of direct range restriction. In the case of indirect range restriction, we use the same formula for a but substitute U_T for U_X. Consider an extreme example: Suppose only the top half of the ability distribution had been selected in a personnel selection study (i.e., direct range restriction). The study population standard deviation is smaller than the reference population standard deviation by the factor $u_X = .60$. The reciprocal of u_X would be $U_X = 1/.60 = 1.67$. If the study correlation (r_{0_i}) were .20, then $a = .94$, and the refining factor would be $a^2 = .88$. That is, the sampling error variance for that study would be 12% smaller than estimated using the simple attenuation factor. (See Bobko, 1983, for an equation for ve that yields values essentially identical to the equation for ve presented here.) Thus, for each study i, we generate four numbers: the corrected correlation r_{c_i}, the sample size N_i, the compound attenuation factor A_i, and the sampling error variance ve_i. These are the numbers used in the meta-analysis proper.

COMBINING ACROSS STUDIES

Meta-analysis reduces sampling error by averaging sampling errors. Thus, an important step in meta-analysis is the computation of certain critical averages: the average correlation, the variance of correlations (the average squared deviation from the mean), and the average sampling error variance. To do this, we must decide how much weight to give to each study.

What weights should be used? The first step in the meta-analysis is to average certain numbers across studies. This averaging can be done in several ways. In averaging corrected correlations, a simple or unweighted average gives as much weight to a study with a sample size of 12 as to a study with a sample size of 1,200. Yet the sampling error variance in the small-sample study is 100 times greater than that in the large-sample study. Schmidt and Hunter (1977); Schmidt, Le, and Oh (2009); and Schulze (2004, 2007) therefore recommended that each study be weighted by its sample size. Hunter et al. (1982, pp. 41–42) noted that this is an optimal strategy when there is little or no variation in population correlations across studies—the "homogeneous" case (Hunter & Schmidt, 2000). They noted that there can be a problem if correlations differ a great deal across studies. The problem is potentially acute if the meta-analysis contains one study with a very large sample size while all the other studies have a much smaller sample size. If the large-sample-size study is deviant in some way, then, because it dominates the meta-analysis, the meta-analysis will be deviant. This case arises rarely in practice.

The homogeneous case was considered in technical detail in Hedges and Olkin (1985, chap. 6). They noted the key mathematical theorem for that case. If the population correlations do not differ from one study to the next, then the optimal weights are obtained by weighting each study inversely to its sampling error variance. In the case of correlations that are not corrected for any artifacts, the sampling error variance is

$$\mathrm{Var}(e_i) = (1 - \rho_i^2)^2 / (N_i - 1)$$

The optimal weight for this homogeneous case would thus be

$$w_i = (N_i - 1) / (1 - \rho_i^2)^2$$

Because the population correlation ρ_i is not known, this optimal weight cannot be used. Although Hedges and Olkin (1985) did not note it, even in the homogeneous case, the substitution of the observed study correlation r_{oi} for the study population correlation ρ_i does not lead to the most accurate alternative weights. As noted earlier in this chapter, a more accurate alternative is to substitute the mean observed correlation $\bar{r}_o$ for each study population ρ_i (Hunter & Schmidt, 1994; Law et al., 1994b; see Chapter 5). Because the resulting multiplicative term

$$1 / (1 - \bar{r}_0^2)^2$$

is the same for all studies, it has no effect and can be dropped. That is, the corresponding weighting can be more easily accomplished by using the weight

$$w_i = N_i - 1$$

As Hedges and Olkin noted, this differs only trivially from the Schmidt and Hunter (1977) recommendation to weight each study by sample size:

$$w_i = N_i \qquad (3.28)$$

The previous discussion is cast in terms of the homogeneous case (i.e., the case where $S_\rho^2 = 0$). However, as noted earlier in this chapter, these weights are also very accurate for the heterogeneous case (where $S_\rho^2 > 0$), so long as the sample size is not correlated with the size of ρ_i (the population correlation). Except for that rare situation, weighting by N_i is very accurate for the heterogeneous case as well as for the homogeneous case (see, e.g., Hall & Brannick, 2002; Schmidt, Oh, & Hayes, 2009). Based on extensive computer simulation studies, Schulze (2004) recommended weighting by N_i in heterogeneous as well as homogeneous cases. This is important because some have maintained that one should not weight by N_i in the heterogeneous case. (See the discussion of study weighting in Chapter 9 and fixed vs. random effects meta-analysis models in Chapters 5 and 8.)

When studies differ greatly on one or more of the artifacts corrected, then more complicated weighting makes better use of the information in the studies. Studies with more information should receive more weight than studies with less information. For example, studies in which one or both of the variables is dichotomized with extreme splits should receive less weight than a study with a near-even split. The same is true if one study has very low reliability while a second study has high reliability.

The sampling error variance of the corrected correlation is

$$\mathrm{Var}(e_C) = [(1-\rho_i^2)^2 / (N_i - 1)] / A_i^2$$

Thus, the weight for each study would be

$$
\begin{aligned}
w_i &= A_i^2 [(N_i - 1)/(1-\rho_i^2)^2] \\
&= [(N_i - 1)A_i^2]/(1-\rho_i^2)^2
\end{aligned}
$$

Because the study population correlation ρ_i is not known, some substitution must be made. As noted previously, the most accurate substitution is to substitute the mean observed correlation $\bar{r}_o$ for each study population correlation ρ_i (Hunter & Schmidt, 1994; Law et al., 1994b). Because $\bar{r}_o$ is a constant, this has the effect of eliminating the term with ρ_i and thus yields the weights

$$w_i = (N_i - 1)A_i^2$$

This, in turn, differs only trivially from the simpler weights

$$w_i = N_i A_i^2 \qquad (3.29)$$

That is, the weight for each study is the product of two factors: the sample size N_i and the square of the artifact attenuation factor A_i. The attenuation factor is squared because to multiply a correlation by the factor $1/A_i$ is to multiply its sampling error variance by $1/A_i^2$. This weighting scheme has the desired effect: The more extreme the artifact attenuation in a given study, the less the weight assigned to that study. That is, the more information contained in the study, the greater its weight. When corrections have been made for study artifacts, the study weights shown in Equation 3.29 are more accurate than weighting by sample size or weighting by the inverse of sampling error. The question of optimal study weights has been discussed extensively in the literature. This question is discussed in more detail in Chapter 9.

Consider two studies with sample size 100. Assume that (1) both variables are measured with perfect reliability and without range restriction, (2) the population correlation ρ is the same in both studies, and (3) the dependent variable is dichotomized in both studies. In Study 1, there is a 50–50 split so the true population correlation ρ is reduced to a study population correlation of $.80\rho$. In Study 2, there is a 90–10 split so the true population correlation ρ is reduced to a study population correlation of $.59\rho$. To correct for the attenuation due to artificial dichotomization, the Study 1 observed correlation r_{o1} must be multiplied by the reciprocal of .80; that is, $1/.80 = 1.25$:

$$r_1 = 1.25 r_{o1}$$

Thus, the sampling error variance is multiplied by the square of 1.25, that is, $1.25^2 = 1.5625$. To correct for the attenuation due to artificial dichotomization, the Study 2 observed correlation r_{o2} must be multiplied by the reciprocal of .59; that is, $1/.59 = 1.695$:

$$r_2 = 1.695 r_{o2}$$

Thus, the sampling error variance is multiplied by the square of 1.695, that is, $1.695^2 = 2.8730$. Before the dichotomization and the correction, the sampling error in both correlations was the same: the sampling error implied by equal sample sizes of 100 and equal population correlations of ρ_i. However, after the correction for dichotomization, the second study has sampling error variance that is $2.8730 / 1.5625 = 1.839$ times larger than the sampling error variance in the first study. Thus, the second study deserves only $1/1.839 = .544$ times as much weight in the meta-analysis. The weights assigned to the studies by the formula

$$w_1 = N_i A_i^2$$

do just that:

$$w_1 = 100(.802)^2 = 100(.64) = 64$$

and

$$w_2 = 100(.592)^2 = 100(.35) = 35$$

where $64/35 = 1.83$. Thus, to use round numbers, the study with twice the information is given twice the weight (1.00 vs. .544).

In summary, there are three typical types of weights that might be used in averaging correlations. First, one could ignore the differences in quality (information content) between studies and give as much weight to high-error studies as to low-error studies. This is the case of equal weights and is represented by $w_i = 1$. Second, one might consider the effect of unequal sample size on quality but ignore the effects of other artifacts. This leads to sample size weighting: $w_i = N_i$. Third, one might consider the weights that take into account both N_i and other artifacts: $w_i = N_i A_i^2$.

We recommend the use of these last weights, because they give less weight to those studies that require greater correction and, hence, have greater sampling error. These weights are used in our Windows-based program for meta-analysis of correlations corrected individually (described in the Appendix).

FINAL META-ANALYSIS ESTIMATION

Once the researcher has corrected each study correlation for artifacts and has decided on the weights, there are three meta-analysis averages to be computed using the corrected rs:

$$\bar{r}_C = \sum w_i r_{C_i} / \sum w_i \tag{3.30}$$

$$\mathrm{Var}(r_C) = \sum w_i [r_{C_i} - \bar{r}_C]^2 / \sum w_i \tag{3.31}$$

$$\mathrm{Ave}(ve) = \sum w_i ve_i / \sum w_i \tag{3.32}$$

The mean actual correlation is then estimated by the mean corrected correlation:

$$\bar{\rho} = \bar{r}_C \tag{3.33}$$

The variance of actual correlations is given by the corrected variance of corrected correlations:

$$\mathrm{Var}(\rho) = \mathrm{Var}(r_C) - \mathrm{Ave}(ve) \tag{3.34}$$

The standard deviation is estimated by the square root of the variance estimate if it is positive. If the standard deviation is actually 0, then the variance estimate will be negative half the time by chance. As discussed earlier in this chapter, a negative variance estimate suggests that the actual variance is 0 (see also Chapters 5 and 9).

AN EXAMPLE: VALIDITY GENERALIZATION WITH INDIRECT RANGE RESTRICTION

We will now consider a hypothetical but realistic validity generalization example for a test of verbal aptitude. The reliability of this test computed in the applicant group (unrestricted group) is $r_{XX_a} = .85$. The 12 studies shown in Table 3.5a have been conducted on job incumbents who have been hired using a variety of procedures of which we have no record; hence, any range restriction would be indirect. The observed validities range from .07 to .49, and only 7 of the 12 validity estimates are statistically significant. The u_X values in the second column in Table 3.5a are all less than 1.00, indicating there has been indirect range restriction. Using Equation (3.16), we convert these u_X values into u_T values, which are shown in the table. The first column of job performance reliabilities (r_{yy_i}) represents the restricted values (i.e., those computed in the incumbent samples). These are the r_{yy} values that are needed for the computations in this example. The r_{yy_a} values—the estimated criterion reliabilities in the *applicant* group—are presented for only general informational purposes. (These values are computed using Equation [5.20] in Chapter 5.) The test reliabilities in Table 3.5a are the restricted (incumbent group) values (i.e., r_{XX_i}). Note that, because of the effects of the indirect range restriction, the r_{XX_i} values are less than the applicant pool value of $r_{XX_a} = .85$. (Test reliabilities are computed from the $r_{XX_a} = .85$ value using Equation [3.17c].) We first correct each observed correlation for measurement error in both variables and then correct for range restriction, using the u_T values in the range restriction correction formula. These corrected correlations are shown in the last column in Table 3.5a. The underlying true score (construct level) correlation used to generate these hypothetical data is $\rho = .57$. However, the true score correlation overestimates operational validity, because in actual test use, we must use observed test scores to predict future job performance and cannot use applicants' (unknown) true scores. Hence, the underlying true validity used to generate this example is $\rho_{xy_t} = \sqrt{.85}(.57) = .53$. In the case of indirect range restriction, meta-analysis must correct for measurement error in both variables prior to the range restriction correction. (The technical reasons for this are given in Hunter et al., 2006.) Thus, the meta-analysis results are those for true score (construct-level) correlations. The mean and *SD* for operational validities are then obtained ex post facto as follows:

$$\text{Mean operational validity:} \quad \rho_{xy_t} = \sqrt{r_{XX_a}} \, (\rho) \qquad (3.35)$$

$$\text{SD of operational validity:} \quad SD_{\rho_{xy_t}} = \sqrt{r_{XX_a}} \, SD_\rho \qquad (3.36)$$

A Worked Example: Indirect Range Restriction

We now proceed with the meta-analysis of the data in our example. Our calculations are the same as those in the computer program VG6-I (for indirect range restriction). (See the Appendix for availability of the software package containing this program.) We weight each study as follows:

$$w_i = N_i A_i^2$$

The worksheet for these calculations is shown in Table 3.5b. The attenuation factor for each study is most easily computed as the ratio of the uncorrected correlation to the corrected correlation. For Study 1,

$$A_1 = .35 \, / \, .80 = .43$$

Thus, the study weight for Study 1 shown in the next to last column is

$$w_1 = 68(.43)^2 = 68(.18) = 12.6$$

The sample size weighted-average uncorrected sample correlation is $\bar{r} = .28$. Thus, the sampling error variance of the uncorrected correlation in Study 1 is

$$\text{Var}(e) = (1 - .28^2)^2 \, / \, 67 = .012677$$

Because all studies in this hypothetical example have the same sample size, this is the estimate of sampling error variance in the uncorrected correlations for every study (not shown in Table 3.5b).

The sampling error variance in the *corrected* correlations can be estimated in two ways. We could use the simple estimate that ignores the nonlinearity of the range restriction correction:

$$\text{Var}(ve') = \text{Var}(e) \, / \, A^2$$

For Study 1, this value is

$$\text{Var}(ve') = .012677 \, / \, (.43)^2 = .068561$$

This estimate is recorded in the column "Simple Error Variance" in Table 3.5b. However, a more accurate estimate is obtained by using the correction factor computed using the derivative of the correction transformation:

$$a_i = 1/[(U_{T_i}^2 - 1)r_{o_i}^2 + 1]$$

For Study 1, the standard deviation ratio is

$$U_T = 1 / u_T = 1 / .468 = 2.1368$$

So the correction factor is

$$a = 1/[(2.1368^2 - 1)(.35)^2 + 1] = 1/1.4368 = .6960$$

Thus, the refined estimate of sampling error variance in Study 1 is

$$\text{Var}(ve) = a^2(.068561) = .033212$$

as shown in the column "Refined Error Variance" in Table 3.5b. (The program VG6 described in the Appendix computes only this more accurate estimate.)

Again, we note that the corrected correlations are denoted by r_C. The three weighted averages are

$$\bar{\rho} = \bar{r}_C = .574$$

$$\text{Var}(r_C) = .034091$$

$$\text{Var}(e) = .048120 \text{ (Simple method)}$$

$$\text{Var}(e) = .035085 \text{ (Refined method)}$$

The estimated mean true score correlation (.574) is very close to the actual value (.570). Because all population correlations were assumed to be the same, the variance of population correlations is actually 0. Thus, the sampling error variance should equal the observed variance. For the simple estimation method, we have

$$\text{Var}(\rho) = \text{Var}(r_C) - \text{Var}(e) = .034091 - .048120 = -.014029$$

which correctly suggests a standard deviation of 0 but is a less accurate estimate than we would like. For the refined estimation method, we have

$$\text{Var}(\rho) = \text{Var}(r) - \text{Var}(e) = .034091 - .035085 = -.000994$$

The value −.000994 is much closer to the true value of 0 and, again, correctly indicates that the true value is 0. Because $SD_\rho = 0$, the credibility interval is .574 to .574. Its width is zero.

Table 3.5 A meta-analysis of hypothetical personnel selection studies with indirect range restriction.

Table 3.5a   Hypothetical validity and artifact information

Study	s_X / S_X (u_X)	s_T / S_T (u_T)	Test Reliability (r_{XX_i})	Criterion Reliability (r_{yy_i})	(r_{yy_a})	Sample Size	Observed Correlation	Corrected Correlation
1	.580	.468	.55	.80	.86	68	.35**	.80
2	.580	.468	.55	.60	.61	68	.07	.26
3	.580	.468	.55	.80	.81	68	.11	.34
4	.580	.468	.55	.60	.70	68	.31*	.81
5	.678	.603	.67	.80	.81	68	.18	.39
6	.678	.603	.67	.60	.67	68	.36**	.75
7	.678	.603	.67	.80	.84	68	.40**	.73
8	.678	.603	.67	.60	.61	68	.13	.33
9	.869	.844	.80	.80	.82	68	.49**	.68
10	.869	.844	.80	.60	.61	68	.23	.38
11	.869	.844	.80	.80	.81	68	.29*	.42
12	.869	.844	.80	.60	.63	68	.44*	.70

Note: r_{yy_a}, the criterion reliability in the applicant group, is not used in the example. It is shown only for informational purposes.

*p < .05 (two-tailed). **p < .01 (two-tailed).

Table 3.5b Meta-Analysis Worksheet

Study	Sample Size	Attenuation Factor	Simple Error Variance	Refined Error Variance	Study Weight	Corrected Correlation
1	68	.43	.0686	.0332	12.6	.80
2	68	.27	.1739	.1670	5.0	.26
3	68	.32	.1238	.1138	7.0	.34
4	68	.38	.0878	.0488	9.8	.81
5	68	.47	.0574	.0319	15.0	.39
6	68	.48	.0550	.0365	15.7	.75
7	68	.55	.0419	.0256	20.6	.73
8	68	.39	.0833	.0785	10.3	.33
9	68	.72	.0244	.0203	35.3	.68
10	68	.60	.0352	.0337	24.5	.38
11	68	.69	.0266	.0233	32.3	.42
12	68	.63	.0319	.0274	27.0	.70

Note: Figures in this table apply to the *corrected* correlations.

The fact that all the variance of the corrected correlations is accounted for by artifacts does not mean there is no sampling error in our mean estimate of .57. How much uncertainty is there in this estimate of the true score correlation? This question can be addressed by placing a confidence interval around it. The standard error of this estimate is the *square root* of the variance of the corrected *r*s (variance = .03409; square root = .1846) divided by the square root of *k*, the number of studies (*k* = 12 here). This standard error is .1846/3.46 = .053. The 95% confidence interval therefore runs from .57 − 1.96(.053) to .57 + 1.96(.053) or .47 to .67. The CI is therefore

$$.47 < .57 < .67$$

The reason this confidence interval is fairly wide is that there are only 12 studies in this example. (All of our examples are based on a small number of studies to keep the computations simple.) Typically, there would be many more than 12. Credibility intervals, unlike confidence intervals, are based on the corrected *SD* (i.e., SD_ρ). The credibility interval here is .57 to .57. Its width is zero, while the width of the confidence interval is .67 − .47 = .20. The 80% credibility is typically used; it ranges from 1.28 SD_ρ below the mean to 1.28 SD_ρ above the mean. Credibility intervals and confidence intervals in meta-analysis are discussed in more detail in Chapters 5 and 8.

Meta-analysis correcting each correlation individually can be carried out on the computer using the program VG6. (See the Appendix for a description of the software package.) This program has separate subroutines for direct and indirect range restriction. In the case of indirect range restriction, as in our example here, the reliabilities entered into the program should be those in the restricted group. (If unrestricted independent variable reliabilities are entered, the program will convert them to restricted group values, using Equation [3.17]. The user must indicate whether the reliabilities are restricted or unrestricted values.) Reliability corrections for both variables are made prior to the correction for range restriction (see Hunter et al., 2006). If range restriction is direct, the reliability correction for the dependent variable can be made prior to the range restriction correction, but the correction for unreliability in the independent variable must be made after the range restriction correction, using the reliability (r_{XX_a}) in the unrestricted population. The reason for this is that direct range restriction on the independent variable causes true scores and measurement errors to be (negatively) correlated in the selected sample, hence violating the critical assumption underlying reliability theory (see Hunter et al., 2006; Mendoza & Mumford, 1987). Under these conditions, the reliability of the independent variable in the selected sample is undefined and undefinable; hence, this correction must be made after the range restriction correction has been made, using an estimate of r_{XX_a} obtained in the unrestricted sample. Mendoza and Mumford (1987) were the first to point out this important fact. Hunter et al. (2006)

incorporated this consideration into their meta-analysis procedures. (The last edition of this book [Hunter & Schmidt, 2004] presented full derivations of the equations for both direct and indirect range restriction; this lengthy exposition is not necessary in the current edition because this material has now been published as Hunter et al. [2006] in a widely read top-tier journal.) Of course, if the meta-analysis is a validity generalization study, there is no need to correct for unreliability in the independent variable, and this correction is simply omitted. (An example of a validity generalization meta-analysis correcting correlations individually under conditions of direct range restriction is presented in Chapter 3 of the 1990 edition of this book.) For further details, see Hunter et al. (2006).

Returning to our example, the mean corrected correlation of .57 that we obtained does not estimate the true validity, because it has been corrected for measurement error in the independent variable (the predictor test). The value .57 is the mean true score correlation, not the mean operational validity (ρ_{xy_t}). Because we know the reliability of this test in the applicant pool (unrestricted) group (i.e., $r_{XX_a} = .85$, as noted at the beginning of our example), we can easily calculate the needed operational validity estimates as follows:

$$\rho_{xy_t} = \sqrt{r_{XX_a}}\,\rho$$
$$\rho_{xy_t} = \sqrt{.85}(.574) = .53$$
$$SD_{\rho_{xy_t}} = \sqrt{.85}\,SD_\rho$$
$$SD_{\rho_{xy_t}} = \sqrt{.85}(0) = 0$$

Again, both these values are correct. Although we need the operational validity estimate for applied work in personnel selection, it is the construct-level correlation of .57 that is needed for theoretical research (theory testing). Most meta-analyses outside the area of personnel selection are theoretical in orientation and hence both independent and dependent variable measures should be corrected for measurement error.

Next, for comparison purposes, we present sampling error corrections for the observed correlations (bare-bones meta-analysis) as well as for the fully corrected correlations (complete meta-analysis). The comparative results are as follows:

Uncorrected Correlations	*Fully Corrected Correlations*
$\bar{r}_o = .28$	$\bar{r}_c = .57$
$\sigma_{ro}^2 = .017033$	$\sigma_{rc}^2 = .034091$
$\sigma_e^2 = .012677$	$\sigma_{e_c}^2 = .035085$

$$\sigma^2_{\rho_{xy}} = .004356 \qquad\qquad\qquad \sigma^2_{\rho_{TU}} = -.000994$$

$$SD_{\rho_{xy}} = .07 \qquad\qquad\qquad\qquad SD_{\rho_{TU}} = 0$$

These results may be checked using the Windows-based program VG6-I (see the Appendix for availability). Program results are the same as those calculated here. The results for uncorrected correlations show an incorrect mean of .28 (vs. the true value of .57) and a standard deviation of .07 (vs. an actual standard deviation of 0). The bare-bones meta-analysis is very inaccurate as an estimate of the actual effect size correlation used to generate these hypothetical data. However, the error in the uncorrected correlation meta-analysis is exactly consistent with the known artifacts. The average attenuation factor is .494 (using the weights that would be used for the meta-analysis of uncorrected correlations, i.e., weighting by sample size). The mean correlation would then be expected to be reduced from .57 to .494(.57) = .282, which matches the mean uncorrected correlation. A check of panel b in Table 3.5 shows considerable variation in the attenuation factors due to variation in the artifact values across studies. In the bare-bones meta-analysis of the standard deviation, this variation of .07 across studies is all artifactual; that is, even after correction for sampling error, the uncorrected correlations vary across studies due to differences in range restriction and test and criterion unreliability.

If the variance beyond sampling error in uncorrected correlations is interpreted to mean that there are real moderator variables present, that is a major substantive error of interpretation. However, if it is correctly noted that no correction for artifacts other than sampling error was made and that the remaining variation might be due to such artifacts, then the substantive error would be avoided. The moral of this story is this: Even meta-analysis will not save a review from critical errors if there is no correction for study artifacts beyond sampling error. Such artifacts are present in virtually every research domain.

In this example, the corrections for indirect range restriction were made using the Hunter et al. (2006) procedure (which is programmed in the VG6-I program). This method of correction for indirect range restriction is based on the assumption that any range restriction that exists on the dependent variable (y) is fully mediated (i.e., caused by) range restriction on the independent variable (x). This means that range restriction on the third variable (called s) is not a direct cause of range restriction on y; the third variable directly causes range restriction only on x. As noted by Hunter et al. (2006), in most contexts, this assumption is likely to hold (or hold to a close enough approximation). But in cases in which this assumption is substantially violated, the Hunter et al. (2006) correction has reduced accuracy (Le & Schmidt, 2006). A method of correcting for indirect range restriction in meta-analysis has recently been developed, based on earlier work by Bryant and Gokhale (1972), that does not require this assumption (Le et al., 2013). However, that method requires the user to know the range restriction ratio (u) for the dependent variable (y), which is not required by the Hunter et al. method. In personnel selection, the y measure is job performance and its *SD* in the applicant population (i.e., its unrestricted *SD*) is virtually impossible to estimate. So this method of correction cannot be used in studies in which the dependent variable is job performance or other behaviors on the job. More generally, it cannot be used with dependent variable measures for which data do not exist on a broader population that allows computation of an unrestricted *SD*. This includes many types of behavioral measures used in psychological research. But in studies focused on the relation between psychological or organizational constructs (e.g., between job satisfaction and organizational commitment), it may be possible to estimate the needed u ratio for the dependent variable based on some broader population *SD* (e.g., from national norms or workforce norms). In such cases, the Le et al. (2013) method can be used, and examples of such applications are presented in Le et al. (2013). If the fundamental assumption underlying the Hunter et al. (2006) method is seriously violated in such a data set, the Le et al. (2013) method will produce more accurate results than will the Hunter et al. method. However, in the example meta-analyses in this book that correct for indirect range restriction, we apply the Hunter et al. (2006) method, because this method is applicable in more situations and because it is rare for its fundamental assumption to be seriously violated.

This method of meta-analysis, in which each study correlation is individually corrected for attenuating artifacts, often cannot be used. The reason is obvious: Many study sets fail to provide all the needed artifact information. For examples of large-scale meta-analyses in which this method could be and was applied, see Carlson et al. (1999) and Rothstein et al. (1990). These studies were both consortium validation efforts in which numerous employers participated. Quite a number of such consortium studies have been conducted (e.g., Dunnette et al., 1982; Dye, 1982; Peterson, 1982). The meta-analysis methods described in this chapter can be applied to the data from these studies. Another example of a meta-analysis in which correlations were corrected individually is the study by Judge et al. (2001) relating job satisfaction to job performance.

When there is no range restriction (and, hence, no corrections for range restriction), meta-analysis correcting each correlation individually is much simpler than the example presented here. When there is no range restriction, sampling error and measurement error are often the only artifacts for which corrections can be made. In such cases, one need not consider the impact of range restriction on the reliabilities. That is, the distinction between reliabilities in the restricted and unrestricted groups does not exist. Also, there is no need for the special step used in our example to compute the "refined" estimate of sampling error variance for the corrected correlations. Hence, such meta-analyses are much easier to compute using a calculator or spreadsheet. However, for these simpler meta-analyses, the same computer program (VG6) can still be used. The user need only indicate that there is no range restriction when the interactive program asks that question. The program output presents the estimates of the same relevant statistics (e.g., $\bar{\rho}$ and SD_ρ) as it does for the case in which there is range restriction.

Version 2.0 of the Hunter-Schmidt meta-analysis programs is now available. This revised version of the programs is easier and more convenient to use. There are 14 major improvements. For example, the programs now allow the researcher to directly import Excel and other files into the programs rather than entering all data by hand. Changes now make it easier to do moderator analysis by subgrouping of studies. There is also now a subroutine that allows one to check for publication bias (see Chapter 13). These and other program improvements are fully described in the Appendix to this book.

In addition to the methods described in this chapter, Raju, Burke, Normand, and Langlois (1991) also developed procedures for conducting meta-analysis on correlations corrected individually for artifacts. Their procedures take into account sampling error in the reliability estimates. These procedures have been incorporated into a computer program called MAIN (Raju & Fleer, 1997), which is available from Michael J. Burke (e-mail: mburke1@tulane.edu). At present, this program is set up to assume that range restriction is always direct, but it could be modified in the future to incorporate the corrections for indirect range restriction described in this chapter. As of this writing, the computer program Comprehensive Meta-Analysis (published by Biostat; www.metaAnalysis.com) does not allow for corrections for measurement error and other artifacts and so does not contain a subprogram for meta-analysis of individually corrected correlations. However, this feature might be added in later versions of the program. Further discussion of available software for meta-analysis can be found in Chapter 11.

Summary of Meta-Analysis Correcting Each Correlation Individually

Correlations are subject to many artifactual sources of variation that we can correct in a meta-analysis: the random effect of sampling error and the systematic attenuation produced by correctable artifacts such as error of measurement, dichotomization, imperfect construct validity, or range variation. Sampling error and error of measurement are found in every study; hence, a full meta-analysis should always correct for both. Some domains are not subject to significant amounts of range variation across studies, but in areas with subject selection, such as personnel selection research and self-selection in volunteers for research, the effects of range restriction can be as large as the effects of error of measurement. The attenuation produced by dichotomization is even larger than the effects produced by error of measurement in most domains. However, measurement error is *always* present while dichotomization is often not present. Failure to correct for these artifacts results in massive underestimation of the mean correlation. Failure to control for variation in these artifacts results in a large overstatement of the variance of population correlations and, thus, in a potential false assertion of moderator variables where there are none.

Some advocate an approach different from that of correcting each correlation in the meta-analysis for artifacts. In this alternative approach, reliabilities, range restriction values, dichotomization, and other artifacts in each study are coded and tested as potential moderator variables in meta-regression (Borenstein et al., 2009, chap. 38). A statistically significant meta-regression coefficient for an artifact indicates that that artifact affects the observed correlations. One problem with this approach is that we know a priori that each of these artifacts has an effect, without need for a significance test. In this connection, a major problem with this approach is low statistical power (Hedges & Pigott, 2004); as a consequence, the results frequently indicate falsely that the artifacts do not have an effect on the observed correlations. Another problem is that this approach does not produce an estimate of the mean corrected correlation and its *SD*. The methods presented in this chapter do not have these problems. The limitations and problems of meta-regression are discussed in Chapter 9.

All meta-analyses can be corrected for sampling error. To do this, we need only know the sample size N_i for each sample correlation r_i. Meta-analysis correcting for only sampling error has come to be called "bare-bones" meta-analysis. However, in this analysis, the correlations analyzed are the correlations between imperfectly measured variables (and so are systematically lowered by error of measurement), the correlations may be computed on restricted rather than reference population samples (so that the correlations are biased by range variation), the correlations may be greatly attenuated by dichotomization, and the correlations may be much smaller than they would have been had the construct validity in each study been perfect. Thus, the mean correlation of a bare-bones meta-analysis is a biased estimate of the desired mean correlation, that is, the correlation from a study conducted without the imperfections that stem from limited scientific resources (Rubin, 1990). Furthermore, although the variance in a bare-bones meta-analysis is corrected for sampling error, it is still biased upward because it contains variance due to differences in measurement error, differences in measure variability (if any), differences in extremity of split in dichotomization (if any), and differences in construct validity. Thus, the "bare-bones" variance is usually a very poor estimate of the real variance.

For any artifact, if the needed artifact information is available from each study, then each correlation can be separately corrected for that artifact. The corrected correlations can then be analyzed by meta-analysis to eliminate sampling error. This chapter presented detailed procedures for this form of meta-analysis: meta-analysis of correlations corrected individually for the effects of artifacts. In most sets of studies to be subjected to meta-analysis, such complete artifact information will not be available. Such study sets do occur, however, and may become more frequent in the future as reporting practices improve. In three cases where this information has been available (Carlson et al., 1999; Dye, 1982; Rothstein et al., 1990), this form of meta-analysis has found virtually all between-study variance in correlations to be due to artifacts. However, if the fully corrected variance of correlations across studies is far enough above 0 to suggest that there is a moderator variable, then appropriate potential moderator variables can be checked by analyzing subsets of studies (as was done in Judge et al., 2001). That is, a separate meta-analysis is conducted for each subset of studies. Alternatively, study characteristics that are potential moderators can be coded and correlated with study correlations. This chapter described methods for both these approaches to moderator analysis.

In many sets of studies, information on particular artifacts is available in some studies but not in others. Because some (often much) artifact information is missing, it is not possible to fully correct each study correlation for the attenuating effects of every artifact. Nevertheless, it is possible to conduct accurate meta-analyses that correct the final meta-analytic results for all artifacts. This is accomplished using distributions of artifact effects compiled from studies that do provide information on that artifact. These methods of meta-analysis are the subject of the next chapter.

Exercise 3.1: Bare-Bones Meta-Analysis: Correcting for Sampling Error Only

These are real data. Psychological Services, Inc. (PSI), of Los Angeles, a selection consulting company, conducted a consortium study that 16 companies participated in. These firms were from all over the United States and from a variety of industries.

The job was mid-level clerical work, and one scale studied was the composite battery score of four clerical tests. The criterion was ratings of job performance based on rating scales specially developed for this study. The same scales were used in all 16 companies.

Following are the sample sizes and observed correlations. Conduct a meta-analysis that corrects only for sampling error (i.e., a bare-bones meta-analysis). Remember to use $\bar{r}$ in the formula for sampling error variance. Give and explain the following:

1. The mean observed correlation ($\bar{r}$)

2. The observed SD and variance (SD_r and S_r^2)

3. The expected sampling error variance

4. The corrected SD and variance ($SD_{\rho_{xy}}$ and $S_{\rho_{xy}}^2$)

5. The percentage of variance accounted for by sampling error and the correlation between sampling error and the observed correlations

6. What observed SD would you expect for these correlations if all observed variance were due to sampling error?

7. What additional corrections need to be made (beyond those that are part of this exercise) before this meta-analysis could be considered complete? Why? What effects would these corrections correct for?

For maximum learning, you should carry out this exercise using a calculator. However, it can also be carried out using either of our computer programs for correlations corrected individually (VG6-D and VG6-I). Both programs provide bare-bones meta-analysis results. You must enter 1.00 for all values of u_x, r_{xx}, and r_{yy}. This requirement makes it clear that a bare-bones meta-analysis makes the unrealistic assumption of perfect reliability and no range restriction. See the Appendix for a description of these programs.

Observed PSI Data

Company	N	Observed Validity of Sum of the Four Tests
1	203	.16
2	214	.19
3	225	.17
4	38	.04
5	34	.13
6	94	.38
7	41	.36
8	323	.34
9	142	.30
10	24	.20
11	534	.36
12	30	.24
13	223	.36
14	226	.40
15	101	.21
16	46	.35

Exercise 3.2: Meta-Analysis Correcting Each Correlation Individually

Find the following journal article in a library or online and make a personal copy of it:

Brown, S. H. (1981). Validity generalization and situational moderation in the life insurance industry. *Journal of Applied Psychology, 66*, 664–670.

Brown analyzed his data as if it were unmatched. That is, even though he had a criterion reliability value and a range restriction value specifically for each observed validity coefficient, he did not correct each observed coefficient individually. Instead, he used an unmatched data approach; that is, he used artifact distribution meta-analysis (see Chapter 4). In fairness to him, at the time he conducted his analysis, we had not yet published a description of methods for correcting each correlation individually.

Assume that range restriction in his data is direct and conduct new meta-analyses of his data correcting each observed validity individually. In the first meta-analysis, weight each study only by sample size (original weighting method). (This analysis cannot be run using the VG6-D program, because it does not weight by N_i.) Then do the meta-analysis again, weighting each study by $N_i A_i^2$ as described in this chapter. The analysis weighting by $N_i A_i^2$ can be done using the program VG6-D (i.e., the program for correcting correlations individually; specify that range restriction is *direct*). This program is described in the Appendix. For each set of analyses, report the following separately for the Group A and Group B companies and for the combined data:

1. Mean true validity

2. Standard deviation of true validities

3. Value at the 10th percentile

4. Percentage variance accounted for and the correlation between artifact effects and the observed correlations

5. Observed standard deviation of corrected validities

6. Standard deviation predicted from artifacts

7. Number of studies (companies)

8. Total N across the studies

Present these items in columns 1 through 8, in the order given here (with the columns labeled). (Each meta-analysis is then one row of your table.)

Compare your values to those obtained by Brown in each case. (Note: Brown did not compute values at the 10th percentile, but you can compute values for his data from information he gives in the study. Be careful to use the correct SD_p in this calculation: Use SD_p for true validity, not SD_p for true score correlations.) How different are the conclusions reached when these two different methods of meta-analysis are applied to the same data? What effect does weighting each study by other artifact indexes in addition to sample size have on the results? Why do you think this is the case? Do your results support Brown's original conclusions?

WORKSHEET—EXERCISE 3.2

Weighted by Sample Size

	1	2	3	4	5	6	7	8
	Mean True Validity	SD True Validity	10th Percentile	% Variance Accounted For	SD_{obs} Corrected Validities (SD_{rc})	SD Predicted From Artifacts	K	N
Overall								
Group A								
Group B								

Weighted by $N_i A_i^2$

	1	2	3	4	5	6	7	8
	Mean True Validity	SD True Validity	10th Percentile	% Variance Accounted For	SD_{obs} Corrected Validities (SD_{rc})	SD Predicted From Artifacts	K	N
Overall								
Group A								
Group B								

Data from S. H. Brown (1981)

	1	2	3	4	5	6	7	8
	Mean True Validity	SD True Validity	10th Percentile	% Variance Accounted For	SD_{obs} Validities	SD Predicted From Artifacts	K	N
Overall								
Group A								
Group B								

Meta-Analysis of 4
Correlations Using
Artifact Distributions

Introduction and Basic Concepts

The preceding chapter assumed that each correlation in each individual study could be corrected for artifacts. However, often every study in meta-analysis does not provide all the information required to correct for attenuation on all the study artifacts that affect that study. In any given meta-analysis, there may be several artifacts for which artifact information is only sporadically available. Indeed, this may be the case for all artifacts other than sampling error. For example, suppose measurement error and range restriction are the only relevant artifacts beyond sampling error. In such a case, the meta-analysis is conducted in three stages. First, the studies are used to compile information on four distributions: the distribution of the observed correlations and their sample sizes, the distribution of the reliabilities of the independent variable, the distribution of the reliabilities of the dependent variable, and the distribution of range departure (i.e., the u values). Second, the distribution of correlations is corrected for sampling error. This step is a bare-bones meta-analysis, as described in the first part of Chapter 3. Third, the distribution corrected for sampling error is then corrected for error of measurement, range variation, and perhaps other artifacts. This fully corrected distribution is the final result of the meta-analysis (unless the data are analyzed by subsets to test for moderator variables). Thus, the broad conceptual outline of meta-analysis based on artifact distributions is very simple. However, there are numerous statistical considerations involved in the third step here. These are examined in this chapter.

There is an important point to be made at the outset. Some have criticized the use of artifact distribution meta-analysis when full artifact data are not available for each study. The problem with this criticism is that only the alternative is making no corrections at all for measurement error and range restriction. The only option for meta-analysis would then be bare-bones meta-analysis (i.e., correcting only for sampling error). It is clear that this option greatly underestimates mean true score correlations in meta-analyses of research literatures in the behavioral and social sciences and in other disciplines. As we show in detail in this chapter, artifact distribution meta-analysis not only avoids such grossly biased meta-analysis results but also produces quite accurate results. This is the important big picture to keep in mind. Some have also argued that improved reporting practices in primary studies (i.e., full reporting of study artifacts in each study) make artifact distribution meta-analysis unnecessary. In fact, reporting practices have not improved to that extent. But more important, vast literatures of older studies need to be included in meta-analyses; most of these older studies typically do not include the information on reliabilities and range restriction needed to allow correction of each effect size individually. Le (2003), in a computer simulation study, showed that even when only 20% of studies report information on study artifacts, the results of artifact distribution meta-analysis are still quite accurate.

In the first section of this chapter, we consider the case in which information on all artifacts (except sampling error) is only sporadically available in the studies. That is, except for sample size, there is no artifact on which information is given in every study. Thus, for every artifact except sampling error, correction is accomplished by use of a distribution of artifact values that is compiled across the studies that do provide information on that artifact. Information on some artifacts may be drawn from studies that do not present any study correlations. For example, the reliabilities of scales measuring the independent and dependent variables (e.g., widely used scales for job satisfaction or work commitment) may be obtained from such studies. Test manuals for personality, interest, and aptitude tests may also provide such information.

In the second section of this chapter, we consider the mixed case. In the mixed case, every study presents information on one or more artifacts, while information on other artifacts is missing from many but not all of the studies. For example, all studies may present information on reliability of the independent variable and on dichotomization of the dependent variable, but only sporadic information on other artifacts. In this case, correlations are first corrected individually for the artifacts for which there is complete information, and an adjusted sample size is computed for each partially corrected correlation. Finally, this information, along with the artifact distributions for the sporadically available artifacts, is used to compute the meta-analysis, usually using an available computer program. This step yields the final meta-analysis results (unless there is a subsequent search for moderators).

An important consideration is the reliability estimates used in making corrections for biases induced in data by measurement error. It is important to use appropriate types of reliability estimates. Use of inappropriate types of reliability estimates leads to incomplete corrections for measurement error. If this is the case, the meta-analysis report should explain that the biasing effects of measurement error were only partially corrected. A detailed guide for selecting appropriate reliability estimates is presented in Chapter 3. We refer the reader to that guide.

Full Artifact Distribution Meta-Analysis

In full artifact distribution meta-analysis, there is no artifact other than sampling error for which information is given in all studies. In this form of meta-analysis, the initial or interim meta-analysis is a meta-analysis of the uncorrected (observed) study correlations, that is, a bare-bones meta-analysis. The questions are these: How can the mean and standard deviation of uncorrected correlations be corrected for the impact of artifacts? How do we restore the mean observed correlation to the value that it would have had had the studies been conducted without design imperfections? How do we subtract the variance in study correlations produced by variation in artifact values across studies? These questions are addressed in this chapter.

In the case of direct range restriction, the methods used in this form of meta-analysis assume that artifact parameters are (1) independent of each other and (2) independent of the actual population correlations. Examination of the substantive nature of artifacts suggests that these independence assumptions are reasonable in the case of direct range restriction; most artifact values are less a matter of scientific choice and more a function of situational and resource constraints. The practical constraints for different artifacts usually have little to do with one another. For example, the dependent variable might be ratings by observers while the independent variable is a commercially available measure of a personality trait. These two types of reliability are unlikely to be correlated. (See Pearlman et al., 1980, and Schmidt, Pearlman, & Hunter, 1980, for a full discussion of the reasons artifacts will usually be independently distributed.) Furthermore, Raju, Anselmi, Goodman, and Thomas (1998), in a computer simulation study under conditions of direct range restriction, found that violations of independence have a negligible effect on meta-analysis results unless artifacts are correlated with the underlying population correlations, an unlikely event. In this unlikely event, mean true score correlation values are accurate while estimates of the *SD* are too large (Raju et al., 1998), creating conservative estimates of credibility intervals (intervals that are too wide). So under conditions of direct range restriction, violations of the independence assumptions do not appear to create serious problems. However, two caveats should be noted here. First, the assumption of independence among artifacts does not hold under conditions of indirect range restriction. The technical reasons for this are presented in Hunter et al. (2006). When there is indirect range restriction, artifacts are, in fact, substantially correlated. However, the interactive meta-analysis procedure described in this chapter has been found via computer simulation studies to be accurate under conditions of indirect range restriction despite violations of the independence assumptions (Le & Schmidt, 2006). Second, in the case of direct range restriction, the assumption of artifact independence, strictly speaking, applies only to the universe of studies and not necessarily to the sample of studies included in the meta-analysis, especially if the number of studies is small. For the studies in hand, independence would be satisfied only to within second-order sampling error. That is, the independence assumptions will become more valid as the number of studies increases. By chance (i.e., sampling error), in a meta-analyses with a small number of studies, the independence assumptions could be violated to a sizable degree. However, in meta-analyses on a small number of studies, second-order sampling error (see Chapter 9) is a more serious problem than are violations of the independence assumption.

Suppose there is sporadic information on some artifact, say the reliability of the independent variable. Some studies report the reliability while other studies do not. Indeed, as we noted previously, we may obtain reliability estimates for some scales in studies that never used the dependent variable studied in the meta-analysis, that is, studies outside the original research domain for the meta-analysis. Data on the construct validity of the independent variable are likely to come predominantly from studies outside the research domain for the meta-analysis. For the artifact values available, we can use the artifact information (e.g., the reliability of our independent variable as reported in that study) to compute the attenuation factor for that artifact (the square root of the reported reliability, symbolized as a in the case of the independent variable and b in the case of the dependent variable). These attenuation factor values can then be compiled across studies to generate a distribution for that artifact. Examination of this distribution can be informative. However, the available computer programs for artifact distribution meta-analysis do not require computation of values of a and b; they allow direct entry of reliability coefficients. The research area of reliability generalization has produced reliability distributions for many different measures used in research (Botella, Suero, & Gambara, 2012; Sanchez-Meca, Lopez-Lopez, & Lopez-Pina, in press; Vacha-Haase & Thompson, 2011). These reliability distributions are a good source for reliability artifact distributions for use in artifact distribution meta-analyses.

Consider then the nature of the meta-analysis to be done. We have the study values to do a meta-analysis of uncorrected correlations. For each of several correctable artifacts, we have the distribution of the artifact values.

These artifact distribution values are then used to correct the initial meta-analysis for the effects of those artifacts.

EARLIER PROCEDURES FOR ARTIFACT DISTRIBUTION META-ANALYSIS

The 2004 edition of this book presented a variety of different equations and procedures for conducting artifact distribution meta-analysis. These included the noninteractive method (cf. Pearlman et al., 1980; Schmidt, Gast-Rosenberg, & Hunter, 1980; Schmidt, Hunter, Pearlman, & Shane, 1979), the Callender and Osburn (1980) multiplicative method, the two Raju and Burke (1983) Taylor Series methods (TSA 1 and TSA 2), the Raju and Drasgow (2003) maximum likelihood methods, and the Hunter and Schmidt (2004) variation on the multiplicative method. This last method was developed in detail in the last edition of this book. However, it turned out not to be as accurate as an alternative method described later.

All of these methods except the Raju and Drasgow (2003) methods have been shown by computer simulation studies to be accurate enough for operational use under conditions of direct range restriction (Callender & Osburn, 1980; Law, Schmidt, & Hunter, 1994a, 1994b; Mendoza & Reinhardt, 1991; Raju & Burke, 1983). These methods all depend on the assumption of independence among artifacts, and so they are not accurate when range restriction is indirect. Computer simulation studies indicate that the interactive procedure with accuracy-enhancing refinements is more accurate under conditions of direct range restriction than the other methods (Law et al., 1994a, 1994b). In addition, computer simulation studies have shown that the interactive method, when modified for indirect range restriction corrections, produces accurate estimates of both the mean corrected (true score) correlation and its standard deviation (Le & Schmidt, 2006). In light of these facts, we incorporated the interactive method as the method for artifact distribution meta-analysis in the Schmidt and Le (2004, 2014) computer programs (described in the Appendix to this book). Because of these advantages, we will focus on the nature and use of the interactive method in this chapter.

In addition to the interactive program, the Appendix also describes other meta-analysis programs: a program for use when correlations are corrected individually, a program for use when d values are corrected individually, and a program for use with artifact distribution meta-analysis of d values. The 2014 version of this program package (Version 2.0) contains a number of improvements. It is now possible to import Excel files into these programs. All the programs now provide confidence intervals, in addition to credibility values. The limit on the number of studies that can be included in a meta-analysis has now been raised to 1,000. Other changes have been made that make the programs easier to use. A full listing of these improvements is included in the Appendix.

THE INTERACTIVE METHOD

The interactive procedure was first presented by Schmidt et al. (1980) and was further developed in Schmidt, Hunter, and Pearlman (1981) and Law et al. (1994a, 1994b). Calculation procedures for the interactive procedure are complex and are done via a computer program. The interactive procedure differs from the noninteractive procedure and other procedures in that variances due to between-study differences in criterion reliability, test reliability, and range restriction are computed simultaneously rather than sequentially. In the case of direct range restriction or when there is no range restriction, this composite step can be summarized as follows:

1. Compute the sample size weighted mean of the observed correlations ($\bar{r}$) and correct this value for criterion unreliability, range restriction, and test unreliability, using mean values of these artifacts. The result is $\bar{\rho}_{TU}$, the estimated mean true score correlation.

2. Create a three-dimensional matrix, the cells of which represent all possible combinations from the artifact distributions of range restriction u values, independent variable reliability, and dependent variable reliability. For example, if there are 10 different u values in that artifact distribution, 15 different values of r_{xx_a}, and 9 different values of r_{yy_a}, the number of cells is $(10)(15)(9) = 1,350$. Typically, the number of cells is large enough to make it impractical to do the calculations described in Steps 3 and 4 by calculator. For this reason, the interactive procedure is applied via computer software.

3. For each cell, attenuate $\bar{\rho}_{TU}$ to compute the expected value of the observed coefficient for that combination of artifacts. The fully corrected mean correlation ($\bar{\rho}_{TU}$) will be attenuated to a different value in each cell.

4. Compute the variance of the resulting coefficients across cells, weighting each cell value by its cell frequency. Cell frequency is determined by artifact-level frequencies; because range restriction values (u_x values) are assumed to be uncorrelated with (applicant pool) reliabilities, and the reliabilities of independent and dependent variables are also assumed to be independent, the joint (cell) frequency is the product of the three marginal frequencies. (Recall that, in each artifact distribution, each artifact value has an associated frequency.) This computed variance of cell correlations is the variance in observed coefficients that would be created by criterion and test reliability differences and range restriction differences

if the true score correlation (ρ_{TU}) were constant and N were infinite in all studies (i.e., if there were no sampling error). Call this value S_{art}^2 .

5. Compute the sample size weighted variance of the observed correlations (S_r^2) and subtract from this value the amount of variance expected from sampling error (S_e^2) and the amount computed in Step 4 (S_{art}^2). The resulting residual variance (S_{res}) is the amount that is not accounted for by artifacts. The square root of this value is the residual standard deviation (SD_{res}). The residual distribution is then described by the mean observed correlation ($\bar{r}$) and SD_{res}.

6. Each value in the residual distribution is then corrected for the downward bias created by measurement error and range restriction. If there is no range restriction, this correction can be made by simply dividing r by the square root of the product of the two mean reliabilities (i.e., by the product ab). This is possible because the two sets of reliabilities are assumed to be independent and because the measurement error correction is a linear correction. However, the range restriction correction is not a linear correction. It is nonlinear because this correction increases small correlations by a larger percentage than large correlations. Therefore, each correlation value in the residual distribution must be individually corrected for range restriction, using the mean value of u_x. The interactive method (the INTNL program) does this (as explained in more detail in Chapter 5). The resulting corrected residual distribution is the distribution of population true score correlations. Its mean is $\bar{\rho}_{TU}$ and its standard deviation is SD_ρ. These two values can then be used to compute a credibility interval. For example, an 80% credibility interval would contain the middle 80% of values in the distribution of population true score correlations. If there is a search for moderators, it is usually run by subgrouping the studies and rerunning the INTNL program on subgrouped studies.

Because the order in which corrections must be made is different for direct and indirect range restriction, there are two separate interactive computer programs: INTNL-D for direct range restriction and INTNL-I for indirect range restriction. These programs and their availability are described in the Appendix. The master program asks the user to indicate whether there is range restriction and, if so, whether it is direct or indirect. It then selects the correct subprogram. When range restriction is indirect, in computing $\bar{\rho}_{TU}$, the reliability corrections must be made *prior to* the range restriction correction, using reliability values for the restricted group. In attenuating $\bar{\rho}_{TU}$ to estimate variance caused by artifacts beyond sampling error, this order must be reversed. The technical reasons for this are given in Hunter et al. (2006). INTNL-I makes the corrections in this order. When range restriction is direct, in $\bar{\rho}_{TU}$, the correction for dependent variable reliability can be made either before or after the range restriction correction; however, it is usually made before because the reliability estimates available for the dependent variable are usually for the restricted group. The INTNL-D program assumes that dependent variable reliabilities are the restricted group values, and makes this correction before the range restriction correction. In direct range restriction, independent variable reliability is undefined in the restricted group because the direct selection on x induces a correlation between true scores and measurement errors in the selected group (Hunter et al., 2006; Mendoza & Mumford, 1987), thus violating the central assumption of reliability theory that true scores and measurement errors are uncorrelated. Hence, in estimating $\bar{\rho}_{TU}$, the correction for measurement error in the independent variable must be made *after* the range restriction correction and must be made using an estimate of reliability in the unrestricted group. Again, see Hunter et al. (2006) for full technical development of these issues. In estimating $\bar{\rho}_{TU}$, the program INTNL-D corrects first for dependent variable reliability, then corrects for range restriction, and corrects last for independent variable reliability using the reliability value in the unrestricted group. In attenuating $\bar{\rho}_{TU}$ to estimate variance caused by artifacts beyond sampling error, this order is reversed.

In addition to somewhat superior accuracy, the interactive procedure has four important advantages over other procedures for artifact distribution meta-analysis. First, unlike other procedures, it takes into account the slight interaction between the effects of measurement error and range restriction (hence the name of the procedure). This interaction occurs because the effect of measurement error on the observed correlation is greater in studies in which there is less range restriction (cf. Schmidt et al., 1980). (This interaction occurs because of the nonlinear nature of the effect of range restriction.) The simultaneous nature of the calculation of artifact effects on observed rs in the interactive procedure allows this interaction to be reflected in the estimate of variance caused by artifacts beyond sampling error. Earlier models discussed do not take this interaction into account.

Second, in the case of direct range restriction, the interactive procedure avoids the problem of lack of independence among the artifact attenuation factors a, b, and c, the range restriction attenuation factor. The term c cannot be completely independent of a and b because the formula for c *contains* both a and b (Callender & Osburn, 1980). Other procedures (except for those of Raju & Burke, 1983) assume that a, b, and c are independent, and because this is not strictly true, there is a slight reduction in their accuracy. The interactive procedure, however, does not assume that a, b, and c are independent. Instead, it assumes that a, b, and u_x are independent. That is, it substitutes u_x for c in the independence assumption. Because there is no mathematical dependency among any of the terms a, b, and u_x, there is no reason they cannot be independent. In fact, it is usually reasonable to assume they are, as noted earlier. This leads to some improvement in accuracy for the interactive procedure. Note that the independence assumption applies to values of a and b in the unrestricted population. Range restriction $[u_X]$ reduces a and b values in the restricted group, and these values are no longer independent of u_X.

Third, the interactive procedure, unlike other procedures, can be used when range restriction is indirect. The only change needed is that u_T values must be entered instead of u_X values when the range restriction corrections are made. (The formula for computing u_T was given in Chapter 3; see Equation [3.16].) The application of the interactive procedure to indirect range restriction is slightly less accurate in estimating S_ρ^2 than it is in the case of direct range restriction because a $(a = \sqrt{r_{xx_a}})$ is not independent of u_T, as can be seen in Equation (3.16). This prediction was verified via computer simulation studies by Le and Schmidt (2006). However, these simulation studies showed that the interactive procedure, when adapted for indirect range restriction, produced reasonably accurate estimates of both the mean corrected correlation and its associated standard deviation. This is important because most cases of range restriction are indirect (Hunter et al., 2006). The other procedures we have discussed produce less accurate results under conditions of indirect range restriction. This result stems from the fact that, under conditions of indirect range restriction, the values of a, b, and c become much more highly intercorrelated (i.e., dependent) than they are under direct range restriction (see Hunter et al., 2006), and this severe violation of the independence assumption causes inaccuracies. The methods of Raju and Burke (1983) may be an exception. It is possible that these methods can be successfully adapted to the case of indirect range restriction (Hunter et al., 2006).

Finally, a fourth advantage of the interactive method is that certain accuracy-enhancing statistical refinements have been developed for it and have been included in the INTNL computer programs; we discuss these refinements later in this chapter and in Chapter 5.

A SIMPLIFIED EXAMPLE OF APPLICATION OF THE INTERACTIVE METHOD

We will be applying the interactive method throughout this chapter. To aid understanding of this procedure, we now present a simplified example application of this method to a hypothetical data set. This example is simplified because there is no range restriction; there is only measurement error in the independent and dependent variable measures. In many research domains, there is no range restriction, so this example is realistic in that sense. This could be a meta-analysis of the correlation between two organizational constructs—for example, the correlation between satisfaction with job tasks (task satisfaction) and satisfaction with one's supervisor. The basic data are as follows:

1. There are $k = 30$ studies and the average N across studies is 43.

2. The sample size weighted average observed correlation is .53 and the SD of the observed rs is .1310; the variance of the observed rs is .017161. Using Equation (3.7) in Chapter 3, we calculate that the amount of sampling error variance expected in this distribution is .012312.

3. The average reliability of the independent variable measure is .77. The square root of $.77 = .877 = a$. There are five values in this artifact distribution, and each value has a frequency of 1.

4. The average reliability of the dependent variable measure is .70. The square root of $.70 = .837 = b$. Again, there are five values in this artifact distribution, and each value has a frequency of 1.

5. The estimated mean true score correlation is $.53/[(.877)(.837)] = .72$. (This estimates the average correlation between these two *constructs*; Schmidt et al., 2013.)

Table 4.1 shows the application of the interactive method. For each cell in the table, the value of .72 is attenuated (reduced) by the square root of the product of the reliabilities in the cell's row and column. We assume that the two sets of reliabilities are independent. As can be seen, these attenuated values range from .394 to .648. The variance across these cell values is .004492. This is the amount of variance in the observed correlations that is

Table 4.1 Simplified example of the interactive method.

			r_{yy}				
			1	2	3	4	5
			.50	.60	.70	.80	.90
	1	.60	.394	.432	.467	.500	.529
r_{xx}	2	.70	.426	.467	.504	.539	.571
	3	.80	.455	.500	.539	.576	.611
	4	.85	.469	.514	.555	.594	.630
	5	.90	.483	.529	.571	.611	.648

produced solely by variation in the reliabilities of the measures. It is the amount of variance that would exist in the total absence of sampling error (i.e., the amount that would exist if every study had an infinite sample size).

The residual variance is the amount of variance left in the variance of the observed correlations (.017161) after subtracting out sampling error variance (.012312) and variance due to variation in the reliabilities (.004492):

$$\text{Residual variance } S_{res}^2 = .017161 - .012312 - .004492 = .000357$$

The proportion of variance accounted for by sampling error is .012312/.017161 = .72 (or 72%). The proportion of variance accounted for by variation in the reliabilities is .004492/.017161 = .26 (or 26%). The total percent of variance accounted for by artifacts is 98%. Only 2% of the variance is not accounted for. The square root of .98 is .99; this is the correlation between the observed correlations and the variations produced by the artifacts of sampling errors and measurement errors.

As noted earlier, the residual variance is *not* the estimate of the variance of the population true score correlations, because the residual variance has been reduced (attenuated) by the average reliability of both measures. The variance of the population correlations is .000357/[(.77) (.70)] = .000662. The *SD* of the corrected correlations (SD_ρ) is the square root of this value, which is .025729. So the final result is as follows: The mean construct-level correlation between job satisfaction and satisfaction with one's supervisor is .72, and this correlation does not vary much; its *SD* is only .026 (rounded). The 80% credibility interval is .69 to .75. Eighty percent of population true score correlations are expected to lie in this interval. This example illustrates the basic processes involved in the interactive procedure.

A WORKED EXAMPLE: ERROR OF MEASUREMENT

Variables in the social sciences are often only poorly measured. Thus, results must be corrected to eliminate error of measurement. Suppose error of measurement is the only artifact that attenuates study correlations in a given area. In many areas of organizational and other research, there is no range restriction, but measurement error (along with sampling error) is always present in all research, so this example is realistic in that respect. The attenuation model for this study is

$$\rho_{xy} = ab\rho$$

where

$$a = \sqrt{r_{XX}}$$
$$b = \sqrt{r_{YY}}$$

Table 4.2 presents the basic computations for the meta-analysis of a hypothetical set of studies of the correlation between organizational commitment and job satisfaction. Table 4.2a presents the basic findings and the artifact information for eight studies. The studies are listed in three groups. The first pair of studies presents no correlational data pertaining to organizational commitment or job satisfaction, but these studies do contain reliability data for the organizational commitment measure. The first is the classic study in which Ermine presented his measure of organizational commitment. The second study is one in which Ferret used "the key items from Ermine" and then correlated commitment with other variables (not including job satisfaction). The second pair of studies contains only reliability information on the job satisfaction scales. Finally, the last four studies contain only correlational information (although each study had the item data and, hence, could have computed at least coefficient alpha reliability coefficients for that study). In Table 4.2a, we see that two of the correlations were statistically significant and two were not.

Table 4.2b presents the meta-analysis worksheet. The column for a presents the attenuation factor for the first correctable artifact, that is, the square root of the reliability of the independent variable. The column for b presents the attenuation factor for the second correctable artifact, that is, the square root of the reliability of the dependent variable. At the bottom of the table, the mean and standard deviation of each entry are given.

Table 4.2   Organizational commitment and job satisfaction (hypothetical results).

Table 4.2a Basic Information

	Organizational Commitment Reliability (r_{xx})	Job Satisfaction Reliability (r_{yy})	Sample Size (N_i)	Sample Correlation (r_{xy})
Ermine (1976)	.70			
Ferret (1977)	.50			
Mink (1976)		.70		
Otter (1977)		.50		
Polecat (1978)			68	.01
Stoat (1979)			68	.14
Weasel (1980)			68	.23*
Wolverine (1978)			68	.34**

Table 4.2b Meta-Analysis Worksheet

Study	a	b	N	r_{xy}
1	.84			
2	.71			
3		.84		
4		.71		
5			68	.01
6			68	.14
7			68	.23
8			68	.34
Ave	.775	.775	68	.180
SD	.065	.065	0	.121

*Significant at the .05 level. **Significant at the .01 level.

Consider first the meta-analysis of the uncorrected correlations:

$$\bar{\rho}_{xy} = \bar{r} = .18$$

$$\sigma_r^2 = .014650$$

$$\sigma_e^2 = \frac{4(1-.18^2)^2}{4(67)} = .013974$$

$$\sigma_{\rho_{xy}}^2 = \sigma_r^2 - \sigma_e^2 = .014650 - .013974 = .000676$$

$$\sigma_{\rho_{xy}} = .026$$

This analysis of sampling error shows that there is little variation in the correlations across studies. The 80% credibility interval is .15 to .21. Thus, the two studies that fail to find statistical significance make Type II errors. Most of the variance of the observed correlations (95%) is attributable to sampling error: $.013974/.014650 = .95$.

We next enter these data into the INTNL (interactive) program. On the computer screen, this programs appears as "*Correlations—Using Artifact Distributions.*" After clicking on this label, the program asks whether your data have range restriction. In this example, the answer is "*No Range Restriction.*" You then enter the correlations and their sample sizes followed by the artifact distributions. In entering the artifact data, note that in this example, the frequency of each of the reliability values is 1.00 for both the independent and independent variable reliabilities. Now let's look at the output of the interactive program:

Mean true score correlation $\bar{\rho} = .279$ (rounding to .28).

Standard deviation of the true score correlations $SD_\rho = .0324$.

The 80% credibility interval for the population true score correlations is .237 to .320.

The sample size weighted variance of the observed $S_r^2 = .014650$.

Variance in observed correlations due to all artifacts combined $S_{pred}^2 = .014202$.

Percent of variation accounted for by sampling error plus reliability variation = .014202/.014650 = 96.9%. The square root of .969 is .98; so the correlation between the effects of artifacts and the observed correlations is .98.

Percent variance in observed rs due to sampling error $S_e^2 = .013974/.014650 = .954$ (or 95%).

Residual variance in observed rs after removal of variance due to both artifacts $S_{res}^2 = .0004479$.

The reader is invited to verify these results by entering the Table 4.2 data into the INTNL program. It is important to remember that only two study artifacts were corrected here: the error of measurement in the independent and the dependent variables. Thus, the residual variation attributed to the actual correlations contains variation due to uncorrected artifacts such as imperfect construct validity or bad data and so on. Therefore, the true standard deviation may be less than the .03 nominal estimate.

Let us consider the impact of artifacts in this example. The impact of sampling error on the mean correlation was assumed to be negligible (although that would not really be true with a total sample size of only 272). However, the impact of sampling error on the variance across studies is massive. The variance of the sample correlations is .014650, of which sampling error is .013974, variance due to variation in reliability is .000228, and "else" is .000448. That is, 95% of the variance in correlations across studies is due to sampling error, about 2% is due to variation in reliability, and about 3% is due to unspecified other determinants.

Variation in reliabilities causes only 2% of the variation in observed correlations, but the impact of measurement error on the mean correlation is very large. Error of measurement caused the *mean* correlation to be depressed from .28 to .18, indicating a 36% downward bias in the mean observed correlation. This pattern is the one that is most common: Measurement errors (and range restriction) create a substantial downward bias in the mean correlation, but they create only a small percentage of the variance of the observed correlations.

A WORKED EXAMPLE: UNRELIABILITY AND DIRECT RANGE RESTRICTION

Suppose we have artifact information on three artifacts: error of measurement in the independent variable, error of measurement in the dependent variable, and direct range restriction on the independent variable. The three attenuation artifacts are

$$a = \sqrt{r_{XX_a}}$$

$$b = \sqrt{r_{YY_a}}$$

$$c = [(1 - u_X^2)\bar{r}^2 + u_X^2]^{1/2} \quad \text{(Callender \& Osburn, 1980)}$$

where r_{xx_a} and r_{yy_a} are the reliabilities in the unrestricted group and $\bar{r}$ is the average observed correlation. The quantity c is the attenuation factor for range restriction. The attenuation formula is

$$\rho_{xy} = abc\rho$$

Table 4.3 presents both the artifact information in raw form and the computed attenuation factors for each artifact for 16 hypothetical studies. The example in Table 4.3 was created by assuming that the population correlation between true scores on the two variables in the reference population is always .58. These two variables could be any two theoretical constructs of research interest. The first five columns of Table 4.3 are the data extracted from the 16 hypothetical studies. The last three columns are the values of a, b, and c, computed from the values of r_{XX_a}, r_{YY_i}, and u_x, respectively. These values are shown for illustrative purposes only. They will be computed internally by the INTNL-D program (the version of the interactive program for direct range restriction). The value of r_{yy} used in this program is the value from the restricted group (r_{yy_i}), and so this is the value in column 4 of Table 4.3. This is also almost always the value given in primary studies.

We now enter the data in Table 4.3 (except for the values of a, b, and c) into the interactive program for direct range restriction (INTNL-D). In doing this, note that the reliability and u_x values in the Table 4.3 can be entered as shown with each having a frequency of 1.00, or these data can be grouped. For example, for the independent variable, the reliability of .49 can be entered once with a frequency of 4. Likewise, the reliability of

Table 4.3 Sixteen hypothetical studies.

Study	N	r_{xx_a}	r_{yy_i}	u_x	r_{xy}	a	b	c
1	68	.49	—	.40	.02	.70	—	.43
2	68	—	.64	—	.26*	—	.80	—
3	68	.49	.64	—	.33*	.70	.80	—
4	68	—	—	.60	.09	—	—	.62
5	68	.49	—	—	.02	.70	—	—
6	68	—	.49	.40	.24*	—	.70	.43
7	68	.49	.49	—	.30*	.70	.70	—
8	68	—	—	.60	.06	—	—	.62
9	68	.64	—	.40	.28*	.80	—	.43
10	68	—	.64	—	.04	—	.80	—
11	68	.64	.64	—	.12	.80	.80	—
12	68	—	—	.60	.34*	—	—	.62
13	68	.64	—	—	.26*	.80	—	—
14	68	—	.49	.40	.02	—	.70	.43
15	68	.64	.49	—	.09	.80	.70	—
16	68	—	—	.60	.33*	—	—	.62

Note: r_{xx_a} is the value in the unrestricted population; r_{yy_i} is the value in the restricted population.

*Significant at the .05 level (two-tailed test).

.64 can be entered once with a frequency of 4. It is usually more convenient to enter artifacts in a grouped format. The output of the program is as follows:

The mean true score correlation $\bar{\rho}$ is .5789 (which rounds to .58).

The standard deviation of the true score correlation SD_ρ is 0. (Sampling error plus variation due to variability of the three artifacts accounts for all the observed variance [102.29%].)

Because SD_ρ is 0, the 80% credibility is .58 to .58.

The variance in observed correlations due to all artifacts = .0154464.

The variance in observed correlations after removal of all variance due to artifacts = 0.

Percent of observed variance accounted for by sampling error = .0140251/.0150999 = .929 (or 93%).

The final conclusion is that these two constructs are highly correlated (.58) but not so highly correlated that they can be concluded to be one and the same construct. They are "correlated but distinct" constructs. This is not always the case, as shown by Le et al. (2009, 2010), who found that certain constructs are redundant (i.e., correlated essentially 1.00). Finally, it is noteworthy that the construct-level correlations (Schmidt et al., 2013) between these two constructs do not vary across studies. All the observed variability in observed correlations between *measures* of these two constructs is apparently due to statistical and measurement artifacts.

A WORKED EXAMPLE: PERSONNEL SELECTION WITH FIXED TEST (DIRECT RANGE RESTRICTION)

Personnel selection is a special case because, in the practical use of a test for hiring, the predictor test is used in imperfect form; that is, observed scores are used. Thus, the relevant population correlation for purposes of assessing the practical impact of the test is corrected for error of measurement in the dependent variable but not in the independent variable. The validity of the test is given by the applicant population correlation between uncorrected test scores and job performance true scores. This means we should correct for measurement error in the job performance measure and correct for restriction in range, but not correct for error of measurement in the test. (Of course, in the *theory* of personnel selection, we would want fully corrected correlations.)

Personnel selection research is vexed by all the artifacts shown in Table 3.1 in Chapter 3. In particular, restriction in range on the independent variable is created by selective hiring. Suppose all studies in a meta-analysis use exactly the same test so there is no variation across studies in the reliability of the independent variable, r_{XX_a}, the reliability of the test in the applicant (unrestricted) group. Suppose $r_{XX_a} = .80$.

Suppose error of measurement in the dependent variable (job performance) and range restriction are the only other artifacts for which artifact information is available. Suppose also that range restriction on the independent variable is direct. The attenuation factors would then be

$$b = \sqrt{r_{YY_a}}$$

$$c = [(1 - u_X^2)\bar{r}^2 + u_X^2]^{1/2}$$

where r_{YY_a} is the reliability of the job performance measure in the applicant pool (the unrestricted group), $\bar{r}$ is the average uncorrected correlation across studies, and c is the attenuation factor for range restriction. The attenuation formula is

$$\rho_{xy} = bc\rho$$

Table 4.4 presents hypothetical data for 12 personnel selection studies of this type. (Note that these data are different from those in Table 3.5 in Chapter 3; the range restriction values are different.) The data in Table 4.4 were generated assuming a mean true validity of .50 with a standard deviation of 0. Table 4.4 presents both the criterion reliabilities in the unrestricted group (r_{yy_a}) and these values in the restricted group (i.e., r_{yy_i} values). Equation (4.2), presented below, transforms between restricted and unrestricted dependent variable reliabilities.

In educational selection, the dependent variable is usually grade point average (often first-year grade point average). In personnel selection, the dependent variable is almost always either job performance or some job behavior such as training performance, accidents, theft, or turnover. Consider performance ratings. All research on performance ratings has been of necessity conducted on incumbents. For example, a review of interrater reliability findings (Viswesvaran et al., 1996) found the average interrater reliability of a multiscale rating scale to be .51. This is the incumbent reliability. The applicant reliability is higher. In principle, the traditional formula relating reliability in two populations (usually called the "homogeneity formula") could be used to compute the applicant reliability from the incumbent reliability:

u_Y = incumbent SD_Y/applicant SD_Y

r_{YY_i} = incumbent reliability

r_{YY_a} = applicant reliability

$$r_{YY_a} = 1 - u_Y^2(1 - r_{YY_i}) \tag{4.1}$$

The problem with this formula is that it requires knowledge of the applicant standard deviation for performance ratings (because $u_Y = SD_{Y_i}/SD_{Y_a}$). Because we have data for job performance ratings only for incumbents, this standard deviation cannot be directly estimated from the data. However, there is another formula that can be used to compute r_{YY_a} (Brogden, 1968; Schmidt et al., 1976):

$$r_{YY_a} = 1 - \frac{1 - r_{YY_i}}{1 - r_{XY_i}^2 [1 - S_{X_a}^2 / S_{X_i}^2]} \tag{4.2}$$

where r_{XY_i} is the observed correlation between X and Y in the incumbent sample. (Callender & Osburn, 1980, p. 549, present a mathematically identical formula.) Consider a realistic case. Let $u_X = SD_{X_i} / SD_{X_a}$ = .70, $r_{XY_i} = .25$, and $r_{YY_i} = .47$. Equation (4.2) then yields $r_{YY_a} = .50$. Hence, the reliability of ratings of job performance would be .03 (6%) higher in the absence of range restriction. Although it is useful to be aware of Equation (4.2), the value of r_{yy} used in the meta-analysis programs for both direct and indirect range restriction is the value in the restricted group (i.e., r_{yy_i}). This is almost invariably the value presented in primary studies.

We will analyze the data in Table 4.4 using the INTNL-D program, and so we must enter the restricted values. Notice that, as expected, all criterion reliabilities are slightly higher in the applicant group. Because complete artifact information is given in Table 4.4 for each observed correlation, the artifact distribution method ordinarily would not be used; instead, each correlation would be corrected individually, using the methods presented in Chapter 3. Here, however, we present an artifact distribution analysis for these data to illustrate the use of artifact distribution meta-analysis using the INTNL-D program. For illustrative purposes, the last two columns of Table 4.4 show the attenuation factors.

We now enter the data in this table (except for the a and c values) in the INTNL-D program, remembering to use only the restricted criterion reliabilities. As noted in the earlier examples, it is more convenient to enter the reliabilities and u_x values in a grouped format. The program output is as follows:

The mean true validity value $\bar{\rho}_{xy_t}$ = .487 (rounding to .49).

The standard deviation of the true validities $SD_{\rho_{xy_t}}$ = .0291.

The 80% credibility interval = .450 to .524.

Sample size weighted variance of observed validities S_r^2 = .017033.

Variance in observed validities due to all artifacts S_{pred}^2 = .016646.

Percent variance in observed rs due to all artifacts = .016646/.017033 = .977 (or 98%).

Percent variance in observed rs due to sampling error = .012678/.017033 = .744 (or 74%).

Residual variance in observed rs after removal of all artifactual variance S_{res}^2 = .000387.

Table 4.4 Meta-analysis of personnel selection validities (direct range restriction).

Study	Selection Ratio	u_x	Criterion Reliability (r_{yy_i})	(r_{yy_a})	Sample Size	Observed Correlation	b	c
1	.20	.468	.80	.86	68	.35**	.928	.529
2	.20	.468	.60	.61	68	.07	.779	.529
3	.20	.468	.80	.81	68	.11	.899	.529
4	.20	.468	.60	.70	68	.31*	.838	.529
5	.50	.603	.80	.81	68	.18	.900	.643
6	.50	.603	.60	.67	68	.36**	.821	.643
7	.50	.603	.80	.84	68	.40**	.919	.643
8	.50	.603	.60	.61	68	.13	.782	.643
9	.90	.844	.80	.82	68	.49**	.904	.857
10	.90	.844	.60	.61	68	.23	.780	.857
11	.90	.844	.80	.81	68	.29*	.898	.857
12	.90	.844	.60	.63	68	.44*	.793	.857

$*p < .05$ (two-tailed test). $**p < .01$ (two-tailed test).

The main conclusion is that this test has a mean validity of .49, and the validity of the test is quite generalizable. The *SD* of the true validities is .03 (rounded), and 80% of all true validities are estimated to fall between .45 and .52. Even the lower bound of .45 represents considerable validity. Almost all the variance (98%) in the observed validities is explained by artifacts, with about three fourths of this variation being due to sampling error. The square root of .98 is .99; so the correlation between the observed correlations and the sum of the sampling and measurement errors is .99.

The mean value of .49 is close to the correct value of .50, and the SD_ρ estimate of .03 is not much different from the correct value of 0. The deviation of our SD_ρ estimate from the correct value of 0 reflects the fact that the meta-analysis methods are necessarily approximations. (Computer simulation studies on this and related methods have consistently shown a tendency to slightly overestimate SD_ρ; see Law et al., 1994b. Hence, these methods can be said to be "conservative.")

The data in Table 4.4 are "matched data." That is, all artifact information is available for every correlation. Therefore, we can meta-analyze these data using the methods described in Chapter 3. That is, we can correct each correlation individually and then do the meta-analysis on the corrected correlations. We can do this by applying the VG6-D (for direct range restriction) program (discussed in Chapter 3 and described in the Appendix) to the data in Table 4.4. In doing this, we enter 1.00s for the reliability of the predictor because we are not correcting for measurement error in the predictor. The program output states that $\bar{\rho}_{xy_t} = .50$ and $SD_\rho = 0$. The estimate of the mean true validity value is correct to two decimal places. The estimated SD_ρ of 0 is the exactly correct value and is more accurate than the .03 value obtained in our worked example based on the interactive method for artifact distribution meta-analysis. This is as would be expected because correction of each correlation individually is a more exact method.

Suppose the type of range restriction affecting the data in Table 4.4 was actually indirect range restriction—and we had falsely assumed it was direct range restriction. In that case, the mean true validity estimates given previously would be underestimates. How large would this underestimation be? We can answer this question by running the data in Table 4.4 through the program INTNL-I (for indirect range restriction). We enter u_X values, which the program converts internally to u_T values, using Equation (3.16). As noted earlier, the unrestricted reliability for the single test used in these studies is $r_{XX_a} = .80$ We enter this value into INTNL-I. Note that in this program, one cannot enter 1.00s for r_{XX_a} values when one does not want to correct for predictor unreliability—because this "convenient fiction" will cause u_X values to be the same as u_T values, because r_{XX_a} values are used in the formula that converts u_X to u_T, Equation (3.16). This problem does not occur when range restriction is direct (i.e., when applying INTNL-D). Running the program, we obtain the following results:

$$\bar{\rho}_{xy_t} = .67$$
$$SD_{\rho_{xy_t}} = 0$$

SD_ρ is 0, the correct value. However, $\bar{\rho}_{xy_t}$, the estimate of mean true validity, is now .67 (vs. the earlier .50 or .49), which is 34% larger. Looked at another way, use of corrections for direct range restriction when the range restriction is actually indirect leads to a 25% underestimate of mean true validity. Hence, it is critical to accuracy of estimates of mean actual correlations to specify and apply the correct type of range restriction correction (Schmidt, Oh, & Le, 2006).

PERSONNEL SELECTION WITH VARYING TESTS

The test used for prediction is usually only specified in terms of the construct to be measured, for example, arithmetic reasoning. There are many arithmetic reasoning tests available that are (nearly) equivalent in general content but different in reliability. This variation in reliability contributes to the variation in correlations across studies if the review covers all studies using a given type of test rather than a fixed test.

There have been two responses to this in the personnel selection literature. In our earliest work, we ignored the variation in the reliability of the predictor (as did Callender & Osburn, 1980). Later, we used a hybrid solution. We corrected the variance across studies for all artifacts, but we corrected the mean correlation only for restriction in range and for error of measurement in job performance. That is, we did not correct the mean for the attenuating effect of error of measurement in the predictor variable. This gives the mean and standard deviation for a distribution of operational validities in which the reliability of the predictor is always fixed at the average value for the study population. If the results are applied in a context in which the actual test used has reliability equal to the average reliability, then our results can be used as such. However, if the results are to be used in a context in which the reliability is different from the average, then the user should modify our reported results. The mean validity and the standard deviation must first be corrected for attenuation using the square root of the mean test reliability. Then the resulting true score validity and true score standard deviation must be attenuated using the square root of the reliability of the actual test to be used (Schmidt et al., 1980).

For example, suppose the validity generalization (VG) results were $\bar{\rho}_{xy_t} = .50$ and $SD_{\rho_{xy_t}} = .10$, and suppose the mean unrestricted reliability in the meta-analysis was $r_{xx_a} = .80$. Now suppose you want to use these results but your test has an $r_{xx_a} = .90$.

First, you correct the VG results to obtain the true score correlation results:

$$\bar{\rho} = \frac{.50}{\bar{a}} = \frac{.50}{\sqrt{.80}} = .56$$

$$SD_\rho = \frac{.10}{\bar{a}} = \frac{.10}{\sqrt{.80}} = .11$$

Next, you attenuate the true scores results so they correspond to a test reliability of $r_{xx_a} = .90$:

$$\bar{\rho}_{xy_t} = .56\sqrt{.90} = .53$$

$$SD_{\rho_{xy_t}} = .11\sqrt{.90} = .10$$

These are the values tailored to your test with a reliability of .90. With a test reliability of .90, mean operational validity is .53 and its standard deviation is .10. Hence, it can be seen that using a more reliable test increases the mean operational validity from .50 to .53, a 6% increase.

There is a more straightforward procedure. Simply compute and report the fully corrected mean and standard deviation in the first place (including correction for error of measurement in the independent variable and including any other artifacts that information is available for). (The procedures presented in this chapter do this as a matter of course.) Then report two means and two standard deviations: (1) the fully corrected mean and standard deviation and (2) a mean and standard deviation attenuated to the level of the mean reliability of the predictor variable. Then if the user's mean predictor reliability is the same as the mean predictor reliability in the meta-analysis, result (2) can be used as is. If the user's predictor reliability is different, however, the user must attenuate the true score results to correspond with the reliability of his or her predictor. For example, suppose the true score results were as above: $\bar{\rho} = .56$, $SD_\rho = .11$, and mean r_{XX_a} is .80. Now suppose the reliability of the user's test is .60. Then, when that test is used, the mean operational validity and its SD are as follows:

$$\bar{\rho}_{xy_t} = .56\sqrt{.60} = .43$$

$$SD_{\rho_{xy_t}} = .11\sqrt{.60} = .09$$

As can be seen, the lower predictor reliability substantially reduces the operational validity (from .50 to .43, a 14% reduction).

PERSONNEL SELECTION: META-ANALYTIC FINDINGS IN THE LITERATURE

As noted in Chapter 1 and in DeGeest and Schmidt (2011), in recent years the meta-analysis methods presented in this book have been applied mostly to organizational research literatures other than personnel selection. But one important early application of artifact distribution meta-analysis was the examination of the validity of tests and other methods used in personnel selection. Meta-analysis has been used to test the hypothesis of situation-specific validity. In personnel selection, it had long been believed that validity was specific to situations; that is, it was believed that the validity of the same test for what appeared to be the same job varied from employer to employer, region to region, across periods, and so forth. In fact, it was believed that the same test could have high validity (i.e., a high correlation with job performance) in one location or organization and be completely invalid (i.e., have zero validity) in another. This belief was based on the observation that observed validity coefficients for similar tests and jobs (and even for the same test and job over time) varied substantially across different studies. In some studies, there was a statistically significant relationship, and in others, there was no significant relationship—which was falsely taken to indicate there was no relationship at all. This puzzling variability of findings was explained by postulating that jobs that appeared to be the same actually differed in important ways in what was required to perform them. This belief led to a requirement for local or situational validity studies. It was held that validity had to be estimated separately for each situation by a study conducted in that setting; that is, validity findings could not be generalized across settings, situations, employers, and the like (Schmidt & Hunter, 1981). In the late 1970s, meta-analysis of validity coefficients began to be conducted to test whether validity might not, in fact, be generalizable (Schmidt & Hunter, 1977; Schmidt, Hunter, Pearlman, & Shane, 1979), and, thus, these meta-analyses were called "validity generalization" studies. These studies indicated that all or most of the study-to-study variability in observed validities was due to artifacts of the kind discussed in this book and that the traditional belief in situational specificity of validity was therefore erroneous. Validity findings did generalize.

Early applications of validity generalization (VG) methods were mostly limited to ability and aptitude tests (e.g., Pearlman et al., 1980; Schmidt, Hunter, Pearlman, et al., 1979), but applications to a wide variety of different selection procedures soon followed: work sample tests (Hunter & Hunter, 1984), behavioral consistency and traditional evaluations of education and experience (McDaniel, Schmidt, & Hunter, 1988b), assessment centers (Gaugler, Rosenthal, Thornton, & Bentson, 1987), integrity tests (Ones, Viswesvaran, & Schmidt, 1993), employment interviews (McDaniel, Whetzel, Schmidt, & Maurer, 1994), job knowledge tests (Dye, Reck, & Murphy, 1993), biographical data measures (Carlson et al., 1999; Rothstein et al., 1990), personality scales (Mount & Barrick, 1995), college grade point average (Roth, BeVier, Switzer, & Shippmann, 1996), and others (Schmidt & Hunter, 1998). In general, validities for these procedures also proved to be generalizable, although interpretation of generalizability was sometimes more complex (see, e.g., Schmidt & Rothstein, 1994). The findings from most of this research are summarized in Schmidt and Hunter (1998).

Selection programs based on validity generalization were introduced by many organizations during the 1980s and 1990s. Examples include the petroleum industry (through the American Petroleum Institute), the electric utility industry (through the Edison Electric Institute), the life insurance industry (through the Association of Insurance Companies), AT&T, Sears, the Gallup Organization, the state of Iowa, ePredix, the Pentagon, and the U.S. Office of Personnel Management (OPM). During this period, VG methods were also used in developing and supporting commercial employment tests (e.g., Psychological Services Incorporated [PSI] and the Wonderlic Company included VG results in their test manuals).

VG methods and findings also resulted in changes in professional standards. The 1985 edition of the AERA-APA-NCME *Standards for Educational and Psychological Testing* recognized validity generalization and the importance of meta-analysis (p. 12). In the most recent edition of this document (the fifth edition; AERA-APA-NCME, 1999), validity generalization plays an even larger role (see pp. 15–16 and Standards 1.20 and 1.21). The 1987 edition of the *Principles for the Validation and Use of Personnel Selection Procedures*, published by the Society for Industrial/Organizational Psychology (SIOP), devoted nearly three pages to validity generalization (pp. 26–28). The current SIOP *Principles* (2003) incorporated newer research and further developments in validity generalization. A report by the National Academy of Sciences (Hartigan & Wigdor, 1989) devoted an entire chapter (Chapter 6) to validity generalization and endorsed its methods and assumptions.

Although, to our knowledge, no up-to-date definitive review is available, validity generalization seems to have fared well in the courts. Sharf (1987) reviewed cases up through the mid-1980s. The most recent case we are aware of is *United States v. City of Torrance*. In that 1996 decision, all basic VG findings were accepted by the court, and the court's rejection of the Department of Justice challenge to the Torrance police and fire tests appears to be based mostly on the court's acceptance of VG and related findings. In addition to U.S. court cases, the use of validity generalization as the basis for selection systems was upheld in Canada in 1987 (*Maloley v. Canadian Civil Service Commission*). A comprehensive review of court decisions related to validity generalization would probably be useful at this point.

The procedures used in most published validity generalization studies were developed for the case of direct range restriction. At the time these procedures were developed, there was no known procedure for correcting for indirect range restriction resulting from selection on a composite of unknown (unrecorded) variables, the type of range restriction that is nearly universal in personnel and educational selection (Linn et al., 1981a; Thorndike, 1949). As a result, published estimates of mean operational validities are underestimates to some extent, and published estimates of SD_ρ are overestimates to some extent (see Hunter et al., 2006; Le & Schmidt, 2006). Hence, published results present a downwardly biased picture of validity and validity generalizability. This fact was demonstrated quantitatively in Schmidt et al. (2006) and Schmidt, Shaffer, and Oh (2008). Of the VG procedures used in the literature, only one—the interactive procedure—can be used in the case of indirect range restriction. This is the INTNL-I program used in this chapter.

A WORKED EXAMPLE: INDIRECT RANGE RESTRICTION

We now present an example illustrating the application of the interactive procedure to data with indirect range restriction. The data are shown in Table 4.5. These are the same data presented in Table 3.5. In Chapter 3, we meta-analyzed these data by correcting each correlation individually. Here, we will analyze the same data, treating the artifact information as distributions—that is, as not being matched to specific observed rs. Because complete artifact information is given in Table 4.5 for each observed correlation, the artifact distribution method ordinarily would not be used; instead, each correlation would be corrected individually, as was done in Chapter 3. However, we present the artifact distribution analysis of these data here because the results can be directly compared to those obtained in Chapter 3 with the same data.

Observed values of u are always u_X values. These are shown in the first data column in Table 4.5. In correcting for indirect range restriction, we must convert u_X values to u_T values, using Equation (3.16). The computer program INTNL-I makes this conversion automatically if you enter u_X values. To make this conversion, the program must have an estimate of

Table 4.5 Indirect range restriction: Hypothetical data for an artifact distribution meta-analysis of 12 personnel selection studies.

Study	s_X/S_X (u_X)	s_T/S_T (u_T)	Test Reliability (r_{XX_i})	Criterion Reliability (r_{YY_i})	Sample Size	Observed Correlation
1	.580	.468	.55	.80	68	.35**
2	.580	.468	.55	.60	68	.07
3	.580	.468	.55	.80	68	.11
4	.580	.468	.55	.60	68	.31*
5	.678	.603	.67	.80	68	.18
6	.678	.603	.67	.60	68	.36**
7	.678	.603	.67	.80	68	.40**
8	.678	.603	.67	.60	68	.13
9	.869	.844	.80	.80	68	.49**
10	.869	.844	.80	.60	68	.23**
11	.869	.844	.80	.80	68	.29*
12	.869	.844	.80	.60	68	.44*

*$p < .05$ (two-tailed test). **$p < .01$ (two-tailed test).

r_{XX_a}, the reliability of the independent variable (predictor) in the unrestricted population. Again, the computer program INTNL-I computes r_{XX_a} automatically from the r_{XX_i} and u_X values entered. In this data set, the same test was used in all studies, and its r_{XX_a} is .85. The calculated u_T values are shown in the second data column in Table 4.5. For the reasons detailed in Hunter et al. (2006), when correcting for indirect range restriction, we must correct observed rs for measurement error *in both variables* before applying the range correction formula. That means, of course, that one must have available the restricted group reliabilities for both variables. The criterion reliabilities shown in Table 4.5 are for the restricted group, as is usually the case in primary studies. The single test used in all 12 studies has an unrestricted group reliability of $r_{XX_a} = .85$. However, range restriction reduces this value in the incumbent groups in the individual studies (Sackett, Laczo, & Arvey, 2002). The restricted group r_{XX_i} values have been computed using the formula for this given in Chapter 3 (Equation [3.17c]) and have been entered into Table 4.5 in the column headed r_{XX_i}.

The formula used is

$$r_{XX_i} = 1 - U_X^2(1 - r_{XX_a})$$

where $U_X^2 = s_{X_a}^2 / s_{X_i}^2$. Note that $s_{X_a}^2$ = the variance of X in the unrestricted group and $s_{X_i}^2$ = the variance of X in the restricted group.

Entering these data into the INTNL-I computer program yields the following results:

$$\bar{r} = .28$$

$$S_r^2 = .017033$$

$$S_e^2 = .012677$$

$$S_{\rho_{xy}}^2 = S_r^2 - S_e^2 = .004356$$

Percentage variance accounted for by sampling error = 74.4%

Percentage variance accounted for by all artifacts = 99.3%

The estimated mean true score correlation is

$$\bar{\rho} = .581$$
$$SD_\rho = .0182$$

The estimate of mean true validity is

$$\bar{\rho}_{xy_t} = .531$$

$$SD_{\rho_{xy_t}} = .0168$$

In Chapter 3, we meta-analyzed this same data set (Table 3.5), correcting each correlation individually. We can compare the present results to those obtained in Chapter 3 using the program VG6-I. In Chapter 3, the estimated mean true score ρ was .57 versus .58 here for artifact distribution meta-analysis. In Chapter 3, the estimate for mean true validity was .530 versus .531 here. In Chapter 3, both SD_ρ and $SD_{\rho_{xy_t}}$ were estimated at 0 (the correct value). Here, $SD_\rho = .0182$ and $SD_{\rho_{xy_t}} = .0168$. These values are close to the correct value of 0 but are slight overestimates. Our estimate here of the total percentage of variance accounted for by artifacts is 99.3% versus the correct value of 100% obtained in Chapter 3. These comparisons show that the INTNL-I artifact distribution meta-analysis program is quite accurate, although not quite as accurate as correcting each coefficient individually. However, the information necessary to correct each correlation individually is often not available, and so artifact distribution meta-analysis must be used. As can be seen here, the resulting level of accuracy is very high in comparison with that of most social science procedures.

In this example, the corrections for indirect range restriction were made using the Hunter et al. (2006) procedure (which is programmed into the INTNL-I program). This method of correction for indirect range restriction is based on the assumption that any range restriction that exists on the dependent variable (y) is fully mediated (i.e., caused by) range restriction on the independent variable (x). This means that range restriction on the third variable (called s) is not a direct cause of range restriction on y; the third variable directly causes range restriction only on x. As noted by Hunter et al. (2006), in most contexts this assumption is likely to hold (or hold to a close enough approximation). But in cases in which this assumption is substantially violated, the Hunter et al. (2006) correction is less accurate (Le & Schmidt, 2006). A method of correcting for indirect range restriction in meta-analysis has recently been developed, based on earlier work by Bryant and Gokhale (1972), that does not require this assumption (Le et al., 2013). However, that method requires the user to know the range restriction ratio (u) for the dependent variable (y), which is not required by the Hunter et al. method. In personnel selection, the y measure is job performance and its SD in the applicant population (i.e., its unrestricted SD) is virtually impossible to estimate. So this method of correction cannot be used in studies in which the dependent variable is job performance or other behaviors on the job. More generally, it cannot be used with dependent variable measures for which data do not exist on a broader population that allows computation of an unrestricted *SD*. This includes many types of behavioral measures used in psychological research. But in studies focused on the relation between psychological or organizational constructs (e.g., between job satisfaction and organizational commitment), it may be possible to estimate the needed *u* ratio for the dependent variable based on some broader population *SD* (e.g., from national norms or workforce norms). In such cases, the Le et al. (2013) method can be used, and examples of such applications are presented in Le et al. (2013). If the fundamental assumption underlying the Hunter et al. (2006) method is known to be seriously violated in a particular data set, the Le et al. method will produce more accurate results than will the Hunter et al. method. However, in the example meta-analyses in this book that correct for indirect range restriction, we apply the Hunter et al. method, because this method is applicable in more situations and because it is rare for its fundamental assumption to be seriously violated.

REFINEMENTS TO INCREASE ACCURACY OF THE SD_ρ ESTIMATE

All quantitative estimates are approximations. Even if these estimates are quite accurate, it is always desirable to make them more accurate if possible. The most complex task performed by meta-analysis methods is the estimation of the *SD* of the population correlations (SD_ρ). One way to make this estimate more accurate is to find a more accurate estimate of the sampling error variance of the correlation coefficient in meta-analysis. Hunter and Schmidt (1994) showed analytically that using mean r ($\bar{r}$) in place of r in the sampling error variance formula for the correlation coefficient increases the accuracy of this estimate in the homogeneous case (i.e., the case in which $SD_\rho = 0$). Because of the complexity of the math, no such analytic demonstration was possible for the heterogeneous case (i.e., the case in which $SD_\rho > 0$). We therefore tested the heterogeneous case using computer simulation and found that there, too, use of mean r improved accuracy over the traditional sampling error variance formula (Law et al., 1994b). Aguinis (2001), again using computer simulation, provided an even more complete and thorough demonstration of this fact. This finding that the traditional formula underestimates the amount of sampling error variance and that its accuracy can be improved by using $\bar{r}$ in the formula instead of the observed r from the individual study at hand is important, because the traditional formula has been accepted throughout statistics since around 1900. However, in studies with range restriction, even the more accurate formula still underestimates (and undercorrects for) sampling error variance. Millsap (1989) showed that the presence of direct range restriction increases sampling error variance and therefore causes the formula to underestimate the amount of sampling variance.

Aguinis and Whitehead (1997) showed the same thing for indirect range restriction. Hence, final corrected SD_ρ estimates are still overestimated in validity generalization studies (and other meta-analyses with range restriction), and validity generalizability is correspondingly underestimated. (However, in non-VG meta-analyses, there may be no range restriction, and, if so, this problem does not occur.)

The preceding improvement increases the accuracy of the estimate of the residual SD (SD_{res}) —the SD of observed rs after variation due to artifacts has been subtracted out. Another opportunity to improve accuracy occurs at the step in which the residual SD is corrected to estimate the SD of operational (true) validities ($SD_{\rho_{xyt}}$). This opportunity occurs with respect to the correction for range restriction. One can think of the range restriction correction as multiplying the observed correlation by a constant. For example, if the correction increases the r by 30%, then the constant of correction is 1.30. In our earlier methods, if the constant of correction for range restriction for *the mean r* was, say, 1.30, we applied that same constant to all the values in the residual distribution. That is, we assumed (as an approximation) that the range restriction correction would increase all values of r by 30%. Actually, the range restriction correction (unlike the measurement error correction) is nonlinear: It increases small r values by *more* than 30% (in this example) and large values by *less* than 30% (in this example). Hence, applying the constant of range restriction correction of the mean r to all rs resulted in overestimation of SD_ρ. We therefore added a refinement that computed the range restriction correction independently for each separate r value in the residual distribution, and we tested this refinement using computer simulation methods. This study (Law et al., 1994a) showed that doing this increased the accuracy of estimates of SD_ρ. Both these accuracy-increasing refinements were then added to the interactive meta-analysis program and that program was then used to reanalyze the extensive database from Pearlman et al. (1980). This research (Schmidt et al., 1993) showed that validity was more generalizable than Pearlman et al. (1980) had concluded. Specifically, the true validity SDs were substantially smaller, 90% credibility values (the lower end of the 80% credibility interval) were considerably larger, and the percentage of variance accounted for by artifacts was substantially larger. These developments show that the accuracy of even well-established methods—methods that are very accurate by the standards of psychological research—can nevertheless be improved. The findings also further undercut the theory of situational specificity of validity. In fact, the average amount of variance accounted for was so large (87%) and the average SD_ρ value was so small (.097) that Schmidt et al. (1993) interpreted their findings as fully disconfirming the situational specificity hypothesis (actually, the hypothesis that $SD_\rho > 0$) for aptitude and ability tests. They reasoned that the tiny amount of remaining variance (.0094, on average) could be explained by the six sources of arti-factual variance that could not be corrected for (see pp. 8–11 of that article; see also Chapter 5). (Note: Because the focus in this study was on SD_ρ and because of space limitations, mean true validity estimates were not reported in this study; however, they can be found in Hunter and Schmidt, 1996.)

It is important to note here that a conclusion that all observed variance is explained by artifacts is not required for validity generalization. Even if $SD_\rho > 0$, validity still generalizes so long as the 90% credibility value in the resulting true validity distribution is greater than 0. However, the fact that in a large validity database (more than 600 studies), created over a span of six decades by a wide variety of researchers, essentially all validity variance can be accounted for by statistical and measurement artifacts is a striking scientific finding. It illustrates the extent to which nature can indeed be parsimonious at its fundamental (deep structure) level despite surface appearances of great variability and complexity.

Accuracy of Corrections for Artifacts

In some validity generalization studies (e.g., Hirsh, Northrop, & Schmidt, 1986; Schmidt, Hunter, & Caplan, 1981a, 1981b), the artifact values used in the artifact distributions were taken directly from the studies that con-tributed validities to the meta-analysis; that is, the procedure described earlier in this chapter was used. In other studies, however, the information on artifacts from the studies analyzed was too sparse. In those studies, artifact distributions were used that were estimated based on familiarity with the personnel selection literature in general. For example, a distribu-tion of u_X values ($u_X = s_X/S_X$) was constructed that was believed to be typ-ical of this research literature as a whole. Later, when it was possible to compare some of these artifact distributions to empirically cumulated distributions from bodies of research studies, the constructed artifact dis-tributions were found to fairly closely match the empirical distributions (Schmidt, Hunter, et al., 1985, Q&A No. 26; Alexander, Carson, Alliger, & Cronshaw, 1989).

The results produced by VG methods would exaggerate the magnitude and generalizability of validity if the artifact distributions used, and the corrections made using them, overcorrect for the effects of artifacts. Com-puter simulation studies do not (and cannot) determine whether the arti-fact distributions are realistic or not; instead, such studies use these artifact distributions along with initial true validity values to generate simulated observed validities and then determine whether the procedures can accu-rately recapture the initial true validity distributions. So the question can be raised: Are the artifact distributions that have typically been used likely to overcorrect for the effects of artifacts?

This question has usually been focused on criterion reliabilities and u_X values. To our knowledge, no one has questioned the artifact distribution values used for the reliability of predictors—because in VG, no correction is made to mean validity for unreliability in the predictors.

Overcorrection could occur in two different ways. First, the mean validity could be overcorrected. That is, if one's estimate of criterion (dependent variable) reliability were too low, or one's estimate of the mean level of range restriction were too severe, then the corrected mean validity estimate (mean true validity estimate) would be too large. Second, even if mean artifact values and corrections were correct, if one's artifact distributions were too variable, then the amount of variance in observed validities attributed to differences between studies in criterion reliability and range restriction would be too great. It appears clear that this second form of overcorrection cannot be a source of serious distortion in results. Hunter and Schmidt (1990b, pp. 224–226) summarized the research showing that even if the artifact distributions are too variable, the effect on the VG final results is negligible. This finding stems from the fact that between-study differences in artifact levels account for very little variance; most between-study variance in validities results from sampling error variance. In addition, empirical studies of range restriction values and criterion reliabilities have found levels of variability similar to those used in VG studies (Alexander et al., 1989; Viswesvaran et al., 1996).

This leaves the question of whether there is overcorrection of mean validity for criterion reliability and range restriction. Criteria include both measures of job performance and measures of training performance. Training performance measures are usually quite reliable, and, to our knowledge, no one has questioned the high reliabilities (and corresponding small corrections) we have estimated for training performance measures. The criterion measure of job performance used in most validity studies is supervisory ratings of job performance. Almost invariably, only one supervisor produces these ratings; it is very rare that the ratings used are the average ratings from two or more supervisors. Also, it is almost always the case that some of the employees in the sample are rated by one rater, others by another rater, and still others by a third rater, and so on, introducing differences in rater leniency effects into the variance of ratings. That is, almost never are all subjects in the study rated by the same rater. Starting with our first VG study, whenever rating reliabilities were not available from the studies in the VG analysis, we have estimated the mean interrater reliability of ratings of this sort at .60. This value was based on our reading of the literature. However, later large-sample and meta-analytic research studies of ratings found smaller mean reliabilities—values at or near .50 (Rothstein, 1990; Viswesvaran et al., 1996). Hence, it is very unlikely that there has been overcorrection for criterion unreliability. In fact, it is likely that there has been undercorrection. (Use of the .60 figure when the correct figure is .50 results in a 9% undercorrection.)

In passing, we note that Murphy and DeShon (2000) argued that interrater reliability is inappropriate for ratings of job performance and stated that intrarater reliability should be used instead. This position entails the rejection of the classical measurement model in industrial-organizational (I/O) research. Schmidt et al. (2000) presented the reasons this position is mistaken. These two articles provide a thorough exploration of the issues involved in this question. This issue is explored further in Viswesvaran et al. (2005).

The final question is whether there is overcorrection for range restriction. There are two ways in which the mean correction for range restriction could be erroneous. First, the mean u_X value used could be too small, leading to an overcorrection for range restriction. When empirical estimates of u_X values were not available, we have typically estimated the mean u_X value at .60 to .70, with these values being based on our reading of the literature. However, as the data became available, we compared these values to quantitative averages from real studies. In the large VG study that Hunter conducted for the U.S. Department of Labor on more than 400 General Aptitude Test Battery (GATB) test validity studies, the average u_X value was .67 (Hunter, 1983b; Hunter & Hunter, 1984). A later empirical study by Alexander et al. (1989) that included available published and unpublished data found an average u_X value of .70. Hence, the empirical evidence indicates that the mean u_X values we have used are close to the appropriate values. These u_X values are for cognitive ability and aptitude measures. Average values of u_X are larger for personality measures, averaging somewhere between .85 and .90 (Barrick & Mount, 1991; Ones & Viswesvaran, 2003). These findings show that organizations do not select or terminate employees based on personality as severely as they do based on mental ability. This is consistent with the fact that personality does not predict job performance as well as mental ability (cf. Schmidt et al., 2008).

The second way in which range restriction corrections can be erroneous is that the range correction formula used can over- or undercorrect. The correction equation we have used until about 2006 has been Thorndike's (1949) Case II formula. This is also the formula used in the models of Callender and Osburn (1980) and Raju and Burke (1983). This formula assumes direct range restriction (truncation) on the predictor. That is, it assumes that all applicants below a certain score on the predictor are rejected for hire and all others are hired. It has long been known that if range restriction is indirect rather than direct, this formula will undercorrect (see, e.g., Linn et al., 1981a), and we have repeatedly pointed out this undercorrection (Schmidt, Hunter, & Pearlman, 1981; Schmidt, Hunter, et al., 1985, p. 751; Schmidt et al., 1993, p. 7). It is clear that if some or all of the primary validity studies in a VG study are characterized by indirect range restriction, the use of this range correction formula will lead to undercorrection, even if one's u_X values are accurate.

This is important because range restriction is indirect in almost all studies (Thorndike, 1949, p. 175). For example, in the General Aptitude Test Battery (GATB) database of the U.S. Department of Labor, *all* of the 515 validity studies were concurrent (i.e., conducted on present employees) and hence range restriction was always indirect. Range restriction is often indirect even in predictive studies: The tests to be validated are often given to *incumbents*, with the criterion measures being taken months or years later, making the study technically predictive. In our research over the years, we have rarely seen a study in which there had been direct selection on the predictor(s) being validated—the only kind of study for which the Case II range correction formula would not undercorrect.

If the Case II range correction formula used in the past in all VG models (ours, Callender and Osburn's, and Raju and Burke's) undercorrects, then why has this undercorrection not shown up in computer simulation studies? As noted most recently by Hall and Brannick (2002), computer simulation studies have shown that these VG methods are quite accurate. In fact, estimates of $\bar{\rho}$ seem to be particularly accurate. The answer is that all computer simulation studies have assumed (and programmed in) only direct range restriction. With the exception of Le and Schmidt (2006), there have to date been no computer simulation studies of VG methods based on indirect range restriction. Hence, the earlier simulation studies, by definition, cannot detect the undercorrection that occurs when range restriction is indirect.

How large is this underestimation of mean true validity? All VG models have, in effect, implicitly assumed that it is relatively small. Linn et al. (1981a) attempted to calibrate empirically the size of the undercorrection in the case of the Law School Admissions Test (LSAT) and concluded that it is probably substantial. Because they were unable to develop an analytical solution, however, their estimates were only suggestive. However, an analytical solution has been developed for the most common case of indirect range restriction: the one in which incumbents have been selected on unknown and unmeasured variables (or on a composite of such variables; Hunter et al., 2006; Mendoza & Mumford, 1987). An example would be a validity study in which there is no formal record of how incumbents were selected but in which $u_x < 1.00$, indicating the presence of range restriction; this example is, in fact, the usual case. Unlike the formula we derived (also derived by Mendoza & Mumford, 1987), other equations for correction for indirect range restriction require knowledge of scores on the measure that produced the indirect range restriction; because of this requirement, it is rarely possible to use these equations (e.g., Thorndike's Case III) with real data.

Our findings indicate that the undercorrection of $\bar{\rho}$ for range restriction is substantial (Hunter et al., 2006). For example, application of the new equation to the GATB database (Hunter & Hunter, 1984) indicates that the mean true validity of measures of general mental ability has been underestimated by 25% to 30% (Hunter et al., 2006). Schmidt et al. (2006) and Schmidt et al. (2008) reanalyzed much wider databases and reached the same conclusion. Hence, the implications of the traditional undercorrection are important.

In summary, the evidence indicates that artifact values used for both criterion reliability and range restriction (the u_X values) do not lead to overcorrection of mean true validities. In fact, there has probably been an undercorrection for criterion unreliability when the criterion was job performance. In addition, even when u_X values are accurate, the Case II range restriction correction equation used in almost all published VG studies to date undercorrects validities for range restriction, resulting in substantial underestimates of mean true validities.

Finally, it is important to note again that those who would reject the use of artifact distribution meta-analysis when full artifact data are not available for each study have only the alternative of making no corrections at all for measurement error and range restriction. Their only option for meta-analysis would then be bare-bones meta-analysis (i.e., correcting only for sampling error). It is clear that this option greatly underestimates actual true validity in validity generalization meta-analyses and greatly underestimates mean true score correlations in meta-analyses of other research literatures in the behavioral and social sciences and in other disciplines. This level of downward bias is much greater than any possible overestimation (upward bias) produced by use of imperfectly estimated artifact distributions. This is the important big picture to keep in mind.

Mixed Meta-Analysis: Partial Artifact Information in Individual Studies

Artifacts differ in terms of the information given in studies. The sample size is almost always given so we can correct for sampling error variance. The same is true for dichotomization whenever it occurs. The degree of split for dichotomization is usually given in the research report. For example, a study may state that 70% were in the successful group and 30% were in the unsuccessful group or that 20% quit their jobs and 80% did not. Thus, it is usually possible to correct individual study correlations for the attenuating effects of dichotomization. Reliability is reported more frequently since meta-analysis has become known, but it is uncommon in older studies and frequently not given even in recent studies. Thus, error of measurement must often be corrected using artifact distributions. The problems are even more serious with the other artifacts, such as range variation, construct validity, attrition artifacts, and extraneous factors. Information is often extremely sporadic. Thus, there are research domains where some correctable artifacts can be corrected for in each individual study while others can be corrected only using artifact distributions. This is the case treated in this section.

There are two ways to conduct meta-analysis in such an area. First, the easiest way is to ignore the fact that information on one or more of the artifacts is available for all studies. One would then use only the distributions of the artifacts and compute the meta-analysis using the artifact distribution methods described earlier in this chapter. Averages across studies would be based on simple sample size weights $w_i = N_i$. As we saw earlier in the worked examples in Tables 4.4 and 4.5, this procedure yields approximate results that are quite accurate. However, the computer programs for meta-analysis described in the Appendix do not allow for entry of dichotomization as one of the study artifacts, so this artifact cannot be directly corrected for within those programs.

The second strategy, the optimal strategy, is to do a two-step meta-analysis. In the first step, the individually known artifacts are corrected. In the second step, the sporadically given artifacts are corrected. This method will now be presented, using dichotomization as the example of the artifact on which information is available in all studies. First, the individually known artifacts are used to correct each observed correlation for dichotomization. Next, the sampling error variance for each corrected correlation is computed; this sampling error variance will be larger as a result of the correction for dichotomization. In the next step, this larger sampling error variance, along with the mean observed correlation and the original study N, is used to compute an adjusted N. The adjusted study Ns will be smaller than the original study's Ns, because the adjusted N is the sample size that corresponds to the sampling error variance after correction for dichotomization. Finally, the correlations corrected for dichotomization and the adjusted sample sizes are entered into the interactive program (INTNL) along with the distributions of the other artifacts (the artifacts available only sporadically). That is, the methods of artifact distribution meta-analysis can then be used to correct for the remaining artifacts.

AN EXAMPLE: DICHOTOMIZATION OF BOTH VARIABLES AND A MODERATOR

Tenure is the length of time that an employee stays with an employer. Termination from the firm can be voluntary or involuntary. We focus here on voluntary termination—people who leave the job of their own accord. Many factors determine tenure, but one of the main factors is performance. People with low performance are frequently under pressure from supervisors and/or peers for a variety of problems that they cause others. This pressure often leads to quitting. So we consider a hypothetical meta-analysis of the correlation between performance and tenure.

If working conditions are poor, workers may also quit for that reason, thus reducing the correlation between tenure and performance. Thus, we postulate that the correlation between performance and tenure will be higher in jobs with good working conditions than in jobs with poor working conditions, and we code the studies for working conditions as a potential moderator variable.

Table 4.6a presents the basic information for 24 hypothetical studies. Information is available on all studies for both the independent and the dependent variable as to whether or not the variable was dichotomized. If it was dichotomized, the resulting split is given. On the other hand, reliability information is sporadic for both variables. No information was available on other potential artifacts, such as imperfect construct validity or extraneous factors. In these data, there is no range restriction, so complications caused by the distinction between direct and indirect range restriction do not arise.

Table 4.6b presents the worksheet for the data in Table 4.6a. The corrected correlations are corrected for dichotomization but not for error of measurement. Thus, they are partially corrected correlations. The compound attenuation factor for each correlation is the product of the dichotomization attenuation factors. We explain this process by using Study 1 (first study in jobs with good working conditions). In Table 4.6a, we see that the dichotomization split on performance ratings for this study is 50–50. In Table 4.6b, we see that this split produces an attenuation factor of .80 (Hunter & Schmidt, 1990a). That is, the observed r is reduced to 80% of its original value. The split on tenure for this study is 90–10 (Table 4.6a), and we see in Table 4.6b that this split produces an attenuation factor of .59 (Hunter & Schmidt, 1990a). The compound attenuation factor is the product of these two attenuation factors: $(.80)(.59) = .472$. The observed (uncorrected) correlation for Study 1 is .46. The corrected r is therefore $.46/.472 = .97$. All 24 correlations are corrected in a similar manner and are shown in Table 4.6b.

The next step is to determine the sampling error of each corrected correlation; this sampling error is needed to compute the adjusted study Ns that will be entered into the interactive program. To do this, we must first compute the sampling error variance of the observed rs and then increase this value to reflect the effect of correcting the correlations for dichotomization. As discussed earlier in this chapter, it has been shown that sampling error variance is more accurately

Table 4.6a Hypothetical meta-analysis of performance and turnover.

Study Number	Sample Size	Ratings Split	Tenure Split	Ratings Reliability	Tenure Reliability	Sample Correlation
Jobs with good working conditions						
1	50	50–50	90–10	.47	—	.46*
2	50	50–50	90–10	—	.81	.08
3	50	Not	90–10	.64	—	.46*
4	50	Not	90–10	—	.81	.18
5	50	50–50	50–50	.47	—	.44*
6	50	50–50	50–50	—	.81	.16
7	50	Not	50–50	.64	—	.52*
8	50	Not	50–50	—	.81	.24
9	50	50–50	Not	.47	—	.51*
10	50	50–50	Not	—	.81	.24
11	50	Not	Not	.64	—	.68*
12	50	Not	Not	—	.81	.40*
Jobs with poor working conditions						
13	50	50–50	90–10	.47	—	.23
14	50	50–50	90–10	—	.64	−.05
15	50	Not	90–10	.64	—	.27
16	50	Not	90–10	—	.64	−.01
17	50	50–50	50–50	.47	—	.26
18	50	50–50	50–50	—	.64	−.02
19	50	Not	50–50	.64	—	.32*
20	50	Not	50–50	—	.64	.04
21	50	50–50	Not	.47	—	.29*
22	50	50–50	Not	—	.64	.01
23	50	Not	Not	.64	—	.36*
24	50	Not	Not	—	.64	.08

Note: "Not" = not dichotomized; *$p < .05$

Table 4.6b Worksheet for the data in Table 4.6a.

Study Number	Sample Size	Ratings Split	Tenure Split	Compound Attenuation	Uncorrected Correlation	Corrected Correlation	Error Variance	Adjusted Study N
Jobs with good working conditions								
1	50	.80	.59	.472	.46	.97	.062903	12
2	50	.80	.59	.472	.08	.17	.062903	12
3	50	1.00	.59	.59	.46	.78	.040258	18
4	50	1.00	.59	.59	.18	.31	.040258	18
5	50	.80	.80	.64	.44	.69	.034213	21
6	50	.80	.80	.64	.16	.25	.004213	21
7	50	1.00	.80	.80	.57	.71	.021897	32
8	50	1.00	.80	.80	.29	.36	.021897	32
9	50	.80	1.00	.80	.51	.64	.021897	32
10	50	.80	1.00	.80	.24	.30	.021897	32
11	50	1.00	1.00	1.00	.68	.68	.014014	50
12	50	1.00	1.00	1.00	.40	.40	.014014	50
Ave					.414	.519	.025788	
Jobs with poor working conditions								
13	50	.80	.59	.472	.23	.49	.086546	12
14	50	.80	.59	.472	−.05	−.11	.086546	12
15	50	1.00	.59	.59	.27	.46	.055389	18
16	50	1.00	.59	.59	−.01	−.02	.055389	18
17	50	.80	.80	.64	.26	.41	.047073	21
18	50	.80	.80	.64	−.02	−.03	.047073	21
19	50	1.00	.80	.80	.32	.40	.030127	32
20	50	1.00	.80	.80	.04	.05	.030127	32
21	50	.80	1.00	.80	.29	.36	.030127	32
22	50	.80	1.00	.80	.01	.01	.030127	32
23	50	1.00	1.00	1.00	.36	.36	.019281	50
24	50	1.00	1.00	1.00	.08	.08	.019281	50
Ave					.167	.208	.035481	

estimated if the average observed $\bar{r}$ is used in the formula than if the study-specific r is used. Consider the jobs with good working conditions. There the average observed r is .414. Also, the original sample size is 50 for all studies. Therefore, the sampling error variance of the observed r is the same for each of these 12 studies:

$$S_e^2 = (1 - \bar{r}^2)^2 / (50 - 1) = .014002$$

The sampling error variance for each of these 12 corrected correlations is then this value of .014002 divided by the square of the compound attenuation factor. For example, for Study 1, the sampling error variance of the corrected r (.97) is

$$S_{e_{adj}}^2 = .014002 / (.472)^2 = .062903$$

The next question is, What is the (adjusted) study N that would produce this value for sampling error variance? The adjusted study N is computed using a formula that is derived by starting with the equation above for the sampling error of an observed correlation, then substituting $S_{e_{adj}}^2$ for S_e^2 and finally solving for N. The value of N is the adjusted N. The formula so obtained is

$$N_{adj} = [(1 - \bar{r}^2)^2 / S_{e_{adj}}^2] + 1 \tag{4.3}$$

For example, for Study 1 in Table 4.5b, this adjusted N is 12. (The formula for the adjusted N can produce fractional N values. For example, for Study 1, the computed value was actually 11.9. All values should be rounded to the next whole number.)

We now have all the information needed to complete the meta-analyses using the interactive program. There is one meta-analysis for the 12 studies with good working conditions and another for the 12 with poor working conditions. Table 4.6c presents this information. This table presents the corrected correlations, their effective sample sizes (adjusted Ns), and the two reliability artifact distributions. This is the information to be entered in the interactive program (INTNL in the Appendix). Note that for the first meta-analysis, the tenure reliability distribution can be a single program entry: .81 with a frequency of 6. For the second meta-analysis, this is .64 with a frequency 6. The reliability artifact distribution for the ratings reliability is the same for both meta-analyses: .47 with frequency = 3 and .64 with frequency = 3.

Table 4.6c   Final data for the interactive program.

Study Number	Corrected Correlation	Adjusted N_i	Ratings Reliability	Tenure Reliability
Jobs with good working conditions				
1.	.97	12	.47	—
2.	.17	12	—	.81
3.	.78	18	.64	—
4.	.31	18	—	.81
5.	.69	21	.47	—
6.	.25	21	—	.81
7.	.71	32	.64	—
8.	.36	32	—	.81
9.	.64	32	.47	—
10.	.30	32	—	.81
11.	.68	50	.64	—
12.	.40	50		.81
Jobs with poor working conditions				
13.	.49	12	.47	—
14.	−.11	12	—	.64
15.	.46	18	.64	—
16.	−.02	18	—	.64
17.	.41	21	.47	—
18.	−.03	21	—	.64
19.	.40	32	.64	—
20.	.05	32	—	.64
21.	.36	32	.47	—
22.	.01	32	—	.64
23.	.36	50	.64	—
24.	.08	50	—	.64

RESULTS

For good working conditions:

The mean true score correlation $\bar{\rho}$ = .777.

The *SD* of true score correlations SD_ρ = .212.

The 80% credibility interval = .505 to 1.00.

For poor working conditions:

The mean true score correlation $\bar{\rho}$ = .350.

The *SD* of true score correlations SD_ρ = .074.

The 80% credibility interval = .256 to .445.

THE MODERATOR EVALUATED

For jobs with good working conditions, the mean correlation is .78 (rounded) with a standard deviation of .21. If the distribution of correlations within this condition is normal, then the 80% credibility interval is .50 to 1.00. This credibility interval is quite wide because the *SD* of true scores is quite large. For jobs with poor working conditions, the mean correlation is .35 with a standard deviation of .07. If the distribution of correlations within this condition is normal, then the 80% credibility interval is .27 to .45.

The mean correlations are quite different, .78 versus .35, and the two credibility intervals do not overlap. This finding suggests that working conditions are a moderator variable. The correlation between job performance and employee tenure is very high in organizations with good working conditions. Low-performing employees are forced out and high-performing employees stay because of the good working conditions. This correlation is much smaller in organizations with poor working conditions, because many employees quit even if their job performance is very good and this reduces the correlation. As is indicated by the credibility intervals, the two distributions do not overlap, supporting the conclusion that the moderator is real. There is remaining variation within each set of studies, although we do not know how much of this remaining variance is due to unknown and uncorrected artifacts. This remaining variation is larger when working conditions are good, and an explanation for this fact should be sought.

The use of the two-step process described in this section will be particularly useful whenever dichotomization of measures is present in some or all the studies included in the meta-analysis. This is because the available computer programs for artifact distribution meta-analysis do not offer a correction for dichotomization. Therefore, unless this two-step process is used, it will not be possible to correct for the dichotomization artifact. If there is no dichotomization in any of the studies and if another artifact, say independent variable reliability, is available for all studies while the dependent variable reliability and the range restriction values are available only sporadically, this two-step process can also be used and will improve accuracy.

However, the option of using full artifact distribution meta-analysis would still be available, and this option would provide accurate results, although not as accurate as the two-step process illustrated here. This option is not available if the artifact given for all studies is dichotomization.

Summary of Artifact Distribution Meta-Analysis of Correlations

Ideally, artifact information on every artifact would be available for every correlation in every study. However, publication practice has not yet reached this level of completeness in reporting research. Typically, artifact information is available at three levels. For some artifacts, information is available for all or nearly all studies. This information can be used to correct studies individually. For some artifacts, information is available on a random subset of studies and/or from other sources not contributing correlations to the meta-analysis (such as the general literature or test manuals), providing enough information to estimate the distribution of artifact values across studies. Although individual studies cannot be corrected, the meta-analysis results can be corrected for those artifacts. For some artifacts, no information is available and no correction can be made. When artifact information is available for all studies on at least one artifact but only sporadically available for other artifacts, meta-analysis should be conducted in two stages, corresponding to the artifact information available.

The first stage corrects for those artifacts for which information is available for all or nearly all studies. This step also computes an adjusted sample size for each partially corrected correlation.

In the second stage, these partially corrected correlations, their adjusted sample sizes, and the artifact distributions for the remaining artifacts are entered into the interactive (INTNL) program for artifact distribution meta-analysis. The main product of the resulting meta-analysis is the mean and standard deviation of population correlations corrected for all artifacts—those that were available for all studies and those for which there was only sporadically available artifact information. However, this program also presents a variety of other outputs, as illustrated earlier. To the extent that important artifacts have not been corrected, the estimate of the mean population correlation will be an underestimate and its standard deviation will be an overestimate, causing the results to be biased in the conservative direction. If the artifacts not corrected have only a small impact, and if we are fortunate enough to have little bad data in the research domain, then the mean and the standard deviation will be reasonably accurate estimates of the true correlation distribution. In any case, the estimates will be much more accurate than the bare-bones meta-analysis results. In conducting artifact distribution meta-analysis, we recommend that you use the interactive meta-analysis method (INTNL) described in the Appendix to this book. This procedure is more accurate than other methods and is the only procedure that can be used when range restriction is indirect.

Exercise 4.1: Artifact Distribution Meta-Analysis

The data presented in this exercise are real data from a selection validity study conducted in one of the largest retailing firms in the United States. Save all your calculations and results from this exercise. The results will be used in the exercise at the end of Chapter 9.

I. First, do a bare-bones meta-analysis of these data (correct *only for* sampling error). You can do this either with a calculator or using the INTNL program (i.e., the program labeled "Correlations—Using Artifact Distributions" in the software package described in the Appendix). You will learn more if you use a calculator. For each test, give

   - The average observed validity $(\bar{r})$
   - The observed variance of validities (S_r^2)
   - The variance expected from sampling error (S_e^2)
   - The residual variance (S_{res}^2)
   - The residual standard deviation (SD_{res})
   - The percentage of variance accounted for

II. We can correct the results of the bare-bones meta-analysis to get the final meta-analysis results. We will do this in two ways: First, we will assume that the range restriction is direct—direct selection on test scores (Thorndike's Case II). Second, we will assume that the range restriction is indirect, being based on some unknown (unrecorded) combination of variables (e.g., the employees were hired based on some unrecorded procedure that, for example, might have included an application blank, an interview, etc.).

   - Direct Range Restriction (Case II). Assume that $u_x = s/S = .65$ in every job family for every test. Assume that the reliability of the job performance measure (supervisory ratings) is .50 (restricted sample value) in each job family. (Note: This means you must make the correction for ratings unreliability first, then the range restriction correction.) Because both of these values are constant across all job families, you can estimate mean true validity $(\bar{\rho}_{xy_t})$ and the standard deviation of true validity (SD_ρ) by just correcting $\bar{r}$ and SD_{res}. (That is, after correcting $\bar{r}$ to estimate $\bar{\rho}_{xy_t}$, you can get an *approximate* estimate of SD_ρ as $SD_\rho = \left[\bar{\rho}_{xy_t} / \bar{r}\right] SD_{res}$.) Compute these estimates in this way. Also, compute the 90% credibility value. Enter your results into the table (under "Direct Range Restriction—Hand Calculations").

     You can also use the INTNL-D program with artifact distributions. This is the program labeled "Correlations—Using Artifact Distributions" in the software described in the Appendix; specify that range restriction is direct when asked by the program. Run the INTNL-D program and enter the results into the accompanying table (under "Direct Range Restriction—Program Calculations").

   - Indirect Range Restriction. Here the employees have been selected by some unknown means, not on the test itself. The reliability of the job performance ratings remains the same, at .50. The value of u_X remains the same at .65 for all tests in all job families. Here you must convert u_X to u_T, using Equation (3.16) in Chapter 3. You then use u_T to make the correction for range restriction. In the case of indirect range restriction, you need to know the reliability of the test—which is not needed in the case of direct range restriction. Assume the reliability of each test is .70 in the incumbent (i.e., restricted) group. (From this value, you can compute the reliability in the unrestricted group using Equation [3.17a] or [3.17b].) You need test reliability for two reasons. First, you need it to compute u_T. Second, you need to enter test reliability into the INTNL-I program, if you use the program. This is the program labeled "Correlations—Using Artifact Distribution"; when asked by the program, specify that range restriction is indirect. (For direct range restriction, you just enter 1.00s for test reliability. For indirect range restriction, however, you must enter the .70 values.) The program will ask you whether the .70 values are from the restricted or unrestricted groups. To get your final estimates, you take the true score values of $\bar{\rho}$ and SD_ρ and attenuate them by the square root of the unrestricted test reliability. This gives the two values for the true validity distribution. (The program provides these values.) (Note that this last step would not be necessary in a nonselection meta-analysis.)

After converting u_X to u_T, do this part of the exercise either using the program INTNL-I or by calculator (or both ways, if you wish). If you use the program, follow the instructions given previously. If you use a calculator, you must first correct r for unreliability in both measures, using *restricted* sample values of reliability, then correct for range restriction, and then attenuate by the square root of *unrestricted* test reliability. Follow the same procedure in computing SD_ρ. You will learn more if you use a calculator rather than the computer program.

Enter your results in the appropriate section of the table. For example, if you use INTNL-I, enter your results under "Indirect Range Restriction—Program Calculations."

III. Now interpret your results:

- Bare-Bones Meta-Analysis. How different across the different tests are the figures for $\bar{r}$, SD_{res}, and percentage variance accounted for? How do you interpret these differences?
- In the data corrected for direct range restriction, compare $\bar{\rho}_{xy_t}$ and SD_ρ computed via the simple-approximation method to these values computed via the computer program. How different are these values?
- Why are these values different? How acceptable is the accuracy of the simple approximation?
- Compare the results obtained when correcting for direct versus indirect range restriction. Do you consider these differences in $\bar{\rho}_{xy_t}$ and SD_ρ large or not? Based on the material in this chapter, explain why these differences occur. Suppose the range restriction in these data is indirect. How serious are the consequences of falsely assuming that it is direct?

- Compare the percentage variance accounted for from the bare-bones analysis to that from the program-calculated direct and indirect range restriction corrections. How different are these? Why are they not more different in this particular data set?

Validity coefficients from the Sears study.

Job Family	N	Test of Mental Alertness			Clerical Battery			
		Linguistic	Quantitative	Total	Filing	Checking	Arithmetic	Grammar
1. Office Support Material Handlers	86	.33*	.20	.32*	.30*	.27*	.32*	.25*
2. Data Processing Clerical	80	.43*	.53*	.51*	.30*	.39*	.42*	.47*
3. Clerical-Secretarial (Lower Level)	65	.24*	.03	.20	.20	.22	.13	.26*
4. Clerical-Secretarial (Higher Level)	186	.12*	.18*	.17*	.07*	.21*	.20	.31*
5. Secretarial (Top Level)	146	.19*	.21*	.22*	.16*	.13*	.22*	.09
6. Clerical With Supervisory Duties	30	.24	.14	.23	.24	.24	.31	.17
7. Word Processing	63	.03	.26*	.13	.39*	.33*	.14	.22*
8. Supervisors	185	.28*	.10	.25*	.25*	.11	.19*	.20*
9. Technical, Operative, Professional	95	.24*	.35*	.33*	.30*	.22*	.31*	.42*
Total Group (Pooled Correlations)		.25*	.25*	.29*	.23*	.24*	.27*	.27*

*$p < .05$.

RESULTS TABLE

	MA Results	Tests						
		Linguistic	Quant.	L & Q Total	Filing	Checking	Arithmetic	Grammar
Calculate Either Way — Bare-Bones Meta Analysis	$\bar{r}$							
	S_r^2							
	S_e^2							
	S_{res}^2							
	SD_{res}							
	% Var							
Hand Calculations — Direct Range Res.	$\bar{\rho}$							
	SD_ρ							
	90% CV							
Hand Calculations — Indirect Range Res.	$\bar{\rho}$							
	SD_ρ							
	90% CV							
Program Calculations — Direct Range Res.	$\bar{\rho}$							
	SD_ρ							
	90% CV							
	% Var.							
Program Calculations — Indirect Range Res.	$\bar{\rho}$							
	SD_ρ							
	90% CV							
	% Var.							

Technical Questions in Meta-Analysis of Correlations

5

This chapter discusses technical questions that arise in the meta-analysis of correlations. These include the question of whether r or r^2 should be used in meta-analysis, and the question of whether meta-analysis of regression slopes and intercepts is preferable to meta-analysis of correlations. Then we look at the Fisher's z transformation of r and show why it should not be used in meta-analysis. Next, this chapter discusses the important distinction between fixed and random models for meta-analysis and concludes that random models should always be used, as recommended by the National Research Council (1992). We then look at the literature on the accuracy of different random effects meta-analysis procedures. Then we discuss the distinction between credibility intervals and confidence intervals in meta-analysis and present methods for computing confidence intervals for estimates of $\bar{\rho}$. Next we examine the practice of using meta-analytic correlation matrices to test causal theories. In earlier chapters, we have stated that estimates of SD_ρ must always be considered upper-bound values. This chapter presents and discusses seven technical factors and shows how they contribute to inflation in SD_ρ estimates.

r Versus r^2: Which Should Be Used?

Chapters 3 and 4 focused on the correlation coefficient as the statistic to be cumulated across studies. Some have argued, however, that it is the squared correlation—r^2—that is of interest, not r itself. They argue that r^2 is the proportion of variance in one variable that is accounted for by the other variable, and this is the figure that provides the true description of the size of the relationship. Further, the advocates of r^2 typically hold that relationships found in the behavioral and social sciences are very small. For example, they maintain that $r = .30$ is small because $r^2 = .09$, indicating that only 9% of the variance in the dependent variable is accounted for. Even $r = .50$ is considered small: Only 25% of the variance is explained.

The "percentage of variance accounted for" is statistically correct but substantively erroneous (Ozer, 1985). It leads to severe underestimates of the practical and theoretical significance of relationships between variables. This is because r^2 (and all other indexes of percentage of variance accounted for) are related only in a very nonlinear way to the magnitudes of effect sizes that determine their impact in the real world (Ozer, 1985).

The correlation is the standardized slope of the regression of the dependent variable on the independent variable. If x and y are in standard score form, then $\hat{y} = rx$. Thus, r is the slope of the line relating y to x. As such, it indexes the predictability of y from x. For example, if $r = .50$, then, for each increase of 1 SD in x, there is an increase of .50 SD in y. The statistic r^2 plays no role in the regression equation. The same principle applies in raw score (unstandardized) regression; here the slope again is based on r, not r^2. The slope is $B = r(SD_y/SD_x)$. The raw score regression equation is

$$Y = \left\{ r \frac{SD_y}{SD_x} \right\} X + C$$

where C is the raw score intercept.

The problem with all percentage variance accounted for indexes of effect size is that variables that account for small percentages of the variance often have very important effects on the dependent variable. Variance-based indexes of effect size make these important effects appear much less important than they actually are, misleading both researchers and consumers of research (Ozer, 1985). Consider an example. According to Jensen (1980) and others, the heritability of IQ true scores is about .80. This means that 80% of the (true) variance is due to heredity and only 20% is due to environmental differences, yielding a ratio of "importance" of .80/.20 or 4 to 1. That is, based on percentage of variance accounted for indexes, heredity is four times more important than environment in determining intelligence. However, this picture is very deceptive. (For purposes of this example, we assume heredity and environment are uncorrelated; that is close to true, and in any event the principle illustrated here is not dependent on this assumption.) The functional relationships between these two variables and intelligence are expressed by their respective standard score regressions, not by the figures of .80 and .20. The correlation between IQ and heredity is $\sqrt{.80} = .894$, and the correlation between environment and intelligence is $\sqrt{.20} = .447$. Thus, the functional equation for predicting IQ from each (when all variables are in standard score form) is

$$Y_{IQ} = .894(H) + .447(E)$$

Thus, for each 1 *SD* increase in heredity (*H*), there is a .894 *SD* increase in *IQ*, and for each 1 *SD* increase in environment (*E*), there is a .447 *SD* increase in *IQ*. This is the accurate statement of the power of *H* and *E* to produce changes in *IQ*; that is, it is the true statement of their effects on IQ. The relative size of these effects is .894/.447 = 2. That is, the true impact of heredity on intelligence is only twice as great as that of environment, not four times as great, as implied by the percentage of variance accounted for indexes. The variance-based indexes underestimate the causal impact of environment relative to heredity by a factor of 2. Further, the absolute causal importance of environment is underestimated. The correct interpretation shows that if environment could be improved by 2 *SD*s, the expected increase in IQ (where $SD_{IQ} = 15$) would be .447(2.00) (15) = 13.4. This would correspond to an increase from 86.6 to 100, which would have very important social implications. This correct analysis shows the true potential impact of environment, while the variance-based statement that environment accounts for only 20% of IQ variance leaves the false impression that environment is not of much importance. (Note: The fact that no one seems to know *how* to increase environment by 2 *SD*s is beside the point here.)

This is not an unusual case. For example, the Coleman (1966) report concluded that, when other variables were controlled for, money spent per student by school districts accounted for only a small percentage of the variance of student achievement. The report concluded that financial resources and facilities, such as libraries and labs, were not very important because they provide little "leverage" over student achievement. Later analyses, however, showed that this small percentage of variance corresponded to a standardized regression coefficient for this variable that was much larger and demonstrated that improvements in facilities could yield increases in student achievement that were significant socially and practically (Mosteller & Moynihan, 1972).

Variance-based interpretations have led to the same sort of errors in personnel selection. There it was said that validity coefficients of, for example, .40 were not of much value because only 16% of the variance of job performance was accounted for. A validity coefficient of .40, however, means that, for every 1 *SD* increase in mean score on the selection procedure, we can expect a .40 *SD* increase in job performance—a substantial increase with considerable economic value. In fact, a validity coefficient of .40 has 40% of the practical value to an employer of a validity coefficient of 1.00—perfect validity (Schmidt & Hunter, 1998; Schmidt, Hunter, McKenzie, & Muldrow, 1979).

Variance-based indexes of effect size are virtually always deceptive and misleading and should be avoided, whether in meta-analysis or in primary research. In meta-analysis, such indexes have an additional disadvantage: They obscure the *direction* of the effect. Being nondirectional, they do not discriminate between an r of .50 and an r of −.50; both would enter the meta-analysis as $r^2 = .25$.

To illustrate that r, and not r^2, is the appropriate index of effect size and to show that "small" rs (e.g., .20–.30) indicate substantial relationships, Rosenthal and Rubin (1979b, 1982c) presented the binomial effect size display (BESD). Although this technique requires that both variables be dichotomous (e.g., treatment vs. control or "survived" vs. "died") and requires 50% on each side of each dichotomy, it does forcefully illustrate the practical importance of "small" correlations. For example, a correlation of .32 ($r^2 = .10$) between treatment with a particular drug and patient survival corresponds to a reduction in the death rate from 66% to 34% (Rosenthal, 1984, p. 130). Thus, a relationship that accounts for only 10% of the variance means a reduction in the death rate of almost 50%. Small correlations can indicate large impacts. The BESD uses a special case— that of truly dichotomous variables—to illustrate the same principle we have presented using the more general regression analysis method.

r Versus Regression Slopes and Intercepts in Meta-Analysis

On the surface, it often appears that some hypotheses or theories could be tested as effectively or more effectively by cumulating raw score slopes and intercepts rather than correlations. For example, a theory advanced by Hackman and Oldham (1975) states simply that the relationship between the "motivating potential" of a job and the job satisfaction of incumbents will be stronger for those incumbents with high "growth need strength" (GNS) than for those low in GNS. Because the theory is not explicit, it seems plausible a priori that it could be tested by cumulation of either regression slopes or correlations. Although some hypotheses or theories specify correlation- or regression-based relationships, most are like the Hackman-Oldham theory. Some have advocated that all such theories should be tested using (raw score) regression analyses. What is the relative feasibility and usefulness of meta-analysis based on slopes and intercepts versus correlations? We show next that the disadvantages of using raw score regression slopes and intercepts rather than correlations outweigh the advantages.

RANGE RESTRICTION

Correlations are affected by range restriction and, therefore, need to be corrected to a common *SD* for the independent variable to remove the resulting differences and the overall attenuation. When range restriction on the independent variable is direct, it has no effect on estimates of raw score slopes and intercepts, and therefore, there is no need for range corrections. This appears to be an important advantage, but unfortunately, range restriction is nearly always indirect, and thus, raw score slopes and intercepts *are* distorted by range restriction. As noted in Chapters 3 and 4 and as discussed in detail later in this chapter, direct range restriction is rare; most range restriction is indirect. So there is no advantage for unstandardized regression with respect to the effects of range restriction.

MEASUREMENT ERROR

Correlations are attenuated by unreliability in the measures of both independent and dependent variables, and they have to be corrected for unreliability in both. These corrections were described in Chapter 3. Raw score regression slopes and intercepts are also attenuated by measurement error, but only measurement error in the independent variable. They are not affected by unreliability in the dependent variable, and thus, one need neither know that reliability nor make that correction. The correction for unreliability in the independent variable is (Hunter & Schmidt, 1977)

$$B_T = B / r_{XX}$$

and

$$C_T = \bar{Y} - (B / r_{XX})\bar{X}$$

where B_T is the estimated true score slope, C_T is the estimated true score intercept, and r_{XX} is the reliability of the independent variable. From these equations, it is apparent that measurement error reduces the observed slope and increases the observed intercept; these corrections reverse those effects. Thus, uncorrected slopes and intercepts can be just as deceptive as uncorrected correlations, underestimating true relationships. In addition, the corrections, with their corresponding increase in sampling error, are often about the same in magnitude. Although B is corrected only for measurement error in the independent variable, division is by r_{XX}, not $\sqrt{r_{XX}}$, and thus, the correction is larger. Both range restriction and reliability corrections increase sampling error; for this reason, it would be better if such corrections were unnecessary. However, this statement is far more important for single studies than for meta-analyses; a major strength of meta-analysis is that, unlike single studies, it corrects for the effects of sampling error. Thus, even if fewer or smaller corrections sometimes have to be made to the slope and intercept, meta-analysis cancels out this advantage.

COMPARABILITY OF UNITS ACROSS STUDIES

A major disadvantage of regression slopes and intercepts is that they are usually not comparable across studies and, thus, cannot be meaningfully cumulated in a meta-analysis. The formulas for the bivariate regression slope (B) and intercept (C) are

$$B = r \frac{SD_y}{SD_x}$$

and

$$C = \bar{Y} - B\bar{X}$$

The values for B are comparable across studies only when all studies have used exactly the same scales to measure X and Y. For example, if X is job satisfaction, then every study must have used the same job satisfaction scale, say, the Job Description Index (JDI). If Y is life satisfaction, again the same scales must have been used in all studies. If different scales are used (usually the case in the literature), slopes are not comparable and so cannot be put into the same meta-analysis, even if those scales correlate 1.00 corrected for unreliability. For example, suppose one study uses a shortened form of the same job satisfaction scale used by another study. Even though the two scales measure the same construct, the short form will have a smaller SD, and that scale difference alone will greatly increase the observed slope. In personnel selection, suppose two studies both use rating scales to measure job performance and use the same test (X). If one study uses a rating scale with 20 subscales and the other a scale with only 7, the SD_y in the first study might be twice as large, causing the slope to be twice as large. This problem makes it impossible to meaningfully compare slopes across the two primary studies. In meta-analysis, it is usually impossible to use slopes and intercepts as the statistic to be cumulated for this reason. The correlation coefficient, on the other hand, is in the same units in all studies and can be cumulated across studies; it is scale independent.

This problem of noncomparable scales is unique to the behavioral and social sciences. In the physical sciences, even if different studies use different scales, all studies can be put on a common scale and the slopes and intercepts can then be cumulated. Pounds can be converted to kilograms, inches to centimeters, quarts to liters, and vice versa. These scales are fully translatable to each other because each has a rational zero point; each is some constant times the other. We can define zero weight, but it is difficult to define zero verbal ability; thus, our studies cannot be converted to the same units of measurement. Instead, we must convert all to the same scale-free unit, the correlation (or the d value; see Chapters 6 and 7). This important distinction between the physical and social sciences has been overlooked by those who have criticized the correlation coefficient and advocated the use of slopes instead (e.g., the Society to Abolish the Correlation Coefficient).

It is sometimes maintained that this comparability problem can be solved by simply standardizing the independent and dependent variables within each study, creating equal standard deviations across studies; but in bivariate regression, the resulting standardized regression weights are then equal to the correlation. There is then no point in not starting with r.

COMPARABILITY OF FINDINGS ACROSS META-ANALYSES

If all available studies have been conducted using the same measurement scales (a very rare event), then one can apply meta-analysis to slopes and intercepts. Methods for doing this have been developed in detail by Raju, Fralicx, and Steinhaus (1986) and have been discussed by Callender (1983). For example, virtually all the studies testing the Hackman-Oldham theory have used the same scales—the original scales developed by Hackman and Oldham. Also, where a consortium study is carried out in many organizations, the same scales are usually used in all organizations. The problem, then, is that the results of such a meta-analysis cannot be compared to other meta-analyses. For example, we cannot ask whether the strength of the relationship between job satisfaction and job performance is the same in the consortium study as in other meta-analyses in the literature. These latter meta-analyses will be in correlation units (or, more rarely, in some *different* raw score unit). As we noted in Chapter 1, the development of theories requires that the results of different meta-analyses can be brought together and integrated into a coherent explanation. Thus, noncomparability of meta-analyses is a serious drawback to cumulation of slopes and intercepts. What it means is that, even in those rare cases in which meta-analysis of slopes and intercepts is statistically possible, one must still do a meta-analysis in correlations to have a set of findings that can be linked to the wider developing nomological net (Callender, 1983).

INTRINSIC INTERPRETABILITY

In addition to the problems mentioned previously, slopes and intercepts are very difficult to interpret. It is easy to grasp the meaning of the correlation—it is the standardized regression coefficient of y or x:

$$\hat{y} = rx$$

For every increase of 1 unit (1 *SD*) on x, there is an increase of r *SD*s on y. If $r = .50$, increasing x by 1.00 *SD* increases y by .50 *SD*. Suppose, however, the raw score regression equation is

$$Y = 3.8X + 13.2$$

It is very hard to see whether this is a strong relationship or a weak one. For every 1-unit increase in X, we get a 3.8-unit increase in Y. But is this a large or small increase? Perhaps SD_y is just very large, so that an increase of 3.8 is actually a small increase. After all, the scaling is arbitrary. To make sense of this equation, one must somehow translate it into standard score units—and then one is back to the correlation!

In summary, the disadvantage of conducting meta-analysis using slopes and intercepts rather than correlations is substantial. Ordinarily, meta-analysts will have few occasions to prefer slopes and intercepts over correlations.

Use of Fisher's z in Meta-Analysis of Correlations

In our original work, we carried out calculations with and without use of Fisher's z. For preliminary calculations done by hand, we averaged the correlations themselves, but on the computer, we used what we thought to be the superior Fisher z transformation. For some of our data sets (e.g., Schmidt et al., 1980), we found that the difference was notable. The average validity using the Fisher z transformation was larger (by about .03) than the average validity when correlations were averaged without this transformation. Careful checking of the mathematics then showed that it is the Fisher transformation that is biased. In meta-analysis results, this bias is minimal when the population correlations do not vary or vary little but can be substantial when the population correlations vary to a nontrivial degree (Strube, 1988).

Although the Fisher z transformation produces an upward bias when it is used in averaging correlations, the transformation does serve its original purpose quite well. The original purpose was not to create a method for averaging correlations. Fisher's purpose was to create a transformation of the correlation for which the standard error (and, therefore, confidence intervals) would depend solely on the sample size and not on the size of the observed correlation (which is affected by sampling error). The standard error of the Fisher z statistic is $1/(N-3)^{1/2}$, and so this goal was achieved. This made the Fisher z transformation useful in statistical tests of the null hypothesis that any two observed correlations are not different. If the test is run in correlation form, the estimated standard error is different for the two correlations even when they are based on equal-sized Ns, because the observed rs differ and the observed r is a component in the sampling error formula. Thus, one would be, in effect, assuming the correlations were different in order to test the hypothesis that they were not different. The Fisher z transformation solved this problem. The situation is different in meta-analysis. The major reason advanced in support of the use of Fisher's z in meta-analysis is likewise this "variance stabilization": The sampling error variances depend only on N and do not depend on the sample estimate of r, which is itself affected by sampling error. However, this variance stabilization via Fisher's z provides no advantage in comparison with the methods presented in this book. As noted in Chapters 3 and 4 and later in this chapter, we have demonstrated that use of *mean r* instead to the individual observed r in computing sampling error variance of each correlation leads to more accurate estimates of sampling error. This procedure also produces variance stabilization, because there is very little sampling error in the mean correlation. Hence, there is no need to use Fisher's z to produce variance stabilization.

There has been considerable confusion in the literature produced by the fact that there is a slight negative bias in the correlation coefficient (a bias that is easily corrected, as noted in Chapter 2). This bias is trivial (i.e., is less than rounding error) unless sample size falls below about 25. There is a widespread false belief that the Fisher z corrects this bias. The fact is that the Fisher z replaces a small (usually tiny) underestimation, or negative bias, by an overestimation, or positive bias. This positive bias is always greater in absolute value than the bias in the untransformed correlation. This bias affects the mean Fisher's z value in meta-analysis and results in a biased estimate of the mean correlation when the mean Fisher's z is back transformed to the correlation metric to estimate the mean meta-analytic r. This upward bias is especially large when there is nontrivial variation in the population correlations across studies (Hunter et al., 1996; Schmidt & Hunter, 2003; Strube, 1988), which is almost always the case. In this case, the bias in Fisher's z can cause estimates of the mean correlation to be biased upward by substantial amounts (Bonett, 2008; Field, 2001, 2005; Hall & Brannick, 2002; Schmidt & Hunter, 2003; Schulze, 2004, 2007; Strube, 1988). This appears to be the reason that the random effects meta-analysis methods of Hedges and Olkin (1985) overestimate the mean correlation (Field, 2001, 2005; Hall & Brannick, 2002; Schulze, 2004). (See the section "Accuracy of Different Random Effects Models" later in this chapter.) Schulze (2004) conducted very extensive computer simulation studies that calibrated in detail the upward bias created by use of the Fisher's z transformation, and he recommended that the Fisher's z transformation not be used in meta-analysis. He later repeated this recommendation (Schulze, 2007). It appears that meta-analysis is never made more accurate by using the Fisher z transformation and can be made substantially less accurate under certain conditions.

Hafdahl (2009, 2010) has presented a procedure for transforming correlations to a metric that is somewhat different from the usual Fisher's z metric. This new transformation is an integral transformation to a sort of *z* metric, in comparison with the traditional direct transformation of *r* to Fisher's *z*. He showed analytically as well as via computer simulation that this new transformation eliminates the Fisher's *z* upward bias in estimates of mean correlations in meta-analysis. However, his results showed that estimates produced by this new procedure are no more accurate than estimates produced when untransformed correlations are used in meta-analysis. Law (1995) presented a transformation of Fisher's *z* based on a Taylor series approach that also eliminates the bias problems with the Fisher's *z* transformation. However, like Hafdahl, he found that the use of the untransformed correlation produced results just as accurate as his transformation of Fisher's *z*. Hence, there appears to be no advantage to using either of these procedures.

Fixed and Random Effects Models in Meta-Analysis

Recently, two questions have received considerable attention in the literature on meta-analysis: (1) the relative appropriateness of fixed versus random effects meta-analysis models (Cook et al., 1992, chap. 7; Hedges & Vevea, 1998; Hunter & Schmidt, 2000; Overton, 1998; Schmidt, Oh, & Hayes, 2009) and (2) the relative accuracy of different random effects models (Field, 2001, 2005; Hall & Brannick, 2002). The second question has been examined mostly with the correlation as the effect size, and this is why we address it here in Chapter 5. But both questions are relevant to both *r*s and *d* values. For this reason, we also discuss this question in Chapter 8, where the focus is on *d* values. Comparison of the accuracy of different random effects models used in meta-analyzing correlations involves consideration of the effects of using the Fisher's *z* transformation of the correlations, which is never used with *d* values.

Fixed Versus Random Effects Models. The basic distinction here is that fixed effects models assume a priori that exactly the same ρ (or δ) value underlies all studies in the meta-analysis (i.e., $SD_\rho = 0$), while random effects models allow for the possibility that population parameters (ρ or δ values) vary from study to study. A major purpose of random effects models is to estimate this variance. The random effects model is the more general one: Fixed effects models are a special case of random effects models in which $SD_\rho = 0$. In fact, when a random effects model is applied to data in which $SD_\rho = 0$, it becomes mathematically a fixed effects model. Application of a random effects model can result in an estimated SD_ρ of 0, indicating that a fixed effects model would be appropriate for those data. Application of a random effects model can detect the fact that $SD_\rho = 0$; however, application of a fixed effects model cannot estimate SD_ρ if $SD_\rho > 0$. That is, random effects models allow for any possible value of SD_ρ, while fixed effects models allow for only one value: $SD_\rho = 0$.

All the models presented in this book, in the three predecessor books (Hunter & Schmidt, 1990b, 2004; Hunter et al., 1982), and in related publications are random effects models (Hedges & Olkin, 1985, p. 242; Hunter & Schmidt, 2000; Schmidt & Hunter, 1999a). These models all assume that population parameters may vary across studies and attempt to estimate that variance. The basic model is subtractive: The estimate of population variance is the variance that is left after variance due to sampling error and other artifacts is subtracted out. Some authors—for example, Field (2001, 2005), Hall and Brannick (2002), and Hedges and Vevea (1998)—pointed out that the weights these procedures apply to studies in computing means and variances across studies are somewhat different from those traditionally applied in random effects models. This is true. The rationale for our study weighting approach (weighting by sample size and, where possible, by the product of sample size and the square of artifact attenuation factors) is presented in Chapters 2 and 3. Field (2005), in a large computer simulation study, found that the differences in results for our method and the Hedges and Vevea (1998) method were not affected by the use of different study weights. Weighting by sample size produces more accurate estimates of population SDs (SD_ρ or SD_δ values), the accuracy of which is critical to meta-analysis. This question is addressed empirically in the studies discussed later that examine the accuracy of different random effects models. These studies show that our random effects models are quite accurate—and more accurate than random effects models with more traditional random effects study weights. Similar to the models in this book and in Hunter and Schmidt (1990b, 2004) and related publications, the Callender-Osburn and Raju-Burke models are also random effects models and also weight studies by sample size. All these models have been shown in computer simulation studies to produce accurate estimates of mean correlations. The question of optimal weighting of studies in a meta-analysis is discussed in more detail in Chapter 9.

Hedges and Olkin (1985) and Hedges and Vevea (1998) presented both fixed and random effects models. However, as a practical matter, their random effects models have until recently rarely been used in the literature. For example, all the applications of the Hedges-Olkin methods of meta-analysis appearing in *Psychological Bulletin* through 1999 used their fixed effects models (Hunter & Schmidt, 2000). (But see Shadish, Matt, Navarro, & Phillips, 2000.) None used their random effects models. (All applications of the Rosenthal-Rubin models in that journal have also used fixed effects models.) Until recently, fixed effects models appeared to be the default choice. Larry Hedges observed in 1990 that "fixed effects models have passionate defenders and far more users than random or mixed models" (Wachter & Straf, 1990, p. 23). A few years later, Cooper observed that "in practice, most meta-analysts opt for the fixed effects assumption because it is analytically easier to manage" (Cooper, 1997, p. 179).

Hedges and Olkin (1985) recommended that, when the fixed effects model is proposed for use, the chi-square homogeneity test should be applied. They stated that only if this test is nonsignificant should one conclude that $SD_\rho = 0$ and proceed to apply the fixed effects model. The National Research Council (1992) pointed out that this chi-square test has low power to detect variation in population values and therefore recommended against the use of fixed effects models and in favor of random effects models. Hedges and Pigott (2001) later showed that the power of the chi-square test is too low to allow its use in detecting between-study variation in population parameters. Not only does the chi-square test often fail to detect real heterogeneity, many users of the Hedges-Olkin fixed effects model apply that model even when the chi-square test *is* significant, indicating the fixed effects model is not appropriate (Hunter & Schmidt, 2000; Schmidt, Oh, & Hayes, 2009). If the fixed effects model is applied when it is not appropriate (i.e., when $SD_\rho > 0$), confidence intervals are erroneously narrow and all significance tests have Type I biases (Kisamore & Brannick, 2008; National Research Council, 1992). These Type I biases are typically quite large (Hunter & Schmidt, 2000; Overton, 1998; Schmidt, Oh, & Hayes, 2009). For example, the actual alpha level can easily be .35 or more when the nominal alpha level is .05. Reported confidence intervals can be only half their actual width (Schmidt, Oh, & Hayes, 2009). The upshot of this is that most of the meta-analyses appearing in *Psychological Bulletin* and a number of other journals, because they are based on fixed effects models, are potentially inaccurate and should be recomputed using random effects models (Hunter & Schmidt, 2000; Schmidt, Oh, & Hayes, 2009). Further discussion of fixed versus random effects models of meta-analysis is presented in Chapter 8.

ACCURACY OF DIFFERENT RANDOM EFFECTS MODELS

Fixed effects models have never been used in validity generalization research and have rarely been used in any research in industrial-organizational (I/O) psychology. So the key question in these areas is which of the random effects models is the most accurate. Actually, because fixed effects models should not be used (National Research Council, 1992), this is the key question in all research areas. This question has been addressed over the years by the many computer simulation studies in the *Journal of Applied Psychology* and *Personnel Psychology* comparing the accuracy of our noninteractive and interactive models, the Callender-Osburn model, the two Raju-Burke models, and other models. The studies by Law et al. (1994a, 1994b) discussed earlier are examples of such studies. The general finding is that all these random effects models are quite accurate by the standards of social science. Law et al. (1994a) showed that the addition of the two accuracy-increasing features discussed later this chapter and in Chapter 4 makes our interactive model (the INTNL program, described in the Appendix) slightly more accurate than the others under most realistic conditions.

One reason so few researchers conducting meta-analyses in social psychology and other non-I/O areas have used the Hedges-Olkin random effects models is that the book by Hedges and Olkin (1985) developed its fixed effects models more completely than its random effects models. Recently, however, Hedges and Vevea (1998) presented a more complete development and discussion of their random effects model, as did the recent book by Borenstein et al. (2009). Schmidt, Oh, and Hayes (2009) found that the use of random effects models has increased in recent years in the major psychology review journal, *Psychological Bulletin*. These developments have stimulated interest in comparing the accuracy of the Hedges-Vevea (1998) and the Hunter-Schmidt (1990b, 2004) random effects models.

Field (2001) compared the accuracy of the Hedges-Vevea (H-V) and the Hunter-Schmidt (H-S) random effects models in estimating $\bar{\rho}$. Field examined only the correlation statistic. He did not compute or compare estimates of SD_ρ, nor did he include or compare the Raju-Burke models or the Callender-Osburn model. He found that when the studies were homogeneous (i.e., $SD_\rho = 0$), the two models had similar accuracy in estimating $\bar{\rho}$ (see his Table 1). However, he found that when the studies were heterogeneous (e.g., $SD_\rho > 0$), the H-V model overestimated $\bar{\rho}$, often by substantial amounts, while the H-S method slightly underestimated these values. For example, when the actual mean was .30, the H-V estimates ranged from .40 to .43, while the H-S estimates were all .29 (all estimates rounded to two places). When the actual mean was .50, the H-V estimates ranged from .64 to .71, while the H-S estimates ranged from .47 to .49. The overestimation produced by the H-V model was much larger than the underestimation produced by the H-S model. We believe that the overestimation produced by the H-V model stems from biases induced by use of Fisher's z transformation (Hunter & Schmidt, 1990b, pp. 213–218; Hunter & Schmidt, 2004; Hunter et al., 1996; Schmidt, Hunter, & Raju, 1988). (See the discussion of Fisher's z transformation in this chapter and the briefer discussion in Chapter 3.) Field also concluded this. Our procedures (like those of the Raju-Burke and Callender-Osburn models) do not use Fisher's z transformation. All calculations are performed directly on the correlation coefficients. In a subsequent study that also focused on the correlation statistic and compared the H-S and H-V methods, Field (2005) employed improved simulation methods. He found that the H-S method "produced estimates of the mean correlation with the least error." He also found that the H-S standard errors of the mean correlation, while accurate enough, were slightly too small, resulting in confidence intervals that were slightly too narrow. Hafdahl and Williams (2009) attempted to replicate the Field (2001) study and reported less overestimation by the H-V model than reported in Field (2001). Inexplicably, they did not replicate the Field (2005) study, the more probative Field study.

Hall and Brannick (2002) also used computer simulation to compare the H-V (1998) and H-S (1990b) random effects models, again for the correlation statistic. Like Field, they also did not examine the Raju-Burke or Callender-Osburn random effects models. However, Hall and Brannick did examine the accuracy of SD_ρ estimates, in addition to $\bar{\rho}$ estimates. Because the H-V method estimates SD_ρ in Fisher's z units, and because there is no way to transform a Fisher's z SD estimate into correlation units, they compared the two methods on the basis of credibility intervals, rather than directly on SD_ρ values. They produced credibility intervals in correlation units for the H-V method by back-transforming the endpoints of the Fisher's z credibility intervals into correlation units. They also separately examined situations in which artifacts attenuated correlations and those in which it was assumed there were no artifacts other than sampling error (i.e., assumed perfect measurement and no range restriction). (The Field studies, by contrast, did not examine any artifacts beyond sampling error.) Whether the studies were homogeneous or heterogeneous, when there were no artifacts other than sampling error, Hall and Brannick found that the H-V method tended to overestimate $\bar{\rho}$ values, while the H-S model produced small underestimates. The H-V model overestimation was less severe in the Hall-Brannick study than in Field (2001) but comparable to that found in Field (2005).

However, when measurement error and range restriction were present, the H-V model produced very large *underestimates* of $\bar{\rho}$ —as would be expected because that model contains no means of correcting for the effects of these artifacts. Hall and Brannick then added the H-S artifact correction methods to the H-V model and then reevaluated that model. With the H-S artifact correction methods grafted on, the accuracy of the H-V model was much improved. However, it still tended to overestimate $\bar{\rho}$ —although not by as large a percentage as in the no-artifact condition. They concluded that the H-S model was generally more accurate than the H-V model.

A major finding in Hall and Brannick (2002) pertained to the credibility intervals produced by the two methods. Hall and Brannick placed considerable stress on credibility values, because they are used to make important practical decisions in applied research. They found that even when the H-V models included the artifact correction modules, the H-S method generally produced more accurate credibility values. The H-V credibility intervals tended to be too wide (compared to the known real values) and to be shifted to the left (see their Figure 1). Again, we believe that this is due to distortions introduced by use of the Fisher's z transformation. The H-S credibility intervals were quite close to the actual values. For these reasons, Hall and Brannick recommended use of the H-S random effects model over the H-V random effects model. Kisamore (2003), in an extensive computer simulation study, reported results similar to those of Hall and Brannick. See also Kisamore and Brannick (2008).

In addition to the use of Fisher's z, there is another difference between the H-V and H-S random effects models that could, in theory, have affected these findings: The two procedures employ different study weights (Schmidt, Oh, & Hayes, 2009). However, Field (2005) found that the difference in study weights did not affect the difference in results. When the H-S weights were applied in H-V model and the H-V study weights were used in the H-S model, the differences between the two models in accuracy did not change. Field concluded that study weights were not critical. The question of study weights in meta-analysis is discussed in Chapter 9.

Although they were not included in these studies, there is good reason to believe that the Raju-Burke (1983) Taylor Series Approximation (TSA) models and the Callender-Osburn (1980) model would perform similarly to the H-S model and would likewise prove more accurate than the H-V model. Again, the use of Fisher's z is the main determinant of this difference in accuracy. These studies also support the conclusion that use of sample size to weight studies in a random effects model—rather than more traditional random effects study weights (Mosteller & Colditz, 1996) used in the H-V model—does not negatively affect accuracy and may improve accuracy. Field (2005) found that these differences in study weights did not affect the results of his comparisons.

Finally, we note that the Hunter-Schmidt random effects model that Hall and Brannick (2002) compared to the Hedges-Vevea random effects model is not our most accurate random effects model. The model these authors evaluated, our multiplicative meta-analysis model, is presented and described in detail in Hunter and Schmidt (1990b; 2004, chap. 4). This model is derived based on the algebra of the products of independent variables (just as the Callender-Osburn, 1980, model is). Unlike our interactive model, this model does not include the accuracy-enhancing refinements discussed later in this chapter and in Chapter 4. In preparing Law et al. (1994b), we found through computer simulation that our multiplicative model was not as accurate as our interactive model, even when the accuracy-enhancing refinements were added to it. Because of length concerns by the editor, we did not include the simulation tests of our multiplicative model in Law et al. (1994b), although we did include the somewhat similar Callender-Osburn multiplicative model. Hence, we believe that our interactive random effects model (i.e., the INTNL program described and applied in Chapter 4 and described in the Appendix) would compare even more favorably with the Hedges-Vevea random effects model. Apparently, Hall and Brannick used the H-S multiplicative model rather than our interactive model because the Hunter and Schmidt (1990b) book they relied on does not contain a detailed mathematical description of the interactive model; this description was omitted because it was available in earlier journal publications. This current book contains a more detailed presentation of the mechanisms of the interactive method.

Credibility Intervals, Confidence Intervals, and Prediction Intervals in Meta-Analysis

The distinction in meta-analysis between credibility intervals and confidence intervals is important. Credibility intervals are formed by use of SD_ρ, not by use of the standard error of $\bar{\rho}$. For example, the 80% credibility interval around a $\bar{\rho}$ value of .50 is $.50 \pm 1.28\ SD_\rho$. If SD_ρ is .10, this credibility interval is .37 to .63. The interpretation of this interval is that 80% of the values in the ρ distribution lie in this interval. The credibility interval refers to the distribution of parameter values, while the confidence interval refers to *estimates* of a single value—the value of $\bar{\rho}$. Confidence intervals express the likely amount of error in our estimate of $\bar{\rho}$ *due to sampling error.* The amount of sampling error is indexed in the standard error of $\bar{r}$ or $\bar{\rho}$ (depending on what artifact corrections are made). The standard error depends on sample size and, hence, sampling error. However, credibility values do not depend on sampling error at all—because variance due to sampling error (and other artifacts) has been removed from the estimate of SD_ρ. The concept of credibility intervals has been viewed by some as Bayesian, because it is based on the idea that parameter values (values of ρ) vary across studies. This discussion of credibility and confidence intervals is presented in terms of correlation values, but credibility and confidence intervals for d values are directly analogous and are discussed in Chapter 8. The concept of credibility values is also critically linked to random effects meta-analysis models, because random effects meta-analysis models (unlike fixed effects models) allow for possible variation in parameters across studies. (In fixed effects models, all credibility intervals would, by definition, have a width of 0.) Credibility intervals provide very important information whenever practical decisions must be made based on the results of a meta-analysis (Rothstein, 2003), because they provide the likely range of population correlations or effect sizes. For example, they reveal whether any of the population correlations or d values are likely to be zero or negative. Confidence intervals do not provide this information. The distinction between credibility intervals and confidence intervals is discussed in Hunter and Schmidt (2000), Schmidt and Hunter (1999a), and Whitener (1990).

Until recently, meta-analyses of medical research studies presented only confidence intervals; credibility intervals were not presented. Medical meta-analysts have now recognized the need for credibility intervals (Higgins & Thompson, 2001; Higgins, Thompson, Deeks, & Altman, 2003). The Borenstein et al. (2009) book presents what the authors term "prediction intervals." Prediction intervals are identical in concept to credibility intervals when they are based directly on the estimate of the SD of the population parameters and are wider than credibility intervals when they are based on both this SD and an estimate of its sampling variance, their usual and recommended usage. The purpose of prediction intervals is to predict the range of possible population parameter values *in a new study* (Higgins, Thompson, & Spiegelhalter, 2009). This is different from the purpose of credibility intervals in our approach, where the focus is on the state of nature in the population and not on the possible results of the next empirical study. Another difference is that prediction intervals are based on correction for only variation due to sampling error; they do not take into account variation produced by other artifacts. Raudenbush (2009) presents what he terms "plausible value intervals," which are identical to the credibility intervals presented here, except that they correct only for sampling error.

All the examples of meta-analysis given in Chapters 3 and 4 were presented with credibility intervals. Confidence intervals were presented only sporadically and were for illustrative purposes. Confidence intervals for many of the example meta-analyses in this book are presented in Chapter 9, in connection with the discussion of second-order sampling error. In meta-analysis, credibility intervals are often more critical and important than confidence intervals. However, for certain questions, confidence intervals are also relevant to the question at hand (as was the case in Viswesvaran, Schmidt, & Ones, 2002). In such cases, the main focus is on the mean value, and there is less interest in the variability of population values around the mean. This is more likely to occur in research testing theories than in applied research.

Computing Confidence Intervals in Meta-Analysis of Correlations

The two most important parameters estimated for random effects models of meta-analysis are $\bar{\rho}$ and SD_ρ. It is perhaps easy to forget that these quantities are *estimates* of the parameters, not the parameters themselves, because in meta-analysis reports, they are rarely topped with a circumflex ($\wedge$). Technically, these values should be written as $\hat{\bar{\rho}}$ and $\hat{SD}_\rho$ but typically are not in the interests of simplifying the symbolism. Every estimate has a standard error (*SE*), known or unknown. Hunter and Schmidt (2000), Schmidt and Hunter (1999a), and Schmidt, Hunter, and Raju (1988) provided formulas for the *SE* of mean observed *r*, but this is not the same statistic. We have derived equations for the *SEs* of $\hat{\bar{\rho}}$ and $\hat{SD}_\rho$ (Hunter & Schmidt, 1987a, 1987b) but have not emphasized these statistics. As noted previously, the use made of the *SE* of the mean in statistics is in placing confidence intervals around the mean. In meta-analysis, unless the estimate of SD_ρ or SD_δ is very small or zero, confidence intervals around the mean are not as important as *credibility* intervals—because it is typically the whole distribution, and not just the mean, that is important. Our focus has therefore been on credibility intervals. Second, *SE*s are rarely given for *SD* estimates in statistical models. This can be seen in the fact that almost all researchers know by heart the formula for the *SE* of the mean $(SD/\sqrt{n})$ but few can even remember seeing the formula for the *SE* of an *SD*. (It is rare to see a confidence interval placed around a reported *SD* or to see an *SD* tested for statistical significance, which also requires the *SE* estimate.) Other random effects models—the Hedges-Vevea (1998) model, the Raju-Burke (1983) models, and the Callender-Osburn (1980) model—also do not provide the *SE* formula for estimates of SD_ρ and SD_δ.

In the case of bare-bones meta-analysis (see Chapter 3), where sampling error is the only artifact corrected for, we have the following (Schmidt, Oh, & Hayes, 2009; Schmidt, Hunter, & Raju, 1988):

$$SE_{\bar{r}} = SD_r / \sqrt{k} \qquad (5.1)$$

This value is then used to place a confidence interval around the mean observed correlation, *r*. Typically, this is the 95% confidence interval, but other widths are equally legitimate.

If correlations are corrected individually (see Chapter 3), then

$$SE_{\bar{\rho}} = SD_{r_c} / \sqrt{k} \qquad (5.2)$$

where $SE_{\bar{\rho}}$ is the *SE* of $\bar{\rho}$, SD_{r_c} is the *SD* of the correlations after each has been individually corrected for measurement error and other artifacts, and *k* is the number of studies. It is important to note that $SD_{r_c} \neq SD_\rho$. SD_{r_c} is much larger than SD_ρ, because SD_{r_c} has not been corrected for sampling error—and r_c values typically have considerable sampling error, in part because the artifact corrections increase sampling error variance. The resulting $SE_{\bar{\rho}}$ is then used to create the confidence interval.

If artifact distribution meta-analysis (see Chapter 4) is used, then

$$SE_{\bar{\rho}} \cong \left[(\bar{\rho}/\bar{r}) SD_r \right] / \sqrt{k} \qquad (5.3)$$

where $SE_{\bar{\rho}}$ is the *SE* of $\bar{\rho}$, $\bar{\rho}$ is the estimate of mean corrected correlation, $\bar{r}$ is the mean observed (uncorrected) correlation, SD_r is the *SD* of the observed (uncorrected) correlations, and *k* is the number of studies. These formulas have been used in published studies (e.g., Judge & Bono, 2001, used Equation [5.2]). In the case of artifact distribution meta-analysis, an alternative to Equation (5.3) can be used to compute confidence intervals for $\bar{\rho}$. First, use Equation (5.1) to compute $SE_{\bar{r}}$, the *SE* of the mean observed correlation. Second, use $SE_{\bar{r}}$ to compute the confidence interval (CI) around $\bar{r}$, as described earlier. Third, correct the endpoints of this CI for mean levels of measurement error and range restriction to yield the CI for $\bar{\rho}$. This method was used in Viswesvaran et al. (2002). When there is range restriction, estimates produced in this manner are slightly more accurate than those produced by Equation (5.3). When there is range restriction, that equation tends to slightly overestimate $SE_{\bar{\rho}}$ because of the nonlinearity of the range restriction correction.

In the case of all three approaches to meta-analysis, use of the Huffcut and Arthur (1995) procedure to eliminate extreme correlation values will usually cause the SE values to be too small and the resulting confidence intervals to be too narrow. Also, in the case of all these approaches, if the number of studies is less than about 30, confidence intervals are slightly more accurate if one uses the t distribution instead of the normal distribution. Li et al. (2010) have presented a bootstrap procedure for estimating confidence intervals when there has been correction for indirect range restriction, which they concluded is slightly more accurate than the methods presented here. However, their procedure is quite complicated and time-consuming. The main purpose of confidence intervals is to provide a general picture of how much potential error there is in an estimate. Therefore, small inaccuracies in the intervals are usually not critical. The formulas for the SE of SD_{ρ} are both more complicated and less useful, and we do not present them here because of space limitations. See Raju and Drasgow (2003) for a treatment of this question.

Technical Issues in Using Meta-Analysis Results in Causal Modeling and Regression

In Chapter 1, in the section "Role of Meta-Analysis in Theory Development," we discussed the use of meta-analysis results in path analyses that test theories. In this section, we discuss some technical issues and questions associated with such usage. This discussion is presented in this chapter because this usage virtually always involves correlations and not d values. Meta-analysis can be used to create correlations among the variables of interest in a theory. An individual meta-analytic study may estimate only a few of these relationships or perhaps only one, but because each meta-analysis can estimate a different cell in the correlation matrix, it is possible to assemble the complete correlation matrix, even though no single meta-analytic study included all the variables of interest (Viswesvaran & Ones, 1995). The literature today contains many studies that use such correlation matrices to test theories in business, education, psychology, and the social sciences. These correlations can be used in path analysis if each correlation has been corrected for the biasing effects of measurement error (always present) and range restriction (present sometimes). If range restriction is present, all meta-correlations must be corrected to the same unrestricted SD value, to ensure they are reflective of the same population. The path analysis methodology assumes the absence of measurement error (Billings & Wroten, 1978), which necessitates correction for measurement error (Coffman & MacCallum, 2005).

In the absence of corrections for measurement error, path analysis results are seriously in error. In path analysis, the path coefficients are standardized regression coefficients. In some cases, the causal model postulates that the multiple independent variables are all direct causes of the dependent variable. Such a model takes the form of a single standardized regression equation. Finally, in some cases, regression analysis is applied *without* hypothesizing causal relations between independent variables and the dependent variable. Hence, our discussion here covers both path analysis and ordinary regression analysis.

PATH ANALYSIS OR SEM?

One question is whether the analyses described here constitute structural equation modeling (SEM) or not. The distinction between SEM and path analysis is that in SEM there are multiple measures of each latent variable (theoretical construct), whereas in path analysis, there is only one measure for each latent variable. In SEM, the multiple measures are used to correct for measurement error in the measures of constructs, while in path analysis, measurement error is corrected using the attenuation correction with the reliability coefficient that is described in Chapters 3 and 4. When a primary data set is used, it is possible to convert a path analysis to an SEM analysis by splitting each measure into several "item parcels," which then become multiple measures of that variable (Coffman & MacCallum, 2005). However, this is not possible when correlations between variables are taken from meta-analyses. Hence, the applications examined here are virtually always path analyses, not SEM analyses. However, such analyses are often erroneously referred to in the literature as SEM analyses.

WHAT SAMPLE SIZE TO USE AND WHAT SOFTWARE?

The different meta-analyses that contribute to the correlation matrix are typically based on different total sample sizes. So the question is, What N should be used for the overall correlation matrix in the path analysis? This question is discussed by Viswesvaran and Ones (1995). Among the options are the arithmetic mean and the harmonic mean. In an important sense, this choice does not really matter, because the most informative indices of model fit do not require an estimate of sample size. These are root mean square error (RMSE) and root mean square error of approximation (RMSEA). These are the two fit indices we recommend, because they are direct *quantitative* indices of the degree of fit. It is only the relatively uninformative fit indices that involve statistical significance tests, such as the chi-square test, that are affected by the figure entered for the overall N. No matter what option for overall N is chosen, all such indices will typically be highly statistically significant because any option for overall N will usually be quite large.

This question interacts with the software used to conduct the path analysis. Recall that all values in the correlation matrix must be corrected for measurement error (and range restriction, if present). These corrections increase sampling error, and hence the effective N is smaller than the overall N estimated based on the total Ns reported in the meta-analyses. To our knowledge, the only software programs that allow for this fact are the path analysis and regression programs in the Hunter (1995) Package set. All other software for path analysis will not make the appropriate downward adjustments in the N entered. If only the two fit indices we recommend here are used, this creates no problem, because these fit indices do not depend on N. Correct use of fit indices that depend on statistical significance tests requires computation and use of an appropriately downwardly adjusted total N. The formula for this computation (Equation [4.3]) is given in the last example application presented in Chapter 4. However, given that the nominal Ns in the original meta-analyses are often large, this adjustment will often not have a large effect.

IS THERE A MIXTURE OF POPULATIONS IN THE CORRELATION MATRIX?

It is possible that the different meta-analyses have been conducted on descriptively different populations. For example, there may be differences in average age, or sex composition, or other variables. Some have argued that this possibility obviates the validity of meta-analytically based path analyses. However, if the correlations do not differ across populations, the inclusion of different populations is not a problem. It simply means that the results properly apply to a super-population that includes all the subpopulations represented in the correlation matrix. Therefore, if the populations sampled in the different meta-analyses differ descriptively, it is incumbent on the researcher to present reasons and evidence supporting the position that the correlations are unlikely to vary by population. For example, there is much meta-analytic evidence in the literature that correlations between ability and personality measures and job performance do not differ across different races and ethnic groups. The widespread belief that correlations of all sorts differ across different populations is usually based on observed differences in correlations that are due to sampling error and other artifacts and therefore are not real.

WHAT ABOUT HETEROGENEITY
WITHIN THE META-ANALYSES?

The correlations entered into the matrix are the average values in the meta-analyses. It is possible there could be considerable heterogeneity within some or all of these meta-analyses (although this was not the case in the example presented in Chapter 1). As we note in Chapters 3 and 4, and in this chapter in the following section, it is possible that much or all of this heterogeneity is due to artifacts that were not corrected for or to incomplete correction of artifacts that were addressed in the meta-analysis. Neverthe-less, to the extent that any of the heterogeneity is real, it suggests the pres-ence of moderators within the meta-analysis. In cases in which there is substantial heterogeneity within the different meta-analyses, the path anal-ysis results provide a picture of the causal model underlying the average correlations. Such results have to be interpreted differently from path anal-ysis results in which there is little or no variability within the contributing meta-analyses. It is incumbent on the researcher to provide a theoretical explication of the meaning of such results.

The last three of these questions were discussed by M. W. L. Cheung and Chan (2005). The methods proposed by these authors rely heavily on statistical tests in their attempt to address these problems. They also pro-posed a generalized least squares (GLS) approach to conducting the path analysis itself. This method also relies heavily on significance tests and also can make no provision for corrections for measurement error or range variation. Their approach is based on fixed effects (FE) model assump-tions. So their approach, while statistically sophisticated in some respects, is not generally helpful to researchers. Becker (2009) and Landis (2013) discuss many of the issues involved in meta-analytic path analysis.

Technical Factors That Cause Overestimation of SD_ρ

Throughout this book, we have stressed that much of the variation in correlations across studies is caused by the operation of statistical and measurement artifacts. These artifacts were defined in Chapter 2, and methods for correcting for many of them were presented in Chapters 3 and 4. This section discusses five additional factors that contribute to overestimation of SD_ρ, the standard deviation of population correlations. These factors lead to an overestimation of the amount of variability in actual correlations. These factors are (1) the presence of non-Pearson correlations in the meta-analysis, (2) the presence of outliers (extremely large or small correlations) in the meta-analysis, (3) the use of study observed correlations in the formula for sampling error variance, (4) the undercorrection for sampling error variance when there is range restric-tion, and (5) the failure to allow for the nonlinearity in range corrections in meta-analyses based on artifact distributions. The first three of these factors apply in all meta-analyses; the fourth applies only when some or all of the correlations have been affected by range restriction; the fifth applies only to meta-analyses that use artifact distributions. However, most meta-analyses to date have used artifact distributions.

PRESENCE OF NON-PEARSON rS

It is well known that commonly used non-Pearson correlation coefficients, such as the biserial and tetrachoric correlations, have larger standard errors than do Pearson rs. Thus, the formula for the sampling error variance of the Pearson correlation underestimates the amount of sampling error variance in these correlations. When such correlations are included in a meta-analysis, they are treated as if their standard errors were those of Pearson rs. This deflates the estimated variance accounted for by artifacts and inflates the estimate of SD_ρ in any distribution of correlations in which biserial and tetrachoric correlations are present. More accurate results can be obtained if non-Pearson rs are deleted prior to the meta-analysis. Of course, such deletion is more feasible when the total number of correlations is large to begin with. In large sets of validity studies, we have found that deleting non-Pearson rs increased the average percentage of variance accounted for by sampling error by almost five percentage points (Schmidt et al., 1993). It should be noted that Spearman's rho is the Pearson r between ranks and has the same sampling error variance as the Pearson r. Hence, it should not be deleted.

PRESENCE OF OUTLIERS AND OTHER DATA ERRORS AND PROBLEMS IN REMOVING OUTLIERS

The use of least squares statistical methods to estimate the mean and variance of the distribution of correlations is based on the assumption that the data contain no aberrant values (i.e., outliers). When this assumption does not hold, the statistically optimal properties (efficiency and unbiasedness) of least squares estimates disappear. Under these circumstances, least squares estimates become very inaccurate because of their extreme sensitivity to outliers (Huber, 1980; Tukey, 1960; see also Barnett & Lewis, 1978; Grubbs, 1969). The presence of even a single outlier can produce a radical increase in the observed standard deviation and a somewhat smaller distortion of the mean. Data sets in any research area are likely to contain data points that are erroneous due to computational, transcriptional, and other errors (Gulliksen, 1986; Wolins, 1962). Even when such errors do not result in outliers, they still produce additional artifactual variance beyond that produced by sampling error and other artifacts.

Based on his extensive experience with data sets of all kinds, Tukey (1960) judged that virtually all data sets contain outliers and other errors. One of our best-known psychometricians expressed the following sentiment:

> I believe that it is essential to check the data for errors before running my computations. I always wrote an error-checking program and ran the data through it before computing. I find it very interesting that in every set of data I have run, either for myself or someone else, there have always been errors, necessitating going back to the questionnaires and repunching some cards, or perhaps discarding some subjects. (Gulliksen, 1986, p. 4)

Unfortunately, the failure to conduct such checks is very widespread. In the physical sciences (e.g., physics and chemistry), extreme values have been routinely eliminated for centuries (Hedges, 1987). The behavioral and social sciences have recently begun to recognize the need for such "trimming" prior to data analysis. Tukey (1960) and Huber (1980) recommended deletion of the most extreme 10% of data points—the largest 5% and the smallest 5% of values. In one study (Schmidt et al., 1989), we found that deletion of only the top and bottom 2% resulted in a five-percentage-point increase in the average percentage of variance accounted for by artifacts.

However, in the case of meta-analysis methods that estimate SD_ρ, the identification and elimination of outliers is a complicated and problematic process. It is difficult to distinguish true outliers from legitimate but extreme values, especially in random effects models (Baker & Jackson, 2008). When sample sizes are small to moderate (the usual case), extreme values can occur simply because of large sampling errors. Such values are not true outliers and should not be eliminated from the data, because the formula for sampling error variance assumes and allows for such occasional large sampling errors. Mosteller and Colditz (1996) take this same position. Elimination of such nonoutlier extreme values can result in overcorrection for sampling error and underestimation of SD_ρ. Because of this, we have generally not removed any but the most extreme "outliers" in conducting our meta-analyses. Huffcutt and Arthur (1995) developed a procedure for identifying and removing outliers in meta-analysis. However, for the reasons discussed here, the use of such procedures is problematic.

Beal, Corey, and Dunlap (2002) have shown the Huffcutt and Arthur (1995) procedure can also lead to overestimation of the mean population correlation by .02 to .04. This occurs when there are few studies (30 or less) in the meta-analysis, study Ns are small, and the uncorrected population correlation is large. This upward bias is caused by the fact that the procedure identifies more false outliers on the low end of the distribution than on the top end. This, in turn, is due to the negative skew in the distribution of r when the population correlation is large. This bias does not occur with d values, because the d value distribution is not skewed.

USE OF r INSTEAD OF r̄ IN THE SAMPLING ERROR FORMULA

The formula for the sampling error variance in a correlation coefficient is

$$S_e^2 = \frac{(1-\rho_{xy}^2)^2}{N-1} \tag{5.4}$$

where N is the sample size and ρ_{xy} is the population (uncorrected) correlation. ρ_{xy} is, of course, unknown, and to use this formula, some method must be found to estimate it. In single studies, the estimate of ρ_{xy} typically used—because it is the only one available—is the observed correlation in the study at hand. In our early meta-analyses of employment test validities, we followed this tradition: The value used to estimate the sampling error variance in every study was the observed correlation in that study. Subsequent simulation studies and studies with real data have shown that this procedure is not optimal. The mean observed r ($\bar{r}_{obs}$)—a good estimate of ρ_{xy}—is typically about .20 in this literature. Sample sizes are usually small, so there are substantial departures in both directions from ρ_{xy}. When the sampling error is large and positive (e.g., +.20, so that $r = .40$), the estimated S_e^2 is substantially reduced (by 23% in this example). However, this effect is not symmetrical. When the sampling error is large and negative (e.g., −.20, so that $r = .00$), the estimated S_e^2 is increased by only a small amount (by 9% in this example). Thus, on balance, the sampling error in a set of correlations is substantially underestimated. The smaller the sample sizes in the studies analyzed, the greater this underestimation will be. Also, the smaller the (attenuated) population correlation, the greater the underestimation will be (because smaller ρ_is have larger sampling error variances, sample sizes being equal). The result is underestimation of the amount of variance accounted for by sampling error and overestimation of SD_ρ. This distortion can be eliminated by using the $\bar{r}$ for the set of studies rather than individual rs in the formula for sampling error. The $\bar{r}$ contains little sampling error, and extreme values are very unlikely. The result is more accurate estimates of SD_ρ. Hunter and Schmidt (1994) showed analytically that use of $\bar{r}$ enhances accuracy in the homogeneous case (where $SD_\rho = 0$). Law et al. (1994b) used computer simulation to show this was also true in the heterogeneous case (where $SD_\rho > 0$). As a result, the methods presented in this book all use $\bar{r}$ in the formula for the sampling error variance of correlations, as do the computer programs available to apply these methods. (See the Appendix for a description of this software package.)

Millsap (1988), in a Monte Carlo study, used r rather than $\bar{r}$ in the formula for sampling error variance. In his study, all ρs were equal so S_ρ^2

was 0, and the variance of the observed rs was solely sampling error variance; that is, $S_r^2 = S_e^2$. However, he found that his formula-derived estimates of S_e^2 were slightly smaller than the S_r^2 figures, and this difference was larger for smaller sample sizes. He attributed this finding to inaccuracy in the formula (the formula is an approximation), but the phenomenon described in this section is in large part the explanation for his findings. He also found that the negative bias in his formula-derived estimates of sampling error variance was larger when scale reliability was lower. This finding is explained by the fact that lower reliability leads to lower values of ρ_i, the operative population correlation (see Chapter 3). Lower ρ_i values have larger sampling error variances for any fixed sample size, thus intensifying the process described previously. Thus, contrary to Millsap's (1988) conclusion, it was not unreliability (measurement error) per se that caused the increase in the underestimation but rather the reduced value of the population correlation and the resulting increase in sampling error.

UNDERCORRECTION FOR SAMPLING ERROR VARIANCE IN THE PRESENCE OF RANGE RESTRICTION

The formula for sampling error variance assumes that the independent and dependent variables are at least approximately normally distributed. Where there is direct range restriction (truncation) on one or both variables, this assumption is violated. For example, in personnel selection, there may be direct restriction on the test (the independent variable). For example, job offers may be made only to those applicants above the mean test score. Millsap (1989), using computer simulation studies, found that under such conditions, the sample (or study) correlations have larger sampling error variances than indicated by the sampling error variance formula. That is, the formula underestimates the true amount of sampling error, leading to undercorrections for sampling variance and, therefore, overestimation of the residual variance and SD_ρ. The undercorrection is largest when sample sizes are 60 or less. As an example, if $N = 60$ and $\rho = .40$ in all studies, and all variance is, in fact, due only to sampling error, then the estimated residual SD (SD_{res}) will, on average, be .046. The estimated SD_ρ value will typically be about .09. The correct value in both cases is, of course, 0. Thus, many nonzero estimates of SD_ρ in the literature could be due, in whole or in large part, to this effect because many are in the .08 to .12 range (see, e.g., Schmidt et al., 1993). Aguinis (2001) reported results similar to Millsap's in the presence of direct range restriction. In most studies, range restriction is indirect rather than direct. Aguinis and Whitehead (1997) showed that indirect range restriction produces a similar downward bias in estimates of sampling error variance. There is no known procedure to adjust for the underestimation of sampling error variance caused by either direct or indirect range restriction. (For a discussion of direct vs. indirect range restriction, see Hunter et al., 2006, or Hunter and Schmidt, 2004, pp. 207–239.)

NONLINEARITY IN THE RANGE CORRECTION

In artifact distribution–based methods of meta-analysis, the mean $(\bar{\rho})$ and standard deviation (SD_ρ) of true correlations are estimated from the mean $(\bar{r}_{res})$ and standard deviation (SD_{res}) of the residual distribution. The residual distribution is the distribution of observed correlations expected across studies if N were always infinite (i.e., no sampling error) and reliability, range restriction, and other artifacts were always constant at their respective mean values. The estimated mean of this distribution is the mean observed r (i.e., $\bar{r}_{res} = \bar{r}$). To correct the residual distribution for the mean level of unreliability, we could divide every value in that distribution by the mean of the square roots of reliabilities. Because that value is a constant, however, we can instead just divide both $\bar{r}_{res}$ and SD_{res} by that constant and get the same result. This is what artifact distribution–based procedures do in correcting for measurement error. However, most of these procedures do exactly the same thing in correcting the residual distribution for the effects of mean range restriction—and here things do not work out so neatly. Using the mean level of range restriction (in the form of the ratio of the restricted to the unrestricted predictor standard deviations), the original procedure corrected $\bar{r}_{res}$. This increases $\bar{r}_{res}$ by some factor, say, 1.50. Then SD_{res} is multiplied by this same factor to estimate the SD of a distribution in which each r has been corrected for the mean level of range restriction. Unlike the reliability correction, however, the range restriction correction is not linear in r. The range correction is not the same for every value of r in the residual distribution: It is larger for smaller rs and smaller for larger rs. Thus, the approximation based on the assumption of linearity in artifact distribution–based meta-analysis procedures leads to overestimates of SD_ρ. Simulation studies (Callender & Osburn, 1980; Raju & Burke, 1983) demonstrated that our original interactive procedure—theoretically, our most sophisticated method (see Chapter 4 and Schmidt et al., 1980)—yields estimates of SD_ρ that are too large by about .02. The same is true for the Callender-Osburn and Raju-Burke procedures. This overestimation occurs in simulated data in which sample sizes are infinite and sources of artifactual variance, such as computational errors, outliers, and non-Pearson rs, do not exist. This overestimation stems from failure to take into account the nonlinearity of range restriction corrections. This nonlinearity can be taken into account by correcting each value in the residual distribution separately for the mean level of range restriction. To take this nonlinearity into account, the following method is used in our INTNL programs for artifact distribution meta-analysis

(Law et al., 1994a, 1994b). (The following applies for direct range restriction; in indirect range restriction, measurement error is corrected before range restriction and S and s values are the true score SDs.) After determining the mean and SD of the residual distribution, identify 60 additional values in that distribution by moving out from the mean in .1 SD units to 3 SD above and below the mean. Then correct each of these values individually for range restriction, using the mean of the s/S ratio. The formula used to correct each value is

$$R = \frac{r(S/s)}{\{([S/s]^2 - 1)r^2 + 1\}^{1/2}} \tag{5.5}$$

where

r = the value of the correlation in the residual distribution,

R = the range-corrected value,

S = the unrestricted standard deviation (for indirect range restriction, the true score value of S is used),

s = the restricted standard deviation (for indirect range restriction, the true score value of s is used).

Each range-corrected r is then corrected for the mean effect of unreliability. (In the case of indirect range restriction, this correction will already have been made.) The relative frequency of each value of r is indexed by the normal curve ordinate associated with its z score in the residual distribution. These frequencies are applied to the corresponding corrected correlations (ρ_i). The frequency-weighted mean of the distribution of the corrected correlations ($\bar{\rho}$) is then determined, and the following (relative) frequency-weighted variance formula is used to find S_ρ^2:

$$S_\rho^2 = \frac{\sum f_i(\hat{\rho}_i - \bar{\rho})^2}{\sum f} \tag{5.6}$$

where f_i is the relative frequency associated with $\hat{\rho}_i$.

Law et al. (1994a, 1994b) showed via computer simulation that this refinement improves accuracy. Schmidt et al. (1993) found that in empirical data sets, the estimated true standard deviations resulting from this improved procedure were smaller than the analogous values derived from the original procedure. Our current computer programs, based on the interactive model for artifact distribution–based meta-analysis of correlations (INTNL-D and INTNL-I), incorporate this refinement. (These programs are described in Chapter 4 and in the Appendix.) The interactive model is described in some detail in Chapter 4. The letters INT in the program label refer to the interactive property. The letters NL stand for "nonlinear," that is, the nonlinear correction (estimation) procedure described here.

SETTING NEGATIVE VARIANCE ESTIMATES TO ZERO

In the meta-analysis methods presented in both Chapter 3 and Chapter 4, the sampling error variance predicted by the appropriate formulas plus the variance produced by other artifacts is subtracted from the observed variance of correlations to estimate the amount of real (nonartifactual) variance. By chance, the amount of variance produced by sampling error is sometimes less in the sample of studies than is predicted by the sampling error variance. This produces a negative estimate of variance. Because a variance cannot be negative, this value is set to zero. The necessity of doing this causes an upward bias in estimates of the SD of the population correlations (Hedges & Vevea, 1998; Overton, 1998; Schmidt, 2008; Schmidt, Oh, & Hayes, 2009). There is no known way to circumvent this inflation in the average estimate of the population correlation SD.

OTHER FACTORS CAUSING OVERESTIMATION OF SD_ρ

Every research area can be expected to have additional factors that cause overestimation of SD_ρ in that particular research literature. The meta-analyst should be alert to this fact and should describe these factors even if no correction can be made for them. This section presents some examples from the meta-analysis of employment test validities. In that literature, some studies used ratings of job performance that had earlier been made for administrative purposes (e.g., pay raises, promotions, etc.), while other studies were based on special ratings that were used solely for the research study. Administrative ratings are known to be strongly influenced by nonperformance considerations (McDaniel et al., 1994; Schmidt & Zimmerman, 2004) and to yield smaller observed correlations with selection procedures than research ratings. This difference is a source of artifactual variance in the observed correlations that could not be corrected for; it thus causes SD_ρ to be an overestimate. Another artifactual source of variance stemmed from the fact that some studies assessed job performance using content-valid work sample measures, while other studies used supervisory ratings of job performance. Work samples are by far the better measure of job performance. We now know that employment tests correlate more highly with work sample measures than with ratings of job performance (Hunter, 1983a; Nathan & Alexander, 1988). This difference between studies inflates estimates of SD_ρ. Another factor causing SD_ρ to be overestimated is inclusion of two or more correlations from the same study whenever the study contains two different tests measuring the same ability in the same sample (e.g., two different tests measuring spatial ability). These correlations are not independent, and the result is inflation of both the observed correlation SD (SD_r) and SD_ρ (see Chapter 10). Finally, we now know that differences between employees in amount of job experience reduce the observed validities of employment tests (McDaniel, Schmidt, & Hunter, 1988a; Schmidt, Hunter, & Outerbridge, 1986). Thus, studies in which employees vary widely in job experience can be expected to report smaller correlations on average than studies in which employees vary little in time on the job. The result is additional variation in correlations across studies that is not corrected for. Again, the effect is to inflate the estimate of SD_ρ.

The specific nature of the factors that cause SD_ρ to be overestimated will vary from one research literature to another. However, they will virtually always be present. Even if no method can be found to correct for their effects, these factors should be described clearly in the meta-analysis report. As we emphasized in Chapter 2, it is important that every meta-analyst and every reader of meta-analyses constantly bear in mind the fact that all estimates of SD_ρ are likely to be overestimates. Even after the meta-analysis is completed, there is still less actual variation across studies than there appears to be.

PART III

Meta-Analysis of Experimental Effects and Other Dichotomous Comparisons

Treatment Effects **6**

Experimental Artifacts and Their Impact

$\mathbf{T}$his chapter presents a substantive discussion of the evaluation of experiments and interventions. The next chapter (Chapter 7) presents the quantitative methods and formulas for meta-analysis and other more technical material. For purposes of simplicity, we consider only a two-group experiment. The principles developed here apply equally to more complicated designs. The more complicated designs are discussed in Chapter 8.

This presentation parallels that for correlational studies in Chapter 2. For typical studies, sampling error causes error in treatment effects and causes studies to appear to be inconsistent with each other. If the usual analysis were based on confidence intervals, the large effects of sampling error would be recognized, and spurious differences between studies would be properly attributed to sampling error. Instead, most investigators rely on the statistical significance test, which aggravates rather than reduces the problem. Meta-analysis can disentangle differences due to sampling error from differences due to real moderator variables. Treatment effects are also distorted by other artifacts: error of measurement in the dependent variable, error of measurement in the treatment variable (i.e., differences between the nominal (intended) treatment and the actual treatment), dichotomization of a continuous dependent variable, range variation on the dependent variable, lack of perfect construct validity in the dependent variable, lack of perfect construct validity in the treatment variable (e.g., confounding of the intended treatment impact with other unintended impacts), bias in the estimation of the treatment effect, as well as bad data due to reporting errors, computation errors, transcription errors, and so on.

The distortions in treatment effects produced by artifacts were camouflaged by the traditional dichotomous description of treatment effects as either "had an effect" or "had no effect." Most artifacts reduce the size of the treatment effect. Had there been no effect to reduce, the artifact would cause no distortion. Thus, under the null hypothesis of "no effect,"

artifacts other than sampling error become irrelevant and were traditionally ignored. However, meta-analysis has shown that the nihilistic
null hypothesis is rarely true. For example, as discussed in Chapters 2, 3,
and 5, Lipsey and Wilson (1993) examined available meta-analyses of
more than 300 psychological interventions (treatment conditions) and
found that only two of the treatments (less than 1%) had essentially no
effect. Based on this massive study, one would estimate the prior probability that the null hypothesis is false in studies of psychological treatments at .993. In most research domains, the null hypothesis is not true
and the reduction in an effect by artifacts has a real and important effect.
Among other things, reduction in the size of the study effect by an artifact increases the error rate of the conventional statistical significance
test (which is high in the best of conditions for most studies). Differences in the extent of artifacts between studies cause apparent differences in effects across studies, producing the appearance of situation (or
setting) by treatment interactions where there are none.

   This chapter begins with a discussion of the quantification of the treatment effect. We then present hypothetical across-study data showing the
effects of sampling error and the failure of the conventional statistical
significance test in the context of the review study. We then present a substantive discussion of artifacts other than sampling error. These other
artifacts can be just as large in size even though they are usually systematic
rather than random in nature.

Quantification of the Treatment Effect:
The *d* Statistic and the Point Biserial Correlation

A key issue is the description of treatment effects as quantitative or
dichotomous. The traditional description is dichotomous: The treatment
either had an effect or had no effect. Methodologists have long argued
that we should instead describe the treatment effect in quantitative form,
that is, estimate the actual size of the treatment effect. A dichotomous
description is poor for several reasons. First, there is a great loss of information, information that can be used (1) to assess the practical importance of a treatment, (2) to compare the effectiveness of treatments, (3) to
determine whether a theory has been confirmed or disconfirmed, and
(4) to test quantitative theories such as path models. Second, the implicit
assumption in dichotomizing the treatment effect is that most treatments
have no effect. If this were true, then there would be important information in the statement that the treatment effect is not 0. However, as discussed previously, meta-analyses have now shown that treatments rarely
have no effect at all. The conclusion, "The treatment had no effect," is
usually erroneous. Thus, the question for a treatment is really not whether
it had an effect but whether the effect is as large as a theory predicts,

whether the effect is large enough to be of practical importance, or whether the effect is larger or smaller than some other treatment or some variation of the treatment. These questions can only be answered by quantifying the size of the treatment effect.

The dichotomization of treatment effects is also related to the statistical analysis of treatments. If it were true that most treatments have no effect, then good statistical analysis would focus on Type I error: falsely concluding that there is an effect when there is no such effect. The conventional significance test guarantees that Type I errors will occur no more than 5% of the time. However, meta-analysis has now shown that this nihilistic null hypothesis is rarely true. If the null hypothesis is false, then all statistical errors will be Type II errors: falsely concluding that there is no effect when there is, in fact, an effect. As we shall see, for typical sample sizes, the Type II error rate is quite high. For sample sizes of 100, the Type II error rate for textbook experiments is around 50%, and the Type II error rate for more subtle follow-up research is higher yet. There are many important research domains where the significance test error rate is as high as 85%.

Because the null hypothesis is false in most research domains, the conventional significance test has a very high error rate. This high error rate means that the conventional significance test is actually counterproductive at the level of review studies. The high error rate for the conventional significance test means that results interpreted using the significance test must necessarily look inconsistent across studies. For example, if the significance test is wrong 50% of the time, then half the studies will have a significant treatment effect, but the other half will falsely appear to show no treatment effect.

This is quite evident in comparing the results of meta-analyses to the conclusions of narrative reviews. For most questions studied, meta-analysis shows that the treatment effect was not 0—although treatment effects are sometimes quite small. Narrative reviews, on the other hand, have been inconsistent. Some reviewers are selective; they throw out studies on "methodological" grounds—frequently of an entirely hypothetical nature. They throw out studies until those that remain have consistent results. They then base their conclusions on the remaining studies. Unfortunately, different reviewers will throw out different studies and, hence, come to different—sometimes opposite—conclusions. Comprehensive reviewers make a different error: They usually conclude that treatment effects are sporadic. They conclude that the treatment effect is present in some studies but absent in others.

The natural quantitative description of the treatment effect is just the difference between the means on the dependent variable. Let Y be the dependent variable. Denote the means for the control and experimental groups as follows:

$$\bar{Y}_E = \text{the mean for the experimental group}$$
$$\bar{Y}_C = \text{the mean for the control group}$$

To say "The treatment increased performance by 3.2 feet," is to say that the difference $\bar{Y}_E - \bar{Y}_C$ is 3.2 feet; that is,

$$\bar{Y}_E - \bar{Y}_C = 3.2$$

If the dependent variable were identically measured in all studies, then the raw score difference between means would be the conventional measure of the treatment effect. However, this is rarely true. Consider the measurement of the job performance of sewing machine operators. One would think that a measure such as "number of garments sewn per week" would be the same variable across studies. However, workers at different places are sewing different kinds of garments. To sew three dresses might be very different from sewing three coats. Thus, typically, the units of the dependent variable vary from one study to the next.

If the dependent variable is the same in two different studies except for units, then it would, in principle, be possible to calibrate the two measures by finding the constant of proportionality between the two units. Consider, however, the problem of matching the units for sewing machine operators in two different studies. In one study, the workers sew dresses, while the workers in the other study sew coats. To transform scores from one metric to the other, the workers at one place would have to sew the other kind of garment. Furthermore, they would have to be given exactly the same training in sewing that other kind of garment to be exactly comparable. This would be prohibitively expensive even if it were possible. Thus, exact calibration of independent variables is also impossible in most research domains.

There is an alternative method of matching across studies, although it depends on a substantive assumption. We can eliminate units within a study by using standard scores instead of raw scores. The treatment effect in standard scores would then be given by

$$d = (\bar{Y}_E - \bar{Y}_C)/\sigma$$

where σ is the standard deviation of the raw scores in that study. The only question is, "Which standard deviation?" This question will be considered in detail in the next chapter. For population data, the natural definition would be to use the population standard deviation of the control group. However, for sample data, the standard deviation is more accurately estimated by using the "within-group variance," that is, by averaging the experimental and control group standard deviations. This sample statistic is Cohen's (1977) d statistic, which is the most widely used statistic in the meta-analysis of experimental or intervention studies. For the population value, we will use the Greek letter for d, that is, δ.

Suppose the distribution of garment sewing performance per month has a mean of 100 and a standard deviation of 25. If a training program increases performance by 10 garments per day, then the treatment effect in standard scores would be

$$d = 10/25 = .40$$

That is, the treatment effect would be .40 standard deviations.

If the outcome (dependent) variable is a true dichotomy (e.g., patient had the disease vs. patient did not have the disease), then another statistic, the odds ratio, can be used. The odds ratio is frequently used in medical research. We do not present procedures for using the odds ratio in this book because it is rarely appropriate and is rarely used in social science research. It is also seriously prone to misinterpretation. Haddock, Rindskopf, and Shadish (1998) provided a discussion of potential uses of the odds ratio in social science research. We discuss the odds ratio in Chapter 9.

A closely related measure of treatment effect will be discussed in detail in the next chapter: the point biserial correlation. The point biserial correlation is actually an ordinary Pearson correlation; the special name comes from the nature of the data on which it is computed. We create a single data set by pooling the data across the control group and the experimental group. We define a treatment variable (sometimes called a "dummy variable" or "contrast variable") by assigning different scores to the people in the two different groups. For example, we might define the variable T by assigning the score 0 to those in the control group and assigning the score 1 to those in the experimental group. The correlation computed on the pooled data between that treatment variable and the dependent variable is the point biserial correlation. The point biserial correlation has the advantage that it can be treated like any other correlation coefficient. In particular, the meta-analysis could be done using the methods of Chapters 3 and 4 on the correlation coefficient (as discussed in Chapter 7). The mathematics is then much easier than that for the d statistic. The correlation is much easier to fit into advanced statistical analyses such as reliability analysis, path analysis, and so on. The point biserial correlation is the second most often used quantification of the treatment effect in meta-analysis. As noted in the next chapter, the two statistics, r and d, can be algebraically transformed back and forth from each other. Thus, it is conceptually arbitrary which statistic is used. However, in this chapter, we primarily use d. For the usual empirical range of d of $-.41 < d < +.41$, the conversion formulas between r and d are trivial.

$$d = 2r \qquad \text{for} -.21 < r < +.21$$
$$r = .5d \qquad \text{for} -.41 < d +.41$$

How close is this approximation? Consider the worst case, $d = .40$. The approximation $.5d$ yields $r = .20$, while the actual correlation is .196.

The *d* statistic is comparable across studies if the standard deviation of the dependent variable (measured in any one set of units) is the same across studies (to within sampling error). This is a typical finding for standardized variables in psychology in the absence of processes producing range restriction. Although means often differ considerably from one setting to the next, standard deviations often differ little. In a research domain where this is not true, the variation in results due to differing units could only be corrected by making a correction for range variation (see Chapter 3).

Sampling Error in *d* Values: Illustrations

Is an argument more effective if it is expressed in intense language or if it is cast in tentative language? A meta-analysis by Hamilton and Hunter (1987) showed the difference in attitude change to be about .20 standard deviations (i.e., $d = .20$ or $r = .10$) favoring strong language. Assume that this is the population value of the *d* statistic for all studies in a hypothetical meta-analysis. What would the review data look like? That depends on the sample sizes used in the studies collected. For simplicity, suppose all studies had used exactly the same sample size. The study results would be approximately distributed as in Table 6.1. (Note: The distributions in Table 6.1 exactly match the sampling distribution for replicated studies. An actual 19-study meta-analysis would find values that depart from this distribution somewhat because the 19 observed sampling errors would not match the exact population distribution of sampling errors.)

CASE 1: N = 30

Suppose 19 studies were done with a total sample size of 30 (15 subjects in each group) in each study. The study treatment effects would distribute themselves as the first column of Table 6.1. Six of the studies would have had negative observed treatment effects. The authors of these studies would believe that intense language is counterproductive and reduces the persuasive effect. On the other hand, six studies would have found treatment effects of $d = .40$ or more, effects as large as textbook examples. These authors would believe that intense language is one of the most powerful persuasive agents known. Both sets of authors would be wrong. Only Study 10—the median study—has an effect size of $d = .20$, the actual population value for all studies.

One classic but crude method of reviewing research is to count the number of studies in the predicted direction. This count is 13 out of 19. This is greater than the .95 out of 19 expected by chance, although not

Table 6.1 Hypothetical meta-analysis data for the effect of language intensity on persuasion (results ordered by magnitude).

Study	N = 30	N = 68	N = 400
1	.80**	.60**	.36**
2	.68*	.50**	.32**
3	.58	.46*	.30**
4	.50	.40*	.28**
5	.44	.36	.26**
6	.40	.32	.26**
7	.34	.30	.24**
8	.30	.26	.22**
9	.24	.24	.22**
10	.20	.20	.20**
11	.16	.16	.18*
12	.10	.14	.18*
13	.06	.10	.16
14	–.00	.08	.16
15	–.04	.04	.14
16	–.10	–.00	.12
17	–.18	–.06	.10
18	–.28	–.10	.08
19	–.40	–.20	.04

Note: In each case, the population effect is $\delta = .20$ in all studies, and all deviation from that value is entirely due to sampling error. The sample size is the total sample size across control (low-intensity) and experimental (high-intensity) groups. Thus, "$N = 30$" means "15 in each group."

*Significant by one-tailed test. **Significant by two-tailed test.

significantly so (using a binomial test). However, had there been 190 studies instead of 19, the expected count of studies in the predicted direction would be 130/190, which is significantly greater than the 9.5 expected by chance. Thus, a count of the studies in the predicted direction would show that intensity increased persuasion more often than chance. However, it would falsely suggest that intensity acted in the *opposite* direction 32% of the time.

The statistical significance test was designed to reduce the impact of sampling error. When the null hypothesis is true, it should reduce errors of inference to 5%. How does the conventional significance test fare in this example? There are two ways to do this significance test. Had each study been analyzed using analysis of variance, it would have been analyzed using a two-tailed significance test, and only the study with $d = .80$ would have been significant. That is, analysis of variance yields the correct inference for only one study, an error rate of 18/19, or 95%. That is, the error rate for the two-tailed significance test is not 5% but 95% in this example.

Had the data been analyzed using the t test, the authors would have had the option of doing a one-tailed test. For a one-tailed test, both Studies 1 and 2 have significant treatment effects. Thus, this significance test yields a correct inference for only 2 of the 19 studies, an error rate of 17/19, or 89%. Thus, for a one-tailed t test, the error rate is not 5% but 89% in this example.

In this example, the two-tailed test (conventional analysis of variance) is correct in only 1 of 19 studies. The one-tailed test is correct in 2 of 19 studies, which doubles the power of the two-tailed test. However, in either case, the error rate is far higher than the 5% error rate that most people believe to be the error rate for the statistical significance test.

Why is the error rate higher than 5%? The conventional statistical significance test assumes a nihilistic null hypothesis of $\delta = 0$. If the null hypothesis were true, then the error rate would be only 5%. However, the null hypothesis is false for this research domain (as it is in most research domains), and thus, the error rate is not constrained to be 5% but will be higher. In this example, the error rate rose to 89% (one-tailed test) or 95% (two-tailed test), which is close to the theoretical maximum error rate.

Consider the position of a reviewer faced with study results such as those in the first column of Table 6.1. If the reviewer counts results in the expected direction, then there is a weak indication of results in the expected direction. It is true that nearly a third of the studies go in the wrong direction, but that is counterbalanced by the third of the studies with effects as large as classic textbook effects in social psychology. That reviewer would probably conclude that intense language is more persuasive most of the time but would warn that there are some settings where, for unknown reasons, intense language is counterproductive. This would be a false interpretation of the data.

Suppose the reviewer ignored the size of the treatment effects and considered only a count of the number of significant findings using a two-tailed test. This reviewer would almost certainly conclude that language intensity has no effect on persuasiveness. That, too, would be a false conclusion. Ironically, the reviewer who uses the significance test—the more "sophisticated" method—is even more in error than the reviewer who naively looks at raw results!

Note that the inferences of reviewers would not materially improve with more data. If the number of studies rose from 19 to 190, the number of studies with results significant by a one-tailed test would rise from 2 to 20. However, the proportion of significant findings would still be the same, $20/190 = 2/19$. Thus, a reviewer who depended on the significance test would still draw the same false conclusions even though there were 10 times as much data.

As we will see, the method of meta-analysis presented in this book deals with these data correctly. This method would estimate the average treatment effect to be $\delta = .20$ to within the sampling error left by using a total sample size of $N = 19(30) = 570$. If there were 190 studies, the error in estimating the mean effect size would drop to that left by a total sample size of $N = 190(30) = 5,700$. As more and more studies become available, this method of meta-analysis has less and less error. This method would also have correctly concluded that all or nearly all the variance in observed study effects was due to sampling error.

Is this example far-fetched? The size of the treatment effect for language intensity is that found in actual studies. On the other hand, the sample size of $N = 30$ is lower than the actual studies ($\bar{N} = 56$). However, there are important research domains with sample sizes this low. For example, Allen, Hunter, and Donahue (1988) did a meta-analysis on studies of the effect of psychotherapy on problems of shyness and fear of public speaking. For the studies using systematic desensitization, the average sample size was 23. For the studies using rational-emotive therapy, the average sample size was only 19.

CASE 2: N = 68

The median sample size of studies in personnel selection is 68 in the pre-1980 literature (Lent, Auerbach, & Levin, 1971a, 1971b). This seems not far from sample sizes in other psychological study domains, although there are exceptions both larger and smaller. The average sample size for the language intensity meta-analysis done by Hamilton and Hunter (1987) was $\bar{N} = 56$, which is about the same as the 68 used in Table 6.1. If all 19 studies were done with a sample size of $N = 68$, then the study values would have an expected distribution like that of the second column of Table 6.1.

A reviewer who looked at the results at face value would now see 15 of 19 values in the expected direction and only 4 of 19 negative values. This split is significantly different from a 50–50 split using a binomial comparison. At the same time, the four large values are not quite as large as textbook examples. This reviewer would probably conclude that the studies in the wrong direction were just sampling errors from a zero effect. Thus, the reviewer would probably conclude that language intensity usually increases persuasion, although there are a minority of cases where it does not. This conclusion is false because the effect is actually $\delta = .20$ in all cases.

The conventional two-tailed statistical significance test of analysis of variance registers only the two largest values as significant. Thus, the conventional two-tailed test is correct in only 2 of 19 cases, an error rate of 17/19, or 89%. A reviewer who counted significant findings would probably conclude that language intensity is irrelevant to persuasion. This conclusion would be a grave error in this example.

The one-tailed significance test registers the top four values as significant. Thus, the one-tailed test is correct four times, which means that the one-tailed test has twice the power of the two-tailed test in this example. However, the one-tailed test is still wrong in 15 of 19 studies, an error rate of 79%. A reviewer who counts one-tailed significant findings would probably conclude that 4 times in 19 is noticeably greater than the 1 in 20 expected by chance. If not, then if the number of studies were raised to 190, the reviewer would certainly notice that 40 out of 190 is much greater than the 190/20 = 9.5 expected by chance. The reviewer would probably conclude that language intensity does have an impact in about $(40 - 9.5)/190$, or 16%, of settings but has no effect otherwise. Note: This reviewer expects 9.5 significant results by chance alone. This is an improvement over the error made by the reviewer who looks at two-tailed tests but is worse than the conclusion drawn by the reviewer who ignores the significance test altogether.

The method of meta-analysis presented here would estimate the treatment effect to within the sampling error left by a total sample size of $N = 19(68) = 1,292$. If there were 190 studies, the error in the mean effect size would be down to that left by a total sample size of $N = 190(68) = 12,920$. The method would also correctly conclude that all or nearly all of the variance across studies is due to sampling error.

CASE 3: N = 400

Most psychologists think of a sample size of 400 as if it were ∞ (i.e., an infinite N). However, pollsters know differently from experience. The typical study results for 19 studies with a sample size of $N = 400$ are shown in the third column of Table 6.1.

A reviewer who looks at the results at face value would now note that all results are in the expected direction, although the smallest results are small indeed. The largest results are still moderate in size. Thus, the reviewer would probably conclude that language intensity always increases persuasion (a correct conclusion), although in some settings, the impact is negligible in magnitude (an incorrect conclusion).

A reviewer who counts two-tailed significance tests would find that 10 of 19 study values are significant. This reviewer would probably conclude that language intensity increases persuasion in about half of the settings but does not work in the other half. This conclusion is quite far from the truth.

A reviewer who counts one-tailed significance tests would find that 13 of 19 study values are significant. Thus, in this example, the one-tailed test is 13/10 times more powerful than the two-tailed test, that is, about 30% more powerful. This reviewer would probably conclude that language intensity increases persuasion in about two thirds of the settings, but does not work in the other third. This conclusion is also quite far from the truth.

Even with a sample size of 400, the reviewer who naively looks at face value results is closer to the truth than a reviewer who counts statistical significance findings. Thus, even with a sample size of 400, the significance test still works so poorly that it is counterproductive in comparison to doing no analysis for sampling error at all.

With an average sample size of 400, our method of meta-analysis would estimate the mean effect size to within the sampling error left by a total sample size of $N = 19(400) = 7,600$. The analysis would also correctly conclude that all or nearly all of the variance across studies is due to sampling error.

From the viewpoint of review studies, the statistical significance test does not correctly deal with sampling error. The statistical significance test works only in a research context in which we know the null hypothesis to be true. If we know the null hypothesis to be true, however, then we need not do the test at all. Thus, we should abandon the use of the statistical significance test in doing review studies. There are now several basically equivalent meta-analysis formulas that take sampling error into account correctly for mean effect sizes, including the method presented here. Our method is also accurate when there is real variance in effect sizes across studies. In addition, we estimate the size of the standard deviation of population effect sizes. Some authors stop with a significance test for homogeneity and present no method for estimating the standard deviation if the significance test indicates that the standard deviation is not 0.

Error of Measurement in the Dependent Variable Measure

Ordinary English interprets the phrase "error of measurement" as having two meanings: systematic and unsystematic error. Systematic error is a departure from measuring exactly what was intended. In psychometric theory, this is called "imperfect construct validity." In psychometric theory, the phrase "error of measurement" is used for unsystematic error, also called "random error" or "unreliability." We follow psychometric terminology here. This section presents the effects of unsystematic or random error of measurement, and a later section covers imperfect construct validity.

In psychology, much of the unsystematic error of measurement is caused by randomness in subject response. This kind of error usually has a mean of 0, that is, is equally likely to be positive or negative, and is uncorrelated with the true value. If we write the observed score on the dependent variable as Y, write the true score as U, and write the error of measurement as e, then

$$Y = U + e$$

where the population mean of e is 0 and the population correlation between e and U is 0.

Because the average error is 0, the mean of errors does not describe the typical size of an error. Rather, the typical size of errors is described by either the error variance—the average squared error—or the error standard deviation. The number σ_e is called the "standard error of measurement" in psychometric theory. The practical impact of error of measurement is relative to the size of differences between people. If two people differ on the dependent variable by 10 points, then errors of size -1 or $+1$ would have little effect on the comparison of those people. On the other hand, if the difference between two subjects were .5, then errors of -1 or $+1$ would completely obscure the comparison. One measure of the relative error of measurement is the "noise to signal" ratio, σ_e/σ_U, although this is not commonly used. Instead, the more useful measure of relative error is the correlation between true and observed score, that is, r_{UY}. By historical convention, the square of this correlation is called the "reliability" of the dependent variable and is denoted r_{UY}^2. That is, we define the reliability of the dependent variable r_{YY} by

$$r_{YY} = r_{YU}^2$$

Different ways of estimating reliability identify and assess different sources of measurement error. It is critical that the researcher use the appropriate reliability estimate. We refer the reader to the extended treatment of this issue presented in Chapter 3. The error standard deviation and the reliability of the dependent variable are related by

$$\sigma_e = \sigma_y \sqrt{(1 - r_{YY})}$$

The size of the reliability depends on the extent of measurement error in the process measured—usually a response in psychology—and on the number of primary measurements used to generate the final response— frequently the number of items on a scale. High-quality measurement often provides reliability in the region of $r_{YY} = .81$. Moderate quality usually falls around $r_{YY} = .64$. Measurement based on a single response frequently has reliability no higher than $r_{YY} = .25$. It should be noted that the reliability of a single response is not determined by the cost of obtaining that response. For example, in equity studies in social psychology, subjects may spend as much as an hour before the criterion act. However, the only measurement of the dependent variable is a single response: the amount of money given to the partner. The reliability of that single response is the correlation between that response and the response that would have been made on some other randomly chosen day. The reliability of single responses is rarely higher than $r_{YY} = .25$

The size of the reliability depends both on the extent of error in the measurement process and on the extent of individual differences on the dependent variable. For instance, Nicol and Hunter (1973) found that the same semantic differential scale that had a reliability of .90 measuring attitudes toward the polarized issue "law and order" had only a reliability of .20 measuring attitudes toward the issue "pollution."

The observed score for a given person p is related to the true score for that person by

$$Y_p = T_p + e_p$$

If we average scores across persons, the mean score is related to the mean true score by

$$\bar{Y} = \bar{T} + \bar{e}$$

That is, errors of measurement are averaged across persons. The population mean of scores across persons averages the errors of measurement across an ∞ (infinity) of errors and is thus 0. That is, at the population level, error of measurement has no impact on the mean.

The raw score treatment effect is defined as the difference between population means:

$$\text{Raw score } \delta_Y = \bar{Y}_E - \bar{Y}_C$$

Because population mean error of measurement is 0, each mean observed score is equal to the mean true score. Thus,

$$\text{Raw score } \delta_U = U_E - U_C = \bar{Y}_E - \bar{Y}_C = \text{Raw score } \delta_Y$$

That is, random error does not alter the raw score treatment effect. This is the reason that traditional statistics has ignored error of measurement in the treatment of experimental design.

However, it is not the raw score treatment effect but rather the standard score treatment effect that is of primary interest in statistics. For purposes of meta-analysis, it is normally necessary to use standard score treatment effects to achieve comparability across studies. However, the standard score treatment effect is also central to traditional statistics because it is the standard score treatment effect that is assessed by the statistical test for significance. In particular, the power of the conventional significance test depends on the standard score treatment effect.

Error of measurement does not affect the mean of the dependent variable, but it *does* affect the variance. The variance of observed scores is related to the variance of true scores by

$$\sigma_Y^2 = \sigma_U^2 + \sigma_e^2$$

That is, error of measurement increases the variance and, hence, the standard deviation of the dependent variable. Consider, then, the experimental versus control group comparison. Adding error does not change the means, but it increases the spread of scores about the mean. This effect is shown in Figure 6.1.

The extent of separation between two groups depends on the extent of overlap between the two distributions. The extent of overlap between the distributions depends on the difference between the means in relation to the extent of spread about the means. The greater the spread about the means, the greater the overlap between the two distributions. Figure 6.1 shows that the extent of overlap is greatly increased by the presence of error of measurement. The lower the reliability, the larger the spread about the means and, hence, the greater the overlap. That is, as the amount of error of measurement increases, the difference is more and more obscure. In terms of statistical power, the more obscure the difference between the means, the more difficult that difference is to detect.

Consider the standardized effect size for true scores and observed scores:

$$\delta_U = (U_E - U_C) / \sigma_U$$
$$\delta_Y = (Y_E - Y_C) / \sigma_Y$$

Because population means are not affected by error of measurement, the numerators are equal. However, error of measurement increases the standard deviation, and hence, the denominators are different. The increase in standard deviation is given by

$$\sigma_Y = \sigma_U / \sqrt{r_{YY}}$$

where we note that to divide by a number less than 1 is to increase the ratio. If this identity is substituted into the equation for δ_Y, we have

$$\delta_Y = \delta_U \sqrt{r_{YY}}$$

Figure 6.1   Effect of error of measurement on the separation between the control and experimental groups for a case in which the true score treatment effect is δ = 1.00.

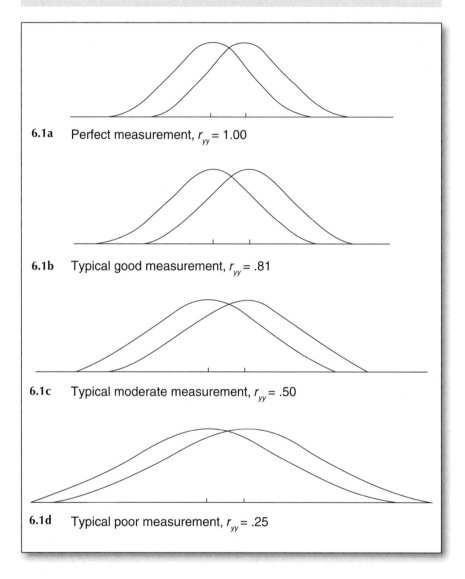

6.1a   Perfect measurement, r_{yy} = 1.00

6.1b   Typical good measurement, r_{yy} = .81

6.1c   Typical moderate measurement, r_{yy} = .50

6.1d   Typical poor measurement, r_{yy} = .25

That is, the standardized effect size for the observed score is the standardized effect size for the true score multiplied by the square root of the reliability. For example, if the reliability were r_{YY} = .81, the effect size would be reduced to

$$\delta_Y = .90\delta_U$$

that is, reduced by 10%.

If the effect size is reduced by error of measurement, the effect is more difficult to detect by the conventional significance test. This is illustrated in Table 6.2. Table 6.2 computes the power of the conventional significance test for studies of sample size $N = 100$, a value roughly typical for empirical studies. An effect size of $\delta = .40$ is about the size of large introductory textbook examples from the social psychology experimental literature. The effect size of $\delta = .20$ is about the size of effects in the more sophisticated research that follows up textbook examples, that is, research that studies variation in textbook manipulations rather than the crude manipulation itself.

Table 6.2 first shows the reduction in the treatment effect produced by different levels of error of measurement. As the reliability decreases from $r_{YY} = 1.00$ to $r_{YY} = .25$, the treatment effect is reduced by half, for example, from $\delta = .40$ to $\delta = .20$ or from $\delta = .20$ to $\delta = .10$. The probability of detecting the effect using a conventional significance test drops correspondingly. For textbook size effects with $\delta = .40$, the power drops from an already low 51% to 17%, a power level only one third the size. Stated the other way, the error rate for the significance test rises from 49% to 83%. For sophisticated research, the initial power level is smaller to begin with, and hence, there

Table 6.2 Power of the conventional significance test for studies with sample size $N = 100$.

I. Reduction in the effect size: the value of δ_y for various values of the reliability of the dependent variable

Reliability	$\delta_U = .10$	$\delta_U = .20$	$\delta_U = .30$	$\delta_U = .40$
1.00	.10	.20	.30	.40
.81	.09	.18	.27	.36
.64	.08	.16	.24	.32
.25	.05	.10	.15	.20

II. Reduction in power: the power of the conventional .05 level statistical significance test for various values of the reliability of the dependent variable, expressed as a percentage

Reliability	$\delta_U = .10$	$\delta_U = .20$	$\delta_U = .30$	$\delta_U = .40$
1.00	7.2	16.6	31.8	51.2
.81	6.5	14.3	26.7	43.2
.64	5.9	12.1	33.0	37.3
.25	4.3	7.2	11.2	16.6

is less distance to fall. If with perfect measurement the effect size is $\delta = .20$, then, if the dependent variable is based on a single response, the observed effect size would be about $\delta = .10$ and the power would drop from 17% to 7%, a reduction of slightly more than half. The error rate for the significance test rises from 83% to 93%.

The next chapter will show that for population effect sizes, the reduction in the treatment effect can be corrected if the reliability of the dependent variable is known. Although the application of that same correction formula to sample values eliminates the systematic effect of error of measurement (Cook et al., 1992, pp. 315–316), the increased sampling error and reduced statistical power cannot be corrected. This shows in the fact that the significance test on the corrected effect size is algebraically equivalent to the significance test on the uncorrected effect size.

Error of Measurement in the Treatment Variable

The treatment variable is defined by group assignment. Because the investigator usually knows exactly which group each subject belongs to, this variable is usually regarded as perfectly measured. However, this definition ignores the interpretation of the results. In interpreting the results, it is not group assignment but the treatment process that is the actual independent variable. From that point of view, the nominal (intended) treatment variable may be quite different from the actual treatment variable.

Consider an attitude change experiment directed to the topic of acid rain. The investigator seeks to manipulate the credibility of the source of the change-inducing message. At one point in the instructions, the sentence "The author of the message is . . ." is completed either with the phrase "a famous scientist in the area" or with "a marine drill instructor." Assume that the instructions are correctly read to each subject so that we do know correctly and exactly the group assignment of each subject. However, suppose 30% of the subjects are not paying careful attention to the instructions. They do not hear the sentence stating the author of the message. They do not think about the author of the message until they read it. Assume that the subjects who did not hear the author's identity then *assume* one. Suppose half the subjects assume the author to be an expert while half the subjects assume the author to be some know-nothing graduate assistant. Then, in this study, 15% of the control group subjects will assume an expert source and will act as if they had been exposed to the experimental group instructions, while 15% of the experimental group subjects will assume a know-nothing source and will act as if they had been exposed to the control group instruction. In this example, the nominal treatment group variable is the reverse of the actual treatment variable 15% of the time. The observed effect size will be correspondingly reduced.

How much will the treatment effect be reduced? The idea is simple, but the computations are complicated. In our example, where 15% of the subjects were misidentified in each group, we could compute the effect of the treatment variable error by assuming each treatment group to be the pooling of 85% from the corresponding true treatment group and 15% from the other true treatment group. The outcome is easily stated in correlational terms. Denote the nominal treatment variable by X and denote the true treatment variable by T; that is,

X = the observed group assignment of the subject, and

T = the actual treatment value for that subject.

If the correlation between X and T is r_{YT}, then the observed treatment effect correlation r_{XY} is related to the true treatment effect correlation r_{TY} by the equation

$$r_{XY} = r_{XT}r_{TY}$$

The formula for the reduction in the d statistic can be obtained by substituting this product into the formula for r to d conversion.

The product rule for the treatment effect correlation is a special case of the attenuation formula from psychometric theory. Let us denote the "reliability of the treatment" by r_{XX} and define it to be the square of the correlation between true and observed treatment identifications; that is, we define r_{XX} by

$$r_{XX} = r_{XT}^2 \qquad (6.1)$$

Then our product formula is a special case of the psychometric formula

$$r_{XY} = \sqrt{r_{XX}r_{TY}} \qquad (6.2)$$

In our attitude change example, we assumed 15% misidentification in each group. The correlation between the observed and true treatment is thus $r_{XT} = .70$, and, hence, the observed treatment effect correlation is

$$r_{XY} = .70r_{TY}$$

That is, the observed treatment effect correlation is reduced by 30%.

If the treatment effect correlation is reduced, then statistical power will be reduced correspondingly. Suppose in our example that the true treatment effect was $\delta_T = .40$ with a sample size of $N = 100$. The true treatment effect correlation would then be $r_{TY} = .20$. The observed treatment effect correlation would then be $r_{XY} = (.70)(.20) = .14$ and the observed treatment effect would be $\delta_X = .28$. Had there been no error in the treatment identification, the statistical power would have been 51%. Instead, it is 28%, reduced by nearly half.

If the reliability of the treatment variable is known, then the attenuation effect can be corrected. The formula is the usual psychometric formula for correction for attenuation due to error in the independent variable:

$$r_{TY} = r_{XY} / \sqrt{r_{XX}} \qquad (6.3)$$

This correction works perfectly at the population correlation level. However, the correction at the sample data level corrects for only the systematic attenuation. It does not correct for the increased sampling error introduced by the measurement error. The significance test on the corrected correlation is algebraically equivalent to the significance test on the uncorrected correlation.

In the previous example of attitude change experiment, errors of measurement in the independent variable had two effects: (1) Within both the experimental and control groups, the within-group variance on the dependent variable was increased, and (2) the raw score mean difference on the dependent variable was reduced, that is, $\bar{Y}_E - \bar{Y}_C$, was reduced. In such a case, the observed d value will be reduced for two reasons: because the numerator is reduced and because the denominator is increased. There are other cases of measurement error in the independent variable in which the numerator, $\bar{Y}_E - \bar{Y}_C$, is unaffected but the denominator, the pooled within-group SD, is inflated, leading to artifactually lowered estimates of d.

For example, suppose an experiment is conducted to determine the effect of personal attention and sympathetic listening by work counselors on the job-related attitudes of problem employees. Each member of the experimental group is supposed to get 12 hours of personal interaction (six 2-hour sessions) with a counselor. However, because of interruptions of scheduled sessions, lateness, and other problems, some people in each study get less than that: some 10 and some 11 hours. Because some counselors run past the stopping time without realizing it, other members of the experimental group get more than 12 hours: some 13 and some 14 hours. The average amount of time might be approximately correct: 12 hours. If the impact of treatment strength differences is approximately linear over the range of variation in the study (true in most cases), then the average effect will be determined by the average treatment strength. The individual variations will cancel out, and the mean of the treatment group will be the same as if there had been no variation in treatment. Thus, the numerator of the effect size formula for d (i.e., $\bar{Y}_E - \bar{Y}_C$) will not be affected. However, the individual variations in treatment strength will cause variations in outcome that will contribute to variation in the dependent variable. Thus, the denominator of the effect size will be larger than would be true if there were no variation in treatment strength. If the denominator of the effect size were increased, then the effect size would be reduced. Thus, within-study variation in treatment strength that has no effect on $\bar{Y}_E - \bar{Y}_C$ nevertheless reduces the effect size.

Furthermore, because the extent of within-study variation is likely to differ from one study to the next, failure to correct for attenuation due to treatment variation will lead to artificial variation in effect size across studies. This uncorrected variation could be falsely interpreted as showing the existence of a nonexistent moderator variable.

Variation in the treatment effect increases the experimental group standard deviation but does not change the control group standard deviation. The increase in the experimental group standard deviation increases the pooled within-group standard deviation and, hence, reduces the observed effect size value. However, this artificial increase in the experimental standard deviation could also cause another error. If there were no true treatment-by-subject interaction and if there were no variation in the treatment effect across subjects, then the control and experimental group standard deviations would be equal. The artificial increase in the experimental group standard deviation might be falsely interpreted as an indication of a treatment-by-subject interaction. That is, it appears that subjects in the experimental group are reacting differently to the same treatment (causing SD_E to be larger than SD_C), when, in fact, the cause of the larger SD_E is the fact that different subjects in the experimental group are by mistake receiving treatments of different intensity or duration.

If there is no true treatment-by-subject interaction, then the increase in the experimental group standard deviation can be used to quantify the impact of treatment variation. If there is no interaction, then the desired effect size is

$$\delta = (\bar{Y}_E - \bar{Y}_C)/SD_C \tag{6.4}$$

The observed population effect size is

$$\delta_o = (\bar{Y}_E - \bar{Y}_C)/SD_W \tag{6.5}$$

The two effect sizes differ by

$$\delta_o = a\delta \tag{6.6}$$

where the attenuation factor a is given by

$$a = SD_C/SD_W \tag{6.7}$$

For equal sample sizes, the attenuation factor can be computed from the ratio comparing the experimental and control group standard deviations. Denote the standard deviation comparison ratio by v. That is, define v by

$$v = SD_E/SD_C \tag{6.8}$$

Then the within-group standard deviation is related to v by

$$SD_W = \sqrt{[(SD_C^2 + SD_E^2)/2]} = SD_C\sqrt{[(1+v^2)/2]} \qquad (6.9)$$

Thus,

$$a = SD_C / SD_W = 1/\sqrt{[(1+v^2)/2]} \qquad (6.10)$$

If v is not much larger than 1, then we have the approximation

$$a = 1 - (v^2 - 1)/2 \qquad (6.11)$$

In summary, within-study variation in treatment strength causes an inflation in the experimental dependent variable standard deviation. Even if there is no real treatment-by-subject interaction, variation in treatment strength causes the experimental group standard deviation to be artificially larger than the control group standard deviation. If treatment variation is not suspected, then this increase could be falsely interpreted as indicating a treatment-by-subject interaction. If it is known that there is no interaction, then the attenuation in the effect size can be computed from a comparison ratio of the experimental to control group standard deviation.

Variation Across Studies in Treatment Strength

In the preceding example, the mean raw score treatment effect, $\bar{Y}_E - \bar{Y}_C$, is the same in all studies. In other cases, however, this value may vary across the studies in a meta-analysis—because the amount of treatment given to the experimental group in different studies might differ, causing $\bar{Y}_E$ to vary across studies. If these differences are known (i.e., if they are given in each study), they can be coded and treated as a potential moderator variable. If the strength of treatment values is not known, however, then variation in treatment strength will produce variation in effect sizes that cannot be accounted for. This variation could cause an actually homogeneous treatment effect to appear to be heterogeneous and, thus, suggest a nonexistent moderator variable. (Alternatively, the effects of variation in treatment strength will be confounded with the real moderator variable.)

Consider an example. Suppose in a *series* of studies evaluating a new training method, the experimental group was supposed to get 10 hours of training in each study. Due to administrative and communications problems, however, the experimental people in some studies get 8, 9, 11, or 12 hours of training; although, *within* each study, each subject received exactly the same number of hours of training, only some of the studies hit exactly the desired 10 hours. If the mean across studies is 10 hours, then the mean effect size for the meta-analysis will not be affected. However, the variation in training time across studies will create additional variance in effect sizes beyond that created by sampling error. The formulas presented in this book do not correct for this. If the number of training hours is given in each study, this variable can be coded and analyzed as a moderator. However, this information would rarely be given because the deviations from 10 hours all represent errors in carrying out the training plan—errors that the experimenters themselves may not even be aware of.

In the example here, average treatment strength across studies was equal to the target value of 10 hours. This is what would be expected if the measurement error were random. If the mean were discrepant from the goal—say, 9 hours instead of 10—then the mean effect size *would* be affected, as well as the variance. However, in this example, we assume a mean (expected value) of 0 for the measurement errors.

This form of measurement error is analogous to unintended differences between studies in range restriction in correlational studies, that is, differences in range restriction (or enhancement) that might appear despite the fact that researchers took special steps to obtain the same variation in all studies, just as the experimenters attempted here to have exactly the same treatment across studies. In many meta-analyses, the strength of treatment conditions will vary across studies, not because of measurement error, but because the different experimenters did not have a common goal for treatment strength to begin with. This condition is closely analogous to the naturally occurring range variation that occurs across correlational studies. (In the experimental studies, the control group is the same in all studies, anchoring the low end of the independent variable, but the high end of the independent variable varies from study to study, and hence the variance of the independent variable varies from study to study.) As noted and illustrated earlier, this problem can be addressed by a moderator analysis when the needed information on treatment strength is given in individual studies. However, this information will often not be given.

Range Variation on the Dependent Variable

The raw score treatment effect is determined by the nature of the treatment process. Thus, if the same process is used in different settings, it should stay about the same. However, the standard deviation of the study group is not determined by the treatment process but by the nature of the selection of the group in question. Thus, the study population might be more homogeneous in some settings than in others. The standardized treatment effect would vary correspondingly.

Consider an attitude change study done on a polarized political topic. Initial attitudes would be much more homogeneous in a group of Republicans than in a politically unselected population. Assume that the standard deviation among Republicans is only half the size of the standard deviation in a mixed population, say $\sigma = 50$ in the mixed population and $\sigma = 25$ for Republicans. If the change produced by the message is 10 points in raw score form, then a study done on a mixed population would produce a standardized effect size of $10/50 = .20$, while the same study done on a Republican population would produce a standardized effect size of $10/25 = .40$, a standardized effect size twice as large.

From the viewpoint of statistical power, there is a considerable advantage to doing a study using a more homogeneous population. Consider the political attitude example again. The investigator doing the study on a general population would have an effect size of $\delta = .20$, while the same study done on a Republican population would have an effect size of $\delta = .40$. Given a study sample size of $N = 100$, the statistical power for the study on a general population would be 17%, while the power on the homogeneous population would be 51%, three times higher.

The investigator studying the general population could have obtained a similar gain in power by breaking his data down into Republicans and Democrats and then properly merging the results from the two within-group comparisons. This is the gain in power that results from analysis of covariance, or use of the "treatment by levels" design.

For purposes of meta-analysis, let us choose some population as a reference population. We want all effect sizes expressed in terms of that reference population. To do so, we must know the ratio of the standard deviation of the study population to the standard deviation of the reference population. Denote the standard deviations of the two populations by

σ_P = standard deviation of the reference population,

σ_S = standard deviation of the study population.

The ratio of study to reference standard deviations is denoted u; that is,

$$u = \sigma_S / \sigma_P \qquad (6.12)$$

If the raw score treatment effect is the same in both populations, then the standardized treatment effect in the study population is given by

$$\delta_S = \delta_P / u \qquad (6.13)$$

That is, the more homogeneous the study population in comparison to the reference population, the larger the study effect size.

To correct for range variation, we need merely use the preceding equation in reverse order; that is,

$$\delta_P = u\delta_S \qquad (6.14)$$

In meta-analysis, this formula could be used to correct each of the study effect sizes to the same reference population value and, thus, eliminate differences in effect size due to differences in homogeneity. However, this correction requires that the same scale of measurement for the dependent variable be used in all studies. This is rarely the case, so this correction usually cannot be made.

Dichotomization of the Dependent Variable Measure

In some studies, a continuous dependent variable is dichotomized. For example, in research on the effect of a realistic job preview on subsequent turnover, most investigators do not use the natural dependent variable of tenure, the length of time the worker stays with the firm. Instead, they dichotomize tenure to create a binary "turnover" variable; for example, they might see whether a worker stays more than 6 months or not. The loss of information inherent in dichotomization causes a reduction in the effect size and a corresponding loss in statistical power (Hunter & Schmidt, 1990b; MacCallum et al., 2002). Within a wide range of values, this artificial reduction in effect size can be corrected. However, within a single study, the statistical correction formula does *not* restore the higher level of statistical power.

Denote the treatment variable by T and denote the continuous dependent variable by Y. Denote the dichotomized dependent variable by Y'. The effect of the dichotomization is to replace the correlation r_{TY} by the correlation $r_{TY'}$, which is lower in magnitude. The statistical significance test is then done on the smaller $r_{TY'}$ with correspondingly lower power. What we seek is a correction formula that restores the value $r_{TY'}$ to the value r_{TY}. There is an approximate formula that works at the population level. Application of that formula at the sample level eliminates the systematic error in the correlation, but does not eliminate the larger sampling error that arises from the loss in information due to dichotomization. The formula works well in meta-analysis because meta-analysis causes the impact of sampling error to be greatly reduced.

For a cross-sectional correlation, dichotomization of the dependent variable reduces the correlation by a product rule formula similar to that for attenuation due to error of measurement. The correction formula is known as that which creates a biserial correlation from a point biserial correlation. This formula does not work for treatment correlations because the dependent variable does not have a normal distribution. The treatment effect causes the distribution of the experimental group to be displaced from that of the control group. When the two groups are pooled, the combination distribution is not normal. To see this, consider the extreme case in which the treatment effect is 3 standard deviations in magnitude. The two distributions hardly overlap, and the combined distribution is distinctly bimodal—one mode at each of the subgroup means.

However, we will show that the biserial correlation formula works quite well as an approximation over the usual range of effect sizes and distribution splits. This corresponds to the fact that the combined distribution is approximately normal unless the treatment effect is very large. Suppose that in the combined groups, the proportion of people in the "high" split is p while the proportion in the "low" split is $q = 1 - p$. For a normal distribution, there would be a z value corresponding to such a split (although the combined distribution is not exactly normal). Call this value the cutoff value and denote it by c. The value of the normal density function or normal ordinate at c is denoted $\varphi(c)$. The attenuation in the treatment correlation is approximately given by the biserial attenuation formula

$$r_{TY'} = a r_{TY} \qquad (6.15)$$

where

$$a = \varphi(c) / \sqrt{pq} \qquad (6.16)$$

The corresponding correction formula is the biserial formula

$$r_{TY} = r_{TY'} / a \qquad (6.17)$$

The range over which the formula is accurate is shown in Table 6.3. Table 6.3 presents the comparison ratio for the actual continuous variable correlation and the attenuated dichotomous variable correlation corrected using the biserial correction formula. The ratio is in the order corrected/actual and is expressed as a percentage. For example, for a population continuous $d = .40$ and a median split on the combined population $p = .50$, the ratio is 101. That is, whereas the actual continuous treatment correlation is $r_{TY} = .20$, the corrected dichotomized correlation is $1.01(.20) = .202$, an error less than rounding error. The error is always less than rounding error for the range of values $-.51 < d < +.51$ and $.09 < p < .91$, the range of values in most current meta-analyses. For the most extreme case in Table 6.3, $d = 1.10$ and $p = .90$, the actual correlation is .48 and the corrected correlation is $.93(.48) = .45$, an error that is visible but still not large in practical terms.

Imperfect Construct Validity in the Dependent Variable Measure

Suppose there is some systematic error in the measurement of the dependent variable; that is, we measure a dependent variable that is different to some extent from the intended dependent variable. What effect will this

Table 6.3   Comparison ratio of corrected/actual correlations—expressed as percentages—where the corrected correlation is the estimated correlation for the continuous dependent variable computed by correcting the dichotomous variable correlation using the biserial correction formula.

	Combined proportion p "high" on the dependent variable								
d	.10	.20	.30	.40	.50	.60	.70	.80	.90
10	100	100	100	100	100	100	100	100	100
.20	100	100	100	100	100	100	100	100	100
.30	100	100	101	101	101	101	101	100	100
.40	99	100	101	101	101	101	101	100	99
.50	99	101	101	102	102	102	101	101	99
.60	98	101	102	103	103	103	102	101	98
.70	97	101	103	104	104	104	103	101	97
.80	96	101	103	105	105	105	103	101	96
.90	95	101	104	106	106	106	104	101	95
1.00	94	101	105	107	107	107	105	101	94
1.10	93	101	105	108	109	108	105	101	93

Note: The statistic *d* is the population effect size for the continuous variable, that is, approximately twice the value of the population continuous variable treatment correlation.

have on the effect size and can it be corrected? A full treatment of this problem requires considerable knowledge of path analysis and knowledge of the nature of the dependent variable and its relationships with other variables. However, certain common cases are relatively straightforward.

The most common case is the use of a dependent variable that is an indirect measure of the desired dependent variable. For example, a good assessment of a juvenile delinquency treatment program would require an objective assessment of the subsequent behavior of the clients. Instead, investigators must often rely on indirect measures such as the subsequent arrest record. Figure 6.2 shows the assumed path model of the relationships between the two measures of behavior and the treatment variable.

Let Y be the measure of the client's actual delinquent behavior and let Y' be the arrest record. The desired treatment effect correlation r_{TY} is related to the observed treatment correlation by the product rule

$$r_{TY'} = r_{TY}\, r_{YY'} \tag{6.18}$$

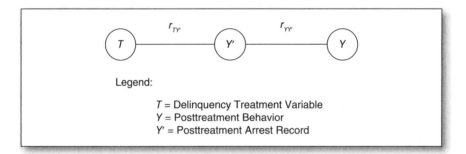

Figure 6.2 Path model for the relationship among the delinquency treatment program, the desired measure of actual posttreatment behavior, and the observed posttreatment arrest record.

Legend:

T = Delinquency Treatment Variable
Y = Posttreatment Behavior
Y' = Posttreatment Arrest Record

If the correlation between behavior and arrest were only $r_{YY'} = .30$, then the treatment correlation would be attenuated to

$$r_{TY'} = .30r_{TY}$$

that is, attenuated by 70%. In this case, the observed correlation could be corrected by reversing the algebraic equation

$$r_{TY} = r_{TY'} / r_{YY'} \qquad (6.19)$$

The corrected d statistic would then be obtained by transforming this corrected correlation. In the delinquency example, the correction would be

$$r_{TY} = r_{TY'} / .30$$

The observed correlation must be more than tripled in this case to correct for the imperfect construct validity. If the observed d statistic were $d_{Y'} = .12$, then $r_{TY'} = .06$, which corrects to $r_{TY} = .06/.30 = .20$ and, hence, to $d_Y = .40$.

Although the treatment correlation, or d statistic, can be corrected to eliminate the systematic reduction in the correlation produced by imperfect construct validity, the effect of increased sampling error cannot be corrected. The confidence interval around the corrected correlation is $1/.30 = 3.33$ times as wide as that for the uncorrected correlation, reflecting the increased sampling error caused by the correction. The significance test for the corrected effect size is algebraically equivalent to the significance test for the uncorrected effect size and, hence, has the same p value.

Imperfect construct validity does not always reduce the size of the effect size. Consider social skills training for supervisors. Assessment of the training program would ideally require measuring the interactive skills of the trainee after the program. Instead, the only available measure might be a measure of how well the person mastered the training program. However, mastery of the material is only antecedent to behavior change; it may take time or special experience for the trainee to put that learning into operation. The path model for this hypothesis is shown in Figure 6.3.

Figure 6.3   Path model for the assumed relationship among the social skills training of supervisors, program mastery, and subsequent interpersonal behavior on the job.

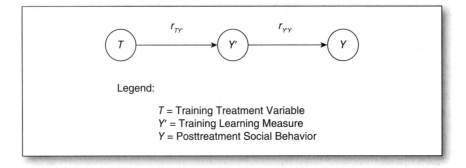

Legend:

T = Training Treatment Variable
Y' = Training Learning Measure
Y = Posttreatment Social Behavior

The desired treatment correlation r_{TY} and the observed treatment correlation $r_{TY'}$ are related by the product rule

$$r_{TY} = r_{TY'} r_{Y'Y} \tag{6.20}$$

If the correlation between the cognitive learning measure and subsequent social behavior was only $r_{Y'Y} = .30$, then the desired correlation r_{TY} would be lower than the observed correlation $r_{TY'}$:

$$r_{TY} = .30 r_{TY'}$$

This product rule is itself the correction formula for the treatment correlation. The correction for the d statistic is obtained by transforming the corrected treatment correlation to a d value.

Imperfect Construct Validity in the Treatment Variable

Imperfect construct validity in the treatment variable is a confounding of the intended treatment effect with an effect due to some other causal agent. This problem can be attacked using path analysis (Hunter, 1986, 1987), and, under certain conditions, it can be corrected in a manner that could be used in meta-analysis. Correction of confounding requires the use of a multiple dependent variable design where an intervening variable is observed that measures the process induced by the confounding causal agent. The desired correlation is then the partial correlation between the treatment variable and the dependent variable with the intervening variable held constant. This approach is a rigorous, quantitative replacement for an analysis of covariance with the intervening variable used as a concomitant variable (Hunter, 1988). Detailed treatment of this method is beyond the scope of the present book.

Bias in the Effect Size (d Statistic)

The effect size statistic is subject to a statistical phenomenon known by the forbidding title "bias." For sample sizes greater than 20, bias is trivial in magnitude. However, there have been articles arguing that a major problem with meta-analysis is the use of "biased methods." This section presents a correction for bias, although the primary intent of the section is to show that the bias is of trivial magnitude.

Consider a set of perfectly replicated studies, all with the same sample size and the same population effect size. The average sample effect size will differ slightly from the population effect size. This discrepancy is called "bias" in the statistical estimation literature. The size of the bias depends on the sample size. The bias is in different directions for the effect size statistic d and the treatment correlation r. The average d is slightly larger than δ while the average correlation is slightly smaller than ρ.

A complete treatment of bias in the treatment correlation is given by Hunter et al. (1996), who showed that the bias is trivial in all but very small sample studies and small for small-sample studies. Some authors have suggested using the Fisher's z transformation to reduce the bias, but the bias using Fisher's z turns out to be even larger, although in the opposite direction, as discussed in more detail in Chapter 5.

The bias in the treatment correlation is given by

$$E(r) = a\rho \tag{6.21}$$

where

$$a = 1 - (1 - \rho^2)/(2N - 2) \tag{6.22}$$

How small is this bias? Consider perfectly replicated studies with a population correlation of $\rho = .20$ and a sample size of $N = 100$. The multiplier for the average observed correlation would be $a = 1 - .00485 = .995$. The average correlation would be .199 instead of .200. The trivial size of the bias in the correlation is the reason that bias has traditionally been ignored. However, for very small sample size meta-analyses (average sample size less than 10), or for very fastidious analysts, it is possible to correct the observed treatment correlation for bias. The nonlinear correction corresponding to the preceding equation would be

$$r' = r / a$$

where

$$a = 1 - (1 - r^2) / (2N - 2) \qquad (6.23)$$

If the meta-analysis is studying treatment correlations below .70 in magnitude (the usual case), then the correction is very closely approximated by the linear correction

$$r' = r/a$$

where

$$a = (2N - 3) / (2N - 2) \qquad (6.24)$$

The linear correction has the advantage that it can be applied *after* the meta-analysis. One need only divide both the estimated mean and the estimated standard deviation of population correlations by the multiplier computed with N set at the average sample size. Note that the corrected correlation will be trivially larger than the uncorrected correlation.

A complete treatment of bias in the d statistic is given in Hedges and Olkin (1985). Although the bias is trivial for all but very small sample studies, they recommend routine correction for that bias. Indeed, they use the symbol d only for the corrected statistic. The bias in d is approximately given by

$$E(d) = a\delta \qquad (6.25)$$

where

$$a = 1 + 3 / (4N - 12) \qquad (6.26)$$

How large is this bias? Consider a study with a textbook-sized effect $d =$ .40 based on a sample size of $N = 100$. The multiplier is $a = 1 + .0077 = 1.0077$. The average study effect size would be .403 instead of .400. On the other hand, consider a study done with an extremely small sample size, say, $N = 10$ (five subjects in each group). The multiplier would be $a = 1 + .107 = 1.107$ and the average effect size would be .443 rather than .400. The correction is straightforward; just divide by a:

$$d' = d / a \qquad (6.27)$$

The programs for *d* value meta-analysis described in the Appendix to this book incorporate this correction. Note that this is a linear correction. Thus, it could be applied *after* the meta-analysis. Just divide both the estimated mean and the estimated standard deviation of corrected *d* values by the multiplier *a*. The *N* used should be the average *N*. The corrected effect sizes will be slightly smaller than the uncorrected effect sizes.

Recording, Computational, and Transcriptional Errors

Meta-analysis will inevitably include some studies with bad data. There might be a recording error in gathering the primary data or in entering it into the computer. The study effect size could be erroneous because of computational error or an error in algebraic sign in the effect size. Finally, error can arise in transcription: from computer output to analyst table, from analyst table to manuscript table, from manuscript table to published table. Some have even suggested that a meta-analyst might miscopy a figure, but it is well known that meta-analysts do not make errors.

Study results should be examined for extreme outliers. This can eliminate the most extreme cases of bad data. However, keep in mind the caveats about outlier analysis in meta-analysis presented in Chapters 3 and 5. Also, even with an outlier analysis, smaller erroneous effect sizes will not be detectable. Thus, any meta-analysis with a very large number of effect sizes will usually have at least a few bad data points.

Because bad data cannot be completely avoided, it is important to consider variation in study results with some caution. A certain percentage of the original observed variation will be due to bad data. A larger proportion of the residual variation—that left after all other study artifacts have been corrected—may be due to bad data.

Multiple Artifacts and Corrections

Unfortunately, there is no rule that says that study results can be distorted by only one artifact. Sampling error will be present in all studies. Error of measurement in the dependent variable will be present in all studies. Imperfect control of the nominal treatment variable will be unavoidable in most studies. Thus, a meta-analysis free of artifact will usually require that effect sizes be corrected for a number of sources of error.

Other than the removal of the most extreme outliers, there is no correction for bad data. Sampling error acts differently from other artifacts in that it is (1) additive and (2) unsystematic. Although a confidence interval for the effect size provides an unbiased estimate of potential sampling error for the single study, there can be no *correction* for sampling error at the level of the single study. We consider correcting the problem of sampling error in meta-analysis in d values in the next chapter.

The artifacts other than sampling error and bad data are systematic in nature and, thus, potentially correctable. Corrections for the biases created by these artifacts are necessary to obtain unbiased estimates of actual d values (Hedges, 2009a; Matt & Cook, 2009; Schmidt, Le, & Oh, 2009). The key is to have the necessary information about the size of the artifact process (e.g., knowledge of the extent of unreliability or the extent of range restriction or the extent of imperfect construct validity). You can correct each artifact where there is adequate artifact information, be this one artifact or seven. Every artifact left uncorrected results in a corresponding underestimate of the true effect size. Furthermore, variation in uncorrected artifacts across studies looks like true variance in treatment effect. This may create the appearance of between-study variation where there is none. If there is true variation in treatment effect, then uncorrected artifacts mask the true differences. That is, variation in apparent effect size due to uncorrected artifacts may override the differences due to true moderator variables and, thus, make it difficult to identify the true moderator variable by examining the studies after the fact.

Correction for artifacts is not difficult if the information on each artifact is given. Consider an example: a study of social skills training for first-line supervisors conducted in a factory setting. The measure of job performance is performance ratings by the immediate manager of each supervisor on a single 100-point graphic rating scale. Because the investigator doubted that performance ratings are measured on a ratio scale (a fact), the investigator decided that parametric statistics could not be used (a statistical error on his part). So the investigator decided to do a sign test on the data. The combined group data were split at the median and a chi-square test was run comparing the proportion of above-average performers among the supervisors with and without the skills training. Assume the treatment effect for training on consensus performance ratings is $d_{TY} = .40$. The true population treatment correlation is thus $r_{TY} = .20$. The interrater reliability of performance ratings by a single supervisor on a single rating scale averages .28 (Hunter & Hirsh, 1987; King et al., 1980). Thus, the effect size is reduced from $d_{TY} = .40$ to

$$d_{TY'} = \sqrt{.28}\, d_{TY} = .53 d_{TY} = .53(.40) = .21$$

For a study with a total sample size of 100, this reduction would reduce statistical power from an already low 51% to a very low 18%. The effect of a dichotomization using a median split for a d value less than .50 is simply to decrease the value by 20%; that is,

$$d_{TY''} = .80 d_{TY'} = .80(.21) = .17$$

This reduces the statistical power from a very low 18% to an even lower 13%. That is, the two artifacts together reduce the effect size from .40 to .17, less than half its proper value. The statistical power is reduced from an already undesirable 51% to only 13%, an increase in the error rate for the significance test from 49% to 87%.

The systematic effect of the artifacts can be eliminated from the study by correction formulas. We have

$$d_{TY} = d_{TY'} / .53 = (d_{TY''} / .80) / .53 = d_{TY''} / .424$$
$$= 2.36 d_{TY''}$$

That is, if the artifacts reduce the size of the effect by 58%, we can restore the value by dividing by the corresponding factor .42. However, while this correction eliminates the systematic error in the effect size, it does not eliminate the increased sampling error. A proper statistical test on the corrected effect size gives the same p values as the test on the uncorrected effect size. Thus, statistical correction formulas do not restore the lost statistical power.

Consider the preceding example in abstract form. The effect of the first artifact is to multiply the effect size by a multiplicative factor a_1 as in

$$d' = a_1 d \qquad (6.28)$$

The effect of the second artifact is to multiply by a second factor a_2 as in

$$d'' = a_2 d' \qquad (6.29)$$

The impact of the two factors is

$$d'' = a_2 d' = a_2 (a_1) d = a_1 a_2 d \qquad (6.30)$$

namely, to multiply the effect size by a multiplicative factor a, which is the product of the two separate artifact multipliers. That is,

$$d'' = ad \qquad (6.31)$$

where

$$a = a_1 a_2$$

The effect size is then restored to its original value by the correction formula

$$d = d'' / a \qquad (6.32)$$

The preceding example is typical of correction for multiple artifacts in effect sizes of moderate size. Each artifact reduces the effect size by a multiplicative factor. The net effect is to reduce the effect size by a multiplicative factor that is the product of the separate multipliers. That is, the attenuating effect of several artifacts is to reduce the effect size by the product of the separate attenuating factors. The corresponding correction restores the effect size to its original size by dividing by the attenuation multiplier.

There is one caveat to the preceding discussion: It is exactly true for the treatment correlation but only an approximation for the effect size d. If a treatment effect is so large that the approximation $d = 2r$ breaks down, then the multiplicative formula above should be applied only to the treatment correlation. The treatment effect d can then be computed by the usual formula for converting r to d.

For example, consider the social skills training example for a very large treatment effect, say, $d = 1.50$. The observed treatment correlation satisfies the attenuation equation

$$r_{TY''} = .42 r_{TY}$$

The effect size $d = 1.50$ corresponds to a treatment correlation of .60. The artifacts reduce this correlation from .60 to

$$r_{TY''} = .42(.60) = .25$$

This attenuated treatment correlation corresponds to an attenuated effect size of $d = .52$. The attenuation in the d statistic is from 1.50 to .52, which is by a factor of .35 rather than the factor .42 for the treatment correlation.

The treatment of multiple artifacts is very straightforward for the treatment correlation. The reduction in the size of the treatment correlation by a series of artifacts is effected by multiplication of the correlation by a total multiplier that is the product of the separate artifact attenuation multipliers. The treatment correlation can be restored to its proper size by correcting for those artifacts by dividing by the attenuation multiplier.

For the d statistic, correction for artifacts is only slightly more difficult. If the unattenuated population d value falls in the moderate range $-.50 < d < +.50$, then the formulas for the treatment correlation apply directly to the d statistic. If the population effect size falls outside the moderate range, then the d value can be converted to a correlation, the correlation can be corrected, and the corrected correlation can be converted to a corrected d value.

These examples refer to single value of d. In the next chapter, we describe how to conduct d value meta-analysis via the meta-analysis methods for correlations described in Chapters 3 and 4. This should always be done whenever any of the observed d values to be meta-analyzed are larger than .50. But this procedure works well even when no d values exceed .50. It is simply easier to correct for multiple artifacts when the meta-analysis is conducted with the correlation as the metric. Afterward, the correlational meta-analysis results can be transformed back to the d values metric. As shown in Chapter 7, both the meta-analytic mean and the corrected SD can be transformed into the d value metric.

Meta-Analysis Methods for *d* Values

7

This chapter presents the meta-analysis formulas for effect sizes from experimental studies. The effect size (or *d* value) is the standardized mean difference between two groups. Effect sizes can also be used to index the size of group differences in observational studies. In this chapter, we considers only the posttest independent groups experimental designs. In such designs, different people are assigned to different treatment groups, hence the label "independent groups" designs. The next chapter considers "within-subjects" or repeated measures designs, ANOVA (analysis of variance) designs, and ANCOVA (analysis of covariance) designs. Studies with more than two levels for a treatment variable could be handled within the present framework using contrasts, but this is beyond the scope of the present book.

As discussed in textbooks on research design, the key difference between experimental and observational studies is that in experimental studies, subjects are randomly assigned to treatments. The control of extraneous influences on study outcomes achieved by random assignment cannot always be fully duplicated by the statistical controls that can be used in observational (nonexperimental) studies. It is random assignment that allows confident inference of causality in single experimental studies. In this chapter, our primary focus is on experimental studies, but the *d* statistic can also be used with observational data, and we discuss such usages in some detail. However, the reader should bear in mind the fundamental distinction between experimental and observational research. Even when the two types of research examine the same questions under apparently similar conditions, the obtained results can sometimes be different (see, e.g., Heinsman & Shadish, 1996; Shadish & Ragsdale, 1996).

In Chapters 5 and 8, we present discussions of the distinction between random effects and fixed effects models of meta-analysis. Briefly, fixed effects models assume a priori that there is no variation in population parameters (in this case, population d values or δ values) across studies. If this assumption is erroneous, meta-analysis results can be very inaccurate. Random effects models, by contrast, allow for variability across studies in underlying population parameter values and provide methods for estimating the magnitude of this variability. As noted in Chapters 5 and 8, most of the meta-analyses published in *Psychological Bulletin* over the past 30 years are based on fixed effects models and for that reason are likely to be inaccurate. *For this reason, we want to emphasize that all the meta-analysis methods presented in this chapter for d values are random effects models.* No fixed effects models are presented.

Independent groups studies could be analyzed using correlations. The size of the treatment effect could be measured by the (point biserial) correlation between treatment and effect. This use of correlation to measure the treatment effect has the advantage of lending itself to multivariate techniques such as partial correlation, multiple regression, and path analysis. However, most meta-analysts have chosen to use a measure of effect size denoted d, the difference between the group means divided by the pooled standard deviation. It matters little because either statistic can be algebraically transformed into the other. Later in this chapter, we will see that the most convenient way to conduct a meta-analysis of d values, especially when there are multiple artifacts to be corrected for, is to first transform the d values to point biserial correlations, conduct the meta-analysis in the r metric, and then transform the results back into the d metric.

Where the outcome (dependent) variable is dichotomous (e.g., died or lived), another statistic, the odds ratio, can be used. The odds ratio is frequently used in medical research, where there are often true dichotomies (e.g., patient lived vs. patient died; has the disease vs. does not have the disease). We do not present meta-analysis methods for the odds ratio statistic in this book, because it is rarely used in social science research. The reason is that our dependent variables are rarely true dichotomies. Another problem with the odds ratio is that research consumers, whether researchers or practicing professionals (e.g., physicians), almost invariably severely misinterpret the meaning of the results (Gigerenzer, 2007; Gigerenzer, Gaissmaier, Kurz-Milcke, Schwartz, & Woloshin, 2007). See Haddock et al. (1998) and Borenstein et al. (2009) for treatment of the odds ratio in meta-analysis. If the original studies to be meta-analyzed report their findings in terms of the odds ratio, there is a simple way to convert the odds ratio to the d value metric for use in meta-analysis (Chinn, 2000). Odds ratios and similar dichotomous statistics are discussed in more detail in Chapter 9.

The reader who starts this book with this chapter is cautioned that many important issues regarding the d statistic are discussed in Chapter 6. Chapter 6 should be read before this chapter. The reader is also cautioned that this chapter is less detailed than Chapters 3 and 4 because many explanations are identical to the corresponding explanation for the meta-analysis of *r* and are not repeated here for want of space. That is, to avoid repetition, many conceptual issues discussed in Chapters 3 and 4 are not repeated in this chapter.

The *d* statistic is affected by all the same artifacts as the correlation, including sampling error, error of measurement, and range variation, but the terminology is the same only for sampling error. Many experimenters believe that error of measurement in the dependent variable is irrelevant in experiments because it averages out in the group means. However, error of measurement enters the variance of the dependent variable and, hence, enters the denominator of *d*. Thus, the value of *d* is systematically lowered by error of measurement, and differences across studies in the reliability of the dependent variable produce spurious differences in the value of *d*.

Error of measurement in the independent variable is also not acknowledged by most experimenters. In their mind, persons are unequivocally assigned to one treatment group or the other. However, those who have used manipulation checks in experiments have found that what is nominally the same treatment for all may be a very different thing to different persons. Some hear the instructions while some do not. Some give one meaning to ambiguous instructions while others give another. Error of measurement in the independent and dependent variables was discussed in Chapter 6. It is also discussed in more detail later in this chapter.

Range variation goes under another name in experimental work, namely, "strength of treatment." In dichotomous experiments, the independent variable is scored 0–1, regardless of how strong the treatment is. However, if differences in treatments across studies can be coded, then treatment effects can be projected onto a common reference strength and the results of different studies become comparable. However, studies often do not give the information needed to code for treatment strength. The resulting problems are discussed later (see also Chapter 6).

Effect Size Indexes: *d* and *r*

Consider an intervention such as training managers in interpersonal skills. The effect of such an intervention might be assessed by comparing the performance of managers who have had such training (the experimental group) with the performance of comparable managers who have not (the control group). The usual comparison statistic is *t* (or *F*, which, in this context, is just the square of *t*, i.e., $F = t^2$). However, this is a very poor statistic because its size depends on the amount of sampling error in the data. The optimal statistic (which measures size of effect in a metric suitable for path analysis or analysis of covariance or other effects) is the point biserial correlation *r*. The great advantage of the point biserial correlation is that it can be inserted into a correlation matrix in which the intervention is then treated like any other variable. For example, the partial correlation between the intervention and the dependent variable with some prior individual difference variable held constant is equivalent to the corresponding analysis of covariance (Hunter, 1988).

Path analysis can be used to trace the difference between direct and indirect effects of the intervention (Hunter, 1986, 1987). For example, training might enhance the interpersonal skills of supervisors. This, in turn, might increase their subordinates' satisfaction with the supervisor, which, in turn, might cause a decrease in subordinate absenteeism. If this is the case, then path analysis would show the training to have a direct effect only on the supervisors' interpersonal skills, even though the intervention was also having second-order and third-order indirect effects on subordinate satisfaction and absenteeism, respectively.

The theory of sampling error for the point biserial correlation is identical to the theory for the Pearson correlation given in the previous section, except that the point biserial correlation may need to be corrected for unequal sample sizes in the two groups before cumulation (as discussed later).

When one variable is dichotomous, the usual formula for the Pearson product moment correlation will yield the point biserial correlation r_{pb}. Thus, popular statistical packages, such as SPSS and SAS, can be used to compute the point biserial correlation. There are also other formulas for r_{pb}:

$$r_{pb} = (\sqrt{pq})\,(\bar{Y}_E - \bar{Y}_C)/SD_y \qquad (7.1)$$

where $\bar{Y}_E$ is the mean of the experimental group on the continuous (usually the dependent) variable, $\bar{Y}_C$ is the mean for the control group, and p and q are the proportion in the experimental and control groups, respectively. It is important to note that SD_y is *not* the within-group SD used in computing d; SD_y is the pooled standard deviation of *all* scores on the dependent variable. The two groups need not be experimental and control groups; they can be any two groups, for example, males and females or high school graduates and nongraduates. Another formula for r_{pb} is

$$r_{pb} = (\bar{Y}_E - \bar{Y}_T)\sqrt{p/q}\,/SD_y \qquad (7.2)$$

where $\bar{Y}_T$ is the total group mean for the continuous variable, and all other terms are as defined for Equation (7.1).

MAXIMUM VALUE OF POINT BISERIAL r

Many texts (e.g., Nunnally, 1978) state that the maximum value of r_{pb} is not 1.00, as it is for the Pearson correlation, but rather .79. They further state that this is the maximum value only when $p = q = .50$; otherwise, the maximum value is lower than .79. However, this theorem is false for experiments. The implicit assumption in this theorem is that the two groups were formed by dichotomizing a normally distributed variable, such as mental ability. This is the case treated in Chapter 2 under the label "dichotomization." Assume that two variables X and Y have a bivariate normal distribution. If a dichotomous variable X' is formed by splitting the distribution of X, then the correlation between the dichotomous variable X' and Y is equal to the original correlation between X and Y multiplied by a constant, which is at most .79. Hence, the statement that the point biserial correlation is at most .79.

Suppose the two groups in the study are defined as those who are above the median on anxiety versus those below the median on anxiety. The question is, Which group will perform better in an assessment center group exercise? Then, if the continuous anxiety variable had a bivariate normal relationship to the dependent variable, the theorem in Chapters 2 and 3 would apply. If the correlation between the anxiety test and performance on the group task is .30, then the point biserial correlation for the two group mean comparisons will be $(.79)(.30) = .24$.

However, in a typical experiment, the dichotomous variable is defined by treatment groups rather than by splitting some continuous variable. The treatment group is defined by some experimental process. For example, at the end of World War II, some Jews migrated to Israel while other Jews remained in Europe. The two groups were then subjected to the impact of radically different environments. Where the groups are defined by process or treatment differences, the theorem given in Chapter 3 does not apply. Instead, the size of the correlation is determined by the size of the treatment effect. The larger the treatment effect, the higher the correlation. As the treatment effect becomes larger and larger, the implied correlation gets closer and closer to 1.00.

In a purely statistical sense, the difference between the two cases lies in the assumption that the continuous independent variable has a bivariate normal relationship to the continuous dependent variable. That constraint places distinct limits on how far apart the two group means on the dependent variable can be. The largest difference occurs if the continuous variables are perfectly correlated. In this case, the two groups are the top and bottom halves of a normal distribution. The largest difference for such groups occurs if the split is at the mean, a difference of 1.58 standard deviations.

If the groups are defined by a treatment process, then there is no mathematical limit on the size of the difference between the two groups. Consider the impact of education on knowledge of history. Consider first two groups of first graders. One group goes to school for the usual 9 months while the other group goes to school for 10 months. The two distributions are likely to overlap substantially, and the point biserial correlation would be low. On the other hand, consider two groups from a Third World country such as India. One group is raised in a mountain village where children rarely go to school, while the other group is educated in Mumbai where they go all the way through college. There is likely to be no overlap between the two knowledge distributions. The difference could be 100 or 1,000 standard deviations, and the point biserial correlation could be arbitrarily close to 1.00.

THE EFFECT SIZE (d STATISTIC)

Cohen (1977) popularized a transform of the point biserial correlation called the effect size statistic d. The effect size d is the difference between the means in standard score form, that is, the ratio of the difference between the means to the standard deviation. The two variants of the effect size statistic are determined by the two different standard deviations used for the denominator. The standard deviation that will be used here is the pooled within-group standard deviation used in analysis of variance. The alternative is the control group standard deviation as used by Smith and Glass (1977). However, because there is rarely a large difference between the control and experimental group (a comparison that can be separately cumulated), it seems reasonable to use the statistic with the least sampling error. The pooled within-group standard deviation has only about half the sampling error of the control group standard deviation.

If the variance for the experimental group is V_E, the variance for the control group is V_C, and the sample sizes are equal, then the within-group variance V_W is defined by

$$V_W = (V_E + V_C)/2 \qquad (7.3)$$

That is, it is the average of the two within-group variances. If the sample sizes are not equal, then a sample size weighted average could be used:

$$V_W = (N_E V_E + N_C V_C)/(N_E + N_C) \qquad (7.4)$$

where N_E and N_C are the sample sizes for the experimental group and control group, respectively. This is the maximum likelihood estimate of the population within-group variance. As it happens, the most common current analysis of variance formula is the modified formula popularized by Fisher, who chose to use slightly different formulas for his analysis of variance. He weighted each variance by its degrees of freedom, that is, by $N - 1$ instead of N:

$$V_W = [(N_E - 1)V_E + (N_C - 1)V_C]/[(N_E - 1) + (N_C - 1)] \qquad (7.5)$$

In view of this convention, we will use the Fisher formula, although it actually makes little difference.

The effect size statistic d is then defined by

$$d = (Y_E - Y_C)/S_W \qquad (7.6)$$

where S_W is the pooled within-group standard deviation, the square root of the within-group variance. That is, d is the difference between the means divided by the within-group standard deviation.

Most researchers are used to comparing group means using the t statistic. However, the t statistic depends on the sample size and, thus, is not a proper measure of the size of the treatment effect. That is, for purposes of testing a difference for statistical significance, it is true that the larger the sample size, the more statistically significant a given observed difference would be. However, the treatment effect we want to estimate is the population treatment effect, which is defined without reference to sample size. The statistic d can be thought of as a version of t that is made independent of sample size.

The three statistics d, t, and r are all algebraically transformable from one to the other. These transformations are shown here for the special case of equal sample sizes in the two groups, that is, for $N_E = N_C = N/2$, where N is the total sample size for that study. The most common statistic reported is t. Thus, in meta-analysis, we often want to convert t to either d or r. The transformation formulas are

$$d = 2t / \sqrt{N} \qquad (7.7)$$

$$r = t / \sqrt{t^2 + N - 2} \qquad (7.8)$$

For example, if the total sample size is $N = 100$ and the study value of t is 2.52, then

$$d = (2/\sqrt{100})(2.52) = .2(2.52) = .504$$
$$r = 2.52/\sqrt{2.52^2 + 98} = 2.52/\sqrt{104.3504} = .247$$

If the d statistic is given, then it can be transformed to either r or t:

$$r = (d/2)/[(N-2)/N + (d/2)^2]^{1/2} \qquad (7.9)$$

$$t = (\sqrt{N}/2)d \qquad (7.10)$$

For example, reverse the previous case for $N = 100$ and $d = .504$:

$$r = (.504/2)/[98/100 + (.504/2)^2]^{1/2} = .247$$
$$t = (\sqrt{100}/2)d = (10/2)(.504) = 2.52$$

If the point biserial correlation r is given, then

$$d = \sqrt{[(N-2)/N]} 2r / \sqrt{(1-r^2)} \qquad (7.11)$$

$$t = \sqrt{(N-2)}[r / \sqrt{(1-r^2)}] \qquad (7.12)$$

For example, given $N = 100$ and $r = .247$, we have

$$d = \sqrt{(98/100)} 2(.247) / \sqrt{(1-.247^2)} = .505$$
$$t = \sqrt{98}(.247) / \sqrt{(1-.247^2)} = 2.52$$

The value for d is off from .504 by rounding error.

The preceding formulas are complicated by the fact that the Fisher estimate of the within-group variance is used. If the maximum likelihood estimate were used, then the formulas relating r and d are

$$d = 2r / \sqrt{(1-r^2)} \qquad (7.13)$$

$$r = (d/2) / \sqrt{[1+(d/2)^2]} = d / \sqrt{(4+d^2)} \qquad (7.14)$$

These formulas are also quite accurate approximations for the Fisher estimate, except for very small sample sizes.

The d to r and r to d conversions are especially simple for the usual small treatment effect sizes. If $-.4 < d < +.4$ or $-.2 < r < +.2$, then, to a close approximation, we have

$$d = 2r \qquad (7.15)$$

$$r = d/2 \qquad (7.16)$$

The preceding formulas are for the equal sample size case. If the control group and experimental group have different sizes, then the number "2" is replaced by

$$\text{"2"} = 1 / \sqrt{(pq)}$$

where p and q are the proportion of persons in the two groups.

Some studies characterize the outcome in statistics other than t, d, or r. Glass et al. (1981) provided transformation formulas for many such cases. However, the transformed value in such cases will not have the sampling error given by our formulas. In particular, probit transformations yield effect sizes with much larger sampling errors than do our formulas for *d* and *r*. This will lead to undercorrections for sampling error variance for such estimates of *d* and *r*.

CORRECTION OF THE POINT BISERIAL
r FOR UNEQUAL SAMPLE SIZES

Conceptually, the effect size is normally thought of as independent of the sample sizes of the control and experimental groups. However, in a natural environment, the importance of a difference depends on how often it occurs. Because the point biserial correlation was originally derived for natural settings, it is defined so as to depend on the group sample sizes. As it happens, for a given size treatment effect, the correlation is smaller for unequal sample sizes. For sample size differences as large as 90–10 or 10–90, the correlation is smaller by a factor of .60, that is, 40% smaller. Thus, extremely uneven sampling can cause substantial understatement of the correlation.

In a typical experiment, any large difference between the sample sizes is usually caused by resource limitations rather than fundamental frequencies in nature. Thus, the point biserial correlation that we want is the point biserial correlation that we would have gotten had we been able to do the study with equal sample sizes. That is, we would like to "correct" the observed correlation for the attenuation effect of unequal sample sizes. (This correction is similar to correcting a correlation for range restriction, as discussed in Chapters 3 and 4.) The formula for this correction of the point biserial correlations is

$$r_c = ar / \sqrt{[(a^2 - 1)r^2 + 1]} \qquad (7.17)$$

where

$$a = \sqrt{[.25 / pq]} \qquad (7.18)$$

For example, if our study were cut short before we had finished the control group, we might have finished with 90 subjects in the experimental group but only 10 in the control group. We thus have $p = .90$, $q = .10$, and

$$a = \sqrt{.25 / [(.90)(.10)]} = \sqrt{2.7777} = 1.6667$$

If the correlation for the unequal groups were .15, then the equal-group correlation would have been

$$r_c = 1.67(.15) / \sqrt{[(1.67^2 - 1)(.15^2) + 1]} = .246$$

Correcting the point biserial correlation in this manner increases its sampling error variance by the factor $(r_c / r)^2$. The sampling error variance of the corrected correlation is

$$S_{e_c}^2 = (r_c / r)^2 S_e^2$$

where r_c is the corrected correlation, r is the uncorrected correlation, and S_e^2 is the sampling error of the uncorrected correlation. Note that if r_c is entered into the meta-analysis without taking this into account, the meta-analysis will be conservative; that is, it will undercorrect for sampling error and, hence, overestimate the corrected standard deviation of r, that is, SD_ρ. One way to avoid this is to enter a smaller N, a value of N that corresponds to $S_{e_c}^2$. The needed value for N can be computed by solving Equation (3.7) in Chapter 3 for N after setting Var(e) equal to $S_{e_c}^2$. In fact, this procedure should be used whenever a correlation or d value has been corrected or adjusted prior to entry into the computer programs. This equation is given in the last example meta-analysis application in Chapter 4 (Equation [4.3]). It is also given as Equation (8.1) in Chapter 8.

The effect size d is already expressed independently of the two sample sizes, although this poses certain problems for natural groups of quite uneven sizes (such as persons with and without migraine headache).

Kemery, Dunlap, and Griffeth (1988) criticized this correction formula and offered an alternative that first converts the point biserial correlation to a biserial correlation and then converts the biserial correlation to a point biserial with a 50–50 split. The Kemery et al. formulas yield accurate results only if the underlying distribution of the dichotomized variable is normal. Where this does not hold, the results are not accurate. As explained earlier, the normal distribution assumption is usually not appropriate in experiments.

EXAMPLES OF THE CONVERTIBILITY OF r AND d

The d statistic is often used to express the difference between treatment and control groups in experimental studies. Indeed, that is our major focus in this chapter. However, d can also be used to express the difference between any two groups. Differences between naturally occurring groups expressed in d form are often very informative, and the same relationships can be expressed using the point biserial r. For example, females average higher than males on measures of perceptual speed; d is approximately .70. What is the correlation in the population between sex and perceptual speed?

$$r = (d / 2) / \sqrt{\{1 + (d / 2)^2\}} = .35 / 1.05948 = .33$$

Thus, the population correlation is .33. Because men and women are about equal in numbers in the population (i.e., $p \cong q \cong .50$), the value of r computed from d is the same as would be computed from representative samples from the population.

As another example, the sex difference on height in the population is approximately $d = 1.50$. This translates into a population correlation between sex and height of $r = .60$.

Consider another example. In the United States, the difference in academic achievement between black and white students is approximately 1 standard deviation; that is, $d = 1.00$. What is the correlation between race and academic achievement? Consider first the formula assuming equal numbers of blacks and whites (Equation [7.4]):

$$r = 1.00 / \sqrt{4 + 1.00^2} = .45$$

This correlation of .45 is the value that would apply if there were equal numbers of black and white students (i.e., $N_W = N_B$). However, this is not the case; black students are only about 13% of the total. Thus, this value must be adjusted to reflect that fact. The correlation reflecting these unequal frequencies is $r = .32$. Thus, for natural populations, if the two groups have greatly different sizes, the natural correlation is substantially smaller.

In some cases in dealing with naturally occurring groups, one encounters a form of range restriction in d. The effect of this is typically to bias the observed d statistic downward. For example, suppose one is interested in estimating the black-white difference on a cognitive ability test among job applicants but has data only for incumbents. Because incumbents are selected (directly or indirectly) at least in part on cognitive ability, the raw score difference is smaller among incumbents than among applicants. Of course, the variances in each group are also smaller, but the decrease in within-group variances is often not sufficient to prevent an overall downward bias when using the d statistic in the selected (incumbent) group as an estimate of the d statistic in the unselected (applicant group). Bobko, Roth, and Bobko (2001) presented procedures for correcting for such range restriction in d. They provided an equation for correcting when the range restriction is direct (e.g., incumbents have been selected directly on cognitive ability) and another equation for correcting when range restriction is indirect (e.g., incumbents have been selected on some variable correlated with cognitive ability). Because range restriction is almost always indirect (see Chapters 3 and 4), this latter equation will typically be the more appropriate and more accurate, while the equation for direct range restriction will undercorrect. Unfortunately, the information needed to apply their equation for correcting for indirect range restriction will rarely be available (it requires information on the third variable on which the range restriction took place). However, in these circumstances, use of the correction for direct range restriction will nevertheless provide estimates that are more accurate than those obtained when *no* correction is made. See also Roth, BeVier, Bobko, Switzer, and Tyler (2001) and Roth, Bobko, Switzer, and Dean (2001). But as discussed in Chapters 3 and 4, Hunter et al. (2006) provide an alternative procedure for correcting for indirect range restriction that depends only on information that is typically available. That procedure can be used in this situation.

PROBLEMS OF ARTIFICIAL DICHOTOMIZATION

Throughout this chapter, we focus on true binary variables such as the control group versus experimental group distinction. If the binary variable is created by dichotomizing a continuous variable—as when people are classified as "high anxious" or "low anxious" using a median split on a continuous anxiety measure—then it is important to remember that the word *correlation* becomes ambiguous. There is the correlation between the continuous variable and the dependent variable—ingenuously called the "biserial" correlation—and the correlation between the binary variable and the dependent variable—called the "point biserial" correlation. The conversion formulas given in this chapter apply to the point biserial correlation. To convert from d to the continuous correlation, one would first convert from d to the point biserial correlation using Equation (7.14). Then one would convert the point biserial correlation to the biserial correlation using the formula to correct for dichotomization given in Chapters 3 and 6.

In experimental studies, it is common for researchers to define a binary variable such as "anxiety" by a median split on a continuous measure of the dependent variable. If the split is the same across studies, there is no problem in simply ignoring the dichotomization for purposes of the initial meta-analysis. The final values for d can be converted to the biserial correlation if desired. However, if the binary variable is created using different splits across studies, then the point biserial correlation and the corresponding d values will vary across studies artifactually because of the variation in split. In the case of "turnover" studies, the variation can be extreme, for example, 50–50 for one author versus 95–5 for another. In such cases, we recommend that the researcher conduct the meta-analysis on correlations and use the correction formulas from Chapters 3, 4 and 6 to correct for dichotomization.

An Alternative to d: Glass's d

Glass has used a variation on the d statistic. He uses the control group standard deviation instead of the within-group standard deviation. His reason for this is that the treatment may have an effect on the experimental group standard deviation as well as on the experimental group mean. That point is well taken; where there is a treatment effect, there may well be a treatment-by-subject interaction. However, if we wish to check for this, there is a much more effective procedure than altering the definition of *d*. We can do a meta-analysis that compares the values of the standard deviations directly.

Let *v* be the ratio of the experimental group standard deviation to the control group standard deviation; that is,

$$v = s_E / s_C \qquad (7.19)$$

The value of *v* will be 1.00 (to within sampling error) if the usual assumptions of the *t* test are met, that is, if there is no treatment-by-subject interaction (assuming all subjects in the experimental group received the same strength of treatment; see the discussion in Chapter 6 of the inflationary effect of measurement error in the independent variable on the treatment group *SD* in experiments). If the meta-analysis produces a mean value other than 1, then this could indicate a treatment-by-subject interaction. The direction of the departure from 1.00 will provide an inkling as to its nature.

Let us use the symbol d_G to denote the Glass variation on the effect size *d*. That is, let us define the symbol d_G by

$$d_G = (\bar{Y}_E - \bar{Y}_C)/s_C \qquad (7.20)$$

If the meta-analysis shows the value of *v* to be 1, then the population values of *d* and d_G are the same. If the meta-analysis shows the value of *v* to be other than 1, then the meta-analysis value for *d* can be transformed into the meta-analysis value of d_G by the following identity:

$$d_G = (s_W / s_C)d = d\sqrt{[(1+v^2)/2]} \qquad (7.21)$$

For example, suppose our meta-analysis found the average *d* to be .20 and the average value of *v* to be 1.50. Then the Glass d_G would be given by

$$d_G = [.20]\sqrt{[(1+1.5^2)/2]} = .255$$

There are two principal advantages to using the within-group standard deviation rather than the control group standard deviation—that is, using *d* rather than d_G. First, the control group standard deviation (and, hence, d_G) has much more sampling error than does the within-group standard deviation (and, hence, *d*). Second, most reports have a value for *t* or *F* and, hence, permit the computation of *d*. Many reports do not present standard deviations, and so d_G cannot be computed. Therefore, we have chosen to develop and present meta-analysis formulas only for *d*. But for those who might want to employ d_G, we note that Hedges (1981) has derived the sampling error variance for it. Using d_G in meta-analysis programs for *d* (or for *r*, if *d* values are first converted to *r* values as described later in this chapter) requires computing the (smaller) effective *N* that corresponds to this larger sampling error variance. The equation for doing this is given in the last worked example in Chapter 4 (Equation [4.3]).

Sampling Error in the *d* Statistic

THE STANDARD ERROR FOR d

Let us denote the population value of the effect size statistic by δ. The observed value *d* will then deviate from δ by sampling error. As with correlations, we can write the sampling error formula as

$$d = \delta + e$$

where *e* is the sampling error. For large samples,

$$E(e) = 0$$

and

$$\text{Var}(e) = (4 / N)(1 + \delta^2 / 8) \tag{7.22}$$

where *N* is the total sample size. This formula assumes that N_1 and N_2 are not extremely discrepant ($N = N_1 + N_2$); it assumes the larger N_i is not more than 80% of the total *N*. This formula is accurate for sample sizes of *N* = 50 (25 in each group) or more. However, more accurate approximations are noted in the next few paragraphs.

The important alteration is a more accurate formula for the sampling error variance. The more accurate estimate is

$$\text{Var}(e) = [(N-1) / (N-3)][(4 / N)(1 + \delta^2 / 8)] \tag{7.23}$$

This formula differs from the large-sample formula only by the multiplier $[(N - 1)/(N - 3)]$. This multiplier differs only slightly from 1.00 for $N > 50$. However, it makes a bigger difference for sample sizes of 20 or less. As with Equation (7.22), Equation (7.23) assumes N_1 and N_2 are not extremely discrepant (i.e., a split no more extreme than 80%–20%).

It will rarely be the case that sample sizes are extremely different in the two groups; as a result, Equation (7.23) is typically quite accurate. If the samples sizes in the two groups are very unequal (i.e., if the *N* in the larger of the two groups is more than 80% of the total N), then a more accurate estimate of the sampling error variance of the d statistic is provided by the following equation (Hedges & Olkin, 1985, p. 86):

$$\text{Var}(e) = \frac{N_1 + N_2}{N_1 N_2} + \frac{d^2}{2(N_1 + N_2)} \tag{7.23a}$$

Laczo, Sackett, Bobko, and Cortina (2005) provided a discussion of cases in which the sample size split is very extreme. This can happen, for example, when computing the standardized difference (*d* value) between two groups in a workforce when one group (the minority group) is less than 20% of the total sample (i.e., there are more than five times as many people in one group than in the other). The Kotov, Gamez, Schmidt, and Watson (2010) study of extreme personality groups is also an example of this. In such cases, Equation (7.23) underestimates sampling error, resulting in conservative meta-analysis results. That is, the result is an undercorrection for sampling error and an overestimation of the corrected standard deviation of the d values (SD_δ). In such a case, this conservative bias in the meta-analysis can be avoided by using Equation (7.23a). However, even in such a case, the conservative bias resulting from using Equation (7.23) is quite small and has little effect on the final meta-analysis results. Nevertheless, we have incorporated Equation 7.23a in our programs for meta-analysis of d values.

An excellent discussion of sampling error in very small sample size values of d is presented in Hedges and Olkin (1985). However, the reader is warned that the statistic that is traditionally denoted d is called g by Hedges and Olkin. They reserve the symbol d for their approximately unbiased estimator. We will denote the approximately unbiased estimator by d^*. The mean value of d across sample replications is

$$E(d) = a\delta \tag{7.24}$$

where, to a close approximation,

$$a = 1 + .75/(N-3) \tag{7.25}$$

For a sample of size $N = 100$, the bias multiplier is

$$a = 1 + .75/97 = 1 + .0077 = 1.01$$

which differs only trivially from 1.00. However, for very small samples—as in therapy research—the bias may warrant correction. For a sample size of $N = 20$, the multiplier a is

$$a = 1 + .75/17 = 1 + .044 = 1.044$$

To correct for the bias, we divide by the bias multiplier. If we denote the (approximately) unbiased estimator by d^*, then

$$d^* = d/a \qquad (7.26)$$

This correction mechanically decreases the value of d, and, hence, the sampling error is similarly decreased. If we define sampling error by

$$d^* = \delta + e^*$$

then we have approximately

$$E(e^*) = 0$$

$$\mathrm{Var}(e^*) = \mathrm{Var}(e)/a^2 \qquad (7.27)$$

There is a small error in Hedges and Olkin (1985) in this regard. They offer the approximation

$$\mathrm{Var}(e^*) = (4/N)(1 + \delta^2/8)$$

This approximation assumes the further approximation

$$[(N-1)/(N-3)]/a^2 = 1$$

This approximation breaks down for sample sizes of 20 or less, where the more accurate approximation

$$[(N-1)/(N-3)]/a^2 = 1 + .25/(N-3)$$

yields the formula that we have given in Equation (7.25).

For a bare-bones meta-analysis, bias can be corrected either study by study or after the meta-analysis has been done. If the meta-analysis is done on the usual d statistic, then the correction for bias would be

$$\mathrm{Ave}(\delta) = \mathrm{Ave}(d^*) = \mathrm{Ave}(d)/a \qquad (7.28)$$

where

$$a = 1 + .75/(\bar{N} - 3)$$

where $\bar{N}$ is the average sample size across studies. This correction is included in the two d value meta-analysis programs described in the Appendix.

The corresponding estimate of the standard deviation of population effect sizes would be

$$\text{Unbiased } SD_\delta = SD_\delta/a \qquad (7.29)$$

Thus, to correct for bias after the fact, we merely divide both the mean and the standard deviation by the bias multiplier computed using the average sample size.

THE CONFIDENCE INTERVAL FOR δ

The *d* statistic has mean δ and sampling variance

$$\text{Var}(e) = [(N-1)/(N-3)][(4/N)(1+\delta^2/8)]$$

The square root of the sampling error variance $\text{Var}(e)$ is the standard error of *d*. Denote the standard error by *S*. Except for very small sample sizes, the *d* statistic is approximately normally distributed. Thus, the 95% confidence interval for δ is given, to a close approximation, by

$$d = 1.96S < \delta < d + 1.96S$$

The exact value of the standard error requires knowledge of δ. Because δ is unknown, we estimate the sampling error variance by substituting *d* for δ. That is, we estimate S^2 by

$$\text{Var}(e) = [(N-1)/(N-3)][(4/N)(1+d^2/8)]. \tag{7.30}$$

The estimated standard error *S* is then the square root of $\text{Var}(e)$.

Cumulation and Correction of the Variance for Sampling Error

At this point, we begin the discussion of the meta-analysis of *d*. We start with a "bare-bones" meta-analysis, which makes no correction to the mean or variance for artifacts such as error of measurement. This form of meta-analysis corrects only for sampling error variance. We consider a meta-analysis that estimates the distribution of uncorrected population effect sizes δ_i from information about the study sample effect sizes d_i. We will return to the consideration of other artifacts in later sections. However, the reader should note that our final coverage of artifacts for the *d* statistic is less extensive than our coverage for correlations. This reflects the greater complexity of correction formulas for *d* than for *r*. Because of this complexity, we recommend that when multiple artifacts are to be corrected for, researchers should first transform the *d* values to correlations, conduct the meta-analysis in the *r* metric, and then convert the results back to the *d* value metric. Methods for doing this are presented later in this chapter. As noted at the beginning of this chapter, all the meta-analysis methods presented in this chapter are random effects models. That is, none of the methods presented here assumes a priori that there is no variability in population delta (δ) values, as fixed effects models do. In fact, a major purpose of the models presented here is to estimate the variability of population δ values across studies. Again, we refer the reader to the discussion of fixed effects versus random effects meta-analysis models presented in Chapters 5 and 8.

BARE-BONES META-ANALYSIS

The basic cumulation process is the same for d values as for correlations: One computes the frequency-weighted mean and variance of the effect size over studies and then corrects the variance for sampling error. Again, we point out that the model to be presented is a random effects model. It assumes there may be real variability in effect sizes across studies and attempts to estimate the size of that variability. This is in contrast to all fixed effects models, which assume a priori that there is no such variability (Hunter & Schmidt, 2000; Schmidt, Oh, & Hayes, 2009). (See Chapters 5 and 8 for a full discussion.)

Consider any set of weights w_i. There are three averages to be computed: (1) the weighted average of d, (2) the correspondingly weighted variance of d, and (3) the average sampling error variance. If we denote the average value of d by $\bar{d}$, then the averages are as follows:

$$\text{Ave}(d) = \Sigma w_i d_i / \Sigma w_i = \bar{d} \qquad (7.31)$$

$$\text{Var}(d) = \Sigma w_i [d_i - \bar{d}]^2 / \Sigma w_i \qquad (7.32)$$

$$\text{Var}(e) = \Sigma w_i \text{Var}(e_i) / \Sigma w_i \qquad (7.33)$$

The tricky computation is the average sampling error variance, $\text{Var}(e)$. The problem is that the sampling error variance within each study requires knowledge of the effect size for that study. That is,

$$\text{Var}(e_i) = (4/N_i)(1 + \delta_i^2/8)$$

depends on the population effect size δ_i, which is unknown. A good approximation in most cases is to substitute the mean value of d for δ_i in each study. In the case of the frequency-weighted average, this leads to the equation

$$\text{Var}(e) = (4/\bar{N})(1 + \bar{d}^2/8) \qquad (7.34)$$

where $\bar{N}$ is the average sample size. That is, if we denote the total sample size by T and the number of studies by K, then

$$T = \sum N_i$$

$$\bar{N} = T / K$$

The more accurate formula for the sampling error variance is

$$\mathrm{Var}(e) = [(\bar{N}-1)/(\bar{N}-3)][(4/\bar{N})(1+\bar{d}^2/8)] \qquad (7.35)$$

where $\bar{N}$ is the average sample size and $\bar{d}$ is the frequency-weighted value of d_i.

The variance of population effect sizes $\mathrm{Var}(\delta)$ is the observed variance of effect sizes corrected for sampling error. The variance of population effect sizes is found by subtracting the sampling error variance from the observed variance. That is,

$$\mathrm{Var}(\delta) = \mathrm{Var}(d) - \mathrm{Var}(e) \qquad (7.36)$$

This difference can be interpreted as subtracting the variance in *d* due to sampling error. That is, subtracting the average sampling error variance corrects the observed variance for the effect of sampling error. The standard deviation of study population effect sizes is the square root of the variance

$$SD_\delta = \sqrt{\mathrm{Var}(\delta)} \qquad (7.37)$$

Thus, for bare-bones meta-analysis, if the observed distribution of effect sizes is characterized by the values $\mathrm{Ave}(d)$ and $\mathrm{Var}(d)$, then the study population effect size is characterized by the following:

$$\mathrm{Ave}(\delta) = \mathrm{Ave}(d) \qquad (7.38)$$

$$\mathrm{Var}(\delta) = \mathrm{Var}(d) - \mathrm{Var}(e) \qquad (7.39)$$

$$SD_\delta = \sqrt{\mathrm{Var}(\delta)} \qquad (7.40)$$

If the effect size is really the same across studies, then the variance of population effect sizes is 0. That is, if there is no real variation in population effect sizes, then the observed variance will in expectation exactly equal the variance due to sampling error. Even if there is some variation across studies, the variance may still be small enough to ignore for practical or theoretical reasons. If the variation is large, especially if it is large relative to the mean value, then there should be a search for moderator variables.

CONFIDENCE INTERVALS FOR $\bar{d}$

Confidence intervals for $\bar{d}$ are completed using the standard error of $\bar{d}$, that is, $SD_d / \sqrt{k}$, where SD_d is the square root of the variance of the observed d values (as given in Equation [7.32]).

$$SE_{\bar{d}} = SD_d / \sqrt{k} \qquad (7.41)$$

where k = the number of studies. The 95% confidence interval is then

$$\bar{d} - 1.96\,(SE_{\bar{d}}) < \bar{d} < \bar{d} + 1.96\,(SE_{\bar{d}}) \qquad (7.42)$$

We present numerical confidence intervals for two of the worked examples presented later in this chapter. Because the examples we use for instructional purposes contain a small number of studies, these confidence intervals are fairly wide.

A WORKED EXAMPLE

The reader is cautioned that discussions of examples in this chapter take certain liberties. To present an example and illustrate computations, we must present examples with a small number of studies. This means that the total sample size in the example is not nearly large enough to eliminate the effect of sampling error. That is, the estimates from the meta-analysis will still have sampling error in them. However, in this chapter, we want to discuss the results as if the sampling error had been removed. Thus, for each example in this chapter, our discussion will be phrased as if the number of studies were much larger than shown in the example. The estimation of sampling error in the estimates from a meta-analysis will be considered in its own right in Chapter 9. That chapter contains sampling error estimates for many of the examples shown here.

Consider the following example for bare-bones meta-analysis:

N	d
100	−.01
90	.41*
50	.50*
40	−.10

*Significant at the .05 level.

Two of the effect sizes are significant and two are not. By the usual logic, a reviewer would assume from this that there is some moderator variable that causes the treatment to have an effect in some settings but have no effect in others. Could this be sampling error?

The bare-bones meta-analysis is

$$T = 100 + 90 + 50 + 40 = 280$$

$$\bar{N} = T/K = 280/4 = 70$$

$$\text{Ave}(d) = [100(-.01) + 90(.41) + 50(.50) + 40(-.10)]/280$$
$$= 56.9/280 = .20,$$

$$\text{Var}(d) = [100(-.01 - .20)^2 + 90(.41 - .20)^2$$
$$+ 50(.50 - .20)^2 + 40(-.10 - .20)^2]/280$$
$$= 16.479/280 = .058854$$

The large-sample estimate of the sampling error variance is

$$\text{Var}(e) = (4/\bar{N})(1 + \bar{d}^2/8) = (4/70)(1 + .20^2/8) = .057429$$

Thus, we estimate the distribution of study population effect sizes by

$$\text{Ave}(\delta) = \text{Ave}(d) = .20,$$
$$\text{Var}(\delta) = \text{Var}(d) - \text{Var}(e) = .058854 - .057429 = .001425$$
$$SD(\delta) = \sqrt{.001425} = .038$$

We now consider an interpretation of this meta-analysis written as if the number of studies were much larger than 4. This meta-analysis has only four studies and a total sample size of 280. Thus, there is actually room for considerable (second-order) sampling error in the meta-analysis estimates. This topic is considered in Chapter 9.

Suppose these meta-analysis estimates were very accurate; for example, assume the number of studies to be 400 rather than 4. If population effect sizes were normally distributed, then the middle 95% of population effect sizes would lie in the interval

$$.20 - 1.96SD_\delta < \delta < .20 + 1.96SD_\delta$$
$$.13 < \delta < .27$$

For a population effect size to be 0, it would represent a standard score of

$$[0 - .20]/.038 = -5.26$$

This is an extremely unlikely possibility. Thus, in this example, meta-analysis shows the usual review logic to be quite wrong. It is not the case that the treatment has no effect in 50% of settings. There are no settings where the treatment effect is 0. Thus, in the two studies with nonsignificant effect sizes, there was a Type II error. That is, in this example, the error rate for the significance test was 50%.

Consider the use of the more accurate formula for the sampling error variance:

$$\text{Var}(e) = [(\bar{N}-1)/(\bar{N}-3)][4/\bar{N}][1+\bar{d}^2/8]$$
$$= [69/67][.057429] = .059143$$

There is little difference in the estimate of the sampling error variance. However, there is a larger difference in the estimate of the study population effect size variance:

$$\text{Var}(\delta) = \text{Var}(d) - \text{Var}(e) = .058854 - .059143 = -.000289$$

Using the less accurate large-sample formula, the difference between observed variance and variance due to sampling error was .001425; that is, the observed variance was larger than expected on the basis of sampling error. However, the more accurate formula shows that the variance was almost exactly equal to the level expected from sampling error. The fact that the difference is negative shows that with only four studies, there is some second-order sampling error in $\text{Var}(d)$ (see Chapter 9). The corresponding estimate of the standard deviation is $SD_\delta = 0$. Thus, using the more accurate sampling error formula generates a description of the study population correlations, which is

$$\text{Ave}(\delta) = .20$$
$$SD_\delta = 0$$

This estimate indicates that there is no variation in the study population effect sizes. That this is true is known from the fact that the authors generated the data using the same population effect size for all studies. In a real meta-analysis based on only four studies, the same finding would be only provisional.

To correct for bias, we first compute the bias multiplier:

$$a = 1 + .75/(\bar{N}-3) = 1 + .75/67 = 1.0112$$

The corrected mean and standard deviation are thus

$$\text{Ave}(\delta) = .20/1.0112 = .1978 = .20$$
$$SD_\delta = 0/1.0112 = 0$$

Thus, for an average sample size of 70, the effect of correction for bias is smaller than rounding error.

ANOTHER EXAMPLE: LEADERSHIP TRAINING BY EXPERTS

Organizational psychologists have long suspected that training in interpersonal or leadership skills improves the performance of managers. Professor Fruitloop decided that he wanted to know the amount of improvement and, therefore, laid out the design of a meta-analysis. He decided that studies should meet two criteria. First, each training program must contain at least three key skills: active listening, negative feedback, and positive feedback. Second, the study should be run under controlled training conditions. To assure this, he used only studies in which the training was done by outside experts (see Table 7.1).

Of the five studies, only one shows a significant effect. Two of the studies show effects in the opposite direction. Thus, using traditional review standards, Fruitloop would be led to conclude that training in interpersonal skills had no impact (or uncertain impact) on performance of supervisors in a majority of settings. Fortunately, however, Fruitloop had heard of meta-analysis. The meta-analysis of the five studies in Table 7.1 is

$$T = 200$$
$$\bar{N} = 40$$
$$\text{Ave}(d) = .20$$
$$\text{Var}(d) = .106000$$

Using the more accurate formula,

$$\text{Var}(e) = [39/37][4/40][1 + .20^2/8] = .105932$$
$$\text{Var}(\delta) = \text{Var}(d) - \text{Var}(e) = .106000 - .105932 = .000068$$
$$SD_\delta = .01$$

The 80% credibility interval here is $.20 - 1.28(.01)$ to $.20 + 1.28(.01) = .187$ to $.213$. Rounding, we have

$$.19 < .20 < .21$$

The credibility interval is very narrow (width = .02). But this is not the case for the confidence interval, which is based on sampling error. For a meta-analysis of five studies with an average sample size of 40, the total sample size is only $T = 200$. Thus, the potential sampling error in the meta-analysis estimates would be about as large as the sampling error in a single study with $N = 200$, and that is very large. Because of this, confidence intervals are wide in this and other examples we present with small numbers of studies. Consider the confidence interval (CI) around the mean d value (.20). SD_d, the square root of the variance of the observed d *values,* is .32557 and the number of studies (k) is 5. So $SE_{\bar{d}} = .32557/\sqrt{5} = .14560$. The lower end of the 95% CI is therefore $.20 - 1.96\,(.14560) = -.085$. The upper end of this CI is $.20 + 1.96\,(.14560) = .480$. This CI is quite wide: .565 d value points, much wider than the .02 width of the credibility interval. This is to be expected in such example meta-analyses. As stated earlier, we use examples with small numbers of studies to make the explication of the meta-analysis methods clearer to readers. This is a bare-bones meta-analysis. Methods for computing CIs when artifacts beyond sampling error are corrected for are presented in Chapters 5 and 8.

It is not our purpose here to focus on the sampling error in meta-analysis with a small number of studies. Rather, we used only a small number of studies so that it would be easy for the reader to replicate the computations in order to understand the formulas. For purposes of argument, assume that the residual variance of .000068 is not due to sampling error; that is, accept the standard deviation of .01 as real. A real standard deviation of .01 would mean that there is real variation in the study population effect sizes. Would that mean, however, that there was real variation in actual population effect sizes? Certainly not. In a bare-bones meta-analysis, we control for only one artifact: sampling error. No control is included for variation in error of measurement, or variation in the degree of imperfection of construct validity, or variation in the strength of the treatment, and so on. Thus, there are many other artifacts that might have caused variance in the study effect size.

It is even more important to remember that this is a bare-bones analysis in interpreting the size of the treatment effect. Most of the artifacts not

Table 7.1   Leadership training (studies with training by outside experts).

Author	Sample Size	Effect Size
Apple	40	−.24
Banana	40	−.04
Cherry	40	.20
Orange	40	.44
Melon	40	.64*

*Significant at the .05 level.

controlled have the effect of lowering the observed effect size. Thus, the observed mean of .20 is almost surely an underestimate and possibly a massive underestimate.

Consider the difference between a narrative review and a meta-analysis, assuming these same results from a meta-analysis of 500 studies. Only 100 of the 500 studies would produce significant results. As many as 200 of the 500 studies would produce results in the wrong direction. Thus, the narrative review would probably conclude that training has an effect in only a minority of settings; on the other hand, 20% of the studies with significant results would find large effect sizes, *d* values of .60 or more. Thus, a narrative review might well conclude that in those settings where training works, it works quite well.

Using meta-analysis, Fruitloop discovered a very different pattern to population effect sizes. He found that virtually all the variation in observed results was actually due to sampling error. Thus, the available studies actually showed perfect consistency in the effect of training, a uniform effect size of $\delta = .20$. Thus, the effect size is never 0, and it is also never as large as .40, much less .60, the levels observed in isolated studies.

Analysis of Moderator Variables

The impact of an intervention might vary from setting to setting. For example, training programs might vary in quality, in quantity, or in the average learning ability of the trainees. If this were so, then the cumulation formulas would yield nonzero variance for the population effect sizes, that is, a nonzero value for SD_δ. The search for and detection of the moderator variables that account for such variation is identical to the procedure followed in looking for moderator variables in correlational studies. Indeed, the general mathematics is identical for both. In particular, if the number of studies is small and the number of coded study characteristics is large, then blind search is highly prone to capitalization on chance. (See the discussion of this at the end of Chapter 2.) Chapter 9 discusses the hierarchical analysis of moderators in meta-analysis, the effect of second-order sampling error on moderator analysis in meta-analysis, and problems in the use of meta-regression.

There are two ways to see if a study characteristic is a moderator variable or not: Use the characteristic to break the data into subsets or correlate the study characteristic with effect size. There have now been enough meta-analyses conducted with both methods to generate an opinion as to which method works better. It is our impression that the correlation method (meta-regression)—which is often touted as "more sophisticated"—is much more often used incorrectly. Thus, for most purposes, we would recommend the subset method be used when possible. See the discussion of this in Chapter 9.

Finally, we note that meta-analysis can examine moderators only at the study level. For example, if some studies have been conducted on males and some on females, then meta-analysis can examine sex as a potential moderator. However, if every study is based on a combination of males and females and reports only the total group results, sex cannot be tested as a moderator.

USING STUDY DOMAIN SUBSETS

If the studies are broken down into subsets, then there is no new computational tool to be learned. The researcher merely performs a separate meta-analysis within each subset. For a bare-bones meta-analysis, there is nothing more to say. However, if artifacts other than sampling error are to be corrected—a critical feature in most research areas—then we have one additional word of advice. Often, artifact information for other artifacts is only sporadically available, and so artifact distribution meta-analysis (discussed later in this chapter) must be used. In most such cases, the artifact distributions are better computed for the entire set of studies rather than computed separately within subsets of studies. The whole domain artifact distribution values are then used in the computation of the within-subsets meta-analyses.

If the data are broken into subsets, then there are two ways that a moderator variable would show itself. First, there should be a difference in the mean effect size between subsets. Second, there should be a reduction in variance within subsets. These are not independent events. We know from an important theorem in analysis of variance that the total variance in effect size is the sum of the variance in mean effect sizes between subsets plus the average within-subset variance. Thus, if there is a large difference between the subset mean effect sizes, then the average within-subset variance must be smaller than the overall variance.

This theorem applies equally well to either observed effect sizes or to population effect sizes. If the usual formula for components of variance is applied to the corrected variances rather than to the uncorrected variances, then the result is the same: A large difference between subset means implies a lower value for average within-subset variance than for overall variance. However, when there are unequal numbers of studies in the two moderator groups and unequal Ns within studies, it becomes difficult to precisely compute the mean within-subset variance, because it becomes difficult to determine the appropriate weight to apply to the two variances. Under these circumstances—which are, in fact, the usual circumstances—it is best to focus solely on differences between the means (here, $\bar{d}_1 - \bar{d}_2$).

USING STUDY CHARACTERISTIC CORRELATIONS

Consider instead the correlation approach to the search for moderator variables. In this approach, we compute a correlation over studies between the coded study characteristic and the observed effect size. The effect of sampling error on this correlation is directly analogous to the effect of error of measurement on a correlation between variables over subjects: The correlation is systematically reduced. Thus, to correct a correlation between effect size and study characteristic for the effect of sampling error is to increase that correlation in proportion to the relative size of the real variation in effect size to the artificial variation caused by sampling error. This is directly analogous to correction for attenuation due to measurement error. This correction of Var(*d*) for sampling error is comparable to correcting the usual within-experiment variance for error of measurement.

If the observed sample effect sizes are correlated with a study characteristic, then the correlation will be attenuated by the sampling error in the observed effect sizes in the same manner that the ordinary correlations across persons are attenuated by error of measurement. Consider the sampling error formula

$$d_i = \delta_i + e_i$$

and consider a study characteristic denoted y_i. Denote the correlation across studies between *d* and *y* as Cor(*d*, *y*). The covariance is

$$\text{Cov}(d,\ y) = \text{Cov}(\delta,\ y) + \text{Cov}(e,\ y) \qquad (7.43)$$

For a large set of studies, the covariance between sampling error and study characteristics will be 0. Thus, in the research domain as a whole, sampling error does not contribute to the covariance of study characteristic and effect size. However, because

$$\text{Var}(d) = \text{Var}(\delta) + \text{Var}(e)$$

sampling error does contribute to the variance of the effect sizes. Thus, the effect of sampling error is to increase the variance in the denominator of the study characteristic correlation while making no corresponding increase in the numerator. Therefore, the effect of sampling error is to decrease the size of the correlation.

The study characteristic correlation can be corrected for sampling error using a formula that is exactly analogous to the formula for correction of a correlation for error of measurement. To do this, we use the error of measurement to define a "reliability" denoted Rel(*d*) and then use it to correct the observed correlation Cor(*d,y*) in the usual manner. In measurement theory, the reliability of a variable affected by random error e_p is the ratio of variance of true scores *T* to observed scores *X*:

$$r_{XX} = \text{Var}(T) / \text{Var}(X)$$

where

$$\text{Var}(X) = \text{Var}(T) + \text{Var}(e)$$

The analogous formula for meta-analysis is

$$\text{Rel}(d) = \text{Var}(\delta) / \text{Var}(d) \tag{7.44}$$

To correct the over-subject correlation between variables X and Y for error of measurement in X, we divide by the square root of the reliability; that is,

$$r_{TY} = r_{XY} / \sqrt{r_{XX}}$$

The corresponding theorem for meta-analysis is

$$\text{Cor}(\delta, y) = \text{Cor}(d, y) / \sqrt{\text{Rel}(d)} \tag{7.45}$$

This formula generates an estimate of the study characteristic correlation that would obtain if all the studies had been done with very large samples.

It is important to note that the preceding formula is derived based on the assumption that sampling error will be uncorrelated with any study characteristic. This theorem is true for the research domain and is approximately true for any meta-analysis done with a large number of studies. However, for a meta-analysis done with a small number of studies, the sampling errors in those particular studies may by chance be correlated with some of the study characteristic values for that sample of studies. This is the problem of capitalization on chance (see Chapters 2 and 9). As one sorts through potential moderator variables, some study characteristics may have a high-chance correlation with the sampling errors. This variable would then look like a strong moderator variable.

For a meta-analysis with a small number of studies, there is no statistical solution to the problem of capitalization on chance. In a research domain with good theories, there is a possible solution. Test first only that moderator variable predicted by a good theory that is well supported by other research. If that variable does not moderate the effect size, then treat all the remaining potential moderators with a very large grain of salt. If there is a theory that supports the discovered moderator variable, then the researcher should check the literature to see if there is any independent corroboration of that theory. For further discussion of this point, see the last part of Chapter 2.

A WORKED EXAMPLE: TRAINING BY EXPERTS VERSUS TRAINING BY MANAGERS

In his dissertation, Jim Russell tested the hypothesis that training of supervisors in interpersonal skills should be conducted by their own managers rather than by outside experts. That idea derived from the proposition that because managers act as role models for supervisors, the supervisors are much more likely to identify with procedures recommended by managers than with those recommended by outside experts.

Consider again the hypothetical cumulative study done by Fruitloop. Fruitloop discarded all studies done by managers as "lacking in experimental control." Thus, Fruitloop analyzed only studies where the training was done by experts. Suppose instead that all studies were analyzed. The results might look like those in Table 7.2. In this collection of studies, only 3 of 10 have significant effects, and 3 of 10 go in the opposite direction. Thus, traditional review practice would probably conclude that the effect of training in interpersonal skills is problematic at best.

The overall meta-analysis for the studies in Table 7.2 is as follows:

$$T = 40 + 40 + \cdots = 400$$
$$\bar{N} = T/10 = 40$$
$$\text{Ave}(d) = .30$$
$$\text{Var}(d) = .116000$$
$$\text{Var}(e) = [39/37][4/40][1 + .30^2/8] = .106591$$
$$\text{Var}(\delta) = .116000 - .106591 = .009409$$
$$SD_\delta = .097$$

Table 7.2   Training in interpersonal skills by managers versus by experts.

Author	Trainer	Sample Size	Effect Size
Apple	Expert	40	−.25
Banana	Expert	40	−.05
Cherry	Expert	40	.20
Orange	Expert	40	.45
Melon	Expert	40	.65*
Cucumber	Manager	40	−.05
Tomato	Manager	40	.15
Squash	Manager	40	.40
Carrot	Manager	40	.65*
Pepper	Manager	40	.85*

*Significant at the .05 level (two-tailed test).

For purposes of computational convenience, we have again presented a meta-analysis with only a small number of studies. A set of 10 studies with an average sample size of 40 represents only a total sample size of 400. Thus, there would still be substantial potential sampling error in the estimates from the meta-analysis. The potential sampling error in the meta-analysis estimates would be about as large as the sampling error in a single study with $N = 400$, and that is large. Because of this, confidence intervals are wide in this and other examples we present with small numbers of studies. Consider the CI around the mean d value (.30) here. SD_d, the square root of the variance of the observed d values, is .34052 and the number of studies (k) is 10. So $SE_d = .34058/\sqrt{10} = .10770$. The lower end of the 95% CI is therefore $.30 - 1.96 (.10770) = .0889$. The upper end of this CI is $.30 + 1.96 (.10770) = .5111$. Rounding, we have

$$.09 < .30 < .51$$

This CI is quite wide: .422 correlation points. This is to be expected in such example meta-analyses. As stated earlier, we use examples with small numbers of studies to make explication of the meta-analysis methods clearer to readers. This example is a bare-bones meta-analysis. Methods for computing CIs when artifacts beyond sampling error are corrected for are presented in Chapters 5 and 8.

Let us assume that we obtained these results not with 10 studies but with 100 studies. The standard deviation of study effect size is .097, which is noticeably greater than 0. The standard deviation of .097 is also large relative to a mean effect size of .30. However, it is not large enough to suggest that there are any settings where the effect size is 0. If variation in effect size were normally distributed (it actually turns out to be dichotomous in this example), the middle 95% of effect sizes (95% credibility interval) would be

$$.30 - 1.96(.097) < \delta < .30 + 1.96(.097)$$
$$.11 < \delta < .49$$

In this example, the confidence interval and the credibility interval differ only a little in width. In practice, many researchers would use the 80% credibility interval, which would be narrower (.18 to .42). However, in either case, this is a substantial range of possible effects, and a search for a moderator variable is justified, especially because a theoretically based potential moderator has been identified a priori (i.e., managers vs. expert trainers).

Consider again the performance of the statistical significance test on this data set. Only 3 of the 10 effect sizes were significant. Yet the meta-analysis shows that all of the population effect sizes were positive. Thus, the (Type II) error rate for the significance test in this example is

70%. Furthermore, the variation in observed effect sizes covered a massive range: from −.25 to +.85. In fact, the meta-analysis shows that most of this variation is due to sampling error. Few values would actually be found outside the interval $.11 < \delta < .49$. On the other hand, there is still quite a bit of variability in results; thus, a search for moderator variables is well advised.

In this example, the moderator was hypothesized before the meta-analysis. Thus, we break the studies down into those where the training was done by outside experts versus those where the training was done by managers. The within-subset meta-analyses are as follows:

Training by Experts

$T = 40 + 40 + \ldots = 200$

$\bar{N} = T / 10 = 40$

$\mathrm{Ave}(d) = .20$

$\mathrm{Var}(d) = .106000$

$\mathrm{Var}(e) = [39/37][4/40][1 + .20^2/8] = .105932$

$\mathrm{Var}(\delta) = .106000 - .105932 = .000068$

$SD_\delta = .008$

Training by Managers

$T = 40 + 40 + \ldots = 200$

$\bar{N} = T / 10 = 40$

$\mathrm{Ave}(d) = .40$

$\mathrm{Var}(d) = .106000$

$\mathrm{Var}(e) = [39/37][4/40][1 + .40^2/8] = .107514$

$\mathrm{Var}(\delta) = .106000 - .107514 = .001514$

$SD_\delta = 0$

Again, we note that the small number of studies was meant only for computational convenience. Assume that there were not 10 but 1,000 studies, 500 studies of each kind. That is, let us interpret the results of the meta-analysis as if there were little or no sampling error in the estimates.

In this example, breaking studies down by type of trainer shows the moderator effect in two ways. First, there is the wide difference between mean effect sizes: $\mathrm{Ave}(d) = .20$ for training by experts versus $\mathrm{Ave}(d) = .40$ for training by managers. Furthermore, the breakdown by type of trainer eliminates virtually all variation in effect size (beyond that due to sampling error). Thus, training by outside experts always has an effect of .20

standard deviations, while training by managers always has an effect of twice that size, .40 standard deviations.

Note that assuming a normal distribution for effect sizes produced a 95% interval from .11 to .49, suggesting that 2.5% of studies would produce values lower than $\delta = .11$ and that 2.5% of studies would produce values higher than $\delta = .49$. In fact, the distribution was not normal. Instead, half the studies had a population effect size of $\delta = .20$ (those with outside expert trainers) and half had a population effect size of $\delta = .40$ (those with manager trainers). Thus, the assumption of normality overestimated the actual spread of effect sizes.

In this case, there was only one moderator. When there are multiple moderators, the moderators may be correlated, and hence, they will be confounded if examined sequentially one at a time. In such cases, it is important to conduct moderator analysis hierarchically to avoid such confounding. See Chapter 9 for a discussion of hierarchical moderator analysis.

ANOTHER WORKED EXAMPLE: AMOUNT OF TRAINING

We now present an example in which the impact of training on interpersonal skills varies as a function of the number of hours of training. The data are shown in Table 7.3. The measure of number of hours is the amount of time that the trainee is in actual interaction with the trainer (as opposed to watching the trainer work with someone else).

In this example, the effect size was significant only 1 in 12 times, and the results were positive in 7 of the 12 studies. That is, nearly half the studies found effects in the opposite direction. Traditional review practice would probably conclude that training in interpersonal skills has no effect.

The meta-analysis results are as follows:

All Studies

$T = 40 + 40 + \ldots = 480$

$\bar{N} = 480/12 = 40$

$\text{Ave}(d) = .15$

$\text{Var}(d) = .109717$

$\text{Var}(e) = .105702$

$\text{Var}(\delta) = .004015$

$SD_\delta = .063$

We leave it as an exercise for the reader to compute the CI around the mean d value of .15. (See the CI computations presented in the examples for Tables 7.1 and 7.2 for guidance.)

Table 7.3 Training in interpersonal skills by hours.

Number of Hours	Sample Size	Effect Size
2	40	−.39
2	40	.54
2	40	.25
2	40	−.05
3	40	−.29
3	40	.00
3	40	.30
3	40	.59
4	40	−.24
4	40	.64*
4	40	.35
4	40	.05

*Significant at the .05 level (two-tailed test).

Again, we duck the issue of the small total sample size of 480 in this example (to which we return in Chapter 9). Suppose there had been not 12 but 1,200 studies. That is, assume that there is essentially no sampling error in the meta-analysis estimates. We describe the distribution of population effect sizes as having a mean of .15 and a standard deviation of .063. How much would study effect sizes vary from one setting to the next? Consider the assumption of a normal distribution of effect sizes. If the variation in effect sizes were normally distributed (it is not), the middle 95% of effect sizes would be

$$.15-1.96(.063) < \delta < .15+1.96(.063)$$
$$.03 < \delta < .27$$

This credibility interval suggests that there are probably no settings in which the training has no effect.

Compare the results of the meta-analysis with the conclusions of a narrative review. Only 100 of the 1,200 studies would have statistically significant effects. This could be interpreted to mean that training only has an effect in about 1 setting in 12. The cumulative analysis shows this to be wrong. At the level of observed study effects, results ranged from −.39 to +.64.

The cumulative analysis shows that most of this variation is due to sampling error.

Thus, the meta-analysis reveals a very different story. The average effect size is a weak .15, but most of the variation is due to sampling error. If variation in effect size were normally distributed, then 95% of settings would have effect sizes in the range $.03 < \delta < .27$.

On the other hand, a range in effect of .03 to .27 would be a whopping difference in impact. Thus, it would be very important to know which studies had the large and which studies had the small effects. Thus, we begin the search for a moderator variable. Consider hours of training as a moderator. Because three levels of amount of training are represented in the domain of studies, we break the total set of studies into three subsets: those with 2 hours, 3 hours, or 4 hours of training. The separate bare-bones meta-analyses follow.

2 Hours of Training

$T = 40 + 40 + \ldots = 160$

$\bar{N} = 160 / 4 = 40$

$\text{Ave}(d) = .10$

$\text{Var}(d) = .108050$

$\text{Var}(e) = .105537$

$\text{Var}(\delta) = .002513$

$SD_{\delta} = .050$

3 Hours of Training

$T = 40 + 40 + \ldots = 160$

$\bar{N} = 160 / 4 = 40$

$\text{Ave}(d) = .15$

$\text{Var}(d) = .108050$

$\text{Var}(e) = .105702$

$\text{Var}(\delta) = .002348$

$SD_{\delta} = .048$

4 Hours of Training

$T = 40 + 40 + \ldots = 160$

$\bar{N} = 160 / 4 = 40$

$\text{Ave}(d) = .20$

$Var(d) = .108050$

$Var(e) = .105932$

$Var(\delta) = .002118$

$SD_\delta = .046$

The moderator analysis shows that the amount of training is an important determinant of the effect of training. As the amount grows from 2 to 3 to 4 hours, the mean treatment effect grows from .10 to .15 to .20. That is, the mean treatment effect is proportional to the amount of training time within the range of training times studied. Thus, even greater impact would be projected if still more time were devoted to the training. On the other hand, the nonlinear learning curves in the literature on learning suggest that we could not just project out linearly; rather, diminishing returns would set in at some point.

We leave it as an exercise for the reader to compute the CIs around each of these three mean *d* values. (See the CI computations presented in the examples in Tables 7.1 and 7.2 for guidance.)

In this example, the one moderator variable does not explain all the variation in results. The overall standard deviation of .063 dropped to .050, .048, and .046 for the three within-subset analyses. This is a decrease in variation, but it is not 0. Consider the 4-hour training studies. The mean effect size is .20, but the standard deviation is .046. If effect sizes varied normally, the middle 95% of the distribution of effect sizes would be

$$.20 - 1.96(.046) < \delta < .20 + 1.96(.046)$$

$$.11 < \delta < .29$$

Thus, if another moderator variable—perhaps job complexity—could be found, it would add to our understanding of interpersonal training.

However, it should be noted that there may not be another moderator variable. A bare-bones meta-analysis corrects only for the effects of sampling error. Other artifacts that cause variation across studies, such as error of measurement, have not been controlled. Thus, it is possible that the residual variation is due to uncontrolled artifacts rather than real differences in training contexts.

THE CORRELATIONAL MODERATOR ANALYSIS

The corresponding correlational moderator analysis defines hours of training as a quantitative variable *H*. This can then be correlated with the observed effect size. The correlation between *H* and *d* in Table 7.3 is

$$Cor(d, H) = .125.$$

The "reliability" is

$$\text{Rel}(d) = \text{Var}(\delta) / \text{Var}(d) = .004015 / .109717 = .0366.$$

Thus, the correlation for population effect sizes would be

$$\text{Cor}(\delta, H) = \text{Cor}(d, H) / \sqrt{\text{Rel}(d)} = .125 / \sqrt{.0366} = .65.$$

That is, the effect of sampling error was to reduce the correlation of .65 between population effect sizes and hours of training to a correlation of only .125. This example makes it clear that the downwardly biasing effect of sampling error on moderator correlations can be very large.

Correcting *d* Value Statistics for Measurement Error in the Dependent Variable

It is now generally recognized that the results of meta-analysis are inaccurate unless one corrects for the effects of measurement error (Hedges, 2009a; Cook et al., 1992, pp. 315–316; Matt & Cook, 2009). In Chapter 6, we showed that error of measurement in the dependent variable reduces the effect size estimate. If the reliability of measurement is low, the reduction can be quite sizable. Failure to correct for the attenuation due to error of measurement yields an erroneous effect size estimate. Furthermore, because the error is systematic, a bare-bones meta-analysis on uncorrected effect sizes will produce an incorrect estimate of the true effect size. The extent of reduction in the mean effect size is determined by the mean level of reliability across the studies. Variation in reliability across studies causes variation in the observed effect sizes above and beyond that produced by sampling error. If the true effect size is actually homogeneous across studies, the variation in reliability produces a false impression of heterogeneity in a bare-bones meta-analysis. A bare-bones meta-analysis will not correct for either the systematic reduction in the mean effect size or the systematic increase in the variance of effect sizes. Thus, even meta-analysis will produce incorrect values for the distribution of effect sizes if there is no correction for the attenuation due to error of measurement.

In meta-analysis, there are two ways to eliminate the effect of error of measurement. Ideally, one could compile information on reliability for all or nearly all the individual studies. In this case, each effect size could be individually corrected and the meta-analysis could be done on the corrected effect sizes. This is the type of *d* value meta-analysis that is calculated by the program D-VALUE described in the Appendix. However, if information on reliability is only available sporadically, then it may only be possible to generate an estimate of the distribution of reliability across studies. If the level of reliability in studies is independent of the level of effect sizes, then it is possible to correct a bare-bones meta-analysis for the effect of error of measurement. That is, if reliability information is only available in the form of a distribution, then we first do a bare-bones meta-analysis, and we then correct the bare-bones meta-analysis estimates for attenuation (the mean effect size) and inflation (the variance of effect sizes) after the fact. This type of meta-analysis is performed by the program D-VALUE1 described in the Appendix.

Some authors would rather incur the error of biased estimates than correct for measurement error. They defend this choice by saying that underestimation of effect sizes is acceptable; only overestimation is bad. That is, some believe that only positive errors count and negative errors do not matter. But the goal of science is to obtain unbiased estimates of all scientifically important parameters (Rubin, 1990). In addition, theoretical work often requires the comparison of effect sizes. If some of the effect sizes have been underestimated, the comparison may be wrong and, thus, lead to false inferences. This is especially likely if different *d* values have been underestimated to different degrees. The history of science shows that negative errors (negative biases) are just as damaging as positive errors. Thus, that correction is always desirable.

The problem in meta-analysis is that some studies do not report the reliability of the measures used. Sometimes this problem can be eliminated by going to studies outside the research domain that use the same measure and report its reliability. If none of the studies that use a given measure ever reports a reliability (often the case in behavioristic studies), then even in meta-analysis no correction can be made. However, even if correction for attenuation is to be ignored, it is important to have some idea of how large the corresponding error in estimation will be. One way to do this would be to look at the reliability of similar measures.

The key to computing the effect of error of measurement on effect sizes is to measure the extent of random measurement error in the dependent variable. This is done in psychometric theory using the reliability coefficient. (See the discussion of estimation of reliability in Chapter 3.) If the reliability of the dependent measure is known, then the extent of the attenuation (downward bias) can be exactly computed. It is then possible to algebraically reverse the attenuation; this process is called "correction for attenuation."

If the true population effect size is δ, then the study population effect size would be as high as δ only if the dependent variable is perfectly measured, which is never the case. The reliability of the dependent variable is always less than 1.00, so there will be a corresponding reduction in the study population effect size. If the reliability of the dependent variable measure is r_{YY}, the attenuated population effect size δ_o is given by

$$\delta_o = a\delta$$

where $a = \sqrt{r_{YY}}$. For example, if the reliability of the dependent variable is $r_{YY} = .64$, then the study population effect size is

$$\delta_o = .80\delta$$

that is, reduced by 20%. If we know that a number has been reduced by 20%, then we can find the original number by division. That is, if we know that $\delta_o = .80\delta$, we can divide by .80 to obtain δ, that is, $\delta = \delta_o / .80$. Thus, the population effect size δ_o could be algebraically corrected for attenuation by dividing both sides of the equation by a. That is,

$$\delta_o / a = (a\delta)/a = \delta$$

If one has the correct type of reliability (see Chapter 3), the formula for correction for attenuation works perfectly with population effect sizes. The sample effect size can also be corrected for attenuation using the same formula. That correction eliminates the systematic attenuation of the sample effect. Thus, in principle, we can use a statistical correction formula to eliminate the effects of random error of measurement. However, there is still sampling error in the corrected effect size; in fact, the correction increases the amount of sampling error. The crucial fact for meta-analysis is that the formula for sampling error in a corrected effect size is different from the formula for the sampling error in an uncorrected effect size. Thus, meta-analysis on corrected effect sizes uses a slightly different formula to correct the variance for sampling error.

If correction for attenuation can eliminate the downward bias produced by measurement error, one might ask why we should bother to try to use good measurement in the first place. The answer lies in the sampling error of corrected effect sizes. A careful analysis of the correction process shows that we pay a price for statistical correction: The sampling error in a statistically corrected effect size is larger than the sampling error in a study done with perfect measurement. The higher the reliability, the less the increase in sampling error. Thus, the better the original measurement, the less the sampling error in the corrected effect size. That is, we can estimate the results for perfect measurement without being able to achieve perfect measurement in our studies, but the price of statistical correction is increased sampling error. The higher the reliability, the lower the price. The price for low reliability in an individual study is very high. However, the larger sample sizes in meta-analysis make it possible to get accurate estimates of effect sizes even if the individual studies in a domain have low reliability. This occurs because the sampling error in the individual studies is averaged out when the mean corrected effect size is computed.

We will now show that correcting the effect size for attenuation increases sampling error. Consider the sample effect size d_o:

$$d_o = \delta_o + e = a\delta + e \qquad (7.46)$$

The attenuated sample effect size can be corrected for the effect of error of measurement. Denote the corrected effect size by d_c:

$$\begin{aligned} d_c &= d_o / a = (\delta_o + e) / a \\ &= \delta_o / a + e / a \\ &= \delta + e' \end{aligned}$$

where e' is the sampling error in the corrected effect size. The sampling error in e' is given by

$$\mathrm{Var}(e') = \mathrm{Var}(e) / a^2 = \mathrm{Var}(e) / r_{YY} \qquad (7.47)$$

To divide by a fraction is to increase the ratio. Thus, the increase in sampling error variance is exactly proportional to the reliability. The standard error of the corrected effect size is the square root of the variance. For the standard error, we have

$$SD_{e'} = SD_e / a \qquad (7.48)$$

That is, to divide the effect size by the attenuation factor is to divide the standard error by the same factor. The lower the reliability, the greater the increase in sampling error.

For example, if the reliability of the dependent variable is .64, then the sampling error variance of the corrected effect size is

$$\mathrm{Var}(e') = \mathrm{Var}(e) / .64 = (1 / .64)\mathrm{Var}(e) = 1.56(e)$$

The corresponding standard error is

$$SD_{e'} = \sqrt{1.56}\,SD_e = 1.25 SD_e$$

That is, if the study reliability is as low as .64, then the corrected effect size has 25% more sampling error than the uncorrected effect size. Thus, to eliminate the 20% systematic error in the uncorrected effect size, we must incur a 25% increase in the unsystematic error.

In meta-analysis, we must worry not only about the extent of reliability in single studies but also about variation in reliability across studies. If there is variation across studies in the reliability of measures of dependent variables, then different effect sizes are attenuated by different factors. This fact will cause variation in observed d values beyond the variation due to sampling error. Thus, in a bare-bones meta-analysis, there will be artifactual variance in the effect sizes that is not subtracted when the variance is corrected for the effect of sampling error. This variation is eliminated if each effect size is individually corrected for unreliability.

META-ANALYSIS OF d VALUES CORRECTED INDIVIDUALLY AND A WORKED EXAMPLE

If the reliability of the dependent variable is known for all individual studies, then each effect size can be individually corrected for attenuation. If the reliability is known for almost all studies, then there is little error in using the average reliability for the missing cases. The meta-analysis is then computed on the corrected effect sizes. The steps in the meta-analysis are the same as those for a bare-bones meta-analysis: (1) Compute the mean and variance of the effect sizes, (2) compute the variance in effect sizes due to sampling error, and (3) subtract that from the variance of the sample effect sizes. However, there is one complication: The weights that are optimal for uncorrected effect sizes are not optimal for corrected effect sizes. Optimal weights are inversely related to the sampling error in the effect size. In an uncorrected effect size, sampling error is primarily determined by the sample size. In a corrected effect size, however, the sampling error also depends on the extent of the correction for attenuation. Studies that require a large correction should get less weight than studies that require only a small correction. For uncorrected effect sizes, the optimal weight for each study is its sample size N_i. For corrected effect sizes, the optimal weight for each study is

$$w_i = N_i a_i^2 = N_i r_{YY_i} \qquad (7.49)$$

That is, the mean effect size is better estimated if we weight each study proportional to its reliability. The lower the reliability in the study, the lower is the optimal weight for that study. (We encountered this same principle in Chapter 3 in the case of corrected correlations.)

For each study, we compute three numbers: (1) the corrected effect size, (2) the weight to be given to the study, and (3) the sampling error variance for that study. The formula for the sampling error variance presents one small problem: It depends on the population effect size. A good approximation is to use the mean effect size in the sampling error formula (see Chapter 5; also see Hunter & Schmidt, 1994; Law et al., 1994b). Thus, the sampling error in the corrected effect size is approximately

$$\mathrm{Var}(e_i') = \mathrm{Var}(e_i)/a_i^2 = \mathrm{Var}(e_i)/r_{YY_i} \qquad (7.50)$$

where

$$\text{Var}(e_i) = [(N_i - 1)/(N_i - 3)][4/N_i][1 + \bar{d}_o^2/8] \qquad (7.51)$$

where $\bar{d}_o$ is the mean uncorrected effect size. Thus, estimation of the sampling error for the corrected effect sizes requires the computation of the average uncorrected effect size.

Let us denote the observed sample effect size by d_o and the corrected effect size by d_c. Denote the population uncorrected effect size by δ_o and the population corrected effect size by δ. Denote the sampling error variance estimate of study i by ve_i and denote the mean corrected effect size by $\bar{d}_c$. Then the three averages required for the meta-analysis are the following three weighted averages:

$$\text{Ave}(d_c) = \sum w_i d_{c_i} / \sum w_i \qquad (7.52)$$

$$\text{Var}(d_c) = \sum w_i (d_{c_i} - \bar{d}_c)^2 / \sum w_i \qquad (7.53)$$

$$\text{Var}(e') = \sum w_i ve_i' / \sum w_i \qquad (7.54)$$

The variance of population effect sizes is then estimated by subtraction:

$$\text{Var}(\delta) = \text{Var}(d_c) - \text{Var}(e') \qquad (7.55)$$

What has just been described here is the analysis conducted by the program D-VALUE described in the Appendix.

Now let us consider an example. Alex Lernmor, a psychologist at New York University, developed a new method of training doppelgängers in the facts they need to operate the machinery on their jobs. His training program has been adopted by many firms in the Northeast that employ doppelgängers. So far, four studies have been done in these firms to evaluate the effectiveness of the program, and the same 100-item measure of job knowledge was used in all four studies. In all cases, there were 20 people in the trained group and 20 in the control group (see Table 7.4). Alphonso Kopikat of the University of Texas learned about this program and, in connection with his consulting work, introduced it into many Texas businesses employing doppelgängers. Four studies evaluating the method have now been completed in Texas. These studies are much the same as the earlier ones, although, to save time, a short 12-item measure of job knowledge was used instead of the lengthy 100-item scale used by Lernmor. The results for this set of studies are also shown in Table 7.4.

Kopikat felt that his studies did not replicate Lernmor's findings. Whereas all of Lernmor's findings were positive, one of Kopikat's studies went in the wrong direction—a finding that greatly bothered the company at which the study was done. Furthermore, where two of Lernmor's

Table 7.4 Bare-bones meta-analyses on hypothetical studies on training doppelgängers.

Research Findings Author	Location	Sample Size	Effect Size
Lernmor	NE	40	.07
Lernmor	NE	40	.36
Lernmor	NE	40	.66*
Lernmor	NE	40	.95*
Kopikat	Texas	40	−.11
Kopikat	Texas	40	.18
Kopikat	Texas	40	.48
Kopikat	Texas	40	.77*
	Within-Subset Bare-Bones Meta-Analysis		
Bare-Bones Meta-Analysis	Texas Studies	Northeastern Studies	
$T = 40 + 40 + \ldots = 320$	$T = 40 + 40 + \ldots = 160$	$T = 40 + 40 + \ldots = 160$	
$N = 320 / 8 = 40$	$N = 160 / 4 = 40$	$N = 160 / 4 = 40$	
$\text{Ave}(d) = .42$	$\text{Ave}(d) = .33$	$\text{Ave}(d) = .51$	
$\text{Var}(d) = .116150$	$\text{Var}(d) = .108050$	$\text{Var}(d) = .108050$	
$\text{Var}(e) = .107730$	$\text{Var}(e) = .106840$	$\text{Var}(e) = .108332$	
$\text{Var}(\delta) = .008420$	$\text{Var}(\delta) = .001210$	$\text{Var}(\delta) = -.000782$	
$SD_\delta = .092$	$SD_\delta = .034$	$SD_\delta = 0$	

*Significant at the .05 level.

findings were significant—half the studies done—this was true for only one of Kopikat's four studies. He interpreted the difference in results in terms of a theory that postulated that Texans were slower learners.

However, a colleague warned Kopikat about sampling error and urged him to do a meta-analysis. Kopikat then did the bare-bones meta-analysis shown in Table 7.4. For the overall analysis, he found a mean of $\text{Ave}(\delta) = .42$ with a standard deviation of $SD = .09$, which, using a normal approximation, implies a middle range of $.24 < \delta < .60$. He also did the meta-analysis corresponding to his belief that the studies in Texas had different results. Those meta-analyses are also reported in Table 7.4. The mean effect was positive in Texas, as in the northeastern states, but the effect size was only a little more than half as large (i.e., .33 vs. .51). Furthermore, the within-subsets standard deviations were .03 and 0, considerably smaller than the overall standard deviation of .09. Thus, Kopikat admitted that the Texas results replicated the northeastern results in sign, but he claimed that the moderator effect confirmed his theory of regional workforce differences in learning ability. Kopikat's study was widely acclaimed as yet another convincing demonstration of the importance of moderator variables when it was published in the *Statistical Artifact Review* (2014, 66: 398–447).

Lernmor did not believe that Texans were slower learners. He was also bothered by the fact that Kopikat used only 12 items in his job knowledge test. Lernmor had found a reliability of .81 with his 100-item test. He used the reverse Spearman-Brown formula (given in the exercise at the end of this chapter and as Equation [7.67]) to compute the reliability of a 12-item test and found the reliability to be only .34. So Lernmor redid Kopikat's meta-analysis, correcting for attenuation. The results are shown in Table 7.5.

Lernmor's overall meta-analysis found a mean effect size of .57 with a standard deviation of .05, an implied middle range of $.49 < \delta < .65$. Lernmor also conducted separate meta-analyses for the two regional areas. He found a mean effect size of .57 in the northeastern studies and a mean effect size of .57 in the Texas studies. He concluded that region is not a moderator variable. Instead, he concluded that Kopikat's low values had resulted from the use of a lower reliability measure of the dependent variable in the studies in Texas. The calculations performed by Lernmor are those performed by the computer program D-VALUE, part of a software package of Windows-based meta-analysis programs available for applying the methods presented in this book. This software package and its availability are discussed in the Appendix. Lernmor performed his calculations by hand. Because there is less rounding error when the program is used, results produced by the D-VALUE program are slightly more accurate than Lernmor's results. We invite the reader to apply the D-VALUE program to the data in Table 7.5. The data in Table 7.5 are included as an example data set in the software described in the Appendix.

ARTIFACT DISTRIBUTION META-ANALYSIS AND A WORKED EXAMPLE

Reliability is sometimes available only on a sporadic basis. In that case, we cannot correct each individual effect size. However, if we can estimate the distribution of reliabilities in the research domain, we can correct the values obtained in a bare-bones meta-analysis for the effects of error of

Table 7.5 Worksheet for meta-analysis of studies in Table 7.4.

Location	N	d_o	r_{YY}	d_c	ve'	w_i
NE	40	.07	.81	.08	.132999	32.4
NE	40	.36	.81	.40	.132999	32.4
NE	40	.66	.81	.73	.132999	32.4
NE	40	.95	.81	1.06	.132999	32.4
Texas	40	−.11	.34	−.19	.316852	13.6
Texas	40	.18	.34	.31	.316852	13.6
Texas	40	.48	.34	.83	.316852	13.6
Texas	40	.77	.34	1.33	.316852	13.6

	Within-Subset Meta-Analysis	
Overall Meta-Analysis	*Texas Studies*	*Northeastern Studies*
Ave(d_c) = .568	Ave(d_c) = .570	Ave(d_c) = .568
Var(d_c) = .189528	Var(d_c) = .322600	Var(d_c) = .133669
Var(e) = .187356	Var(e) = .316852	Var(e) = .132999
Var(δ) = .002172	Var(δ) = .005748	Var(δ) = .000670
SD_δ = .047	SD_δ = .076	SD_δ = .026

measurement. The methods for this are developed fully in Chapter 4 (for correlations) and will be only sketched here. The method of meta-analysis of d values presented here is the method implemented by the program D-VALUE1 described in the Appendix.

The Mean True Effect Size

The key to the analysis is to look at the effect of error of measurement on the statistics computed in a bare-bones meta-analysis: the mean and variance of uncorrected effect sizes. The formula relating the actual effect size and the sample effect size is

$$d_o = \delta_o + e = a\delta + e \tag{7.56}$$

where δ is the actual effect size, a is the attenuation factor (the square root of the reliability), and e is the sampling error. Across a research domain, the mean observed effect size is

$$E(d_o) = E(a\delta + e) = E(a\delta) + E(e) \qquad (7.57)$$

If we ignore the slight bias in d (discussed earlier and in Chapter 6), then the mean sampling error is 0:

$$E(d_o) = E(a\delta) \qquad (7.58)$$

If the level of reliability of measurement is independent of the true effect size, then the mean of the product is the product of the means:

$$E(d_o) = E(a)E(\delta) \qquad (7.59)$$

The desired mean true effect size is thus attenuated by the average of the attenuation factors for individual studies. If the mean attenuation factor is known, then we can correct the observed mean effect size using the same formula we would use to correct an individual effect size:

$$E(\delta) = E(d_o) / E(a) \qquad (7.60)$$

Thus, to compute the mean effect size, we do not need to know the attenuation factor for each individual study; we need only know the mean attenuation factor across studies.

Note that the factor a is not the reliability but its square root. Thus, from the distribution of reliabilities, we must extract the distribution of attenuation factors. If the reliabilities are given individually, we merely transform to square roots before computing the mean and standard deviation. The D-VALUE2 program does this automatically; the user enters the reliability coefficients.

The Variance of True Effect Sizes

The variance of observed effect sizes is given by

$$\text{Var}(d_o) = \text{Var}(\delta_o + e) = \text{Var}(\delta_o) + \text{Var}(e) \qquad (7.61)$$

The bare-bones meta-analysis uses this to compute the variance of study population effect sizes $\text{Var}(\delta_o)$ by subtracting the sampling error variance $\text{Var}(e)$ from the variance of observed effect sizes $\text{Var}(d_o)$. That residual variance has been corrected for sampling error but not for error of measurement. The corrected variance from the bare-bones meta-analysis is connected to the desired variance of true effect sizes $\text{Var}(\delta)$ by

$$\text{Var}(\delta_o) = \text{Var}(a\delta) \qquad (7.62)$$

If the level of reliability is independent of the true effect size across studies, then, to a close approximation,

$$\mathrm{Var}(\delta_o) = [E(a)]^2 \mathrm{Var}(\delta) + [E(\delta)]^2 \mathrm{Var}(a) \qquad (7.63)$$

This equation can be solved for the desired variance $\mathrm{Var}(\delta)$:

$$\mathrm{Var}(\delta) = \{\mathrm{Var}(\delta_o) - [E(\delta)]^2 \mathrm{Var}(a)\} / [E(a)]^2 \qquad (7.64)$$

The right-hand side of this equation has four entries. The entry $\mathrm{Var}(\delta_o)$ is the corrected variance from the bare-bones meta-analysis. The entry $E(a)$ is the average attenuation factor across studies. The entry $\mathrm{Var}(a)$ is the variance of the attenuation factor across studies. The entry $E(\delta)$ is the average true effect size as computed in the previous section. The numerator

$$\mathrm{Var}(\delta_o) - [E(\delta)]^2 \mathrm{Var}(a) \qquad (7.65)$$

shows the subtraction of the variance in observed effect sizes due to variation in reliability from the bare-bones meta-analysis estimate of variance. In Chapter 4, the resulting variance was referred to as the residual variance. That is, the variance in study effect sizes can be partitioned

$$\begin{aligned} \mathrm{Var}(\delta_o) &= [E(a)]^2 \mathrm{Var}(\delta) + [E(\delta)]^2 \mathrm{Var}(a) + \mathrm{Var}(e) \\ &= A + B + C \end{aligned} \qquad (7.66)$$

where

A is the variance due to variation in true effect size (residual variance),

B is the variance due to variation in reliability, and

C is the variance due to sampling error.

An Example of Artifact Distribution Meta-Analysis

One of the oldest hypotheses in psychology is that a failure experience produces anxiety. For example, this is the hypothesis that links job stress to health problems, such as high blood pressure or stomach ulcers. Stress produces fear of failure, which produces anxiety, which produces autonomic arousal, which causes high levels of blood pressure and high levels of stomach acid. This has been studied in the laboratory by putting subjects in a situation where it is predetermined that they will fail and then measuring the resulting level of state anxiety. Table 7.6 presents the database for a meta-analysis of eight hypothetical experimental studies.

Jones (1992) located the eight studies but did only a bare-bones meta-analysis of the data. Thus, Jones saw only the columns for sample size and effect size in Table 7.6. His results are given as the first meta-analysis in Table 7.7. He found a mean effect size of .31 and a standard deviation of .075. Using the normal distribution as a guide, he estimated the 95% range to be $.16 < \delta < .46$. He concluded that the effect is always positive, but that the size of the effect varied across studies by as much as 3 to 1. Jones looked for a moderator variable but found none.

Smith (1996) had read the meta-analysis book by Hunter et al. (1982), and he worried about the reliability of the measurement of anxiety in these studies. He went back to the eight studies to see which studies reported the reliability of the dependent variable. Two studies reported reliability, the two studies with values listed in Table 7.6. He then did a meta-analysis correcting for reliability using the values found in the studies. This is the second meta-analysis shown in Table 7.7.

Table 7.6 Meta-analysis of hypothetical studies examining the effect of a failure experience on state anxiety.

Effect Size Studies Author	Sample Size	Effect Size	Number of Items	Reliability	Attenuation Factor
Callous (1949)	40	.82	5	—	—
Mean (1950)	40	.23	5	.60	.77
Cruel (1951)	40	−.06	5	—	—
Sadistic (1952)	40	.53	5	.65	.81
Villainous (1983)	40	.38	1	—	—
Vicious (1984)	40	−.20	1	—	—
Fiendish (1985)	40	.68	1	—	—
Diabolical (1986)	40	.10	1	—	—
Reliability Studies Author	Number of Items		Reliability	Reliability of One Item	
Uneasy (1964)	2		.45	.29	
Nervous (1968)	2		.35	.21	
Concerned (1972)	4		.60	.27	
Anxious (1976)	4		.54	.23	
Distressed (1980)	6		.68	.26	
Paralyzed (1984)	6		.66	.24	
Average reliability of one item = .25 or a = .50					
Implied reliability of five items = .625 or a = .79					

Table 7.7 Meta-analyses performed on the studies of failure and anxiety in Table 7.6.

Bare-Bones Meta-Analysis (Jones, 1992)
$T = 320$
$\bar{N} = T / 8 = 40$
Ave(d) = .310
Var(d) = .112225
Var(e) = .106672
Var(δ_0) = .005553
$SD_{\delta_O} = .075$
Bare-Bones Analysis Corrected for Error of Measurement Using the Reliability Information Given in the Experimental Studies (Smith, 1996)
Ave(a) = [.77 + .81] / 2 = .79
Var(a) = [$(.77 - .79)^2 + (.81 - .79)^2$] / 2 = .000400
Ave(δ) = Ave(d) / Ave(a) = .31 / .79 = .392
Var(δ) = {Var(δ_o) − [Ave(δ)]^{2}Var(a)} / {Ave(a)}^{2}
= {.0005553 − $(.392)^2(.00040)$} / $(.79)^2$ = .008799
$SD_\delta = .094$
Bare-Bones Meta-Analysis Corrected Error of Measurement Using the Information From the Reliability Studies (Black, 2002)
Ave(a) = [.79 + .50] / 2 = .645
Var(a) = [$(.79 - .645)^2 + (.50 - .645)^2$] / 2 = .021025
Ave(δ) = Ave(δ_o) / Ave(a) = .310 / .645 = .481
Var(δ) = {Var(δ_o) − [Ave(δ)]^{2}Var(a)} / {Ave(a)}^{2}
= {.0005553 − $(.481)^2(.021025)$} / $(.645)^2$ = .001655
$SD_\delta = .041$

For the two studies that reported reliability, the attenuation factors are .77 and .81, which have a mean of .79 and a standard deviation of .02. The corrected meta-analysis yielded a mean effect size of .39 with a standard deviation of .09. The normal distribution middle 95% range would be

.21 < δ < .57. Smith then noted that Jones was right in asserting that the effect is always positive, but Jones had underestimated the strength of the mean effect by 21%. On the other hand, Smith, too, found that the size of the effect varied by as much as 3 to 1.

Black (2002) thought that Smith was right to worry about reliability, but he worried that the two studies that reported reliability might not have been representative of the domain as a whole. Black looked at each report to see what was said about the nature of the measurement. What he found was that the four older studies were done before behavioristic methodology had had much impact on personality research. Those studies all worried about the quality of measurement and constructed multi-item scales to assess state anxiety. Each older study used a five-item scale to measure anxiety. The four later studies were done after behavioristic methodology became dominant in personality research. These studies were unconcerned with the quality of measurement and assessed state anxiety by a single response, that is, a one-item scale. Black then looked up six studies that reported the reliabilities of various scales measuring state anxiety. The reported reliabilities are shown in Table 7.6. The reliabilities are not comparable because the scales vary in the number of items. So Black used the reverse Spearman-Brown formula to compute the reliability of one item, a common reference point for all studies. This formula is

$$r_i = [r_n / n] / [1 - (1 - 1/n)r_n] \qquad (7.67)$$

where n is the number of items on the scale with reliability r_n. The one-item reliabilities are reported in Table 7.6. All one-item reliabilities are close to .25, and the variation in reliabilities is no more than would be expected from sampling error. From this, it was apparent to Black that the reliability in the newer one-item studies was only .25. Based on this fact, he used the Spearman-Brown formula (given in the exercise at the end of this chapter) to compute a reliability of .625 for the older five-item studies, a value that agrees with the two reliabilities reported. He then used that information to do the third meta-analysis shown in Table 7.7. Black found a mean effect size of .48 with a standard deviation of .04. The normal distribution middle range would be .40 < δ < .56. Black noted that Jones had underestimated the mean effect of failure by 35% while Smith had underestimated it by 19%. He also noted that both authors had very greatly overestimated the extent of variation across studies. Variation in reliability produced a variance of

$$[E(\delta)]^2 \text{Var}(a) = (.481)^2(.021025) = .004864$$

in study population correlations whose variance was $S_{\delta_o}^2 = .005553$. That is, variation in reliability accounts for .004864 / .005553 or 88% of the variance in study population effect sizes. Black noted that it would be quite possible that variation in other artifacts that could not be corrected might account for the remaining 12% of the variance. That is, it is reasonable to suspect that the actual treatment effect is actually approximately constant across studies.

The artifact distribution methods for *d* value meta-analysis illustrated in this example are the basis of the computer program D-VALUE1, one of the six Windows-based interactive programs in the program package available for applying the methods described in this book. This meta-analysis software package and its availability are described in the Appendix.

Measurement Error in the Independent Variable in Experiments

The preceding section shows that error of measurement in the dependent variable can have a considerable impact on the effect size, both in terms of reducing the apparent size of the mean effect and in terms of producing artificial variation in effect sizes across studies. The analysis in Chapter 6 showed that error of measurement in the independent variable can have just as large an effect. The important point is to remember that group membership is a *nominal* designation. It represents what the experimenter *intended* to happen to the subject and may or may not represent actual processes. If the subject is not listening closely to the instructions, then an experimental difference in instructions may not apply to many of the nominally experimental group subjects. In naturalistic dichotomies, such as "schizophrenic" versus "normal," some of the nominal schizophrenics may not be psychotic and some of the nominal normals may be schizophrenic. The practical problem for meta-analysis is that in most current studies, there is no information on the extent of misidentification on the independent variable. Without such information, there can be no analysis of its impact. This is unfortunate, because the fact that experimenters ignore such an error does not make the error disappear. Thus, in the typical meta-analysis, there will be no correction for error of measurement in the independent variable. It is important to remember this in the interpretation of the meta-analysis. If this artifact is ignored, then the mean treatment effect is correspondingly underestimated and the variance of treatment effects is correspondingly overstated.

If the correlation between nominal and actual identification is denoted *a*, then the population study effect size correlation is

$$\rho_o = a\rho \tag{7.68}$$

where ρ is the actual treatment correlation (attenuated for the other artifacts in the study). Thus, if the meta-analysis were done measuring the treatment effect as a correlation, the analysis would be directly symmetric to the analysis of the impact of error of measurement in the dependent variable. The analysis of the d statistic is complicated by the nonlinearity of the transformation from r to d:

$$d = 2r / \sqrt{(1-r^2)} \qquad (7.69)$$

In the present case, we have

$$\delta_o = 2\rho_o / \sqrt{(1-\rho_o^2)} = 2(a\rho) / \sqrt{(1-a^2\rho^2)} \qquad (7.70)$$

where

$$\rho = \delta / \sqrt{(4+\delta^2)} \qquad (7.71)$$

In most contemporary meta-analyses, the population treatment effects are not large. Those of textbook social psychology experiments are rarely larger than $\delta = .40$ (Richard et al., 2003). Those for more sophisticated research domains are smaller yet. We will show that, for domains where the population treatment effects are no larger than .40, we have the close approximation

$$\delta_o = a\delta \qquad (7.72)$$

This approximation is perfectly symmetric to the equation for the impact of error of measurement in the dependent variable. Thus, the mathematics of the meta-analysis is the same except for the change in the meaning of the attenuation factor a. For the present case, a is the correlation between nominal and actual group membership. For the case of error in the dependent variable, a was the square root of the reliability of the dependent variable. This difference is less than it might seem. The square root of the reliability of the dependent variable is the correlation between observed dependent variable score and the dependent variable true score. Thus, the meaning of a is actually symmetric between the case of the independent variable and the case of the dependent variable.

It is important to note that the approximation is used here for population effect sizes and not for sample effect sizes. Sample effect sizes will often be larger than .40 because of sampling error. If the population effect size were $\delta = .20$ and the sample size were $N = 40$, it would not be unusual to see a sample effect size as large as $d = .64$. However, sampling error is not a part of the approximation process. Rather, sampling error is added *after* the attenuation effect. That is, the sampling error equation is additive:

$$d_o = \delta_o + e$$

Thus, the sampling error equation uses the approximation

$$d_o = \delta_o + e = a\delta + e$$

which does not alter the value of e.

In most real meta-analyses, the study population effect size is attenuated by other artifacts, such as error of measurement in the dependent variable. In this case, the extraneous attenuation has the effect of extending the range of the linear approximation. Suppose the true treatment effect is $\delta = .60$, but it is attenuated to $\delta_1 = .40$ by error of measurement in the dependent variable. The linear approximation applies to the attenuated effect size .40 rather than the unattenuated effect size .60. Thus, we have the approximation

$$\delta_o = a\delta_1 \tag{7.73}$$

which becomes

$$\delta_o = ab\delta \tag{7.74}$$

with the substitution $\delta_1 = b\delta$, where b is the attenuation factor for error of measurement in the dependent variable. Thus, in this case, the linear approximation is still quite close even though the true effect size is as large as .60.

Finally, we show that, for effect sizes no larger than .40, the impact of nonlinearity is slight. Suppose $\delta = .40$. Then

$$\rho = \delta / \sqrt{(4 + \delta^2)} = .40 / \sqrt{(4 + .16)} = (.40 / 2) / \sqrt{1.04}$$

which, to a close approximation, is

$$\rho = (\delta / 2)(1.02) = \delta / 2 \tag{7.75}$$

That is, for population treatment effects in the usual range, the transformation from d to ρ is approximately linear. Using this approximation, we have the approximation

$$\delta_o = [2a(\delta / 2)] / \sqrt{[1 - a^2(\delta / 2)^2]} \tag{7.76}$$

$$= [a\delta] / \sqrt{[1 - .25\delta^2 a^2]} \tag{7.77}$$

For population treatment effects no larger than $\delta = .40$, the denominator satisfies the following inequality:

$$\sqrt{[1 - .25\delta^2 a^2]} \quad > \sqrt{[1 - .04a^2]}$$
$$> 1 - .02a^2 > 1 - .02$$

Thus, if the population treatment effect is no larger than .40, there is little error in the approximation

$$\delta_o = [a\delta] / 1 = a\delta \tag{7.78}$$

Thus, for population treatment effects no larger than .40, we have the close approximation

$$\delta_o = a\delta \qquad\qquad (7.78a)$$

Other Artifacts and Their Effects

In this chapter, we have considered the following artifacts: sampling error, random measurement error in the dependent variable, and random measurement error (causal misidentification) in the independent or treatment variable. Other artifacts were discussed in Chapter 6: imperfect construct validity of the dependent variable, imperfect construct validity (confounding) in the independent or treatment variable, dichotomization of a continuous dependent variable, variation in the strength of treatment, and attrition artifacts. Given certain information about the extent and nature of the artifact, it is possible to correct the meta-analysis for the effects of that artifact. We have shown how to do this for a meta-analysis of correlations, but we have not presented the corresponding computations for the *d* statistic. The computations can be done, although the correction formulas for the *d* statistic are usually nonlinear and more cumbersome than the formulas for *r*. The simplest method is to convert the *d*s to *r*s and do the meta-analysis on *r*, as we noted earlier in this chapter. The methods for doing this are presented later in this chapter.

We would like to emphasize that the reason that we did not present the formulas is not because the artifact effects are small. Where such artifacts have been tracked, they have often proved to be large. Of special concern is the effect of imperfect construct validity in experimental studies. Experimental treatments, especially in lab experiments in social psychology, are often metaphorical in nature. For example, the investigator codes helping someone pick up his or her dropped papers as measuring altruism and, thus, treats that dependent variable measure as if it were equivalent to signing up for the Peace Corps. Or the investigator believes that a failure experience is an attack on self-esteem and, thus, treats failure at a laboratory problem-solving task as if it were the same as the effect of flunking out of college. In the organizational literature, there is often a considerable gap in the construct validity of lab and field studies. This has shown up in many meta-analyses conducted on organizational interventions.

It is important to correct for as many artifacts as possible, even if the formulas to do so are not given in this chapter for the *d* statistic. Finally, it is important to remember that there is an artifact that is difficult to detect and, thus, is rarely corrected: bad data. There can be error in coding raw data, error in computing statistics or recording the numbers computed, error in typing manuscripts, error in printing numbers, and, according to certain cynics, error in meta-analytic data recording (especially in converting from some strange statistic to d or r). At a minimum, one should be on the lookout for extreme outliers, that is, effect sizes that are extremely different from other studies. Unfortunately, in many research domains, the average sample size is so small that it is difficult to distinguish between an outlier and a large sampling error. For these reasons, it is always wise to consider residual variance with a large grain of salt. The residual variance virtually always contains the effects of uncorrected artifacts, even if the meta-analyst has convinced himself or herself that the artifact does not exist.

Correcting Individual d Values for Multiple Artifacts

The previous sections of this chapter treated error of measurement in the independent and dependent variable as if one or the other occurred, but not both. The fact is that both errors often occur in a given study. Furthermore, any given study may also be affected by the many artifacts listed in Chapter 6 that have not been considered in this chapter to this point. Thus, a proper meta-analysis will have to correct for multiple artifacts.

In Chapter 6, we noted that quantifying the effect of multiple artifacts on the effect size statistic d requires very complicated formulas. These complicated formulas make it cumbersome in a primary study to correct a d value for several artifacts jointly. The complicated artifact formulas create serious problems for meta-analysis when meta-analysis with multiple artifacts is conducted in the d value metric. The solution is to transform ds into rs, correct for the multiple artifacts, and then transform the corrected rs back into the d value metric. In this section, we derive formulas based on the correlational transform of d values for the correction of *individual* d values for multiple artifacts. Methods for using the correlational transform of d values in meta-analysis with multiple artifacts are given in a later section.

Attenuation Effect of Multiple Artifacts and Correction for the Same

The artifacts other than sampling error are systematic. At the level of population statistics, the attenuation produced by the study artifacts can be algebraically computed. That algebra can be reversed. Thus, it is possible to start with the attenuated effect size and compute the true effect size. In the form of an equation, this process would be called "correction for attenuation." The classic formulas were developed for random error of measurement, but similar correction formulas could be generated for any systematic artifact.

Observed study effect sizes are influenced not only by the systematic artifacts but by sampling error as well. The algebraic formulas that work exactly for population statistics do not work exactly for sample statistics. Instead, there is a more complicated interaction between sampling error and the systematic effect of the other artifacts. This section describes the attenuating effect of systematic errors on population statistics. The effects of sampling error are considered in the following section.

The complication of artifact formulas for *d* is in sharp contrast to the simple formulas for artifact effects on the correlation. For the artifacts currently identified, the effect on the correlation is to multiply the correlation by a constant that measures the impact of the artifact. In many of the cases in Chapter 6, we capitalized on this fact to indirectly compute the effect of an artifact on *d*. There are three steps to this method. First, transform the actual treatment effect *d* into the corresponding treatment effect correlation ρ. Second, compute the effect of the artifact on the treatment correlation, that is, compute the attenuated treatment correlation ρ_o. Third, transform the attenuated treatment correlation ρ_o back into the *d* statistic form as δ_o. We will now use this same strategy to compute the attenuating effect of multiple artifacts.

For correlations, it is as easy to handle multiple artifacts as it is to handle one. Each of the artifacts currently listed can be quantified in the form of a product in which the unaffected correlation is multiplied by a constant. This process was explored in detail in Chapter 3. Denote the actual population correlation by ρ and the artifactually attenuated population correlation by ρ_o. Then the effect of any one artifact is quantified as

$$\rho_o = a\rho$$

where *a* is an artifact multiplier (such as the square root of the reliability) that measures the effect of that artifact on the correlation. If the correlation is affected by several artifacts, then the study correlation is simply multiplied by the several corresponding artifact multipliers. For example, if three artifacts were measured by *a*, *b*, and *c*, then

$$\rho_o = abc\rho.$$

The net impact of the several artifacts can be combined into one artifact multiplier as in

$$\rho_o = A\rho$$

where the combined artifact multiplier *A* is given by the product

$$A = abc$$

That is, the combined artifact multiplier *A* is the product of the individual artifact multipliers. Except for the change of notation from *a* to *A*, the math of the compound effect of several artifacts is no different from the math of a single artifact.

We will now derive a procedure to compute the attenuated study effect size δ_o from the actual treatment effect δ. This is done in three steps. First, we transform δ to ρ. Second, we use the simple multiple-artifact formulas for correlation to compute the attenuated study treatment correlation ρ_o. Third, we transform the attenuated study correlation ρ_o into the attenuated study effect size δ_o. The complexity of formulas for the d statistic stems from the nonlinearity of the relationship between d and r. Consider the true treatment effect size δ and the corresponding true treatment correlation ρ. The relationship between them is given by the conversion formulas

$$\delta = 2\rho / \sqrt{(1-\rho^2)}$$
$$\rho = \delta / \sqrt{(4+\delta^2)}$$

Note that sample size does not appear in these conversion formulas because they are formulas for population parameters.

Attenuation

To compute the attenuating effect of several artifacts, we first transform the unattenuated effect size δ to obtain the unattenuated treatment correlation ρ:

$$\rho = \delta / \sqrt{(4+\delta^2)} \tag{7.79}$$

We then compute the attenuated treatment correlation ρ_o. The combined impact of several artifacts is computed for the treatment correlation by the product

$$\rho_o = A\rho$$

where A is the combined artifact multiplier (the product of the individual artifact multipliers). We now compute the attenuated treatment effect size δ_o. The study population effect size δ_o is given by

$$\delta_o = 2\rho_o / \sqrt{(1-\rho_o^2)} \tag{7.80}$$

Correction for Attenuation

For the systematic artifacts, the attenuation effect can be computed algebraically. This algebra can be reversed to produce a formula that corrects the observed treatment effect for attenuation. That is, we can produce an algebraic procedure that takes the study effect size δ_o, which has been reduced in size by the study artifacts, and algebraically restores it to the size of the actual treatment effect δ. This is most easily done for the treatment effect statistic by transforming to treatment correlations. The steps are as follows: (1) Transform the attenuated study effect size δ_o to the attenuated study treatment correlation ρ_o; (2) correct the study treatment correlation for attenuation, that is, algebraically restore the attenuated value ρ_o to the correct treatment correlation ρ; and (3) transform the disattenuated correlation ρ into the disattenuated treatment effect δ.

Suppose we are given the attenuated study treatment effect δ_o. The attenuated study treatment correlation is computed by the conversion formula to be

$$\rho_o = \delta_o / \sqrt{(4 + \delta_o^2)} \tag{7.81}$$

From the fact that the study artifacts reduced the treatment correlation ρ to

$$\rho_o = A\rho$$

we algebraically deduce the fact that

$$\rho = \rho_o / A \tag{7.82}$$

This is the formula for the correction of the treatment correlation for attenuation due to the artifacts measured by the compound artifact multiplier A. The true treatment effect δ is then computed by transforming the true treatment correlation ρ:

$$\delta = 2\rho / \sqrt{(1 - \rho^2)} \tag{7.83}$$

Meta-Analysis of *d* Values With Multiple Artifacts Using the Correlation Metric

For meta-analysis in the *d* value metric with multiple artifacts (i.e., with artifacts beyond sampling error and measurement error in the dependent variable), we need a method that enables us to compute sampling error variance and relate it to the variation in effect sizes across studies. That is, we need a formula relating the sample study *d* statistic to the true effect size δ. To get this formula, we would need a formula for the attenuated study effect size as a function of the attenuation multiplier A and the true treatment effect *d*. The exact formula is intractable for meta-analysis because of the nonlinearity of the relationship of *d* to *r*. However, close

approximations yield formulas that can be used for meta-analysis of
d values, and these approximation formulas are presented in Hunter and
Schmidt (2004, chap. 7). However, these equations are complicated and as
a result are not often used. Instead, most meta-analysts have converted
d values to r values and conducted the meta-analysis on these r values,
using the program illustrated and discussed in Chapter 3 (VG6) when each
value is corrected individually and the program illustrated in Chapter 4
(INTNL) when artifact distribution meta-analysis is employed. This
approach is simpler, more convenient, and easier than carrying out the
meta-analysis in the d value statistic when there are multiple artifacts. This
approach is widely used in the literature today.

There are four steps in conducting a meta-analysis of d values correcting for multiple artifacts using the r statistic:

1. Convert all the ds to rs using the formula given earlier in this chapter. The maximum likelihood formula is

$$r = d / \sqrt{(4 + d^2)} \tag{7.84}$$

2. Use the methods described in Chapters 3 and 4 to conduct the
   meta-analysis on r, correcting for all possible artifacts. The sample
   size (N) is the total N from the d study.

3. Convert the final results for the mean correlation to a mean effect
   size using the conversion formula for r to d. The maximum likelihood formula is

$$\bar{d}_c = 2\bar{\rho} / \sqrt{(1 - \bar{\rho}^2)} = \bar{\delta} \tag{7.85}$$

4. Convert the standard deviation of correlations to the standard deviation for effect sizes using the formula

$$SD_\delta = a SD_\rho$$

where

$$a = 2 / (1 - \bar{\rho}^2)^{1.5} = 2 / \left[\left(1 - \bar{\rho}^2\right) \sqrt{1 - \bar{\rho}^2} \right] \tag{7.86}$$

For example, suppose the meta-analysis in the r metric yields a mean
treatment correlation of Ave(ρ) = .50 and a standard deviation of SD_ρ = .10.
The conversion to mean d value effect size is then

$$Ave(\delta) = 2(.50) / \sqrt{[1 - (.50)^2]} = 1.1547$$
$$SD_\delta = a(.10)$$

where $a = 2/(1-.25)^{1.5} = 2/.6495 = 3.0792$. The final result is Ave(δ) = 1.15 and $SD_\delta = .31$.

As explained in Chapters 3 and 4, the output of these two programs (VG6 and INTNL) also includes many other items of information (e.g., percent of variance accounted for by artifacts and percent by sampling error alone). Credibility and confidence intervals will be given in the ρ metric. Their endpoints can be translated to the *d* value metric using Equation (7.85) presented earlier.

Summary of Meta-Analysis of *d* Values

Although statisticians have consistently warned against it, the conventional evaluation of experiments and programs has been by use of the statistical significance test. In a two-group design, this means that the number most likely to be published is the *t* statistic. The value of *t* does not answer the most relevant question: How large was the treatment effect? Instead, the value of *t* answers the question, How far out is the observed treatment effect under the assumption that the population treatment effect is 0? This chapter began by presenting alternative measures of the size of the treatment effect: the raw score mean difference, the standard score mean difference (*d* or δ), and the point biserial correlation (*r* or ρ). Because different authors use different measures of the dependent variable, the raw score difference is not usually workable for meta-analysis. Nor is the odds ratio an appropriate statistic in most social science research. Thus, the usual statistics used to characterize the size of the treatment effect are *d* and *r*. If the point biserial correlation is used (and it is the easier of the two in terms of formulas), then the relevant chapters are Chapters 2 through 4. This chapter presented formulas for bare-bones meta-analysis using the *d* statistic. The *d* statistic is influenced by a number of error factors or artifacts as listed in Chapter 6: sampling error, error of measurement in either variable, imperfect construct validity in either variable, artifactual dichotomization of the dependent variable, and so on. For each such artifact, there is artifact information that would make it possible to control for that artifact in meta-analysis. However, primary researchers are only just beginning to orient publication practices to include the collection and presentation of the information needed to control for the effects of artifacts. Thus, it is often the case that the only piece of artifact information available is the sample size *N*, the number needed to control for the effect of sampling error.

If sample size is the only piece of artifact information available in a given research area, then the only meta-analysis that can be conducted is a bare-bones meta-analysis that controls for no artifact other than sampling error. This type of meta-analysis is part of the output of both of the *d* value meta-analysis programs described in the Appendix: D-VALUE (for individual correction) and D-VALUE1 (for artifact distributions). Because other artifacts are not controlled, the bare-bones meta-analysis will greatly underestimate the mean treatment effect and will overestimate the standard deviation of treatment effects across studies, especially in relation to the mean (i.e., the coefficient of variation of treatment effects will be greatly overestimated). The key formula for the bare-bones meta-analysis of the d statistic is the sampling error variance formula for d. The bare-bones meta-analysis is very straightforward. The mean population d is estimated by the mean d statistic across studies, where the mean is computed by weighing each study by its sample size. The variance of population effect sizes is estimated by subtracting the sampling error variance from the observed variance of d statistics across studies. The subtraction of the sampling error variance is the statistical control for sampling error that completely eliminates the effects of sampling error once the number of studies in the meta-analysis becomes large enough. For a meta-analysis with a small number of studies, there is still sampling error in the meta-analysis values (second-order sampling error, a topic considered in Chapter 9). Thus, bare-bones meta-analysis uses the mean observed effect size, the standard deviation of observed effect sizes, and the sample size for each study to produce an estimate of the mean and standard deviation of study population effect sizes. For most purposes, the key question is this: Is the standard deviation of effect sizes small in comparison to the effect size? If the answer is yes, then most inferences about the treatment effect will be correctly made if the mean effect size is used as "the" effect size. However, it is important to remember that the mean effect size from a bare-bones meta-analysis underestimates the actual effect size because there is no correction for attenuation due to study artifacts other than sampling error. It is also important to remember that the standard deviation of population effect sizes in a bare-bones meta-analysis is *not* corrected for variation in the other artifacts and, thus, overestimates the extent of real variation in the attenuated effect sizes across studies. If a theory predicts that effect sizes will vary between certain kinds of studies, or if the standard deviation of population effect sizes is large in proportion to the mean effect size, then the meta-analysis should be extended to analyze potential moderator variables. If the theory predicts that studies of Type A will yield effect sizes larger than those of Type B, that distinction is the moderator variable to be tested. Otherwise, the moderator variable must be sought by trial and error, usually starting with some set of study characteristics that are coded for each study for descriptive purposes. As described near the end of Chapter 2, this process can result in disastrous capitalization on chance (sampling error). This problem is discussed in detail in Chapter 9.

The use of bare-bones meta-analysis to study a potential moderator variable requires no new statistical mathematics. The potential moderator variable is used to break the studies into subsets. A bare-bones meta-analysis is then run on each subset separately. The impact of the potential moderator is registered in two ways: the difference in the mean effect size across subsets and a reduction in the standard deviation of effect sizes within subsets. Because the number of studies within subsets is smaller, the theory of second-order sampling error in Chapter 9 shows that the difference in means is better estimated than is the reduction in variance within subsets. In the case of the theoretically predicted moderator variable, the subset strategy works well. However, as discussed in Chapter 9, if multiple potential moderators are examined, it is important to avoid confounding of moderators; this can be achieved via hierarchical moderator analysis. In the case of a trial-and-error search for moderators, there is a further problem of capitalization on sampling errors. As discussed in Chapters 2 and 9, if you analyze a large number of potential moderator variables, then at least one will appear to be statistically significant by chance. If one uses regression analysis of moderators (i.e., meta-regression), there will almost always be a combination of potential moderator variables that appears to account for variation in effect size, but this "explanation" could be a result of capitalization on the specific sampling errors in specific studies.

If there is information on artifacts other than sampling error (and experience has shown that where the data are available, these artifacts prove to be large and important), then the meta-analysis can be considerably more accurate than a bare-bones meta-analysis. Beyond sampling error, the artifact most commonly corrected for in meta-analyses of experiments is measurement error in the dependent variable. If artifact information is known for all or almost all studies, then each observed *d* value can be corrected individually for artifacts and the meta-analysis can be conducted on the corrected *d* values. Examples of this were presented. This type of *d* value meta-analysis is conducted by the program D-VALUE described in the Appendix. If artifact information is available only sporadically across studies, then artifact distribution meta-analysis can be performed. Again, examples of this were presented. This procedure for meta-analysis is performed by the program D-VALUE1 described in the Appendix.

In meta-analysis of *d* values, when artifacts beyond sampling error and measurement error in the dependent variable are corrected for, it is simpler and easier to transform all *d* values to point biserial correlations, conduct the meta-analysis on correlations using the methods described in Chapters 3 and 4, and then transform the final results back to the *d* value metric. This is because the formulas for correlations are less complicated than those for *d* values. If artifact information is available for some artifacts for all studies and only sporadically available for other artifacts, then a mixed meta-analysis of the type described in the example near the end of Chapter 4 can be conducted. In all cases in which artifacts beyond sampling error are corrected for, potential moderators can be examined using the same methods described for use with bare-bones meta-analysis.

Exercise 7.1: Meta-Analysis of *d* Values

Meta-Analysis of d Values: Studies of Gender Differences in Conformity

Study	Total Sample Size	Effect Size Estimate d Value	Number of Items
1	254	.35	38
2	80	.37	5
3	125	−.06	5
4	191	−.30	2
5	64	.69	30
6	90	.40	45
7	60	.47	45
8	20	.81	45
9	141	−.33	2
10	119	.07	2

A hypothetical researcher conducted a review of experimental studies of gender differences in conformity. The 10 studies summarized here are called "other conformity studies." Because all these studies use an experimental paradigm involving a nonexistent norm group, they are called "fictitious norm group" studies.

These studies measure conformity by examining the effect of knowledge of other people's responses on an individual's response. Typically, an experimental subject is presented with an opportunity to respond to a question of opinion. Before responding, the individual is shown some "data" on the responses of other individuals. The "data" are manipulated by the experimenters, and the "other individuals" are the fictitious norm group. For example, the subject might be asked for an opinion on a work of art and told that 75% of art majors liked the work "a great deal."

Positive *d* values indicate females were more conforming; negative values indicate males were more conforming.

Except for Step 2, this exercise can be worked using the program D-VALUE, which corrects *d* values individually for artifacts. Alternatively, you can convert all *d* values to correlations and apply the program VG6, which uses the methods presented in Chapter 3 to correct correlations individually and then performs meta-analysis on the corrected correlations. You would then convert these results back into the *d* value metric using equations given in this chapter. Both these programs are included in the Windows-based package of programs available for applying the methods presented in this book. Details about this software package can be found in the Appendix. However, you will learn more if you carry out the exercise using a calculator or a spreadsheet.

INSTRUCTIONS FOR EXERCISE

1. Perform a bare-bones meta-analysis of these 10 studies. Correct the *d* values for their small positive bias, as discussed in this chapter. In estimating sampling error variance, use the most accurate formula given in this chapter. Create a table showing the mean *d*, the observed variance of *d*, the variance predicted from sampling error, the variance corrected for sampling error, and the standard deviation of the *d* values corrected for sampling error. In addition, present the percentage variance accounted for by sampling error variance, the square root of the *proportion of variance accounted for,* and the 80% credibility interval.

   What percentage of variance is accounted for by sampling error? What is the correlation between sampling errors and the observed *d* values? How would these results be interpreted by someone with no knowledge of measurement error? That is, give the "face value" interpretation of these results.

   From these results, in what percentage of groups would you expect males to be more conforming? Females? Note that if $\bar{d}$ were 0, males would be more conforming in 50% of the groups and the same for females. Use the properties of the normal curve to compute the percentages implied by your $\bar{d}$ value. First, compute $z = (0 - \bar{d}) / SD_{\delta_{xy}}$. Then look this *z* value up in a normal curve table and record the percentages above and below this *z* value. These are the needed percentages.

2. Determine the importance of correcting the observed *d* values for their positive bias. Rerun the analysis in Step 1 but do not correct for this bias. How different are your results? What do you conclude about the bias correction?

3. Reliabilities for the conformity measures were not given in these studies. However, the number of trials (or "items") *was* given. An example of a trial (or item) was given previously: The subjects were shown a piece of art and told that 75% of art majors liked the work "a great deal." Some studies had only two such trials; the largest number of trials was 45. (Three studies had this many.) The number of items in each study is given in the data table.

   The average correlation between trials is .10 (i.e., $\bar{r} = .10$). Use this information and the Spearman-Brown formula to compute the reliability of the conformity measure used in each study, based on the number of "items" (trials) used in that study. In the exercise, the Spearman-Brown formula can be written as

   $$\text{Reliability} = n\bar{r} / [1 + (n - 1)\bar{r}]$$

   where *n* is the number of trials and $\bar{r}$ is the average correlation between trials.

4. Use these reliability estimates to correct each *d* value for measurement error. (Use the *d* values corrected for positive bias.) Then conduct a meta-analysis of the corrected *d* values. Report the r_{yy} values computed.

Present the same information as in the bare-bones meta-analysis, except this time for the corrected d values. That is, present the following in a table:

a. The mean corrected d value

b. The observed variance of the corrected d values

c. The sampling error variance for the corrected d values

d. The variance of the corrected d values corrected for sampling error variance, that is, the estimated variance of the population (δ) values

e. The estimated standard deviation of δ

f. The percentage of variance accounted for by the two artifacts (sampling error and measurement error) and the square root of the *proportion* of variance accounted for.

g. The 80% credibility interval

Interpret these findings as you did those for the bare-bones meta-analysis. How different is the percentage of variance accounted for compared to the bare-bones meta-analysis? What is the correlation between the corrected d values and the combined effects of the two artifacts? Does the correction for measurement error lead to any differences in substantive conclusions? Compute the estimated percentage of groups in which males are more conforming than females and vice versa. Is the estimated percentage of groups in which males are more conforming than females different from the figure obtained in the bare-bones meta-analysis? What about the estimated percentage of groups in which the females are more conforming? Why are these percentages different from those computed from the bare-bones meta-analysis results? What conclusions do you draw about the importance of correcting for measurement error?

Technical Questions in Meta-Analysis of *d* Values

8

This chapter discusses technical questions that arise in the meta-analysis of experimental effect sizes. The most important of these questions is the effect of different experimental designs on the properties of the resulting *d* values. The other technical issues we address include (a) empirical research findings on the accuracy of different designs for repeated measures research, (b) threats to internal and external validity of repeated measures experiments that do not have a control group, (c) the slight positive bias in observed *d* values, (d) confidence and credibility intervals in *d* value meta-analysis, and (e) fixed versus random effects models in *d* value meta-analysis.

Alternative Experimental Designs: General Considerations

The methods presented in Chapter 7 are for independent groups design. In this design, subjects are assigned randomly to experimental and control groups. Different subjects are assigned to different groups, and hence, the design is called "independent subjects," "between-subjects," or "independent groups" design. This is the most commonly used design, but a number of other possible study designs are sometimes used: (a) analysis of covariance (ANCOVA) designs (in which the effects of certain variables are partialled out), (b) factorial analysis of variance (ANOVA) independent groups designs, (c) repeated measures designs without a control group and matched groups designs, and (d) repeated measures designs with a control group. We also provide references for methods of dealing with more statistically complex designs (e.g., nested ANOVA designs) that are less commonly used.

In most meta-analyses based on *d values,* the *d* values to be included in the meta-analysis will mostly come from studies using the independent groups design. But some of the relevant studies will often have used other experimental designs. In order to include these studies in the meta-analysis, *d* values must be computed for these studies that are in the same metric as that of the independent groups *d* values. That is, they must be expressed in the standard deviation units of the independent groups *SD*. In the case of each of these alternative designs, there are two critical questions; First, how does one compute *d* values that estimate the same population parameter estimated by the *d* value in the independent groups design? Second, what is the correct formula for the sampling error variance of each of these (correctly computed) *d* values? Consider the question of how to estimate the correct *d* value. In ANCOVA models, the pooled standard deviation is usually reduced by partialling out the covariates; hence, the *d* value is over-estimated if the usual formula for a *d* value is used. Special formulas must be used to ensure that this does not happen. In repeated measures designs, the standard deviation is the standard deviation of change scores (gain scores or difference scores); this *SD* is typically much smaller than the standard deviation of raw scores across individuals in the population. Again, special formulas are needed to ensure that the *d* value used represents the standardized mean group difference expressed in the metric of population standard deviation units of the raw scores on the measure. If these adjustments are not made, the result can be the reporting of erroneously large mean *d* values in a meta-analysis. An example of this is the meta-analysis of experimenter expectancy effects by Rosenthal and Rubin (1978). This article included a number of meta-analyses of different subareas of this literature, with mean *d* values (uncorrected for measurement error) often in the range of 2.00 to 4.00 for different meta-analyses. These are strikingly large mean effect sizes, especially for a subtle influence such as experimenter expectancy effects. However, they were interpreted as ordinary *d* values; that is, they were interpreted as if they were in the metric of the within-group standard deviation. However, many of the studies were repeated measures designs and the *d* values were computed using the standard deviation of gain scores in the denominator. Hence, reported *d* values were much larger than actual *d* values. This example shows why this is a serious issue. This error resulted from an erroneous equation given in Rosenthal (1991). Dunlap, Cortina, Vaslow, and Burke (1996) showed that this erroneous equation was incorporated into a set of software programs for meta-analysis (Johnson, 1989; Mullen, 1989; Mullen & Rosenthal, 1985) and led to serious overestimates of *d* values in a number of published meta-analyses. Burke and Landis (2003) and Dunlap et al. (1996) elaborate in some detail on the inaccuracies in various published meta-analyses caused by this error in these programs.

A number of articles and books discuss these issues for different experimental study designs and present the formulas for computing appropriate *d* values from different designs (Arvey, Cole, Hazucha, & Hartanto, 1985; Borenstein et al., 2009; Dunlap et al., 1996; Grissom & Kim, 2012; Hedges, 2009a; Morris, 2008; Morris & DeShon, 1997, 2002; Nouri & Greenberg, 1995). This chapter presents many of the needed conversions formulas. There is also a computer program called *ES* (for Effect Size; Shadish, Robinson, & Lu, 1999) that is useful for computing effect sizes from a variety of such research designs, including ANCOVA designs, ANOVA factorial designs (both between- and within-subjects designs), repeated measures designs, and other designs. This program also allows computation of *d* values from studies that report limited information—for example, studies that report only significance tests. In this connection, the program includes more than 40 different methods of computing *d* values. It can be used to make the transformations into appropriate *d* values that are described in this chapter. This program is available at no cost from William Shadish (wshadish@ucmerced.edu).

Once the appropriate *d* values and their sampling error variances are computed, the meta-analysis of the resulting database proceeds in the same way as described in Chapter 7. The methods—including corrections for sampling error and measurement error in the dependent variable measure—are identical. The computer programs for meta-analysis of *d* values (D-VALUE and D-VALUE1) contained in the Windows-based software package described in the Appendix can be used to conduct such meta-analyses when sampling error and measurement error in the dependent variable measure are the only artifacts that the meta-analyst corrects for. This is the most common case. When artifacts in addition to these two are corrected, the *d* values should be transformed to *r* values, with the meta-analysis being performed on the *r* values and the results then transformed back to the *d* value metric, as described near the end of Chapter 7.

In most cases, the sampling error variance for these *d* values is the same as that for the independent groups *d* value (as given in Chapter 7). However, this is not the case for *d* values transformed from repeated measures designs; in those cases, special equations must be used to compute sampling error variance. One must be certain to enter into the programs a sample size *(N)* value that will lead the program to produce correct sampling error variance values. This is achieved as follows. Once the sampling error variance for each such *d* value has been computed, the needed value for *N* can be computed by solving Equation (7.22) for *N*. The result is Equation (8.1):

$$N_{adj} = 4(1+d^2/8)/S_{ed}^2 \qquad (8.1)$$

where *d* is the appropriate *d* value computed to have the same meaning as an independent groups *d* value (or, better, the mean observed *d* value in the meta-analysis), and S_{ed}^2 is the appropriately computed sampling error variance for that *d* value. This value of *N* (the adjusted *N*, or N_{adj}) is then entered into the database for the computer program. This step is necessary because even when unbiased estimates of d values are obtained from repeated measures designs, these d values do not have the same sampling error variances as d values from the independent groups design. In ANCOVA models, the pooled standard deviation is usually reduced by partialling out the covariates; hence, the d value is overestimated if the usual formula for a d value is used. Special formulas must be used to ensure that this does not happen. The programs are set up to use the sampling error variance formulas for d values from independent groups designs. Hence the meta-analyst must enter into the program the N that produces that same sampling error variance from the sampling error variance equation for the independent groups design. In Chapter 7, we recommended that when artifacts beyond sampling error and measurement error in the dependent variable measure are corrected, d values should be transformed into correlations and the meta-analysis then conducted on the r statistic, with the final results being transformed back into the d or δ metrics. It is important to note that when d values are transformed to the r metric, the N for the resulting correlation must be the adjusted N described here.

Analysis of Covariance (ANCOVA) Designs

The typical ANCOVA design, like the independent groups design, has an experimental group and a control group. The difference is that in ANCOVA designs, variables believed to be extraneous to the hypothesis being tested are partialled out of the dependent variable; that is, their effects (if any) are statistically "controlled." For example, the researcher might want to statistically partial out the effects of education on political beliefs. There may be only one such covariate or there may be several. In ANCOVA models, the pooled standard deviation is usually reduced by partialling out the covariates; hence, the d value is overestimated if the usual formula for a d value is used. Special formulas must be used to ensure that this does not happen. At minimum, we need an estimate of the within-group SD unadjusted for the partialled covariates. The formula for the desired d value is

$$d = (\bar{Y}_1' - \bar{Y}_2') / SD_{pooled} \tag{8.2}$$

The denominator in Equation (8.2) must be computed using within-groups SDs without the covariates being partialled out. The values given and used in the ANCOVA study must be the SDs with the covariates partialled out, which are usually smaller than the needed SDs. In Equation (8.2), two Y means have the effects of the covariate or covariates partialled out. However, if we can assume that the covariate means are the same in the two groups, then the Y means can be the unadjusted observed Y means; that is, in this case, the effects of the covariates are equal on both means and so do not affect the difference between them. This assumption is tenable when subjects have been randomly assigned to the two groups, especially when Ns are large, and is usually made in the case of experimental studies. Equation (8.2) then becomes

$$d = (\bar{Y}_1 - \bar{Y}_2) / SD_{pooled} \qquad (8.3)$$

where $\bar{Y}_1$ and $\bar{Y}_2$ are the observed group means prior to any partialling. The assumption of equal covariate effects on the two groups, while usually reasonable for experiments, is less likely to hold in the case of naturally occurring groups, such as gender, racial, or occupational groups. If this assumption is not tenable, then Equation (8.2) must be used. The adjusted means in Equation (8.2) are usually given in the primary study.

Now consider the denominator, SD_{pooled}. To get this value, we must first compute the within-group $SD(SD_{within})$ in the experimental and control groups as they exist prior to controlling for the covariates. Within each group, this value is

$$SD_{within} = SD_{adj} / \sqrt{1-R} \qquad (8.4)$$

where SD_{adj} is the SD adjusted for the covariates and R is the correlation between the covariate and the dependent variable. If there are multiple covariates, R is the multiple correlation predicting the dependent variable from the covariates. The two values of SD_{within} are then combined using Equation (7.4) in Chapter 7 to produce the estimate of SD_{pooled} to be used in Equation (8.2) or (8.3).

The sampling error variance of the resulting d value is the same as that for an independent groups d value, as described in Chapter 7. Therefore, in using either of our programs for meta-analysis of d values (DVALUE or DVALUE1), the meta-analyst can enter the sample size in the same manner as for independent groups d values; that is, $N = N_1 + N_2$, where N_1 and N_2 are the sample sizes in the experimental and control groups, respectively. There is no need to compute an adjusted N, as described earlier (Equation [8.1]), and as required for d values computed from repeated measures designs.

The d value described here can also be computed from the t test from the ANCOVA, from the F statistic from the ANCOVA, and from the p values of one- and two-tailed tests. Borenstein et al. (2009, Table 12.3) provide some of these formulas. These values can be most easily computed from the program *ES* (Effect Size) by Shadish et al. (1999), described earlier. In fact, the use of this program is a convenient way to transform the results of all the research designs described in this chapter to the statistics needed for meta-analysis of *d* values.

Factorial Independent Groups ANOVA Designs

Consider a 2×2 independent groups factorial ANOVA design. There are two levels of each factor, an experimental group and a control group, and subjects are assigned randomly to each of the four cells. Suppose the subjects are people suffering from anxiety disorder, and Factor A is rational emotive psychotherapy and Factor B is an experimental anti-anxiety drug that can be used only in research studies. It is not approved for general use. Now suppose we are interested only in computing a d value for Factor A, because we are conducting a meta-analysis on the effectiveness of rational emotive therapy. Factor A has two levels: (a) the experimental condition, where people in this cell (Cell 1) receive rational emotive therapy, and (2) a control condition, where people in this cell (Cell 2) receive no treatment. The needed d value is then

$$d = (\bar{Y}_1 - \bar{Y}_2) / \sqrt{MS_{within}} \tag{8.5}$$

where $\bar{Y}_1$ is the mean on the dependent variable in Cell 1, and $\bar{Y}_2$ is the mean in Cell 2. The denominator is the square root of mean square within (MS_{within}), which is the square root of the pooled within-cell variance. MS_{within} is in the same metric as SD_{pooled} in a single-factor independent groups design. This d has the same sampling error variance as the d value from an independent groups design and can be entered into the DVALUE or DVALUE1 meta-analysis computer programs with $N = N_1 + N_2$ as the sample size. If cell means are not given in the study, this same d value can be computed from other statistics given in the study (e.g., from F statistics and their degrees of freedom), using the Shadish et al. (1999) program.

In this example, we have completely ignored Factor B and the variance it creates in computing the relevant d value. The reason this is appropriate is that Factor B does not vary in the population to which we wish to generalize. The population of interest is people who suffer from anxiety disorder. Members of this population will not receive the drug being evaluated as Factor B, because it cannot be used except in experiments. Therefore, variance created between the control and experimental groups by this drug in this experiment does not exist in our population of interest. As a result, we want an estimate of the pooled within-group variance that does not include this variance. The pooled within-cell variance (MS_{within}) is this value. This situation is probably the most common case.

Now consider a design in which Factor A is the same (psychotherapy) but now Factor B is gender. In Level 1 of Factor B, all subjects are men, and within Level 2, all subjects are women. Now we have a Factor B that does vary in the population. If our population of interest consists of men and women, then any variance created by the sex of subjects factor must be included in the estimate of the pooled within-group SD used in the denominator of our *d* value computation. The equation given by Glass et al. (1981) for computing this pooled *SD* is

$$SD_{pooled} = [(SS_B + SS_{AB} + SS_W)/(df_B + df_{AB} + df_W)]^{\frac{1}{2}} \quad (8.6)$$

where

SS_B = sum of squares for Factor B,

SS_{AB} = sum of squares for the interaction term,

SS_W = the within-group sum of squares (error term),

df_B = degrees of freedom for Factor B,

df_{AB} = degrees of freedom for the interaction term,

df_w = degrees of freedom for SS_W (error term).

The SD_{pooled} value is then used to compute the *d* value:

$$d = (\bar{Y}_1 - \bar{Y}_2)/SD_{pooled} \quad (8.7)$$

where $\bar{Y}_1$ and $\bar{Y}_2$ are defined as in Equation (8.5).

Morris and DeShon (1997) and Nouri and Greenberg (1995) present different formulas for computing the needed SD_{pooled} for this case. However, these formulas are more complicated and/or require information less often given in published studies. The information required by Equation (8.6) is most often presented in experimental studies with this design. (Also, Morris and Deshon, 1997, and Nouri and Greenberg, 1995, do not provide formulas for the case in which the second factor does not vary in the population of interest [our first example here].) Procedures for calculating *d* values from more complex ANOVA designs are given in Cortina and Nouri (2000), Morris and DeShon (1997), and Nouri and Greenberg (1995). Hedges (2009a) presents equations for computing *d* values from nested ANOVA designs. Most such *d* values can be conveniently computed using the Shadish et al. (1999) program.

Repeated Measures Designs

The previous edition of this book (Hunter & Schmidt, 2004) provided an in-depth treatment of repeated measures designs, demonstrating in detail their advantages in precision of estimates and statistical power over the independent groups design. We do not reproduce that treatment here, but we refer the interested reader to the earlier book for that information. Here we simply provide the information necessary to extract from repeated measures studies d values that are in the same metric as d values from the independent groups design, so that these d values can be entered into a meta-analysis along with independent groups d values.

REPEATED MEASURES DESIGNS WITHOUT CONTROL GROUP AND MATCHED GROUPS DESIGNS

In this section, we consider pre-post repeated measures designs with no control group and also matched group designs (because they require the same conversion equations). In the pre-post design, there is only one group, the experimental group. This group is first measured on the dependent variable (e.g., job knowledge), then the treatment is administered (e.g., a training program or a drug), and finally the posttest measure of the dependent variable is administered. The focus of interest is on the gain or change between the pretest and posttest. If this gain is expressed as the mean pre-post difference divided by the SD of the *gain* (or *difference* or *change*) scores, the resulting d value will be inflated, because the correlation between pre- and postscores (which is usually positive and often large) reduces this SD. In order to compute the needed within-group SD, we must adjust for this effect. If only the SD *of the gain scores is reported*, the formula for the needed SD is (Borenstein et al., 2009, p. 227)

$$SD_{within} = SD_{gain} / \sqrt{2(1-r)} \qquad (8.8)$$

where SD_{gain} is the SD of the gain scores and r is the correlation between pretest and posttest scores. This correlation is sometimes not provided in the study but can often be estimated from other, similar studies (Cortina & Nouri, 2000; Morris & DeShon, 2002). If the pretest SD is given, that is used as the within-group SD. In either case, the needed d value is then

$$d = (\bar{Y}_2 - \bar{Y}_1) / SD_{within} \qquad (8.9)$$

where $\bar{Y}_2$ is the mean posttest score and $\bar{Y}_1$ is the mean pretest score. The sampling error variance of this d value is given by

$$S_e^2 = [(N-1)/(N-3)][1/N][\beta + \{d^2/2\}\{N/(N-1)\}] \qquad (8.10)$$

where

$$\beta = 2[1 - r_{12}]/r_{YY} \qquad (8.10a)$$

where r_{12} is the pretest-posttest correlation, r_{yy} is the reliability of the dependent variable measure, and d is the d value from Equation (8.9). If there is no treatment-by-subjects interaction, the test-retest correlation is equal to the test-retest reliability of the dependent variable measure; that is,

$$r_{12} = r_{YY}$$

For large samples with no treatment-by-subjects interaction,

$$\text{Var}(e) = [\beta + d^2/2]/N \qquad (8.10\text{b})$$

For small samples with no treatment-by-subjects interaction,

$$\text{Var}(e) = [(N-1)/(N-3)][\beta + (d^2/2)(N/\{N-1\})]/N \qquad (8.11)$$

Note that Equation (8.11) is the same as Equation (8.10). The sampling error in this *d* statistic is not the same as the sampling error of *d* for the independent groups design. If the meta-analysis includes both within-subjects (repeated measures) and between-subjects (independent groups) designs, the sampling error must be computed separately for the two sets of studies. The programs compute sampling error variance using the independent groups design sampling error formula. To obtain the appropriate *N* to enter into the DVALUE programs for this *d* value, the sampling error variance from Equation (8.10) or (8.11) must be entered into Equation (8.1) and solved for the adjusted *N*, which is then entered into the program.

These equations apply also to matched group designs. In that design, pairs of subjects are matched on a variety of characteristics (e.g., age, sex, IQ, education), and then members of each pair are randomly assigned to the experimental and control groups. Difference scores are then computed within each pair, and the average of these difference scores is the mean gain (or change) due to the treatment. The *r* in Equations (8.8) and (8.10a) is the correlation between the scores of matched pairs. (In the matched groups design, this correlation is a between-persons *r*, while in the repeated measures design, it is a within-persons *r*.)

In the pre-post repeated measures design, if the *SD* of the pretest scores (SD_{pre}) is given, then the needed *d* can be computed as follows:

$$d = (\bar{Y}_2 - \bar{Y}_1)/SD_{pre} \qquad (8.12)$$

where $\bar{Y}_1$ and $\bar{Y}_2$ are as defined in Equation (8.9). The sampling error variance for this *d* value is essentially the same as that for the independent groups *d* (as given in Chapter 7). Hence, the *N* reported in the study can be entered into the DVALUE programs. (Actually, the sampling error variance is slightly larger than would be indicated by the reported study *N* [Hedges, 1981], so use of the study-reported *N* slightly underestimates sampling error variance, producing a slight conservative effect. This effect is very small.) The reader may wonder why we shouldn't just pool the pre- and posttest *SDs*. One problem is that these are not independent estimates of the *SD*, because they are computed on the same individuals. This causes the degrees of freedom to be unknown, making it impossible to compute an exact sampling error variance (Morris, 2008; Morris & DeShon, 2002). Perhaps more important, use of such a pooled *SD* might cause underestimation of the *d* value, because, as discussed in a later section of this chapter, the posttest *SD* is typically larger than the pretest *SD*, which would cause the pooled *SD* to be too large.

Equation (8.12) can also be applied to matched groups by replacing SD_{pre} with the dependent variable *SD* in the control group, if that is reported in the study. As with the pre-post repeated measures design, the *SDs* in the two matched groups are not independent (because of the matching process) and therefore should not be pooled. Again, we remind the reader that the Shadish et al. (1999) program can be used to compute *d* values for these two designs. It is especially useful in this respect when the studies in question report only limited information (e.g., report only significance tests).

REPEATED MEASURES DESIGNS WITH A CONTROL GROUP

The repeated measures design with a control is a stronger design than the pre-post design with no control group. This design controls for factors that might intervene between pretest and posttest that affect the dependent variable. Any such factors are captured in the pre-post gain scores in the control group. There is empirical evidence that control groups do often show mean gains (Carlson & Schmidt, 1999). The focus of interest in this design is on the difference between the mean change or gain in the experimental group and the mean gain or change in the control group. A key question is, What *SD* should be used in the denominator of the *d* value equation we need for our meta-analysis? Ideally, a study using this design should report not only the difference between these two change scores and the *SD* of this difference (SD_{dif}) but also four *SDs* based directly on the dependent variable measures (i.e., not change scores or differences between change scores). These are the pretest *SDs* in each group (SD_{pre-e} and SD_{pre-c}) and the posttest *SDs* in each group (SD_{post-e} and SD_{post-c}). Within each group, the pretest and posttest *SDs* are not independent and so should not be pooled. This leaves two possibilities: We can compute a pooled *SD* based on the two pretest *SDs* (which are independent of each other [$SD_{pooled-pre}$]), or we can compute a pooled *SD* based on the two posttest *SDs* ($SD_{pooled-post}$). On both statistical grounds (Becker, 1988; Cortina & Nouri, 2000; Morris, 2008; Morris

& DeShon, 2002) and empirical grounds (Carlson & Schmidt, 1999), the consensus is that $SD_{pooled-pre}$ should be used. The equation for the desired *d* value is therefore

$$d = (M_{g-e} - M_{g-c}) / SD_{pooled-pre} \qquad (8.13)$$

where $SD_{pooled-pre}$ is computed as in the pooled *SD* for the independent groups design (i.e., using Equation [7.14] in Chapter 7), and M_{g-e} and M_{g-c} are the mean pre-post gains (or changes) in the experimental and control groups, respectively. This *d* value is the difference between two *d* values: the *d* value for the amount of gain (or change) in the experimental group and the *d* value for the amount of gain (or change) in the control group, and these two *d* values are computed on independent groups. Hence, the sampling error variance of the *d* value in Equation (8.13) is the sum of the sampling error variance of the two component *d* values (Becker, 1988). So the sampling error variance is twice the value given in Equation (8.10) or (8.11), which expresses the sampling error variance for the single gain score–based *d* value given in Equation (8.9). An alternative formula for this sampling error variance is given in Morris (2008).

Again, this is not the sampling error variance of an independent groups *d* value. This sampling error variance must be entered into Equation (8.1) to compute the adjusted *N* (N_{adj}) to be entered into the DVALUE or DVALUE1 meta-analysis programs for *d* values. If this *d* value is converted to a correlation, the sample size for this correlation will also be this adjusted *N*. More complex repeated measures designs are discussed by Cortina and Nouri (2000), Morris and DeShon (2002), and Nouri and Greenberg (1995).

EMPIRICAL COMPARISON OF THE TWO REPEATED MEASURES DESIGNS

It is possible to examine empirically some questions about the two repeated measures designs. Carlson and Schmidt (1999) examined the vast literature on evaluation of training programs in work organizations. Many of these studies used the independent groups design or the pre-post design with no control group, but there were 248 evaluations of various dependent variables based on the pre-post design with a control group. The design is considered the "gold standard" of accuracy when the *SD* used in the denominator of the *d* value equation is the pooled *SD* of the two pretreatment *SD*s (as shown in Equation [8.13]). However, with this design, one can also compute a simple pre-post *d* value without use of the control group, producing two estimates of *d* from the same study and based on the same dependent variable. As noted earlier, in the pre-post design without a control group, one can use either the pre-*SD* or the post-*SD* in computing the *d* value. And in the pre-post design with a control group, the *SD* used in the denominator of the *d* value equation can be either the pooled pre-*SD*s or the pooled post-*SD*s. This set of data allowed Carlson and Schmidt (1999) to address a number of questions. One question is whether *d* values are larger when based on the pre-post design without a control group than when the control group is used. They found that this was in fact the case for most dependent variables of training outcome and, in particular, for measures of job knowledge. The reason was that the control group, as well as the experimental group, made gains on the dependent variable. Hence, the pre-post design with no control group tended to overestimate the *d* value in comparison to the *d* value produced by the pre-post design with a control group.

Another question was whether pretest and posttest *SD*s are equal in each of the designs. They found that posttest *SD*s were on average somewhat larger in the experimental group for both designs, meaning that use of posttest *SD*s (whether alone or pooled) caused *d* values to be somewhat underestimated in comparison to the "gold standard" of accuracy described earlier. Hence, they recommended that for both designs, only pretest *SD*s be used in computing *d* values. There are at least two reasons why posttest *SD*s could be larger in the experimental groups. First, there could be a subject-by-treatment interaction; different people might respond differently to the training, causing an increase in variance compared to the pretest *SD*. Second, as we noted in Chapters 6 and 7, the treatment condition may not be the same for different individuals in the experimental group. For example, some trainees but not others might have had to leave the training session early or might have been tired and dozed during parts of the training. This would be an example of measurement error in the independent variable, and it would cause an increase in variability. Hence, we can understand why the posttest *SD* might be larger than the pretest *SD* in the experimental group. However, Carlson and Schmidt found that posttest *SD* also averaged somewhat larger than the pretest *SD in the control groups* (although the difference was not as large). They stated that there was no obvious explanation for this finding. It is possible that there is a sort of "subjects-by-treatment" interaction in the control groups. That is, different individuals may react differently to being in the control group, with some but not others seeking to learn on their own some of the material taught in the training program. This would cause increased variability.

The reader should bear in mind that these findings, although based on a large database, are all based on studies evaluating training programs in work organizations. The dependent variables assessed were limited to job knowledge, work behavior changes, attitude changes, and on-the-job efficiencies produced by the training. Findings in other research areas and for other types of treatments might be different. But these findings can be viewed as suggestive of what might be found in other areas when and if similar research is conducted in those areas. However, the next section presents an argument that the problems found by Carlson and Schmidt (1999) for the repeated measures design with no control group may not occur in many other research areas.

Threats to Validity in Repeated Measures Designs With No Control Group

There are many who reject the pre-post repeated measures design without a control group before considering issues such as the often very low statistical power and precision of the independent groups design and the much higher power and precision of the pre-post design (Hunter & Schmidt, 2004, chap. 8). This higher power and precision is especially important in the detection of interactions in primary studies. The common rejection of the pre-post repeated measures design stems primarily from a misreading of the deservedly famous monograph by D. T. Campbell and Stanley (1963). The more recent version of this monograph (Shadish, Cook, & Campbell, 2002) is very similar to Campbell and Stanley and is subsumed in our comments here. In Table 1 of that monograph, they listed "sources of invalidity" for various designs, including seven sources for the within-subjects (repeated measures) design without a control group. However, at the bottom of the table is the reminder that these are only *potential* threats to validity and that they may not apply to any given study. Many have dropped the adjective *potential* in the phrase "potential threats to validity" and, thus, state that the within-subjects design has "threats to validity." Worse yet, some researchers have dropped the word *threat* and interpret Campbell and Stanley as having said that the within-subjects design is "fundamentally flawed because it lacks internal and external validity." This is not what Campbell and Stanley wrote, and they themselves said so several times. Yet the topic of this within-subjects design can hardly come up in a group without someone citing Campbell and Stanley as stating that the within-subjects design is riddled with uncontrolled sources of internal and external invalidity.

D. T. Campbell and Stanley (1963) viewed potential threats to validity as source ideas of possible rival theories to explain an observed effect. They stipulated, however, that one must argue for the rival hypothesis—the claim that a threat was realized—with carefully documented evidence of the same sort that is used for the original hypothesis. For example, on page 7 they say, "To become a *plausible* rival hypothesis, such an event should have occurred to most of the students in the group under study." Note that they are interested only in *plausible* threats, not in vague hypothetical possibilities, and that they cast their argument in terms of a specific concrete event, not as an abstract argument such as "the within-subject design is flawed by failure to control for history."

The purpose of this section is not to criticize Campbell and Stanley but to remind researchers of what Campbell and Stanley actually said. Their intention was this: If you are planning to do a pre-post within-subjects design with no control group, check these potential problems to see if any apply to that study. If so, then change the study procedures to eliminate that problem by, for example, adding a pre-post control group. This design controls for most of the potential threats to validity listed by D. T. Campbell and Stanley (1963). The purpose of this section is to show that often the pre-post repeated measures design with no control group does not suffer from potential threats to validity. The frequent false conclusion is that the Campbell and Stanley checklist is a statement of problems that apply to every within-subjects design. We attempt to dispel these false beliefs by presenting a series of examples. On one hand, we will take a typical example of a pre-post study in organizational psychology and show that not one of the Campbell-Stanley threats actually exists for that study. On the other hand, for each threat, we will cite a study for which that threat would exist. Thus, we will be true to the actual content of Campbell and Stanley: a checklist of *possible* problems, not a list of charges in an indictment of the design.

Some would argue that showing that a given example is free of the threats listed by Campbell and Stanley does not save the within-subjects design. They would say that only a rare study would be free of flaws, and thus, it is a waste of time to consider such a design in the first place. It is true that the logical conclusions that can be drawn from a couple of examples are limited. However, we believe that the probability implication in this argument is wrong. In our experience, the probability of each threat on the Campbell-Stanley list is actually low.

D. T. Campbell and Stanley (1963, p. 8) listed the following potential threats to the internal validity of the within-subjects design: history, maturation, testing, instrumentation, regression, and interactions of these factors. They listed the following potential threats to the external validity of the within-subjects design: interaction of testing and treatment, interaction of selection and treatment, and reactive arrangements (with a question mark). We will show by example that a within-subjects design could indeed suffer from a flaw of each kind. However, we will also show by example that there can be a study that suffers from none of these potential problems. The Campbell-Stanley list is intended to be a list of potential problems to consider, not a list of problems to assume.

The part of the psychological literature in which the within-subjects design is most commonly used is field studies of interventions, that is, program evaluation. Two frequent examples are evaluation of training programs in organizations and educational programs in schools and colleges. In most such studies, the subjects understand the program's objectives and know that they are part of an intervention. However, it is also true that the dependent variable in most interventions is a behavior or event that is very difficult to change without intervention. These aspects of the study usually rule out most of the Campbell-Stanley potential threats to validity.

Consider a management training program. Supervisors are to be given a training experience that explains how to apply certain skills, such as active listening, to supervisor problems. The dependent variable is the performance rating of the supervisor by the manager who is the supervisor's immediate superior. The pre-post design compares performance ratings before and after the training experience.

HISTORY

In this design, the experimenter interprets the change in the dependent variable as being caused by the intervention. But perhaps there was some concurrent event outside the scope of the study that actually caused the improvement. For example, suppose that we introduce goal setting to a group of small-car salesmen. During the test interval, there is a massive oil price increase in the Middle East that drives buyers from the large cars they had bought before to smaller cars. An increase in sales could be due to the oil price increase rather than to the goal-setting intervention. Thus, there could be a study in which history made the interpretation of the study result false. Of course, use of a repeated measures design with a control group would produce correct results—and would have higher precision and statistical power than an independent groups design.

How often are there natural events that produce a large change in important dependent variables? How often would such an event be overlooked by a seasoned scientific researcher working in an area that he or she knows well? Consider the skills training study. There is a long history of supervisory behavior study, which has found that even with intervention, it is difficult to produce change in supervisory social behavior. What real event could change these supervisors that the experimenter would not be aware of?

MATURATION

Perhaps the change observed in the study could be due to some internal process in the subject that would have taken place whether the intervention was carried out or not. Consider a psychologist studying psychomotor skills training in children. He argues that the change he observed between ages 5 and 6 was due to the special training program that he administered. However, psychomotor systems between the ages of 5 and 6 improve because of brain maturation. In this study, we would need some additional evidence to show that the increase in skills was not due to maturation rather than training. A repeated measures study with a control group could provide that evidence.

But how often would a psychologist overlook the process of maturation? For most dependent variables, there is ample evidence showing that the variable changes little for adults unless there is some major event that causes a reorganization of that behavior domain. Consider the social skills training example. Most people change their basic social behavior little over the adult years. Thus, we know before doing the study that there is no maturation process for the behavior in question.

TESTING EFFECTS

Perhaps the observed change could be due to the pretest rather than to the intervention. For example, suppose we believe that teaching mathematical reasoning will improve a person's problem-solving skills. We create a problem-solving test to assess skills. We see if the test score improves from before the reasoning module to after the reasoning module. The problem is memory. If people remember how they solved the problem the first time, they can use that same method of solution much more rapidly. So it is possible that the observed improvement was due to memory for the specific problems rather than due to the use of the skills taught. Thus, it is possible for the results of a study to be due to testing rather than to the intervention.

How often does a researcher have so little understanding of the dependent variable being used that he would overlook practice effects? In some social psychology experiments, subjects are deceived or misled as to the purpose of the study, and it is critical to the study that they not figure out that purpose. In such cases, the testing is a clue to the purpose and, hence, produces undesired effects. In field studies, however, the subject is usually told the purpose of the intervention, and hence, there is no secret to be revealed. Thus, testing rarely alerts the subject to anything not already known and provides no opportunity for practice. Again, a repeated measures design with a control group would control this threat to validity and, as noted earlier, would bring with it the same benefit of higher power and precision than the independent groups design.

Consider the social skills training example. The supervisors in the study have had performance ratings all of their working lives. Why should the performance rating before the training program change their fundamental social behavior? Testing is not a plausible rival theory for change in that study.

INSTRUMENTATION

Perhaps the change in a value is due to a change in the measuring instrument. If a spring is used to weigh a very heavy object, it may not spring all the way back to its original position. Consider studies in which the dependent variable is obtained from the subjective judgment of an observer. The observer may be tired or may have different standards after the study than he or she had before the study. For example, suppose that, unlike in our example, both the supervisor and his manager are put through the same training experience. Suppose the supervisor does not improve, but the manager now has new standards for acceptable performance. The manager evaluates the unchanged supervisor behavior negatively against the new standards and gives lower ratings after the training. So it is possible that a change in the instrument could produce a change in value, which is falsely attributed to the intervention.

In many studies, the instrument is not a subjective observer. In such studies, it is not likely that the instrument will change. If the dependent variable is a judgment, is it likely that a scientist familiar with the research area would overlook the possibility of change in the observer? In most studies with human observers, researchers go to a great deal of trouble to train the observers. One typical criterion for training is that the observer must learn to give consistent responses to equivalent stimuli. Thus, even with subjective judgment, change in the instrument is rarely a plausible hypothesis.

Consider our social skills training study example. Managers usually have long experience in making performance ratings. They are not likely to change their standards because of a study in which they do not participate. In fact, studies have shown that it is difficult to change performance ratings even with extensive training on the rating process. Thus, in our example, change in the instrument is not a threat to validity.

REGRESSION TOWARD THE MEAN

Suppose that people are preselected for the study. Perhaps the preselection biases the pretest scores and causes a false change effect when unbiased scores are obtained after the study. One such change is regression toward the mean due to error of measurement. Consider an example from psychotherapy to reduce anxiety about public speaking. The study begins by giving a public speaking anxiety test to a large class of subjects. The 20 out of 100 students with the highest anxiety scores are put through a special program that uses stimulus desensitization to reduce anxiety. At the end of the class period, the same anxiety instrument is used to assess change. The problem is this: No instrument is without error of measurement. In particular, the anxiety test has less than perfect reliability. To pick out unusually high scores is to select people for positive errors of measurement. Thus, the selected group will not have an average measurement error of 0 on the pretest; the average error will be positive. Suppose there is no change in anxiety produced by the desensitization. After the study, each subject will have the same true score on anxiety. However, the new measurement will produce new errors of measurement. For each subject, the new error of measurement is as likely to be negative as positive. Thus, for the group of subjects, the average posttest error of measurement is 0. The change in average error of measurement from positive to 0 produces a decrease in mean anxiety score that could be falsely attributed to therapy. Thus, regression to the mean could cause a change to be falsely interpreted.

On the other hand, there is no preselection of subjects in most studies and, hence, no possibility of regression effects. If there is preselection, then there is an easy way to eliminate a possible regression effect: Use a double pretest. That is, use a first pretest for selection. Then use a second pretest to assess the preintervention level. The errors of measurement will be resampled on the second pretest, and hence, the mean error will be 0 on the second pretest, as on the posttest, thus eliminating the regression problem. Also, if the reliability of the dependent variable is known, and if the extent of selection is known, then it is possible to use a procedure similar to range restriction correction to correct the observed change for regression to the mean (Allen, Hunter, & Donohue, 1989), even without a double pretest. Another solution is to include a control group. The subjects will be preselected in the same manner in both groups, and hence the effect of regression toward the mean will not affect the results.

Consider the social skills training study. All supervisors are to be given the training. There is no preselection and, hence, no possibility of a regression effect.

REACTIVE SITUATIONS

Reactive situations are interventions in which some seemingly trivial aspect of the treatment procedure causes a change that is not anticipated in the interpretation of the treatment as such. There are two possibilities: reactive measurement and reactive procedure.

Consider an example of potential reactive measurement. (What D. T. Campbell and Stanley, 1963, called "interaction between testing and treatment" is here called "reactive measurement.") Suppose we believe that a certain dramatic movie (e.g., *Guess Who's Coming to Dinner?*) will produce altruistic thoughts on racial issues. We use a sentence completion test to assess racial imagery. A typical item is "Black people are . . ." We look to see whether the person expresses more racial altruism after the movie than before the movie. The problem is this: What will the person think when he or she (1) is given a test that taps attitudes toward blacks and (2) is then presented with a movie about prejudice? It may be that the person would then try to do a self-evaluation in the form of "I'm not that prejudiced, am I?" The person would search his or her memory for instances of nonprejudiced behavior. These biased memories might then form the substance of the apparently altruistic thoughts that register in the posttest. This would then lead the experimenter to a false conclusion.

Consider an example of reactive procedure. As part of a quality circle experiment, randomly selected workers are taken to a room off the factory floor. They might wonder why this is happening and might form paranoid theories about assessment for labor union sympathies or dislike of them by their supervisor, or whatever. They might then be preset to have a negative reaction to the quality circle presentation. Thus, the reactive procedure could produce a spurious change. This is again a potential threat to validity that can be controlled by adding a control group to the pre-post design.

Consider the question of reactive measurement. Most field studies in political, organizational, or clinical psychology use measurements of important dependent variables, variables that are well known to the experimenters and are reasonably well understood by the participants. Thus, reactive measurement is rare in these fields.

Consider the question of reactive procedure. In laboratory experiments that depend critically on deception, this is a serious problem. In most field studies, however, the subjects are told the objectives of the study, and the nature of the measurements is obviously consistent with those objectives. Thus, the measurement cannot reveal secrets and cannot produce bizarre subject theories as to the experimenter's unknown objectives. That is, reactive procedures are rare in most areas of psychological research.

Consider the social skills training example. The subjects are told that they will be participating in a training exercise. They are told that the objective is to improve their skills as supervisors. The training exercise tells them what they are supposed to do, and instructors tell them why. Thus, both reactive measurement and reactive procedures are unlikely or impossible.

INTERACTION BETWEEN SELECTION AND TREATMENT

The problem discussed by D. T. Campbell and Stanley (1963) under the rubric "interaction between selection and treatment" is not a problem of erroneous interpretation of the results of the study itself. That is, it is not a threat to "internal validity." Rather, they were worried about a generalization from the results of the study to some other context that might turn out to be erroneous, that is, a threat to "external validity." The interaction in question represents the assumption that the effect of a treatment might differ from one setting to the next. If there is such variation, then an experimenter who generalizes from one setting to another may make a false inference. However, if there is variation in results across settings, the independent groups design will *not* work any better than the within-subjects design. If people in a given setting are randomly assigned to control and experimental groups, the mean difference will be the same as if a pre-post study had been done in that same setting. Thus, variation in treatment effects across settings creates the same logical problem for single-setting studies—usually the only feasible study—for between-subjects designs as for within-subjects designs. This problem would also exist for a repeated measures design with a control group.

Bias in Observed d Values

Hedges (1981, 1982a) and Rosenthal and Rubin (1982a) showed that there is a slight positive bias in the d value statistic presented in Chapters 6 and 7. That is, the computed d value is slightly larger on average than the population value (δ). The size of this bias depends on δ (the population value) and N (the sample size). This bias is typically small enough to be ignored. For example, if $\delta = .70$ and $N = 80$, the bias is .007. Rounded to two places, this would be .01, a bias of no practical or theoretical significance. (Also, if the d value is converted to a correlation using the formulas given in Chapter 7, the bias in the correlation will be only about half as large.) The bias is large enough to be of concern only when the sample size is quite small. Green and Hall (1984) stated that the bias can be ignored unless the sample size for a study is 10 or less. In the previous example, if N were 20 instead of 80, the computed d value would average approximately .03 too large, that is, about a 4% upward bias. Both Hedges (1981) and Rosenthal and Rubin (1982a) presented formulas that provide approximate corrections for this bias. We also present such a correction in Chapters 6 and 7, and this correction is built into our computer programs for meta-analysis of d values. If study sample sizes are very small, these corrections should be used. Otherwise, this tiny bias can safely be ignored. This upward bias is small in comparison to the ever-present downward bias created by measurement error in the dependent variable. For example, if the reliability of the measure of the dependent variable were .75 in our example in which $\delta = .70$, then the average observed d value would be $(.75)^{1/2} (.70) = .61$; then if no correction were made for measurement error (often the case in published meta-analyses), the negative bias would be .09. This is 9 times greater than the upward bias of .01 identified by Hedges (1981) and Rosenthal and Rubin (1982a) when $N = 80$ and three times larger than the bias when $N = 20$. This places the upward bias in d values in its proper perspective. It is strange to obsess over the tiny bias in the d statistic while at the same time ignoring the much larger biases created by measurement error.

Credibility Intervals, Confidence Intervals, and Prediction Intervals in Meta-Analysis of d Values

The distinction in meta-analysis between credibility intervals and confidence intervals is very important. Credibility intervals are formed by use of SD_δ, not by use of the standard error of δ. For example, the 80% credibility interval around a $\bar{\delta}$ value of .50 is $.50 \pm 1.28\, SD_\delta$. If SD_δ is .10, this credibility interval is .37 to .63. The interpretation of this interval is that 80% of the values in the δ distribution lie in this interval. The credibility interval refers to the distribution of parameter values, while the confidence interval refers to *estimates* of a single value—the value of $\bar{\delta}$. Confidence intervals express the likely amount of error in our estimate of $\bar{\delta}$ *due to sampling error.* The amount of sampling error is indexed in the standard error of $\bar{d}$ or $\bar{\delta}$ (depending on what artifact corrections are made). The standard error depends on sample size and, hence, sampling error. However, credibility values do not depend on sampling error—because variance due to sampling error (and other artifacts) has been removed from the estimate of SD_δ. The concept of credibility intervals has been viewed by some as Bayesian, because it is based on the idea that parameter values (values of δ) vary across studies. The concept of credibility values is also critically linked to random effects meta-analysis models, because random effects meta-analysis models (unlike fixed effects models) allow for possible variation in parameters across studies. In fixed effects models, all credibility intervals would, by definition, have a width of 0. Credibility intervals provide very important information whenever practical decisions must be made based on the results of a meta-analysis (Rothstein, 2003), because they provide the likely range of population correlations or effect sizes. For example, they reveal whether any of the population correlations or *d* values are likely to be zero or negative. Confidence intervals do not provide this information. The distinction between credibility intervals and confidence intervals is discussed in Hunter and Schmidt (2000), Schmidt and Hunter (1999a), and Whitener (1990). Until recently, meta-analyses of medical research studies presented only confidence intervals; credibility intervals were not presented. Medical meta-analysts have since recognized the need for credibility intervals (Higgins & Thompson, 2001). The Borenstein et al. (2009) book presents what the authors term "prediction intervals." Prediction intervals are identical in concept to credibility intervals when they are based directly on the estimate of the *SD* of the population parameters and are wider than credibility intervals when they are based on both this *SD* and an estimate of its sampling variance, their recommended usage. The purpose of prediction intervals is to predict the range of possible values *in a new study.* This is different from the purpose of credibility intervals, which is to describe the state of nature. Another difference is that prediction intervals correct study effect size variation only for sampling error; they do not correct for variation across studies produced by other artifacts.

All the examples of meta-analysis given in Chapter 7 (and Chapters 3 and 4) were presented with credibility intervals. Confidence intervals were presented only sporadically and were for illustrative purposes. In meta-analysis, credibility intervals are usually more critical and important than confidence intervals. However, for certain questions, confidence intervals are relevant to the question at hand (as was the case in

Viswesvaran et al., 2002). In such cases, the main research focus is on the mean value, and there is less interest in the variability of population values around the mean. This is more likely to occur in research testing theories than in applied research.

Computing Confidence Intervals in Meta-Analysis of d Values

The two most important parameters estimated for random effects models of meta-analysis of d values are $\bar{\delta}$ and SD_δ. It is perhaps easy to forget that these quantities are *estimates* of the parameters, not the parameters themselves, because in meta-analysis reports, they are rarely topped with a circumflex ($\wedge$). Technically, these values should be written as $\hat{\bar{\delta}}$ and $\hat{SD_\delta}$ but typically are not in the interests of simplifying the symbolism. Every estimate has a standard error (SE), known or unknown. As noted previously, the use made of the SE of the mean in statistics is in placing confidence intervals around the mean. In meta-analysis, unless the estimate of SD_δ is very small or zero, confidence intervals around the mean are not as important as *credibility* intervals—because it is typically the whole distribution, and not the just the mean, that is important. Our focus has therefore been mostly on credibility intervals.

In the case of bare-bones meta-analysis of d values (see Chapter 7), where sampling error is the only artifact corrected for, we have the following:

$$SE_{\bar{d}} = SD_d / \sqrt{k} \tag{8.14}$$

where SD_d is the SD of observed d values and k is the number of studies. This value is then used to place a confidence interval around the mean observed d value, $\bar{d}$. Typically, this is the 95% confidence interval, but other widths are equally legitimate (e.g., the 90% confidence interval).

If d values are corrected individually (see Chapter 7), then

$$SE_{\bar{\delta}} = SD_{d_c} / \sqrt{k} \tag{8.15}$$

where $SE_{\bar{\delta}}$ is the SE of $\bar{\delta}$, SD_{d_c} is the SD of the d values after each has been individually corrected for measurement error and other artifacts, and k is the number of studies. It is important to note that $SD_{d_c} \neq SD_\delta$. SD_{d_c} is much larger than SD_δ, because SD_{d_c} has not been corrected for sampling error—and d_c values typically have considerable sampling error, in part because the artifact corrections increase sampling error variance. The resulting $SE_{\bar{\delta}}$ is then used to place a confidence interval around $\bar{\delta}$.

If artifact distribution meta-analysis of d values (see Chapter 7) is used, then

$$SE_{\overline{\delta}} = \left[\left(\overline{\delta} / \overline{d} \right) SD_d \right] / \sqrt{k} \qquad (8.16)$$

where $SE_{\overline{\delta}}$ is the *SE* of $\overline{\delta}$, $\overline{\delta}$ is the estimate of mean corrected *d* value, mean $\overline{d}$ is the mean observed (uncorrected) *d* value, SD_d is the *SD* of the observed (uncorrected) *d* values, and *k* is the number of studies. In the case of artifact distribution meta-analysis, an alternative to Equation (8.16) can be used to compute confidence intervals for $\overline{\delta}$. First, use Equation (8.14) to compute $SE_{\overline{d}}$, the *SE* of the mean observed *d* value. Second, use $SE_{\overline{d}}$ to compute the confidence interval (CI) around mean observed *d*, as described above. Third, correct the endpoints of this CI for mean levels of measurement error to yield the CI for $\overline{\delta}$. Estimates produced in this manner are just as accurate as those produced by use of Equation (8.16).

In the case of all three approaches to computing CIs in meta-analysis, use of the Huffcut and Arthur (1995) procedure or any similar procedure to eliminate extreme *d* values will usually cause the *SE* values to be too small and the resulting confidence intervals to be too narrow. Also, in the case of all these approaches, if the number of studies is less than about 30, confidence intervals are slightly more accurate if one uses the *t* distribution instead of the normal distribution. The main purpose of confidence intervals is to provide a general picture of how much potential error there is in an estimate. Therefore, small inaccuracies in the intervals are usually not critical.

Fixed Effects and Random Effects Models in Meta-Analysis of d Values

Two questions that have received considerable attention in the meta-analysis literature are (1) the relative appropriateness of fixed versus random effects meta-analysis models (Cook et al., 1992, chap. 7; Hedges & Vevea, 1998; Hunter & Schmidt, 2000; Overton, 1998; Schmidt, Oh, & Hayes, 2009) and (2) the relative accuracy of different random effects models (Field, 2001, 2005; Hall & Brannick, 2002). The second question has been examined mostly with the correlation as the effect size, and for this reason we addressed it in Chapter 5, where the focus is on correlations. As noted in Chapter 5, comparison of the accuracy of different random effects models used in meta-analyzing correlations involves consideration of the effects of using the Fisher's *z* transformation of the correlations, which cannot be used with *d* values. But both questions are relevant to both *r*s and *d* values.

Fixed Versus Random Effects Models. The basic distinction is that fixed effects models assume a priori that exactly the same δ value underlies all studies in the meta-analysis (i.e., $SD_\delta = 0$), while random effects models allow for the possibility that population parameters (δ values) vary from study to study. A major purpose of random effects models is to estimate this variance. The random effects model is the more general one: Fixed effects models are a special case of random effects models in which $SD_\delta = 0$. In fact, when a random effects model is applied to data in which $SD_\delta = 0$, it becomes (in expectation) mathematically a fixed effects model. Application of a random effects model can result in an estimated SD_δ of 0, indicating that a fixed effects model would be appropriate for those data. Application of a random effects model can detect the fact that $SD_\delta = 0$; however, application of a fixed effects model cannot estimate SD_δ if $SD_\delta > 0$. That is, random effects models allow for any possible value of SD_δ, while fixed effects models allow for only one value: $SD_\delta = 0$.

Fixed effects models have never been used in validity generalization research and have rarely been used in any meta-analyses in industrial-organizational (I/O) psychology. As noted below, the opposite is true in many other research areas. All the models presented in this book, in the three predecessor books (Hunter & Schmidt, 1990b, 2004; Hunter et al., 1982), and in related publications are random effects models (Hedges & Olkin, 1985, p. 242; Hunter & Schmidt, 2000; Schmidt & Hunter, 1999a). These models all assume that population parameters may vary across studies and attempt to estimate that variance. The basic model is subtractive: The estimate of population variance is the variance that is left after variance due to sampling error and other artifacts is subtracted out. Some authors—for example, Field (2001, 2005), Hall and Brannick (2002), and Hedges and Vevea (1998)—have pointed out that the weights these procedures apply to study d values in computing means and variances across studies are somewhat different from those traditionally applied in random effects models. This is true. The rationale for our study weighting approach (weighting by sample size and, where possible, by the product of sample size and the square of artifact attenuation factors) is presented in Chapters 2 and 3. Field (2005), in a large computer simulation study, found that the differences in results for our method and the Hedges and Vevea (1998) random effects method were not affected by the use of different study weights. This question is addressed empirically in the studies discussed in Chapter 5 that examine the accuracy of different random effects models. These studies show that our random effects models are quite accurate—and more accurate than random effects models with more traditional random effects study weights. As with the models in this book and in Hunter and Schmidt (1990b, 2004) and related publications, the Callender-Osburn and Raju-Burke models are also random effects models and also weight studies by sample size. All these models have been shown in computer simulation studies to produce accurate estimates. The question of the optimal weighting of studies in meta-analysis is explored further in Chapter 9. That chapter also presents a discussion of so-called mixed effects meta-analysis models.

Hedges and Olkin (1985) and Hedges and Vevea (1998) presented both fixed and random effects models. However, as a practical matter, their random effects models have until recently rarely been used in the literature. For example, all the applications of the Hedges-Olkin methods of meta-analysis appearing in *Psychological Bulletin* through 1999 used their fixed effects models (Hunter & Schmidt, 2000; but see Shadish et al., 2000). None used their random effects models. All applications of the Rosenthal-Rubin models in that journal also used fixed effects models. Larry Hedges observed in 1990 that "fixed effects models have passionate defenders and far more users than random or mixed models" (Wachter & Straf, 1990, p. 23). A few years later, Cooper observed that "in practice, most meta-analysts opt for the fixed effects assumption because it is analytically easier to manage" (Cooper, 1997, p. 179). Schulze (2004, p. 35) noted that the fixed effects model has been much more frequently used than the random effects model. One reason so few researchers conducting meta-analyses in social psychology, education, and other non-I/O areas have used the Hedges-Olkin random effects models is that the fixed effects model is simpler and easier to implement. The National Research Council (1992) stated that many users of meta-analysis prefer fixed effects models because of "their conceptual and computational simplicity" (p. 52). Another important reason for widespread use of the fixed effects procedure is that the book by Hedges and Olkin (1985) developed its fixed effects models more completely than its random effects models. Later, however, Hedges and Vevea (1998) presented a more complete development and discussion of their random effects model, as does the recent book by Borenstein et al. (2009). Schmidt, Oh, and Hayes (2009) found that the use of random effects models has increased somewhat in recent years in the major psychology review journal, *Psychological Bulletin*. These developments have stimulated interest in comparing the accuracy of the Hedges-Vevea (1998) and the Hunter-Schmidt (1990b, 2004) random effects models. The results of this work are summarized in Chapter 5 because these studies have typically been conducted using the *r* statistic. Similarities and differences between the Hedges and Vevea (1998) and the Hunter and Schmidt random effects models for *d* value meta-analysis are examined in detail in Schmidt, Oh, and Hayes (2009).

Hedges and Olkin (1985) recommended that, when the fixed effects model is proposed for use, the chi-square homogeneity test should be applied. They stated that only if this test is nonsignificant should one conclude that $SD_\delta = 0$ and proceed to apply the fixed effects model. The National Research Council (1992) pointed out that this chi-square test has low power to detect variation in population values and therefore recommended against the use of fixed effects models and in favor of random effects models. Hedges and Pigott (2001) later showed that the power of the chi-square test is too low to allow its use in detecting between-study variation in population parameters. Not only does the chi-square test often fail to detect real heterogeneity, but many users of the Hedges-Olkin fixed effects model apply that model even when the chi-square test *is* significant, indicating the fixed effects model is not appropriate (Hunter & Schmidt, 2000; Schmidt, Oh, & Hayes, 2009). If the fixed effects model is applied when it is not appropriate (i.e., when $SD_\delta > 0$), confidence intervals are erroneously narrow and all significance tests have Type I biases (Kisamore & Brannick, 2008; National Research Council, 1992). These Type I biases are typically quite large (Hunter & Schmidt, 2000; Overton, 1998; Schmidt, Oh, & Hayes, 2009). For example, the actual alpha level can be .35 or more when the nominal alpha level is .05 (Hunter & Schmidt, 2000). Reported confidence intervals can be only half their actual width. Schmidt, Oh, and Hayes (2009) reanalyzed 68 fixed effects meta-analyses based on the *d* statistic that were published in *Psychological Bulletin;* their reanalysis applied both the Hunter-Schmidt and Hedges-Vevea (1998) random effects meta-analysis models to the data in these studies. They then compared the random effects confidence intervals to the fixed effects confidence intervals reported in the original studies. They found that the fixed effects confidence intervals were on average 52% narrower than their actual width, with similar results being produced by the two random effects procedures. The nominal 95% fixed effects confidence intervals were found to be on average 56% confidence intervals. This study reviewed all the meta-analyses published in *Psychological Bulletin* from 1977 (when the first meta-analysis appeared in the journal) through 2006. During this period, 199 meta-analyses were published; however, only 169 presented enough information to allow classification as either fixed effects or random effects models. Of these 169, 129 (76%) used only the fixed model. Of these 129, 91 (71%) used the fixed effect procedures of Hedges and Olkin (1985), 24 (19%) used the Rosenthal and Rubin (1982a, 1982b) fixed effects procedure, and 14 (11%) used combinations or did not provide enough information to allow classification. The upshot of this is that most of the meta-analyses appearing in *Psychological Bulletin* and other journals, because they are based on fixed effects models, are almost certainly inaccurate and should be recomputed using random effects models (Hunter & Schmidt, 2000; Schmidt, Oh, & Hayes, 2009). The erroneously narrow confidence intervals create the impression of much greater certainty about mean *d* values than is in fact the case. This distortion could bias beliefs about the strength of support for certain theories and could skew decisions on whether to implement applied treatments (e.g., in education) or to adopt certain social policies. So the problems created by the use of the fixed effects meta-analysis model when the random effects model should have been used are serious.

PART IV

General Issues
in Meta-Analysis

General Technical Issues in Meta-Analysis

9

This chapter discusses technical issues that are general to meta-analysis. That is, these issues apply whether meta-analysis is applied to correlations, to d values, or to other statistics (e.g., odds ratios). Also, these issues apply whether the methods used are those presented in this book, those of Hedges and Olkin (1985), Borenstein et al. (2009), those of Rosenthal (1984, 1991), or any other methods. The issue of fixed versus random effects meta-analysis models is general in nature but is not included in this chapter because it has been fully addressed in Chapters 5 and 8. New developments in meta-analysis methods occur with some frequency (Schmidt, 1988). Some of these developments are explored in this chapter.

First, we discuss the contention that large-sample studies are a substitute for meta-analysis and show why this view is incorrect. Second, we discuss the various methodological issues involved in detecting moderators (interactions) in meta-analysis, including subgrouping of studies and meta-regression. Next, we introduce second-order sampling error (the sampling error remaining in the results of a meta-analysis), and we present methods for second-order meta-analysis (meta-analysis of meta-analyses) that address some of the problems created by second-order sampling error. We then provide a complete technical treatment of second-order sampling error and its effect on confidence intervals in meta-analysis. In this connection, we point out differences in the way confidence intervals for random effects meta-analyses are computed in the Hedges-Olkin and Hunter-Schmidt methods. Next, the technical issue of how to update a meta-analysis when new studies become available and the question of optimal study weights in meta-analysis are discussed. This is followed by a discussion of a more informative way to view and interpret percent variance accounted for in a meta-analysis. Finally, we present a discussion of a statistical index of effect sizes not treated elsewhere in this book: the odds ratio. Last, we present the reader with three exercises: conducting second-order meta-analysis in two different ways.

Large-*N* Studies Versus Meta-Analysis

Some have argued that the need for meta-analysis is merely a consequence of small-sample studies with their typically low levels of statistical power. The argument is made that researchers should conduct only large-sample studies (i.e., studies with *N*s of 2,000 or more) and that such studies, with their higher statistical power, would make meta-analysis unnecessary (see, e.g., Bobko & Stone-Romero, 1998; Murphy, 1997). We question this position for three reasons: (1) It leads to a reduction in the total amount of information available in the literature for the calibration of correlations and effect sizes, (2) it reduces the ability to detect the presence of potential moderators, and (3) it does not eliminate the need for meta-analysis.

Loss of Information. For practical reasons, many researchers cannot obtain large sample sizes, despite their best efforts. If a requirement for large *N*s is imposed, many studies that would otherwise be conducted and published will not be conducted—studies that could contribute useful information to subsequent meta-analyses (Schmidt, 1996). This is what has happened in the area of validity studies in personnel psychology. After publication of the study by Schmidt et al. (1976) showing that statistical power in traditional validity studies averaged only about .50, the average sample sizes of published studies increased from around 70 to more than 300. However, the *number* of studies declined dramatically, with the result that the total amount of information created per year or per decade (expressed as *N*s in a meta-analysis) for entry into validity generalization studies decreased. That is, the total amount of information generated in the earlier period from a large number of small-sample studies was greater than that generated in the later period for a much smaller number of larger-sample studies. Hence, there was a net loss in ability to calibrate validities.

Reduced Ability to Detect Potential Moderators. The situation described previously creates a net loss of information *even if there are no moderator variables* to be detected, that is, even if $SD_\rho = 0$ in all validity domains studied. Although $SD_\rho = 0$ is a viable hypothesis in the predictor domains of ability and aptitude tests (Schmidt et al., 1993), this hypothesis may not be viable in some other predictor domains (e.g., assessment centers, college grades). And it is certainly not viable in many research areas outside personnel selection. If $SD_\rho = 0$, the total number of studies does not matter; all that matters in determining the accuracy of the meta-analysis study is the total *N* across all studies in the meta-analysis. As described previously, this total *N* has been reduced in recent years. If $SD_\rho > 0$, however, it is critical to have an accurate estimate of SD_ρ. In estimating SD_ρ, *N* is *the number of studies*. Hence, holding the total *N* in the meta-analysis constant, a small number of large studies provides a less accurate estimate of SD_ρ than does a large number of small studies. A large number of small studies samples a much more numerous array of potential moderators—in fact, each small study samples different potential moderators that might contribute to $SD_\rho > 0$. For example, suppose total N for the meta-analysis is 5,000. If this total N consists of four studies each with $N = 1,250$, then the estimate of SD_ρ is based on *only four data points:* four samples from the distribution of ρ. On the other hand, if this total N consists of 50 studies of $N = 100$ each, then the estimate of SD_ρ is based on 50 data points sampled from the ρ distribution—and is therefore likely to be much more accurate. This greatly increases what Cook and Campbell (1976, 1979) called "external validity."

Bobko and Stone-Romero (1998) argued that this same level of precision of estimation for SD_ρ can be obtained with a single large-N study by, in effect, dividing the one large study into many smaller ones. This is unlikely to be true. The single large study reflects the way a single researcher or set of researchers conducted that one study: same measures, same population, same analysis procedures, and so forth. It is unlikely to contain within itself the kinds of variations in the methods and potential moderator variables that are found in 50 independently conducted studies. Another way to see this is to consider the continuum of different types of replications of studies (Aronson, Ellsworth, Carlsmith, & Gonzales, 1990). In a literal replication, the same researcher conducts the new study in exactly the same way as in the original study. In an operational replication, a different researcher attempts to duplicate the original study. In systematic replication, a second researcher conducts a study in which many features of the original study are maintained but some aspects (e.g., types of subjects) are changed. Literal and operational replications contribute in only a limited way to external validity (generalizability) of findings, but systematic replications are useful in assessing the generalizability of findings across different types of subjects, measures, and so on. Finally, in the case of constructive replications, the researcher attempts to vary most of the aspects of the initial study's methods, including subject type, measures, and manipulations. Successful constructive replication adds greatly to the external validity of a finding. Breaking up a large study into "pieces" is similar to the creation of several smaller literal replications and does not contribute to external validity or generalizability of findings. However, in a meta-analysis of a large number of small studies, the studies in the meta-analysis constitute systematic or constructive replications of each other; that is, many study aspects vary across studies. In these circumstances, a finding of a small SD_ρ (or a small SD_δ) provides strong support for generalizability—that is, this result is strong evidence of external validity of the finding. As discussed in Chapter 4, this finding is common in the personnel selection area. If the number of studies in the meta-analysis is small, even if each study is a large-sample study, the meta-analysis is weaker because the number of systematic or constructive replications underlying the final results is smaller, and hence, external validity is more questionable. This is another approach to understanding why a large number of small studies are better than a small number of large studies.

Meta-Analysis Still Necessary. Finally, even if all studies conducted are large-sample studies, it is still necessary to integrate findings across studies to ascertain the meaning of the set of studies as a whole. Because meta-analysis is the statistically optimal method for doing this, meta-analysis is still necessary. In concluding that meta-analysis would no longer be necessary, advocates of the position we are critiquing appear to be thinking of the fact that large-N studies, with their high statistical power, will show agreement on statistical significance tests: If there is an effect, all studies should detect it as statistically significant. However, this does not mean meta-analysis is unnecessary. What is important is the estimates of effect size magnitudes. Effect size estimates will still vary across studies, and meta-analysis is still necessary to integrate these findings across studies. Hence, we cannot escape the need for meta-analysis.

We conclude therefore that a movement to a smaller number of larger N studies would not contribute to the advancement of cumulative knowledge in any area of research. In fact, it would be detrimental to knowledge generation and discovery. And it would not eliminate the need for meta-analysis.

Detecting Moderator Variables in Meta-Analysis

A variety of issues arise when meta-analysis is used to detect moderators (or interactions). One of these issues is capitalization on sampling error when focusing on only those potential moderators that show statistical significance when a larger number of potential moderators are examined. This issue was explored in some detail near the end of Chapter 2. The related issues discussed in this chapter include (a) detecting moderators not hypothesized a priori, (b) use of hierarchical meta-analysis in moderator detection, (c) meta-regression in moderator detection (including "mixed models" of meta-analysis), and (d) multilevel meta-analysis and hierarchical linear models (HLM).

DETECTING MODERATORS NOT HYPOTHESIZED A PRIORI

When the moderator variable is not specified or hypothesized in advance by theory, the statistical power of a meta-analysis with respect to the variance of ρ or δ is the probability that the meta-analysis will detect variation in ρ or δ values across studies when such variation does, in fact, exist. One minus this probability is the probability of a Type II error: concluding that all the variance across studies is due to artifacts when, in fact, some of it is real. When all variance is indeed artifactually caused, there is no possibility of a Type II error, and there can be no statistical power question. Just as second-order sampling error becomes more of a problem as the number of studies becomes smaller, statistical power also becomes lower. A number of statistical tools have been used to make the decision about whether any of the observed variance is real. In our meta-analytic research on test validities, we have used the 75% rule of thumb: If 75% or more of the variance is due to artifacts, we conclude that all of it is, on grounds that the remaining 25% is likely to be due to artifacts for which no correction has been made. Another method is the chi-square test of homogeneity. As pointed out in Chapters 5 and 8 and again in this chapter, this test has low power under most realistic circumstances (Hedges & Pigott, 2001; National Research Council, 1992). In addition, it has all the other disadvantages of significance tests, as discussed in Chapter 2. Callender and Osburn (1981) presented a third method, one based on simulation.

Extensive computer simulation studies have been conducted to estimate the statistical power of meta-analyses to detect variation in ρ using these decision rules (Aguinis et al., 2008; Osburn, Callender, Greener, & Ashworth, 1983; Sackett, Harris, & Orr, 1986; Spector & Levine, 1987). These estimates have been obtained for different combinations of (1) numbers of studies, (2) sample size of studies, (3) amount of variation in ρ, (4) mean ρ values, and (5) levels of measurement error. The findings of the Sackett et al. (1986) study are consistent with the others and are probably the most relevant to meta-analysis in general. Sackett et al. found that, under all conditions, the 75% rule had "statistical power" greater than (or equal to) the other methods, including the Q statistic (although the 75% rule also showed a higher Type I error rate: concluding there was a moderator when there was not). The term *statistical power* is placed in quotation marks here because that term applies only to significance tests, and the 75% rule is not a significance test but rather a simple "rule of thumb" decision rule. The advantage in statistical power for the 75% rule was relatively the greatest when the number of studies was small (4, 8, 16, 32, or 64) and the sample size of each study was small (50 or 100). However, when the assumed population variance to be detected (s_ρ^2) was small, and both the number of studies and the sample size of the studies were small, all methods had relatively low statistical power. For example, if there were four studies ($N = 50$ each) with $\rho = .25$ and four studies ($N = 50$ each also) with $\rho = .35$ (corresponding to $s_\rho^2 = .01$), and if $r_{xx} = r_{yy} = .80$ in all studies, statistical power was .34 for the 75% rule and only .08 for the other methods. However, a total sample size of 8(50) = 400 is very small, and 8 is a small number of studies for a meta-analysis. Also, a difference of .10 is very small. If the difference in this example is raised to .30, power rises to .75. This difference between ρs is more representative of the moderators that it would be theoretically and practically important to study. Nevertheless, it is true that individual meta-analyses have less than optimal statistical power in some cases. As the reader of this book is by now aware, we recommend against the use of significance tests (see, e.g., Chapter 2). These simulation studies show that our simple 75% rule typically is more accurate than significance tests used to assess homogeneity. However, no decision rule for judging homogeneity versus heterogeneity in meta-analyses of realistic sets of studies has perfect accuracy.

The preceding discussion applies to "omnibus" tests for moderator variables—moderator variables that are not specified in advance by theories or hypotheses. In such cases, the existence of moderators must be detected by determining whether the variance of study effect sizes is larger than can be accounted for by the presence of variance-generating artifacts. The story is very different when the moderator hypotheses are specified in advance. In such cases, the studies in the meta-analysis can be subgrouped based on the moderator hypothesis (e.g., studies done on blue- vs. white-collar employees), and credibility and confidence intervals can be placed around the means ($\bar{\delta}$ or $\bar{\rho}$) of the subgroup meta-analyses, as described in earlier chapters (Chapters 3, 4, 5, 7, and 8) and later in this chapter. Confidence intervals are most relevant in assessing moderator variables if the main focus of interest is on mean differences. Credibility intervals are most relevant if the focus of interest is on whole distributions of parameters. This procedure is much more effective in identifying moderators than operating without a priori moderator hypotheses and attempting to assess the presence of moderators by testing for heterogeneity in observed d or r values.

In most areas of research, there should be sufficient development of theory to generate hypotheses about moderators. However, in one major meta-analytic research area—the generalizability of employment test validities—this has not been the case. It has not been possible to use the subgrouping approach to test the "situational specificity" hypothesis in personnel selection. To use this approach, the moderators must be specified. There must be a theory, or at least a hypothesis, that is specific enough to postulate that, for example, correlations will be larger for females than for males, or larger for "high-growth-need" individuals than for "low-growth-need" individuals, or larger in situations where supervisors are high in "consideration" than where supervisors are low in consideration. The situational specificity hypothesis does not meet this criterion; it postulates merely that there are unspecified subtle but important differences from job to job and setting to setting in what constitutes job performance, and that job analysts and other human observers are not proficient enough as information processors to detect these critical elusive differences (Albright, Glennon, & Smith, 1963, p. 18; Lawshe, 1948, p. 13). When the operative moderators are actually unknown and unidentifiable, it is not possible to subgroup studies by hypothesized moderators. However, if one can show that all observed validity variance is due to artifacts, one has shown that no moderators can possibly be operating. This approach does not require that the postulated moderators be identified or even identifiable. Given that there is a broad and heterogeneous range of situations represented in one's meta-analysis, one can show that the postulated moderators do not exist, even without knowing what the moderators might be.

However, some might make statements like the following: "There are many factors that could affect outcomes. Supervisory style may have important effects; group membership, geographical location, type of industry, and many other variables would be expected to be moderators." Such statements are usually not based on theoretical reasoning or empirical evidence. They are usually just unsupported speculations and, thus, are not scientifically useful. Because the number of hypothesized potential moderators is essentially unlimited, it will never be possible to test them all using the second, more effective, procedure. However, the first procedure—the omnibus procedure we have used to test the situational specificity hypothesis—can be used to test all such moderators simultaneously, even those that have not yet been named by the critic. If the meta-analysis is based on a *large* group of studies that is heterogeneous across all potential moderators, then a finding that artifacts account for all between-study variance in correlations or effect sizes indicates that none of the postulated moderators are, in fact, moderators. Even when all the variance is not accounted for by artifacts, the remaining variance may often be small, demonstrating that even if some moderators might exist, their effect is far more limited in scope than implied by the critic. In fact, the results may often indicate that the moderators have at best only trivial effects (Schmidt et al., 1993). In this connection, it should always be remembered that the variance remaining after correction for artifacts indicates the *upper bound* of the effects of the moderators. This will almost always be true because, as described in Chapters 3, 4, 5, and 7 there will almost always be some artifacts operating to create variance for which no corrections will be possible.

The facts of second-order sampling error and less than perfect "statistical power" in individual meta-analyses point to another reason for the importance of a principle we stated in Chapters 1 and 2. The results of a meta-analysis should not be interpreted in isolation but rather in relation to a broader set of linked findings from other meta-analyses that form the foundation for theoretical explanations. Estimating a particular relationship is only the immediate objective of a meta-analysis; the ultimate objective is to contribute pieces of information that can be fitted into a wider developing mosaic of theory and understanding. However, just as the results of a meta-analysis can contribute to this bigger picture understanding, so also can the resulting bigger picture understanding contribute to the interpretation of particular meta-analysis results. Results of "small" meta-analyses (those based on few studies and small-sample studies) that are inconsistent with the broader cumulative picture of knowledge thereby become suspect, while the credibility of those that are consistent is enhanced. This is the universal pattern in science of reciprocal causation between data and theory.

Some have worried that the inadequate ability of meta-analysis to detect moderators might be an almost insurmountable problem limiting scientific progress (even while admitting that better alternatives to meta-analysis do not exist). The critical difficulty with this argument is that it focuses on single meta-analytic studies. Just as earlier researchers focused on the individual study, failing to realize that single studies cannot be interpreted in isolation, this position focuses on single meta-analyses—in particular, on the some-times weak ability of single meta-analyses to identify moderators—not seeing that it is the overall pattern of findings from many meta-analyses that is important in revealing the underlying reality.

Consider an example in which the overall pattern of findings was criti-cal. In personnel selection, the theory of situational specificity holds that the true (population) validity of any employment test varies substantially from one organization to another even for highly similar or identical jobs. This is the hypothesis that $S_\rho^2 > 0$. In meta-analysis (called validity gener-alization when used in personnel selection), this hypothesis is tested by determining whether artifacts such as sampling error account for the vari-ation of observed validity coefficients across studies conducted in different organizations on similar jobs using measures of the same ability (e.g., arithmetic reasoning). In the initial validity generalization studies, the average percentage of the observed validity variance accounted for by arti-facts was less than 100%. However, these meta-analyses were based on published and unpublished studies from a wide variety of sources and researchers, and we pointed out in all our studies that there were several sources of between-study variance that we could neither control for nor correct for (e.g., programmer errors, transcriptional errors; see Chapter 5 and Schmidt et al., 1993). When all studies going into a validity general-ization analysis are conducted by the same research team, strong efforts can be made to control these sources of errors. In two large-scale, nation-wide consortium studies, such efforts were made (Dunnette et al., 1982; Peterson, 1982). In both cases, these studies found that, on average, all variance across settings (i.e., companies) was accounted for by artifacts. The same was found to be true in data from studies conducted in 16 com-panies by Psychological Services, Inc. (Dye, 1982). Thus, our prediction that improved control of sources of error variance would show that all between-study variance is due to artifacts was borne out. These findings are strong evidence that there is no situational specificity in the validity of employment tests of cognitive ability.

There were more aspects to the pattern of evidence against situational specificity, however. The situational specificity hypothesis predicts that if the situation is held constant and the tests, criteria, and job remain unchanged, validity findings should be constant across different studies conducted in that setting. That is, because the setting is constant, observed validities should be constant because it is differences between settings that are hypothesized to cause differences in observed validities. Meta-analytic principles predict that such observed validities will vary substantially, mostly because of sampling error. We tested these predictions in two studies (Schmidt & Hunter, 1984; Schmidt, Ocasio, et al., 1985) and found that observed validities within the same situation varied markedly, disconfirming the situational specificity hypothesis. In the second of these studies, the data from a large-sample validity study ($N = 1,455$) were divided into smaller, randomly identical studies (21 studies of $n = 68$ each). Because situational variables were held constant, the specificity hypothesis predicted that all the smaller studies would show the same observed validity. This was not the case, however. Instead, there was great variance among studies in both magnitude of validity and statistical significance level, as predicted by the theory of artifacts, which is the basis of meta-analysis and validity generalization. A key finding was that the variation in validities was as great as that typically found across similar studies conducted in entirely different settings.

The final piece of evidence that fits into this framework is this: Recent refinements in validity generalization methods have led to the conclusion that published validity generalization studies substantially underestimate the percentage of observed validity variance that is due to artifacts, further undercutting the situational specificity hypothesis. There are three such refinements. First, non-Pearson validity coefficients are removed, because the sampling error formula for Pearson correlations substantially underestimates the sampling error in non-Pearson correlations such as the biserial and the tetrachoric (see Chapter 5). Second, within each meta-analysis, the population observed correlation used in the sampling error formula is estimated by the mean observed validity instead of the individual observed validity from the study at hand. This provides a more accurate estimate of sampling error (see Chapter 5). Third, the problem created by nonlinearity in the range restriction correction (cf. Chapter 5 and Law et al., 1994a, 1994b) is solved by a new set of computational procedures. Schmidt et al. (1993) applied these improvements in the massive validity database in Pearlman et al. (1980), which consisted of approximately 3,600 validity coefficients from published and unpublished studies from many organizations, researchers, and more than periods ranging over 70 years. Each of these methodological refinements resulted in increases in the percentage of validity variance accounted for and smaller estimates of SD_ρ. Even in this heterogeneous group of studies, almost all validity variance (nearly 90%) was found to be due to artifacts. This research is discussed in more detail in Chapter 5.

All these pieces of interlocking evidence point in the same direction: toward the conclusion that, for employment tests of cognitive abilities, the situational specificity hypothesis is false. The only conclusion consistent with the total pattern of evidence is that there is no situational specificity (or that situational effects are so tiny that it is reasonable to consider them to be 0; some prefer this latter conclusion, which we regard as scientifically identical).

In some research areas, there may be no related meta-analyses with which one's meta-analytic results can be cross-referenced and checked for consistency. In such cases, one's results should be compared with the broader pattern of general research findings. Where even this is not possible, meta-analyses based on small numbers of studies should indeed be interpreted with caution, even though the meta-analysis provides the most accurate summary possible of existing research knowledge at that point in time. We stress that, in cases such as this, the problem is created not by meta-analysis methods but by the limitations of the research literature. These limitations do not have to be permanent. Consider an example. McDaniel et al. (1988b) found that only 15 criterion-related studies had ever been conducted on the validity of the behavioral consistency method of evaluating applicants' past job-related achievements and accomplishments. Based on these 15 studies, mean true validity is estimated at .45 (SD = .10; 90% credibility value = .33; percentage variance accounted for = 82%). The appropriate interpretation of these findings is different from the interpretation that would be appropriate for exactly the same findings based on exactly the same number of studies in a meta-analysis of cognitive ability. There are literally hundreds of meta-analyses of cognitive abilities and job performance to which the latter findings could be cross-referenced to check for consistency. In the case of the behavioral consistency method, there are no other meta-analyses. Furthermore, we have very little information as to precisely what the behavioral consistency procedure measures. For example, there are no reported correlations between cognitive ability test scores and behavioral consistency scores. Behavioral consistency scores are not yet part of a rich, structured, complex, and elaborated network of established knowledge as cognitive abilities are. Therefore, this meta-analysis must stand alone to a much greater extent. We cannot be really certain that the results are not substantially influenced by outliers or by second-order sampling error. (For example, the actual amount of variance due to artifacts may be 100%, or it may be 50%.) For these reasons, McDaniel et al. (1988b) stated that these findings must be considered preliminary and recommended that additional validity studies be conducted, not to estimate "local validities" from local studies for local settings but to have more studies to combine into the meta-analysis.

There are other areas of research in industrial-organizational psychology completely outside the area of personnel selection and many areas outside the field of industrial-organizational psychology where (1) the number of studies now available is small, and (2) there is no elaborated structure of empirical and theoretical knowledge against which the meta-analytic results can be checked. When meta-analytic results have less evidentiary value because the number of individual studies in the meta-analysis is small *and* there is no related structure of empirical and theoretical knowledge against which the meta-analytic results can be checked, the alternative is neither reversion to reliance on the single study nor a return to the narrative review method of integrating study findings; both are vastly inferior to meta-analysis in information yield. The appropriate reaction is to accept the meta-analysis provisionally while conducting (or awaiting) additional studies, which are then incorporated into a new and more informative meta-analysis. During this time, other forms of evidence bearing on the hypothesis in question may appear—forms of evidence analogous to the within-setting studies (Schmidt & Hunter, 1984; Schmidt, Ocasio, et al., 1985) in the area of situational specificity, in that they represent different approaches to the same question. Such evidence then constitutes the beginning of the kind of structured pattern of evidence described previously.

HIERARCHICAL ANALYSIS OF MODERATOR VARIABLES VIA SUBGROUPING

One approach to detection of moderators is subgrouping of studies. But the results of subgrouping can be deceptive if moderators are correlated. In searching for moderator variables using meta-analysis, some authors have used partially hierarchical subgrouping. First, all studies are included in an overall meta-analysis. The studies are then broken out by one key moderator variable, then the studies are recombined and broken out by another key moderator variable, and so on. The meta-analysis of assessment center validities by Gaugler et al. (1987) is an example of this approach. This type of analysis, however, is not fully hierarchical because the moderator variables are not considered in combination, which can result in major errors of interpretation. These errors are analogous to problems in analysis of variance due to confounding and interaction. An analysis of each moderator separately may lead to quite misleading results. In a meta-analysis by Rodgers and Hunter (1986) of the effects of management by objectives (MBO) on productivity, the initial analysis suggested two moderator variables: top-level management commitment and length of the intervention period. Their initial analysis suggested that MBO programs with the strong support of top management increased productivity by an average of 40%, while programs without the strong support of top management had little effect. Their initial analysis also suggested that studies based on an assessment period of more than 2 years showed much larger effects than studies based on less than 2 years. However, when the studies were broken down by the two moderator variables together, the effect of time virtually vanished. Most of the long-term studies were studies with strong top-management commitment, while most of the short-term studies were studies with weak top-management commitment. Thus, the apparent impact of time horizon as a moderator variable was due to the fact that it was confounded with managerial commitment. The difficulty in conducting fully hierarchical moderator analyses in meta-analysis is often that there are too few studies to yield adequate numbers of studies in cells beyond the two-way breakout. This simply means that it is not possible to address all moderator hypotheses at that time. As more studies accumulate over time, more complete moderator analyses can be performed.

The MBO meta-analysis illustrates the potential problems of confounding between moderators, that is, "spurious" (in the language of path analysis) mean differences for one potential moderator are produced by real differences on another. Thus, confounding results from the fact that the moderators are correlated.

The second problem is potential interaction between moderator variables. Suppose two moderator variables A and B have been found to moderate effect sizes when analyzed separately, and assume the moderator variables are independent (uncorrelated) across studies. Can we then conclude that A and B always moderate effect size? We cannot. Consider an example. Suppose the mean effect size is .30 when A is present versus .20 when A is absent, and suppose the mean effect size is .30 when B is present versus .20 when B is absent. Assume that the frequency of A is 50% and the frequency of B is 50% and that A and B are independent. Then each of the four cells obtained by considering A and B together will have a 25% frequency. Consider the mean effect sizes in the following joint breakdown table:

		Moderator A		
		Present	*Absent*	*Ave.*
Moderator B	Present	.40	.20	.30
	Absent	.20	.20	.20
	Ave.	.30	.20	.25

Consider the 50% of studies in which moderator B is absent. Within those studies, the presence or absence of A does not matter; the mean effect size is .20 in either case. Thus, A is a moderator variable only for the studies in which B is present. The statement that "A moderates the effect of X on Y" is false for the 50% of the studies where B is absent. Consider the 50% of studies in which moderator A is absent. Within those studies, the presence or absence of B does not matter; the mean effect size is .20 in either case. Thus, B is a moderator variable only for the studies in which A is present. To say "B moderates the effect of X on Y" is false for the 50% of the studies where A is absent. This means that A and B are inextricably linked as moderator variables. Within the 75% of studies in which one or the other is absent, the mean effect size is .20, regardless of whether either variable is present or absent. The only moderating effect is that studies in which both *A* and *B* are present together differ from the other studies.

There is a rule in analysis of variance that states "If there is an interaction between two or more factors in the design, then interpretation of lower order main effects or interactions may be quite erroneous." This same rule applies to interaction between moderators. If moderators have interacting effects, then the interpretation of separate effects may be erroneous.

If the hierarchical breakdown reveals moderator variables, then the overall analysis without moderator variables is likely to be misleading. If the hierarchical analysis shows that moderator variables are correlated and/or interact, then the analysis of moderator variables separately is likely to be misleading. Thus, if a hierarchical breakdown is presented, it is critical to focus the interpretation solely on the full breakdown of the data.

Consider the partially hierarchical analysis in the meta-analysis of personnel selection validities by Schmitt, Gooding, Noe, and Kirsch (1984). These researchers first pooled correlations across all predictors (biodata, tests, interviews, and more) and all criterion measures (performance ratings, tenure, advancement, etc.). They then broke the data down by predictor and criterion separately, and finally by the two together. The combinatorial breakdown showed a strong interaction between predictor and criterion variables as moderators—as had been found in past analyses. Had they based their conclusions solely on that last analysis, they would have made no error of interpretation. Unfortunately, they based some of their conclusions on the earlier global analyses. For example, they claimed that their meta-analysis yielded results at odds with the comparable meta-analysis by Hunter and Hunter (1984). However, Hunter and Hunter broke their data down by both predictor variable and criterion variable from the beginning. Thus, the only table in Schmitt et al. comparable to the analysis of Hunter and Hunter is their final table, the combinatorial breakdown. There is no contradiction between their results in that analysis and that of Hunter and Hunter. This was brought out in a side-by-side presentation in Hunter and Hirsh (1987) that showed the analyses to be in agreement.

The analysis of multiple moderator variables separately (i.e., one by one) will be correct only if one can correctly make two assumptions: One must assume that (1) the moderator variables are independent and (2) the moderator variables are additive in their effects. In the MBO analysis of Rodgers and Hunter (1986), the commitment and time moderator variables were correlated across studies. Thus, the large difference due to the commitment variable produced a "spurious" mean difference between studies of different time lengths. If the two potential moderator variables had been independent, there could have been no spurious effect for time produced by commitment. The *AB* combination example showed that interactive moderators must always be considered together to generate correct conclusions.

If a fully hierarchical analysis is presented, it is critical to base conclusions on the highest level of interaction (i.e., the full hierarchical analysis). Schmitt et al. (1984) made an error of interpretation because they went back to an analysis with confounded interactions for one of their conclusions. Finally, it is important to recognize that one often will not have enough studies to conduct a fully hierarchical moderator analysis. If the number of studies in the cells of the fully hierarchical analysis is very small, the conclusions about moderators can only be tentative. Firmer conclusions must await the accumulation of a larger number of studies.

Use of Multiple Regression in Moderator Analysis and Mixed Meta-Analysis Models

This section explores meta-regression, multilevel meta-analysis, hierarchical linear modeling (HLM), and the mixed effects (ME) meta-analysis model. As we will see, these procedures are all closely related to one another.

META-REGRESSION: ADVANTAGES AND DISADVANTAGES

In meta-regression, r or d values are regressed onto measures of potential moderator variables that have been coded as study characteristics. This procedure has been used in meta-analyses of psychotherapy outcome studies (Smith & Glass, 1977) and the effects of class size (Smith & Glass, 1980) and many other more recent meta-analyses. Glass (1977) was the first to advocate using multiple regression to identify moderator variables in meta-analysis. He recommended and used ordinary least squares (OLS) regression, but others (e.g., Hedges & Olkin, 1985) later recommend weighted least squares regression (WLS). The use of meta-regression has the advantage that it controls (at least in theory) for any potential correlations among moderator variables, hence avoiding the problems that can plague nonhierarchical subgrouping of studies in meta-analysis. It also has the advantage of being better able to deal with continuous moderators.

The same considerations that apply to other applications of regression apply to meta-regression. Unless sample sizes are sufficiently large relative to the number of variables (predictors) in the regression equation, there is a great deal of sampling error in regression weights. As a result, simulation studies have found that the multiple Rs produced by regression weights are often less accurate in estimating population multiple R values than simple equal weighting of the predictor variables (Schmidt, 1971), even when there is no ex post facto selection of predictors. Under realistic conditions, with two predictors, one must have an N of at least 50 for regression weights to be superior to equal weights. With six predictors, N must be at least 100. With

8 predictors, N must be at least 150, and with 10 predictors, at least 200 (Schmidt, 1971). Keep in mind that in meta-regression, $N = k$, the number of studies. How many meta-regression studies that examine 8 potential moderators have $k = 150$ studies? Most do not. The extent of sampling error in regression weights can be illustrated by drawing multiple samples from the same realistic population, computing regression weights on each sample, and then computing the average correlation of regression weights across samples. That is, the regression weights are treated as a vector of scores whose reliability is measured by the average correlation between these vectors of weights across samples. With four predictors, it requires an N of 500 to produce a correlation of .85 (Schmidt, 1972, Table 1). For a larger number of predictors, larger Ns are required to attain this level of reliability for the regression weights. These findings apply to meta-regression as well as to other applications of regression analysis.

Meta-regression has eight serious disadvantages. The first and most serious is the potential for massive capitalization on chance resulting in inflated multiple Rs (Raudenbush, 2009), as described near the end of Chapter 2. The square of the multiple R is then falsely interpreted as the proportion of variance in r or d values explained by the "moderators." In meta-regression applications in the literature, the appropriate shrinkage formula to adjust for the inflation in the multiple R (Cattin, 1980) is almost never applied. Even if a shrinkage formula is applied, the multiple R is still inflated if there is any ex post facto selection of the potential moderators included in the meta-regression, a frequent practice. As noted in Chapter 2, some who use this procedure focus not on the multiple R but on the statistically significant regression weights. But these are also distorted by capitalization on chance if there is any ex post facto selection of the potential moderators to be included in the regression. For example, this occurs when only those potential moderators with a large or statistically significant correlation with the effect sizes are included in the meta-regression equation, a common practice. The second major problem is that statistical power is typically low, because the number of studies (k is the relevant N) is almost never large. Because of low power, the regression weights for most *real* moderators will be nonsignificant. At least they should be, given known statistical principles, yet most moderators in the literature *are* significant, which raises suspicions about capitalization on chance and/or selective reporting (see Chapter 13). The third disadvantage is susceptibility to distortion by outlier data points. This consideration exists in all applications of regression, but it is much more serious when sample sizes are small in relation to the number of predictors (Stevens, 1984). In meta-regression, the sample size (the number of studies, k) is often as small as 15, 20, or 30, and the number of potential moderators (predictors) may be as large as 5 or 10 (or more). The fourth disadvantage stems from the fact that the obtained regression weights are unstandardized (raw score) regression weights. Because of this, they are difficult or impossible to interpret in any substantive way and any given weight cannot be compared with other regression weights in the meta-regression, as discussed in the second section of Chapter 5. For example, the size of the regression weight on any hypothesized moderator depends on how that moderator is scaled or measured. Because different moderators are measured on different scales with different SDs, the magnitudes of the regression weights are not comparable and their magnitudes cannot be compared to each other, so it is not apparent which are the most important moderators. This fact leads users of meta-regression to focus almost entirely on p values in comparing moderators, an undesirable emphasis; p values become an inappropriate index of importance.

The fifth disadvantage is the fact that meta-regression results are inaccurate when the d or r values have not been corrected for measurement error (and for range restriction, where applicable) (Ones, Viswesvaran, & Schmidt, 2012). While all the values will be biased downward by measurement error, some will be biased more than others, undercutting the construct validity of the observed d s or r s as measures of the real effects and, hence, artifactually reducing the apparent strength of all true moderators. It is rare in published meta-regressions for these corrections to be made. The correction for measurement error that is necessary for accuracy of meta-regression results causes significance tests, standard errors, and confidence intervals for regression coefficients to be inaccurate with most computer programs. Hunter (1995) developed special software that yields accurate standard error values when the data have been corrected for measurement error. (Corrections to individual r or d values are not possible when artifact distribution meta-analysis is used, which makes the use of meta-regression even more questionable in such cases.) The sixth problem is measurement error in the measures of the hypothesized moderator variables. As noted in Chapter 3, Orwin and Cordray (1985) showed that failure to correct for measurement error in the measures of the moderator variables leads to serious errors in the meta-regression results. This finding is important because almost no meta-analyses in the literature using meta-regression make this correction, meaning their moderator results are suspect (see also Cordray & Morphy, 2009). Seventh, even if the d or r values are corrected for measurement error and other artifacts, there is still the problem created by the fact that much (often most, sometimes all) of the variance in the d values or rs (i.e., the dependent variable) is due to sampling error and other artifacts, creating low reliability for the dependent variable and, hence, low statistical power to detect moderator effects (as discussed in Chapters 2, 3, and 7; Cook et al., pp. 325–326). (Aloe, Becker, and Pigott, 2010, have proposed an adjustment for the sampling error in the effect sizes [which functions as measurement error in meta-regression]. This adjustment partials the effects of sampling error out of the multiple correlation and is similar to the correction for effect size unreliability illustrated in Chapter 3 in the Tibetan Employment Service example.) The eighth disadvantage stems from problematic data requirements. Use of meta-regression requires estimates of the correlations among the potential moderators (predictors). Often, estimates of some of these correlations are not available and must be guessed at or somehow imputed. This potential adds additional error to the meta-regression results.

In articles and textbooks, meta-regression is often presented and described without any mention of these disadvantages (e.g., Lipsey & Wilson, 2001). In light of these serious limitations, it can be seen that it is only under rare and unusual circumstances that meta-regression will produce reliable and valid results. Meta-regression is used quite frequently in the literature today, and it is highly likely that most of the results are not trustworthy.

Hedges and Olkin (1985, pp. 11–12, 167–169) argued for use of weighted least squares (WLS) regression rather than OLS in meta-regression. They pointed out that the assumption of homogeneity of sampling error variances is usually not met in meta-analysis data sets. The sampling error variance of each "observation" (i.e., each d or r value) depends on the sample size on which it is based (and on the size of the observed d or r value). If these sample sizes vary substantially, as they usually do, then different effect size estimates will have different sampling error variances. In meta-regression, study sampling error variance plays the same role as measurement error in a primary study analysis. Heterogeneity of variances can affect the validity of significance tests; actual alpha levels may be larger than nominal levels (e.g., .10 vs. the nominal .05). Estimates of the regression weights of moderators and multiple correlations can also be affected. Hedges and Olkin (1985, chap. 8) described a WLS regression procedure that circumvents these potential problems by weighting each study by the inverse of its sampling error variance. However, when Hedges and Stock (1983) used this method to reanalyze the Smith and Glass (1980) studies on class size, they obtained results that were quite similar to the original results, suggesting that the problem identified by Hedges and Olkin (1985) may not be serious when the number of d or r values is large (which was the case in the Smith and Glass, 1980, study). The general finding has been that most statistical tests are robust with respect to violations of the assumption of homogeneity of variance (see, e.g., Glass, Peckham, & Sanders, 1972; or Kirk, 1995).

In an attempt to address this question, Steel and Kammeyer-Mueller (2002) compared OLS and WLS using computer simulation. They focused only on continuous moderators and only on the accuracy of the multiple R resulting from predicting observed effect sizes from the continuous moderator variables. They did not look at the accuracy of the standardized regression weights, which provide the needed information on the size and importance of each individual moderator variable. They found that when the distribution of study sample sizes (N) was approximately normal, there was little difference in the accuracy of OLS and WLS. However, when the distribution of study Ns was skewed to the right, WLS produced more accurate estimates of the multiple R. However, the level of skew they examined was somewhat extreme (skew = 2.66) and might occur only infrequently in real research literatures. The Steel and Kammeyer-Mueller study did not address or discuss the problem of capitalization on sampling error in the use of either type of regression weighting. Nor did the study address the other disadvantages of meta-regression discussed above.

There are reasons to be cautious about the use of WLS. If there is an outlier (in either direction) with an extremely large N, the WLS estimates will be greatly influenced by such a study. Hence, with WLS, it is especially important to be concerned with outliers. There are also potential problems in the weighting of studies with small N s. When N is small, very large r or d values can occur due to large sampling errors. The observed value of r or d affects the computed sampling error variance (as can be seen by inspecting the formulas for sampling error variance for r and d) and, therefore, affects the weight the study gets. As Steel and Kammeyer-Mueller (2002) noted, a study based on $N = 20$ with an r of .99 would be given the same weight as a study based on $N = 20,000$ but with an r of .60! One solution to this latter problem is to use mean r or d in the sampling error variance formulas for r and d, in place of the r and d values from the individual study, as discussed and recommended in Chapters 3, 4, 5, and 7. Because both OLS and WLS regression methods have (different) problems, Overton (1998) recommended applying both and comparing the results. If they are similar, one's confidence in the results is supported. However, the eight disadvantages of meta-regression discussed above remain whether WLS or OLS is used. Modification of the study weights does not make these problems go away.

With these cautions in mind, when moderators are continuous and the decision has been made to use regression, it is probably advisable in typical cases to emphasize WLS results in preference to OLS results. In most meta-analyses that use meta-regression, the meta-regression analysis is conducted after the main meta-analysis. However, some applications of meta-analysis consist of only a meta-regression analysis. In general, this is not an approach that we recommend because it does not produce an overall corrected mean and standard deviation for the population parameters. In addition, the results produced by this approach will be stable only if k, the number of studies, is very large. The meta-analysis by Nye, Su, Rounds, and Drasgow (2012) used this approach effectively. This meta-analysis included 568 correlations, so sampling error in the regression analysis was greatly reduced. Such large k values are rare, however. An example of this approach to meta-analysis is the structural equation modeling (SEM)–based meta-analysis methods of M. W. L. Cheung (2008), discussed in Chapter 11. In practice, this form of meta-analysis, including Cheung's approach, is usually a mixed effects meta-analysis (discussed later). This approach to meta-analysis can be viewed as a form of hierarchical linear modeling (discussed later).

If moderators are dichotomous or categorical (e.g., sex or race), the subgrouping approach to moderator analysis is superior. However, it is important to bear in mind that moderators are often correlated and that it is important to use hierarchical moderator analysis to avoid confounding of correlated moderators. When moderators are continuous, the subgrouping method has the disadvantage of requiring dichotomization of the continuous variables to produce the subgroups, thus losing information. When there is only one hypothesized moderator to be examined and it is continuous, simple correlation can be used, as described in Chapters 3 and 7. That correlation is then the standardized regression weight for predicting the effect sizes or correlations. In this case, there is no capitalization on chance. When there is more than one continuous moderator, simple correlation is maximally informative only if the moderators are uncorrelated. If the continuous moderators are correlated, OLS or WLS can be used to assess the moderators (bearing in mind the limitations of meta-regression). Hierarchical meta-analysis via subgrouping can also be used, but it requires dichotomizing (or perhaps trichotomizing) the continuous moderator variables, which is not desirable. It is not clear which of these two options is to be preferred in a case like this. Some advice on use of meta-regression in moderator detection is provided by Aguinis and Gottfredson (2010) and Aguinis and Pierce (1998).

MULTILEVEL MODELS IN META-ANALYSIS AND HLM

The use of meta-regression as described in the previous section is often referred to as "multilevel" meta-analysis. In this nomenclature, the first level is the meta-analysis of d or r values, and the second level is the regression of the effect sizes onto a set of potential moderator variables. In a sense, this is a form of hierarchical linear modeling (HLM; Raudenbush, 2009; Raudenbush & Bryk, 2002). But HLM is typically used when effect sizes are not independent. For example, in educational research, teachers are nested within classrooms, and therefore the academic achievement scores of students within the same classroom are not independent (Raudenbush & Bryk, 2002), because the achievement of all the students is affected by the competence of their particular teacher. In meta-analysis, HLM is typically restricted to the case in which the same sample or study contributes multiple r or d values, which creates a similar violation of the assumption of independence. HLM can handle this problem. Freund and Kasten (2012) is an example of such an application of HLM in a meta-analysis. However, as seen in Chapter 10, we recommend that steps be taken to ensure that the effect sizes within a meta-analysis are statistically independent of each other. We also present evidence that violations of the independence assumption have less of a distorting effect on meta-analysis results than is usually assumed. It has been suggested that the HLM can be viewed as a general approach to conducting meta-analyses (Raudenbush & Bryk, 2002). As such, it is a form of linear mixed effects meta-analysis (discussed in the next section). However, in practice, HLM has typically been restricted to cases in which the independence assumption has been violated. Hedges, Tipton, and Johnson (2010a, 2010b) have presented an approach to HLM that is simpler to use and is robust to the distributional assumptions made by other HLM approaches. A major limitation of HLM in general is that it is very difficult, if not impossible, to correct for the distorting effects of measurement error and range restriction or enhancement, causing inaccuracy in the results. HLM has all of the eight disadvantages of meta-regression discussed in the previous section. In addition, most applications of HLM use maximum likelihood (ML) estimation methods, which require larger sample sizes. As in the case of meta-regression, it is only under rare circumstances that one has data sufficient to cause HLM to produce accurate results.

MIXED EFFECTS MODELS IN META-ANALYSIS

In Chapters 5 and 8, we presented discussions of fixed effects (FE) and random effects (RE) models in meta-analysis. There is a related concept called the "mixed effects (ME) model." The ME model is viewed as a mixture of RE and FE models. Suppose a meta-analyst applies the RE model to a set of effect sizes and stops after calibrating the variation in the population effect sizes, with no attempt to test or identify moderators. This occurs when the meta-analyst views this variation as completely random; that is, produced by unknown (and maybe unknowable) factors. This is referred to by Hedges (1982c, 1983b) as the "simple random effects model." Alternatively, the meta-analyst might hypothesize that certain specific factors account for at least some of the between-study variability in population values. The meta-analyst would then attempt to test these hypotheses using meta-regression (Raudenbush, 2009). According to Hedges (1983b), if these hypothesized moderators are related to study outcomes, they are then viewed as "fixed factors," meaning that they constitute all the potential moderators that the researcher is or would ever be interested in. This is the definition of fixed factors in analysis of variance (National Research Council, 1992). Therefore, in the weighted meta-regression, the studies are weighted by the inverse of their FE sampling error variances and not by the inverse of their larger RE sampling error variances (Overton, 1998; Raudenbush, 2009), which would be the study weights used if the moderators were viewed as just a sample of possible moderators. If there is no further variation in population effect sizes beyond sampling error in the subgroups in which these moderators are held constant (i.e., if the hypothesized moderators produce a [properly adjusted] multiple R of 1.00 with the actual study effect sizes), then the overall model is said to be an FE model, because there is no unexplained variation left. This outcome is rare in real data, if it exists at all. If, on the other hand, the postulated moderators account for some but not all the variation in the rho or delta values, the resulting model is said to be an ME model. The RE part of this conclusion stems from the fact that there is still remaining unexplained variance in population parameters, variance not accounted for by the moderators. The FE part of this conclusion stems from the fact that the postulated moderator variables are assumed to be fixed factors (FE factors). Vevea and Citkowicz (2008) showed via simulation that this approach often results in "seriously inflated Type I errors" in testing potential moderators that are in fact unrelated to the effect sizes. But in addition to this statistical problem there is also a conceptual problem here. If variance in population parameters remains after controlling for the fixed factors, there must be other moderators operating. This fact casts doubt on the definition of the fixed factors as constituting all the moderators that the researcher is interested in or could ever be interested in (National Research Council, 1992). The SEM-based methods of M. W. L. Cheung (2008) are ME meta-analysis methods, as noted earlier.

This way of thinking about meta-analysis models stemmed from an early conception of meta-analysis models in the 1985 Hedges and Olkin meta-analysis book. At that time, the hope was that the FE model as described above would turn out to be the case. That is, the hope was that postulated moderator variables would account for all the variation beyond sampling error in study population values. If so, then the FE model as defined above would actually apply. However, as meta-analyses accumulated in the literature, it became apparent that postulated moderators almost never explained all the variance in population parameters. (This result could be due in part to the fact that these meta-analysis methods do not control for variation due to artifacts such as measurement error; see Chapter 11. It is possible that these artifacts account for the remaining variance.)

Second-Order Sampling Error: General Principles

The outcome of any meta-analysis based on a small number of studies depends to some extent on which studies randomly happen to be available; that is, the outcome depends in part on study properties that vary randomly across studies. This is true even if the studies analyzed are all that exist at that moment. This phenomenon is called "second-order sampling error." It affects meta-analytic estimates of standard deviations more than it affects estimates of means. This is also the case with ordinary, or first-order, sampling error and ordinary statistics: Ordinary sampling error affects standard deviations more than means. Ordinary, or first-order, sampling error stems from the sampling of subjects within a study. Second-order sampling error stems from the sampling of studies in a meta-analysis.

Consider a hypothetical example. Suppose there were only 10 studies available estimating the relationship between Trait A and job performance. Even if the mean sample size per study were only 68 (the median for published validity studies reviewed by Lent et al., 1971a, 1971b), the mean validity would be based on $N = 680$ and would be reasonably stable. The observed variance across studies would be based on only 10 studies, however, and this variance, which we compare to the amount of variance expected from sampling error, would be based on only 10 data points. Now suppose sampling error were, in fact, the only factor operating to produce between-study variance in observed correlations (validities). Then, if we randomly happened to have one or two studies with large positive sampling errors, the observed variance across studies would likely be larger than the variance predicted by the sampling error variance formula, and we might falsely wind up concluding, for example, that sampling error accounts for only 50% of the observed variance of validities across studies. On the other hand, if the observed validity coefficients of, say, five or six of the studies randomly happened to be very close to the expected value (population mean), then the observed variance across studies would likely be very small and would underestimate the amount of variance one would typically (or on the average) observe across 10 such randomly drawn studies (from the population of such hypothetical studies that could be conducted). In fact, the observed variance might be smaller than the variance predicted from sampling error. The computed percentage variance accounted for by sampling error would then be some figure greater than 100%, for example, 150%. Of course, in this case, the correct conclusion would be reached: All the observed variance could be accounted for by sampling error. However, some people have been troubled by such outcomes. They are taken aback by results indicating that sampling error can account for more variance than is actually observed. Sometimes they are led to question the validity of the formula for sampling error variance (see, e.g., H. Thomas, 1988, and the reply by Osburn & Callender, 1990). This formula correctly predicts the amount of variance sampling error will produce on average. However, sampling error randomly produces more than this amount in some samples and less in other samples. The larger the number of studies (other things being equal), the smaller the deviations of observed from expected sampling variance. If the number of studies is small, however, these deviations can be quite large *on a percentage basis* (although *absolute* deviations are usually small even in such cases).

Negative estimates of variances occur using other methods of statistical estimation. In one-way analysis of variance (ANOVA), for example, the variance of sample means is the sum of two components: the variance of population means and the sampling error variance. This is directly analogous to the meta-analytic breakdown of the observed variance of sample correlations across studies into the variance of population correlations (the real variance) and the sampling error variance (the false or spurious variance). In estimating the variance of population means in ANOVA, the first step is to subtract the within-group mean square from the between-group mean square. This difference can be, and sometimes is, negative, as a result of sampling error. Consider a case in which the null hypothesis is true; the population means are then all equal and the variance of population means is 0. The variance of observed means (i.e., sample means) is then determined entirely by sampling error. This observed between-group variance will vary randomly from one study to another. About half the time, the within-group mean square will be larger than the between-group mean square, while half the time, the within-group mean square will be smaller. That is, if the variance of population means is 0, then in half of the observed samples, the estimated variance of population means will be negative. This is exactly the same as the situation in meta-analysis if all the population correlations are equal: The estimated variance will lie just above 0 half the time and will lie just below 0 half the time. The key here is to note that the variance of population correlations is estimated by subtraction: The known sampling error variance is subtracted from the variance of sample correlations, which estimates the variance of sample correlations across a population of studies. Because the number of studies is never infinite, the observed variance of sample correlations will depart by sampling error from the expected value. Thus, when the variance of population correlations is 0, the difference will be negative half the time.

Another example is the estimation of variance components in generalizability theory. Cronbach and his colleagues (Cronbach, Gleser, Nanda, & Rajaratnam, 1972) proposed generalizability theory as a liberalization of classical reliability theory, and it is now widely used to assess the reliability of measuring instruments in situations where the techniques of classical reliability theory are considered inadequate. Generalizability theory is based on the well-known ANOVA model and requires estimated variance components for its application. One or more of the estimated variance components may be negative, as noted by Cronbach et al. (1972, pp. 57–58) and Brennan (1983, pp. 47–48), even though, by definition, population variance components are nonnegative. The same phenomenon was also noted by Leone and Nelson (1966). Cronbach et al. (1972) recommended substituting 0 for the negative variance, and Brennan (1983) agreed with this recommendation.

Negative estimated variances are not uncommon in statistical estimation. The occurrence of negative estimates of variance in empirical research does not call into question a statistical theory such as ANOVA or a psychometric theory such as meta-analysis. As described previously, existing statistical sampling theory provides a sound rationale for observed negative estimates of variance in meta-analysis when the actual variance of true validities is 0 or close to 0. W. A. Thompson (1962) provides an analytical discussion of negative variance estimates.

Second-Order Meta-Analyses
Across Different Independent Variables

A second-order meta-analysis is a meta-analysis of meta-analyses. A form of second-order meta-analysis can be applied in cases in which the different meta-analyses have nonidentical in dependent variables to which the same theoretical and methodological considerations apply. In such cases, the effect sizes cannot be combined because the in dependent variables are different, but the problem of second-order sampling error can be addressed by computing the average percent variance accounted for by artifacts. Validity generalization research on cognitive ability tests is an example. Under the situational specificity hypothesis, the hypothesized situational moderators would be essentially the same for different abilities (e.g., verbal, quantitative, reasoning, spatial), and under the alternate hypothesis, all variance would be hypothesized to be artifactual for all abilities. The second-order meta-analysis would involve computing the average percentage of variance accounted for across the several meta-analyses. For example, in a large consortium study conducted by Psychological Services, Inc., in 16 companies, the percentage of variance accounted for by sampling error ranged over different abilities from about 60% to more than 100%. The average percentage accounted for across abilities was 99%, indicating that once second-order sampling error was considered, all variance of validities across the 16 companies was accounted for by sampling error for all the abilities studied.

Such a finding indicates that the meta-analyses with less than 100% of the observed variance accounted for are explained as cases of second-order sampling error (specifically, secondary second-order sampling error, as defined later in this chapter). The same is true of meta-analyses with more than 100% of the observed variance accounted for. It should be clear that in conducting a second-order meta-analysis, figures greater than 100% should not be rounded down to 100%. Doing so would obviously bias the mean for these figures, because those that are randomly lower than 100% are not rounded upward.

There is an important technical issue in this form of second-order meta-analysis: The average percentage of variance accounted for must be computed in a particular way or it will be inaccurate. This technical issue is best illustrated by a study conducted by Spector and Levine (1987). Spector and Levine conducted a computer simulation study aimed at evaluating the accuracy of the formula for the sampling error variance of r. In their study, the value of ρ was always 0, so the formula for the sampling error variance of observed rs was $S_e^2 = 1/(N-1)$. They conducted simulation studies for various values of N, ranging from 30 to 500. The number of observed rs per meta-analysis was varied from 6 to 100. For each combination of N and number of rs, they replicated the meta-analysis 1,000 times and then evaluated the average value of S_e^2 / S_r^2 across 1,000 meta-analyses. That is, they focused their attention on the average ratio of variance predicted from the sampling error formula to the average observed variance of the r s across studies. They did not look at $S_r^2 - S_e^2$, the difference between predicted and observed variances. They found that for all numbers of rs less than 100, the ratio S_e^2 / S_r^2 averaged more than 1.00. For example, when there were 10 rs per meta-analysis and $N = 75$ in each study, the average ratio was 1.25. Kemery, Mossholder, and Roth (1987) obtained similar results in their simulation study. The smaller the number of rs per meta-analysis, the more the ratio exceeded 1.00. They interpreted these figures as demonstrating that the formula for S_e^2 overestimates sampling variance when the number of correlations in a meta-analysis is less than 100. Their assumption was that if the S_e^2 formula were accurate, the ratio S_e^2 / S_r^2 would average 1.00.

The Spector-Levine (1987) study was critiqued by Callender and Osburn (1988), who showed that if one assessed accuracy by the difference $S_r^2 - S_e^2$, the sampling error variance formula was shown to be extremely accurate, as had also been demonstrated in their numerous previous simulation studies. There was no bias. They also demonstrated why the average ratio S_e^2 / S_r^2 is greater than 1.00 despite the fact that S_e^2 is an unbiased estimate of sampling variance. When the number of correlations in a meta-analysis is small, then, by chance, the S_r^2 will sometimes be very small; that is, by chance, all observed rs will be very similar to each other. Because S_r^2 is the denominator of the ratio, these tiny S_r^2 values lead to very large values for S_e^2 / S_r^2, sometimes as large as 30 or more. Furthermore, if S_r^2 should, by chance, be 0, the ratio is *infinitely large*. These extreme values raise the mean ratio above 1.00; the *median* ratio is very close to 1.00. The analysis by Callender and Osburn (1988) fully explains the startling conclusions of Spector and Levine (1987) and demonstrates that the fundamental sampling variance formula for the correlation is, in fact, accurate.

It should be noted that Spector and Levine would not have reached the conclusion they reached had they used the reciprocal of their ratio. That is, if they had used S_r^2 / S_e^2 instead of S_e^2 / S_r^2, they would have found that the mean ratio was 1.00. With this reversed ratio, the most extreme possible value is 0 (rather than infinity), and the distribution of ratios is much less skewed. This point has important implications for second-order meta-analyses of the sort discussed in this section. As noted earlier, this form of second-order meta-analysis is conducted by averaging the percentage of variance accounted for by artifacts over similar meta-analyses. In any given meta-analysis, this percentage is the ratio of artifact-predicted variance (sampling variance plus variance due to other artifacts) to the observed variance. One over this ratio is the reversed ratio, S_r^2 / S_e^2. In second-order meta-analysis, this reversed ratio should be averaged across studies, and then the reciprocal of that average should be taken. This procedure prevents the upward bias that appeared in the Spector-Levine study and results in an unbiased estimate of the average percentage of variance across the meta-analyses that is due to artifacts. For an example application, see Rothstein et al. (1990).

Meta-analysis has made clear how little information there is in single studies because of the distorting effect of (first-order) sampling error. An examination of second-order sampling error shows that even several studies combined meta-analytically contain limited information about between-study variance (although they provide substantial information about means). Accurate analysis of between-study variance requires either meta-analyses based on a substantial number of studies (we have had up to 882; cf. Pearlman et al., 1980) or meta-analyses of similar meta-analyses (second-order meta-analyses). These are the realities and inherent uncertainties of small-sample research in the behavioral and social sciences (or in any other area, e.g., the biomedical area). There is no perfect solution to these problems, but meta-analysis is the best available solution. As the number of studies increases, successive meta-analyses will become increasingly more accurate.

Second-Order Meta-Analysis With a Constant Independent Variable

When there are number of independent meta-analyses that focus on the same independent and dependent variables, another form of second-order meta-analysis becomes possible (Schmidt & Oh, 2013). For example, Oh (2009) conducted separate meta-analyses of the validity of five personality traits for predicting job performance in four East Asian countries. Each meta-analysis contained only studies conducted in that country, so there were no overlapping studies between meta-analyses. Mean validity values differed across countries but a second-order meta-analysis using the methods described in this section showed that most of the between-country variance in mean correlation values was due to second-order sampling error. For one personality trait—Conscientiousness—all the between-country variability was due to second-order sampling error, indicating that this trait has the same mean validity in all the countries. Schmidt and Oh (2013) present other such applications. The number of meta-analyses of the same independent and dependent variables conducted in different countries or regions is increasing, and so this form of second-order meta-analysis is becoming more important.

In this section, we present the essential equations and computations for second-order meta-analysis applied to (a) bare-bones meta-analyses (as described in Chapter 3), (b) meta-analyses that corrected each value individually (as described in Chapter 3), and (c) meta-analyses that used the artifact distribution method to correct for artifacts (as described in Chapter 4). The presentation is in terms of correlations, but analogous equations apply when the outcome statistic is the d value.

SECOND-ORDER META-ANALYSIS OF BARE-BONES META-ANALYSES

Equation (9.1) is the fundamental equation when the first-order meta-analyses entering the second-order meta-analysis have corrected only for sampling error:

$$\hat{\sigma}^2_{\bar{\rho}_{xy}} = S^2_{\hat{\bar{r}}} - E(S^2_{e_{\hat{\bar{r}}_i}}) \tag{9.1}$$

where the term on the left side of the equation is the estimate of the population variance of the uncorrected mean correlations ($\hat{\bar{\rho}}_{xy}$) across the meta-analyses after second-order sampling error has been subtracted out. The first term on the right side of Equation (9.1) is the weighted variance of the mean correlations across the m meta-analyses, computed as follows:

$$S^2_{\hat{\bar{r}}} = \sum_1^m w_i \left(\hat{\bar{r}}_i - \hat{\bar{\bar{r}}} \right)^2 / \sum_1^m w_i \tag{9.1a}$$

where

$$\hat{\bar{\bar{r}}} = \sum_1^m w_i \hat{\bar{r}}_i / \sum_1^m w_i \tag{9.1b}$$

and

$$w_i = \left(\frac{S^2_{r_i}}{k_i} \right)^{-1} \tag{9.1c}$$

and where $S^2_{r_i}$ is the variance of the observed correlations (rs) in the ith meta-analysis, $\hat{\bar{r}}_i$ is the estimate of the mean effect size for the ith meta-analysis, $\hat{\bar{\bar{r}}}$ is the estimate of the (weighted) grand mean effect size across the m meta-analyses, k_i is the number of primary studies included in the ith meta-analysis, and the w_i is the weight applied to the ith meta-analysis. The second term on the right side of Equation (9.1) is the expected (weighted average) second-order sampling error variance across the m meta-analyses:

$$E(S^2_{e_{\hat{\bar{r}}_i}}) = \sum_1^m \left(w_i \frac{S^2_{r_i}}{k_i} \right) / \sum_1^m w_i$$

(9.1d)

Equation (9.1d) reduces to Equation (9.1e):

$$E(S^2_{e_{\hat{\bar{r}}_i}}) = m / \sum_1^m w_i$$

(9.1e)

To summarize, each meta-analysis will have reported a mean uncorrected (i.e., mean observed) correlation, $\hat{\bar{r}}_i$. The first term on the right in Equation (9.1) is the weighted variance of these mean correlations. This computation is shown in Equations (9.1a) and (9.1b). The weights (w_i) used in Equations (9.1a), (9.1b), (9.1d), and (9.1e) are as defined in Equation (9.1c). Each weight is the inverse of the random effect (RE) sampling error variance for the mean correlation in the ith meta-analysis (Schmidt, Oh, & Hayes, 2009). The second term on the right in Equation (9.1) is the sampling error variance of these mean correlations. Each of the meta-analyses will have reported the variance of the observed correlations in that meta-analysis. Dividing each such variance by k_i (the number of studies in that meta-analysis) yields the RE sampling error variance of the mean r ($\hat{\bar{r}}_i$) in that meta-analysis (Schmidt, Oh, & Hayes, 2009). (This reflects the well-known principle that the sampling error variance of the mean of any set of scores is the variance of the scores divided by the number of scores [and the standard error of the mean is the square root of this value.]) The weighted average of these values across the m meta-analyses estimates the RE sampling error variance of the mean rs as a group, as shown in Equations (9.1d) and (9.1e). The square root of this value divided by the square root of m is the standard error ($SE_{\hat{\bar{r}}}$) and can be used to put confidence intervals around the estimate of the (weighted) grand mean ($\hat{\bar{\bar{r}}}$; computed in Equation [9.1b]). Also, using the square root of the value on the left side of Equation 9.1 ($\hat{\sigma}_{\bar{\rho}_{xy}}$), one can construct a credibility interval (see Chapters 5 and 8) around the grand mean correlation across the m meta-analyses, within which a given percentage of the first-order population meta-analytic (mean) effect sizes ($\hat{\bar{\rho}}_{xy}$) is expected to lie. For example, 80% would be expected to lie within the 80% credibility interval. If the value on the left side of Equation (9.1) is zero, the conclusion is that the mean population correlation values are the same across the meta-analyses. In that case, all the observed variance is accounted for by second-order sampling error, and the conclusion is that there are no moderators. If it is greater than zero, one can compute the proportion of variance between meta-analyses that is due to second-order sampling error. This is computed as the ratio of the second term on the right side of Equation (9.1) to the first term on the right side, that is,

$$\text{Proportion Var} = \frac{E(S^2_{e_{\hat{r}_i}})/S^2_{\hat{r}}}{}$$
(9.1f)

and $1 - \text{Proportion Var}$ denotes the proportion of the variance across first-order meta-analytic (bare-bones) mean correlations that is "true" variance (i.e., variance not due to second-order sampling error). As such, this number is the reliability of the meta-analytic correlations (considered as a set of values, one for each first-order meta-analysis; see Chapters 3 and 7). This follows because reliability is the proportion of total variance that is true variance (Magnusson, 1966; Nunally & Bernstein, 1994). As discussed later, this value can be used to produce enhanced accuracy for estimates of these mean (meta-analytic) correlations from the first-order meta-analyses by regressing them toward the value of the grand mean correlation (the mean across the first-order meta-analyses). Both of these analyses are unique to second-order meta-analysis and cannot be performed using other analysis methods.

SECOND-ORDER META-ANALYSIS WHEN CORRELATIONS HAVE BEEN INDIVIDUALLY CORRECTED

Measurement error is present in all research, and it biases all relationships examined in research. Therefore, it is important to include corrections for these biases. One approach in meta-analysis is to correct each correlation individually for the downward bias created by measurement error and other artifacts as appropriate (see Chapter 3). When the first-order meta-analyses entering the second-order meta-analysis have corrected each correlation individually for measurement error (and range restriction and dichotomization, if applicable), the fundamental equation for second-order meta-analysis is

$$\hat{\sigma}^2_{\bar{\rho}} = S^2_{\hat{\bar{\rho}}} - E(S^2_{e_{\hat{\bar{\rho}}_i}})$$
(9.2)

where the term on the left in Equation (9.2) is the estimate of the actual (nonartifactual) variance across the m meta-analyses of the population mean disattenuated correlations ($\hat{\bar{\rho}}$), that is, the variance after variance due to second-order sampling error has been subtracted out. The first term on the right side of Equation (9.2) is the variance of the mean individually corrected correlations across the m meta-analyses, computed as follows:

$$S^2_{\hat{\bar{\rho}}} = \sum_1^m w_i^* \left(\hat{\bar{\rho}}_i - \hat{\bar{\bar{\rho}}} \right)^2 / \sum_1^m w_i^*$$
(9.2a)

where

$$\hat{\bar{\bar{\rho}}} = \sum_1^m w_i^* \hat{\bar{\rho}}_i / \sum_1^m w_i^*$$
(9.2b)

and

$$w_i^* = \left(\frac{S^2_{r_{c_i}}}{k_i} \right)^{-1}$$
(9.2c)

and where $S^2_{r_{c_i}}$ is the weighted variance of the disattenuated (individually corrected) correlations in the ith meta-analysis, $\hat{\bar{\rho}}$ is the mean meta-analytic disattenuated correlation in that meta-analysis, $\hat{\bar{\bar{\rho}}}$ is the (weighted) grand mean effect size across the m meta-analyses, k_i is the number of primary studies included in the ith meta-analysis, and the w_i^* is the weight applied to the ith meta-analysis. The second term on the right side of Equation (9.2) is the weighted average second-order sampling error variance across the m meta-analyses:

$$E(S^2_{e_{\hat{\bar{\rho}}_i}}) = \sum_1^m w_i^* \left(\frac{S^2_{r_{c_i}}}{k_i} \right) / \sum_1^m w_i^*$$
(9.2d)

Equation (9.2d) reduces to Equation (9.2e):

$$E(S^2_{e_{\hat{\bar{\rho}}_i}}) = m / \sum_1^m w_i^*$$
(9.2e)

where the w_i^* are as defined in Equation (9.2c).

To summarize, each first-order meta-analysis will have reported an estimate of the mean disattenuated correlation (the meta-analytic mean correlation, $\hat{\bar{\rho}}_i$). The first term on the right side of Equation (9.2) is the variance of these meta-analytic mean correlations across first-order meta-analyses. This computation is shown in Equations (9.2a) and (9.2b). Equation (9.2c) shows the weights that are used in Equations (9.2a) and (9.2b). The second term on the right side of Equation (9.2) is the expected value of the second-order sampling error variance of these meta-analytic correlations. Each meta-analysis will have reported an estimate of the variance of the corrected correlations it included, preferably to four decimal places, for precision. Dividing this value by k (the number of studies in the meta-analysis) yields the RE sampling error variance of the meta-analytic correlation for that meta-analysis (Schmidt, Oh, & Hayes, 2009). (As noted earlier, this reflects the well-known statistical principle that the sampling error variance of the mean of any set of scores is the variance of the scores divided by the number of scores [and the standard error of the mean is the square root of this value].) As shown in Equations (9.2d) and (9.2e), the weighted mean of these values across the m meta-analyses yields the second-order sampling error variance needed in Equation (9.2).

The square root of this value divided by the square root of m is the standard error ($SE_{\bar{\bar{\rho}}}$) and can be used to put confidence intervals around the grand mean ($\bar{\bar{\rho}}$; shown in Equation [9.2b]).

The term on the left side of Equation (9.2) is the estimate of the actual (nonartifactual) variance across meta-analysis of the population mean disattenuated correlations (the $\bar{\hat{\rho}}_i$), that is, the variance across first-order meta-analytic estimates after removal of variance due to second-order sampling error. Using the square root of this value ($\hat{\sigma}_{\bar{\rho}}$), credibility intervals can be placed around the grand mean computed in Equation (9.2b).

If the value on the left side of Equation (9.2) is zero, the indicated conclusion is that the mean population correlation values are the same across the multiple meta-analyses. All the variance is accounted for by second-order sampling error. If this value is greater than zero, one can compute the proportion of variance across meta-analyses that is explained by second-order sampling error. This is computed as a ratio of the second term on the right side of Equation (9.2) to the first term on the right side, that is,

$$\text{ProportionVar} = E(S^2_{e_{\bar{\hat{\rho}}_i}}) / S^2_{\bar{\hat{\rho}}} \tag{9.2f}$$

and 1 − ProportionVar denotes the proportion of the variance across the first-order meta-analysis mean population correlation values that is true variance (i.e., variance not due to second-order sampling error). As such, this number is the reliability of the estimated mean first-order population correlations (see Chapter 3), because reliability is the proportion of total variance that is true variance (Magnuson, 1966; Nunnally & Bernstein, 1994). This value can be used to refine the estimates of these first-order meta-analysis mean values by regressing them toward the value of the grand mean disattenuated correlation (the mean across the m meta-analyses, computed in Equation [9.2b]). In addition, when $S^2_{\bar{\hat{\rho}}}$ is zero, the ProportionVar is 100% and the reliability of the vector of m first-order meta-analytic mean estimates is zero (e.g., Conscientiousness in Table 2 of Schmidt & Oh, 2013). This is the same as the situation in which all examinees get the same score on a test, making the reliability of the test zero.

SECOND-ORDER META-ANALYSIS WITH ARTIFACT DISTRIBUTION META-ANALYSES

Often the information needed to correct each correlation individually for measurement error is unavailable for many or most of the studies. In such literatures, meta-analysis can nevertheless correct for measurement error by use of measurement error estimates (reliability estimates) from other credible sources, as indicated earlier. This method of meta-analysis is called artifact distribution meta-analysis (see Chapter 4). Equation (9.3) is the fundamental equation for second-order meta-analysis when the first-order meta-analyses have applied the artifact distribution method of meta-analysis.

$$\hat{\sigma}^2_{\bar{\hat{\rho}}} = S^2_{\bar{\hat{\rho}}} - E(S^2_{e_{\bar{\hat{\rho}}_i}}) \tag{9.3}$$

where the term on the left side of Equation (9.3) is the estimate of the nonartifactual variance of the population meta-analytic (disattenuated) correlations (population parameter values) across the m first-order meta-analyses. This is the variance remaining after variance due to second-order sampling error has been subtracted out. The first term on the right side of Equation (9.3) is the variance of the mean disattenuated correlations across the m meta-analyses, computed as follows:

$$S^2_{\bar{\hat{\rho}}} = \sum_1^m w_i^{**} \left(\hat{\bar{\rho}}_i - \hat{\bar{\rho}} \right)^2 / \sum_1^m w_i^{**} \tag{9.3a}$$

where

$$\hat{\bar{\rho}} = \sum_1^m w_i^{**} \hat{\bar{\rho}}_i / \sum_1^m w_i^{**} \tag{9.3b}$$

and

$$w_i^{**} = \left[\left(\frac{\hat{\bar{\rho}}_i}{\bar{r}_i} \right)^2 \left(\frac{S^2_{r_i}}{k_i} \right) \right]^{-1} \tag{9.3c}$$

and where $S^2_{r_i}$ is the variance of the observed correlations within a given meta-analysis, $\hat{\bar{\rho}}_i$ is the mean disattenuated correlation in that meta-analysis, $\bar{r}_i$ is the meta-analytic (bare-bones) mean correlation in that meta-analysis, $\hat{\bar{\rho}}$ is the (weighted) grand mean effect size across the m meta-analyses, k_i is the number of primary studies included in the ith meta-analysis, and w_i^{**} is the weight applied to the ith meta-analysis. The second term on the right side of Equation (9.3) is the weighted average second-order sampling error variance across the m meta-analyses:

$$E(S^2_{e_{\hat{\rho}_i}}) = \sum_1^m w_i^{**} \left[\left(\frac{\hat{\bar{\rho}}_i}{\bar{r}_i} \right)^2 \frac{S^2_{r_i}}{k_i} \right] / \sum_1^m w_i^{**}$$

(9.3d)

Equation (9.3d) reduces to Equation (9.3e):

$$E(S^2_{e_{\hat{\rho}_i}}) = m / \sum_1^m w_i^{**}$$

(9.3e)

The w_i^{**} are as defined in Equation (9.3c). Equation (9.3) has the same form as Equation (9.2), but some of the terms in it are estimated differently, so some explanation is indicated. The first term on the right side of Equation (9.3) is the computed variance across the meta-analyses of the first-order meta-analytic mean disattenuated population correlations. Computation of this value is shown in Equations (9.3a) and (9.3b). Equation (9.3c) shows the weights that are applied in Equations (9.3a) and (9.3b). The second term on the right in Equation (9.3) is the sampling error variance of these estimates. As shown in Equations (9.3d) and (9.3e), this sampling error is estimated as the weighted average across meta-analyses of the product of the square of the mean correction factor and the mean sampling error variance of the bare-bones (uncorrected) meta-analytic correlations ($S^2_{e_{\bar{r}}}$; see Equation [9.1d]). Each meta-analysis will have reported the variance of the observed correlations it included. Dividing this variance by k (the number of studies in the meta-analysis) yields the RE sampling error variance of the mean of the observed (uncorrected) correlations in that meta-analysis. As shown in Equations (9.3d) and (9.3e), the weighted average of the product of these values and the square of the correction factors across the m meta-analyses is the random effects sampling error variance estimate needed for Equation (9.3) (see Chapter 4). (As noted in the discussion of first-order artifact distribution-based meta-analysis in Chapter 4, this is based on the well-known principle that if one multiples a distribution of scores by a constant, the standard deviation is multiplied by that constant and the variance is multiplied by the square of that constant. Here the constant is the mean measurement error correction [$\hat{\bar{\rho}}/\bar{r}_i$].) The square root of the value on the left side of Equation (9.3d) divided by the square root of m is the standard error ($SE_{\hat{\bar{\rho}}}$) and can be used to put confidence intervals around the grand mean ($\hat{\bar{\bar{\rho}}}$; computed in Equation [9.3b]).

The value on the left side of Equation (9.3) is the estimate of the nonartifactual variance of the population disattenuated correlations across the m
meta-analyses. This is the variance remaining after subtraction of variance
due to second-order sampling error. When this value is negative (i.e., second-
order sampling error variance is greater than the observed variance across
the first-order meta-analytic mean estimates), it is set to zero. Using the
square root of this value ($\hat{\sigma}_{\bar{\rho}}$), credibility intervals around the grand mean
correlation can be computed, as described earlier. If the value on the left
side of Equation (9.3) is zero, the indicated conclusion is that these mean
population correlations are the same across the m meta-analyses. All variance is accounted for by second-order sampling error, leading to the conclusion that there are no moderators. If this value is greater than zero, one
can compute the proportion of between meta-analyses variance that is
accounted for by second-order sampling error variance. This is computed
as the ratio of the second term on the right side of Equation (9.3) to the
first term; that is,

$$\text{ProportionVar} = E(S^2_{\hat{e}_{\bar{\rho}_i}}) / S^2_{\hat{\bar{\rho}}} \tag{9.3f}$$

where 1 − ProportionVar denotes the proportion of the variance of the
population disattenuated correlations that is true variance (i.e., variance
not due to second-order sampling error). Because of this, this number is
the reliability of the vector of mean corrected correlations across the m
first-order meta-analyses. This follows from the fact that reliability is
defined as the proportion of total variance that is true variance (i.e., variance not due to error; Magnusson, 1966; Nunnally & Bernstein, 1994).
This reliability reflects the extent to which the mean first-order corrected
correlations discriminate between the first-order meta-analysis results.

MIXED SECOND-ORDER META-ANALYSIS

In some cases, some of the first-order meta-analyses might have corrected each correlation individually while others applied the artifact distribution method. How, then, should the second-order meta-analysis be
conducted? The meta-analyses that corrected each coefficient individually
can be "converted" to artifact distribution meta-analyses, and the equations for second-order artifact distribution meta-analysis can be applied to
all the first-order meta-analyses. The quantities needed in these equations
(Equations [9.3] and [9.3a] through [9.3f]) are typically reported in
meta-analyses that have corrected each correlation individually, making
this conversion possible.

CONSIDERATIONS IN SECOND-ORDER META-ANALYSIS

One limitation of second-order meta-analysis methods is that the requirement for statistical independence of meta-analysis may limit the frequency with which the methods can be applied. The extent to which moderate violations of this assumption affect the results is unknown, but Cooper and Koenka (2012), in discussing an older, cruder form of second-order meta-analysis, suggest that minimizing the lack of independence might be sufficient to produce reasonably accurate results, and they give several examples of such published second-order meta-analyses. Tracz, Elmore, and Pohlmann (1992), in a simulation study, found that violations of the assumption of independence in first-order meta-analyses had minimal effect on the accuracy of results. Issues related to the importance of the independence assumption are discussed further in Chapter 10.

Second-order meta-analysis is not directly concerned with the variability of study population correlations *within* each of the first-order individual meta-analyses. To be sure, this variability within meta-analyses (i.e., nonartifactual variability between primary studies in first-order meta-analyses) is taken into account mathematically in second-order meta-analysis methods, as can be seen in Equations (9.1a), (9.1b), (9.1c), (9.2a), (9.2b), (9.2c), (9.3a), (9.3b), and (9.3c). But a finding that second-order sampling error accounts for all of the variability in the mean values across first-order meta-analyses does not imply that population parameters do not vary within first-order meta-analyses. Such a finding simply means that the *mean* values are equal across the different first-order meta-analyses. For example, the Schmidt and Oh (2013) finding that the mean meta-analytic operational validity for Conscientiousness is the same across different East Asian countries does not mean that this validity cannot vary somewhat across subpopulations within, for example, South Korea. If this is the case, this variability will be reflected in the results of the first-order meta-analysis. It is the purpose of the original first-order meta-analyses to address this nonartifactual variability between primary studies within each first-order meta-analytic context. The purpose of second-order meta-analysis is to gauge the true (nonartifactual) variability between meta-analyses (e.g., cross-country, cross-region, cross-criterion, cross-setting) for *mean values* of ostensibly the same relationship and to use this information to improve accuracy of estimation for each first-order meta-analytic mean estimate.

A possible objection to second-order meta-analysis is the following: Instead of second-order meta-analysis, why not conduct an overall meta-analysis, pooling all primary study data from all meta-analyses (which will yield the same grand mean as the second-order meta-analysis), and then break out into sub-meta-analyses based on hypothesized moderators (which yields the same subgroup means as those used in the second-order meta-analysis)? First, this is often an impossible or impractical alternative, because the primary studies used in all first-order meta-analyses are often not available. Some journals (e.g., *Journal of Applied Psychology*) in the fields of organizational behavior and human resource management have only recently required that meta-analyses report all data from primary studies used in the meta-analysis (Aytug, Rothstein, Zhou, & Kern, 2012; Kepes, Banks, McDaniel, & Whetzel, 2012). As mentioned, second-order meta-analysis can be conducted using only first-order meta-analytic results (k, mean observed r, mean corrected r, and variance across observed or corrected rs), and thus it can be applied to most if not all previous first-order meta-analyses. Second, and perhaps more important, this procedure does not allow one to estimate the variance (and the percentage of variance) across subgroup meta-analyses that is (and is not) due to second-order sampling error variance, because second-order sampling error variance is not computed (or computable) in the omnibus meta-analysis approach. This is because omnibus meta-analyses and their subgroup meta-analyses are both first-order meta-analyses. For example, application of this approach to the Conscientiousness validity data in our first example would not have revealed that all the variance across the four East Asian countries in meta-analytic operational validity values was due to second-order sampling error. Instead, the values would have been taken at face value. So the omnibus meta-analysis procedure is not a substitute for second-order meta-analysis.

A variation on this objection is the following: Why not just conduct an omnibus, pooled meta-analysis along with subgroup meta-analyses based on hypothesized moderators and then look at the relative variances? The difference between the estimated population parameter variance in the omnibus meta-analysis and the average of this figure across the subgroup meta-analyses estimates the variance of the subgroup means (the variance of means across subgroup meta-analyses). This statement reflects the well-known ANOVA principle that total variance is the sum of between-group variance and average within-group variance. However, knowing the variance of the subgroup means does not allow one to estimate *how much* of this variance is (or is not) due to second-order sampling error and therefore does not allow computation of the proportion of this variance that is due to second-order sampling error. As a result, the analyses presented in the example in Schmidt and Oh (2013) cannot be conducted. For example, if all the between-mean variance was accounted for by second-order sampling error (as was the case with Conscientiousness in our first example application), there would be no way for one to know this. The procedure advocated here allows one to compute the percentage of *total variance* that is accounted for by between-group variance in mean values, but this is not the same as the percentage of between-group variance in mean values that is due to second-order sampling error variance. So again, this is a procedure that is not a substitute for second-order meta-analysis.

Another possible objection is this: Why not just compute a meta-regression in which coded hypothesized moderators are used to predict the primary study correlations pooled across all the first-order meta-analyses? (These correlations can be either observed correlations, as in bare-bones meta-analysis, or correlations corrected for measurement error.) This procedure fails for the same reason as above: The squared multiple correlation will reveal the percentage *of the total variance* that is accounted for by the hypothesized moderator or moderators. But it will not reveal the percentage of the variance in the mean values that is explained by second-order sampling error, and therefore the analyses allowed by second-order meta-analysis cannot be done. So this procedure is also not capable of being a substitute for second-order meta-analysis.

In conclusion, the methods of second-order meta-analysis provide unique information that cannot be obtained using the more traditional methods of first-order meta-analysis. The methods are particularly useful in conducting cross-culture generalization studies (i.e., synthesizing first-order meta-analyses conducted in different countries for the same relationship using within-country studies) and meta-analytic moderator analyses (i.e., comparing first-order meta-analytic results of the same relationship across different settings and/or groups; e.g., racial or social class groups). This unique information can be important from the point of view of cumulative knowledge and understanding, as illustrated in the several empirical examples presented in Schmidt and Oh (2013).

Second-Order Sampling Error: Technical Treatment

This section presents a more technical and analytical treatment of second-order sampling error and statistical power in meta-analysis. For the sake of simplifying the presentation, the results are presented for "bare-bones" meta-analyses, that is, meta-analyses for which sampling error is the only artifact that occurs and for which a correction is made. However, the principles apply to the more complete forms of meta-analysis presented in this book.

If a meta-analysis is based on a large number of studies, then there is little sampling error in the meta-analytic estimates. However, if the meta-analysis is based on only a small number of studies, there will be sampling error in the meta-analytic estimates of means and standard deviations. This is called second-order sampling error. There are potentially two kinds of second-order sampling error: sampling error due to incompletely averaged sampling error in the primary studies and sampling error produced by variation in effect sizes across studies. We will call unresolved sampling error from the primary studies "secondary second-order sampling error," or "secondary sampling error" for short. We will call sampling error due to variation in effect sizes "primary second-order sampling error." Table 9.1 shows the circumstances in which the two types of second-order sampling errors occur. The key to this table is whether we have the homogeneous or heterogeneous case in the population. In the homogeneous case, there is no variance in ρ or δ in the population. In the heterogeneous case, the population values of ρ or δ do vary. As we noted in Chapters 5 and 8, the heterogeneous case is much more common in real data. Note that regardless of whether the set of studies is homogeneous or heterogeneous, there is always secondary second-order sampling error. This occurs because, in real data sets, it is never the case that the number of studies is infinite or that all studies have infinite sample size—the only conditions that can completely eliminate secondary second-order sampling error. However, primary second-order sampling error occurs only in the heterogeneous case. That is, when there is variance in ρ or δ, then primary second-order sampling error will be produced by the sampling of particular values of ρ_i or δ_i in individual studies. This cannot happen in the homogeneous case, because different values of ρ or δ cannot be sampled, because there is only a single value of ρ or δ in all studies. Because the homogeneous case is rare in real data, however, there will typically be both kinds of second-order sampling error in real meta-analyses. That is, typical real-world meta-analyses fall into the bottom row of Table 9.1.

Table 9.1 Second-order sampling error: Schematic showing when the two types of second-order sampling error occur.

	Secondary Second-Order Sampling Error	Primary Second-Order Sampling Error
Homogeneous Case $(S_\rho^2 = 0; S_\delta^2 = 0)$	Yes	No
Heterogeneous Case $(S_\rho^2 > 0; S_\delta^2 > 0)$	Yes	Yes

For simplicity, the following discussion will be written for analyses of the d statistic, but analyses based on correlations or other statistics are also subject to second-order sampling error when the number of studies is not large. In particular, second-order sampling error for correlations is directly analogous to that for d values.

Consider secondary sampling error. Meta-analytic estimates are averages. Thus, the sampling error in individual studies is averaged across studies. If enough studies are averaged, then the average sampling error

effects become exactly computable and, hence, exactly correctable. However, if the number of studies is small, then the average sampling error
effects will still be partly random. For example, consider the mean effect
size. Ignoring the small bias in the d statistic (see Chapters 7 and 8), the
average d for the meta-analysis is

$$\text{Ave}(d) = \text{Ave}(\delta) + \text{Ave}(e) \qquad (9.4)$$

If the number of studies is large, then the average sampling error across
studies, $\text{Ave}(e)$, will equal its population value of 0. That is, if we average
across a large number of particular sampling errors, the sampling errors
will cancel out exactly and yield an average of 0. If $\text{Ave}(e) = 0$, then

$$\text{Ave}(d) = \text{Ave}(\delta) \qquad (9.5)$$

That is, if the average sampling error in the meta-analysis is 0, then the
average observed effect size in the meta-analysis is equal to the average
population effect size in the meta-analysis. If $\text{Ave}(e)$ differs from 0, that is
the effect of secondary sampling error.

If secondary sampling error were 0, then the average effect size in the
meta-analysis would equal the average population effect size in the studies included in the meta-analysis. The number that we want to know,
however, is the average population effect size across the entire research
domain. The average effect size in the meta-analysis might differ from
the average for the whole domain. If there were no variance in effect
sizes across studies (the homogeneous case), then $\text{Ave}(\delta) = \delta$ for any
meta-analysis, and there can be no difference between the mean for the
meta-analysis and the mean for the research domain. If there is variation
across studies (the heterogeneous case), however, then the mean in the
meta-analysis could differ by chance from the mean in the domain as a
whole. This is primary second-order sampling error.

If the number of studies is large and if the studies are representative of
the research domain, then the average population effect size in the
meta-analysis, $\text{Ave}(\delta)$, will differ little from the average effect size across
the research domain. That is, if the number of studies is large, then the
$\text{Ave}(d)$ value in the meta-analysis will be almost exactly equal to the average across the entire potential research domain. Thus, for a large number
of studies, there will be no primary second-order sampling error in the
meta-analysis mean.

In the next section, we will derive a confidence interval to estimate the
potential range of second-order sampling error in the meta-analysis mean.

Both the mean (i.e., $\hat{\bar{\rho}}$ or $\hat{\bar{\delta}}$) and the standard deviation (i.e., SD_ρ or
SD_δ) estimated in meta-analysis have second-order sampling error,
although the exact relationship is more complicated in the case of standard deviations than it is for means. If the number of studies is large, then

the variance of the particular sampling errors in the meta-analysis, Var(e), will equal the value predicted from statistical theory. If the number of studies is small, then the observed sampling error variance may differ from the statistically expected value. Similarly, if the number of studies is large, then the variance in the particular effect sizes included in the meta-analysis, Var(δ), will equal the variance for the research domain as a whole. However, if the number of studies is small, then the variance of study population effect sizes in the meta-analysis may differ by chance from the variance of population effect sizes. This can also be stated as follows: If the number of studies is large, then the covariance between effect size and sampling error will be 0, but if the number of studies is small, then this covariance in the meta-analysis may differ by chance from 0.

Let us consider primary second-order sampling error in more detail. One key question is whether there is any primary second-order sampling error. There are two possible cases. First, there is the "homogeneous case" in which the population effect sizes do not differ from one study to the next (i.e., $S_\delta^2 = 0$). Second, there is the "heterogeneous case" where there is variation in population effect sizes across studies (i.e., $S_\delta^2 > 0$). Consider first the case in which the population study effect, δ_i, does not vary across studies. That is, in the homogeneous case, we have

$$\delta_i = \delta \text{ for each study } i \text{ in the domain}$$

As discussed in Chapters 5 and 8 and earlier in this chapter, the homogeneous case is probably rare in real data. In the homogeneous case, it is possible to speak of "the" population effect size δ. Because δ_i is the same for each study,

$$\text{Ave}(\delta_i) = \delta \text{ for any set of studies from the domain}$$
$$\text{Var}(\delta_i) = 0 \text{ for any set of studies from the domain}$$

The meta-analysis mean observed effect size is

$$\begin{aligned} \text{Ave}(d_i) &= \text{Ave}(\delta_i) + \text{Ave}(e_i) \\ &= \delta + \text{Ave}(e_i) \end{aligned} \tag{9.6}$$

Thus, the meta-analytic average effect size differs from the effect size δ only to the extent that the average of the sampling errors in the meta-analysis differs from 0. That is, the only second-order sampling error in the mean effect size in the meta-analysis is the secondary sampling error, the sampling error resulting from primary sampling errors that by chance do not average to exactly 0.

In the homogeneous case, the population effect size is constant across studies. Thus,

$$\text{Var}(d_i) = \text{Var}(e_i)$$

If the number of studies were large, then the variance of the particular sampling errors in the meta-analysis would equal the variance predicted by the statistical theory for the research domain as a whole. However, if the particular sampling errors in the meta-analysis have a variance that is different by chance from the domain variance, then that unresolved primary sampling error will not have been eliminated from the meta-analysis. Thus, in the homogeneous case, the only second-order sampling error in the variance of observed effect sizes will be secondary sampling error, that is, unresolved first-order study sampling error.

Now let us consider the heterogeneous case in which population effect sizes *do* differ from one study to the next (i.e., $S_\delta^2 > 0$). The average observed effect size in a meta-analysis is

$$\text{Ave}(d_i) = \text{Ave}(\delta_i) + \text{Ave}(e_i) \tag{9.7}$$

If the number of studies is small, then there can be error in each of the two terms: the average sampling error, $\text{Ave}(e_i)$, and the average population effect size, $\text{Ave}(\delta_i)$. Consider the average sampling error, $\text{Ave}(e_i)$. By chance, the average sampling error for that meta-analysis, $\text{Ave}(e_i)$, is likely to depart from 0 by at least some small amount. That is secondary sampling error. Secondary sampling error always converges to 0 if the number of studies is large enough. However, it is possible for secondary sampling error to be small even if the number of studies is small. If the sample sizes in the primary studies were all very large—an unlikely event in psychological research—the average of the individual sampling errors would be near 0. The average sampling error would then be near 0 even though the number of studies is small.

Now consider the other term in the average effect size, $\text{Ave}(\delta_i)$, the average population effect size for the meta-analysis. If the number of studies is large, then the average population effect size in the meta-analysis will differ little from the average population effect size for the whole research domain. However, if the number of studies is small, then the particular values of (δ_i) observed in the meta-analysis are only a sample of the effect sizes from the domain as a whole. Thus, by chance, the average effect size in the meta-analysis may differ by some amount from the average effect size for the entire research domain. This departure is primary second-order sampling error. Even if all primary studies were done with an infinite number of subjects (i.e., even if every primary study sampling error e_i were 0), then the particular effect sizes in the meta-analysis need not have an average that is exactly equal to the domain average.

Thus, in the heterogeneous case, both the mean and the standard deviation of population effect sizes in the meta-analysis will depart from the research domain values because the studies observed are only a sample of studies. This is "primary second-order sampling error."

THE HOMOGENEOUS CASE

In defining the word *homogeneity*, it is important to distinguish between actual treatment effects and study population treatment effects. There are few studies that are methodologically perfect and, thus, few studies in which the study population treatment effect is equal to the actual treatment effect. In a research domain in which the actual treatment effect is the same for all studies, artifact variation across studies (e.g., varying levels of measurement error in different studies) will produce artifactual differences in study effect sizes. In most current textbooks on meta-analysis, the definition of *homogeneous* is obscured by implicit statistical assumptions. The definition of homogeneity requires that the study population effect sizes be exactly uniform across studies. In particular, most current chi-square homogeneity tests thus assume not only that the actual treatment effect is constant across studies but also that there is no variation in artifact values (e.g., measurement error) across studies. This assumption is very unlikely to hold in real data.

Most contemporary meta-analyses of experimental treatments have been bare-bones meta-analyses; no correction has been made for error of measurement or variation in strength of treatment, or variation in construct validity, or other artifacts. For a bare-bones meta-analysis, it is very unlikely that the study population effect sizes would be exactly equal for all studies. To have uniformity in the study effect sizes, the studies would have to be not only uniform in actual effect size but uniform in artifact values as well. All studies would have to measure the dependent variable with exactly the same reliability and the same construct validity. All studies would have to have the same degree of misidentification—inadvertent treatment failure—in group identification, and so on. (See the discussion of fixed vs. random meta-analysis models in Chapters 5 and 8; fixed effects meta-analysis models assume the homogeneous case; see also Chapters 2 and 6.) However, it may be useful in some cases to think of the homogeneous case as an approximation.

For purposes of this exposition of second-order sampling error, we assume homogeneity, and we denote the uniform study effect size by δ. Assume the average sample size to be 50 or more so that we can ignore bias in mean d values. Then, for each study individually, the treatment effect differs from δ only by sampling error. That is,

$$d_i = \delta + e_i \tag{9.8}$$

We then have

$$\text{Ave}(d) = \delta + \text{Ave}(e_i) \tag{9.9}$$

$$\text{Var}(d) = \text{Var}(e_i) \tag{9.10}$$

The average differs from δ only if the average sampling error is not the expected value of 0, that is, only if the number of studies is too low for errors to average out to the expected value (to within rounding error). The variance of observed effect sizes differs from $\text{Var}(e)$ only if the variance of sampling errors $\text{Var}(e_i)$ differs from the expected variance $\text{Var}(e)$. This would not occur for a meta-analysis on a large number of studies. However, the sampling error in the variance estimate $(\hat{S}_\delta^2)$ is larger than the sampling error in the estimate of the mean $(\bar{\delta})$. Thus, in most meta-analyses, the sampling error in the estimate of the variance of effect sizes is much more important than the sampling error in the estimate of the average effect size.

In the homogeneous case, the sampling error in the mean effect size for a bare-bones meta-analysis is obtained from the sampling error equation

$$\bar{d} = \delta + \varepsilon$$

where $\bar{d}$ is the mean effect size and ε is the average sampling error. The distribution of meta-analytic sampling error ε is described by

$$E(\varepsilon) = 0$$

$$\text{Var}(\varepsilon) = \text{Var}(e)/K \tag{9.11}$$

where K is the number of studies and $\text{Var}(e)$ is the average sampling error variance across the studies in the meta-analysis. $\text{Var}(\varepsilon)^{\frac{1}{2}} = SD_\varepsilon$. Thus, under the assumption of homogeneity, the 95% confidence interval for the mean effect size in a *bare-bones meta-analysis* is

$$\text{Ave}(d) - 1.96 SD_\varepsilon < \delta < \text{Ave}(d) + 1.96 SD_\varepsilon$$

(See Chapters 5 for and 8 methods of computing this confidence interval when artifacts beyond sampling error are corrected for.)

The sampling error in the estimated variance of effect sizes for a bare-bones meta-analysis is obtained by considering a variance ratio. For a large number of studies, the condition of homogeneity could be identified by computing the following ratio:

$$\text{Var}(d) / \text{Var}(e) = 1$$

For a small number of studies, this ratio will depart from 1 by sampling error. Many writers recommend that a chi-square test be used to assess the extent to which there is variance beyond sampling error variance. The statistic Q is defined as

$$Q = K\mathrm{Var}(d) \,/\, \mathrm{Var}(e)$$

We recommend that you not use the Q statistic. The Q statistic is the comparison variance ratio multiplied by the number of studies. Under the assumption of homogeneity, Q has a chi-square distribution with $K - 1$ degrees of freedom. This is the most commonly used "homogeneity test" of contemporary meta-analysis. The homogeneity test has all the serious flaws of any significance test. These flaws were discussed in Chapter 2. If the number of studies is small, then a real moderator variable must be enormous to be detected by this test. That is, the power of the test is low unless the moderator effect (interaction) is very large (Hedges & Pigott, 2001; National Research Council, 1992). On the other hand, if the number of studies is large, then any trivial departure from homogeneity, such as departures from artifact uniformity across studies, will suggest the presence of a moderator variable where there may be none. Because of these problems, we recommend against use of the homogeneity test.

THE HETEROGENEOUS CASE

If the research domain is heterogeneous (i.e., $S_\delta^2 > 0$), then there can be primary second-order sampling error—error due to the fact that the number of studies is not infinite. In a real meta-analysis in the heterogeneous case, there will therefore be two kinds of error: secondary sampling error and primary second-order sampling error. For purposes of discussion, we will focus first on just primary second-order sampling error. To do this, we will make a very unrealistic assumption: We will assume either (1) that all studies are done with infinite size or (2) (which is the same thing) that all study population effect sizes are known. After consideration of the special case, we will return to the realistic case of primary as well as second-order sampling error.

To make primary second-order sampling error clearly visible, let us eliminate first-order sampling error. That is, we assume all study Ns are infinite. Suppose population effect sizes do vary across studies (i.e., $S_\delta^2 > 0$). The individual study effect size is δ_i. Under these assumptions, meta-analysis will compute the average and variance of the study effect sizes in the studies located:

$$\mathrm{Ave}(d) = \mathrm{Ave}(\delta_i)$$
$$\mathrm{Var}(d) = \mathrm{Var}(\delta_i)$$

However, if the number of studies is small, the average population effect size in the studies in the meta-analysis is only a sample average of the population effect sizes across all possible studies in the research domain.

The simplest case of a moderator variable is the binary case, for example, studies done with males versus studies done with females. The statistical description of a binary variable includes four pieces of information: the two values that are taken on by the binary variable and the probability of each value. Denote the two values by X_1 and X_2 and denote the respective probabilities by p and q. Because the sum of probabilities is 1, $p + q = 1$ and, hence, $q = 1 - p$. The mean value is

$$E(X) = pX_1 + qX_2 \qquad (9.12)$$

Let D denote the difference between the values; that is, define D by

$$D = X_1 - X_2$$

The variance of the binary variable is

$$Var(X) = pqD^2 \qquad (9.13)$$

Suppose a research domain has a moderator variable such that for 50% of studies, the effect size is $\delta = .20$, while for the other 50% of studies, the effect size is $\delta = .30$. For the research domain as a whole, the mean effect size is

$$Ave(\delta) = .50(.20) + .50(.30) = .25$$

The variance is given by

$$Var(\delta) = pqD^2 = (.50)(.50)(.30 - .20)^2 = .0025$$

Thus, the standard deviation is $SD_\delta = .05$. Consider a meta-analysis with $K = 10$ studies. If the studies are split 5 and 5, then for that meta-analysis, the mean effect size would be .25 and the standard deviation would be .05. Suppose, however, the studies by chance are split 7 and 3. The mean would be

$$Ave(d) = (7/10)(.20) + (3/10)(.30) = .23$$

rather than .25. The variance would be

$$Var(d) = (7/10)(3/10)(.30 - .20)^2 = (.21)(.01) = .0021$$

instead of .0025. That is, the standard deviation would be .046 rather than .05. These deviations in the mean and standard deviation of effect sizes are primary second-order sampling error, variation due to the fact that the sample of studies has chance variations from the research domain, which is the study population.

How large is primary second-order sampling error? The answer is simple for the mean effect size:

$$\text{Var}[\text{Ave}(\delta)] = \text{Var}(\delta) / K \qquad (9.14)$$

The primary second-order sampling error variance of the variance estimate ($\hat{S}_\delta^2$) depends on the shape of the effect size distribution. That discussion is beyond the scope of the present book.

Consider now the case of a real meta-analysis with a small number of heterogeneous studies. There will be both primary and second-order sampling error. For the mean effect size in a bare-bones meta-analysis, each can be computed separately and easily:

$$
\begin{aligned}
\text{Var}[\text{Ave}(d)] &= \text{Var}[\text{Ave}(\delta)] + \text{Var}[\text{Ave}(e)] \\
&= \text{Var}(\delta) / K + \text{Var}(e) / K \\
&= [\text{Var}(\delta) + \text{Var}(e)] / K \qquad (9.15) \\
&= \text{Var}(d) / K
\end{aligned}
$$

The square root of this quantity is the standard error of $\bar{d}$ and is used to create confidence intervals around $\bar{d}$. This formula holds for whatever set of weights is used in the basic estimation equations (see Hunter & Schmidt, 2000; Schmidt, Hunter, & Raju, 1988; Schmidt, Oh, & Hayes, 2009). Equation (9.15) applies to bare-bones meta-analysis; see Chapter 8 and 5 for methods of computing confidence intervals for $\hat{\bar{\delta}}$ or $\bar{\rho}$, respectively, in the heterogeneous case (random effects model) when measurement error and other artifacts in addition to sampling error are corrected for. The standard error of the standard deviation (or of $\hat{S}_\delta^2$) is much more complex and is beyond the scope of this book (cf. Raju & Drasgow, 2003).

A NUMERICAL EXAMPLE

Consider the first numerical example presented in Chapter 7:

N	d
100	.01
90	.41
50	.50
40	−.10

*Significant at the .05 level.

The meta-analysis using the more accurate formula found the following:

$$T = 280$$
$$K = 4$$
$$\bar{N} = 70$$
$$\text{Ave}(d) = .20$$
$$\text{Var}(d) = .058854$$
$$\text{Var}(e) = .059143$$

Here all observed variance is accounted for by sampling error, so the standard deviation of effect sizes is 0. Thus, the only second-order sampling error would be the secondary sampling error in the mean effect size. As described earlier, for the homogeneous case, the sampling error in the mean for a bare-bones meta-analysis is given by

$$\text{Var}[\text{Ave}(d)] = \text{Var}(e) / K = .059143 / 4 = .014786$$

and thus, the standard error of the mean is .12. The 95% confidence interval for the effect size δ is

$$.20 - 1.96(.12) < \delta < .20 + 1.96(.12)$$
$$-.04 < \delta < .44$$

Thus, the sampling error in this meta-analysis is substantial. We cannot be sure that the effect size is actually positive.

The problem in the previous meta-analysis is the total sample size. A total sample size of 280 would be a small sample size even for a single study. Thus, this meta-analysis can be expected to have considerable sampling error. To make this very explicit, suppose the number of studies was $K = 40$ rather than $K = 4$. The total sample size would then be $T = 2,800$, which is far from infinite but still substantial. The sampling error variance would be

$$\text{Var}[\text{Ave}(d)] = \text{Var}(e) / K = .059143 / 40 = .001479$$

and the standard error would be .04. The confidence interval would be

$$.20 - 1.96(.04) < \delta < .20 + 1.96(.04)$$
$$.12 < \delta < .28$$

Thus, given 40 studies with an average sample size of 70, the average value of δ is known to be positive and the width of the 95% uncertainty interval shrinks from .48 to .16.

If the number of studies were 400, the total sample size would be 28,000 and the 95% confidence interval would shrink to

$$.18 < \delta < .22$$

Thus, under these assumptions, meta-analysis will eventually yield very accurate estimates of effect sizes. However, if the average sample size in the primary studies is very small, the number of studies required may be quite large.

ANOTHER EXAMPLE: LEADERSHIP TRAINING BY EXPERTS

Consider the leadership bare-bones meta-analysis from Table 7.1 in Chapter 7. Let us illustrate the computation of confidence intervals about those estimates. We have a heterogeneous case here, so we must use Equation (9.15) to compute the sampling error variance of our estimate of the mean. The sampling error variance in the mean effect size is

$$\text{Var}[A\text{ve}(d)] = \text{Var}(d)/K = .106000/5 = .021200$$

and the corresponding standard error is .146. The 95% confidence interval for the mean effect size is thus

$$.20 - 1.96(.146) < A\text{ve}(\delta) < .20 + 1.96(.146)$$
$$-.09 < A\text{ve}(\delta) < .49$$

This is a random effects standard error and a random effects confidence interval. Thus, with a total sample size of only 200, the confidence interval for the mean effect size is very wide.

This would also be true, however, for a single study with a sample size of only 200. For a single study with a sample size of 200 and an observed d of .20, the sampling error variance would be

$$\text{Var}(e) = [199/197][4/200][1 + .20^2/8] = .020304$$

The corresponding standard error would be .142, and the 95% confidence interval would be

$$.20 - 1.96(.142) < \delta < .20 + 1.96(.142)$$
$$-.08 < \delta < .48$$

The key to accuracy in the estimate of the mean effect size is to gather enough studies to generate a large total sample size.

For this example with a total sample size of 200, the 95% confidence interval for the mean effect size is $-.09 < A\text{ve}(\delta) < .49$. In particular, because the confidence interval extends below 0, we cannot be sure that the mean effect size is positive. On the other hand, it is equally likely to be off in the other direction. Just as the mean effect size might be .00 rather than the observed mean of .20, so with equal likelihood it could be .40 rather than the observed value of .20.

Assume now that we obtained similar results not for 5 studies but for 500 studies. For 500 studies with an average sample size of 40, the total sample size would be $500(40) = 20,000$. There would be little sampling error in the meta-analysis estimates. The sampling error in the mean effect size would be

$$\text{Var}[Ave(d)] = \text{Var}(d)/K = .106000/500 = .000212$$

and the standard error would be .015. The 95% confidence interval for the mean effect size would be

$$.20 - 1.96(.015) < Ave(\delta) < .20 + 1.96(.015)$$
$$.17 < Ave(\delta) < .23$$

MODERATOR EXAMPLE: SKILLS TRAINING

Consider the overall bare-bones meta-analysis of the studies in Table 7.2 of Chapter 7. We have

$$T = 40 + 40 + \cdots = 400$$
$$K = 10$$
$$\bar{N} = T/10 = 40$$
$$Ave(d) = .30$$
$$\text{Var}(d) = .116000$$
$$\text{Var}(e) = [39/37][4/40][1 + .30^2/8] = .106591$$
$$\text{Var}(\delta) = .116000 - .106591 = .009409$$
$$SD_\delta = .097$$

This is again a heterogeneous case. The estimated standard deviation of effect sizes is .097, which is large relative to the mean of .30. However, the total sample size is only 400.

Because the total sample size is only 400, we should worry about the sampling error in the mean effect size. The sampling error in the mean effect size is thus

$$\text{Var}[Ave(d)] = \text{Var}(d)/K = .116000/10 = .011600$$

and the standard error is .108. The confidence interval for the mean effect size is thus

$$.30 - 1.96(.108) < Ave(\delta) < .30 + 1.96(.108)$$
$$.09 < Ave(\delta) < .51$$

That is, with a total sample size of 400, there is a large amount of sampling error in the mean effect size.

On the other hand, suppose we obtained these results not with 10 studies but with 1,000 studies. The total sample size would be 1,000(40) = 40,000, and there would be very little sampling error in the mean effect size. The 95% confidence interval for the mean effect size would be

$$.30 - 1.96(.0108) < \text{Ave}(\delta) < .30 + 1.96(.0108)$$
$$.28 < \text{Ave}(\delta) < .32$$

Confidence Intervals in Random Effects Models: Hunter-Schmidt and Hedges-Olkin

The way in which the standard error of the mean r or d is estimated in a random effects meta-analysis differs between the methods presented in this book and the method presented by Hedges and Vevea (1998).

Estimation procedures are simpler for the Hunter-Schmidt (H-S) approach (Schmidt, Hunter, & Raju, 1988), so we present those procedures first.

The Hunter-Schmidt Random Effects (RE) Procedure. Our presentation is in terms of the d statistic, but procedures are similar and analogous for r and other indices of effect size. In the H-S RE procedure, the sampling error variance of the mean d is estimated as the variance of the observed ds across studies divided by k, the number of studies:

$$S^2_{e_{\bar{d}}} = \frac{\bar{V}_e}{k} + \frac{S^2_\delta}{k} = \frac{S^2_d}{k} \tag{9.16}$$

The square root of Equation (9.16) is the *SE* that is used in computing CIs:

$$SE_{\bar{d}} = \frac{SD_d}{\sqrt{k}} = \sqrt{\frac{\bar{V}_e + S^2_\delta}{k}} \tag{9.17}$$

In this model, $\bar{V}_e$ is conceptualized as the sample size weighted mean of the V_{e_i} values. The equation for S^2_d is

$$S^2_d = \sum N_i (d_i - \bar{d})^2 \ / \ \sum N_i \tag{9.18}$$

where

$$\bar{d} = \sum N_i d_i \ / \ \sum N_i \tag{9.19}$$

The rationale for this procedure can be seen in the fact that $S^2_d = S^2_e + S^2_\delta$. That is, the expected value of S^2_d is the sum of simple sampling error variance and the variance of the study population parameters (Chapters 3 and 7; Field, 2005; Hedges, 1989). Hence, S^2_d divided by k is the sampling error variance of the mean. Osburn and Callender (1992) showed that this equation holds both when $S_\delta^2 > 0$ and when $S_\delta^2 = 0$ (i.e., when the assumption underlying the FE model holds). The study weights in the H-S RE model are (total) study sample sizes, N_i, used because these weights closely approximate the inverse of the simple sampling error variances ($1 / V_{e_i}$) (see Chapter 3) and are less affected by sampling error variance (Brannick, 2006). Hedges (1983b) stated that in the heterogeneous case ($S_\delta^2 > 0$), weighting by sample size "will give a simple unbiased estimator [of the mean] that is slightly less efficient than the optimal weighted estimator" (p. 392). Osburn and Callender (1992) showed via simulation that weighting by sample size produces accurate *SE* estimates both when $S_\delta^2 = 0$ and when $S_\delta^2 > 0$. Also using simulation, Schulze (2004) found that for heterogeneous population data sets, the H-S RE procedure weighting by sample size produced accurate (more accurate than other procedures evaluated) estimates of CIs (see his Table 8.13, p. 156); estimates for the mean correlation were also acceptably accurate (with a tiny median negative bias of .0022, much less than rounding error; Table 8.4, p. 134; see pp. 188–190 for a summary). Brannick (2006) reported similar results. Further details can be found in Osburn and Callender (1992) and Schmidt, Hunter, and Raju (1988). We note here that in the H-S RE method, when the *d*s are corrected for measurement error, the procedure is analogous except that S_d^2 is now the variance of the corrected *d*s. The same is true for *r* value meta-analyses. Standard errors of the mean for corrected mean values are given in Chapter 5 for *r* values and Chapter 8 for *d* values. The Hedges-Vevea (H-V) procedure does not include corrections for artifacts.

The Hedges-Vevea RE Procedure. The Hedges and Vevea (1998) RE procedure estimates the two components of RE sampling error variance separately. The simple sampling error variance component is estimated exactly as it is in the FE model:

$$S_{e_{\bar d}}^2 = 1 / \Sigma w_i \tag{9.20}$$

where the w_i are $1 / V_{e_i}$.

The second component, $\hat\sigma_\delta^2$ (symbolized as $\hat\tau^2$ by Hedges and Vevea), is estimated as follows:

$$\hat\sigma_\delta^2 = \begin{cases} \dfrac{Q - (k-1)}{c} & \text{if } Q \geq k-1 \\ 0 & \text{if } Q < k-1 \end{cases} \tag{9.21}$$

where $Q = \chi^2$ overall homogeneity test and c is a function of the study weights and is given in Equation (11) from Hedges and Vevea (1998):

$$c = \sum w_i - \frac{\sum (w_i)^2}{\sum w_i} \tag{9.22}$$

where the study weights w_i are the FE study weights as defined in our Equation (9.20).

The estimated mean value is then

$$\hat{\delta} = \bar{d} = \sum w_i^* d_i \ / \ \sum w_i^* \tag{9.23}$$

The sampling error variance is

$$S^2_{e_{\bar{d}}} = 1 \ / \ \sum w_i^* \tag{9.24}$$

where the w_i^* are $1 \ / \ [\ V_{e_i} + \hat{\sigma}^2_{\delta} \ ]$.

When the effect size statistic is the correlation, this RE procedure first converts rs to the Fisher's z transformation, conducts the calculations in that metric, and then back transforms the resulting means and CIs into the r metric (Hedges & Olkin, 1985). The Fisher's z transform is discussed in Chapter 5. See Hedges and Vevea (1998), Field (2005), and S. M. Hall and Brannick (2002) for a complete technical description of this RE procedure.

$\hat{\sigma}^2_{\delta}$ in Equation (9.21) is set to zero when $Q - (k - 1)$ yields a negative value, because by definition a variance cannot be negative. Hedges and Vevea (1998) discuss the positive bias that characterizes this estimate as a result of setting negative values to zero, and they tabulate this bias in their Table 2 for various conditions. This bias causes the SE to be upwardly biased, causing the resulting CIs to be too wide; that is, the probability content of the CIs is larger than the nominal value (Hedges & Vevea, 1998, p. 496). Overton (1998, pp. 371, 374) found this same bias for this procedure and also for an iterative procedure he used to estimate S^2_{ρ} and S^2_{δ}. Hedges and Vevea state that bias becomes smaller as k (the number of studies) increases and is generally small when k is 20 or more. However, Overton (1998) pointed out that the bias also depends on the actual size of S^2_{δ} (or S^2_{ρ}). For example, if this value is zero, then 50% of the estimates are expected to be negative due to sampling error, creating a positive bias regardless of the number of studies. If this value is small but not zero, then less that 50% of the estimates of S^2_{δ} are expected to be negative, and the positive bias is smaller. When S^2_{δ} is large, the positive bias is negligible.

Overton (1998) stated that when S^2_{δ} is small, the RE model overestimates sampling error variance and produces CIs that are too wide. This effect is not due to any inherent property of the RE model; it is due to the positive bias in the procedures he examined for estimating the standard error of the mean

meta-analysis value. Some researchers have mistakenly cited Overton's statement as a rationale for preferring the FE model to the RE model in their
meta-analyses (e.g., Bettencourt, Talley, Benjamin, & Valentine, 2006).

Because of its different mode of estimating the sampling error variance
(described earlier), the H-S RE procedure does not have this upward bias.
As shown earlier, in the H-S RE procedure, the two components of the RE
sampling error variance are estimated jointly rather than separately. Note
that if S_δ^2 is in fact zero, the H-S RE estimate of sampling error variance
has the same expected value as the FE estimate of sampling error variance
(Osburn & Callender, 1992; Schmidt, Hunter, & Raju, 1988; Schmidt, Oh,
& Hayes, 2009). As shown by Hedges and Vevea (1998), this is not the case
for the H-V RE procedure.

Updating a Meta-Analysis When a New Study Becomes Available

When a new study becomes available, there are two ways in which one
can update the meta-analysis to include this study. First, one can rerun
the meta-analysis including the new study. Second, one can take a
Bayesian approach. In that approach, one would treat the existing fully
corrected meta-analysis mean and *SD* as the Bayesian prior distribution
and multiply this distribution times the likelihood function from the
new study, using the usual Bayesian equation. The likelihood function
or distribution has as its mean the fully corrected *r* or *d* value from the
new study, and its *SD* is the standard error (*SE*) of that estimated corrected *r* or *d* value (i.e., the square root of the sampling error variance
of the corrected value from the study). Either of these procedures can
also be applied when there are multiple new studies. Schmidt and Raju
(2007) have examined the properties of these two procedures in detail.
They conclude that it is virtually always best to rerun the meta-analysis
including the new study or studies.

What Are Optimal Study Weights in Random Effects Meta-Analysis?

Considerable attention has been devoted in the literature to the question
of how the studies in a meta-analysis should be weighted. In the H-V procedure, because of the nature of the study weights used to produce the
weighted mean *d* value (or *r* value), it is necessary when using these
weights to have a separate estimate of σ_δ^2 (Field, 2005; Hedges & Vevea,
1998). As noted earlier, the weight applied to each study is $w_i^* = 1 / [\, V_{e_i} +$
$\hat{\sigma}_\delta^2\,]$, where V_{e_i} is the simple sampling error variance for that study.
The H-S procedure weights each study by its (total) sample size (N_i) and

therefore does not require a separate estimate of σ_δ^2. (As noted in Chapter 3, when correlations are corrected individually, the H-S procedure weights studies by the product of the study N and the compound attenuation factor.) Of course, the H-S RE model does estimate σ_δ^2 for other purposes (such as credibility intervals), and this estimate does have a positive bias (discussed in Chapter 5), but this estimate is not used in the weights applied to the studies and so does not affect the computation of weighted mean values, SEs, or confidence intervals (Schmidt, Hunter, & Raju, 1988; Schmidt, Oh, & Hayes, 2009; see also Schulze, 2004, p. 190). The H-V weights were derived within the context of large sample statistical theory, that is, under the assumption the number of studies and study Ns are very large. In such a hypothetical situation, the H-V study weights are in expectation more accurate for RE models (Hedges, 1983a, 1983b; Hedges & Vevea, 1998; Raudenbush, 1994; Schulze, 2004, 2007). But even within large sample theory, this advantage is slight (Hedges, 1983b, p. 393). The problem in using these weights with actual data is that the small theoretically expected advantage for these study weights is not realized with the smaller numbers of studies and study Ns that are typical in real meta-analyses, because of inaccuracies induced by sampling error in the estimates of the σ_δ^2 component of the weights (e.g., see Brannick, 2006; Raudenbush, 1994, p. 317; and Schulze, 2004, pp. 84 and 184; 2007). Because of this effect, Schulze (2004, pp. 193–194), based on the results of his extensive Monte Carlo studies, recommended weighting studies by sample size in the heterogeneous case (i.e., σ_δ^2 or $\sigma_\rho^2 > 0$), as well as the homogeneous case. Kulinskaya, Morgenthaler, and Staudte (2010) reached this same conclusion, as did Shuster (2009). Brannick (2006) conducted an extensive simulation study in the r metric. He found that sample size study weights produced estimates that were less biased and had smaller root mean square error than weighting by inverse sampling error variances. He concluded that the accuracy problems of the inverse study weights stemmed from the fact that sampling error often causes the r statistic to take on extreme values, which cause extreme study weights, which, in turn, cause inaccurate estimates of mean correlations. In a later study, Brannick, Yang, and Cafri (2011) confirmed these results favoring N-weighting for the r metric but found that in the case of the d metric, weighting by inverse variance had a slight advantage over weighting by N. Marin-Martinez and Sanchez-Meca (2010) also reported this result. However, Sanchez-Meca and Marin-Martinez (1998), in another simulation study in the d metric, found that weighting studies by sample size resulted in unbiased estimates of mean d under all conditions, while inverse sampling variance weights produced slightly (negatively) biased estimates. At the same time, weighting by inverse variance was slightly (2.8%) more statistically efficient. In the case of the d metric, the differences between the two weighting methods appear to be very tiny and not of practical significance in research.

The random effects study weights used in the Hedges procedure are less unequal across studies than sample size weights. Hence, that procedure gives relatively more weight to studies based on small sample sizes, which can cause problems in applying widely used methods for the detection of publications bias (see Chapter 13).

Bonett (2008, 2009) has challenged both these approaches to weighting of studies when used with the RE meta-analysis model. He argues that the RE model is based on the assumption that the studies in the meta-analysis are a random sample of a defined population of studies and that this assumption cannot be justified because meta-analysts cannot appropriately define or delimit such a population. Because of this problem, he advocates that all studies be weighted equally. He is correct that in the RE model, the studies in the meta-analysis are viewed as a random sample from a larger universe of studies that exist or could be conducted. Hedges and Vevea (1998) pointed out that this larger universe is often poorly defined and ambiguous in nature. However, Schulze (2004, pp. 40–41) noted that this is not a problem specific to meta-analysis or RE models in meta-analysis but one that characterizes virtually all samples used in primary and other research. Rarely in research is the target population of subjects fully enumerated and delimited; in fact, data sets used frequently consist of something close to convenience samples (i.e., a set of subjects for whom it was possible to obtain data). Viewed in this light, this problem appears less serious. We can ask how different meta-analytic results would be using equal study weights. Brannick et al. (2011) evaluated equal weights in their simulation study. They found that both sample size weights and inverse variance weights were more accurate and efficient than equal weights, but the differences were often negligible from a practical point of view. However, this study does not speak directly to Bonett's (2008, 2009) objection, because in the Brannick et al. simulation study, there was in fact a clearly defined population of studies from which studies were sampled.

The Meaning of Percent Variance Accounted for in Meta-Analysis

In the first part of Chapter 5, we presented the case against percent variance accounted for as a useful statistic in any kind of research. Yet in Chapters 3, 4, and 7, we often presented figures for the percentage of variance in r or d values accounted for by sampling error and other artifacts in meta-analysis. In doing this, we have tried to point out a more meaningful interpretation of this meta-analytic result: The square root of the

proportion of variance explained is the correlation between the observed
r or d values, on one hand, and the sampling errors and other artifactual
perturbations in the effect sizes, on the other. For example, if 81% of the
variability across effect sizes is explained by artifacts, then the observed
effect sizes are correlated .90 (the square root of .81) with artifact-produced
perturbations in the observed values. If 50% is accounted for, this correlation is .71 ($r = \sqrt{.50}$). The correlation is much easier for readers and
research users to understand than percent variance. Correlations (i.e.,
linear relations) exist in the real world while variances do not; a variance
is a quadratic statistic created by squaring data points of interest and is in
that sense artificial. In addition, as noted in Chapter 5, the percent variance statistic is highly susceptible to misinterpretation, because small
percent variance figures are often wrongly dismissed as unimportant when
the effect sizes underlying them are fairly large and of practical significance. So we recommend that in meta-analysis, the final percent variance
accounted for figures be converted to correlations.

The Hedges and associates meta-analysis methods as presented in
Borenstein et al. (2009) include an index of percent variance called I^2,
which is attributed to Higgins et al. (2003). This index represents the
proportion of variance *not* explained by sampling error (the only artifact
addressed by that method). In a Hunter-Schmidt bare-bones meta-analysis, 1 minus the proportion of variance accounted for equals I^2. Both
indices are affected by the Ns of the studies in the meta-analysis, because
sampling error causes most artifactual variance. Other things constant, if
study Ns are small, percent variance explained tends to be large, I^2 tends
to be small, and the correlation between observed values and perturbations due to artifacts tends to be large. The opposite tends to be the case
when the Ns of the studies in the meta-analysis are large. This depen-
dence on study Ns should be borne in mind in interpreting both these
indices.

It is also important to remember that the proportion of variance
explained is less informative when the observed variance of the meta-
analytic correlations or d values is small. A percent-based estimate can be
misleading when it is interpreted blindly without considering the size of its
denominator. For example, a proportion of variance figure of 50% could
be .1000 / .2000 or .00010 / .00020. The latter case would not suggest the
existence of moderator(s), given the tiny amount of observed variation to
begin with and the even smaller amount of nonartifactual variance. For
purposes of detecting the likely presence of moderators, the absolute
amount of true variance (nonartifactual variance) in the study effects sizes
(or even better, its square root, the SD) can be more important than the
relative percent of variance attributable to artifacts. We suggest that
meta-analysts consider both estimates.

The Odds Ratio (OR) in Behavioral Meta-Analyses

In medical research, both the independent and dependent variables are often true dichotomies—for example, vaccinated versus not vaccinated (independent variable) and contracted the disease versus did not contract the disease (dependent variable), creating a 2×2 table. The favored and most widely used ratio measure in medical research is the odds ratio (Haddock et al., 1998). The odds ratio (OR) is the ratio of two probabilities:

$$OR = P(I/E)/ P(I'E),$$

where $P(I/E)$ (in our example) is the probability of getting the disease in the group that did not get the vaccine, and $P(I'E)$ is the probability of getting the disease in the group that got the vaccine. These probabilities are estimated via ratios between cells in the 2×2 table. Primary studies and meta-analyses using the OR statistic analyze the natural logs of the ORs (ln(OR)), with the final results then being converted back to the OR metric. The OR is seldom used in psychological or behavioral research because it is rare that both variables are true dichotomies. In fact, in many studies, both variables are continuous; this is especially frequent in correlational studies. Of course, in experiments, the independent variable is often dichotomous: the treatment group versus the control group. However, the dependent variable is almost always continuous or at least not dichotomous. Some examples are amount learned in the training program, degree of change in racial attitudes, and amount of reduction in anxiety. It is rare in behavioral research to have a truly dichotomous dependent variable. Of course, dependent variables that are actually continuous can be artificially dichotomized to allow application of the OR, but it is well known that doing this is not good practice because it causes a major loss of information (Cohen, 1983; Hunter & Schmidt, 1990a; MacCallum et al., 2002). In their explication of the OR, Haddock et al. (1998) present an example in which the independent variable is a psychosocial treatment for drug addiction (experimental vs. control group) and the dependent variable is "successful" or "not successful" in reducing drug use. This is an example of what MacCallum et al. (2002) warned against: an artificial dichotomization of a continuous variable. There are degrees of success in reducing drug usage. We believe that this sort of consideration is the reason why the use of the OR is still rare in behavioral research 15 years after Haddock et al. (1998) advocated its use for behavioral research in the journal *Psychological Methods*.

There is another important reason to avoid using the OR: Most people find it difficult to understand the meaning of an OR—not only laypeople but also medical practitioners (to whom the medical research is directed) and even medical researchers themselves. The OR is not an intuitive statistic (Borenstein et al., 2009). In fact, as demonstrated by Gigerenzer and his associates (Gigerenzer, 2007; Gigerenzer et al. 2007), the vast majority of practicing medical doctors routinely seriously misinterpret the meaning of outcome statistics used in medical research. Patients would be quite concerned if they were aware of this fact.

Suppose some of the studies relevant to one's meta-analysis present results in the form of ORs. Must these studies be omitted? Actually, it is quite easy to covert OR to either d or r values. These conversion formulas are given by Bonett (2007), Borenstein et al. (2009), and Chinn (2000). Both OR values and their sampling error variances can be converted. So such studies can be included in a meta-analysis conducted in the r or d metrics. If *all* relevant primary studies use the OR statistic, all can be converted to the r or d metric prior to meta-analysis. This is the procedure we recommend in both cases.

Exercise 9.1: Second-Order Meta-Analysis Across Different Independent Variables With the Same Dependent Variable

This exercise is based on the data used in the exercise at the end of Chapter 4. That exercise required you to conduct separate bare-bones meta-analyses for each of six tests. This results in an estimate of the percentage of variance accounted for by sampling error for each test. These are the first set of figures needed for this exercise. We hope you have retained them.

These data meet the requirements for a second-order meta-analysis, as described in this chapter. That is, the six meta-analyses are very similar substantively, and there is no reason to believe that there are different nonartifactual sources of variance (i.e., moderators) for the different tests.

Conduct a second-order meta-analysis across these six tests using the methods described in this chapter for second-order meta-analysis across different in dependent variables.

What is the average percentage of variance accounted for by sampling error across these six tests? What is your interpretation of this finding?

In the exercise at the end of Chapter 4, you also computed the percentage of variance accounted for by *all* artifacts—sampling error plus the other artifacts. This was computed not as part of the bare-bones meta-analysis but as part of the full meta-analyses, which corrected for measurement error and range restriction, as well as for sampling error. There were two such meta-analyses—one correcting for direct and one correcting for indirect range restriction. Conduct a separate second-order meta-analysis for each of these sets of percentage of variance figures.

Are these values different from those computed earlier based only on sampling error variance? Why is this difference in this particular set of data not larger than it is? What is your interpretation of these values?

Exercise 9.2: Second-Order Meta-Analysis With Constant Independent and Dependent Variables

Chanchal Tamrakar (2012) conducted separate, independent meta-analyses on the relationship between customer satisfaction and customer loyalty for (1) the retail industry, (2) the tourism industry, and (3) the telecom industry. He also conducted separate, independent meta-analysis by geographical area: (1) Asia, (2) Europe, and (3) North America. He used the artifact distribution method of meta-analysis in all six of his meta-analyses. His first-order meta-analysis results that you need for this exercise are shown in the first four columns in the following table. Conduct two second-order meta-analyses on his results—one for the industry categories and one for the geographical areas. To conduct these analyses, you need to use the following equations: (9.3) and (9.3a) through (9.3f) (a total of seven equations). Columns 5 through 12 are for your answers. The headings on these columns are as defined in the discussion in the text of equations listed here. They are also defined in the notes to the table.

Explain your results.

1. How much different are the mean corrected correlations after adjustment for second-order sampling error (column 12) in comparison with the values originally reported by Tamrakar (column 4)? Make this comparison separately for the two sets of meta-analyses.

2. Compare the percent of variance in his mean corrected correlations explained by second-order sampling error (column 10) for the industry category versus the geographical region category. What might be the explanation for this difference?

Exercise 9.2 Second Order Meta-Analysis of the Relationship between Customer Satisfaction and Customer Loyalty (Tamrakar, 2012, Table 1)

Predictor	(1)	(2)	(3)	(4)	(5)	(6)	(7)	(8)	(9)	(10)	(11)	(12)
Moderator	k	$\bar{r}_i$	S_r^2	$\hat{\bar{\rho}}_i$	$S_{e_{\hat{\rho}_i}}^2$	$\hat{\bar{\bar{\rho}}}$	$E(S_{e_{\hat{\rho}_i}}^2)$	$S_{\hat{\bar{\rho}}}^2$	$\sigma_{\bar{\rho}}^2$	ProVar	$r_{\rho\rho}$	$\hat{\bar{\rho}}_{ir}$
Industry												
Retail	10	.55	.01605	.67								
Tourism	14	.69	.01415	.85								
Telecom	7	.59	.00335	.71								
Region												
Asia	13	.59	.02503	.72								
Europe	12	.69	.00881	.83								
North America	15	.61	.02211	.72								

Note. Columns (1) though (4) are input values (italicized) available from first order meta-analyses. (1) Number of samples; (2) Sample size weighted mean observed validity; (3) Sample size weighted observed variance across observed validities; (4) First order meta-analytic mean validity estimates; ; (5) Second order sampling error variance for each first order meta-analytic validity estimate (see discussion of Eq. 7d); (6) Second order, grand mean validity estimates (Eq. 7b); (7) Expected (average) second order sampling error variance (Eq. 7d) and standard error (in parentheses); (8) Observed variance and SD (in parentheses) across first order mean operational validity estimates (Eqs. 7a, 7b, and 7c); (9) Estimated true variance and SD (in parentheses) across first order mean operational validity estimates after expected second order sampling error variance is subtracted out from the observed variance (Eq. 7); negative values are set to zero; (10) The proportion (percentage if multiplied by 100) of the observed variance across first order mean operational validity estimates that is due to second order sampling error variance; values greater than 1 are set to 1; (11) The reliability of the first order meta-analytic validity vectors; these values are computed as 1 minus the values in Column 10; (12) Regressed first order validity estimates based on the reliability of the original validity vectors shown in Column 11.

431

Exercise 9.3: Second-Order Meta-Analysis With Constant Independent and Dependent Variables

Van Iddekinge, Roth, Putka, and Lanivich (2011) meta-analyzed relationships between job-related interests and job turnover. They examined this relationship for three different types of interest measures: (1) job and vocation focused scales, (2) construct-focused interest scales, and (3) basic interest scales. They also meta-analyzed the relationship between job interests and three different types of turnover: (1) voluntary, (2) involuntary, and (3) "other turnover." In all six of these first-order meta-analyses, they used the artifact distribution meta-analysis method. Their first-order meta-analysis results that you need for this exercise are shown in the first four columns in the following table. Conduct two second-order meta-analyses on their results—one for the type of interest scale meta-analyses and one for type of turnover meta-analysis. To conduct these analyses, you need to use the following equations: (9.3) and (9.3a) through (9.3f) (a total of seven equations). Columns 5 through 12 are for your answers. The headings on these columns are as defined in the discussion in the text of equations listed here. They are also defined in notes to the table.

Explain your results.

1. How much different are the mean corrected correlations after adjustment for second-order sampling error (column 12) in comparison with the values originally reported by Iddekinge et al. (2011) (column 4)? Compare separately for the two sets of first-order meta-analyses.

2. Compare the percent of variance in the Iddekinge et al. mean corrected correlations explained by second-order sampling error (column 10) for the type of interest scale category versus the type of turnover category. Why do you think these values are so different?

Exercise 9.3 Second Order Meta-Analysis of the Relationship between Customer Satisfaction and Customer Loyalty (Tamrakar, 2012, Table 1)

Predictor	(1)	(2)	(3)	(4)	(5)	(6)	(7)	(8)	(9)	(10)	(11)	(12)
Moderator	k	$\bar{r}_i$	S_r^2	$\hat{\rho}_i$	$S_{e_{\hat{\rho}_i}}^2$	$\hat{\bar{\rho}}$	$E(S_{e_{\hat{\rho}_i}}^2)$	$S_{\hat{\bar{\rho}}}^2$	$\sigma_{\hat{\rho}}^2$	ProVar	$r_{\rho\rho}$	$\hat{\hat{\rho}}_{ir}$
Type of Interest scale												
Job and vocation focused	10	-.16	.00467	-.17								
Construct focused	11	-.11	.00602	-.12								
Basic Interest scales	6	-.11	.00280	-.13								
Nature of Turnover												
Voluntary	15	-.20	.01363	-.22								
Involuntary	2	-.13	.00004	-.15								
Other turnover	15	-.11	.00351	-.11								

Note. CFP = corporate financial performance; CSP = corporate social/environmental performance. Columns (1) though (4) are input values (italicized) available from first order meta-analyses. (1) Number of samples; (2) Sample size weighted mean observed validity; (3) Sample size weighted observed variance across observed validities; (4) First order meta-analytic mean validity estimates; (5) Second order sampling error variance for each first order meta-analytic validity estimate (see discussion of Eq. 7d); (6) Second order, grand mean validity estimates (Eq. 7b); (7) Expected (average) second order sampling error variance (Eq. 7d) and standard error (in parentheses); (8) Observed variance and SD (in parentheses) across first order mean operational validity estimates (Eqs. 7a, 7b, and 7c); (9) Estimated true variance and SD (in parentheses) across first order mean operational validity estimates after expected second order sampling error variance is subtracted out from the observed variance (Eq. 7); negative values are set to zero; (10) The proportion (percentage if multiplied by 100) of the observed variance across first order mean operational validity estimates that is due to second order sampling error variance; values greater than 1 are set to 1; (11) The reliability of the first order meta-analytic validity vectors; these values are computed as 1 minus the values in Column 10; (12) Regressed first order validity estimates based on the reliability of the original validity vectors shown in Column 11.

433

Cumulation of Findings Within Studies

10

It is often possible to obtain more than one correlation or estimate of effect size from within the same study. Should these estimates be included in the meta-analysis as independent estimates? Or should they be combined somehow within the study so that only one value is contributed? There is no single answer to these questions because several different kinds of replications can take place within studies. This chapter surveys the most frequent cases.

Many single studies have replication of observation of a relationship within the study. Thus, there can be cumulation of results within, as well as across, studies. However, the method of cumulation depends on the nature of the replication process used in the study. Three kinds of replication will be considered here: fully replicated designs, conceptual replication, and analysis of subgroups.

Fully Replicated Designs: Statistical Independence

A fully replicated design occurs in a study if that study can be broken into parts that are conceptually equivalent but statistically independent. For example, if data are gathered at several different organizations, then statistics calculated within organizations can be regarded as replicated across organizations. The outcome measures from each organization are statistically independent and can be treated as if they were values from different studies. That is, the cumulation process for these values is the same as that for cumulation across entirely different studies. This is the statistical definition of independence: If statistics (e.g., rs or d values) are computed on different samples, then their sampling errors cannot be correlated. Some writers go further and state that, even if the samples are different, the studies are not independent because they were all conducted by the same researcher, who may have biases that could have affected the results of all three studies. This is not the typically accepted definition of independence and is certainly not the definition of statistical independence. Also, this concept of independence is subject to being carried to extremes. For example, one could contend that the studies included in a meta-analysis were not independent because they were all carried out during one period (e.g., 1980–2002) or because they were all conducted in English-speaking countries. That is, this concept of independence is so vaguely defined that it is subject to indefinite expansion. In this chapter, we focus only on the statistical concept of independence.

Conceptual Replication and Lack of Statistical Independence

Conceptual replication occurs within a study when more than one observation that is relevant to a given relationship is made on each subject. The most common example is replicated measurement, the use of multiple indicators to assess a given variable: for example, the use of several scales to assess job satisfaction; the use of training grades, selection test scores, and job knowledge to assess cognitive ability for work performance; or the use of peer ratings, supervisor ratings, and production records to assess job performance. The second most common example is observation in multiple situations. For example, a participant in an assessment center may be asked to show problem-solving skills in Task A, Task B, and so on. The observation in the various situations can be regarded as replicated measurements of problem-solving skills.

The replication within the study can be used in either of two ways: (1) Each conceptual replication can be represented by a different outcome value, and these separate outcome values can either be averaged and entered into the meta-analysis or entered separately, or (2) the measurements can be combined, and the resulting single-outcome measure can be used to assess the relationship in question.

Suppose three variables are used as indicators of job performance: peer rating, supervisor rating, and a job sample measure. Any potential test could then have three correlations that are conceptually all validity coefficients: the correlation between test and peer rating, the correlation between test and supervisor rating, and the correlation between test and job sample measure. These values are often entered into a meta-analysis in one of two ways: (1) The three correlations could be entered as three separate values, or (2) the three correlations could be averaged and the average could be contributed as the one value representing the study.

If these three correlations are entered separately into the meta-analysis, then there is a problem for the cumulation formulas presented in Parts II and III of this book. These formulas assume that the values used are statistically independent of each other. This is guaranteed if the values come from different samples but is only true in the present example if the correlations between peer rating, supervisor rating, and job sample test are all 0 (as population values for that study), which is impossible if the measures are even approximately equivalent measures, as they are assumed to be. If the number of correlations or d values contributed by each study is small in comparison to the total number of correlations or d values, then there is little error in the resulting cumulation. However, if a very large number of values are contributed from one small sample, then the result can be undercorrection for sampling error in the meta-analysis, according to statistical theory.

To the extent that a meta-analysis contains groups of correlations or d values that come from the same sample, the formulas for sampling error presented in Chapters 3, 4, and 7 will underestimate the sampling error variance component in the observed variance of effect sizes (S_r^2 or S_d^2). This means that there will be an undercorrection for sampling error and that the final estimate of S_ρ^2 or S_δ^2 will be too large. To this extent, the obtained meta-analysis results will be conservative; that is, they will underestimate the degree of agreement (or generalizability) across studies.

One way to understand how violations of statistical independence cause sampling error variance to be larger than predicted by sampling error variance formulas is as follows. If sampling errors are uncorrelated across two independent samples (i.e., $r_{e_1e_2} = 0$), then

$$Total\,sampling\,variance = \Sigma S_{e_i}^2 = S_{e_1}^2 + S_{e_2}^2 \tag{10.1}$$

$$\overline{S}_e^2 = \frac{\Sigma S_{e_i}^2}{k} \tag{10.2}$$

where k is the number of independent samples or studies ($k = 2$ here) and $\overline{S}_e^2$ is the size of the sampling error component in the variance of observed rs or ds in the meta-analysis (S_r^2 or S_d^2).

If the r or d values are computed on the same sample, however, sampling errors *are*, to some degree, correlated (i.e., $r_{e_1e_2} > 0$). Then,

$$Total\,Sampling\,variance = S_{e_1}^2 + S_{e_2}^2 + 2r_{e_1e_2}S_{e_1}S_{e_2} \tag{10.3}$$

and

$$\overline{S}_e^2 = [S_{e_1}^2 + S_{e_2}^2 + 2r_{e_1e_2}S_{e_1}S_{e_2}]/2 \tag{10.4}$$

The standard formulas for sampling error variance used to estimate the amount of sampling error variance in S_r^2 or S_d^2 are Equations (10.1) and (10.2). When independence is violated, however, the actual amount of sampling error is the larger amount given by Equations (10.3) and (10.4). Hence, sampling error is underestimated. Note that it is usually not possible to estimate the correlation $r_{e_1 e_2}$, and so it is not possible to avoid the underestimation for sampling error by just using Equation (10.4) in conducting the meta-analysis.

In our own earlier research on the validity of ability tests in personnel selection, whenever it was the ability (e.g., verbal ability) that had multiple measures, we included the individual correlations in the meta-analysis. Most studies contained only one measure of each ability and, thus, contributed only one correlation to the meta-analysis for that ability. A minority of studies had two measures (e.g., two measures of spatial ability). Therefore, this decision rule contributed only a slight conservative bias to our estimates of SD_ρ. Whenever a study contained multiple measures of job performance, these measures were combined into a composite as described later; if that was not possible, then the correlations were averaged and only the average correlation was entered into the meta-analysis. This decision rule ensured complete independence on the job performance side of the correlation.

It should be noted that while violations of the assumption of independence affect (inflate) the observed variance of effect sizes across studies, such violations have no systematic effect on the mean d or mean r values in a meta-analysis. Thus, violations of independence cause no bias in estimates of mean values in meta-analysis. The truth of this theoretical expectation has been demonstrated via simulation studies (S. F. Cheung & Chan, 2004; Tracz et al., 1992). However, the methods described in this book focus strongly on estimating the true (population) variance (and SD) of study effects. The accuracy of estimates of SD_δ and SD_ρ is important because these estimates play a critical role in the interpretation of the results of the meta-analysis, via credibility intervals. Violations of independence create an upward bias in estimates of SD_δ and SD_ρ because they lead to underestimation of sampling error; recall that the sampling error variance estimate is subtracted from the observed variance in the r or d values. Therefore, the question of statistical independence in the data deserves careful attention in applications of our meta-analysis methods.

The second alternative is to average the d or r values computed on the same sample. If the average correlation is entered into the meta-analysis, then there is no violation of the independence assumption. However, what are we to use for the sample size of the average correlation? If we use the total number of observations that go into the average correlation (i.e., the product of sample size times the number of correlations averaged), then we greatly underestimate the sampling error because this alternative assumes that we have averaged independent correlations. This will cause overestimation of SD_ρ or SD_δ, because of the resulting undercorrection for sampling error variance. On the other hand, if we use the sample size of the study, then we overestimate the sampling error because the average correlation has less sampling error than a single correlation. This then leads to underestimation of SD_ρ or SD_δ because of the resulting overcorrection for sampling error variance.

The value of N that corresponds to the correct amount of sampling error variance lies between these two values. S. F. Cheung and Chan (2004) presented a procedure to estimate this value. Use of this procedure requires one to have an estimate of the correlation between the correlations within studies, and they provide a method of estimating this value. This procedure would be useful when the mean r or d must be used because the information needed to compute the more desirable composite correlation (described later) cannot be obtained or estimated. However, this is rare.

There is another potential problem with the average correlation. In those rare cases in which there is a strong moderator variable—that is, cases in which there is a large, real, corrected standard deviation across studies—the moderator variable may vary within studies as well as across studies. In such a case, the average correlation would be conceptually ambiguous. For example, there is strong evidence that measures of ability have higher true score correlations with job sample measures than with supervisory ratings (Hunter, 1983a; Nathan & Alexander, 1988). Identification of this difference in any meta-analysis would require that these two measures not be combined. In fact, it would require separate meta-analyses for each dependent variable measure. Of course, this is even more true when the different measures reported in the primary study samples are intended to measure different constructs, as discussed later.

Research on Effects of Violation of Statistical Independence

So far in this chapter, we have discussed the abstract statistical principles related to violations of independence. The conclusions presented are derived logically from statistical theory. This is what statisticians focus on. These conclusions are statistically correct, but they do not empirically address the question of how serious the problems created by violations of independence are in real data. Taveggia (1974) addressed this question in a large research project in educational research. He first conducted a meta-analysis on only the independent statistical estimates and then conducted the same analysis by adding in the data points that violated the assumption of independence. He found that the two sets of results did not differ. However, his main focus was on mean values, which we know are not biased by violations of independence. The simulation study by Tracz et al. (1992) suggests that under realistic data conditions, violations of independence have little or no effect, not only on mean values but also on standard deviations and confidence intervals. This study examined the case in which the underlying population correlation was constant. Hence, the variance of the observed correlations was sampling error variance only. As the degree of violation of independence increases, we would expect the variance of the observed r values (S_r^2) to increase, because the effect of correlated sampling errors should be to increase sampling error variance, as demonstrated logically earlier in this chapter. However, there was no observable increase in this value (S_r^2) as the number of nonindependent rs from each study increased from 0 to 5 and as the correlation between the nonindependent outcome measures increased from 0 to .70. The study concluded that "combining statistics from nonindependent data in a correlation meta-analysis does not have an adverse effect on the results" (p. 886). And "Therefore, proceeding under the assumption of independence is not as risky as previously thought, because means, medians, standard deviations and confidence intervals in a correlational meta-analysis are not affected by nonindependence of data" (pp. 886–887). Bijmolt and Pieters (2001) also addressed this question in their computer simulation study. In one condition in their study, the multiple nonindependent measures from the same sample were entered into the meta-analyses as if they were statistically independent; the lack of independence was ignored. In another condition, a special statistical procedure that adjusts for the fact that measures are nested within studies (i.e., are not statistically independent) was applied to these same data. (This procedure was similar to that discussed by Hedges, 2009b.) They found that the correlations between the true parameter values and the estimated values were very similar for the two procedures. The correlation was only .02 larger on average for the complex adjustment procedure (about 2% larger). Both procedures showed a tiny negative bias in parameter estimation, and the absolute size of this bias was slightly smaller for the complex adjustment procedure. Overall, the tiny improvement resulting from use of the complex adjustment procedure appears insufficient to justify its use in most situations. Bijmolt and Pieters (2001) concluded that "the commonly used method of treating all measurements as independent performs reasonably well" (p. 157).

So it is possible that violations of independence in real data are not as serious a threat to accuracy as is widely believed. However, this conclusion rests on only two studies. We could locate no other such studies. It would be useful to know whether additional simulation studies confirm these findings.

As noted above, when the means of nonindependent rs or ds are entered into the meta-analysis, use of the study N in the meta-analysis to compute the sampling error leads to an overestimation of sampling error, leading to an underestimation of SD_ρ or SD_δ. This was demonstrated in two simulation studies (S. F. Cheung & Chan, 2004; Martinussen & Bjornstad, 1999). Both studies stated that this finding indicated that the Hunter-Schmidt procedures underestimate these SDs (by a small amount). However, their results are explained by their use of study *N*s with mean *r*s and in fact could have been predicted in advance from statistical principles and from the discussion of this in Hunter and Schmidt (1990a, 2004). Use of study *N*s with mean values of nonindependent effect sizes is not part of psychometric meta-analysis methods, and we have advised against it Note that this research did not deal with violations of statistical independence. There was no violation of independence in these studies because they entered the *means* of nonindependent *r*s into their simulated meta-analyses, not the individual *r*s. Neither of these studies considered the more desirable composite correlations, which we discuss in the next section.

Conceptual Replication and Composite Scores

There is a third alternative that is superior to both entering dependent effect sizes separately and using the mean effect size. If the different outcome measures computed on the same sample all measure the same construct (e.g., all are measures of job skills), then it is possible to combine them into a composite measure, compute the correlation of the independent variable with this composite measure, and enter that composite correlation into the meta-analysis. If the *d* value is the outcome statistic, the *d* values can be converted to the *r* metric, and this composite correlation can be computed and then transformed back into the *d* metric. By the principle of multiple indicators familiar from confirmatory factor analysis, we know that the composite has higher construct validity than the individual measures. And the composite correlation solves both the problem of lack of independence and the problem of what to enter as the sample size. There is only one entry for that sample, so there is no violation of independence; the study *N* indexes the correct amount of sampling error, and the composite correlation has the same sampling error variance as any other independent correlation.

The correlation of a variable with the sum of other variables can be computed using familiar formulas for the correlation of variables with composites (Nunnally, 1978, chap. 5), and this composite correlation can later be corrected for measurement error and other artifacts. The basic formula for the Pearson correlation between any two variables *a* and *b* is

$$r_{ab} = \frac{\text{Cov}(a,b)}{SD_a SD_b} \tag{10.5}$$

If one variable, say *b*, is a composite, then we need only replace SD_b with the expression for the standard deviation of a composite and replace Cov(*a*, *b*) with the expression for the covariance of a variable with a composite. Suppose we want to compute r_{xY}, where *x* is a single variable and *Y* is a composite that is the sum of the measures y_1, y_2, and y_3. Then, if the

y_i measures are all in z score form (i.e., if $SD = 1$ for all y_is), the value S_Y^2, the variance of the composite, is merely the sum of all the values in the intercorrelation matrix of the y_i measures. This sum is denoted by $\underline{1}'R_{yy}\underline{1}$ in matrix algebra, where R_{yy} is the correlation matrix among the y_i measures (including the 1.00s in the diagonal). The $\underline{1}$s in the expression above are vectors that indicate that values in R_{yy} are to be summed. The square root of this value is SD_Y, that is, $(\underline{1}'R_{yy}\underline{1})^{1/2} = SD_Y$, the standard deviation of the composite.

The covariance of a variable with a composite is the sum of the covariances of the variable with each of the component measures of the composite. In our example, this would be $\text{Cov}(xy_1)+\text{Cov}(xy_2)+\text{Cov}(xy_3)$. Because all variables are standardized, however, this is $r_{xy_1}+r_{xy_2}+r_{xy_3}$. This is denoted in matrix algebra as $\underline{1}'r_{xy_i}$. Thus, we have

$$r_{xY} = \frac{\underline{1}'r_{xy_i}}{SD_x\sqrt{\underline{1}'R_{yy}\underline{1}}} = \frac{\Sigma r_{xy_i}}{(1)\sqrt{n+n(n-1)\bar{r}_{y_iy_j}}} \tag{10.6}$$

where $\bar{r}_{y_iy_j}$ is the average off-diagonal correlation in the correlation matrix R_{yy}.

Suppose, for example, a measure of perceptual speed (x) were correlated in the same sample of people with three measures of job performance: supervisory ratings of job performance ($r = .20$), peer ratings of job performance ($r = .30$), and records of output ($r = .25$). Suppose the correlations among the job performance measures are reported and the average of these is .50; that is, $\bar{r}_{y_iy_j} = .50$. Then,

$$r_{xY} = \frac{(.20+.30+.25)}{\sqrt{3+3(2)(.50)}} = .31$$

The obtained value of .31 is larger than the average $r\,(\bar{r}_{xy_i} = .25)$, as expected. Also, the sampling error variance of r_{xY} is known; it is $S_e^2 = (1-.31^2)^2/(N-1)$. If the meta-analysis is to be conducted using artifact distributions (see Chapter 4), this value of .31 should be entered directly into the meta-analysis, using the INTNL program. However, the reliability of the composite measure of job performance should be computed, using the methods discussed below, and entered into the artifact distribution of reliabilities. If the meta-analysis is to be based on correlations individually corrected for unreliability (see Chapter 3), then the correction for unreliability (and range restriction if appropriate) will be applied to the .31 value in the VG6 program described in the Appendix. In particular, for this particular study, the meta-analyst would enter the .31 correlation, the study N, the reliability of the Y composite, and the range restriction ratio u (if there is range restriction). In theoretically oriented meta-analyses, r_{xY} would also be corrected for unreliability in x (using the appropriate estimate of r_{xx}).

The formula given previously assumes that the y_i measures are to be weighted equally. All weights are unity and all variables are in standard score form; therefore, each y_i measure makes an equal contribution the final Y composite. If the meta-analyst makes the calculations with the variance-covariance matrix instead of the correlation matrix, the y_i measures will be weighted by their standard deviations. If the meta-analyst makes the calculations with the correlation matrix, the researcher can still weight the y_i measures differentially, by assigning unequal weights instead of unity weights. For example, suppose that, based on construct validity considerations, you decide to assign twice as much weight to production records as to supervisory ratings and three times as much weight to peer ratings as to supervisory ratings. This leads to the weight vector $w' = [1\,3\,2]$. The correlation between the independent variable x and the weighted composite Y is then

$$
r_{xY_2} = \frac{\underline{w}'\, r_{xyi}}{\sqrt{\underline{w}'\, R_{yy}\, \underline{w}}} = \frac{[1\,3\,2]\begin{bmatrix}.20\\.30\\.25\end{bmatrix}}{\sqrt{[1\,3\,2]\begin{bmatrix}1.00 & .50 & .50\\.50 & 1.00 & .50\\.50 & .50 & 1.00\end{bmatrix}\begin{bmatrix}1\\3\\2\end{bmatrix}}}
$$

$$
= \frac{(1)(.20)+(3)(.30)+2(.25)}{\sqrt{[3.5\ 4.5\ 4.0]\begin{bmatrix}1\\3\\2\end{bmatrix}}} = \frac{1.6}{5.0} = .32
$$

Thus, the weighted correlation is .32, while the unweighted correlation is .31. This is a typical result; when measures in a composite are substantially positively correlated, weighting usually has little effect on the correlation of the composite with other variables. If some measures in a composite have higher construct validity, however, differential weighting should be considered. The weighted mean correlation is

$$
\bar{r}_w = \frac{(1)(.20)+(3)(.30)+2(.25)}{1+3+2} = .26
$$

Again, the mean correlation is smaller than the composite correlation.

Sometimes a study sample will have multiple measures of both the independent and dependent variables. If the correlations among all measures are given, you can compute the correlation between the sum of the independent variable measures (composite X) and the sum of the dependent variable measure (composite Y). The measure within each composite can be weighted equally or differentially. If the k measures in the independent variable composite are $x_1, x_2 \ldots x_i \ldots x_k$ and the m measures in the dependent variable composite are $y_1, y_2 \ldots y_i \ldots y_m$, then the correlation between the two composites when all variables are equally weighted is

$$r_{XY} = \frac{\mathbf{1}'R_{xy}\mathbf{1}}{\sqrt{\mathbf{1}'R_{xx}\mathbf{1}}\sqrt{\mathbf{1}'R_{yy}\mathbf{1}}} \tag{10.7}$$

Note that the first term in the denominator is SD_X and the second is SD_Y; these are the SDs of the two composites. R_{xy} is the matrix of cross-correlations between the x_i measures and the y_i measures. The sum of these correlations is the covariance of composite X with composite Y. Thus, this formula corresponds to the fundamental formula for the Pearson r; that is,

$$r_{XY} = \frac{\text{Cov}(X,Y)}{SD_X SD_Y}$$

The measures contained in each composite can also be differentially weighted. If the vector of (unequal) weights to be applied to the y_i is $\underline{w}$, as before, and the vector of weights to be applied to the x_i measures is $\underline{v}$, then the correlation between the two weighted composites is

$$r_{XY} = \frac{\underline{v}'R_{xy}\underline{w}}{\sqrt{\underline{v}'R_{xx}\underline{v}}\sqrt{\underline{w}'R_{yy}\underline{w}}} \tag{10.8}$$

If the measures in one composite are to be weighted unequally, but not the measures in the other composite, then the differential weights can be replaced by a vector of 1s for the composite whose measures are to be equally weighted. For example, if the x_is are to be equally weighted, then $\underline{v}$ should be replaced by the vector of 1s.

The formulas for the correlation of variables with composites and composites with other composites can be used to compute a better estimate of the correlation from a study with conceptual replications. Entering these correlations into the meta-analysis instead of the individual measure correlations, or the mean r, improves the precision of the meta-analysis. We have used these formulas repeatedly in our work; typically, the composite correlations can be computed with a hand calculator when one is reading and coding data from the study. The meta-analysis program package described in the Appendix contains a subprogram that computes composite correlations.

Composite correlations require an estimate of the correlation between the measures or an estimate of the average of these correlations. One sometimes hears the objection that the correlations between the different study outcomes or measures are often not reported in the study. When this is the case, it is usually possible to obtain estimates of these correlations from other studies in the literature. Many such measures have been widely used in research, and their intercorrelations can be found in other studies, in test manuals, or in other sources, including unpublished sources. This process is illustrated in McDaniel et al. (1988b). Even if such estimates are only approximate, the resulting meta-analysis results are more accurate than if composite correlations are not used to address the independence issue. This situation is directly analogous to the use of artifact distributions from a variety of sources in artifact distribution meta-analysis (Chapter 4). In both cases, the final results are made more accurate than they would otherwise be.

These formulas are also useful in data interpretation in general. For example, suppose you are reading a journal research report that employs three measures of job satisfaction that are all correlated with a measure of organizational commitment. It may be clear that the best measure of job satisfaction would be the sum of the three measures. If the study reports the correlations among measures, you can use the formulas in this section to quickly compute the correlation between the job satisfaction composite and the organizational commitment measure, thus extracting an important piece of information not reported by the study's authors. If the study does not report the correlations among the measures, you can often get estimates of these correlations from other studies and use these to compute the composite correlation; McDaniel et al. (1988b) presented an example of this. You can also check reported research for errors. If the study reports correlations for composites, these rs should be as large as or larger than the rs for individual measures. If they are not, that indicates an error in the reported results.

After computing composite correlations, the meta-analyst should next compute the reliability of the composite measure. If you are using the meta-analysis procedure that corrects each correlation individually (see Chapter 3), you should use this reliability to correct the correlation computed (i.e., enter it into the data set for that study that is entered into the meta-analysis program). If you are using artifact distribution meta-analysis (see Chapter 4), then you should enter this reliability into the distribution of reliabilities.

The Spearman-Brown formula can be used to compute the reliability of the composite, based on the $\bar{r}$ among the measures in the composite. In our example, this would be

$$r_{yy} = \frac{n\bar{r}_{yy}}{1+(n-1)\bar{r}_{yy}}$$

$$= \frac{3(.50)}{1+(3-1)(.50)} = .75 \tag{10.9}$$

An identical estimate of reliability would be produced by Cronbach's alpha. (Both estimates are a little too large because they do not capture transient measurement error [as described in Chapter 3].) The corrected correlation is then

$$r_{xY_T} = \frac{.31}{\sqrt{.75}} = .36$$

In most meta-analyses, one would correct for unreliability in the x measure also. This would further increase the correlation. But this correction would not be made in a personnel selection meta-analysis.

See the discussion of reliability in Chapter 3. Use of Spearman-Brown or alpha reliabilities assumes that the specific factors measured by each component measure in the composite are unrelated to the construct measured by the other variable (in this case x, a measure of perceptual speed) and can be treated as random error. In our example, this would be the assumption that the specific factors in supervisory ratings, peer ratings, and production records are unrelated to perceptual speed (as well as unrelated to each other). It also assumes that these specific factors are not part of true job performance, that is, are irrelevant to the construct of job performance. This distinction is discussed in more detail in Schmidt and Kaplan (1971). If either or both of the assumptions appear to be implausible, then each measure in the composite may be measuring some aspect of actual or true job performance that is not measured by the other y_i measures. If so, then a different measure of reliability must be used, one that treats specific factor variance as true variance. This is the Mosier reliability. (The Mosier reliability is computed by an auxiliary program in the program package described in the Appendix.) The appropriate formula is given by Mosier (1943):

$$r_{yy} = \frac{\underline{1}'(R_{yy} - D + D_{rel})\underline{1}}{\underline{1}'R_{yy}\underline{1}} \tag{10.10}$$

The denominator of this formula is the total variance of the composite, as explained earlier. Because reliability is always the ratio of true to total variance, the numerator is true variance. The matrix D is a k-by-k diagonal matrix with 1s in the diagonal (all other values are 0). Subtracting D from R_{yy} takes all the 1s out of the diagonal of the R_{yy} matrix. Then adding the matrix D_{rel} (also k by k) back in replaces all the diagonal values with the reliabilities of the individual y_i measures. D_{rel} is a diagonal matrix that contains only these reliabilities.

Suppose in our example the reliability of the y_is is as follows:

$$\text{Supervisory ratings}: r_{y_1 y_1} = .70$$

$$\text{Peer ratings}: r_{y_2 y_2} = .80$$

$$\text{Production records}: r_{y_3 y_3} = .85$$

Then the Mosier reliability is

$$
r_{yy} = \frac{\underline{1}' \left(\begin{bmatrix} 1.00 & .50 & .50 \\ .50 & 1.00 & .50 \\ .50 & .50 & 1.00 \end{bmatrix} - \begin{bmatrix} 1 & 0 & 0 \\ 0 & 1 & 0 \\ 0 & 0 & 1 \end{bmatrix} + \begin{bmatrix} .70 & 0 & 0 \\ 0 & .80 & 0 \\ 0 & 0 & .85 \end{bmatrix} \right) \underline{1}}{\underline{1}' \begin{bmatrix} 1.00 & .50 & .50 \\ .50 & 1.00 & .50 \\ .50 & .50 & 1.00 \end{bmatrix} \underline{1}}
$$

$$
r_{yy} = \frac{.70 + .80 + .85 + 6(.50)}{3 + 6(.50)}
$$

$$
r_{yy} = \frac{5.35}{6.00} = .89
$$

Because the Mosier reliability treats the specific factor variance in each measure as true variance, the reliability estimate is larger than our Spearman-Brown estimate of .75. Therefore, the correlation corrected for unreliability is smaller:

$$
r_{xY_T} = \frac{.31}{\sqrt{.89}} = .33
$$

This value is 8% smaller than the previous value of .36. Thus, you should give careful consideration to the question of whether specific factors should be treated as measurement error variance or true construct variance. In general, the larger the number of measures contained in a composite, the less likely it will be that specific factor variance should be treated as true variance. However, the final answer depends on the definition and theory of the construct being measured, and so no general answer can be given. In many cases, however, theory does provide fairly clear answers. For example, verbal ability may be *defined* as what different measures of verbal ability have in common, thus implying that the specific factor variance in different verbal measures is measurement error variance. Other constructs, for example, job satisfaction and role conflict, are often defined theoretically in the same way. In most cases that we have encountered, specific factor variance should be treated as measurement error.

Conceptual Replication: A Fourth Approach and Summary Conclusions

So far, we have discussed three possible ways in which conceptual replications might be handled. First, one can enter the nonindependent correlations or *d* values individually into the meta-analysis and just ignore the lack of independence. The result is an underestimation of sampling error leading to an overestimation of the *SD* of population parameters. Second, one can enter the average *r* or *d* value into the meta-analysis. In that case, if one enters the study *N* as the sample size, the result is overestimation of sampling error, leading to underestimation of the *SD* of population parameters. Alternatively, the meta-analyst could enter as the sample size the study *N* times the number of correlations or *d* values, resulting in underestimation of sampling error and overestimation of the *SD* of population parameters. Finally, the meta-analyst could compute composite correlations or *d* values, with the result being measures with greater construct validity and accurate estimation of sampling error variance. This third approach is what we recommend. There is also a fourth approach; that approach calls for entering the nonindependent correlations or *d* values individually into the meta-analysis while using special statistical methods to estimate sampling error variance in the presence of nonindependence (robust sampling error estimation methods). For example, Hedges et al. (2010a, 2010b) present a robust variance estimation procedure that estimates these sampling error variances empirically. Their simulation studies show this method is accurate. Gleser and Olkin (2009) present a detailed analysis of such methods of dealing with violations of statistical independence. Similar methods were used in the Bijmolt and Pieters (2001) study, discussed earlier in this chapter. These methods are quite complicated and are beyond the scope of this book. Shah, Barnwell, and Bieler (1995) present software that allows a researcher to use statistically dependent data. As illustrated earlier, lack of independence causes standard errors (*SE*s) to increase. This software adjusts all *SE*s (and sampling error variances) upward to account for the lack of independence, resulting in correct *SE*s for use in confidence intervals and in meta-analysis. The adjusted sampling error variances could be used in Equation (4.3) (in Chapter 4) to calculate the adjusted *N*s to be entered into the meta-analysis.

How do these methods compare to use of composite correlations? The different *r*s or *d* values from the same sample either measure or reflect the same construct, or measure or reflect different constructs. If they measure different constructs or latent variables, then they should not be included in the same meta-analysis. They should be entered into different meta-analyses; there should be a separate meta-analysis for each different construct. In that case, the statistical methods described here obviously should not be used. On the other hand, in conceptual replication, the different measures all measure the same underlying construct or latent variable. If this is the case, then as shown earlier, combining them into a single composite measure yields a more construct valid measure, as well as providing accurate estimation of sampling error variance. So in conceptual replication, the use of composites is superior to use of these robust sampling variance estimation procedures.

Replication by Analysis of Subgroups

For many, it has now become routine to compute correlations separately by race and sex, even though there is usually no reason to believe that either will act as a moderator. This practice stems in part from a common confusion between additive and moderator effects. For example, some have hypothesized that the technology of an organization sets limits on its managerial philosophy. For example, large-scale manufacturing requires rigid coordination of work and, hence, provides fewer opportunities for power sharing with subordinates. This leads to the prediction that the level of consideration will be lower in manufacturing organizations. Even if this is true, however, within such organizations, it may still be true that those who bring workers into their decision-making structure will have higher production. Thus, the *correlation* need not be lower in such plants even though the mean is. We have seen many examples in which differences between groups *in means* lead researchers to believe that group membership is a moderator of correlational relationships. This is not logically justified.

However, in those cases in which there is solid reason to believe that demographic membership is a real and substantial moderator, then the subgroup correlations can be entered into the larger cumulation as independent outcome values. Statistically, outcome values for non-overlapping (statistically independent) groups have the same properties as values from different studies.

SUBGROUPS AND LOSS OF POWER

The analysis of subgroups exacts a price. Consider an example in which 100 persons are evenly split by race and by sex. There will then be four subgroups: 25 black females, 25 black males, 25 white females, and 25 white males. An outcome value for a sample size of 25 has much more sampling error than an outcome based on 100 cases. In fact, the confidence interval for 25 cases is about twice as wide as that for 100 cases. For example, for the full sample, an observed correlation of .20 would have a confidence interval of $.00 \leq \rho \leq .40$. For each subsample, the confidence interval would be $-.20 \leq \rho \leq .60$. There is actually very little information in an observed correlation based on as few as 25 cases (although it can be cumulated with other small-sample correlations and make a contribution in this way).

The immense statistical uncertainty and sampling error in subgroup analysis leads to massive capitalization on chance. For simplicity, suppose there is no moderating effect. If the population correlation is 0, then there are four opportunities to make a Type I error instead of one, and the actual Type I error rate would not be .05 but .19. If the population correlation is not 0, then there are four opportunities to make a Type II error rather than just one. However, the situation is worse than that. The probability of a Type I error is always .05 for each individual test regardless of the sample size, but the probability of a Type II error increases drastically with a decrease in sample size. For example, if the population correlation is .20 and the sample size is 100, then the probability of statistical significance and a correct inference is only .50. If the sample size is 25, however, then the probability of significance drops to .16; that is, the investigator will be wrong 84% of the time. Furthermore, the probability of correctly concluding significance in all four subgroups is $(.16)^4 = .0007$, which is less than 1 in 1,000. That is, analysis by subgroups for a population correlation of .20 raises the Type II error rate from 50% to 99.9%.

SUBGROUPS AND CAPITALIZATION ON CHANCE

The situation is even worse for the many investigators who select the data to present using significance tests. If there were 10 variables in the study, then the correlation matrix would have 45 entries. If all population correlations were 0, then the analysis of the whole sample would provide for a search through 45 entries to capitalize on sampling error. At least 2 such correlations would be expected to be significant by chance, and it would not be incredibly unlucky to get 5. For a sample size of 100, the largest correlation in a chance matrix would be expected to be .23. However, for a subgroup, the largest correlation among 45 would be expected to be .46. Furthermore, the analysis by subgroups provides a search list of $4(45) = 180$ elements on which to capitalize on sampling error and, hence, a greater expected error and an expected 8 and possibly 20 false significant readings.

Even if the null hypothesis were false for every correlation (in which case, every failure to find significance would be Type II error of about 84% frequency), the handful pulled out would be completely unrepresentative of the population correlations. The true value of each correlation is .20, but with a sample size of 25, only correlations of .40 or greater will be significant (two-tailed test, $p \leq .05$). Therefore, only those correlations that by chance are much larger than the true population value will be statistically significant. The conclusion that these correlations are not 0 will be correct; that is, in this 16% of cases, there will be no Type II error. However, these significant observed correlations will greatly overestimate actual population correlations. The significant observed correlations will, in fact, be about twice as large as the actual value.

SUBGROUPS AND THE BIAS OF DISAGGREGATION

If the moderator effect is nonexistent or trivial in magnitude, then the desired correlation for cumulation is the total group correlation. For practical purposes, however, it is the average correlation that is entered into the larger cumulation. That is, if there is no moderator effect, then the larger cumulation will ultimately average all entries and, hence, implicitly average the entries for each study. As it happens, the average correlation in this case may be quite biased as an estimate of the total sample correlation. This bias is always in the direction of the average correlation being smaller in magnitude than the total sample correlation. This bias is produced by restriction in range in the subgroups.

Assume that the covariance structures are the same in each subgroup; that is, assume that the regression line is the same in all groups. Then the correlation is smaller in a subgroup to the extent that the standard deviation in the subgroup is smaller than the total population standard deviation. Let u be the ratio of standard deviations; that is, let u be defined by

$$u = \frac{\sigma_{subgroup}}{\sigma_{total}}$$

Let r_t be the correlation in the total group and let r_s be the correlation in the subgroup. Then the formula for direct restriction in range yields

$$r_s = \frac{ur_1}{((u^2-1)r_t^2 + 1)^{1/2}}$$

For small correlations, this formula differs little from $r_s = ur$; that is, the subgroup correlation is lower by a factor of u. To show that u is less than 1, we note that

$$u^2 = \frac{\sigma_{subgroup}^2}{\sigma_{total}^2} = 1 - \eta^2 \qquad (10.11)$$

where η^2 is the correlation ratio between the grouping variable and the causally prior variable of the two being correlated. If the range restriction is indirect, then, for the same value of u, the downward bias in the subgroup correlations will be greater (see Chapters 3, 4, and 5).

Conclusion: Use Total Group Correlations

If the moderating effect of the demographic variable is to be studied, then, of course, subgroup correlations should be entered into the cumulation. However, once the demographic variable is known to have little or no moderator effect, the major cumulative analysis should be done with total group correlations.

Summary

There are three common forms of replication within studies: fully replicated designs, conceptual replication, and replication via analysis of independent subgroups. Each requires a different strategy for meta-analysis.

A fully replicated design is a study in which there are subparts that are independent replications of the study design. For example, the same study design might be carried out in three organizations. Results from each organization can then be entered into the meta-analysis as if the results were from three separate studies. If results are averaged rather than entered separately, then the average should be treated as if the sample size were the sum of the sample sizes across the three organizations.

Conceptual replication is multiple measurement of a construct in the same sample. Either the independent or the dependent variable or both could be measured by several instruments or methods. Each such measure then produces its own correlation or effect size. Ideally, these alternate measures should be combined by using formulas for the correlations of composites to yield a single correlation or effect size. The study then contributes one value to the meta-analysis with a minimum of measurement error (because reliability is higher for the composite) and a known sampling error variance. If the study does not report the between-measure correlations needed to compute composite correlations, and if estimates of these correlations cannot be obtained from other studies (rarely the case), then one alternative is to average the conceptually equivalent correlations or effect sizes. The average value will be an underestimate of the value that would have been produced by use of composite correlations or confirmatory factor analysis. However, it is difficult to obtain a correct estimate of the sampling error variance of the average value, and, according to statistical theory, the resulting under- or overestimation of sampling error variance logically causes biases in estimates of SD_ρ or SD_δ. The other alternative is to ignore the lack of independence and enter the dependent measures into the meta-analysis as if they were independent. According to statistical theory, this alternative should logically lead to overestimation of the SDs of population parameters. However, recent research indicates that this distortion is probably negligible.

Different Methods of Meta-Analysis and Related Software

11

This chapter presents and discusses 11 different methods for integrating study results across studies. These methods are presented and discussed in their approximate order of efficacy (from least to most efficacious) in extracting the information needed from the studies reviewed. Available computer programs for applying these methods are discussed at the end of this chapter.

The Traditional Narrative Review

The oldest procedure is the narrative review. The narrative review has been described as "literary," "qualitative," "nonquantitative," and "verbal." In this procedure, the reviewer takes the results reported in each study at face value and attempts to find an overarching theory that reconciles the findings. If there are few studies to be interpreted, this integration might be feasible. If the number of studies is large (50 to 1,000), however, the studies will almost never be precisely comparable in design, measures, and so forth, and findings will typically vary across studies in seemingly bizarre ways. As a result, the information-processing task becomes too taxing for the human mind. The result is usually one of three outcomes. First, the result may be "pedestrian reviewing where verbal synopses of studies are strung out in dizzying lists" (Glass, 1976, p. 4). That is, the reviewer may not even attempt to integrate findings across studies. Second, the reviewer may simplify the integration task by basing his or her conclusions on only a small subset of the studies. Reviewers often reject all but a few of the available studies as deficient in design or analysis and then "advance the one or two acceptable studies as the truth of the matter" (Glass, 1976, p. 4). This approach unjustifiably wastes much information and, in addition, may base conclusions on unrepresentative studies. Third, the reviewer may actually attempt the task of mentally integrating findings across all studies—and fail to do an adequate job. Cooper and Rosenthal (1980) showed that even when the number of studies reviewed is as small as seven, reviewers who use narrative-discursive methods and reviewers who use quantitative methods reach different conclusions.

The Traditional Voting Method

The traditional voting method was one of the first techniques developed to ease the information-processing burden on the reviewer. In its simplest form, it consists merely of a tabulation of significant and nonsignificant findings. Light and Smith (1971) described this approach as follows:

> All studies which have data on a dependent variable and a specific independent variable of interest are examined. Three possible outcomes are defined. The relationship between the independent and dependent variable is either significantly positive, significantly negative, or there is no significant relationship in either direction. The number of studies falling into each of these three categories is then simply tallied. If a plurality of studies falls into any of these three categories, with fewer falling into the other two, the model category is declared the winner. This model categorization is then assumed to give the best estimates of the direction of the true relationship between the independent and dependent variable. (p. 433)

The voting method is sometimes also used in an attempt to identify correlates of study outcomes. For example, the proportion of studies in which training method A was superior to training method B might be compared for males and females.

An example of a review based on this method is Eagly (1978). The voting method is biased in favor of large-sample studies that may show only small effect sizes. Even where variation in sample size does not cause problems in interpreting significance levels, and where the voting method correctly leads to the conclusion that an effect exists, the critical question of the size of the effect is still left unanswered. However, the most important problem with the voting method is that it can and does lead to false conclusions. Consider an example. Based on a meta-analysis of 144 studies, Pearlman et al. (1980) found the correlation of general intelligence and proficiency in clerical work to be .51. That is, if a perfect study were done using the entire applicant population and a perfectly reliable measure of job proficiency, then the correlation between measured intelligence and performance would be .51. However, proficiency measures cannot be obtained on applicants; performance can be measured only on those who are hired. Most organizations hire fewer than half of those who apply. Suppose those hired are those in the top half of the distribution on intelligence. Then, because of restriction in range, the correlation between test and performance will only be .33, rather than .51. It is also impossible to obtain perfect measures of job performance. Typically, the best feasible measure is the rating of the single supervisor who knows the person's work well enough to rate it. According to the review of Viswesvaran et al. (1996), the average interrater reliability of a rating by a single supervisor using a multi-item rating scale is .50. This means that the correlation between test and performance would drop to $(.50)^{1/2}(.33) = .23$. With an underlying population correlation of $\rho_{xy} = .23$, the average statistical power in a series of studies can easily be less than .50. Suppose it were .45. Then, in expectation, 55% of the studies—a majority—would find no significant relationship, and the traditional voting method would falsely conclude there was no relationship—despite the fact that the relationship is $\rho_{xy} = .23$ in every study.

Hedges and Olkin (1980) showed that if there is a true effect, then in any set of studies in which mean statistical power is less than about .50, the probability of a false conclusion using the voting method *increases as the number of studies increases*. That is, the more data examined, the greater the certainty of a false conclusion about the meaning of the data! Thus, the traditional voting method is fatally flawed statistically and logically. The typical conclusion of reviewers using the voting method is that the research literature is in deplorable shape. Some researchers get results; others do not. Sometimes a given researcher gets significant results, sometimes not. These reviewers almost invariably conclude that more research is needed and issue calls for better research designs, better experimental controls, better measures, and so on (Glass, 1976). Bushman and Wang (2009) provide an extended technical discussion of the flaws in the traditional voting method.

Cumulation of *p* Values Across Studies

This procedure attempts to cumulate significance levels across studies to produce an overall *p* value (significance level) for the set of studies as a whole. If this value is small enough, the reviewer concludes that existence of the effect has been established. These methods were developed by Mosteller and Bush (1954) from earlier work by Stouffer, Suchman, DeVinney, Star, and Williams (1949). The most recent advocates of this method have been Rosenthal and his associates (Cooper & Rosenthal, 1980; Rosenthal, 1978). As discussed in Chapter 13, in this method, the *p* value from a one-tailed significance test from each study is converted to a standardized normal deviate, denoted z. These z values are either summed directly or used to compute a weighted sum of the zs. Then the average of these zs is computed and the significance level (p value) of the average z value is determined. This is the p value for the set of studies as a whole.

An important problem with this method is that it assumes the homogeneous case (Hunter & Schmidt, 2000, pp. 286–287). That is, it assumes that $S_\rho^2 = 0$ (or that $S_\delta^2 = 0$). This means that it is a fixed effects model and, therefore, has all the problems of fixed effects meta-analysis methods, as discussed in Chapters 5 and 8. In particular, if the fixed effects assumption does not hold and $S_\rho^2 > 0$ (or $S_\delta^2 > 0$), then the alpha level of the test is inflated. For example, the combined p value for a set of studies might be computed as $p = .01$ when, in fact, it is .10. As noted in Chapters 5 and 8, the fixed effects assumption of homogeneity is rarely met in real studies.

Another major problem with this method is that in most sets of studies, the combined p value will be significant, but that fact tells nothing about the magnitude of the effect. Obviously, the practical and theoretical implications of an effect depend at least as much on its size as on its existence. Rosenthal (1978, p. 192) recognized the necessity for analysis of effect sizes along with p values, and in his later substantive reviews, he used a combination of p value and effect size analysis.

This method—cumulation of p values along with computation of the mean effect size ($\bar{r}$ or $\bar{d}$)—has been labeled the combined probability method by Bangert-Drowns (1986). Bangert-Drowns noted that the combined probability method is best regarded as a "transitional" form of meta-analysis. The introduction of the mean effect size resulted from the recognition by Rosenthal and his colleagues (Rosenthal, 1978; Rosenthal & Rubin, 1982a, 1982b) of the need for an index of the magnitude of study outcomes; at the same time, however, the method provides no information about the variability of effect sizes across studies and, therefore, lacks an important component available in some other forms of meta-analysis. With the introduction of the combined probability method, the method of cumulating p values alone was left with no major advocates. Rosenthal (1984) provided an extensive discussion of methods for cumulating p values across studies. Additional information can be found in Rosenthal (1983) and Rosenthal and Rubin (1979a, 1983). In Chapter 13, we present a discussion of the specific method of combining p values favored by Rosenthal (the Stouffer method), but we do not emphasize these methods in this book because of the problems just discussed. Others have also discussed problems with the combined p value methods (see, e.g., Becker, 1987; Becker & Schram, 1994; National Research Council, 1992). As a result of these problems, the National Research Council (1992) report recommended that the use of p value methods "be discontinued" (p. 182). In fact, these methods are rarely used in the literature today.

In passing, we note a technique developed by Rosenthal as a result of his work in cumulating p values across studies. This technique was developed to address the so-called file drawer problem. Suppose a researcher has demonstrated that the combined p value across the studies reviewed is, say, .0001 and concludes that a real effect exists. A critic could then argue that this finding is due to nonrepresentativeness of the studies reviewed, on grounds that studies not showing an effect are much less likely to have been located by the reviewer. That is, the studies with negative findings are apt to have been tucked away in file drawers rather than circulated or published. Using Rosenthal's (1979) technique, the researcher can calculate the number of missing studies showing zero effect size that would have to exist in order to bring the combined p value down to .05, .10, or any other level. This number typically turns out to be very large, for example, 65,000 (Rosenthal & Rubin, 1978). It is highly unlikely that there are 65,000 "lost" studies on any topic. The statistical formulas and the rationale for this form of file drawer analysis are given in Chapter 13. However, the file drawer technique, like the combined p value method, is a fixed effects model and, therefore, yields accurate results only if the underlying correlation (or d value) is identical in all studies. If population values of ρ and δ vary across studies (which is usually the case, as noted in Chapters 5 and 9), the number of studies needed to make the combined p value just barely significant is much smaller than the number provided by the file drawer analysis. Another source of inaccuracy is the fact that the initially computed p value for the set of studies also depends on the fixed effects assumption and, therefore, is typically inaccurate also. Other important criticisms of the Rosenthal file drawer analysis are given by Begg (1994, p. 406). These problems reduce the usefulness of the file drawer analysis.

Statistically Correct Vote-Counting Procedures

Although the traditional vote-counting method is statistically and logically deficient, there are methods of cumulating research findings across studies based on vote counting that are statistically correct. These methods fall into two categories: (1) those that yield only a statistical significance level for the body of studies and (2) those that provide a quantitative estimate of the mean effect size. These methods are discussed in technical detail by Bushman and Wang (2009). Here we provide a less technical treatment of them.

VOTE-COUNTING METHODS
YIELDING ONLY SIGNIFICANCE LEVELS

If the null hypothesis is true, then the population correlation or effect size is, in fact, 0. Thus, when study results are given in the form of *p* values, half would be expected to be larger than .50 and half smaller than .50. The sign test can be used to test whether the observed frequencies of findings in the positive and negative directions depart significantly from the 50–50 split expected under the null hypothesis (Hedges & Olkin, 1980; Rosenthal, 1978). Alternatively, the reviewer can use a count to determine the proportion of studies reporting statistically significant findings that support the theory (positive significant results) and test this proportion against the proportion expected under the null hypothesis (typically, .05 or .01). The binomial test or the chi-square statistic can be used for this test (Brozek & Tiede, 1952; Hedges & Olkin, 1980; Rosenthal, 1978). Hedges and Olkin (1980) noted that some reviewers believe that most, if not the majority, of studies should show a positive significant result if the true effect size or true correlation is nonzero. In fact, this is typically not true. When the true effect size or true correlation is in the range of magnitude typically encountered, only a minority of studies will usually report significant positive findings because of low statistical power in the individual studies (National Research Council, 1992). Hedges and Olkin (1980) also pointed out that the proportion of positive significant findings required to reject the null hypothesis is much smaller than is commonly believed. For example, if 10 studies are run using alpha = .05, the probability of three or more positive significant findings is less than .01. That is, 3 positive significant findings out of 10 are sufficient to reject the null hypothesis.

These vote-counting methods, however, are most useful when the null hypothesis is true, not when it is false. For example, Bartlett, Bobko, Mosier, and Hannan (1978) and Hunter, Schmidt, and Hunter (1979) showed that the frequency of significant differences in employment test validities for blacks and whites did not differ from the chance frequencies expected under the null hypothesis and the alpha levels used. Bartlett et al., for example, examined over 1,100 such tests at the alpha = .05 level and found that 6.2% were significant. Coward and Sackett (1990) examined thousands of ability-performance relationships and found that the frequency of statistically significant departures from linearity at the .05 alpha level was about 5%. When the null hypothesis is not rejected in cumulative studies with high statistical power, this method does provide an estimate of population effect size or population correlation: 0. However, when the null hypothesis is false (the usual case), the binomial or sign tests provide no estimate of effect size. This is a serious disadvantage. In addition, because they are statistical significance tests, the binomial and sign tests have all the disadvantages of significance tests, as discussed in detail in Chapter 2. However, it is possible to use these correct vote-counting methods without using a significance test. For example, in the studies of Bartlett et al. (1978) and Coward and Sackett (1990), the numerical findings make it perfectly apparent what the conclusion should be without using a significance test.

VOTE-COUNTING METHODS
YIELDING ESTIMATES OF EFFECT SIZES

The probability of a positive result and the probability of a positive significant result are both functions of the population effect size and study sample size. If sample sizes are known for all studies, then the mean effect size underlying a set of studies can be estimated from either the proportion of positive results or from the proportion of positive significant results. Hedges and Olkin (1980) derived formulas for both of these methods of estimating effect size. They also presented formulas that can be used to compute confidence intervals around the mean effect size estimate. These confidence intervals are, in general, wider than those resulting when effect sizes can be and are computed individually for each study and then averaged. In the latter case, confidence intervals are based on the standard error of the mean. Confidence intervals are wider for the Hedges-Olkin estimates of the mean effect size because estimation of effect sizes from counts of positive results (regardless of statistical significance) or positive significant results uses less information from the studies than the usual direct procedure. Therefore, vote-counting-based estimates of effect sizes should typically be used only when the information needed to determine effect sizes in individual studies is not available or retrievable.

Most studies provide either r or d values or enough information to compute these values. If a few studies do not, ordinarily one would just omit these studies from the meta-analysis. If the entire set does not, one would have to use one of the methods presented by Hedges and Olkin (1980); however, that would be unusual. It would be more likely that one would have a subset of studies (say, 10 studies) that do not provide enough information to compute r or d. One could then use the Hedges-Olkin method to derive an estimate of $\bar{d}$ for this subset of studies and thereby avoid losing these studies. Also, if you are reading a traditional review that gives only statistical significance and the direction of significance for each study, you can use one of these methods to get an estimate of the $\bar{d}$ for the studies in the review; in effect, this would be an incomplete and less precise— but quick and convenient—meta-analysis of these studies.

Counting Positive Significant Findings

Suppose one has 10 studies in which $N_E = N_C = 12$ in each study and suppose 6 of the 10 have significant positive results $(\hat{p} = 6/10 = .60)$. Then, from Table A2 of Hedges and Olkin (1980), one can determine that the estimated $\hat{\delta} = .80$. The researcher can also derive an estimate of the standard error of this $\hat{\delta}$ using the formula given by Hedges and Olkin for the confidence intervals for the p value. The 90% confidence interval for $\hat{p}$ is

$$\frac{(2m\hat{p}+c_\alpha^2)\pm\sqrt{c_\alpha^4+4mc_\alpha^2\,\hat{p}(1-\hat{p})}}{2(m+c_\alpha^2)}$$ (11.1)

where m is the number of studies (10 here) and $c_\alpha = 1.645$. The 90% confidence interval in our example is then

$$\frac{\{2(10)(.6)+1.645^2\}\pm\sqrt{1.645^4+4(10)(1.645)^2(.60)(1-.60)}}{2(10+1.645^2)}$$

$$= .35 < \hat{p} < .81$$

This confidence interval applies to $\hat{p}$. We must next transform the endpoints of this confidence interval to $\hat{\delta}$ values, again using Table A2 of Hedges and Olkin (1980). By linear interpolation, $\hat{\delta}$ for $\hat{p} = .81$ is 1.10 and $\hat{\delta}$ for $\hat{p} = .35$ is .53. The approximate standard error of $\hat{\delta}$ is then

$$SE_{\hat{\delta}} = \frac{1.10-.53}{2(1.645)} = .1733$$

and the sampling error variance of $\hat{\delta}$ is $(.1733)^2$ or .03003. Thus, for the 10 studies combined, there is only one entry into the meta-analysis: $\hat{\delta} = .80$ and $S_e^2 = .03003$.

Note that the SE_δ here is the SE of the $\bar{d}$, not the standard error of ds from each individual study. This SE is analogous to the standard error of the mean (i.e., $SE_{\bar{d}} = SD_d/\sqrt{m}$) from an ordinary meta-analysis of observed (and uncorrected) d s. (Recall that m is the number of studies in the Hedges-Olkin notation.) The analogous estimate of SE_d for individual d values would be $\sqrt{m}\,SE_{\bar{d}}$, which here is $\sqrt{10}(.1733) = .548$. This is the estimate of the observed SD of individual d values across the 10 studies, when the estimate of $\bar{d}$ is based only on the significance information. Here we have, in effect, combined the 10 studies into one "study" for entry into the meta-analysis. Hence, the sampling error variance value that should be used is $S_{e_{\hat{\delta}}}^2$, which is .03003 here. This estimate, like the Hedges-Olkin vote-counting methods in general, assumes that d does not vary across studies. If δ does vary, the estimate of SE_δ is only approximate.

This procedure allows us to salvage some, but not all, of the information potentially in the 10 studies. We can compute how much information is lost by our inability to compute a d value for each study. The actual total N in the 10 studies is $10(12)(2) = 240$. We can solve the following equation for N to determine the effective N in this analysis:

$$S_e^2 = \frac{4}{N}\left(1 + \frac{\bar{d}^2}{8}\right)$$

$$.03003 = \frac{4}{N}\left(1 + \frac{.8^2}{8}\right)$$

$$N = 144$$

Thus, the effective N, when only significance is known, is reduced from 240 to 144; 40% of the information in the studies is lost because the researchers did not report enough information to allow computation of d values.

This example assumed that $N_E = N_C =$ some constant across all studies. This will virtually never be true. If sample sizes vary, some form of the average sample size should be used. Hedges and Olkin (1980) suggested the geometric mean, the square mean root, or the simple average sample size. The geometric mean is

$$GM = \sqrt[m]{N_1 N_2 \ldots N_m} \tag{11.2}$$

The square mean root is

$$SMR = \left[\sum_1^m\left[\frac{\sqrt{N_i}}{m}\right]\right]^2 \tag{11.3}$$

If sample sizes do not vary dramatically across studies, the simple average N will be reasonably accurate. The reader should note that in Hedges and Olkin's Table A2, n is the number in the control *or* experimental group. Total N is $2n$. Thus, when sample sizes are not equal, one should average both the N_E and N_C values together.

Hedges and Olkin did not provide a separate table for correlations. However, their Table A2 will yield approximately correct values for r if (1) one converts the δ values at the top of the table to r (actually ρ), using Equation (7.9) in Chapter 7, and (2) one remembers to use one half of the N in entering the table.

Counting Positive Results

An estimate of $\bar{d}$ or $\bar{r}$ for a group of studies that does not provide enough information to compute d and r in individual studies can also be derived from the number of outcomes that favor the experimental group— whether they are significant. If the null hypothesis is true, and there are no differences between experimental and control groups, this expected frequency is 50%. This method uses departures from the expected 50% to estimate $\bar{d}$ or $\bar{r}$. Suppose you have 10 studies for which $N_C = N_E = 14$ in each study, and 9 of 10 results are in the positive direction (i.e., favor the experimental group whether they are significant or not). Entering this information into Table A1 of Hedges and Olkin (1980) yields $\hat{\delta} = .50$. Confidence intervals and the SE and S_e^2 of $\hat{\delta}$ are computed in the same way as illustrated previously for counts of positive significant results.

Counting Positive and Negative Results

This method is more useful than the previous two methods when you suspect that publication or other availability bias is distorting the sample of studies, that is, when you believe that significant results—both positive and negative—are being published or located and nonsignificant results are not being published or located. This occurs when there are two competing theories that make opposite predictions. (See the example of this situation from economics in Chapter 13.) This situation means the available set of studies is unrepresentative of all studies that have been conducted. This method is based on the proportion of all significant findings that are *positive* significant results, that is,

$$\hat{p} = \frac{\text{Number of positive significant results}}{\text{Number of positive plus negative significant results}}$$

If the null hypothesis is true, the expected value of $\hat{P}$ is .50. Departures from .50 are the basis for the estimate $\hat{\delta}$. For example, suppose you have 20 studies, each with $N_E = N_C = 10$. Ten studies report significant results, and of the 10, 8 are significant positive findings. Thus, $\hat{p} = .80$. Table A3 of Hedges and Olkin (1980) shows that $\hat{\delta}$ is then .15. Confidence intervals and standard errors can be estimated in the same way as described previously for counts of positive significant results. This method should be used only when (1) publication bias based on significance only (not direction) is suspected, and (2) the studies do not allow computation of d or r values.

The Hedges-Olkin (1980) methods of estimating effect size based on vote counting assume that the population effect size (δ) does not vary across studies. If δ varies substantially across studies, these methods yield only approximate estimates of mean effect size and variance of effect sizes.

Meta-Analysis of Research Studies

In this book, we have limited the term *meta-analysis* to methods that focus on the cumulation of effect sizes or correlations, rather than significance levels, across studies. Much early systematic work on combining p values across studies can be found in the literature (e.g., R. A. Fisher, 1932, 1938; Pearson, 1938). Although systematic methods for meta-analysis have been presented and advocated only recently, many of the basic concepts underlying meta-analysis have been employed by individual researchers and research teams over the decades. Thorndike (1933) cumulated test-retest reliability coefficients for the Binet intelligence test from 36 studies and even went so far as to correct the observed variance of these coefficients for the effects of sampling error. He found that much of the observed variance could be explained by sampling error but not all; some of the variation was due to the length of the interval between test and retest. Ghiselli (1949, 1955, 1966) cumulated validity coefficients from numerous studies for different types of tests and different jobs, presenting the results in the form of median values. Although he did not systematically analyze the variances of coefficients, he did cumulate a vast amount of information, which he presented in his 1966 book, followed later by an update (Ghiselli, 1973). Despite his later emphasis on the cumulation of significance levels across studies, Rosenthal was computing and publishing mean correlations as early as 1961 (Rosenthal, 1961, 1963). Bloom (1964) averaged correlation coefficients to summarize the large number of studies that had accumulated on the stability (and instability) of human traits and abilities. Erlenmeyer-Kimling and Jarvik (1963) used kinship correlations for intelligence test scores from many studies to piece together a picture of hereditary influences on mental ability. Taveggia (1974) recognized the importance of sampling error and underpowered significance tests in creating the appearance of conflicting findings in the literature and advocated and applied an approach to meta-analysis similar to that of Glass (1977). Fleishman and Levine and their associates cumulated effect sizes across experimental studies to determine the relationship between alcohol intake and decrements in task performances dependent on different abilities (Levine, Kramer, & Levine, 1975) and to determine the effectiveness of an abilities classification system in the vigilance area of human performance (Levine, Romashko, & Fleishman, 1973). None of these authors, however, advanced a systematic body of meta-analysis methodology for use in solving the general problem of integrating findings across studies to produce cumulative knowledge. It was not until the 1970s that systematic quantitative techniques for integrating research findings across studies were introduced. Glass (1976) advanced the first such set of procedures. Unaware of Glass's work, we published our first article on meta-analysis methods the following year (Schmidt & Hunter, 1977). Glass coined the term *meta-analysis* to refer to the analysis of analyses (studies). One reason he introduced this term was to distinguish such analyses from secondary analysis. In secondary analysis, the researcher obtains and reanalyzes the original data on which an earlier study was based (Light & Smith, 1971). Meta-analysis is the quantitative cumulation and analysis of effect sizes and other descriptive statistics across studies. It does not require access to original study data.

Meta-analysis methods fall into three broad categories, as depicted graphically in Figure 11.1. The purely descriptive methods (the Glass methods and the study effects meta-analysis methods) paint a descriptive picture of what is in the research literature but do not attempt to analyze, correct for, or otherwise address any of the artifacts that distort study findings. Next are meta-analysis methods that address only the artifact of sampling error. These include the homogeneity test–based methods of Hedges and Olkin (1985) and Rosenthal and Rubin (1982a, 1982b), the "bare-bones" meta-analysis methods described in the early part of Chapter 3, and Cheung's structural equation modeling (SEM)–based methods (M. W. L. Cheung, 2008, 2010, 2012a, 2012b, in press). These methods do not address the effects of artifacts other than sampling error. In particular, they do not address measurement error. Finally, there are meta-analysis methods that address and correct for the effects of not only sampling error but also a variety of other artifacts that distort study results. These methods estimate the results that would have been obtained had all the studies been conducted in a methodologically unflawed manner. That is, they attempt to reveal the scientific reality underlying a group of imperfect real-world studies. This is the purpose that Rubin (1990) stated meta-analysis methods should serve. These methods, called psychometric meta-analysis methods, are the focus of this book. In addition to the methods that we have presented, beginning in 1977 (Schmidt & Hunter, 1977), Callender and Osburn (1980) and Raju and his associates (e.g., Raju & Drasgow, 2003) have also made important contributions, as noted in Chapters 3, 4, and 5 and elsewhere in this book.

PURELY DESCRIPTIVE META-ANALYSIS METHODS: GLASSIAN AND RELATED METHODS

Glassian Meta-Analysis Methods and Criticisms

For Glass, the purpose of meta-analysis is descriptive; the goal is to paint a very general, broad, and inclusive picture of a particular research literature (Glass, 1977; Glass et al., 1981). The questions to be answered are very general; for example, does psychotherapy—regardless of type—have an impact on the kinds of outcomes that therapy researchers consider important enough to measure, regardless of the nature of these outcomes (e.g., self-reported anxiety, count of emotional outbursts, etc.)? Thus, Glassian meta-analysis often combines studies with somewhat different independent variables (e.g., different kinds of therapy) and different dependent variables. As a result, some have criticized these methods as

Figure 11.1   Schematic illustrating methods of meta-analysis.

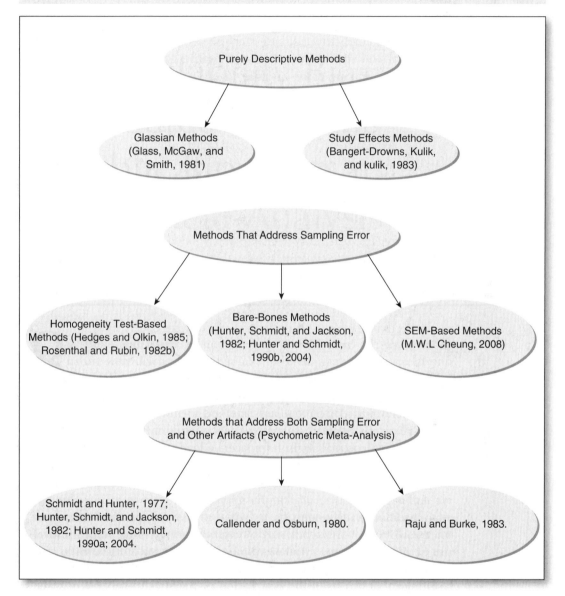

combining apples and oranges. Glassian meta-analysis has three primary properties:

1. *A strong emphasis on effect sizes rather than significance levels.* Glass believed the purpose of research integration is more descriptive than inferential and that the most important descriptive statistics are those that indicate most clearly the magnitude of effects. Glassian meta-analysis typically employs estimates of the Pearson *r* or estimates of *d*. The initial

product of a Glassian meta-analysis is the mean and standard deviation of observed effect sizes or correlations across studies.

2. *Acceptance of the variance of effect sizes at face value.* Glassian meta-analysis implicitly assumes that the observed variability in effect sizes is real and should have some substantive explanation. There is no attention to sampling error variance in the effect sizes. The substantive explanations are sought in the varying characteristics of the studies (e.g., sex or mean age of subjects, length of treatment, date of publication, and more). Study characteristics that correlate with study effects are examined for their explanatory power. The general finding in applications of Glassian meta-analysis has been that few study characteristics correlate significantly with study outcomes. Problems of capitalization on chance and low statistical power associated with this step in meta-analysis were discussed in Chapters 2 and 9.

3. *A strongly empirical approach to determining which aspects of studies should be coded and tested for possible association with study outcomes.* Glass (1976, 1977) felt that all such questions are empirical questions, and he de-emphasized the role of theory in determining which variables should be tested as potential moderators of study outcome (see also Glass, 1972). One result was that numerous study characteristics were coded, magnifying the opportunities for capitalization on change in the meta-regression.

In later sections of this chapter, we argue that Glassian meta-analysis is incomplete in important respects and that the methods presented in this book extend and complete Glass's methods. However, others have also advanced criticisms of Glass's methods. As a result of these criticisms, new approaches to meta-analysis have been advanced, approaches that are essentially variations on the Glass methods. These new approaches are discussed later. The major criticisms of Glassian methods are the following:

1. In Glassian meta-analysis, the study effect size estimate is the unit of analysis. Studies based on a single research sample often report several (sometimes numerous) estimates of effect sizes; in such cases, Glass and his associates typically include all such estimates in the meta-analysis, resulting in violations of the assumption of statistical independence (see Chapter 10). The effect of this is to cast doubt on the validity of any inferential statistical tests that might be applied in the meta-analysis, for example, tests of the significance of the $\bar{d}$ value. This criticism is statistically correct, but it overlooks the important fact that, for Glassian meta-analysis, the purpose of research integration is more descriptive than inferential. Although statistical tests are usually used, they are secondary to the descriptive purpose. We agree with the de-emphasis of significance testing in Glassian meta-analysis. As shown in Chapters 1 and 2, overreliance on statistical significance tests in psychology and the other social

sciences has led to extreme difficulties in drawing correct conclusions from research literatures. Also, in most cases, violations of independence have a conservative effect on meta-analysis outcomes; they lead to overestimates of what the observed variance of study outcomes would be if all study effects were independent. Another important consideration is that violations of independence can be expected to have no systematic effect on $\bar{d}$ or $\bar{r}$ values, and the main focus of the Glass method is on these two summary statistics. Nevertheless, when a very small percentage of studies contributes a large percentage of the effect sizes, the credibility of the meta-analysis is called into question. Technical issues related to this problem are discussed in Chapter 10. There is now evidence that violations of independence cause only minimal distortions of meta-analysis results.

2. The second criticism holds that Glass is mistaken in including all studies in the meta-analysis regardless of methodological quality (Bangert-Drowns, 1986; Slavin, 1986). Slavin (1986), for example, called for replacement of Glass's method by what he referred to as "best evidence synthesis," in which all but the studies judged to be methodologically strongest are excluded from the meta-analysis. We discuss this question in more detail in Chapter 12. Glass's position—one that we agree with—is that judgments of overall methodological quality are often very subjective, and inter-evaluator agreement is often low. Therefore, the question should be decided empirically by meta-analyzing separately the studies judged methodologically strong and weak and comparing the results. If they differ, one should rely on the "strong" studies; if they do not, then all studies should be used.

3. The third criticism is that the Glass methods mix very different independent variables in the meta-analysis, thereby masking important differences in the mean outcomes for different independent variables. For example, the Smith and Glass (1977) meta-analysis of the effects of psychotherapy included 10 different kinds of therapy (e.g., rational-emotive along with behavior modification therapies). The argument is that if some of these therapy methods are more effective than others, such a meta-analysis would never reveal that fact. This criticism ignores the fact that application of Glass's methods usually includes a separate meta-analysis for each independent variable type as a second step, allowing any such differences in treatment effects to emerge. However, Glass correctly argued that whether such finer grained meta-analyses are necessary depends on the purpose of the meta-analysis. If the research question is, "What is the relative effectiveness of different types of therapy?" clearly they are. However, if the research question is whether therapy in general is effective, then the overall analysis may be more appropriate (Wortman, 1983). Glass's critics are theoretically and analytically oriented and, therefore, find it hard to see why anyone would ever ask such a broad research question. In our research, we have typically asked narrower questions, and, therefore, our independent variables have been quite homogeneous.

4. The last major criticism is that Glassian methods mix measures of very different dependent variables. For example, in studies of educational interventions, d values for measures of attitudes, beliefs, disciplinary behavior, and academic achievement may all be included in the same meta-analysis. The critics are correct in contending that the results of such meta-analysis are difficult or impossible to interpret. It does not seem likely that the impact of, say, the open classroom would be the same on such conceptually diverse dependent variables. Again, however, there is nothing inherent in Glass's methods that precludes conducting separate meta-analyses for each dependent variable construct. The problem is that this has often not been done. In our research, we have confined the dependent variable measures within a single meta-analysis to measures of a single construct. In our validity generalization research, for example, the dependent variable has always been a measure of overall job performance.

Most of these criticisms do not stem from the nature of the Glassian statistical methods for meta-analysis per se. Instead, they are criticisms of the applications of these methods made by Glass, his associates, and some others. The criticisms stem from the fact that Glass and his critics have very different concepts of the purpose of meta-analysis. For Glass, the purpose of meta-analysis is to paint a very general, broad, and inclusive picture of a research literature. The questions to be answered are very general; for example, does psychotherapy—regardless of type—have an impact in general on the kinds of things that therapist-researchers consider important enough to measure, regardless of the nature of the construct (e.g., self-reported anxiety and counts of emotional outbursts and . . .)? His critics believe meta-analysis must answer much narrower, more specific questions if it is to contribute to cumulative knowledge, understanding, and theory development. Actually, meta-analysis can be used for both purposes. A more general quantitative summary may be useful as a first step. For those who believed that there was no cumulativeness—and indeed no order whatsoever other than randomness—in social science research literatures, the results of such meta-analysis could be (and probably have been) a heartening step back from epistemological despair. However, they can only be a first step; further advances in scientific understanding do require that meta-analysis answer more specific questions. For example, we must look separately at the impact of a given organizational intervention on job satisfaction and job knowledge.

Study Effects Meta-Analysis
Methods as a Response to Criticisms

One variation on Glass's methods has been labeled study effects meta-analysis by Bangert-Drowns (1986). It attempts to address some of the criticisms directed against Glassian methods. These methods differ from Glass's procedures in several ways. First, only one effect size from each study is included in the meta-analysis, thus assuring statistical independence within the meta-analysis. If a study has multiple dependent measures, those that assess the same construct are combined (usually averaged), and those that assess different constructs are assigned to different meta-analyses. These steps are similar to those we have followed in our research. Second, this procedure calls for the meta-analyst to make at least some judgments about study methodological quality and to exclude studies with deficiencies judged serious enough to distort study outcomes. In reviewing experimental studies, for example, the experimental treatment must be at least similar to those judged by experts in the research area to be appropriate, or the study will be excluded. This procedure seeks to determine the effect of a particular treatment on a particular outcome (construct), rather than to paint a broad Glassian picture of a research area. Some of those instrumental in developing and using this procedure are Mansfield and Busse (1977), Kulik and his associates (Bangert-Drowns, Kulik, & Kulik, 1983; Kulik & Bangert-Drowns, 1983–1984), Landman and Dawes (1982), and Wortman and Bryant (1985).

META-ANALYSIS METHODS FOCUSING ONLY ON SAMPLING ERROR

As noted earlier, numerous artifacts produce the deceptive appearance of variability in results across studies. The artifact that typically produces more false variability than any other is sampling error variance. Glassian meta-analysis and study effects meta-analysis implicitly accept variability produced by sampling error variance as real variability. Three types of meta-analyses move beyond Glassian methods in that they attempt to control for sampling error variance.

Homogeneity Test–Based Meta-Analysis: Hedges-Olkin Methods and Rosenthal's Methods

The first of these methods is homogeneity test–based meta-analysis. This approach has been advocated independently by Hedges (1982c; Hedges & Olkin, 1985) and by Rosenthal and Rubin (1982a, 1982b). Hedges (1982a) and Rosenthal and Rubin (1982a, 1982b) proposed that chi-square statistical tests be used to decide whether study outcomes are more variable than would be expected from sampling error alone. If these chi-square tests of homogeneity are not statistically significant, then the population correlation or effect size is accepted as constant across studies and there is no search for moderators. Use of chi-square tests of homogeneity to estimate whether findings in a set of studies differ more than would be expected from sampling error variance was originally proposed by Snedecor (1946).

The chi-square test of homogeneity typically has low power to detect variation beyond sampling error (Hedges & Pigott, 2001; National Research Council, 1992). Hence, the meta-analyst will often conclude that the studies being examined are homogeneous when they are not; that is, the meta-analyst will conclude that the value of ρ_{xy} or δ_{xy} is the same in all the studies included in the meta-analysis when, in fact, these parameters actually vary across studies (Hedges & Pigott, 2001). A major problem is that, in these circumstances, the fixed effects model of meta-analysis (see Chapters 5 and 8) is then used in almost all cases. Unlike random effects meta-analysis models, fixed effects models assume zero between-study variability in ρ_{xy} or δ_{xy} in computing the standard error of $\bar{r}$ or $\bar{d}$, resulting in underestimates of the relevant standard errors of the mean. This, in turn, results in confidence intervals around $\bar{r}$ or $\bar{d}$ that are erroneously narrow—sometimes by large amounts. This creates an erroneous impression that the meta-analysis findings are much more precise than they really are. This problem also results in Type I biases in all significance tests conducted on $\bar{r}$ or $\bar{d}$, and these biases are often quite large (Hunter & Schmidt, 2000; Schmidt, Oh, & Hayes, 2009). As a result of this problem, the National Research Council (1992) report on research synthesis and meta-analysis methods recommended that fixed effects models be replaced by random effects models, which do not suffer from this problem. We have also made that recommendation (Hunter & Schmidt, 2000, 2004; Schmidt, Oh, & Hayes, 2009). However, the majority of published meta-analyses using the Rosenthal-Rubin methods and the Hedges-Olkin methods have used their fixed effects models. For example, as noted in Chapters 5 and 8, most of the meta-analyses that have appeared in *Psychological Bulletin* are fixed effects meta-analyses. Most of these analyses used the Hedges-Olkin (1985) fixed effects meta-analysis model.

Both Rosenthal and Rubin and Hedges and Olkin presented random effects meta-analysis models as well as fixed effects methods, but traditionally meta-analysts have rarely employed their random effects methods, although a trend toward use of their random effects model appears to have started after 2007 (Schmidt, Oh, & Hayes, 2009). The methods presented in this book are all random effects methods.

Hedges (1982b) and Hedges and Olkin (1985) extended the concept of homogeneity tests to develop a more general procedure for moderator analysis based on significance testing. It calls for breaking an overall statistically significant chi-square statistic down into the sum of within- and between-group chi-squares. The original set of effect sizes in the meta-analysis is divided into successively smaller subgroups until the chi-square statistics within the subgroups are nonsignificant, which is taken as indicating that sampling error can explain all the variation within the last set of subgroups. Often it is not possible to attain this outcome. This problem is discussed in the section on mixed effect (ME) meta-analysis models in Chapter 9.

Homogeneity test–based meta-analysis represents a return to the practice that originally led to the great difficulties in making sense out of apparent conflicting findings in research literatures: the practice of relying on significance tests. We discussed these problems in detail in Chapter 1. As noted previously, the chi-square test typically has low power (Hedges & Pigott, 2001; National Research Council, 1992). Hedges and Olkin (1985, pp. 2–6) warn against the dangers of reliance on significance tests in primary studies under conditions of low power. This warning is equally applicable to the use of significance tests in meta-analysis. Another problem is that the chi-square test has a Type I bias (Schmidt & Hunter, 2003; Schmidt, Oh, & Hayes, 2009). Under the null hypotheses, the chi-square test assumes that all between-study variance in study outcomes (e.g., rs or ds) is sampling error variance, but there are other purely artifactual sources of variance between studies in effect sizes. As discussed earlier, these include computational, transcriptional, and other data errors; differences between studies in reliability of measurement and in levels of range restriction; and others (see, e.g., Chapters 2 and 6). Thus, even when true study effect sizes are actually the same across studies, these sources of artifactual variance will create variance beyond sampling error, sometimes causing the chi-square test to be significant and, hence, to falsely indicate heterogeneity of effect sizes. This is especially likely when the number of studies is large, increasing statistical power to detect small amounts of such artifactual variance. Another problem is that, even when the variance beyond sampling error is not artifactual, it often will be small in magnitude and of little or no theoretical or practical significance. Hedges and Olkin (1985) recognized this fact and cautioned that researchers should not merely look at significance levels but should evaluate the actual size of the variance; unfortunately, however, once researchers are caught up in significance tests, the usual practice is to assume that if it is statistically significant, it is important (and if it is not significant, there is no relation). We have seen in Chapter 1 how erroneous such interpretations are. Once the major focus is on the results of significance tests, effect sizes are usually ignored.

Homogeneity-based meta-analysis methods do address sampling error, although perhaps not in the most effective manner. However, they do not include corrections for measurement error, range variation, dichotomization, or other artifacts that distort study results. However, some researchers using or studying these methods have added corrections for artifacts to these methods. Examples include Aguinis et al. (2008) and Hall and Brannick (2002). But the originators of these methods have not done this.

Hunter-Schmidt Bare-Bones Meta-Analysis

The second approach to meta-analysis that attempts to control only for the artifact of sampling error is what we referred to earlier as bare-bones meta-analysis (see, e.g., Chapters 3, 4, and 7). This approach can be applied to correlations, *d* values, or any other effect size statistic for which the standard error is known. For example, if the statistic is correlations, $\bar{r}$ is first computed. Then the variance of the set of correlations is computed. Next the expected amount of sampling error variance is computed and subtracted from this observed variance. If the result is 0, then sampling error accounts for all the observed variance, and the mean *r* value accurately summarizes all the studies in the meta-analysis. If not, then the square root of the remaining variance is the index of variability remaining around the mean *r* after sampling error variance has been removed. Chapters 3, 4, and 7 present examples of bare-bones meta-analysis.

Because there are always other artifacts (such as measurement error) that should be corrected for, we have consistently stated in our writings that the bare-bones meta-analysis method is incomplete and unsatisfactory. It is useful primarily as the first step in *explaining* and *teaching* meta-analysis to novices. However, meta-analyses based on bare-bones methods alone have been published; the authors of these studies have invariably claimed that the information needed to correct for artifacts beyond sampling error was unavailable to them. In our experience, this is rarely the case. Estimates of artifact values (e.g., reliabilities of scales) are usually available from the literature, from test manuals, or from other sources, as indicated earlier. These values can be used to create distributions of artifacts for use in artifact distribution–based meta-analysis (described in Chapter 4) or used to correct individual *r*s or *d*s, thus correcting for the biasing effects of measurement error and other artifacts in addition to sampling error.

Cheung's SEM-Based Meta-Analysis Method

Michael Cheung has developed a method that incorporates meta-analysis as a form of SEM (Cheung, 2008, 2010, 2012b, in press; Cheung & Chan, 2005). In Cheung's view, regression analysis, path analysis, factor analysis, and meta-analysis are all special cases of SEM. He likens this position to the demonstration by Jacob Cohen (Cohen, Cohen, West, & Aiken, 2003) that analysis of variance can be viewed as a special case of regression analysis. The articles by Cheung cited above explain how meta-analysis can be conducted as a form of SEM, and Cheung (2012a) presents a computer program for carrying out meta-analysis in this manner. Cheung (personal communication, February 21, 2013) states that his method is statistically and mathematically the same as the mixed effects (ME) meta-regression method discussed in Chapter 9. However, he believes it is better to have a uniform frame for meta-analysis, regression analysis, path analysis, and factor analysis, and he argues that the uniform framework is SEM. This raises the question of what the value added is of conceptualizing all these methods under the umbrella of SEM modeling.

In his earlier articles (e.g., Cheung, 2008; Cheung & Chan, 2005), this method relied heavily on low-powered significance tests, but he has since modified the method so that it produces approximate confidence intervals for all parameter estimates (Cheung, 2009). This method does address sampling error but does not provide an index of the amount or percent of variance accounted for by sampling error. Cheung's initial work in this area (Cheung & Chan, 2005) was limited to the fixed effects (FE) meta-analysis model, but later work, starting with Cheung (2008), expanded the method to cover random effects (RE) models. Because this method is a form of SEM, it can make use of advanced techniques built into many SEM programs. These include methods for handling missing data and missing covariates (potential moderators not coded in some primary studies), SEM-type goodness-of-fit indices, and other data techniques. Cheung (2008; personal communication, February 21, 2013) argues that this is a major advantage stemming from placing meta-analysis under the SEM umbrella.

However, this approach has several limitations. First, mean effect sizes (whether in the r or d metric) and moderator effects are given as raw score (unstandardized) regression weights. Such weights are affected by differences in scaling between regression variables and thus are not comparable. This problem was discussed in detail in Chapter 5 and mentioned in the section on meta-regression in Chapter 9. For example, if two moderators are measured on different scales, their regression weights cannot be compared. This noncomparability of estimates leads users to rely on p values when attempting to compare moderator effects. Cheung (personal communication, February 21, 2013) is aware of this and says he will attempt to modify the procedure so it produces the more interpretable standardized regression weights. Second, even beyond the unstandardized metrics, the methods are complex and difficult to understand for researchers who are not experts in SEM. Third, at present this method addresses only sampling error (which is why it is in the present category in our classification scheme). However, Cheung says he plans to work in the future on incorporating corrections for measurement error (Cheung, personal communication, February 21, 2013). The absence of correction for measurement error is perhaps surprising, because the major strength of SEM over path analysis is correction for measurement error via multiple measures of each latent variable. But the SEM meta-analysis method lacks multiple measures; in this respect, it is essentially a form of path analysis rather than what most people think of as SEM. It may be difficult to incorporate corrections for range variation into these methods. However, the large-scale meta-analysis of Nye et al. (2012) employed an ME meta-regression method similar to Cheung's methods in which they corrected all correlations for both measurement error and range restriction prior to the meta-regression.

Psychometric Meta-Analysis:
Correction for Multiple Artifacts

The third type of meta-analysis is psychometric meta-analysis. These methods correct not only for sampling error (an unsystematic artifact) but for systematic artifacts, such as measurement error, range restriction or enhancement, dichotomization of measures, and so forth. These other artifacts are said to be systematic because, in addition to creating artifactual variation across studies, they also create systematic downward biases in the results of all studies. For example, measurement error systematically biases all correlations and d values downward. Psychometric meta-analysis corrects not only for the artifactual variation across studies but also for the downward biases. Psychometric meta-analysis is the only meta-analysis method that takes into account both statistical and measurement artifacts. Two variations of these procedures were described earlier in Chapters 3, 4, and 7. In the first, each r or d value is corrected individually for artifacts; in the second, correction is accomplished using artifact distributions. Callender and Osburn (1980) and Raju and Burke (1983) also developed methods for psychometric meta-analysis. These methods differ slightly in computational details but have been shown to produce virtually identical results (Law et al., 1994a, 1994b).

Every method of meta-analysis is of necessity based on a theory of data. It is this theory (or understanding of data) that determines the meta-analysis methods used to analyze the data. A complete theory of data includes an understanding of sampling error, measurement error, biased sampling (range restriction and range enhancement), dichotomization and its effects, data errors, and other causal factors that distort the raw data we see in research studies. Once a theoretical understanding of how these factors affect data is developed, it becomes possible to develop methods for correcting for their effects. In the language of psychometrics, the first process—the process by which these factors (artifacts) influence data—is modeled as the attenuation model. The second process—the process of correcting for these artifact-induced biases—is called the disattenuation model. If the theory of data on which a method of meta-analysis model is based is incomplete, that method will fail to correct for some or all of these artifacts and will thus produce biased results. For example, a theory of data that fails to recognize measurement error will lead to methods of meta-analysis that do not correct for measurement error. Such methods will then perforce produce biased meta-analysis results. As discussed in this chapter, some current methods of meta-analysis do not, in fact, correct for measurement error. But in research methodology, the pressure is always toward increased accuracy, and so eventually these other methods will have to incorporate corrections for measurement error and perhaps other distorting artifacts. This has already happened to some extent, because users of these other methods have "appended" these corrections to those methods (e.g., Aguinis et al., 2008; Hall & Brannick, 2002).

Sampling error and measurement error have a unique status among the statistical and measurement artifacts with which meta-analysis must deal: They are always present in all real data. Other artifacts, such as range restriction, artificial dichotomization of continuous variables, or data transcription errors, may be absent in a particular set of studies being subjected to meta-analysis. There is always sampling error, however, because sample sizes are never infinite. Likewise, there is always measurement error, because there are no perfectly reliable measures. In fact, it is the requirement of dealing simultaneously with both sampling error and measurement error that makes even relatively simple psychometric meta-analyses seem complicated. Most researchers are used to dealing with these two types of errors separately. For example, when psychometric texts (e.g., Lord & Novick, 1968; Nunnally & Bernstein, 1994) discuss measurement error, they assume an infinite (or very large) sample size, so that the focus of attention can be on measurement error alone, with no need to deal simultaneously with sampling error. When statistics texts discuss sampling error, they implicitly assume perfect reliability (the absence of measurement error), so that they and the reader can focus solely on sampling error. Both assumptions are highly unrealistic, because all real data simultaneously contains both types of errors. It is admittedly complicated to deal with both types of errors simultaneously, yet this is what meta-analysis must do to produce accurate results (Cook et al., 1992, pp. 315–316, 325–328).

The question of what theory of data underlies a method of meta-analysis is strongly related to the question of what the general purpose of meta-analysis is. Glass (1976, 1977) stated that the purpose is simply to summarize and describe the reported results of studies in a research literature. Our view, the alternative view, is that the purpose is to estimate as accurately as possible the construct-level relationships in the population (i.e., to estimate population values or parameters), because these are the relationships of scientific interest. This is an entirely different task; this is the task of estimating what the findings would have been if all studies had been conducted perfectly (i.e., with no methodological limitations). Doing this requires correction for sampling error, measurement error, and other artifacts (if present) that distort study results. Simply describing the contents of studies in the literature requires no such corrections but does not allow estimation of parameters of scientific interest.

Rubin (1990) critiqued the common, descriptive concept of the purpose of meta-analysis and proposed the alternative offered in this book. He stated that, as scientists, we do not really care about the population of imperfect studies per se; hence, an accurate description or summary of these studies is not really important. Instead, he argued that the goal of meta-analysis is to estimate the true effects or relationships—defined as "results that would be obtained in an infinitely large, perfectly designed study or sequence of such studies." According to Rubin,

> Under this view, we really do not care *scientifically* about summarizing this finite population (of observed studies). We really care about the underlying scientific process—the underlying process that is generating these outcomes that we happen to see—that we, as fallible researchers, are trying to glimpse through the opaque window of imperfect empirical studies. (p. 157, emphasis in original)

This is an excellent summary of the purpose of meta-analysis as we see it and as embodied in the methods presented in this book—the methods of psychometric meta-analysis.

Unresolved Problems in Meta-Analysis

In all forms of meta-analysis, including psychometric meta-analysis, there are unresolved problems. First, when effect size estimates are correlated with or regressed on multiple-study characteristics (i.e., meta-regression), capitalization on chance operates to increase the apparent number of significant associations for those study characteristics that have no actual associations with study outcomes. Because the sample size is the *number of studies* and many study properties may be coded, this problem is potentially severe (see discussion in Chapters 2 and 9). There is no purely statistical solution to this problem. The problem can be mitigated, however, by basing choice of study characteristics and final conclusions not only on the statistics at hand but also on other theoretically relevant findings (which may be the results of other meta-analyses) and on theoretical considerations. Results should be examined closely for substantive and theoretical meaning. Capitalization on chance is a threat whenever the (unknown) correlation or regression weight is actually 0 or near 0. Second, when there is, in fact, a relationship, there is another problem: Statistical power to detect the relationship is usually low (see discussion in Chapters 2 and 9). Thus, true moderators of study outcomes (to the extent that such exist) may have only a low probability of showing up as statistically significant. In short, this step in meta-analysis is often plagued with all the problems of small-sample studies. For a discussion of these problems, see Schmidt et al. (1976) and Schmidt and Hunter (1978). Other things being equal, conducting separate meta-analyses on subsets of studies to identify a moderator avoids some of these problems but not all and may lead to additional problems of confounding of moderator variables (see Chapter 9). In short, despite perceptions to the contrary, the task of identifying and calibrating moderator variables (interactions) is complex and difficult (Schmidt & Hunter, 1978).

Summary of Methods of Integrating Studies

We have reviewed 11 different methods for integrating research findings across studies. These methods form a rough continuum of efficacy in revealing hidden facts that can be proved by the cumulative weight of previous studies. The narrative method is unsystematic, is haphazard, and imposes an impossible information-processing burden on the reviewer. The traditional voting method uses only part of the available information, provides no information about effect size, and, worst of all, logically leads to false conclusions under circumstances that are quite common. Cumulating p values across studies does not logically lead to false conclusions but has all the other disadvantages of the traditional voting method. Statistically correct vote-counting methods that yield only an overall statistical significance level (p value) for the group of studies reviewed have all the disadvantages of cumulating p values across studies. In particular, these methods provide no estimate of effect size. Other vote-counting procedures presented by Hedges and Olkin (1980, 1985) do provide estimates of effect size, but the uncertainty in such estimates is substantial because these methods are based on only a part of the information that individual studies should present. These methods require the assumption that effect sizes are equal across studies; if this assumption is not met, then these methods yield only approximate estimates.

Glassian meta-analysis is a quantum improvement over these research integration methods. It uses more of the available information from the individual studies and provides a more accurate estimate of mean effect size, it does not require the assumption that effect sizes are constant across studies, and it provides an estimate of the variance of observed effect sizes. It also provides for correlating study effect sizes with study characteristics in an attempt to determine the causes of variation in study findings.

For most purposes of scientific research, study effects meta-analysis is an improvement over Glassian meta-analysis. It allows clearer conclusions about relationships between specific independent and dependent variable constructs, permitting finer tests of scientific hypothesis. Homogeneity test–based meta-analysis, bare-bones meta-analysis, and Cheung's SEM-based method have the additional advantage of addressing sampling error in study findings. However, these methods fail to address or correct for the effects of any artifacts beyond sampling error. In particular, they ignore the biases created by measurement error, which are present in all studies. In this respect, they are based on an incomplete, and therefore erroneous, theory of data, as noted earlier.

Only psychometric meta-analysis methods are based on a complete theory of data—that is, an understanding of data that includes not only the effects of sampling error on data but also the effects of measurement error and other artifacts such as range restriction, dichotomization, imperfect construct validity, and others discussed in this book. Psychometric meta-analysis corrects not only for the artifactual variation across studies created by these artifacts but also for the downward biases created by them on the mean correlation or mean d value. Psychometric meta-analysis can be accomplished either by correcting each r or d individually or by use of distributions of artifacts when artifact values are not available for each r or d value. Psychometric meta-analysis estimates what research findings would have been had it been possible to conduct studies without methodological flaws. As Rubin (1990) noted, this is what we, as scientists, want to know, and, therefore, the production of such estimates should be the purpose of meta-analysis.

Computer Programs for Meta-Analysis

In conducting their meta-analyses, some researchers prefer to write their own programs, often using spreadsheet programs. This is feasible for simple meta-analysis procedures such as bare-bones or basic homogeneity-based meta-analysis methods but is a complex (and maybe error-prone) task for more complex forms of meta-analysis. Some researchers prefer to use commercially available programs for the PC. Still others elect to use one of the many freeware meta-analysis programs. There are many programs available today for conducting the different types of meta-analysis discussed in this chapter. If you Google "meta-analysis software," you will get more than 11 *million* hits. Although there are not 11 million different meta-analysis programs listed, the number is large. Obviously, we cannot review them all here. Many of the freeware programs found online have been published in medical journals and are oriented toward meta-analysis of medical studies, especially controlled randomized trials. The programs used in this book appeared in our web search, but we were not able to locate online any other programs that make possible corrections for measurement error, range restriction, or other artifacts. However, such programs do exist, and we discuss some of them later in this section. In this section, we briefly discuss some of the commercially available programs for the PC along with some of the freeware programs that allow corrections for research artifacts. A more complete description of available software for meta-analysis is given in Rothstein et al. (2001).

PROGRAMS FOR GLASSIAN META-ANALYSIS

We are not aware of any commercially available programs for Glassian meta-analysis or study effects meta-analysis. However, the key statistical step in these methods is the computation of effect sizes. A program called ES (for Effect Size) is available (Shadish et al., 1999) that computes effect sizes from a wide variety of reported statistics and study designs. As we noted in Chapter 8, this program is useful for computing effect sizes from repeated measures designs, analysis of variance factorial designs (both between- and within-subjects designs), and a variety of other research designs. This program also allows computation of effect sizes from studies that report limited information—for example, studies that report only specific significance tests. The program includes over 40 different methods of computing effect sizes. (However, the program does not provide sampling error variance formulas for the estimates.) The utility of this program is by no means limited to applications of Glassian or study effects meta-analysis. The program is a useful adjunct in preparing a database for any type of meta-analysis. This program is available free of charge from William Shadish (wshadish@ucmerced.edu).

PROGRAMS FOR HOMOGENEITY-BASED META-ANALYSIS

There are a large number of programs available for homogeneity test–based meta-analysis, more than for any other type of meta-analysis. None of these programs allow for correction for measurement error or other study artifacts. Many of these are freeware and others are sold commercially. We are aware of four commercial programs. The first is D-Stat (Johnson, 1989), marketed by Lawrence Erlbaum. This program is based on the Hedges-Olkin (1985) meta-analysis methods. The second is Advanced BASIC Meta-Analysis (Mullen, 1989), also marketed by Lawrence Erlbaum. This program is based on the Rosenthal-Rubin methods of meta-analysis, although it can be used to conduct approximate Hedges-Olkin meta-analyses. In Chapter 8, we discussed the error in this program that can cause d values to be greatly overestimated (Dunlap et al., 1996). This program is available in DOS only. Both of these programs are limited to fixed effects meta-analysis models. Next, there is Meta-Win (Rosenberg, Adams, & Gurevitch, 1997; www .sinauer.com). This program uses a Windows interface. Unlike D-Stat and Advanced BASIC Meta-Analysis, this program allows for both fixed and random effects meta-analysis models in the Hedges-Olkin framework. It also has a number of other additional features. Finally, there is the Comprehensive Meta-Analysis (CMA) program, marketed by Biostat (www .Meta-Analysis.com). This program is considerably more costly than the other programs discussed here (cost is $1,295 as of this writing). This program is based on Hedges-Olkin (1985) homogeneity test–based meta-analysis (fixed , random, and mixed effects models). It addition to r and d value meta-analysis, it allows meta-analysis of odds ratios and risk ratios. It has a large number of convenient features for data entry, calculation of effect sizes, confidence intervals for individual study results, forest plots, and other statistics from individual studies. The resulting data can be displayed in a variety of clarifying and informative ways, and there are features that allow for the creation, management, and updating of the resulting databases.

This program does not allow for psychometric meta-analysis of correlations or *d* values, and so users cannot correct meta-analysis results for biases due to measurement error or other artifacts. Because of this, one might question the word *comprehensive* in the CMA title. But it is possible that corrections for study artifacts may be incorporated into the program in the future.

There are many freeware programs for homogeneity-based meta-analysis. One that should not be overlooked is RevMan (which stands for "Review Manager"). This is the meta-analysis program used by the Cochrane Collaboration, the U.K. group that publishes meta-analyses online on the effectiveness of numerous medical treatments and procedures. The Cochrane Collaboration was discussed in Chapter 1. RevMan has many (but not all) of the same features as the Comprehensive Meta-Analysis program and is available for free. An Internet search for RevMan reveals considerable information on this program. The statistical package R is an increasingly popular set of flexible programs for many different statistical applications (R Development Core Team, 2010). Among these applications are at least three for conducting homogeneity-based meta-analysis: *metafor* (Viechtbauer, 2010), *rmeta* (Lumley, 2009), and *meta* (Schwarzer, 2010). Viechtbauer (2010) compares and contrasts these three programs. All these programs have an impressive number of features, especially considering that they are free. There are also macros available for homogeneity-based meta-analysis for the Stata package (StataCorp, 2007; Sterne, 2009), SPSS (SPSS, Inc., 2006; see Lipsey & Wilson, 2001), and SAS (SAS Institute, Inc., 2003).

PROGRAMS FOR PSYCHOMETRIC META-ANALYSIS

There are several programs available for psychometric meta-analysis. The first is the software package (Version 2.0) written to accompany this book: Hunter-Schmidt Meta-Analysis Programs (see the Appendix). This Windows-based program package is available commercially from Huy Le and Frank Schmidt. It includes six programs that implement the methods presented in this book. The first two programs are for correlations corrected individually (discussed in Chapter 3). The first subprogram here is for studies in which range restriction is direct, while the second is for data in which range restriction is indirect. (If there is no range restriction in one's study set, either program can be used; the programs will produce identical output.) The second two programs conduct artifact distribution meta-analysis for correlations, based on the interactive method described in Chapter 4. The first of these is for studies in which range restriction is direct; the second, for studies with indirect range restriction. (Again, if there is no range restriction in one's studies, either program can be used.) The fifth program is for *d* values corrected individually, while the sixth program is for artifact distribution meta-analysis of *d* values. Both these programs correct for sampling error and measurement error in the dependent variable. Both these approaches to meta-analysis of d values are discussed in Chapter 7. Data files for data analyzed as examples in Chapters 3, 5, and 7 are included in the programs, and the user can run these analyses to become familiar with the programs. All these programs include the accuracy-enhancing procedures discussed in Chapters 5, 7, and other chapters. In addition to psychometric meta-analysis results, all six programs also report bare-bones meta-analysis results for comparison purposes. For all these programs, the Windows format allows for easy data input on the screen or from stored data files. The most important output is presented automatically on the screen. However, users usually elect to print the output; the printed output is more complete and detailed. Output and data files can be saved on the program site. The program set also includes a number of utility programs for computing statistics for entry into meta-analysis (e.g., a program for converting point biserial correlations to biserial correlations and a program for computing correlations of sums [composite correlations] and reliabilities of composites, as described in Chapter 10). A review of Version 1.1 of these programs is presented by Roth (2008). Reviews of the methods used in the programs (and of Hunter & Schmidt, 2004) are presented by Morris (2007) and Oh (2007).

The current version of these programs (Version 2.0) incorporates improvements not available at the time of the Roth (2008) review. The programs now allow direct importation of data files from spreadsheet programs like Excel. The output now includes confidence intervals around mean values, in addition to the credibility values provided in the earlier version (Version 1.1). The program now makes it easier to do moderator analyses by subgrouping studies. The maximum number of studies includable in a meta-analysis has been raised to 1,000. The programs also include a program for cumulative meta-analysis to detect publication bias (see Chapter 13) and a program for forest plots. The programs now present meta-analysis results in the tabular form needed for publication, as illustrated in Chapter 12. Additional improvements are described in the Appendix.

The computer program MAIN (Raju & Fleer, 1997) is another program for psychometric meta-analysis. This PC program is limited to correlations. It corrects correlations individually and applies psychometric meta-analysis to the corrected correlations. This method, described in Raju et al. (1991), takes into account sampling error in the reliability estimates, as well as in the correlations. It is set up for use only with direct range restriction, although it may be modified in the future to also handle indirect range restriction. This program does not conduct artifact distribution meta-analysis for correlations, nor does it perform meta-analysis of d values. However, noncommercial programs for artifact distribution psychometric meta-analysis of correlations based on the two Taylor series approximation (TSA) procedures (Raju & Burke, 1983) (discussed in

Chapter 4) are available from Michael Burke at no charge. As of this writing, these programs are limited to studies with direct range restriction. They are quite accurate for data with direct range restriction (as shown in Law et al., 1994a, 1994b).

Another program that performs psychometric meta-analysis is that of McDaniel (1986a, 1986b). This PC program accepts only correlation coefficients. It consists of a series of SAS macros that perform both artifact distribution meta-analysis and meta-analysis correcting correlations individually. It corrects for measurement error in both variables and for direct range restriction but not indirect range restriction. The artifact distribution program is based on the interactive model (discussed in Chapter 4) but does not include the accuracy-enhancing refinements discussed in Chapter 5. This program is available free of charge from Michael McDaniel (mamcdani@vci.edu).

Finally, there is the psychometric meta-analysis program created by Huffcutt, Arthur, and Bennett (1993). This program is also based in SAS. It uses SAS PROC MEANS to compute its meta-analysis results. This program is limited to correlations and to artifact distribution meta-analysis. It uses the noninteractive artifact distribution meta-analysis procedure (see Hunter & Schmidt, 2004), an older method that is less accurate than the interactive procedure described in detail in Chapter 4. This program corrects for measurement error and direct range restriction. We have found that there is an error in this program in the standard error for mean effect sizes. There is also a mislabeling of credibility intervals as confidence intervals. The program is available free of charge from Allen Huffcutt at Bradley University. Huffcutt et al. (1993) compared results from their program and the McDaniel program for artifact distribution meta-analysis and found the differences in output were small.

This discussion of software for meta-analysis is by no means comprehensive. New programs for meta-analysis appear with some frequency, and we have undoubtedly missed some existing programs. Readers interested in a more complete picture will find that an Internet search turns up additional programs of interest.

Locating, Evaluating, Selecting, and Coding Studies and Presentation of Meta-Analysis Results

12

Because of the explosive expansion of the literature on meta-analysis over the past 35 years, no single book can today cover all aspects of meta-analysis. The primary focus of this book is on statistical and psychometric methods for data analysis in meta-analysis. However, the less quantitative processes of locating, selecting, evaluating, and coding studies are also important. The topic of reporting standards for meta-analyses is also important. We cannot cover these topics in detail, but fortunately good published treatments of these topics are readily available. The material in this chapter is selective rather than comprehensive. It is intended to supplement other published discussions of this topic. We have included in this chapter mostly material we have found to be absent from other published treatments.

Conducting a Thorough Literature Search

Many topics not addressed in detail in this book are covered in more detail in H. Cooper (1998, 2010). For this reason, we recommended the H. Cooper (1998, 2010) books as supplements to this book in graduate courses in meta-analysis. We have used these books successfully in that capacity. Chapter 3 in each of these books presents considerable detail on how to conduct a thorough literature search, including discussion of the following methods for locating studies: the World Wide Web, conference papers, personal journals, libraries, electronic journals, research report reference lists, research bibliographies, and reference databases (such as PsycINFO, ERIC, Dissertation Abstracts International, and Social Sciences Citation Index). Cooper also provides a discussion of the limitations of computer-based literature searches and gives methods for assessing the adequacy and completeness of a literature search. Other useful sources include Cook et al. (1992, pp. 289–305), Reed and Baxter (2009; using reference databases), Rothstein (2012), Rothstein and Hopewell (2009; locating "grey" literature), and White (2009; literature retrieval in meta-analysis). A thorough literature search is important in ensuring the most representative sampling of studies for the meta-analysis and hence the accuracy and unbiasedness of the meta-analysis results. In particular, searches limited to only certain journals or only published studies are more likely to be distorted by publication or source bias. Publication and source bias are discussed in Chapter 13.

There are two important reasons for carefully describing the literature search process in a review article. First, it allows the reader to judge the comprehensiveness and representativeness of the sources that are the subject of the review and thereby to assess the threat, if any, of distortion due to publication or source bias. Second, detailing the literature search process in a meta-analysis report allows future reviewers of the topic to extend the meta-analysis without duplicating it. If it is known that most of the articles included in the review were those listed under certain descriptors of certain years of certain indexes, or found in the bibliographies of specified sources, it is easy for a subsequent reviewer to broaden or deepen the search for relevant sources without duplicating the earlier work.

What to Do About Studies With Methodological Weaknesses

Many reviewers wish to eliminate from their analyses studies that they perceive as having methodological inadequacies. An example of this is Slavin (1986). This often is not as reasonable and desirable as it may seem. The assertion of "methodological inadequacy" always depends on theoretical assumptions about what might be true in a study. These assumptions may well be false and are rarely tested in their own right. Those who believe the assumptions usually feel no need to test them. That is, the hypothesis of "methodological inadequacy" is rarely tested empirically. No research study can be defended against all possible counterhypotheses; hence, no study can be without "methodological inadequacy." However, methodological inadequacies do not always cause biased findings, and, prior to the analyses of the full set of studies on the topic, it is difficult to determine reliably when methodological inadequacies have caused biased findings and when they have not.

Some reviewers are inclined to use the simple strategy of eliminating all studies believed to have methodological inadequacies. This is the approach advocated by Slavin (1986). (See "The Myth of the Perfect Study" in Chapter 1.) Because most studies have some weaknesses, these reviewers often end up reporting meta-analyses based on only a few studies. When there is good a priori evidence that the eliminated studies had substantially biased results, this strategy would be justified, but that seldom is the case.

The hypothesis of methodological inadequacy should be tested only after two prior hypotheses have been rejected. First, one should determine if the variation across all studies can be accounted for by sampling error and other artifacts, such as differences in reliability. If the variation is due solely to artifacts, then there can be no variance due to methodological inadequacy. Second, if there is substantial variation across studies, then theoretically plausible moderator variables should be tested. If the moderator variables account for all nonartifactual variance, there can be no variance across studies due to methodological inadequacy. If the theoretically plausible moderator variables do not explain the variance, methodological inadequacies may be present. One can then rate the internal and external validity of the studies or code the characteristics that might produce inadequacy and test these characteristics as moderator variables. Turner, Spiegelhalter, Smithe, and Thompson (2009) present a method of doing this intended for use in the medical meta-analyses.

Two methodological inadequacies discussed throughout this book are low reliability of the measures used and range restriction. But as shown in Chapters 3 and 4, meta-analysis methods can correct for the effects of these methodological weaknesses. Hence, these limitations can never be a reason for excluding a study (although they do lead to lower weighting of such studies).

It is important to recognize that the actual threat to the internal and external validity of a study is not determined exclusively or even primarily by the design of the study. D. T. Campbell and Stanley's monograph (1963) on experimental and quasi-experimental designs shows which threats are controlled by various research designs if none of the controlled factors interact. However, the monograph does not indicate which threats are likely to be trivial in a given study or which threats can be reasonably controlled by other means (see the discussion of these threats and their plausibility in Chapter 8).

Some have suggested that there is a counterexample to our argument: violations of construct validity across studies. The fact that the same variable name is used in different studies does not mean that the same variable is measured in those studies. We believe that construct validity is potentially an empirical question, as well as a theoretical question. Ideally, one would do an empirical study in which alternative instruments or methods are used to measure the independent and dependent variables. Confirmatory factor analysis could then be used to see if the alternate measures differ by more than error of measurement. That is, do the different measures correlate approximately 1.00 after correcting for measurement error? A test of the construct invalidity hypothesis can be run within a meta-analysis. If several instruments are really measuring different things, then it would be unlikely that they would have the same correlation with the second variable in the meta-analysis (or, in the case of an experiment, that the treatment effect would be identical across the different variables). If the meta-analysis shows no variance across studies, then that would suggest that the alternate measures are substantially equivalent. On the other hand, if the meta-analysis does find variance across studies, the hypothesized nonequivalence of variables can be tested as a moderator variable. If this moderator variable does explain variance across studies, this finding is confirmation of the hypothesis of construct invalidity. In any case, it is our belief that the *assertion* of construct invalidity is not the same as the *fact* of construct invalidity. We believe that methodological hypotheses are less likely to be true than substantive hypotheses because they are usually based on a much weaker database.

If meta-analysis shows that the studies evaluated as methodologically superior yield different results from the studies rated methodologically poorer, then final conclusions can be based on the superior studies. If there is no difference in results, this finding disconfirms the methodological hypotheses. In such cases, all studies should be retained and included in the final meta-analysis to provide the largest possible database.

The question of construct validity can be complex. It is possible that measures with different names and that are intended to measure different constructs actually measure the same construct. Le et al. (2010) found that after the proper correction for measurement error, measures of job satisfaction and organizational commitment correlate .92, meaning that these two constructs are empirically redundant. In addition, the pattern of correlation of these two measures with other variables is identical to within-sampling error. Construct redundancy may be quite common in organization behavior and other areas of psychology. Because of this condition of construct redundancy, it may be possible and appropriate to combine in one meta-analysis measures that were originally intended to measure different constructs but have been shown to measure the same construct. In addition to Le et al. (2010), see also Le et al. (2009) on issues involved in construct redundancy and also the discussion later in this chapter on combining measures of different cognitive abilities in the same meta-analysis. Future studies of construct redundancy may reveal that many constructs believed on conceptual or theoretical grounds to be different are actually empirically redundant as measured.

Cooper (1998, pp. 81–84) pointed out another reason for caution in attempts to exclude methodologically weak studies. To make such decisions, evaluators must judge and rate each study on methodological quality. Cooper noted that research on interrater agreement for judgments of research quality shows that the average correlation between experienced evaluators is at best about .50, illustrating the subjectivity of assessments of methodological quality. Based on the Spearman-Brown formula, it would require use of six evaluators to yield a reliability of approximately .85 for ratings of methodological quality. Most meta-analyses will not be able to draw on the considerable time and effort of six experienced judges of methodological quality. Use of fewer judges would usually result in the erroneous elimination of a prohibitive number of acceptable studies.

The question of methodological weaknesses must be separated from the question of relevant and irrelevant studies. Relevant studies are those that focus on the relationship of interest. For example, if one is interested in the relationship between role conflict and employee turnover, studies that report only correlations between measures of role conflict and organizational identification should be excluded because they are irrelevant. (If enough such studies are encountered, one can, of course, conduct a separate meta-analysis of the relationship between role conflict and organizational identification.) Measures of different dependent variable constructs should ordinarily not be combined in the same meta-analysis (see Chapter 11), but if they are, separate meta-analyses should also be reported for each conceptually different dependent variable. But complexities may arise. As found by Le et al. (2010), it is possible that measures believed to assess conceptually different constructs are really assessing the same construct. However, such a conclusion requires an appropriate empirical foundation (Le et al., 2009). Glass and his associates do combine different dependent variable constructs, and they have been severely criticized on this account (see, e.g., Chapter 11 and Mansfield & Busse, 1977). While it is true that meta-analyses that "mix apples and oranges" are difficult to interpret, little harm is done as long as separate meta-analyses are presented later for each dependent variable construct. In general, meta-analyses that do not mix different *independent* variables are more likely to be informative. However, the question is not a simple one. For example, in our meta-analyses of the relationship between verbal ability and job performance, we excluded job performance correlations based on other abilities (e.g., quantitative ability measures). For our purposes, such correlations were irrelevant because different abilities represented different constructs. However, we later found that the mean and standard deviation of correlations for verbal ability were very similar to the mean and standard deviation for quantitative ability (see, e.g., Pearlman et al., 1980). We also found that the validity of both kinds of measures stemmed entirely from the fact that they were both measures of general mental ability (see, e.g., Hunter, 1986; Schmidt, 2002). Although we have not yet conducted such an analysis, these findings provide a rationale for a meta-analysis that includes both kinds of measures—a meta-analysis of the relationship between equally "g-loaded" tests and job performance. The point is that measures that assess different constructs from one theoretical perspective may assess the same construct from the perspective of another theory. Furthermore, the second theory may represent an advance in understanding. Thus, the question of how varied the independent and dependent variable measures included in a meta-analysis should be is a more complex and subtle one than it appears to be at first glance. The answer depends on the specific hypotheses, theories, and purposes of the investigator. Glass has stated that there is nothing objectionable about mixing apples and oranges if the focus of the research interest is fruit. This statement is consistent with our position. However, Glass goes beyond the theory-based rationale presented here in arguing that it may be appropriate to include in the same meta-analysis independent and dependent variable measures that appear to be different constructs. Specifically, he argues that such broad, mixed meta-analyses may be justified and useful in summarizing a research literature in broad strokes (see Chapter 11). However, most researchers—ourselves included—do not usually find such broad-brush research summaries as informative as more focused meta-analyses. At least initially, meta-analyses in a given research area should probably be narrow and focused enough to correspond to the major constructs recognized by researchers in that area. Then, as understanding develops, later meta-analyses may become broader in scope if that is shown to be theoretically appropriate.

Additional considerations in evaluating studies for meta-analysis can be found in Chapter 7 of Cook et al. (1992), Chapter 4 of Cooper (1998), in Valentine (2009), and in Wortman (1994).

Coding Studies in Meta-Analysis

The process of coding data from primary studies can often be complex, tedious, and time-consuming. Nevertheless, it is a critical component of meta-analysis, and it is essential that it be done appropriately and accurately. Wilson (2009) and Orwin and Vevea (2009) present detailed discussions of the many considerations, decisions, and subtasks that can be involved in coding information from primary studies. Chapter 4 of Cooper (1998, 2010) presents a shorter discussion of some issues in coding. The complexity of the needed coding depends on the hypotheses and purposes underlying the meta-analysis, making any general detailed discussion of coding issues difficult. If studies differ on many dimensions, the meta-analysis focuses on several different relationships, and there is reason to believe many study characteristics may affect study results, the coding task will usually be quite complex. On the other hand, coding can be relatively simple in research literatures in which studies are quite similar, the focus is on a single bivariate relationship, and there is reason to believe that there will be few, if any, moderators of this relationship. In such a case, few study characteristics need to be coded, greatly reducing the scope of the coding task. This distinction bears on the issue of coder agreement. Whetzel and McDaniel (1988) found that, for studies of the latter type, intercoder agreement and intercoder reliability were virtually perfect. The conclusion of their study was that for such research literatures, there was no need to report intercoder agreement or reliability. Even in more complex coding tasks, the general finding has been that coder agreement and reliability have typically been quite good (Cooper, 1998, pp. 95–97). However, these findings apply to the coding of more objective aspects of studies. As noted previously, subjective evaluations such as assessments of overall study methodological quality produce much lower agreement. However, one study (Miller, Lee, & Carlson, 1991) found that coders could reliably make inferential judgments about psychological mediators in studies based on reading the methods sections of studies and that these judgments revealed important moderator variables in the meta-analyses.

As discussed in Chapters 3 and 4, the initial application of the methods presented in this book in the 1970s and 1980s was to the area of personnel selection, specifically, to the estimation of the validity of selection methods such as ability tests, structured interviews, and personality tests. The coding schemes needed in research of this sort are usually closer to the simple end of the continuum than has been the case for many subsequent applications of these methods to other research literatures (see Chapter 1). However, even these coding schemes can be somewhat complex. To illustrate this, the Appendix to this chapter presents the coding scheme used by the U.S. Office of Personnel Management for validity generalization meta-analyses, along with the instructions and decision rules for the coding task. Despite the apparent complexity of the instructions, this coding scheme is far simpler than many used in meta-analyses in organizational behavior and other areas today. There is no such thing as the perfect illustrative coding scheme, because each coding scheme must be tailor-made to the purposes of the particular meta-analysis. However, this coding scheme nevertheless provides some general guidance for approaching the task of constructing a coding scheme.

Reporting the Results of a Meta-Analysis: Standards and Practices

A widely held precept in all the sciences is that reports of research ought to include enough information about the study that the reader can critically examine the evidence and, if desired, replicate the study. At a minimum, the report ought to describe the research design, sampling, measurement, analyses, and findings. Where unusual procedures have been used, it is expected that they will be described in some detail. The

American Psychological Association (2008) has published standards for the reporting of research in general, and this document includes a section on standards for reporting of meta-analyses. That section includes a detailed checklist of information that should be reported (Table 4 in that document). Clarke (2009) and Borman and Grigg (2009) provide detailed suggestions for the proper and effective structuring of meta-analysis reports. We recommend these sources to readers seeking guidance on what to report in their meta-analyses.

There has been some research evaluating the quality of meta-analysis reports in the literature. Aytug et al. (2012) examined 198 meta-analyses published between 1995 and 2008 in 11 top journals in organizational behavior and industrial-organizational psychology and evaluated them on 54 items of reporting. They found that, on average, the meta-analyses reported only 53% of the information needed to replicate the meta-analysis or assess its validity. They found a trend toward improvement, with the more recent meta-analyses reporting more of the needed information. Dieckmann et al. (2009) conducted a similar analysis but with a broader scope. They selected a random sample of 100 meta-analyses from all areas of psychology and related fields that were published between 1994 and 2004. They too found a wide variation in the quality of the meta-analysis reports (and, indeed, in the quality of the meta-analyses themselves). Like Aytug et al., they found some indication that reporting practices were improving over time. A third study, Geyskens et al. (2009), was focused on meta-analyses published between 1980 and 2007 in 14 management journals (none of which were psychology journals). Like Aytug et al. and Dieckmann et al., they found that published meta-analyses generally fell short of desirable reporting practices. For example, they found that only 49% of the meta-analyses corrected for statistical artifacts. (Interestingly, of those that did, 56% used the artifact distribution methods presented in Chapter 4.) They provided a breakout of the percentage of meta-analyses that corrected for measurement error, range restriction, and dichotomization. Like the American Psychological Association (2008) standards discussed earlier, they provide a checklist of items of information that should be reported in every meta-analysis (their Table 5).

The Geyskens et al. (2009) study went further and created demonstrations of the difference in meta-analysis results due to practices used in the data analysis. They reanalyzed the data from four earlier meta-analyses, and for each of these data sets, they conducted multiple meta-analyses with each one varying in the quality of meta-analysis practices. The first was a "full-fledged" meta-analysis, conducted properly with all appropriate corrections, study weighting, and so on. Another was the same but omitted corrections for measurement error. Still another weighted the studies inappropriately (studies were equally weighted). The finding was that the quality of the data analysis practices usually had a substantial percentage effect on the mean estimated correlation. They concluded that, contrary to some contentions, meta-analysis reporting practices and standards do make an important difference in research conclusions. Another study (Aguinis, Pierce, Bosco, Dalton, & Dalton, 2011) reached the opposite conclusion, surprisingly concluding that the methodological choices and judgment calls made in published meta-analysis had little or no effect on final meta-analysis results. This study was based on 196 meta-analyses with 5,581 effect size estimates published in five top industrial-organizational and organizational journals between 1982 and 2009. Mean effect sizes were found not to differ across variations in 20 meta-analytic practices, including whether or not there were corrections for range restriction or measurement error. The explanation for these findings appears to be that the average effect sizes reported are taken across a wide variety of different kinds of research areas and relations that differed in typical effects sizes, whether corrected or not. Unlike the Geyskens et al. (2009) study, this study did not reanalyze the same data set repeatedly using better and worse meta-analysis practices. Instead, they pooled the 5,581 effect sizes across the meta-analyses and based their reported mean effect sizes on these. The different kinds of relations addressed in these effect sizes very likely had different effect sizes, both corrected and uncorrected. Hence, it not possible to draw conclusions from this study.

The direction and magnitude of each primary study finding or of the mean or variance of the set of findings is important information. Without it, the reader often cannot make a confident judgment about the validity of the conclusions of a meta-analysis unless he or she laboriously consults the original reports of each study. Many meta-analyses do not cover more than 40 or 50 studies. In such cases, it is often possible to provide substantial data on each study in a single-page table. The table should include the author and date of each study, the sample size, and the d value or correlation. This is, in fact, often done today in published meta-analyses. If sources of spurious variance do not account for most of the variation in the rs or d values, other characteristics of each study should be included in the table, such as the status characteristics of the subjects, subjects' average pretreatment scores on the criterion (when applicable), level and duration or scope conditions (such as region of the country, occupations of subjects, and the like), strength of the study design with respect to internal and external validity, and other study characteristics. If there is not enough space for this table in the publication, there should be a reference indicating where it can be obtained. Today supplementary information that cannot be included in a published article due to space constraints can be (and increasingly is) posted online, where it can easily be accessed by readers.

In addition to information on the individual studies included in a meta-analysis, certain quantitative information on the meta-analysis results should be provided in tabular form. This required quantitative information differs somewhat depending on whether effect sizes are corrected individually (Chapters 3 and 7) or artifact distribution methods are used (Chapters 4

Table 12.1 Quantitative results that should be reported in a meta-analysis

Reporting Meta-Analytic Results When Individual-Correction Methods Are Used (Chapter 3)

Variable	k	N	$\bar{r}$	SD_r	$\hat{\bar{\rho}}$	SD_ρ	CV_{LL}	CV_{UL}	CI_{LL}	CI_{UL}	%Var
X and Y Variables	6	1,063	−.53	.1531	−.63	.1476	[−.82	−.43]	[−.76	−.50]	15%

Note: k = number of independent samples; N = total sample size; $\bar{r}$ = sample size weighted mean observed correlation; SD_r = sample size weighted standard deviation of observed correlations (the sample size weighted standard deviation of corrected correlations prior to correction for sampling error should also be reported, either in this table or in the text.); $\hat{\bar{\rho}}$ = mean true score correlation (corrected for unreliability in both variables); SD_ρ = true score standard deviation; CV_{LL} and CV_{UL} = lower and upper bounds, respectively, of the 80% credibility interval; CI_{LL} and CI_{UL} = lower and upper bounds, respectively, of the 95% confidence interval around the mean true score correlation; %Var = percentage of variance attributable to statistical artifacts.

Reporting Meta-Analytic Results When Artifact Distribution Methods Are Used (Chapter 4)

Variable	k	N	$\bar{r}$	SD_r	SD_{pre}	SD_{res}	$\hat{\bar{\rho}}$	SD_ρ	CV_{LL}	CV_{UL}	CI_{LL}	CI_{UL}	%Var
X and Y Variables	12	2,337	.29	.1253	.0840	.0931	.33	.1278	[.16	.50]	[.25	.42]	25%

Note: k = number of independent samples; N = total sample size; $\bar{r}$ = sample size weighted mean observed correlation; SD_r = sample size weighted standard deviation of observed correlations; SD_{pre} = standard deviation of observed correlations predicted from all artifacts; SD_{res} = standard deviation of observed correlations after removal of variance due to all artifacts ; $\hat{\bar{\rho}}$ = mean true score correlation (corrected for unreliability in both variables); SD_ρ = true score standard deviation; CV_{LL} and CV_{UL} = lower and upper bounds, respectively, of the 80% credibility interval; CI_{LL} and CI_{UL} = lower and upper bounds, respectively, of the 95% confidence interval around the mean true score correlation; %Var = percentage of variance attributable to statistical artifacts.

and 7). Using the correlation as the illustrative statistic, the required information is shown in Table 12.1. Analogous results should be reported for *d* values. (The actual numbers presented in Table 12.1 are for illustrative purposes only.) The notes to Table 12.1 provide definitions of each of the symbols given in the table headings. These are the definitions given throughout this book. This is an area in which improvements in reporting practices are needed, because many meta-analyses omit some of these important quantitative results. They are all needed for the reader to have a full understanding of the meaning of the meta-analysis. In addition, they are needed for subsequent second-order meta-analyses (as discussed in Chapter 9). To ensure accuracy in future second-order meta-analyses, all *SD* estimates should be reported to four decimal places; variance estimates should be reported to five decimal places. We believe that all the information illustrated in Table 12.1 should be reported in published articles (and in technical reports), but if space limitations imposed by the journal or journal editor necessitate omitting some of these items of information, they should at least be posted online so as to be easily accessible by readers.

Additional guidance and issues to consider in preparing the final report of a meta-analysis are presented in the following publications: the APA research reporting standards (American Psychological Association, 2008), Aytug et al. (2012), Clarke (2009), Cooper (1998; 2010, chap. 6), Geyskens et al. (2009), Halvorsen (1994), and Light, Singer, and Willett (1994).

Information Needed in Reports of Primary Studies

The conduct of a meta-analysis requires certain kinds of data from each primary study that is to be included in the cumulation. Unfortunately, some of those data are usually missing from at least some of the studies being reviewed. This forces the reviewer to track down authors and try to secure the data from them and, when this fails, to attempt to estimate the data using statistical approximations of the sort recommended by Glass et al. (1981). Often, the missing data would lengthen the report of the study by only one fourth to one half a page, and in all cases, these data would provide the readers important information about the study as well as provide the information needed for a valid meta-analysis. Large correlation matrices may be awkward to include in some reports, but these primary data can often be reported in appendixes or made available online. At the very least, they should be preserved for later analysis and referenced in the report.

CORRELATIONAL STUDIES

Consider correlation studies. If reported study findings are to be usable in cumulative studies, then the mean, standard deviation, and reliability of each variable should be published. The mean is necessary for the cumulation of norms, for the cumulation of regression lines (or for the assessment of possible nonlinearity over extreme ranges), or for the identification of very special populations. The standard deviation is necessary for the same reasons and for an additional one. If the relationship between two variables is linear, then there is little variation in the correlation produced by variation in the mean from study to study. However, this is quite different for the standard deviation. Differences in variability from study to study can have dramatic effects on intercorrelations between variables. If a study is being done in a homogeneous population in which the standard deviation is only half the size of the standard deviation in other studies, then, in that population, the correlations for that variable will be much smaller than the correlations observed in other populations. Similarly, if the variance is inflated by observing only high and low extreme groups on a given variable, then correlations for that study will be larger than those in populations with the middle range included. This is the problem of range restriction and range enhancement discussed in detail in Chapters 3 to 5. Estimates of reliability of the measures used are needed for two reasons. First, variations in standard deviation produce differences in reliability. Second, and more important, the variable used in the study may not be identical to that used in published norm studies. For example, a study might include a measure of "authoritarianism," but that scale might consist of a subset of eight items chosen by the investigator; the reliability of this subscale may be quite different from the reliability of the complete scale published in norm studies. In the case of new scales, reliabilities may not have been established on large norm populations; in such cases, the reliabilities can be established by cumulating reliability estimates across studies. As noted in Chapter 4, such meta-analyses of reliability coefficients have been reported in the literature and can serve as a source of reliability information for meta-analyses (Vacha-Haase & Thompson, 2011). Some of these reliability estimates, however, may have to be adjusted for *SD* differences using the equations presented in Chapters 3 and 4.

It is imperative that the entire matrix of zero-order correlations between all variables be published (the means, standard deviations, and reliabilities can be easily appended as extra rows or columns of this matrix). Each entry in this table may be used in entirely unrelated meta-analyses. Correlations that are not statistically significant should still be included; one cannot average a "—" or a "*ns*" or whatever. If only significant correlations are printed, then cumulation is necessarily biased. This is even more the case for correlations that are not only excluded from the table but are not even mentioned because they are not statistically significant.

EXPERIMENTAL STUDIES

What about experimental studies in which analysis of variance is used instead of correlation? In the independent groups design, the F value that is conventionally computed is an exact transformation of the point biserial correlation, as explained in Chapter 7. The significance test on the point biserial correlation is exactly equivalent to the F test. In a 2-by-2-by-2-by . . . design, every effect in the analysis of variance is the comparison of two means and could thus be represented by a point biserial correlation. In fact, the square of that point biserial correlation is the "eta square," or percentage of variance accounted for by that effect. In designs with more than two categories for a facet, the categories are frequently ordered (indeed, frequently quantitative). In such cases, there is rarely any important effect beyond the linear trend. In such cases, the square root of eta can be used as the correlation between the corresponding variables, after assignment of the appropriate positive or negative sign to eta. Thus, everything stated previously, including considerations of restrictions in range and reliability, applies to experimental as well as correlational studies.

STUDIES USING MULTIPLE REGRESSION

A multiple regression analysis of a primary study is based on the full zero-order correlation (or covariance) matrix for the set of predictor variables and the criterion variable. Similarly, a cumulation of multiple regression analyses must be based on a cumulative zero-order correlation matrix (as demonstrated in Chapter 5). However, many reports of multiple regression fail to report the full correlation matrix, often omitting the zero-order correlations among the predictors and sometimes even the zero-order correlations between each predictor and the criterion. Reporting practices are sometimes even worse. Some studies report only the multiple regression weights for the predictors. (These bad reporting practices are particularly common in the areas of labor and industrial relations, labor economics, and other areas of economics.) However, cumulation leading to optimal estimates of multiple regression weights requires cumulation of the predictor intercorrelations as well as of the predictor-dependent variable correlations. That is, the formula for each multiple regression weight uses all the correlations between the predictors, and hence, they must be cumulatively estimated.

The practice of ignoring the predictor intercorrelations is extremely frustrating even if large samples are used. Given the predictor intercorrelations, path analysis can be applied to the primary study data to test hypotheses about direct and indirect causes. If the predictor intercorrelations are not given, one cannot distinguish between a predictor that makes no contribution and a predictor that makes a strong but indirect contribution. In short, one cannot do the desired path analysis unless the predictor intercorrelations are given as well as the predictor-criterion correlations.

Finally, it should be noted that, as discussed in Chapter 5, regression weights are typically not suitable for cumulation. Suppose Y is to be predicted from $X_1, X_2, \ldots, X_m$. The beta weight for X_1 depends not only on the variables X_1 and Y but on all the other variables $X_2, X_3, \ldots, X_m$ contained in the same regression equation. That is, beta weights are relative to the set of predictors considered and will replicate across studies only if the exact set of predictors is considered in each. If any predictor is added or subtracted from one study to the next, then the beta weights for all variables may change. Although it may be worthwhile to calculate beta weights within a study, it is crucial for cumulation purposes that the zero-order correlations be included in the published study. *After* cumulation of zero-order correlations, a multiple regression can be run using a set of predictors that may never have occurred together in any one study (see J. M. Collins et al., 2003, for an example of this).

For example, suppose we wanted to predict job performance from three abilities, *a*, *b*, and *c*. To cumulate beta weights, we would have to find multiple studies that computed beta weights for the *a*, *b*, and *c* combination and included no other predictors. There may be few such studies. On the other hand, cumulation from zero-order correlations greatly expands the set of studies that can contribute estimates of one or more of the needed correlations. In fact, any predictive study containing any combination of two of these variables (*a* and *b*, *a* and *c*, or *b* and *c*) would contain a correlation of interest. In order for r_{ab} to be estimated, there must be at least one study with both *a* and *b*; estimation of r_{ac} requires at least one study with both *a* and *c*; and estimation of r_{bc} requires at least one study with both *b* and *c*. However, there need be no study in which all three predictors occur together. See Chapters 1 and 5 for a more complete discussion of this process.

STUDIES USING FACTOR ANALYSIS

Factor analyses are often published with the zero-order correlation matrix omitted, presumably to conserve journal space. However, zero-order correlations can be meta-analyzed across studies while factor loadings cannot be. First, the factors that appear in a given study are not determined by the single variables that appear but by the sets or clusters of variables that occur. For example, suppose a study contains one good measure of motivation and 10 cognitive ability measures. Then it is likely that the communality of the motivation variable will be 0, and a motivation factor will not appear in the factor analysis. Factors are defined by *redundant* measurement; no factor will appear unless it is measured by at least two redundant indicators (and preferably by three or more). Second, the factors in an exploratory factor analysis (such as principal axis factors followed by VARIMAX rotation) are not defined independently of one another. For example, suppose that in the initial output, one cluster of variables defines G_1 and another cluster defines G_2, and the correlation between G_1 and G_2 is *r*. Then, if factor scores are standardized, the VARIMAX factors will be defined by

$$F_1 = G_1 - \alpha G_2$$
$$F_2 = G_2 - \alpha G_1$$

where

$$\alpha = \frac{1-\sqrt{1-r^2}}{r}$$

Thus, each orthogonal factor is defined as a discrepancy variable between natural clusters, and the loading of an indicator of G_1 on factor F_1 will depend not only on the other indicators of G_1 in its own set but also on what other factors appear in the same study (Hunter & Gerbing, 1982). Cluster analysis results and confirmatory factor analysis results present a different picture. If a cluster analysis or confirmatory factor analysis model fits the data (Hunter, 1980; Hunter & Gerbing, 1982), then the factor loading of an indicator on its own factor is the square root of its reliability and is independent of the rest of the variables and is thus subject to cumulation. For this reason, confirmatory factor analysis and cluster analysis are preferable to exploratory factor analysis.

STUDIES USING CANONICAL CORRELATION

Canonical correlation begins with a set of predictor variables and a set of dependent measures and is thus conceptually a situation suitable for multiple regression. In canonical correlation, however, two *new* variables are formed: a weighted combination of the predictor variables and a weighted combination of the dependent measures. These combinations are formed in such a way as to maximize the correlation between the two weighted composites.

Canonical correlations cannot be cumulated across studies. Neither can the canonical weights. In multiple regression, each beta weight depends on the dependent variable and on the specific set of predictors. Thus, it generalizes only to other studies in which exactly the same set of predictors is used (which is rare indeed). However, each canonical regression weight depends not only on the exact set of predictors in the study but on the exact set of dependent measures as well. Thus, it will be very rare that the results of canonical regression (i.e., the canonical correlations) would be comparable across studies and so could be cumulated in a meta-analysis. In addition, even if multiple canonical correlation primary studies using the same independent and dependent variable sets existed and could be subjected to meta-analysis, interpretation of the results would be conceptually difficult or impossible. That is, there would be no way to know what the two constructs being related were, because each variable is a weighted combination of different constructs (and with each set of weights being chosen solely to maximize the correlation with the other composite). For this same reason, canonical correlations are theoretically meaningless in primary studies as well as in a meta-analysis. On the other hand, the zero-order correlation matrices from such studies can be cumulated across studies and the results can be interpreted as revealing relationships between known theoretical constructs.

STUDIES USING MULTIVARIATE ANALYSIS OF VARIANCE (MANOVA)

Statistically, MANOVA is a canonical regression, with the treatment contrast variables as "independent" variables and with measured variables as "dependent" measures. Consequently, the data needed for cumulation across studies are the set of zero-order correlations between contrasts, between contrasts and other measured variables, and between other measured variables. These data should be reported but rarely are. Hence, data from studies using MANOVA can rarely be meta-analyzed.

General Comments on Reporting in Primary Studies

For multiple regression, factor analysis, and canonical correlation analyses, the zero-order correlation matrices are essential for cumulation across studies. Once these data are secured, the reviewer is able to analyze the cumulative correlation matrix using any appropriate statistical procedure. For example, data gathered for multiple regression can be used in path analysis.

If journals required the publication of confidence intervals in place of levels of statistical significance, three benefits would ensue. First, researchers would be alerted to how much uncertainty there is in estimates derived from most individual social science studies. The common small-sample studies will generally have wide confidence intervals. Second, the results across studies would correctly appear to be in greater agreement than they usually do when focusing on the proportions of studies that are statistically significant (Schmidt, 1996). For instance, if there are five studies, each with a sample size of 50 and with correlations of .05, .13, .24, .33, and .34, only two of the five are statistically significant at the .05 level, but the 95% confidence intervals of all five correlations would overlap substantially. Finally, in the case of two-sample tests, reports of the confidence interval and sample sizes are all that is needed for computing standardized effect scores.

The correlations between measures should be corrected for attenuation due to error of measurement. It is clear from measurement theory and methods that the reduction in correlations due to the use of imperfect measurement is purely a matter of artifact. Reliability of measurement is a matter of feasibility and practicality independent of the theoretical and psychological meaning of the variables measured. Therefore, it is correlations between perfectly measured variables that are of theoretical importance (Schmidt, Le,

& Oh, 2013); that is, it is the corrected correlations that should be used in multiple regression or path analysis when theories are being tested (Cook et al., 1992, chap. 7; MacMahon et al., 1990). As noted earlier (see Chapter 3), correction increases the sampling error in the estimated correlation, and therefore, the formulas for the correction of variance due to sampling error in uncorrected correlation coefficients are not appropriate for correlations corrected for attenuation. Instead, the formulas given in Chapter 3 for corrected correlations should be used to compute the sampling error in corrected correlations. Most commercial regression and path analysis programs do not incorporate these formulas and so provide erroneous standard errors, confidence intervals, and significance tests when used with corrected correlations. The PACKAGE programs of Hunter (1995) do incorporate these formulas and so do provide correct results.

Appendix

Item-by-Item Instructions for Validity Coding Sheet

1. STUDY ID

   The study ID is the ID number assigned to a research report. This ID number is also referenced in the bibliography data file. If the study has not been entered into the bibliography data file, it needs to be entered. This field cannot be blank. Use leading zeros as needed.

2. SAMPLE WITHIN STUDY

   The "SAMPLE WITHIN STUDY" number assigns a number to each sample within the research report. Samples are numbered consecutively starting with number 1. If validity data are available for a sample and for one or more racial or gender subgroups of the sample, a separate coding sheet should be completed for the total sample and for each racial or gender subgroup that reports a validity coefficient. The assigned number for the "SAMPLE WITHIN STUDY" for a racial/gender subgroup is the *same* as the number assigned to the total sample. This field cannot be blank. This allows the data analyst to know which race or gender subsample is a subset of which total sample.

   EXAMPLE: The validity for a clerical test is given for two samples of stenographers. For the first sample, validity coefficients are available for the total sample and separately by gender. For the second sample, only the validity coefficient for the total sample is reported. A value of 1 is assigned as the SAMPLE WITHIN STUDY number for the three coefficients for the first sample. A value of 2 is assigned for the coefficient from the second sample.

   EXAMPLE: A validity study has two criteria for one sample. It is judged that it is best to consider the two criteria as separate. Two coding sheets are completed, one for each criterion. The SAMPLE WITHIN STUDY code for each coding sheet is 1.

   EXAMPLE: A validity study has two predictors for one sample. It is judged that it is best to consider the two predictors as separate. Two coding sheets are completed, one for each predictor. The SAMPLE WITHIN STUDY code for each coding sheet is 1.

3. RACE SUBGROUP?

   If a validity coefficient for a sample is given for the total sample, and given separately for racial subgroups, leave this field blank on the coding sheet for the total sample and enter Y (Y for "Yes, this is a race subsample.") on the coding sheets for the racial subsamples. If a validity coefficient is only available for a racial subgroup and not for a total sample, leave this field blank. If the total sample is composed of individuals who all have the same race, leave this field blank.

4. SEX SUBGROUP?

   If a validity coefficient for a sample is given for the total sample, and given separately for gender subgroups, leave this field blank on the coding sheet for the total sample and enter Y (Y for "Yes, this is a gender subsample.") on the coding sheets for the gender subsamples. If a validity coefficient is only available for a gender subgroup and not for a total sample, leave this field blank. If the total sample is composed of individuals who all have the same gender, leave this field blank.

5. RACE

   Code the race of the sample or subsample for which the sheet is completed. If unknown, leave blank.

6. SEX

   Code the sex of the sample or subsample for which the sheet is completed. If unknown, leave blank.

7. SAMPLE SIZE

   Enter the sample size of the sample or subsample for which the sheet is completed. This is the actual sample size and not an adjusted sample size. This field cannot be blank. If the coefficient is a mean or a composite of several coefficients, use the mean of the sample sizes.

   EXAMPLE: A study contains two criteria for one sample. The first criterion is a performance rating on quantity of work, and the second criterion is a performance rating on quality of work. A decision was made to consider the two performance ratings as subscales of one criterion. Thus, the reported r is the correlation between one predictor and a composite of the two criteria. The sample size for the first performance rating is 100. Data on only 90 of these 100 people were available for the second performance rating. An average (e.g., 95) of these two sample sizes was coded.

8. OCCUPATIONAL CODE

Enter the occupational code for the sample. Use the fourth edition of the DOT. This field cannot be blank.

9. VALIDITY COEFFICIENT (UNCORRECTED)

Enter the uncorrected validity coefficient. See "Sign Reversal" under "Other Notes." This field cannot be blank.

EXAMPLE: A coefficient of .50 is coded *0. 5 0.*

A coefficient of −.50 is coded *− . 5 0.*

10. VALIDITY COEFFICIENT (CORRECTED FOR RANGE RESTRICTION)

Code this coefficient only if it is reported in the study. Do not compute this coefficient. Leave blank if missing.

11. VALIDITY COEFFICIENT (CORRECTED FOR CRITERION UNRELIABILITY)

Code this coefficient only if it is reported in the study. Do not compute this coefficient. Leave blank if missing.

12. VALIDITY COEFFICIENT (CORRECTED FOR CRITERION UNRELIABILITY AND RANGE RESTRICTION)

Code this coefficient only if it is reported in the study. Do not compute this coefficient. Leave blank if missing.

13. TYPE OF COEFFICIENT

Enter the type of coefficient. If the coefficient is a composite or a mean coefficient, enter the type of coefficient used to compute it. If the type of correlation coefficient is not specified, the coefficient is probably a Pearson correlation coefficient. Note that a rank coefficient is a Rho. This field cannot be blank.

EXAMPLE: The validity coefficient is a Pearson correlation coefficient. Code 03.

EXAMPLE: The validity coefficient is the mean of four Pearson correlation coefficients. Code 03.

14. SAMPLE SIZE FOR MEAN *r*

If the reported validity coefficient is a *mean* of several coefficients, code the sum of the sample sizes for the several coefficients. Leave this field blank unless the validity coefficient coded in Item 10 is a mean of two or more coefficients. If the validity coefficient is a composite, leave this field blank.

EXAMPLE: The validity coefficient reported in Item 10 is a mean of two coefficients. While data on 200 individuals were available for one of the coefficients, data on only 199 of the 200 individuals were available for the second coefficient. The sample size for the mean r is reported as 399.

15. STUDY TYPE

There are two types of predictive studies: (1) predictive studies where the predictor is not used in the selection of the employees and (2) predictive studies where the predictor is used in the selection of employees. Code 1 for the first case and 2 for the second case. Code 3 if the study is predictive, but one does not know if the predictor was used in the selection of employees. Code 4 for a concurrent study.

16. TIME IN MONTHS BETWEEN COLLECTION OF PREDICTOR AND CRITERION DATA

If the study is predictive, enter the number of months between the collection of predictor and criterion data. If the time varies across the subjects in a sample, report the mean or median time. Leave blank if missing.

17. PREDICTOR CODE

Enter the four-digit predictor code.

18. PREDICTOR RELIABILITY COEFFICIENT—EMPLOYEE GROUP

If the predictor reliability computed on the employee (restricted) group is given, code it here.

EXAMPLE: A reliability of .95 is coded 9 5.

If the predictor is the sum of the mean of two or more measures, you may need to adjust the reliability with the Spearman-Brown formula.

EXAMPLE: The predictor is an interview. The predictor score is the sum of ratings by two independent raters. The interrater reliability coefficient is .80. This coefficient is the reliability of scores for one rater. Because the predictor is the sum of two independent raters, the Spearman-Brown formula is used to boost the reliability to reflect this fact. The coded reliability is .89.

19. PREDICTOR MEAN—EMPLOYEE GROUP

Code the predictor mean for the employee (restricted) group. Leave blank if not given.

20. PREDICTOR STANDARD DEVIATION—EMPLOYEE GROUP

Code the predictor standard deviation for the employee (restricted) group. Leave blank if missing.

21. TYPE OF PREDICTOR RELIABILITY—EMPLOYEE GROUP

Code the type of reliability. Note that coefficient alpha is an internal consistency reliability.

22. TIME INTERVAL BETWEEN TESTING FOR PREDICTOR RELIABILITY ESTIMATE (in weeks)—EMPLOYEE GROUP

For reliabilities using two ratings (e.g., rate-rerate or interrater), code the number of weeks between the two ratings.

23. PREDICTOR RELIABILITY COEFFICIENT—APPLICANT GROUP

If the predictor reliability computed on the applicant (unrestricted) group is given, code it here.

EXAMPLE: A reliability of 95 is coded 9 5.

If the predictor is the sum or the mean of two or more measures, you may need to adjust the reliability with the Spearman-Brown formula.

EXAMPLE: The predictor is an interview. The predictor score is the sum of two independent ratings. The interrater reliability coefficient is .80. This coefficient is the reliability of scores for one rater. Because the predictor is the sum of ratings by two independent raters, the Spearman-Brown formula is used to boost the reliability to reflect this fact. The coded reliability is .89.

24. PREDICTOR MEAN—APPLICANT GROUP

Code the predictor mean for the applicant (unrestricted) group. Leave blank if not given.

25. PREDICTOR STANDARD DEVIATION—APPLICANT GROUP

Code the predictor standard deviation for the applicant (unrestricted) group. Leave blank if missing.

26. TYPE OF PREDICTOR RELIABILITY—APPLICANT GROUP

Code the type of reliability. Note that the coefficient alpha is an internal consistency reliability.

27. TIME INTERVAL BETWEEN TESTING FOR PREDICTOR RELIABILITY ESTIMATE (in weeks)—APPLICANT GROUP

For reliabilities using two ratings (e.g., rate-rerate or interrater), code the number of weeks between the two ratings.

28. RATIO RESTRICTED/UNRESTRICTED *SD*

    If the ratio of the restricted to unrestricted standard deviation of the predictor is given, code it. Do not compute this statistic. If not given, leave it blank.

29. CRITERION CONTENT

    Code the type of criterion content. If the criterion is wages, promotion/demotion, or commendations/reprimands, code it as such; do not code it as job performance. Note: Grade level is not a criterion unless it reflects promotion/demotion decisions.

30. CRITERION MEASUREMENT METHOD

    Code the measurement method used to collect the criterion data. Typically, this item is relevant only when the criterion content is job performance or training performance. If this item is not relevant to the criterion, leave it blank.

    EXAMPLE: If the criterion content is wages, none of the measurement categories is relevant. This item is left blank.

    Production data include counts of quantity (e.g., widgets produced), error counts, and amount of time to process a given quantity of product (time to complete 10 widgets).

31. CRITERION: ADMINISTRATIVE VS. RESEARCH

    If a criterion is collected solely for a validity study, it should be coded as a "research" criterion. If the criterion is collected as part of a routine administrative procedure, code it as an "administrative" procedure.

    EXAMPLE: Supervisors rate each of their employees as part of a concurrent validity study. This criterion is coded as "research."

    EXAMPLE: Performance evaluations that are routinely completed every year are used as criteria in a validity study. Code this criterion as "administrative."

    EXAMPLE: A tenure or wage criterion is always administrative.

32. CRITERION RELIABILITY

    Code the criterion reliability if it is given. If the criterion is missing, leave Items 33 to 35 blank. If the criterion is a composite, and the reliabilities of the components are given, one should compute the reliability of the composite. Note that this reliability may need to be boosted. See the examples for details.

EXAMPLE: A reliability of .95 is coded *9 5*.

EXAMPLE: The criterion is a performance appraisal. Only one rater's evaluation is used as the criterion. The reliability is an interrater reliability. This reliability is not boosted via the Spearman-Brown formula.

EXAMPLE: The criterion is a performance appraisal. The criterion is the sum of two raters' evaluations. The reliability is an interrater reliability. This reliability is boosted ($k = 2$) via the Spearman-Brown formula.

33. TYPE OF CRITERION RELIABILITY

Code the type of criterion reliability.

34. TOTAL NUMBER OF RATERS FOR RELIABILITY ESTIMATE (if ratings or rankings)

Code the number of raters who rated each subject.

EXAMPLE: If the criterion reliability applies to ratings by two supervisors (i.e., each ratee was rated by two raters), Item 34 is coded *0 0 2*.

EXAMPLE: The criterion reliability is the correlation between the same supervisor's ratings made 1 week apart. There is only one rater, so Item 34 is coded *0 0 1*.

35. TIME INTERVAL BETWEEN CRITERION RATINGS (in weeks)

If the criterion rating used two or more ratings (e.g., rate-rerate or interrater), code the time interval in weeks between the two ratings.

36. IDS OF OTHER STUDIES COVERING SAME DATA (not shown on coding sheet)

If the data in a particular study are reported in more than one report, code the other study IDs. This will prevent the data from being coded twice.

37. RACE AND GENDER PREDICTOR DATA

These items request means and standard deviations for racial and gender subgroups. Code these data here only if a validity for the subgroup is not reported. If subgroup data are reported, the subgroup information is placed on its own coding sheet and the mean and standard deviation data are coded in Items 19, 20, 24, and 25.

38. DOES THE STUDY REPORT INTERCORRELATIONS AMONG PREDICTORS?

    If the study reports intercorrelations between two or more predictors, code 1 (1 = *yes*). Then complete the intercorrelation coding sheet.

39. ADDITIONAL INFORMATION #1, #2, #3.

    This space is left for future information needs whose content is at present unanticipated.

At present, this space is only used when coding interviews. See the separate instruction sheets for additional information.

Decision Rules for Coding Validity Studies

Multiple Correlations in Each Study: Introduction

One goal of this coding scheme is to code one validity coefficient for each predictor/job combination using the entire study sample. In addition, when validity data are available, separate coding sheets should be completed for each racial or gender subgroup.

A problem arises when there are separate validity coefficients for multiple predictors or multiple criteria. A judgment is needed as to whether multiple predictors are truly separate predictors or are repeated measures of the same predictor. Likewise, when there are two or more criteria, one must decide if a separate coefficient is warranted for each criterion or if the several validity coefficients are best expressed as one coefficient. To assist in making these judgments, a set of decision rules is provided.

Refer to "Multiple Predictor Decision Rules" for guidelines and examples of multiple predictor problems. Refer to "Multiple Criterion Decision Rules" for guidelines and examples of multiple criterion problems. Once a decision has been made to combine coefficients, refer to "Combining Coefficients Decision Rules."

Multiple Predictor Decision Rules

General Rule: When in doubt, consider multiple predictors to be separate predictors and code each coefficient separately.

Examples of predictors to be viewed as subscales of the same predictors:

- A performance score and a time-to-completion score from an MT&E (miniature training and experience)
- Assessment center dimensions

Examples of predictors to be viewed as separate predictors:

- Predictors with the same item type (e.g., if the study involved two reading comprehension tests, two coefficients would be coded)
- Predictors measuring different construct types
- An interview conducted by one person and an interview conducted by a panel

Multiple Criterion Decision Rules

General Rule: When in doubt, combine the coefficients for different criteria in order to report one coefficient.

Note the criterion categories in Item 29. Do not combine across these categories. While wages, promotions, and commendations can be considered job performance measures, they probably have different reliability distributions than job performance ratings.

If multiple coefficients are reported for the same sample for the same criteria at two or more points in time, code the coefficients separately. If these data are reported for many points in time, use judgment.

EXAMPLE: Two validity coefficients are reported for the same sample. The two criteria are training ratings made at 3 months and 6 months into training. Complete two coding sheets. Note that the sheets will have the same SAMPLE WITHIN STUDY code and will have different values for TIME IN MONTHS BETWEEN COLLECTION OF PREDICTOR AND CRITERION DATA.

Examples of criteria to be viewed as subscales of the same criterion:

- Subscales of a performance appraisal form. If there is an overall performance rating that is the sum (or composite) of the subscales, use the overall performance rating. If the overall performance rating is a single rating, consider it a subscale and combine with the other subscale coefficients.

Examples of criteria to be viewed as separate criteria:

- A performance measure and a training measure
- A performance appraisal rating and a work simulation exercise

Combining Coefficients Decision Rules

Note that combining coefficients is acceptable only when it is appropriate to view multiple predictors as subscales of the same predictor or when it is appropriate to view multiple criteria as subscales of the same criterion. When separate validity coefficients are reported and a decision has been made to report only one coefficient, select the best choice available:

First choice: Use a composite correlation. Unless the author presents a meaningful reason for unequal weighting of components, the composite correlation should be based on equally weighted components. If two or more components are to be unequally weighted, and a composite is to receive very little weight, examine the component. It may be reasonable to exclude the component from the composite.

To compute a composite correlation, use the composite correlation program in the SPSS software or in the computer program described in the Appendix to this book. For small calculations, one might calculate the composite by hand (using the methods presented in Chapter 10).

Second choice: Shrink the multiple R. Use the formulas described in Cattin (1980).

Third choice: Use the one coefficient that best represents the correlation between the overall test performance and the overall job performance.

Fourth choice: Compute a mean validity.

Other Notes

Clerical Tests

Written examinations, labeled "clerical," are often composites of verbal, quantitative, and perceptual speed items. If so, code them as a combination ($V + Q + PS$). If not, determine what construct(s) the test is measuring and code them accordingly.

Right-Justify, Leading Zeros

Right-justify and use leading zeros for all codes that do not fill up the entire item field.

EXAMPLE: The value for Item 2, SAMPLE WITHIN STUDY, is 1. Code it as *0 0 1*.

Sign Reversal

One may need to reverse the sign of a correlation. A positive correlation should indicate that a high score on a measure is associated with better job performance.

EXAMPLE: The criterion is a count of errors. A correlation is reported as −.2, indicating that the higher the predictor score, the lower the number of errors. This coefficient is coded as +.2.

Who Is an Employee, and What Is a Job?

Coding sheets are to be completed for predictors of job or training performance for employees.

Examples of studies that should be coded:

- Subjects are interns in an agency
- Subjects are employees in an agency

Examples of studies that should not be coded:

- Subjects are students
- Subjects are psychiatric patients
- The criterion measure is job satisfaction

Instruction Sheet for Coding Intercorrelations among Predictors

Intercorrelations among predictors are being recorded for subsequent data analysis. These intercorrelations are needed to estimate the validity of a composite selection system.

1. PREDICTOR CODE—FIRST PREDICTOR

   Enter the predictor code for the first of two predictors.

2. RELIABILITY—FIRST PREDICTOR

   Enter the reliability of the first predictor.

3. PREDICTOR CODE—SECOND PREDICTOR

   Enter the predictor code for the second predictor.

4. RELIABILITY—SECOND PREDICTOR

   Enter the reliability for the second predictor.

5. OBSERVED CORRELATION

   Code the observed correlation between the two predictors.

6. CORRECTED CORRELATION

   If reported, code the corrected correlation between the two predictors. Do not compute this value; only code if it is reported.

7. SAMPLE SIZE

   Code the sample size for the correlation coefficient.

8. STUDY ID

   Code the study ID.

Availability Bias, Source Bias, and Publication Bias in Meta-Analysis

13

Q uestions and issues related to meta-analysis that are technical in nature were discussed in Chapter 5 for meta-analyses of correlations, in Chapter 8 for meta-analyses of *d* values, and in Chapter 9 for general meta-analysis issues. This chapter explores the general issue of availability bias in meta-analysis. One of the most frequent criticisms leveled against meta-analysis is the argument that the studies available for analysis will typically be a biased sample of all existing studies. This is often referred to as *publication bias*, defined as existing when published studies are a biased sample of all existing studies. However, publication bias is not necessarily the only source of bias. Even among unpublished studies, those that are retrievable may not be representative of all unpublished studies. So we favor the more general terms *availability bias* and *source bias*. However, for ease of exposition, we use all three of these terms interchangeably in this chapter. (Comparable terms used by others are *retrieval bias* and *selection bias*.) In the case of publication bias, it is often suspected that published studies will show results that are more often statistically significant and have larger effect sizes than unpublished studies (see, e.g., Begg & Mazumdar, 1994; Coursol & Wagner, 1986; Dickersin, 2005; McNemar, 1960). Thus, it is contended, effect size estimates from meta-analysis will be biased upward. This criticism applies equally well to the narrative review, the usual alternative to meta-analysis. The fact that the narrative review is not quantitative in no way mitigates the effects of any bias in the sample of studies. Thus, to the extent that source or availability bias is a problem, it is a completely general one and is not limited to meta-analysis.

In fact, it applies to even an informal assessment of the literature by a research user or practitioner. However, the key role now played by meta-analysis in all areas of science has created a focus on the effects of availability bias on meta-analytic results.

Smith (1980) presented a dramatic example of publication bias. This meta-analysis focused on the degree of sex bias against women clients on the part of both male and female psychotherapists and counselors. Smith found that the meta-analysis of all published studies showed a substantial average bias against women clients. She next conducted a meta-analysis of only unpublished dissertations and masters theses. This meta-analysis showed a substantial sex bias *against men* clients. When both published and unpublished studies were included in the meta-analysis, there was on average no bias against either sex. Most of the studies were conducted in the late 1960s and the 1970s, a time when it was fashionable to view women as victims and to focus on discrimination against women. As a result, there was strong publication bias favoring studies showing women as victims of therapist bias.

The detection of availability bias and adjustment for it can be a difficult and complex problem in meta-analysis (J. L. Peters, Sutton, Jones, & Abrams, 2010; Sutton, 2009). It is often difficult to determine whether such bias exists in a set of studies, and, if it is detected, some methods of adjusting for it are complex and not easy to use. In addition, some of the assumptions on which the methods are based may be questionable. The main problem is that the mechanisms or processes causing publication bias in any given literature are never known with certainty, and the accuracy of any particular method to address it depends on how closely the method's assumptions about this mechanism are to the truth (Sutton, 2009). As discussed later, one response to this problem is the emphasis on triangulation using multiple methods of addressing publication bias. The issue of publications bias is an important one, has generated a large literature, and will undoubtedly continue to receive attention. One sign of this fact is the recent publication of a book devoted entirely to this subject (Rothstein, Sutton, & Borenstein, 2005).

Effects of Source Bias: Type I Errors versus Inflation of Effect Sizes. If the null hypothesis is true, and there is no effect or relationship, publication bias can lead to a Type I error in meta-analysis—a conclusion that a relationship exists when it does not. However, as noted in Chapter 2 and elsewhere in this book, there is much evidence that the null hypothesis is rarely true in most areas of applied psychological research. For example, Lipsey and Wilson (1993) found that less than 1% of psychological interventions (2 out of 302) produced no effect. Richard et al. (2003) examined 322 meta-analyses in psychological research and found that only 8 of these (2.5%) produced a zero or near-zero mean effect size. Even allowing for the possibility of some Type I errors produced by publication bias in the meta-analyses these two studies reviewed, it would still appear that the null hypothesis is rarely true in social science literatures. Hence, the usual effect of publication bias would be to inflate the size of mean correlations and d values, rather than producing Type I errors. Hence, the conclusions of meta-analyses affected by publication or other availability bias would be qualitatively correct but quantitatively incorrect. However, it is typically important to have accurate estimates of the size of effects; it is rarely sufficient merely to know that an effect exists. Also, in some other research areas, it is probably not the case that the null hypothesis is rarely or never true. For example, in the lab experiments conducted in social psychology and related areas, the null may often be true, as discussed later in this chapter. It is possible in such areas for Type I errors to lead to the conclusion that an effect or relation exists when it does not.

There is evidence that availability bias may not exist in some literatures. Also, apparent differences in mean effect sizes by source (e.g., journals, books, and unpublished reports) may at least in part reflect the artifactual effects of differences in measurement error and other artifacts among sources. If so, then a meta-analysis that corrects for methodological weaknesses (such as measurement error) will correct for these differences. However, there is now substantial evidence that one form of source bias—publication bias—is a serious problem in some research literatures (e.g., see Dickersin, 2005). Methods are now available to help detect and control for these effects. None of these methods is perfect; all depend on assumptions about the mechanisms that produce publication bias that may or may not hold for any given data set. Some methods may yield incorrect conclusions when effect sizes are heterogeneous due to binary or bimodal moderators. As discussed later, a major deficiency of all currently available methods is inability to take into account study differences due to the biases created by measurement error and other distorting artifacts, a deficiency that often renders results questionable. Nevertheless, these methods can be useful in many cases, especially when multiple methods are used to triangulate and when sensitivity analyses for publication bias are carried out.

Some Literatures May Have Little or No Publication Bias

The publication bias hypothesis holds that unpublished studies have two important properties: (1) They have smaller effect sizes, and (2) they are less frequently available to be included in meta-analysis. If the first of these were not true, then even if the second were true, no bias would be introduced into meta-analysis results. The question of whether effect sizes are smaller in unpublished studies has been addressed empirically for some literatures.

Based on data presented in Glass et al. (1981), Rosenthal (1984, pp. 41–45) examined the effect sizes from 12 meta-analyses on different topics to determine whether mean effect sizes differed depending on their sources. Based on several hundred effect sizes, he found there was virtually no difference on the average between those published in journals and those from unpublished reports. The mean d value was .08 *larger* for the unpublished reports; the median d value was .05 larger for the published journal articles. Thus, the mean and median differences were in the opposite directions, and neither was statistically or practically significant. His overall conclusion was that the effect sizes from journal articles, unpublished reports, and books are "essentially indistinguishable from each other" (p. 44). On the other hand, Rosenthal did find that doctoral dissertations and masters theses yielded average d values that were 40% or more smaller than those from other sources. The problem created by this difference for theses and dissertations is mitigated by the fact that most dissertations are retrievable by meta-analysts through *Dissertation Abstracts*. Also, the lower average d values may in part be due to lower reliability of measurement in dissertations and theses (as explained below), and thus the difference in actual (corrected) d values may be smaller or even nonexistent.

In our meta-analytic research on the validity of employment tests (see Chapter 4), we examined that vast literature to determine whether correlations (validities) from published and unpublished studies differ. We found that they do not. Where it was possible to compare data sets like that of Pearlman et al. (1980) to other large data sets, the two data sets were found to be very similar. For example, the data of Pearlman et al. are very similar to the unpublished U.S. Department of Labor General Aptitude Test Battery (GATB) data set (525 studies) used by Hunter (1983b) in terms of validity means and variances (controlling for sample sizes) of observed validity coefficients. The same is true when the comparison is with large-sample military data sets. Military researchers routinely report all data, and the reported validity means and variances correspond closely to those from other data sets for the same criterion measures. Also, mean observed validities in our data sets are virtually identical to Ghiselli's (1966) reported medians, based on decades of careful gathering of both published and unpublished studies. Hedges (1992b) and Vevea, Clements, and Hedges (1993) applied their method of detecting availability bias to the large GATB data set and concluded that there was no evidence of availability bias. (The U.S. Department of Labor made this data set available to researchers. Availability bias would have existed if studies with weaker results had been withheld from the database.)

There are other indications of a lack of source bias in validity generalization data sets. For example, in the Pearlman et al. (1980) data set for measures of performance on the job, 349 of the 2,795 observed validities (12.5%) were 0 or negative; 737 (26.4%) were .10 or less. Furthermore, 56.1% of the 2,795 observed validities were nonsignificant at the .05 level. This figure is consistent with our estimate (Schmidt et al., 1976) that the average criterion-related validity study has statistical power no greater than .50. If selectivity or bias in reporting were operating, many of the nonsignificant validities would have been omitted, and the percentage significant would have been much higher than 43.9%.

Even more striking was the close comparability of the percentage of observed validities that were nonsignificant in the published studies reviewed by Lent et al. (1971a, 1971b)—57%—and the percentage non-significant in the mostly unpublished data set (68% of the sources were unpublished) of Pearlman et al. (1980)—56.1%. The Pearlman et al. data almost perfectly match the published data, an empirical indication that the unpublished data were not different from the published data. (Note: To provide comparability with Lent et al., 1971a, all figures for Pearlman et al., 1980, are for two-tailed tests. Using one-tailed tests, 49.1% of the Pearlman et al. proficiency coefficients are nonsignificant at the .05 level.)

We have examined hundreds of unpublished studies in the personnel selection research domain and have found no evidence that data were suppressed or omitted. Studies typically reported results for all tests tried out (even poorly constructed experimental instruments with well below-average reliabilities). In the typical scenario, the study is an explor-atory one designed to determine the optimal test battery. A multitest bat-tery is tried out on a variety of jobs and/or criteria. Full tables of validities against all criteria for all jobs were reported. We found no evidence that reporting the full set of results (usually including many low and nonsignif-icant validities) was viewed negatively by the sponsoring organization, or that it allowed or encouraged either their own psychologists or outside consultants to partially or fully suppress the results. Thus, this evidence also indicates that the results of unpublished studies are essentially identi-cal to those of published studies, indicating that there is no problem of availability bias in the literature on the validity of cognitive ability mea-sures. McDaniel, Rothstein, and Whetzel (2006) examined validities found in test manuals from four test vendors for publication bias using the trim-and-fill method (discussed later). Four of the five measures of cognitive abilities showed little or no evidence of publication bias. The other mea-sures examined were personality tests. Vendor A's personality tests showed essentially no evidence of publication bias. Vendor B's personality tests showed evidence of modest publication bias in two of its three personality scales. Vendor C's four personality test validities showed no evidence of publication bias.

However, the situation is potentially different in different research areas, and as we will see later, there is substantial evidence for publication bias in some research literatures, especially in small-sample experiments (lab experiments) in social psychology, general experimental psychology, management, marketing, and other areas, and in studies of all kinds in pharmacology, medicine, and the biomedical area in general.

Effects of Methodological Quality on Mean Effect Sizes From Different Sources

If published studies do have larger observed effect sizes than unpublished studies in a particular research literature, that fact need not indicate the existence of a publication bias in favor of large or significant effect sizes. Instead, the publication "bias" could be in favor of methodologically stronger research studies. Reviewers are often selected by journal editors based on their judged methodological expertise, and it is therefore to be expected that their evaluations will focus heavily on the methodological quality of the study. Many methodological weaknesses have the effect of artifactually reducing the expected study effect size. For example, unreliability of measurement reduces study effect sizes in both correlational and experimental studies. Thus, publication decisions based on methodological quality alone would be expected to produce, as a side effect, differences in mean observed study effect sizes between published and unpublished studies, given only that the null hypothesis of no relationship is false, the usual case today, at least in most areas of applied psychology research (see, e.g., Lipsey & Wilson, 1993). This would be expected to be the case even though the actual effect size is the same in published and unpublished studies.

Table 13.1 shows the approximate mean observed d values found by Smith and Glass (1977) for books (.80), journals (.70), dissertations (.60), and unpublished reports (.50) in studies on the effectiveness of psychotherapy. The difference between the largest and smallest $\bar{d}$ is $.80 - .50 = .30$, a considerable difference. Suppose, however, the mean reliabilities of the dependent variables were as indicated in the second column of numbers in Table 13.1. Then the true effect sizes (effect sizes corrected for the attenuating effects of measurement error, which is what is of interest scientifically) would be the same in all sources, and the apparent "source effect" on study outcomes would be shown to be entirely artifactual. The point is that the effects of methodological quality on study outcomes should be carefully examined before accepting the conclusion that real study findings differ by study source. This example also clearly illustrates the importance and necessity of making the appropriate corrections for measurement error in conducting meta-analyses.

A severe limitation of all of the methods of detecting, and adjusting for, source or publication bias discussed later in this chapter is the fact that none of these methods—either in concept or in applications to date—addresses the effects of measurement error or other study artifacts. As a result, they may indicate source or publication bias where none exists. This problem is discussed in more detail later.

Table 13.1 Hypothetical example of observed and true mean effect sizes for four sources of effect sizes.

Source	Observed Mean ($\overline{d}$)	Mean Dependent Variable Reliability ($\overline{R}_{yy}$)	True Mean d Value $\overline{\delta}$
Books	.8	.90	.84
Journals	.7	.70	.84
Dissertations	.6	.51	.84
Unpublished	.5	.35	.84

Multiple Hypotheses and Other Considerations in Availability Bias

An important consideration in understanding availability bias was pointed out by Cooper (1998, p. 74) and earlier by Schmidt, Hunter, et al. (1985). Most studies examine multiple hypotheses, and, hence, there are multiple significance tests. This reduces the possibility of publication bias based on statistical significance, because the probability that all such tests would be significant is quite low. Likewise, the probability that all such tests will be nonsignificant is also low. Hence, the vast majority of studies register in the minds of evaluators not as "significant" or "nonsignificant," but as "mixed" (Maxwell, 2004), making it difficult to create publication bias based on statistical significance. If only studies with all significant results were published, only a tiny fraction of studies would be published. Likewise, if only studies with no significant results were not published, only a tiny fraction of all studies would not be published. Most discussions of publication bias—and most methods for detecting and correcting for this bias—appear to ignore this consideration. In effect, they assume that there is only one significance test per study or at least that there is only one important significance test. However, not all studies in any discipline test multiple hypotheses. For example, studies in industrial-organizational psychology of the structured employment interview typically examine only one relation: the correlation of the structured interview with job performance. Oh, Postlethwaite, and Schmidt (2013) found evidence of publication bias in this literature.

It is possible that authors may be motivated to include in their report only the results for hypotheses that were statistically significant. If reviewers are appropriately familiar with the theory being tested, they will be able to see that tests of some hypotheses that flow from the theory have been omitted, and may therefore be able to ask for their inclusion. However, there is no certainty that this would always be done. There is evidence that in medical research, there is often publication bias within studies. That is, researchers report some but not all outcomes in randomized clinical trials (A. W. Chan & Altman, 2005; A. W. Chan, Hrobjartsson, Haahr, Gotzsche, & Altman, 2004). We are not aware of any such evidence for social science or psychological research, although Maxwell (2004) speculated that in psychological research, there may be some selective reporting within studies.

In the health sciences areas, particularly in medical and pharmaceutical research, studies frequently examine only one hypothesis—or at least only one hypothesis that is considered important. This is especially true for randomized controlled trials (RCTs) in medical and pharmaceutical research. In the typical RCT study, either a treatment is compared with a placebo or with no treatment, or two treatments are compared with each other. Hence, there is essentially only one hypothesis of interest—and therefore the protection against publication bias afforded by multiple hypotheses is absent. In fact, the evidence for publication bias is quite strong for RCTs: When the results of the single hypothesis are nonsignificant, they are far less likely to be submitted for publication and also less likely to be accepted if they are published (see, e.g., Dickersin, 2005; Dickersin, Min, & Meinert, 1992; Easterbrook, Berlin, Gopalan, & Matthews, 1991). This evidence is not based on surveys of attitudes or statements of what researchers and editors say they would do; it is based on the empirical history of actual RCT studies. While this suggests that publication bias can be severe in literatures in which studies test only one hypothesis, literatures in psychology and the social sciences often consist of studies with multiple hypotheses, and most or all the hypotheses are considered important.

A related consideration is that many meta-analyses focus on questions that were not central to the primary studies from which data are taken. For example, sex differences (in traits, abilities, attitudes, etc.) are rarely the central focus of a study; instead, they tend to be reported on an incidental basis, as supplementary analysis. Hence, these results tend not to be subject to publication bias because they are close to irrelevant to the central hypotheses of the research study (Cooper, 1998, p. 74). As noted later, one index of publication bias is the correlation between sample size (an index of study precision) and study effect sizes. If there is publication bias, the correlation should be negative, because smaller studies will have larger effect sizes (due to the fact that most small-N studies with smaller effect sizes did not reach statistical significance and so were not published). Schmidt, Oh, and Hayes (2009) examined five meta-analysis publications, each reporting 13 to 14 separate independent meta-analyses. Within each publication, they computed the correlation between sample size and effect size. They found that the average of these five correlations across the five meta-analyses of sex differences in cognitive abilities was mean $r = 0$, indicating an *overall* absence of publication bias. In addition, the variability of these *r*s across the meta-analyses was explained entirely by sampling error, indicating the absence of publication bias *in any of the individual* meta-analysis. The focus of these five meta-analyses was on sex differences in mental abilities, but in the studies that went into these meta-analyses, such differences were not a focus and were of an incidental nature.

In the next section, we examine recent evidence suggesting a crisis of confidence in scientific research findings across a wide range of sciences and research areas.

Is There a Crisis of Confidence in Scientific Research Today?

We have presented evidence suggesting that source and/or publication bias may not be a problem in some research literatures. In some other areas, it is viewed as a major problem (Rothstein, 2008; Rothstein et al., 2005). But before we look at this evidence, we examine a broader phenomenon. In recent years, one focus of attention has moved beyond publication bias per se to the various mechanisms and processes that engender both publication bias and other distortions in research literatures, ranging all the way from reporting unexpected findings as having been hypothesized a priori ("harking") to outright fraud in research. These efforts and findings have raised serious questions about the soundness and credibility of research findings in many scientific areas—the physical and biomedical sciences as well as the social sciences and psychology. Many today view these developments as creating a crisis of confidence in research findings. Most of these developments do not focus on meta-analysis per se, but rather on individual studies, studies that may eventually cause biased results when included in a meta-analysis. We will first review these developments and then review the evidence indicating how they contribute to publication bias and other distortions that can skew the results of meta-analyses.

SCIENTIFIC FRAUD

A very serious form of "publication bias" is outright research fraud; this occurs when individuals publish studies based on data that they have simply made up. A very serious recent case of this is that of Diederik Stapel, a prominent social psychologist in the Netherlands who has admitted to publishing numerous studies, often in top journals like *Psychological Science,* based on data he fabricated. Even his coauthors were unaware of this fraud, because he always "collected the data" himself (Carey, 2011; *Nature,* 2001, *479,* p. 15; Stroebe, Postmes, & Spears, 2012). Often such frauds come to light when someone notices a highly improbable sequence of statistical results in small-sample studies. For example, if in a sequence of eight studies, each with an N of 40 or less, the SDs of a particular measure are all identical or nearly identical across the studies, this is a very low-probability outcome given the reality of sampling error. As we saw in Chapter 2 (in the section "A More Detailed Examination of Statistical Power"), there is evidence that researchers underestimate the amount of variability produced by sampling error (Schmidt, Ocasio, et al., 1985). So, if people fabricate data, they are likely to build in less variability than sampling error would really produce. This lack of expected variability can potentially be detected in fraudulent data.

Uri Simonsohn of the University of Pennsylvania is a prominent "data detective" who looks for such suspicious research results. After he flagged questionable data in the publications of social psychologist Dirk Smeesters, Smeesters resigned from his faculty position at Erasmus University in the Netherlands (Yong, 2012), and the Erasmus University investigative committee concluded that several of his articles should be retracted. After a similar finding by Simonsohn in the case of the publications of Lawrence Sanna, a social psychologist at the University of Michigan, Sanna resigned his position there (Yong, 2012). It may be noteworthy that in all three cases, the individuals in question were social psychologists who "conducted" small-sample laboratory experiments. John, Loewenstein, and Prelec (2012) surveyed more than 2,000 psychologists about their use of questionable research practices (discussed later) and the defensibility of such practices. The rate of admission of using such practices was highest among social psychologists (40%) as was their rating of the defensibility of such practices. When broken out by type of research, the admission rates and defensibility ratings were highest for laboratory and experimental research, the domains of social psychology and general experimental psychology. Stroebe et al. (2012) set out to investigate whether the rate of research fraud was higher in social psychology than in other disciplines. They were able to locate 41 cases of proven research fraud. Of these, 33 (80%) were in the biomedical field. (In one of these cases, biomedical researcher Yoshitaka Fujii was found to have fabricated data in at least 172 journal articles; Yong, 2012.) Only 3 of the fraud cases were in social psychology. This suggests that the *number* of research fraud cases (if not the *rate* of fraud) is greater in the biosciences than in social psychology. (The annual number of published biomedical studies is far greater than the number of social psychology studies.) However, this study did not compare social psychologists to psychologists in other areas. The Stroebe et al. study and the John et al. study appeared in a special issue of the journal *Perspectives on Psychological Science* devoted to questionable research practices and the question of whether research articles in the psychological literature are replicable.

In 2011, the journal *Nature* reported that the number of retractions of scientific articles in all areas had increased tenfold in the previous decade, while the number of published articles had increased only 44% (Zimmer, 2012b). The articles in question were mostly in the physical and biomedical sciences. It had usually been thought that retractions were the result of the discovery by the authors or others of honest errors in data or data analysis. However, an analysis of 2,047 retracted articles in the biomedical and life sciences found that research misconduct was the reason for retraction in 75% of the cases in which the cause could be determined (Zimmer, 2012a). Another striking finding was that journals with higher impact factors had higher retraction rates than lower tier journals (Zimmer, 2012b). The journal with the highest retraction rate was the *New England Journal of Medicine*, one of the leading medical journals in the world. This correlation might be due to the fact that top-tier journals seek to publish papers with dramatic and surprising findings. In light of what we now know about retractions and research fraud, it appears that for some researchers, the pressure to publish in order to obtain tenure, promotions, raises, and research grants is sufficient to lead them into data fabrication. While most scientists continue to believe that outright research fraud is quite rare, there is no way to know for certain what the actual frequency is (Fanelli, 2009). No one knows how frequently research fraud goes undetected.

DATA MANIPULATION SHORT OF OUTRIGHT FRAUD

In an article that has attracted much attention, Simmons, Nelson, and Simonsohn (2011) outlined the ways in which empirical psychologists often use flexibility in data collection, analysis, and reporting to enhance the chances of obtaining statistical significance. One example is adding subjects to the lab study one at a time until statistical significance is reached and then stopping. Another is failing to report experimental conditions in which the treatment failed—that is, reporting the results for only the conditions in which the treatment produced statistically significance results (in the desired direction). A third example is "harking": hypothesizing after the results are known. These authors emphasize the potential of such practices, while widely accepted and used, to produce Type I errors in the literature. As noted earlier, the work of Lipsey and Wilson (1993) suggests that Type I errors are very rare in applied psychological interventions, because the null hypothesis is rarely true. However, this may not be the case in certain other areas, particularly in laboratory experiments in social psychology and related areas such as experimental marketing and experimental economics. In such areas, the hypotheses tested sometimes seem far-fetched, for example, the hypothesis that people in a lab study will walk more slowly after seeing words related to old age, an example of the "priming effect." There are many reported examples of priming effects in the social psychology literature. Failed attempts to replicate such priming effects have led to questions about the credibility of this research. In response, Daniel Kahneman, a Nobel Prize–winning cognitive psychologist, called on the field to make serious replication efforts in this area to address these questions (Yong, 2012). The outcome of this effort is not yet known. Another example of a potentially implausible priming effect hypothesis in social psychology is the proposition that white people are more likely to stereotype and discriminate against black people when they are in a messy environment than when in a neat environment (Carey, 2011). Simmons et al. showed via a series of simulation studies how easy it is to produce statistical significance for a relationship that does not exist. But even if the null hypothesis is false (making Type I errors impossible), the commonly employed practices cited by Simmons et al. (2011) lead to inflated correlations and d values, which would, in turn, create bias in subsequent meta-analyses. Bakker, van Dijk, and Wicherts (2012) focused their simulation study on cases in which the null hypothesis was wrong (and a relationship did in fact exist and so Type I errors were not possible), as well as cases in which the null was true and there was no relationship. In the latter case, they showed how easy it is to get statistical significance by employing widely used questionable research practices (QRPs), as had Simmons et al. (2011). In the case in which a relationship actually exists, they demonstrated that use of QRPs greatly inflated the obtained d values. More important, they showed how use of QRPs when a real relationship exists produces a rate of statistical significance that is highly improbable given the (computable) statistical power of the individual studies. We discuss this phenomenon in more detail later. How common are QRPs among psychological researchers? John et al. (2012) surveyed more than 2,000 academic psychologists and found that large percentages of researchers admitted to engaging in QRPs. The following are some examples. Fifty-six percent admitted to deciding whether to collect more data after looking to see whether the results were significant. Fifteen percent admitted to stopping data collection earlier than planned because they found the result they were looking for. Forty-five percent admitted to selectively reporting only studies that "worked." And 38% stated that they had decided whether to exclude data after looking at the impact of doing so on the results. These percentages were slightly higher in the group that was given an incentive to be honest.

Fiedler (2011) presented another set of practices that researchers often use to bias study outcomes to get statistical significance. Unlike the practices addressed by Simmons et al. (2011), Bakker et al. (2012), and John et al. (2012), most of these practices are nonstatistical or at least less obviously statistical. One example is the practice of pretesting independent variable stimuli for use in an experiment so as to be able to select and use only those stimuli that produce the largest effect with the dependent variable. Unlike Simmons et al., Fiedler does not focus only on Type I errors. Like Bakker et al., he demonstrated that even if we assume the null hypothesis is always false, common research practices lead to inflated effect sizes. Articles such as these have increased in frequency and have touched nerves among some researches, particularly among those in the areas in which small-N laboratory experiments are the rule.

Most of the questionable procedures cited by Simmons et al. (2011), Bakker et al. (2012), and John et al. (2012) operate via capitalization on sampling errors. Recall our discussion of capitalization on sampling error ("chance") near the end of Chapter 2 and again in Chapter 9 (in correction with meta-regression). One research area in which capitalization on chance has been rampant is in neuroscience studies that attempt to relate functional magnetic resonance imaging (fMRI) patterns to behavior, traits, or emotions. There are an extremely large number of pixels (or voxels) in each fMRI screen picture, and researchers typically select these to maximize the correlation with the dependent variable (emotion, personality, cognition, etc.), often with the study being based on 15 to 20 people. (The first author of this book once resigned from the dissertation committee of a neuroscience PhD student because this was the paradigm to be used in that dissertation.) Vul, Harris, Winkielman, and Pashler (2009) pointed out this problem in an article with the sharply worded title "Puzzlingly High Correlations in fMRI Studies of Emotion, Personality, and Social Cognition." They point out that this literature is almost certainly filled with relationships that will not replicate because they are not real, and that even when they are real, they are highly inflated. This article gave rise to the phrase "voodoo correlations." Another area with this same problem is research attempting to link specific genes with particular diseases, behaviors, personality traits, or abilities. The number of genes surveyed is extremely large, and the number of people in the study small enough that the ex post facto identification of genes appearing to be related to the criterion capitalizes greatly on sampling error. As a result, the vast majority of such identified linkages fail to appear in subsequent replication studies (Trikalinos & Ioannidis, 2005). Both of these examples are similar to the capitalization on chance depicted in Table 2.4 in Chapter 2 of this book.

Publication bias has traditionally been defined as a situation in which studies showing statistical significance are more likely to be published than those not showing statistical significance. This definition does not include questionable research practices beyond that. The research practices discussed in the articles cited above go beyond this definition and examine a wider range of influences that distort research literatures. These findings show that the problems involved in ensuring that the studies available for entry into meta-analyses are not biased go beyond the traditional conception of publication bias. The widespread nature of these research practices has raised questions about the reality and replicability of research findings in some literatures. John Ioannidis, a prominent critic of research practices in the biomedical area, has published a widely cited article titled "Why Most Published Research Findings Are False" (Ioannidis, 2005b).

In another article (Ioannidis, 2005a), he explores the disquieting fact that initially reported effect sizes for treatments in the medical area are usually large and then decline in size in subsequent replications, sometimes to zero. In sequential meta-analysis, as more recent studies are added to the meta-analysis, the mean effect declines. Lehrer (2011) describes this phenomenon not only in biomedical research but also in social psychology experiments. These findings indicate serious problems in the epistemology of research, at least in the biomedical and social psychology areas, and they must be resolved if meta-analyses of studies in these areas are to have credibility.

EVIDENCE FOR PUBLICATION BIAS (TRADITIONALLY DEFINED)

Most research in this area has focused on one type of source bias: publication bias. In this section, we examine the evidence, much of it quite recent, that publication bias is an important problem in some research literatures. The first type of evidence offered for the importance of publication bias consists of surveys of the beliefs and attitudes of researchers, reviewers, and editors about the role of statistical significance in making decisions about manuscripts. In these surveys, most researchers say they are more likely to submit a study if the results are statistically significant. Also, most reviewers say they are more likely to evaluate a study favorably if the results are significant. Finally, many editors state that they are more likely to accept a paper if the results are significant. Studies reporting findings of this sort include Chase and Chase (1976), Coursol and Wagner (1986), Greenwald (1975), and John et al. (2012). The questions in these surveys are worded in terms of a significant versus nonsignificant study outcome. Essentially, they measure the attitude a researcher, reviewer, or editor would have if (a) the study tested only one hypothesis (a rare event today) and the result was either significant or nonsignificant or (b) multiple hypotheses were tested but the result was either that all tests were nonsignificant or all were significant (again, a highly improbable event). To our knowledge, no studies of this sort on publication bias have attempted to assess what the role of statistical significance in decisions about manuscripts would be for typical real-world studies—studies in which several hypotheses are tested and some tests are significant and some are nonsignificant. Hence, surveys of this sort are of limited evidentiary value in illuminating the extent of publication bias.

A second type of evidence comes from empirical studies. Emerson et al. (2010) created two artificial biomedical studies that were identical except that in one, the result for the main hypothesis was statistically significant, and in the other it was not. Reviews were returned by 210 medical journal reviewers. Reviewers were more likely to recommend publication for the version with statistically significant results (97% vs. 80%). This study focused on evaluations by reviewers. Olson et al. (2002) focused on final decisions by editors of *JAMA* (*Journal of the American Medical Association*) made over a period of 3.5 years. They found that studies not reporting a statistically significant finding had only a slightly lower probability of being accepted for publication (.19 vs. .20). They concluded that publication bias, at least in case of *JAMA*, occurs in researcher decisions to submit a study to the journal and does not result from editorial action.

The third type of evidence offered in support of the proposition that publication bias is a serious problem consists of reports that the frequency of statistical significance in published articles is suspiciously high. For example, Sterling (1959) and Bozarth and Roberts (1972) found that 92% to 97% of published articles reported significant results for their main hypothesis. In a follow-up study more than 35 years after Sterling (1959), Sterling, Rosenbaum, and Weinkam (1995) found that the rate of statistical significance was still about 97% in the medical and experimental psychology journals that they examined. Given the evidence (discussed in Chapter 1) that the average level of statistical power in psychological research is somewhere around 50%, these percentages would seem to suggest massive publication bias. These findings might explain what has been a puzzling aspect of research in many areas. In a series of important articles and books, Cohen (1962, 1977, 1988) showed that statistical power is low (around 50%) in many research literatures and urged researchers to increase statistical power. However, Sedlmeier and Gigerenzer (1989) and Maxwell (2004) showed that researchers had not increased statistical power in response to Cohen's efforts. Cohen (1992) expressed puzzlement as to the reasons for this failure. The problem created by low statistical power is a high frequency of Type II errors—failure to detect relationships that are present. Yet such failures appear to be rare (i.e., missing) in many literatures. This raises the possibility that the reason researchers have apparently been unconcerned about low statistical power in their studies is that they found they could employ questionable research practices that capitalize on sampling error to avoid most nonsignificant results and to produce a frequency of statistical significance that corresponds to a much higher level of statistical power than their studies actually have. A more likely explanation is that researchers looked and simply did not see, in their studies or in their literatures in general, the high frequency of nonsignificant results predicted by Cohen, and so they concluded that statistical power was not really a problem. In this scenario, they were unaware that their research practices were capitalizing on sampling error and were producing the high rate of statistical significance despite low statistical power. This scenario is likely because there is much evidence that researchers do not understand sampling error—neither its magnitude nor its susceptibility to being capitalized on (as discussed in Chapters 1, 2, and 9). This could explain why John et al. (2012) found that many questionable research practices that capitalize on sampling error were rated as defensible by researchers.

Statistical power analysis has recently been developed as a method for detecting publication bias in a series of studies by the same author or group of authors. In recent years, some journals have become concerned about the need for replication of research findings, so they have begun to require multiple studies (usually experiments) in each article they publish as a way to ensure that the findings are replicated and hence are presumably real. In such a series of statistically independent studies, it is possible to compute both the statistical power of each study and the average statistical power in the series of studies. For example, if the average statistical power is .50, then the probability that five studies would all show statistical significance is $(.50)(.50)(.50)(.50)(.50) = .03$. If all five studies show statistical significance, this is evidence of some form of publication bias, because the statistical probability of this outcome is so small. The picture is even more suspicious if this type of outcome is repeatedly observed in a given literature. This is an approach to publication bias that has nothing to do with Type I errors; it is based on the missing Type II errors (the missing nonsignificant results) that should be in the literature but are not because they failed to reach statistical significance. That is, given the low power of the studies to detect the relationship, there should be quite a few failures to detect it (i.e., nonsignificant results). And these nonsignificant results are missing. This procedure was originally presented by Ioannidis and Trikalilnos (2007) for application to biomedical studies and has been extended for use with psychology and social science studies by Francis (2012a, 2012b, 2013) and by Schimmack (2012). Applications by Francis and Schimmack have found strong evidence of publication bias in all the multiple replications they have examined, typically laboratory experiments. This method has not yet been used to detect publication bias in the set of studies to be included in a meta-analysis, but it could be (as discussed later).

It may be the case that top-tier research journals are more susceptible to publication bias than other journals (Fiedler, 2011). Their journal pages are limited and so they attempt to favor papers that have novel and surprising findings and have large effects (Kepes & McDaniel, 2013). These are the kinds of studies that are most susceptible to publication bias and failure to replicate (Ioannidis, 2005a, 2005b). They are also more likely to be Type I errors, especially in the case of typical small-sample laboratory experiments. And as discussed earlier, top-tier journals, at least in the biomedical area, have higher retraction rates than lower tier journals.

Publication Bias in Economics

Doucouliagos and Stanley (2011) examined the research literature in economics and concluded that it contained substantial publication bias in areas in which there was a single dominant, widely accepted theory. In such cases, findings that supported that theory were published, but studies contradicting the theory were rarely published and hence were missing from the literature. In areas in which there were two or more competing theories that made different and opposing predictions, there was little evidence of publication bias. As an example of the effects of a single dominant theory, T. D. Stanley, Jarrell, and Doucouliagos (2010) and Doucouliagos and Stanley (2009) cite the economic theory holding that an increase in the minimum wage leads to a decrease in the number of (lower wage) jobs. The majority of published studies reported findings supporting this dominant theory. However, after adjusting for the publication bias favoring such studies (using the trim-and-fill method), the results indicated that there was no effect on employment from raising the minimum wage. Ioannidis and Doucouliagos (2013) presented a broader survey of economic research and concluded that there is reason to suspect publication bias in many areas of empirical economics.

Publication Bias in Industrial-Organizational Psychology

J. P. Campbell (1990) and his associates attempted to gauge publication bias in industrial-organizational (I/O) psychology by personally visiting many researchers and examining their "file drawers," looking for unpublished studies with nonsignificant results. Campbell et al. reported that they were unable to find any evidence of publication bias. In the last edition of this book, your first author was dubious about whether publication bias was important in I/O psychology, based on the evidence indicating a lack of publication bias in studies of test validity and the widespread requirement in this and other I/O areas for testing multiple theoretically derived hypotheses in published studies and the apparent absence of studies testing only a single hypothesis. But then he discovered an I/O literature in which each study tested only one hypothesis: the validity of the structured employment interview. Researchers who conducted these studies were perhaps typically inclined to have positive attitudes toward structured interviews. In any event, application of the trim-and-fill method (Duval, 2005) indicated publication bias in this literature; there was an apparent absence of small-sample studies with low validity estimates. Adjustment for this apparent publication bias led to noticeably smaller estimates of interview validity (Oh et al., 2013). Banks, Kepes, and McDaniel (2012), Kepes et al. (2012), and Kepes and McDaniel (2013) make a strong case that meta-analyses published in I/O psychology journals tend to not include meaningful attempts to detect publication bias. These articles do not present evidence that publication bias is a problem in this area of psychology, but they argue that there is no reason to believe that the incentives toward publication bias that have spawned publication bias in some other research areas (as discussed earlier) are absent from the I/O area. In light of this, they urge those conducting I/O meta-analyses to apply multiple methods of detecting publication bias, and they explicate these methods in some detail for readers.

In contrast, Dalton, Aguinis, Dalton, Bosco, and Pierce (2012) did attempt to provide empirical evidence on the question of publication bias in the I/O research literature. These authors focused only on non-experimental (observational) research articles. In a series of studies focusing on correlation matrices, they found that the percentage of nonsignificant correlations was about the same in published and unpublished correlation matrices (about 45% in each). This finding is not really reassuring since the correlations were not selected to be those related to the hypotheses tested in these studies. However, they also examined nearly 7,000 correlations used as input to 51 published I/O meta-analyses and found that 44% of these were nonsignificant, closely matching both the published and unpublished averages mentioned above. This suggests that the correlations going into I/O meta-analyses may not have been affected by publication bias. It is important to note that this study omitted all experimental studies (which would typically be small-sample laboratory studies), which, as we saw earlier, seem to be more susceptible to both questionable research practices and to publication bias. Such studies are only a small minority in the I/O literature, but they should still be considered. Bedeian, Taylor, and Miller (2010) conducted a survey on questionable research practices among researchers in management departments in business colleges, a group that includes some I/O psychologists. Respondents were asked whether they had knowledge of faculty engaging in a variety of questionable research practices in the past year. Their results suggested that questionable research practices were quite widespread. For example, 91% reported knowing of a case in which a researcher reported unexpected results as having been hypothesized in advance (harking). Nearly 80% said they had observed researchers withholding data that contradicted their previous research. And 27% reported knowledge of fabrication of research results. These are sobering findings. More recently Kepes, Banks, and Oh (in press) examined the studies contained in four published I/O meta-analyses and found evidence of at least some degree of publication bias in three of the four meta-analyses. However, the effects of the apparent publication bias on final meta-analysis results were often small, and the different methods of detecting publication bias that they applied sometimes disagreed with each other. Renkewitz, Fuchs, and Fiedler (2011) found some evidence of publication bias in a research area that overlaps somewhat with I/O—the judgment and decision-making area. And Banks, Kepes, and Banks (2012) found some evidence of publication bias in educational research.

Methods for Dealing With Availability Bias

Some methods for addressing availability bias allow one only to detect or judge whether source bias is present or not but do not allow quantification of the amount of bias or adjustment for the bias. Other methods allow detection, calibration of the amount of bias, and adjustment for bias. Different methods are based on different assumptions about the processes that produce availability bias. There is wide agreement that researchers should employ multiple methods to triangulate. There is also wide agreement that the results of application of these methods should be viewed as sensitivity analyses. If multiple methods all suggest the absence of publication or source bias, the researcher has a strong basis for concluding that the results of the meta-analysis are unbiased. If multiple methods indicate the presence of source bias, the meta-analysis should not "correct" for this bias but rather should "adjust" for the possibility of bias and should report the original results as well as the adjusted results.

FILE DRAWER ANALYSIS BASED ON p VALUES

Rosenthal's (1979) file drawer analysis estimates the number of unlocated ("file drawer") studies averaging null results (i.e., $\bar{d} = 0$ or $\bar{r} = 0$) that would have to exist to bring the significance level for a set of studies down to the "just significant" level, that is, to $p = .05$. The required number of studies is often so large as to have very little likelihood of existing, thus supporting the conclusion that the study findings, taken as a whole, are indeed unlikely to have resulted from biased sampling of studies. The first step in applying file drawer analysis is computation of the overall significance level for the set of studies. One first converts the p value for each of the k effect sizes to its corresponding z value using ordinary normal curve tables, for example,

Study	p Value	z Value
1	.05	1.645
2	.01	2.330
3	.50	.000
.	.	.
.	.	.
.	.	.

This test is directional (one-tailed), so the researcher must determine the direction of the hypothesized difference. For example, if females are hypothesized to have higher average levels of perceptual speed than males, then a finding that favors *males* at the .05 level (one-tailed) would be entered with a p value of $1.00 - .05 = .95$ and its z value would be -1.645.

When variables are uncorrelated, the variance of the sum is the sum of the variances. If the z values are from k independent studies, then each has a variance of 1.00, and the variance of the sum of the zs across the k studies is k. Because the variance of Σz_k is K, the $SD = \sqrt{k}$. The z_c, the z score corresponding to the significance level of the total set of studies, is then

$$z_c = \frac{\Sigma z_k}{\sqrt{k}} = \frac{k\bar{z}_k}{\sqrt{k}} = \sqrt{k}\,\bar{z}_k$$

For example, if there were 10 studies ($K = 10$) and $\bar{z}_k = 1.35$, then $z_c = \sqrt{10}(1.35) = 4.27$, a highly significant z_c value. ($p = .0000098$).

In a file drawer analysis, the researcher computes the number of additional unlocated studies averaging $z = 0$ needed to bring z_c down to 1.645 (or $p = .05$). Denote this additional number of studies by x. Because these studies have $\bar{z} = 0$, $\Sigma z_{k+x} = \Sigma z_k$. However, the number of studies will increase from k to $k + x$. Thus, the knew SD for Σz_{k+z} will be $\sqrt{k+x}$. If we set $z_c = 1.645$, the desired value, we can then solve the following equation for x:

$$1.645 = \frac{k\bar{z}_k}{\sqrt{k+x}}$$

Solving for x,

$$x = k/2.706[k(\bar{z}_k)^2 - 2.706] \tag{13.1}$$

This is the file drawer formula when the critical overall significance level is $p = .05$. Returning to our earlier example where $k = 10$ and $\bar{z}_k = 1.35$, we obtain

$$x = \frac{10}{2.706}[10(1.35)^2 - 2.706] = 57$$

Thus, there would have to be 57 unlocated studies averaging null results to bring the combined probability level for the group of studies up to .05. If in this example, there were originally 100 studies ($k = 100$) instead of 10, then $x = 6,635$! More than 6,000 studies would be required to raise the combined P value to .05. In most research areas, it is inconceivable that there could be more than 6,000 "lost" studies.

An important problem with this method is that it assumes the homogeneous case (Hunter & Schmidt, 2000, pp. 286–287). That is, it assumes $S_\rho^2 = 0$ (or that $S_\delta^2 = 0$). This means it is a fixed effects model and therefore has all the problems of fixed effects meta-analysis methods, as discussed in Chapters 5 and 9. In particular, if the fixed effects assumption does not hold (and it rarely does), then the number of missing studies needed to make the combined p value just barely significant is much smaller than the number yielded by the file drawer analysis (Iyengar & Greenhouse, 1988). This method also has an ironic feature: The more publication bias there is, the more the method indicates there is no publication bias. That is, extreme levels of publication bias lead to very small p values in the available studies, which leads to an extremely small combined p value for the set of studies as a whole. This, in turn, results in an estimate that a very large number of missing studies must exist to bring the overall significance level down to the just significant value of $p = .05$, which suggests the absence of publication bias. Other important criticisms of the Rosenthal file drawer analysis are given by Begg (1994, p. 406), Iyengar and Greenhouse (1988, pp. 111–112), and Becker (2005), who concluded that this method should be discontinued as a publication bias method. As a result, the Rosenthal file drawer analysis is no longer widely used.

FILE DRAWER ANALYSIS BASED ON EFFECT SIZE

Another problem with the file drawer analysis of Rosenthal (1979) is that, even accepted at face value, it yields a very weak conclusion. The combined study results can be highly significant statistically even though the mean effect size is small or even tiny. Neither the combined probability method in general (see Chapter 11) nor the file drawer analysis in particular provides any information on effect size. It would be more informative to know how many missing studies averaging null findings would have to exist to bring $\bar{d}$ or $\bar{r}$ down to some specific level. The formulas given here for this calculation were derived by the authors in 1979 and used extensively by Pearlman (1982). Later, we learned that Orwin (1983) had independently derived the same formulas. These equations do not depend on the fixed effects assumption; in effect, they represent a random effects model.

If k is again the number of studies, then

$$\bar{d}_k = \frac{\Sigma d_k}{k}$$

We want to know how many "lost" studies (x) must exist to bring $\bar{d}_k$ down to $\bar{d}_c$, the critical value for mean d (which may be the smallest mean value that we would consider theoretically or practically significant). Thus, the new total number of studies will again be $k + x$. Σd_k will remain unchanged, because $\Sigma d = 0$ for the x new studies. We again set $\bar{d}_k$ equal to $\bar{d}_c$ and solve for x:

$$\bar{d}_c = \frac{\Sigma d_k}{k + x}$$
$$x = k\bar{d}_k / \bar{d}_c - k$$
$$x = k(\bar{d}_k / \bar{d}_c - 1)$$

(13.2a)

The corresponding formula for $\bar{r}$ is

$$x = k(\bar{r}_k / \bar{r}_c - 1)$$

(13.2b)

For example, if $\bar{d}_k = 1.00$, $k = 10$, and $\bar{d}_c = .10$, then

$$x = 10(1.00 / .10 - 1)$$
$$x = 90 \ studies$$

If $k = 100$ but the other numbers remain the same, then $x = 900$. The number of missing studies averaging null results needed to reduce the effect size to some specified level is usually much smaller than the number required to reduce the combined probability value to $p = .05$. Nevertheless, in many research areas, it is unlikely that there are even 90 "lost" studies, and it is highly unlikely that there are 900. McNatt (2000) provided an example of the use of this procedure in a published meta-analysis. He found that it would take 367 missing studies averaging zero effect size to reduce his observed $\bar{d}$ of 1.13 (a large effect) to $\bar{d} = .05$ (a trivial effect). Like the Rosenthal file draw analysis, this procedure has an ironic feature. The more publication bias there is, the larger will be the mean d or mean r value, which will cause the method to indicate that a large number of missing studies must exist to bring the mean value down to a trivial value—which is interpreted as indicating the absence of publication bias.

SUBGROUPING OF PUBLISHED AND UNPUBLISHED STUDIES

One way to quickly check for publication bias per se (as opposed to other forms of source bias) is to conduct separate meta-analyses on the published and unpublished studies. A larger mean effect size in the published study meta-analysis would be taken as suggesting publication bias. However, such a conclusion could be erroneous unless certain cautions are observed. First, the appropriate corrections for measurement error and other artifacts must be made, as discussed earlier in this chapter. If the measures used in the unpublished studies are less reliable, then when there is no publication bias, the observed (uncorrected) mean effect size will be lower in the unpublished studies. It is also possible that range restriction is more severe in the unpublished studies, which would likewise create the false appearance of publication bias. After the appropriate corrections, the two mean effect sizes might be equal (as in the example at the beginning of this chapter). So in comparing the published and unpublished studies, it is critical to first make the appropriate artifact corrections. An unequal partition of moderators could also cause a deceptive appearance of publication bias. If a moderator that increases the effect size is more often present in the published studies than in the unpublished studies, the difference in mean effect size might not be due to publication bias per se. So the published and unpublished studies should be matched as well as possible on study characteristics that might affect study outcomes. If this does not appear to be the case in the initial subgroups, further subgrouping into smaller groups might be required.

THE FUNNEL PLOT

Light and Pillemer (1984) introduced a simple graphic method of detecting publication or other availability bias. This technique is based on the fact that, in the absence of availability bias, the average effect size is expected to be the same in large- and small-sample studies, while varying more widely in small-sample studies due to greater sampling error. In applying this technique, one graphs effect sizes (d values or correlations) against study sample size (or the standard error of the study estimate, which is an inverse function of sample size). In the absence of bias, the resulting figure should take the form of an inverted funnel, as shown in Figure 13.1. Note that in Figure 13.1, the average effect size is approximately the same regardless of study sample size. However, if there is publication or other availability bias based on the statistical significance (p value) of the studies, then small-sample studies reporting small effect sizes will be disproportionately absent, because these studies fail to attain statistical significance. These are the studies in the lower left-hand corner of the funnel plot. Figure 13.2 shows a funnel plot that suggests the presence of availability bias. Note that in Figure 13.2, the average effect size of the small-sample studies is larger than that for the large-sample-size studies.

Although the concept underlying the funnel plot method is simple and direct, it has a problematic aspect. If all nonsignificant studies are unavailable due to publication or other availability bias, it is easy to see the evidence of bias. However, if only some are missing (say, 20%–60%), it is much harder to detect the bias (Greenhouse & Iyengar, 1994). This is especially true if the number of studies is not large (often the case). It is highly unlikely that 100% of all nonsignificant studies will be missing. Significance tests are available as a substitute for judgment in evaluating the funnel plot (Sterne & Egger, 2005), but these tests have all the problems

Figure 13.1   Example of funnel plot showing no evidence of availability bias.

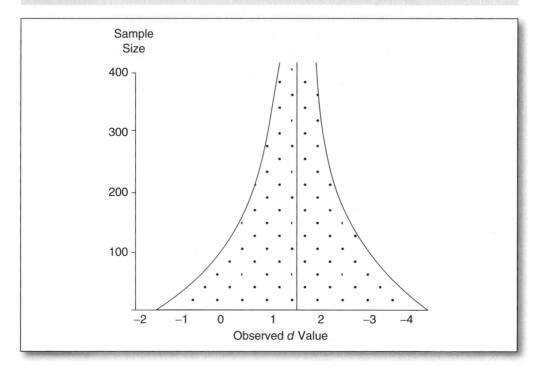

Figure 13.2   Example of funnel plot showing evidence of availability bias.

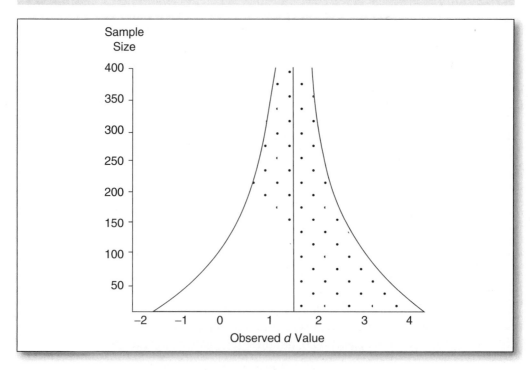

of significance tests discussed in Chapter 1. In particular, they have low power. Therefore, we recommend against their use.

When the funnel plot suggests availability bias, some have suggested basing the meta-analysis only on the large-N studies (e.g., Begg, 1994), under the assumption that all or nearly all of these would have been statistically significant (and therefore published), and hence, these studies would provide an unbiased estimate of the mean effect size. This is probably the case if the underlying mean effect size is large and there is little or no real variance in this parameter. (These two conditions together contribute to high statistical power in the larger N studies, helping to ensure the larger N studies will not be a biased sample of studies.) Another important condition is that the *number* of large-N studies should itself be large, because the situation is different if there is heterogeneity in study parameters (the usual case). If there are only a small number of large sample size studies, there will be only a few data points on which to estimate the variability of the parameters rho and delta (i.e., SD_ρ and SD_δ). An extreme recommendation for reliance on only the large-N studies was made by T. D. Stanley et al. (2010). They recommend that in order to avoid publication bias, one should include in the meta-analysis only the 10% of studies with the largest sample sizes. In most cases, this would be far too few studies to allow accurate estimation of SD_ρ or SD_δ. In addition, even the estimate of the mean might be inaccurate because the small number of studies runs the risk of a randomly unrepresentative sampling of the underlying distribution of rho or delta values.

Note also that the bias shown in Figure 13.2 appears larger than it actually would be in the meta-analysis, because studies are weighted by their sample size, and so the small-N studies (which have the biased estimates) receive little weight in the meta-analysis average. This is the case for the random effects models presented in this book. However, as discussed in Chapter 9, the study weights used in the Hedges-Olkin random effects model are different; in comparison to sample size study weights, they increase the relative weight given to small-N studies. As seen in the next section, this fact has implications for how the trim-and-fill method is applied by those using the Hedges-Olkin random effects meta-analysis model.

Palmer, Peters, Sutton, and Moreno (2008) have recommended that funnel plots be "enhanced" by adding contour lines of statistical significance as aids in interpreting the funnel plot. The combinations of effect size and sample size on one side of the contour line would always be statistically significant at the .05 level (at minimum); all combinations of effect size and sample size on the other side of the line would be nonsignificant. If studies appear to be missing in areas that cannot produce statistical significance, this suggests that the asymmetry is due to publication bias. If studies appear to be missing in the areas where studies would be statistically significant, then it is unlikely that the cause of this is publication bias. This approach assumes that lack of statistical significance is the only cause of publication bias, which may not be the case. This procedure makes interpretation of funnel plots easier, but it is not essential. This procedure can also be used with the trim-and-fill method, discussed next.

THE TRIM-AND-FILL METHOD

Duval and Tweedie (2000) and Duval (2005) noted that some methods of addressing publication bias are complex, difficult to understand, and highly computer intensive to run and, as a result, are rarely used. They presented a relatively simple, nonparametric method based on the properties of the Wilcoxon distribution and using the funnel plot. In this method, one first computes the mean effect size based on all studies. Next, this method trims off the studies that cause the funnel plot asymmetry, usually (but not always) in the lower right corner of the funnel plot, and then computes a mean effect size based on the remaining studies. This method then estimates the number of missing studies, assumed to be from the lower left corner of the funnel plot. They present three different nonparametric estimators of the number of missing studies, all of which seem to provide similar estimates. Based on the estimate of the number of missing studies, their method provides an estimate of what $\bar{\rho}$ and $\bar{\delta}$ would have been had there been no availability bias. This is done by "filling in" the missing studies on the lower left side with a mirror image of the studies on the lower right side of the funnel plot and then recomputing $\bar{\rho}$ and $\bar{\delta}$ based on the original studies plus the imputed studies. For example, it can be seen in Figure 13.2 that small-sample studies are missing in the lower left-hand corner. In Figure 13.1, these missing studies have been "filled in" to create a mirror image of the lower right-hand corner of the figure. This is a method for adjusting for the effects of publication bias, not a method for determining whether it exists. It is assumed that determination will be made by examination of the funnel plot or by other means. Duval and Tweedie (2000) and Duval (2005) recommend that this method be used to create a form of sensitivity analysis. An absence of publication bias is indicated if the difference between the untrimmed estimate of the mean and the adjusted estimate is small or zero. (It is expected that the "trimmed" estimate and the adjusted estimate would be close in value.)

This method was derived under the assumption that all studies estimate the same parameter (i.e., a fixed effects assumption). A question concerning this method is whether it works well when studies are heterogeneous. If SD_ρ or SD_δ is nonzero but small, the method appears to work well. If these SDs are larger but the distribution is normal or symmetrical in shape, the method still works well (Peters et al., 2010). However, if there is substantial heterogeneity and large moderators, the method may indicate publication bias where none exists (Duval, 2005; Peters et al., 2010; Terrin,

Schmid, Lau, & Olkin, 2002). An example of this could be a large binary moderator with unequal numbers of studies in the two moderator categories. Another example would be a continuous moderator with a bimodal distribution with unequal modes. In such cases, the studies must be subgrouped into relatively more homogeneous groups on the moderators, with the trim-and-fill analysis then being applied to these subgroups. This could result in subgroups with only a small number of studies, making application of the trim-and-fill method questionable. More generally, any factor related to both study outcomes and study sample size has the potential to distort the appearance of the funnel plot and destroy its symmetry. The trim-and-fill method detects and adjusts for funnel plot asymmetry, regardless of the reason for such asymmetry.

The question of study weighting is important in connection with the trim-and-fill method when there is heterogeneity in the studies (the usual case). As discussed in Chapters 5 and 9, random effects (RE) meta-analysis models should be used when studies are heterogeneous. As discussed in Chapter 9, the study weights used in the Hedges-Olkin RE model give relatively more weight to small-N studies compared to the sample size weighting used in the methods presented in this book. The Hedges-Olkin procedure causes study sampling errors, and therefore study weights, to be less unequal. The standard errors of large-N studies are increased by a larger percentage than for small-N studies. The increased weight given to small studies distorts the results of the trim-and-fill method (Duval, 2005; Sutton, 2005; Terrin et al., 2002). As a result, most researchers using Hedges-Olkin methods use their fixed effects (FE) model study weights when applying the trim-and-fill method, while using the Hedges-Olkin RE model for their main meta-analysis. This inconsistency raises a question: If the Hedges-Olkin RE study weights give too much weight to small-N studies in the trim-and-fill method (Sutton, 2005), do they not also give those studies too much weight in the overall meta-analysis? The methods presented in this book are all RE methods but do not experience this study weighting inconsistency when using the trim-and-fill method.

Duval and Tweedie (2000) presented examples showing that their method gives results very similar to more complex methods. In particular, they showed that both their method and the more complex methods indicate that, after the adjustment for publication bias, there is little evidence that second-hand smoke (environmental tobacco smoke) is harmful. (See Cordray and Morphy, 2009, for a detailed critique of the meta-analysis on environmental tobacco smoke.) Duval (2005) presents several additional informative example applications of the trim-and-fill method to real data sets. This method is much easier to program for use by meta-analysts than the other methods of adjusting for availability bias discussed here. This method is now widely used in both behavioral science and biomedical meta-analyses. As is the case with other methods, trim and fill can produce erroneous results and conclusions if the proper corrections for measurement error and other artifacts are not made prior to applying the method. Applications of trim and fill in the literature have rarely included these corrections and so are of questionable accuracy. As described in Chapter 3, these corrections increase the standard error in each r or d value, and these adjusted values must be used on the vertical axis of the funnel plot.

CUMULATIVE META-ANALYSIS

In a cumulative meta-analysis aimed at detecting publication bias, studies are ranked on sample size (or the inverse of their standard error, which is essentially equivalent). Studies are then added to the meta-analysis one at a time starting with the study with the largest sample size. The sequence of mean effect sizes can then reveal evidence for or against publication bias. If there is publication bias, the addition of the smaller N studies will cause the mean effect size to trend upwards (Borenstein et al., 2009; McDaniel, 1990). The sequence of meta-analyses is usually presented as a moving forest plot, allowing users to easily compare the effect size based on only the large-N studies to that based on all studies. The assumption underlying the method (Borenstein et al., 2009, chap. 30) is that publication bias, if it exists, will be concentrated in the small-sample studies—the same assumption that underlies the funnel plot and the trim-and-fill methods. There is evidence of publication bias (or availability bias) if the mean effect size based on all studies is larger than the mean effect size based only on the large-N studies. The adjustment for publication or availability bias is then to drop the small-N studies from the main meta-analysis (while also presenting the results obtained when the small-N studies are included). The meta-analysis computer programs discussed in the Appendix to this book include this method of analysis for publication bias. Unlike other programs that apply this method, this program corrects for measurement error and range restriction (if present) in each cumulative sequential meta-analysis. (See the Appendix for more details.)

The inconsistency in the weighting of studies that we discussed in connection with the trim-and-fill method also occurs here. As we saw in Chapters 5 and 9, the RE model is almost always the appropriate meta-analysis model. The RE study weights used in the Hedges-Olkin methods give relatively more weight to small-N studies than do the RE methods presented in the book. As a result, in a cumulative meta-analysis, the Hedges-Olkin RE model and study weights are more likely to produce an erroneous conclusion that publication bias exists, because this RE model gives too much weight to small-N studies (Sutton, 2005). As a result, most users of the Hedges-Olkin methods use their FE model study weights when applying cumulative meta-analysis to test for publication and use their RE model as the basis for their final meta-analytic results. This inconsistency does not occur with the RE models presented in this book.

CORRELATION AND REGRESSION-BASED METHODS

Begg and Mazumdar (1994) argued that small-sample studies tend to be published only if they yield a correlation or *d* value of large magnitude (which is required for statistical significance, given the small *N*), while large-sample studies tend to be published regardless of the size of their *r* or *d* values (because their results will almost always be statistically significant). This is the assumption underlying the funnel plot, and Figure 13.2 illustrates the expected outcome under this assumption: The missing studies are those with both small *N*s and small *d* values. They therefore suggested a simple test for publication bias: the rank order correlation between the *d* (or *r*)values and their standard errors. (The Pearson correlation can also be used.) In the absence of publication bias, this correlation should be zero. A positive correlation indicates publication bias. This procedure can be viewed as a way of quantifying the outcome of a funnel plot as a substitute for subjective interpretation of the funnel plot. McDaniel and Nguyen (2002) provided an example of use of this procedure. Earlier in this chapter (in the section "Multiple Hypotheses and Other Considerations in Availability Bias"), we present an example of an application of this method. Schmidt, Oh, and Hayes (2009) examined five meta-analysis publications, each reporting 13 to 14 separate independent meta-analyses. Within each publication, they computed the correlation between sample size and effect size. They found that the average of these five correlations across the five meta-analyses of sex differences in cognitive abilities was mean $r = 0$, indicating the absence of publication bias. In addition, the variability of the five correlations across the meta-analyses was found to be attributable to sampling error, indicating there was no publication bias in *any* of the meta-analyses.

Egger, Smith, Schneider, and Minder (1997) and Sterne and Egger (2005) proposed a somewhat similar method, albeit one that is more difficult to understand. In this method, precision (the inverse of the study standard error) is used in a regression equation to predict the so-called standardized effect—the *r* or *d* value divided by its standard error. If there is no publication bias, the intercept of this regression line will be zero (i.e., the line will run through the origin). The intercept is the slope of effect sizes on their standard errors. A positive value for the intercept indicates that small-*N* studies have larger effect sizes, suggesting the presence of publication bias. For most researchers, this method is less intuitive than the Begg and Mazumbar (1994) method. Both these methods have been criticized because they have low statistical power. However, the same criticism can be made of other methods of detecting publication bias. And as we have argued throughout this book (and especially in Chapter 1), it is counterproductive for researchers to rely on significance tests. A more relevant criticism of these two methods is that (a) they assess only whether bias is present and do not calibrate the amount of bias, and (b) unlike the trim-and-fill method and the cumulative meta-analysis method, they provide no estimate of what the meta-analysis results would be in the absence of publication bias; that is, they do not allow an adjustment for the bias.

THE STATISTICAL POWER METHOD AND THE p-HACKING METHOD

As discussed earlier in this chapter (in the section "Evidence for Publication Bias (Traditionally Defined)"), the frequency of statistical significance in a set or subset of studies can be inconsistent with the statistical power of those studies. For example, if the statistical power in a group of studies is .50, then we expect that about half these studies will report significant results and half nonsignificant results. If 90% or 100% of these studies report significant results, this is strong evidence of publication bias: Type II errors that should be there are missing from the set of studies. That is, because of the low statistical power, there should be many more studies with statistically nonsignificant findings. As discussed earlier, this method for detecting questionable research results was first proposed by Ioannidis and Trikalilnos (2007) for application to biomedical literatures and was later applied to primary psychology studies by Francis (2012a, 2012b, 2013) and Schimmack (2012). So far, this method has been applied only to multiple studies conducted by a single author or a group of authors; typically, there have been 5 to 10 studies in such a group. As of this writing, this method has not yet been used to test for publication bias in studies to be included in a meta-analysis, but it could become an important application in that respect. This method would differ from other methods in that its application would not include all the studies in a meta-analysis but only the small-N (i.e., low-powered) studies. Meta-analysis would first be applied to the large-N studies to create an unbiased estimate of the mean effect size. The statistical power analysis would then be applied, using this effect size, only to those studies with sample sizes small enough to potentially be affected by publication bias. A more lenient test for publication bias would result if one computed the mean effect size based only on the small-N studies, because this effect size would be expected to be biased upwards, thus reducing the improbability of a large number of significant findings. The same would be true if the effect size is estimated separately for each small-N study and then used to compute statistical power in that study. The application of this method is straightforward, and the steps are presented by Francis (2012a, 2012b, 2013) and Schimmack (2012). A finding of a frequency of significance in these studies that has a low statistical probability of occurring given the prevailing statistical power in the studies indicates publication bias. This method allows only detection of bias; it does not allow an adjustment for any detected bias. A finding of publication bias would lead to the exclusion from the meta-analysis of the biased studies. This method answers the following question: Should small-N (i.e., imprecise be) studies included in the meta-analysis or omitted?

A related method, presented by Simonsohn, Nelson, and Simmons (in press), focuses on the detection of groups of studies that are the product of Type I errors. It is less useful in the detection of publication bias in studies in which the true relationship is nonzero. As discussed earlier in this chapter, there is concern among some that in certain areas of research, particularly small-sample laboratory experiments in social psychology and related areas, the statistically significant findings in the literature are due to Type I errors. Simonsohn et al. showed that the p values in such a literature will bunch up and peak around .05, with few p values that are much smaller (i.e., few values of .01, .005, etc.). On the other hand, if a relationship actually exists, the distribution of p values is quite different: There is no bunching up around the .05 value, and there are many more p values smaller than .05. Unlike the statistical power method, this method must be applied to all the studies in the meta-analytic data set. If the distribution of p values is severely bunched up around the value of .05, the conclusion would be that the true mean effect size is zero. The difference between this value of zero and the mean effect size resulting from a meta-analysis of all the studies is then the quantification of the amount of publication bias. It is probably rare for an entire research literature to consist of Type I errors, but it could occur.

SELECTION MODELS

Selection methods are based on the p values of the primary studies; that is, they assume that the probability of publication depends (via some weight function) on the p value of that study. For example, a selection model might indicate that the probability of publication of a study with $p = .10$ is .50, while the probability for a study with $p = .001$ is .95. There is no provision for the possibility that other properties of studies might affect the probability of publication (e.g., the effect size reported, methodological qualities of the study, the reputation of the authors, etc.). This would appear to make these methods somewhat unrealistic (Duval & Tweedie, 2000). Another potential criticism is that all these methods seem to implicitly assume that each study tests only one hypothesis (or only one main hypothesis) and hence has only one relevant p value to be considered. As a result, the applicability of these methods to studies in which several hypotheses are tested, resulting in several significance tests and p values, may be questionable. As noted earlier, studies with multiple hypotheses are the majority in many research literatures today. Beyond these broad assumptional questions, these methods depend on a variety of additional statistical assumptions that may or may not hold in real data (see, e.g., Hedges, 1992b). However, as noted earlier, such assumptions are common to all publication bias methods. Earlier we noted that substantial heterogeneity in study population values (e.g., large dichotomous moderators) can make application of the trim-and-fill method and other methods problematic. A major advantage of selection models is that they are much less susceptible to distortion due to study heterogeneity (Duval, 2005; Vevea & Woods, 2005). And, as described later in this section, there have been important improvements in selection models in recent years.

Nevertheless, because publication bias has the potential to seriously distort conclusions from research reviews, including meta-analytic reviews, these methods have received considerable attention but have not been widely used to date. It is possible that recently introduced improvements in these methods (Hedges & Vevea, 2005; Vevea & Woods, 2005) will make these methods substantially more important in meta-analysis in the future. Early versions of the selection model required that the p value–based selection function be estimated empirically based on the set of studies at hand. These estimation procedures are satisfactory only when the number of studies is large. More recent versions of the selection model do not require this estimation procedure. These methods have evolved over time, and in the following, we present these methods in the approximate chronological order in which they appeared. Because of the highly technical nature of these methods and because of space constraints, we present only overviews and summary descriptions of these methods.

The Original Hedges-Olkin (1985) Method

The initial method presented by Hedges (1984) and Hedges and Olkin (1985) was based on the assumption that all significant studies were published (regardless of the direction of significance) and none of the nonsignificant studies was published. That is, they started with the simplest of "weight functions": All significant studies were weighted 1 and all nonsignificant studies were weighted 0. Later methods employed more complex—and less unrealistic—assumptions and weighting functions.

If, in a given research literature, only published studies were available and only studies reporting significant results were published, then, if the null hypothesis were true, there would be approximately equal numbers of statistically significant positive and negative d or r values in the published literature, and $\bar{r}$ and $\bar{d}$ would, on the average, be 0, and there would be no effect of publication bias on estimates of $\bar{r}$ and $\bar{d}$ (although estimates of S_ρ^2 and S_δ^2 would be biased upwards). Significant and extreme results in either direction would be equally likely. However, if the null hypothesis were false (e.g., $\bar{\delta} > 0$), the mean effect size computed from such studies would not equal its true value but instead would be biased upward. The amount of this bias would depend on the underlying δ and on study sample size.

Based on maximum likelihood methods, Hedges and Olkin (1985) estimated and tabled the estimates of δ for different study sample sizes and values of g^*, where g^* is the observed value of d from a study in a set of studies from which all nonsignificant d s have been eliminated (censored). In a set of studies that excludes all nonsignificant ds, there is a bias in each d value. These biased d values (symbolized g^*) can be converted to approximately unbiased estimates of δ by use of Hedges and Olkin's Table 2 (pp. 293–294). For example, if $N_E = N_C = 20$ and $g^* = .90$, this table shows that the maximum likelihood estimate of $\delta(\hat{\delta})$ is .631. This conversion from g^* to $\hat{\delta}$ can be made for each of the g^* values in the set of studies. The table is based on the assumption that $N_E = N_C$, but Hedges and Olkin (p. 292) noted that when the experimental and control group sample sizes are unequal, one can use the average of the two to enter the table with minimal loss of accuracy. Once all observed d values have been corrected for the bias induced by the reporting of only significant results, Hedges and Olkin recommended that the resulting $\hat{\delta}$ values be weighted by study sample sizes and averaged to estimate the (almost) unbiased mean effect size $(\bar{\delta})$. Thus, it is possible to obtain an unbiased estimate of mean effect size even when only studies that report significant effect sizes are available for analysis. Note that this estimate, $\bar{\delta}$, will be considerably smaller than the observed mean effect size, $\bar{g}^*$. The formulas for this method were derived under the assumption that the population effect size δ does not vary across studies (i.e., it is a fixed effects model). If δ varies substantially across studies, this method yields only an approximate estimate of the mean effect size $(\bar{\delta})$.

The sampling error variance of the $\hat{\delta}$ values is considerably larger than that given for ordinary d values in the formula in Chapter 7. This is true unless the actual δ is less than about .25 or both sample size and δ are "large" (e.g., $N_E = N_C = 50$ and $\delta = 1.50$). For most data sets that occur in meta-analysis, the sampling error variance formulas in Chapter 7 would underestimate actual sampling error variance by about one third to one half. Thus, the resulting estimate of SD_δ would be too large. However, as noted previously, the estimate of $\bar{\delta}$ should be approximately unbiased.

Ordinarily, the censoring of studies is not complete. Some nonsignificant studies will be found among the significant ones. In these cases, Hedges and Olkin (1985) suggested that the researcher eliminate the nonsignificant studies and then proceed to use the methods described here. However, methods developed subsequently allow for less than total publication bias. That is, they allow for the possibility that some nonsignificant studies are published and some significant studies are not published. This eliminates the need to exclude nonsignificant studies from the analysis.

The Iyengar-Greenhouse (1988) Method

Iyengar and Greenhouse (1988) extended the original Hedges-Olkin method to allow for nonzero probabilities of publication for nonsignificant studies. They retained the assumption that all significant studies would be published, regardless of direction of significance (i.e., their selection model was two-tailed, like the Hedges-Olkin model). Their method assumes that all nonsignificant studies have the same nonzero probability of being published, although it can be extended to include different probabilities of publication for nonsignificant studies with different p values. Similar to the Hedges-Olkin method, this method uses maximum likelihood (ML) methods to estimate the values of $\bar{\rho}$ or $\bar{\delta}$ that would have been observed had there been no publication bias. Sensitivity analyses can be conducted to determine whether different weights for different p values have large or small effects on the final estimates of $\bar{\rho}$ or $\bar{\delta}$. Although more realistic than the original Hedges-Olkin method, this method, like that one, is a fixed effects model and, hence, will rarely be appropriate for real data (as noted by several commentators in the same issue of the journal). Also, the assumption of two-tailed publication bias is probably unrealistic in many cases.

The Copas Selection Model

Selection models considered up to this point assume that publication bias depends only on the p values of studies. The Copas (1999; Copas & Shi, 2001) selection model assumes that publication bias is driven by study effect size and the standard error of the effect size, and in this sense may be more realistic. This selection model is similar to both the Iygenar-Greenhouse model and the early Hedges-Olkin model (Hedges, 1984) in that the selection function must be empirically estimated from the studies at hand. The estimation process is more problematic in this model than in those previously discussed, especially when the number of studies is small. Often the maximum likelihood procedure does not converge to a solution. Schwarzer, Carpenter, and Rucker (2010) present a clear description of the Copas selection model.

Further Work by Hedges and Associates

Hedges (1992b) generalized the Iyengar-Greenhouse method to include study weights reflecting probabilities of publication that are based on research findings about how researchers view p values. For example, researchers see little difference between p values of .05 and .04 but view the difference between .06 and .05 as very important. Hedges used this information to create a discrete step function of study weights based on p values.

Again using ML methods, these initial weight estimates are iterated to refine the estimates, and the refined weight estimates are then used to produce estimates of the values of $\overline{\rho}$ or $\overline{\delta}$ that would have been observed had there been no publication bias. This estimation procedure appears to work well only when the number of studies is large (Hedges, 2005). This is a random effects model, and so estimates of S_ρ^2 and S_δ^2 are also produced. Based on these estimates, this method can estimate the distribution of p values that would be expected in the absence of publication bias. This distribution can then be compared with the observed distribution of p values in the set of studies. Discrepancies indicate the presence of publication bias. In addition to the improved methods for estimating study weights, this method is more realistic in being a random effects model. However, it still assumes two-tailed selection based on p values.

In Hedges (1992b) and in Vevea et al. (1993), this method was applied to the 755-study database of validity studies for the General Aptitude Test Battery (GATB) of the U.S. Department of Labor. Although the two applications were slightly different in detail, both indicated there was essentially no availability bias in this data set. This is exactly what would be expected when multiple hypotheses are tested. Each GATB study estimates the validity of the 12 different tests in the battery and also estimates the validity of nine different abilities measured by different combinations of these 12 tests. Almost no studies reported only partial results. As discussed earlier, under these conditions, it is highly unlikely that there could be any availability bias based on p values. The probability of all 21 significance tests being nonsignificant is vanishing small, as is the probability that all would be significant. Almost all studies must have a mixture of significant and nonsignificant results, which would make the attainment of availability bias difficult even for someone deliberately intent on producing such a bias. Hence, we would not expect to see availability bias in such a literature, and this was the conclusion of the Hedges bias detection and correction method.

Vevea and Hedges (1995) further refined the preceding set of methods. Recognizing that the assumption of two-tailed publication bias is probably unrealistic in most situations, they modified the method to assume one-tailed publication bias. The major improvement, however, is the provision for moderator variables that might be correlated with study effect sizes (and hence with study p values). For example, one type of psychotherapy might be particularly effective (large effect sizes) and, at the same time, typically be studied with small sample sizes. This situation calls for a random effects model with weighted least squares used to predict study outcomes from study characteristics (coded moderators) to (in effect) partial out the effect of the moderators on the bias-corrected estimates of $\overline{\rho}$ and S_ρ^2 (or $\overline{\delta}$ and S_δ^2). That is, this method allows one to distinguish between publication bias and the effects of moderators of study outcomes. Vevea and Hedges (1995) illustrated this method by applying it to a subset of Glass's studies on psychotherapy. The two moderators were type of therapy (behavioral vs. desensitization) and type of phobia (simple vs. complex). Even after controlling for these moderators, their analysis still detected publication bias; the bias-corrected estimates of $\bar{\delta}$ were 15% to 25% smaller than the original uncorrected estimates. The reason availability bias was detected in these studies, and not in the GATB studies, may be that most of the psychotherapy studies focused on a single hypothesis (or a single important hypothesis) rather than on multiple hypotheses, as in the GATB study set. Although smaller, the bias-corrected mean effect sizes were still substantial, ranging from .48 to .76.

In this analysis, there was no correction for measurement error in the measure of the dependent variable (the therapy outcome measure). If the publication bias-corrected mean d values had been corrected for measurement error, this would likely have raised them to values larger than the original mean observed d values (uncorrected for publication bias). Hence, as estimates of the actual effects of psychotherapy, the original reported values might have been fairly accurate—and might be more accurate than the bias-corrected values of Vevea and Hedges (1995). As with most other methods of addressing publication bias, there is no recognition in this method of the importance of measurement error as a bias-creating artifact.

Although this procedure appears to remove the effects of publication bias, the price is an increased standard error (SE) of the mean estimate. In this application, the average SE of the mean d values more than doubled, increasing from .07 to .15. This is similar to what we saw in the case of corrections for measurement error and range restriction: The correction removes the bias but increases the uncertainty in the estimate of the mean.

A major limitation of all selection models up to this point is the necessity of estimating the weight function empirically based on the set of studies at hand. These estimates can be inaccurate unless the number of studies is large. Recently, Hedges and associates have proposed a way of circumventing this problem, making it possible to apply the selection model in meta-analyses with a small number of studies (Hedges & Vevea, 2005; Vevea & Woods, 2005). In this newer procedure, the researcher prespecifies a number of plausible weight functions on the study p values (i.e., patterns of possible publication bias), eliminating the need to empirically estimate the pattern. Comparison of the resulting effect size estimates obtained using the different weight functions provides a sensitivity analysis. If all or almost all of the prespecified weight function suggest the absence of publication bias, the researcher has a strong case for the accuracy of his or her meta-analysis results. Vevea and Woods (2005) provide several examples of applications with such a result. If some of the weight patterns suggest publication bias, the researcher can report the results produced under all the selection models (including the no-selection model). This modified method allows for the partialing out of moderator effects, as did the previous selection model. As noted earlier, selection models have been criticized as being computationally complex and difficult to apply. This may no longer be a valid criticism: Vevea and Woods (2005) provide links to online software for application of this method. In light of these developments, it is quite possible that selection models—or at least this newest selection model—will become more important and more widely used.

Study Artifacts and Publication Bias Analyses

This is good place to again warn readers that the results produced by all of the publication bias methods discussed in this chapter are distorted by failure to correct for measurement error and other biasing artifacts prior to application of the methods. For example, when subgrouping published and unpublished studies, lower reliability of measurement among unpublished studies will lead to smaller observed effect sizes than in published studies, giving a false impression that the published studies are providing an upwardly biased estimate of effect size when in fact the true magnitude of effect sizes is the same in unpublished and published studies. When applying the trim-and-fill and funnel plot methods, the user should first correct all correlations or d values for measurement error and other artifacts and adjust each study's standard error appropriately upward for this correction (as explained in Chapter 3) before applying these methods. If sample size rather than standard errors are used on the vertical axis, then adjusted sample sizes should be used, as described in connection with Equation (4.3) in Chapter 4. When applying cumulative meta-analysis, the appropriate corrections for measurement error (and range restriction, if applicable) should be applied in each of the sequential meta-analyses or the results may be distorted. For example, if measures tend to more reliable in small-N studies and measurement error corrections are not made, this would create a false appearance of publication bias—because the observed (uncorrected) effect sizes would be larger on average in the small-N studies, which would be falsely interpreted as publication bias. The same principle applies, of course, to moderator analysis. The literature on the validity of structured and unstructured employment interviews provides a good example of this. Before the coefficients were appropriately corrected for range restriction, the observed validities of structured interviews were substantially larger than those for unstructured interviews. After the appropriate range restriction correction, this difference disappeared (Oh et al., 2013). The general failure to take into account the distorting effects of study artifacts on study outcomes is a serious deficiency in the general literature on publication bias.

Software for Publication Bias Analysis

Software for conducting meta-analysis was discussed in Chapter 11. Most of the program packages discussed there include programs for assessing publication bias. These include Comprehensive Meta-Analysis (CMA), Meta-Win, Stata, RevMan, and M. Borenstein (2005) provides a review of these programs as they relate to publication bias analysis. It appears that overall, the CMA program package provides for the largest number of methods and is the most convenient to use. However, as noted in Chapter 11, it is also the most expensive. The program package that applies psychometric meta-analysis (see the Appendix) includes the cumulative meta-analysis method. This program, unlike others, does include corrections for measurement error (and range variation, if present) in the cumulative meta-analyses.

Attempts to Prevent Publication Bias Before It Happens

In the biomedical area, the potential problems created by publication bias are viewed as so serious that there is a movement toward research registries, which are now increasingly being required by medical journals and some federal funding agencies (Krakovsky, 2004). Under this procedure, researchers are required to register (and describe) their studies in a public database prior to beginning them. The assumption underlying this requirement is that if studies that later when conducted get negative (nonsignificant) results do not appear in the literature, this system makes it possible to detect and reveal that publication bias. It is assumed that this procedure will reduce publication bias in medical research. However, so far this approach has been only partly successful (Berlin & Ghersi, 2005). Dickersin (1994) provides a good discussion of research registries. This requirement has been applied mostly to large-sample federally funded biomedical randomized clinical trials. At present, it appears unlikely to be used in behavioral and social science research. A potentially important recent development is that some large pharmaceutical companies have agreed to release detailed information and data on all their drug trials (K. Thomas, 2013). Previously, the practice was to release only limited information of these trials. Another procedure that has been suggested is the two-stage review. Under this procedure, journal reviewers and editors would first evaluate and rate a study based only on the introduction and the methods sections; they would not have access to the results at this point. Later they would see the whole paper and make a final evaluation. It is thought that this procedure would reduce the tendency to heavily emphasize positive, statistically significant outcomes when making acceptance decisions. Although this procedure has been proposed for psychology and social science journals, to our knowledge it has not yet been adopted by any journal editors. In general, it is our impression that proposals for methods of preventing publication bias—beyond general educational efforts—would be difficult or infeasible to implement.

Summary of Methods for Correcting Availability Bias

Kepes et al. (2012) provide a clear description of most of the methods discussed in this chapter along with example applications of most of them. As noted at the beginning of this chapter, the area of availability bias is one of the most difficult and complex in meta-analysis. It is often difficult to determine whether such bias exists in a set of studies, and, if it does, many methods for detecting it and adjusting for it are complex and not easy to use (Sutton, 2009). In addition, some of the assumptions on which many of them are based may be questionable. Nevertheless, the issue is an important one and will undoubtedly continue to receive attention. There is evidence that availability bias may be relatively unimportant in some literatures used in meta-analysis and quite important in other literatures. In connection with the choice of methods of checking for publication or source bias, it is our judgment that the cumulative meta-analysis method and the trim-and-fill method are the two most informative and useful, although it is desirable to apply more than two methods in order to triangulate. The meta-analysis programs that go with this book (see the Appendix) include a program for the cumulative meta-analysis method, a program that takes into account measurement error (and range variation, if present). Both these methods allow not only the detection of publication bias, but also the quantification of the amount of bias (if any), and an adjustment for the bias. However, it may be useful to include methods beyond these two because of the potential value of triangulating with several methods. The recently improved selection method (Hedges & Vevea, 2005; Vevea & Wood, 2005) would be a good choice. If all methods suggest the absence of bias, the researcher can make a strong case for acceptance of his or her meta-analytic results as being accurate and unbiased. If all or most methods suggest publication bias, then the researcher has a strong case for emphasizing and preferring the results that are adjusted for that bias.

Summary of Psychometric Meta-Analysis

14

Meta-Analysis Methods and Theories of Data and Theories of Knowledge

Every method of meta-analysis is of necessity based on a theory of data. It is this theory (or understanding of data) that determines the nature of the resulting meta-analysis methods. A complete theory of data includes an understanding of sampling error, measurement error, biased sampling (range restriction and range enhancement), dichotomization and its effects, data errors, and other causal factors that distort the raw data results we see in research studies. Once a theoretical understanding of how these factors affect data is developed, it becomes possible to develop methods for correcting for their effects. The necessity of doing so is presented in detail in Schmidt, Le, and Oh (2009), as well as in this book. In the language of psychometrics, the first process—the process by which these factors (artifacts) influence data—is modeled as the attenuation model. The second process—the process of correcting for these artifact-induced biases—is called the disattenuation model. If the theory of data on which a method of meta-analysis is based is incomplete, that method will fail to correct for some or all of these artifacts and will thus produce biased results. For example, a theory of data that fails to recognize measurement error will lead to methods of meta-analysis that do not correct for measurement error. Such methods will then perforce produce biased meta-analysis results. Most current methods of meta-analysis do not, in fact, correct for measurement error, as noted in Chapter 11. But in research methodology, the thrust is always in the direction of increased accuracy, so eventually methods for meta-analysis that do not correct for study artifacts that distort empirical findings will have to incorporate these corrections. This has already happened to some extent in that some users of these methods have "appended" these corrections to those methods (e.g., Aguinis et al., 2008; S. M. Hall & Brannick, 2002). One's theory of data is also part of one's theory of knowledge or theory of epistemology. Epistemology is concerned with the ways in which we can attain correct knowledge. One requirement of an effective epistemology in empirical research is proper correction for the artifacts that distort the empirical data.

Sampling error and measurement error have a unique status among the statistical and measurement artifacts with which meta-analysis must deal: They are always present in all real data (Schmidt, 2010). Other artifacts, such as range restriction, artificial dichotomization of continuous variables, or data transcription errors, may be absent in a particular set of studies being subjected to meta-analysis. There is always sampling error, however, because sample sizes are never infinite. Likewise, there is always measurement error, because there are no perfectly reliable measures. In fact, it is the requirement of dealing simultaneously with both sampling error and measurement error that makes even relatively straightforward psychometric meta-analyses seem complicated to many. Most of us are used to dealing with these two types of errors separately. For example, when psychometric texts (e.g., Lord & Novick, 1968; Nunnally & Bernstein, 1994) discuss measurement error, they assume an infinite (or very large) sample size, so that the focus of attention can be on measurement error alone, with no need to deal simultaneously with sampling error. When statistics texts discuss sampling error, they implicitly assume perfect reliability (the absence of measurement error), so that they and the reader can focus solely on sampling error and can ignore issues of measurement error. Both assumptions are highly unrealistic, because all real data simultaneously contain both sampling error and measurement error. It is admittedly more complicated to deal with both types of error simultaneously, yet this is what meta-analysis must do to be successful, as the content of this book has made clear. In an important statement, Cook et al. (1992, pp. 315–316, 325–328) also acknowledge this necessity, as does Hedges (2009b).

Another critical component of a complete theory of data capable of providing a foundation for meta-analysis methods is recognition of the fact that it is highly likely that study population correlations or effect sizes will vary from study to study. The assumption that these parameters are identical across all studies in a meta-analysis—the assumption made by all fixed effects meta-analysis models—is unrealistic and typically erroneous, as discussed in Chapters 5 and 9. Fixed effects and random effects models are both (partial) theories of the nature of data. Evidence and observation disconfirm the fixed effects theory and support the random effects theory. Fixed effects models can lead to serious errors in meta-analytic results, and this is not the case for random effects models (Schmidt, Oh, & Hayes,

2009). Therefore, the theory of data underlying meta-analysis methods should include the random effects model but not the fixed effects model.

What Is the Ultimate Purpose of Meta-Analysis?

The question of what theory of data (and therefore of knowledge) under-lies a method of meta-analysis is strongly related to the question of what the general purpose of meta-analysis is. As discussed in Chapter 11, Glass (1976, 1977) stated that the purpose is simply to summarize and describe in a general way the reported results of studies in a research literature. In the Hedges-Olkin (1985) and the R. Rosenthal (1984, 1991) approaches to meta-analysis, the purpose of meta-analysis is more analytic: The focus is on examination of relationships between measures of particular constructs or between measures of specific types of treatments and measures of spe-cific outcomes. However, the purpose is still to summarize the findings reported in a specific research literature (Rubin, 1990). Our view of the purpose of meta-analysis is different: The purpose is to estimate as accu-rately as possible the construct-level relationships in the population (i.e., to estimate population values or parameters), because these are the rela-tionships of scientific interest (Schmidt et al., 2013). This is an entirely different task; this is the task of estimating what the findings would have been if all studies had been conducted perfectly (i.e., with no methodolog-ical limitations). Doing this requires correction for sampling error, mea-surement error, and other artifacts (when present) that distort study results. Simply quantitatively summarizing and describing the contents of studies in the literature requires no such corrections and does not allow estimation of parameters of scientific interest. In the methods presented in this book, construct-level relationships are estimated by true score rela-tionships. Schmidt et al. (2013) showed that in the measures used in behavioral research, true score relationships almost always reflect construct-level relationships very closely.

Rubin (1990, pp. 155–166) critiqued the common, descriptive concept of the purpose of meta-analysis and proposed the alternative offered in this book. He stated that, as scientists, we are not really interested in the popula-tion of imperfect studies per se; hence, an accurate description or summary of these studies is not really important. Instead, he argued that the goal of meta-analysis should be to estimate the true effects or relationships—defined as "results that would be obtained in an infinitely large, perfectly designed study or sequence of such studies." According to Rubin,

> Under this view, we really do not care *scientifically* about summarizing this finite population (of observed studies). We really care about the underlying scientific process—the underlying process that is generating

these outcomes that we happen to see—that we, as fallible researchers, are trying to glimpse through the opaque window of imperfect empirical studies. (p. 157, emphasis in original)

Rubin stated that all studies in the finite population of existing studies, or in a hypothetical population of studies from which these studies are drawn, are flawed in various ways. Therefore, in order to understand the underlying scientific realities, our purpose should not be to summarize their typical reported effect sizes or correlations but rather to use the flawed study findings along with other available information to estimate the underlying unobserved relationships among constructs. This is an excellent statement of the purpose of meta-analysis as we see it and as embodied in the methods presented in this book. M. E. Chan and Arvey (2012) have documented the fact that this approach to meta-analysis has in fact achieved this objective in a wide variety of research areas.

Psychometric Meta-Analysis: Summary Overview

The goal of research in any area is the production of an integrated statement of the findings of the many pieces of research done in that area. This means an analysis of how the many facts fit together, that is, the development of theory. However, this broad theoretical integration cannot be put on a sound footing until a narrower integration of the literature has taken place. We must first establish the basic facts about relationships before those facts can be integrated. The purpose of meta-analysis is to calibrate these basic relationships at the construct level. That is, the purpose is to estimate what these relationships would be found to be in perfectly conducted studies.

Consider a theoretical question such as "Does job satisfaction increase organizational identification?" Before we can answer such a question, we must consider the more mundane question, "Is there a correlation between satisfaction and organizational identification?" Such questions cannot be answered in any one empirical study. Results must be pooled across studies to eliminate sampling error, and corrections must be made for measurement error. Furthermore, the correlation between satisfaction and identification might vary across studies. That is, we must compare the population correlations in different settings. If there is variation across settings large enough to be theoretically important, then we should identify the moderator variables that produce this variation. To compare correlations across settings, we must correct these correlations for other artifacts such as measurement error and range variation (if present).

Consider error of measurement. Job satisfaction can be measured in many ways. These different methods may not measure exactly the same construct, or they may differ in the extent of measurement error. Differences in measurement error can be assessed by differences in the appropriate reliability coefficients. If the reliability of each measure is known in each study, then the effect of error of measurement can be eliminated from each study by correcting the correlation for attenuation and performing the psychometric meta-analysis on these corrected correlations. If only the distribution of reliability coefficients across studies is known, then the effect of random error of measurement can be eliminated using the artifact distribution methods of psychometric meta-analysis.

Systematic differences between measures with the same name require examination of the construct validity of the different methods. If there are large systematic differences between measures, then these must be assessed in multimeasure studies using techniques such as confirmatory factor analysis or path analysis. These studies require replication of results within studies as well as across studies and require special treatment.

Range variation on the independent variable produces differences of an artifactual nature in correlations and in effect size statistics. Even if the basic relationship between variables is the same across studies, variation in the size of the variance on the independent variable will produce variation in the correlation with the dependent variable. The larger the variance on the independent variable, the higher will be the correlation. Range variation (or range restriction) can be either direct or indirect. Indirect range restriction is by far the more common type in all literatures and produces more severe data distortions than direct range restriction. In experimental studies, range variation is produced by differences in the strength of the treatment. If the range size in each study is known (i.e., if standard deviations are published or if treatment strengths are measured), then all correlations or effect sizes can be corrected to the same standard value, eliminating the impact of range variation across studies. Psychometric meta-analysis can then be carried out on these corrected correlations or d values. If only the distribution of range variation is known, then this effect can be eliminated using artifact distribution meta-analysis methods.

Meta-analysis begins with all studies that an investigator can find that provide empirical evidence that bears on some particular fact, such as the relationship between job satisfaction and organizational identification. The key findings of each study are expressed in a common statistic, such as the correlation between identification and satisfaction or the d statistic, which measures the difference between experimental and control groups for the treatment of interest. Each such statistic can be examined across studies. The mean value of the statistic across studies is a good estimate of the mean attenuated population value across studies. However, the variance across studies is inflated by sampling error. Thus, the first task in artifact distribution meta-analysis is to correct the observed variance across studies to eliminate the effect of sampling error. Then the mean and variance of population values are corrected for the effect of error of measurement and range variation. This mean and standard deviation have thus been corrected for three sources of artifactual variation across studies: sampling error, error of measurement, and range variation. The largest source of variation not corrected for is often reporting errors, such as incorrect computations, typographical errors, failure to reverse score, and the like. However, there are numerous other potential sources of artifactual variation.

In many of our meta-analyses, we have found little or no remaining variance in results across studies once artifacts have been eliminated (e.g., Schmidt et al., 1993). In such cases, the theorist is provided with a very straightforward fact to weave into the overall theoretical picture. In such a case, one way to reveal theoretical implications is to review all the reasons that have been cited as explanations for the apparent but actually artifactual variation across studies. Most such explanations are based on more general theoretical ideas or propositions. Hence, the disconfirmation of the explanation leads to disconfirmation of the more general theoretical propositions underlying the explanation. For example, meta-analysis has shown that the correlation between cognitive ability factors and job performance essentially does not vary across settings for a given job or for different jobs with the same mental complexity level. This means that it is unnecessary and wasteful for practitioners in personnel selection to conduct detailed behavioristic job analyses to equate jobs in different organizations on the specific tasks performed in those jobs, because meta-analysis has disconfirmed the theory that specific task differences cause validity differences.

If there is variation across studies, it may not be large enough to warrant an immediate search for moderator variables. For example, suppose meta-analysis had shown the mean effect of interpersonal skills training on supervisor performance to be $\bar{\delta} = .50$ with a standard deviation of .05. It would be wise for an employer to institute a program of training immediately rather than wait to find out which programs work best. On the other hand, if the mean effect were $\bar{\delta} = .10$ with a standard deviation of .10, then the arbitrary choice of program might incur a loss. There is a 16% chance that the program would be counterproductive and another 34% chance that the program would cause a positive but nearly trivial improvement.

Meta-analysis provides a method for establishing the relevance of a potential moderator variable. The moderator variable is used to split the studies into subsets, and meta-analysis is then applied to each subset separately. Mean differences will appear if a moderator is present. If there are large differences in subset means, then there will be a corresponding reduction in within-subset variation across studies. Meta-analysis can then show how much of any remaining variation is due to artifacts.

The extent of variation is in part a question of the scope of the research review. If we start with all studies on psychotherapy, it would be no surprise to find moderator effects. However, if we consider only studies using desensitization on simple phobias, then we might expect to find no differences. However, this is an empirical question. The a priori assumption that there are no differences—made by all fixed effects meta-analysis methods—is virtually never justifiable (Schmidt, Oh, & Hayes, 2009). For meta-analysis, scope is an empirical question. If we have the resources for a wide scope, then meta-analysis can be used to assess a wide scope of results. If meta-analysis shows only small differences over a very wide set of studies, that finding indicates that many moderator hypotheses are at most of only minor importance. If the wide-scope study shows large differences, then meta-analysis can be applied to subsets of studies with smaller scope. Meta-analysis then shows which aspects of scope (i.e., which potential moderators) are truly important and which are only erroneously thought to be important. The general finding of meta-analysis studies is that true differences across studies are much smaller than researchers believe them to be. These beliefs derive in large part from the cumulative psychological effects of sampling error, that is, repeated observations of large but spurious differences in the observed results from small-sample studies.

Restriction of scope in meta-analysis should be theory based rather than methodological. The most misleading reviews are those in which the author cites only "key" studies selected based on the author's judgments of methodological quality. First, reviews that selectively ignore studies with contrary findings may falsely suggest that there are no moderator variables. Second, even if there are no real variations across studies, there are still spurious variations due to sampling error and other artifacts. Studies selected because they have particularly "sharp" findings are likely to be studies that capitalize on between-study variation that meta-analysis shows to be due mostly to sampling error and other artifacts. In particular, consideration of only studies with statistically significant findings leads to great bias in the estimate of correlations or effect sizes.

Many authors justify selective reviews on the basis of the "methodological deficiencies" in the studies not considered. However, the assertion of "deficiency" is usually based on a personal theory that is itself empirically untested. Agreement between researchers on overall methodological quality is typically quite low. Two reviewers could select mutually exclusive sets of "best studies" from the same literature on the basis of "methodological quality." Meta-analysis provides an empirical procedure for the identification of methodological deficiencies if there are any. First, one should gather a comprehensive set of studies. Second, one should identify those believed to be "methodologically flawed." Third, one should apply meta-analysis to all studies. If there is no nonartifactual variation across studies, then there is no difference between the "defective" studies and the "competent" studies. Fourth, if there is variation across all studies, then that variation may or may not be explained by separate meta-analyses of the "defective" and "nondefective" studies, the next analysis to be conducted.

It is our experience that many real methodological problems beyond sampling error are captured by the rubrics "error of measurement" and "range variation." Error of measurement, in particular, is universal, although some studies may have much poorer measurement than others. The solution to these methodological problems is to *measure* the deficiency and correct for it rather than to discard the data.

Appendix

Windows-Based Meta-Analysis Software Package Version 2.0

The Hunter-Schmidt Meta-Analysis Programs Package includes six programs that implement all basic types of Hunter-Schmidt psychometric meta-analysis methods. Information on how to obtain this program package is provided at the end of the Appendix. Brief descriptions of the six programs are provided in Section 4, "Types of Analyses." A full description of the output of each program is given in Section 11, "Full Description of Output of Individual Programs." These programs are intended to be used in conjunction with this book (henceforth referred to as "the text").

In response to feedback from users, we have made a number of improvements to the current version of these programs (Version 2.0) that were not available in previous versions (Versions 1.0 and 1.1). These include the following:

1. The programs now allow importation of data files from Excel.

2. The programs now will produce forest plots. Forest plots can be useful in examining the studies prior to the meta-analysis.

3. Confidence intervals (in addition to credibility intervals) are now provided for all mean values except bare-bones meta-analysis means.

4. Output for corrected r and d values is now presented in tabular form, as well as in the more detailed output form. The tabular form output includes the values that should be reported in tables of meta-analytic results in papers submitted for publication. (Tabular form is not provided for bare-bones meta-analysis results.)

5. Studies can now be coded for analysis of potential moderators, making it more convenient to subgroup studies for moderator analysis.

6. The programs now include a method of checking for publication bias—cumulative meta-analysis. See Chapter 13 for a discussion of this procedure.

7. Output now includes the correlation between observed r or d values and artifact effects on these values.

8. The maximum number of studies in a meta-analysis has been raised from 200 to 1,000.

9. It is now possible to select saved data files for analysis by just clicking on the file name. (In older versions, the file name had to be typed in.)

10. It is now easier for users to access the supplementary programs for computing composite correlations and for converting point-biserial correlations to biserial correlations. These programs are no longer password protected. They can now be accessed by clicking on the appropriate icon.

11. The programs can be downloaded from the Internet. Alternatively, a program package CD can be provided.

12. Three small technical adjustments have been made. First, in the previous version, if an r or d value was entered as zero, the program would not run. This has been corrected. Second, the correction for the small bias in observed rs has been added. Third, in computing the sampling error variance of d values, the programs now use Equation (7.23a) instead of Equation (7.23). (These equations are in Chapter 7.) Use of Equation (7.23a) produces greater accuracy in those cases in which the sample size for one group is very small compared to the other group. It is also accurate when the group sample sizes are less unequal or equal in size.

The programs are provided on a CD or downloaded from the Internet and are compatible with Microsoft Windows operating systems (Windows 95, 98, 98SE, ME, 2000, XP, and Windows 7). Program interface is logically and intuitively arranged so that people with basic familiarity with Windows-based applications can easily learn to use the program functions. Navigating through the different steps (pages) of the programs is achieved by single-clicking appropriate buttons or icons. Throughout all the steps (pages), there are built-in help functions in the form of roll-over pop-ups (i.e., help statements that appear when the cursor is rolled over certain predetermined areas) explaining the options and instructing the user in how to execute his or her desired tasks.

1. What Is in the Download or the CD Program Package?

In addition to the core meta-analysis programs, the program package contains (1) the Setup file (Setup Meta Program.exe), (2) the Readme.doc file (the file you are now reading), and (3) three utility programs in the form of Microsoft Excel templates (Composites.xls and Point-Biserial.xls; details of these programs are described in the "Extras" section). Two of these auxiliary programs help users convert correlations in the primary studies to appropriate forms before inputting them into the meta-analysis programs. The third auxiliary program produces forest plots of the studies in a meta-analysis.

2. Installation

If you have an earlier version of the program package (Version 1.0 or 1.1), you should uninstall it before installing the current version. Uninstallation can easily be done by using the "Remove Hunter-Schmidt Meta Analysis Programs" option available in the Windows Programs taskbar.

The installation process starts by double-clicking the Setup file on the CD or following the downloading instructions you receive via an e-mail. You will be asked to provide a serial number to continue. The main programs and all the supporting files will be copied to folder "C: \ Meta Analysis Programs" on your hard drive (unless you specify a different drive).

3. Starting the Program

The programs can be activated by selecting the "Hunter & Schmidt Meta Analysis Programs" in the Windows Programs taskbar. Alternatively, you can start the programs by using the icon "Hunter & Schmidt MA" on your desktop. You will be presented with the Start Page, where you can access the Readme file by clicking on the book icon at the upper right corner of the page. There are also links that allow you to get access to the extra programs for computing composite correlations or point-biseral correlations or for creating the forest plots. To move on to the next page, in which you can select types of meta-analyses to be run, click on the red arrow icon at the lower right corner of the page. The "Type of Analyses" page will appear, presenting you with four options of analyses (described next).

4. Types of Analyses

The programs in this package do the following types of meta-analysis:

1. Meta-analysis of correlations corrected individually for the effects of artifacts. (These two programs are collectively referred to in the

text as VG6.) These programs are used when (1) the user desires to estimate the correlation between variables, and (2) information on the statistical and measurement artifacts (i.e., range restriction, reliabilities on both variables) is available in all (or the majority) of the primary studies. These programs are illustrated in Chapter 3 of the text.

There are two subprograms under this type of meta-analysis:

A. Program that corrects for direct range restriction: To be used when range restriction is direct (i.e., selection occurs on one of the two variables being correlated). (This program is referred to in the text as VG6-D; see Chapter 3.)

B. Program that corrects for indirect range restriction: To be used when range restriction is indirect (i.e., selection occurs on a third variable that is correlated with both the variables of interest). (This program is referred to in the text as VG6-I; see Chapter 3.)

(Note: Both programs ask the user if there is any range restriction. If the answer is no, the data entry field for the range restriction statistic [the u value] does not appear. When there is no range restriction, the results provided by the subprograms 1A and 1B are identical.)

2. Meta-analysis of correlations using artifact distributions. These programs are used when (1) the user desires to estimate the correlation between variables, and (2) information on the statistical and measurement artifacts is *not* available in most of the primary studies. (These two programs are collectively referred to in the text as INTNL; see Chapter 4.)

This meta-analysis program also includes two subprograms:

A. Program that corrects for direct range restriction: To be used when range restriction is direct (i.e., selection occurs on one of the two variables being correlated). (This program is referred to in the text as INTNL-D; see Chapter 4.)

B. Program that corrects for indirect range restriction: To be used when range restriction is indirect (i.e., selection occurs on a third variable that is correlated with both the variables of interest). (This program is referred to in the text as INTNL-I; see Chapter 4.)

(Note: Both programs ask the user if there is any range restriction. If the answer is no, the data entry field for the range restriction statistic [the u value] does not appear. When there is no range restriction, the results provided by the subprograms 2A and 2B are identical.)

3. Meta-analysis of *d* values corrected individually for measurement error.

    This program is used when (1) the meta-analysis is based on the effect size (*d* value; standardized difference between groups), and (2) information on the reliability of the measure of the dependent variable is available in all (or most) of the primary studies. (This program is referred to in the text as D-VALUE; see Chapter 7.)

4. Meta-analysis of *d* values using artifact distributions.

    This program is used when (1) the meta-analysis is based on the effect size (*d* value; standardized difference between groups), and (2) information on the reliability of the measure of the dependent variable is *not* available in most of the primary studies. (This program is referred to in the text as D-VALUE1; see Chapter 7.)

The "Type of Analyses" page of the program shows four types of meta-analysis (1 to 4, listed above), and the user selects the most appropriate analysis. If the user selects option 1 or 2, the subprograms (1A and 1B or 2A and 2B) will appear on subsequent pages (under the Analysis section) for further choice of the exact program to be used (depending on whether range restriction is direct or indirect). As noted earlier, the user can also indicate that there is no range restriction.

5. Data Management

After selecting the appropriate type of analysis, the user is presented with the "Setting Up the Data" page. Here the user can opt to input (enter) new data, load existing (previously saved) data files, or import data files from Excel (when selecting this option, the user will be provided with an Excel template for entering data). In all programs, users can elect to code studies by potential moderators to make subsequent moderator subgroup analysis more convenient. This is done by following the instructions in the programs (described in Section 9, "Moderator Analysis"). The users can also conduct analysis to examine publication bias based on the cumulative meta-analysis method described in Chapter 13 of the book.

a. Entering Data

    For meta-analysis type 1 (i.e., meta-analysis for correlations, with information on statistical and measurement artifacts available in most primary studies; VG6 programs), the user need only enter data into one general data file. This data file can be imported from Excel or created with the program. The "Enter data from primary studies" page has a spreadsheet-like layout with six fields (spaces) so that relevant information for each study (i.e., code for moderator analysis [explained later in Section 9, "Moderator Analysis"], correlation, sample size, reliability of variable X [independent variable reliability, R_{xx}], reliability of variable Y [dependent variable reliability, R_{yy}], and range restriction ratio [u]) can be entered accordingly. Data are entered sequentially for each study. When corrections are needed, the user can click on the "Modification" buttons available in front of the data holder for each study. All the data fields must be filled. When there is no range restriction in a particular study, "1" should be entered in the range restriction (u) cell. Similarly, when a variable is assumed to be perfectly measured (very rare case), "1" should be entered in the corresponding reliability cell. In situations where information on an artifact (R_{xx}, R_{yy}, or u) of a study is not available, the user can simply enter "99" into the corresponding cell. The program will then automatically use the mean of all the relevant artifact values provided in other studies to replace the missing value.

There are spaces to enter data for eight studies in each page. After entering the data for each page, the user clicks on the "Continue" button to proceed to the next page. The two buttons, "Back" and "Continue," can be used to navigate through the pages to modify and/or enter data. The maximum number of studies is 1,000. After completing data entry, the user can press the "Done" button to exit to the previous page and start analysis (or choose other options, such as printing, saving, or modifying the data, as described later).

For meta-analysis type 2 (i.e., meta-analysis for correlations when information on statistical and measurement artifacts is *unavailable* in most primary studies; INTNL programs), the user enters data separately into several data files: The first data file consists of the code for moderators, correlations, and the corresponding sample sizes of the primary studies (r and N). The second data file consists of the distribution of reliability coefficients of the independent variable (R_{xx} and freq of each). The third data file consists of the distribution of reliability coefficients of the dependent variable (R_{yy} and freq of each). And the fourth data file consists of the distribution of range restriction (u and freq of each u). These data files can also be imported from Excel. If information is not available (or the artifact is not applicable) for an artifact distribution (e.g., when there is no range restriction), the program will assume that such artifacts have values fixed at 1.00 and automatically place 1.00s in the relevant data file(s). This means no correction will be made for these artifacts.

For meta-analysis type 3 (i.e., meta-analysis for effect sizes [d values], with information on statistical and measurement artifacts available in most primary studies; D-VALUE program), the procedures are similar to those of the type 1 meta-analysis described previously, except that the user enters only information on dependent variable reliability (R_{yy});

information on independent variable reliability (R_{xx}) and range restriction (u) is not required. This data file can be imported from Excel.

For meta-analysis type 4 (i.e., meta-analysis for effect sizes [d values] when information on statistical and measurement artifacts is *unavailable* in most primary studies; D-VALUE1 program), the procedures are similar to those of the type 2 meta-analysis described previously, except that the user enters only information on the distribution of dependent variable reliability (R_{yy} and freq); information on distributions of independent variable reliability (R_{xx}) and range restriction (u) is not required. Hence, there are only two data files rather than the four data files required for meta-analysis type 2. Again, these data files can be imported from Excel.

  b. Saving Data

  After completing the entry of the data (by clicking on the "Done" button), the user is taken back to the previous page where several options are presented: "Save," "Print," "Analysis," and "Exit." Selecting the "Save" option allows the user to save the data file he or she has just entered. The user will be asked to provide the name for the data set so that it can be easily retrieved when needed. The data will then be saved at the following location: C:\ Meta Analysis Programs \ Data i\"datasetname," with i being the number corresponding to the type of meta-analysis.

Alternatively, the user can simply start analyzing the data. After the meta-analysis results are presented, the user is given another opportunity to save the current data set.

  c. Loading Previously Saved Data

  To load the previously saved data, select the "Load" option in the "Setting Up the Data" page. The user will be presented with names of all the previously saved data sets. He or she can select the appropriate data set to load into the program by clicking on the name of that data file.

  d. Viewing/Modifying Saved Data

  After loading/entering data, the user can view the data by selecting the "Entering/Modifying" option. Data will be presented in the spreadsheet-like layout. Modifications (corrections) can be made by clicking the icon in front of each individual study.

  e. Printing Data

  The user can print the current data set (i.e., the data that have just been entered, loaded, or imported from Excel) for easy reviewing by selecting the "Print" option.

  f. Conducting Publication Bias Analysis

  Selecting the link "Publication bias analysis" will open a new page (instructions will be given by the program), which enables the users to conduct publication analysis based on the cumulative meta-analysis method described in Chapter 13 of the book.

6. Analyzing Data

After entering/loading/modifying the data, the user can start analyzing the data by clicking on the "Analyzing the Data" button. For correlation-based meta-analysis (i.e., types 1 and 2; VG6 and INTNL programs), if the user has previously indicated there is range restriction, the user will next be asked to indicate the nature of range restriction existing in his or her data (i.e., direct or indirect, which means selecting between type 1A [VG6-D program] or 1B [VG6-I program] or selecting between 2A [INTNL-D program] or 2B [INTNL-I program]).

Both direct range restriction programs (VG6-D and INTNL-D) automatically assume that the independent variable reliabilities (R_{xx}) are from the unrestricted samples, and the dependent variable reliabilities (R_{yy}) are from the restricted samples. These assumptions agree with the nature of data available in research and practice. (See the text, Chapters 3, 4, and 5, for a more detailed discussion.)

Both indirect range restriction programs (VG6-I and INTNL-I) require the user to specify whether (1) the independent variable reliabilities (R_{xx}) are from the restricted or unrestricted samples and (2) whether the range restriction ratios are for true scores (u_T) or observed scores (u_X). For all cases, the program assumes that the dependent variable reliabilities are from the restricted samples. (See the text, Chapters 3, 4, and 5, for a detailed discussion.)

When there is no range restriction, it does not matter which type of analysis (A or B) the user chooses; the programs will provide identical results.

The user will be asked to provide the title for the analysis (e.g., "Interviews and job performance—Meta-analysis 1") and the name of the output file where results will be saved.

7. Reporting Results

Results of the analyses are provided three different ways: (1) on screen (partial output), (2) on disk (at C: \Meta Analysis Programs\Output\ "filename", with "filename" being the name the user provided for the current analysis), and (3) print out (optional; which can be activated by clicking on the "Printer" option). As noted earlier, the printed output is present both in table form (some of the output) and in the more traditional output format (complete output). Due to space limitations, only partial output is presented on the screen. Complete output is saved to disk and printed with the print-out option.

A full listing and description of the output of each program is given later. The following are *some* of the items provided as output of the analysis:

1. Number of correlations (or *d* values) and total sample size.

2. Mean true score correlation (or mean corrected *d* value), the corresponding standard deviation (true score correlation SD_ρ or true effect size SD_δ), and the corresponding variances. These values are corrected for the biasing effects of all the artifacts considered in the meta-analysis. These values are estimates of mean construct-level relationships. Credibility intervals and confidence intervals are also provided.

3. Weighted mean observed correlation (or *d* values), observed variance and observed standard deviation, and variance and standard deviation corrected for sampling error only. This is the bare-bones meta-analysis output.

4. Sampling error variance, percentage of the observed variance due to sampling error variance, variance accounted for by all artifacts combined, and percentage of the observed variance due to all the artifacts combined.

5. The correlation between observed values and artifact effects is also presented. This is the square root of the proportion of variance accounted for by all artifacts combined.

6. For types 1 and 2 analyses (i.e., correlation-based meta-analyses), certain output is provided that is relevant to employment or educational selection research. The VG6 and INTNL programs provide the mean true validity and its standard deviation. Credibility intervals and confidence intervals are also provided. The true validity (also called operational validity) is the correlation between the predictor (*X*) and the criterion (*Y*) corrected for all the artifacts except for the attenuating effect of measurement error in the predictor *X*. This value represents the mean correlation of the predictor *measures* with the criterion of interest. (In contrast, the true score correlation represents the mean construct-level correlation between the independent variable and the dependent variable.)

8. Illustrating Examples

The programs include several data sets used as examples in Chapters 3, 4, and 7. There are examples representing all six types of meta-analyses discussed previously. The user can practice doing analyses based on these data sets to familiarize himself or herself with the programs.

9. Moderator Analysis

The programs allow users to conduct analyses separately for each moderator value/category. Results will be presented for each value/category of the moderator. To specify moderator analysis, the user can enter values of the moderator of interest at the field labeled "Moderator value" when entering the data. Values of the moderator should be entered using a number from 1 to k (with k being the number of categories of the moderator) for each study. If no moderator analysis is needed, the user can leave the field for "Moderator Value" blank.

10. Extras (Auxiliary Programs)

There are three utility programs in the form of Microsoft Excel templates that aid in examining and processing data before entering data into the meta-analysis programs. The user must have Microsoft Excel to use these programs. During the process of installing the main (meta-analysis) programs, these three utility programs will be automatically copied onto your hard drive at the following location: "C: \Meta Analysis Programs\ Extras." The first program ("Composite.xls") combines correlations within a study; it computes the correlation between a composite (summed) independent or dependent variable and the other variable. This program also computes the reliability of the composite measure. (Both these procedures are described in Chapter 10 of the text.) The second program ("Formula to compute biserial r.xls") computes the biserial correlation from a point-biserial correlation provided in a primary study. This conversion should be carried out when a continuous (and normally distributed) variable has been artificially dichotomized in a primary study (as described in Chapters 4, 6 and 7 of the text). The third program allows users to create the forest plots to examine their data. As noted earlier, these programs can be accessed at the start page that users find when first starting the program packages.

11. Full Description of Output of Individual Programs

The standard program output is divided into three sections: (1) Main Meta-Analysis Output, which presents results corrected for all artifacts; (2) Bare-Bones Meta-Analysis Output, which presents results corrected for sampling error only; and (3) Validity Generalization Output, which presents validity results relevant to tests and other procedures used in employment and educational selection. Section 3 is provided only for meta-analyses of correlations (i.e., type 1 meta-analysis [based on the VG6 programs] and type 2 meta-analyses [based on the INTNL programs]). It is not provided for meta-analyses of d values (type 3 meta-analysis [based on the D-VALUE program] and type 4 meta-analysis [based on the D-VALUE1 program]). The sections of program output always appear in the same order: The main output is always presented first, followed by the bare-bones output, followed by the validity generalization output (if applicable). The bare-bones output is identical for VG6 and INTNL program output. Hence, to avoid repetition, we present this first below.

A. Bare-bones output for VG6 (type 1 meta-analysis) and INTNL (type 2 meta-analysis)

1. Sample size weighted mean observed correlation.

2. Variance of correlations after removing sampling error variance.

3. Standard deviation (*SD*) of correlations after removing sampling error variance. (This is the square root of Item 2.)

4. Sample size weighted variance of observed correlations.

5. Sample size weighted *SD* of observed correlations. (This is the square root of Item 4.)

6. Variance due to sampling error variance.

7. *SD* predicted from sampling error alone. (This is the square root of Item 6.)

8. Percentage variance of observed correlations due to sampling error variance.

9. The correlation between observed values of *r* and their sampling errors. (This is the square root of the proportion of variance accounted for by sampling error; see Item 8.)

B. Main output for VG6 programs (type 1 meta-analysis)

1. Number of correlations in the meta-analysis.

2. Total sample size. (Sum of study sample sizes.)

3. Mean true score correlation ($\bar{\rho}$).

4. Variance of true score correlations (S_ρ^2).

5. *SD* of true score correlations (SD_ρ). (This is the square root of Item 4.) Note: For most purposes, the key output is Items 3 and 5.

6. Eighty percent credibility interval for true score correlation distribution (see Chapter 5).

7. Ninety-five percent confidence interval around the mean true score correlation (see Chapter 5).

8. Observed variance of the corrected correlations ($S_{r_c}^2$). (Each correlation is first corrected for measurement error and other artifacts; then the variance of these corrected correlations is

computed. This is the variance of the corrected correlations before sampling error variance is removed. As described in Chapter 3, the corrections for artifacts, while eliminating systematic downward biases, increase sampling error.)

9. *SD* of the corrected correlations SD_{r_c}. (This is the square root of Item 8.)

10. Variance in corrected correlations due to sampling error. (Note: This figure is larger than the variance in *uncorrected* [*observed*] correlations due to sampling error variance, which is reported in the bare-bones output section. This is because the artifact corrections, while removing systematic downward biases, increase sampling error variance. Note: Variance due to other artifacts is included in this variance because the effects of these artifacts have been previously corrected for.)

11. *SD* of corrected correlations predicted from sampling error. (This is the square root of Item 10.)

12. Percentage variance in corrected correlations due to sampling error and other artifacts.

13. The correlation between the corrected *r*s and their sampling errors. (This is the square root of the proportion of variance in the corrected correlations accounted for by all artifacts; see Item 12.)

C. Validity generalization output for VG6 programs (type 1 meta-analysis)

1. Mean true validity. (Same as mean true score correlation, except it is not corrected for the attenuating effects of measurement error in the independent variable; see Chapter 3 of text.)

2. Variance of true validities.

3. *SD* of true validities. (This is the square root of Item 2.)

4. Eighty percent credibility interval for true validity distribution (see Chapter 5).

5. Ninety-five percent confidence interval around mean true validity (see Chapter 5).

6. Observed variance of the corrected validities. (Each validity is first corrected for measurement error in the dependent variable and for range restriction; then the variance of these corrected validities is computed. This is the variance of the corrected validities before sampling error is subtracted out. As described in Chapter 3, the corrections for artifacts, while eliminating systematic downward biases, increase sampling error.)

7. *SD* of the corrected validities. (This is the square root of Item 6.)

8. Variance in corrected validities due to sampling error. (Note: This figure is larger than the variance in uncorrected [observed] validities due to sampling error variance, which is reported in the bare-bones output section. This is because the artifact corrections, while removing systematic downward biases, increase sampling error. Note: Variance due to other artifacts is included in this variance because the effects of these artifacts have previously been corrected for.)

9. *SD* of corrected validities predicted from sampling error and other artifacts. (This is the square root of Item 8.)

10. Percentage of variance accounted for by sampling error. (Note: Variance due to other artifacts is included in this because these artifacts have previously been corrected for.)

11. The correlation between corrected *r*s and artifact effects. (This is the square root of the proportion of variance in the corrected *r*s accounted for by artifacts; see Item 10.)

D. Main output for INTNL programs (type 2 meta-analysis)

1. Number of correlations in the meta-analysis.

2. Total sample size. (Sum of study sample sizes.)

3. Mean true score correlation ($\bar{\rho}$).

4. Variance of true score correlations (S_ρ^2).

5. *SD* of true score correlations (SD_ρ). (This is the square root of Item 4.) Note: For most purposes, the key output is Items 3 and 5.

6. Eighty percent credibility interval for true score correlation distribution (see Chapter 5).

7. Ninety-five percent confidence interval around mean true score correlation (see Chapter 5).

8. Variance in observed correlations due to all artifacts combined (see Chapter 4).

9. *SD* of observed correlations predicted from all artifacts. (This is the square root of Item 8.)

10. Variance of observed correlations after removal of variance due to all artifacts (residual variance [SD_{res}]; see Chapter 4).

11. Percentage variance of observed correlations due to all artifacts.

12. Correlation between observed *r*s and artifact effects. (This is the square root of the proportion of variance in observed *r*s accounted for by artifacts; see Item 10.)

E. Validity generalization output for INTNL programs (type 2 meta-analysis)

  1. Mean true validity. (Same as mean true score correlation, except not corrected for the attenuating effects of measurement error in the independent variable.)

  2. Variance of true validities.

  3. *SD* of true validities. (This is the square root of Item 2.)

  4. Eighty percent credibility interval of true validity distribution (see Chapter 5).

  5. Ninety-five percent confidence interval around mean true validity (see Chapter 5).

  6. Variance of observed validities due to all artifacts combined (see Chapter 4).

  7. *SD* of observed validities predicted from all artifacts. (This is the square root of Item 6.)

  8. Variance in observed validities after removal of variance due to all artifacts (residual variance [SD_{res}]; see Chapter 4).

  9. Percentage variance in observed validities due to all artifacts.

  10. Correlation between observed validities and artifact effects. (This is the square root of the proportion of variance in observed validities accounted for by artifacts; see Item 9.)

F. Bare-bones output for D-VALUE and D-VALUE1 programs (meta-analysis types 3 and 4; bare-bones output is identical for these two types of meta-analyses)

  1. Sample size weighted mean effect size (mean *d* value).

  2. Variance of *d* values after removing sampling error variance.

  3. *SD* of *d* values after removing sampling error variance. (This is the square root of Item 2.)

  4. Sample size weighted variance of observed *d* values.

  5. Sample size weighted standard deviation of observed *d* values. (This is the square root of Item 4.)

  6. Variance in observed *d* values due to sampling error variance.

  7. *SD* predicted from sampling error variance alone. (This is the square root of Item 6.)

  8. Percentage variance in observed *d* values due to sampling error variance.

9. Correlation between observed d values and their sampling errors. (This is the square root of the proportion of variance accounted for by sampling error; see Item 8.)

G. Main output for D-VALUE program (type 3 meta-analysis)

1. Number of effect sizes (d values) in the meta-analysis.

2. Total sample size. (Sample sizes summed across studies.)

3. Mean true effect size ($\bar{\delta}$)

4. Variance of true effect sizes (S_δ^2)

5. SD of delta (SD_δ). (This is the square root of Item 4.) Note: For most purposes, the key output is Items 3 and 5.

6. Eighty percent credibility interval for delta distribution (see Chapter 8).

7. Ninety-five confidence interval around the mean delta (see Chapter 8).

8. Observed variance of corrected d values ($S_{d_c}^2$). (Each d value is corrected for measurement error in the dependent variable; then the variance of these corrected d values is computed. This is the variance of the corrected d values before sampling error variance is removed. As described in Chapter 7, the correction for measurement error, while eliminating the systematic downward bias, increases sampling error variance.)

9. Observed SD of the corrected d values (SD_{d_c}). (This is the square root of Item 8.)

10. Variance in corrected d values due to sampling error. (Note: This figure is larger than the variance in *uncorrected* [*observed*] d values due to sampling error variance, which is presented in the bare-bones output section. This is because the correction for measurement error, while removing the systematic downward biases, increases the sampling error variance. Note: Variance due to measurement error differences is included in this variance figure, because measurement error has previously been corrected for.)

11. SD of corrected d values predicted from sampling error variance. (This is the square root of Item 10.)

12. Percentage variance in corrected d values due to sampling error variance. (Note: Variance due to measurement error differences is included in this value because the effects of this artifact have previously been corrected for.)

13. Correlation between corrected d values and their sampling errors. (This is the square root of the proportion of variance accounted for by sampling error; see Item 12.)

H. Main output for D-VALUE1 program (type 4 meta-analysis)

1. Number of effect sizes (d values) in the meta-analysis.
2. Total sample size. (Sample sizes summed across studies.)
3. Mean true effect size ($\bar{\delta}$).
4. Variance of true effect sizes (S_δ^2).
5. *SD* of delta (SD_δ). (This is the square root of Item 4.) Note: For most purposes, the key output is Items 3 and 5.
6. Eighty percent credibility interval for delta distribution (see Chapter 8).
7. Ninety-five percent confidence interval around mean delta (see Chapter 8).
8. Variance in observed d values due to sampling error and measurement error differences between studies (see Chapter 7).
9. *SD* of observed d values predicted from sampling error and measurement error differences. (This is the square root of Item 8.)
10. Variance in observed d values after removal of variance due to sampling error and between-study measurement error differences (residual variance [S_{res}^2]; see Chapter 7).
11. Percentage variance in observed d values due to sampling error and differences in measurement error.
12. Correlation between observed d values and the combined effects of sampling error and differences in measurement error. (This is the square root of the proportion of variance due to all artifacts in Item 11.)

This program package can be ordered by contacting Huy Le, Department of Management, University of Nevada at Las Vegas. Electronic mail: huyanhle@gmail.com. (Frank Schmidt can be contacted at: frank-schmidt@uiowa.edu.) A website for this program is being prepared and will be available soon.

References

AERA-APA-NCME. (1985). *Standards for educational and psychological testing* (4th ed.). Washington, DC: American Educational Research Association.

AERA-APA-NCME. (1999). *Standards for educational and psychological testing* (5th ed.). Washington, DC: American Educational Research Association.

Aguinis, H. (2001). Estimation of sampling variance of correlations in meta-analysis. *Personnel Psychology, 54,* 569–590.

Aguinis, H., & Gottfredson, R. K. (2010). Best practice recommendations for estimating interaction effects using moderated multiple regression. *Journal of Organizational Behavior, 31,* 776–786.

Aguinis, H., & Pierce, C. A. (1998). Testing moderator variable hypotheses meta-analytically. *Journal of Management, 24,* 577–592.

Aguinis, H., Pierce, C. A., Bosco, F. A., Dalton, D. R., & Dalton, C. M. (2011). Debunking myths and urban legends about meta-analysis. *Organizational Research Methods, 14,* 306–331.

Aguinis, H., Sturman, M. C., & Pierce, C. A. (2008). Comparison of three meta-analytic procedures for estimating moderating effects of categorical variables. *Organizational Research Methods, 11,* 9–34.

Aguinis, H., & Whitehead, R. (1997). Sampling variance in the correlation coefficient under indirect range restriction: Implications for validity generalization. *Journal of Applied Psychology, 82,* 528–538.

Albright, L. E., Glennon, J. R., & Smith, W. J. (1963). *The use of psychological tests in industry.* Cleveland, OH: Howard Allen.

Alexander, R. A., Carson, K. P., Alliger, G. M., & Carr, L. (1987). Correcting doubly truncated correlations: An improved approximation for correcting the bivariate normal correlation when truncation has occurred on both variables. *Educational and Psychological Measurement, 47,* 309–315.

Alexander, R. A., Carson, K. P., Alliger, G. M., & Cronshaw, S. F. (1989). Empirical distributions of range restricted SDx in validity studies. *Journal of Applied Psychology, 74,* 253–258.

Allen, M., Hunter, J. E., & Donahue, W. A. (1988). *Meta-analysis of self report data on the effectiveness of communication apprehension treatment techniques.* Unpublished manuscript, Department of Communication, Wake Forest University.

Allen, M., Hunter, J. E., & Donahue, W. A. (1989). Meta-analysis of self-report data on the effectiveness of public speaking anxiety treatment techniques. *Communication Education, 38,* 54–76.

Alliger, G. M., Tannenbaum, S. I., Bennett, W., Traver, H., & Shotland, A. (1997). A meta-analysis of the relations among training criteria. *Personnel Psychology, 50*(2), 341–358.

Aloe, A. M., Becker, B. J., & Pigott, T. D. (2010). An alternative to *R*-squared for assessing linear models of effect sizes. *Research Synthesis Methods, 1,* 272–283.

American Psychological Association. (2001). *Publication manual of the American Psychological Association* (5th ed.). Washington, DC: Author.

American Psychological Association. (2008). Reporting standards for research in psychology. *American Psychologist, 63,* 839–851.

American Psychological Association. (2009). *Publication manual of the American Psychological Association* (6th ed.). Washington, DC: Author.

Antman, E. M., Lau, J., Kupelnick, B., Mosteller, F., & Chalmers, T. C. (1992). A comparison of results of meta-analyses of randomized control trials and recommendations of clinical experts. *Journal of the American Medical Association, 268,* 240–248.

Aronson, E., Ellsworth, P., Carlsmith, J., & Gonzales, M. (1990). *Methods of research in social psychology* (2nd ed.). New York: McGraw-Hill.

Arthur, W., Bennett, W., Edens P. S., & Bell, S. T. (2003). Effectiveness of training in organizations: A meta-analysis of design and evaluation features. *Journal of Applied Psychology, 88*(2), 234–243.

Arvey, R. D., Cole, D. A., Hazucha, J., & Hartanto, F. (1985). Statistical power of training evaluation designs. *Personnel Psychology, 38,* 493–507.

Aytug, Z. G., Rothstein, H. R., Zhou, W., & Kern, M. C. (2012). Revealed or concealed? Transparency of procedures, decisions, and judgment calls in meta-analysis. *Organizational Research Methods, 15,* 103–133.

Baker, R., & Jackson, D. (2008). A new approach to outliers in meta-analysis. *Health Care Management Science, 23,* 151–162.

Bakker, M., van Dijk, A., & Wicherts, J. M. (2012). The rules of the game called psychological science. *Perspectives on Psychological Science, 7,* 543–554.

Bangert-Drowns, R. L. (1986). Review of developments in meta-analysis method. *Psychological Bulletin, 99,* 388–399.

Bangert-Drowns, R. L., Kulik, J. A., & Kulik, C.-L. C. (1983). Effects of coaching programs on achievement test performance. *Review of Educational Research, 53,* 571–585.

Banks, G. C., Kepes, S., & Banks, K. P. (2012). Publication bias: The antagonist of meta-analytic reviews and effective policy making. *Educational Evaluation and Policy Analysis, 34,* 259–277.

Banks, G. C., Kepes, S., & McDaniel, M. A. (2012). Publication bias: A call for improved meta-analytic practice in the organizational sciences. *International Journal of Selection and Assessment, 20,* 182–196.

Barnett, V., & Lewis, T. (1978). *Outliers in statistical data.* New York: John Wiley.

Barrick, M. R., & Mount, M. K. (1991). The Big Five personality dimensions and job performance: A meta-analysis. *Personnel Psychology, 44,* 1–26.

Bartlett, C. J., Bobko, P., Mosier, S. B., & Hannan, R. (1978). Testing for fairness with a moderated multiple regression strategy: An alternative to differential analysis. *Personnel Psychology, 31,* 233–241.

Beal, D. J., Corey, D. M., & Dunlap, W. P. (2002). On the bias of Huffcutt and Arthur's (1995) procedure for identifying outliers in the meta-analysis of correlations. *Journal of Applied Psychology, 87,* 583–589.

Becker, B. J. (1987). Applying tests of combined significance in meta-analysis. *Psychological Bulletin, 102,* 164–171.

Becker, B. J. (1988). Synthesizing standardized mean-change measures. *British Journal of Mathematical and Statistical Psychology, 41,* 257–278.

Becker, B. J. (1989, March). *Model-driven meta-analysis: Possibilities and limitations.* Paper presented at the annual meeting of the American Educational Research Association, San Francisco.

Becker, B. J. (1992). Models of science achievement: Forces affecting male and female performance in school science. In T. D. Cook, H. Cooper, D. S. Cordray, H. Hartmann, L. V. Hedges, et al. (Eds.), *Meta-analysis for explanation: A casebook* (pp. 209–282). New York: Russell Sage.

Becker, B. J. (1996). The generalizability of empirical research results. In C. P. Benbow & D. Lubinski (Eds.), *Intellectual talent: Psychological and social issues* (pp. 363–383). Baltimore: Johns Hopkins University Press.

Becker, B. J. (2005). Failsafe *N* or file drawer number. In H. R. Rothstein, A. J. Sutton, & M. Borenstein (Eds.), *Publication bias in meta-analysis: Prevention, assessment, and adjustments.* Chichester, UK: John Wiley.

Becker, B. J. (2009). Model based meta-analysis. In H. Cooper, L. V. Hedges, & J. C. Valentine (Eds.), *Handbook of research synthesis and meta-analysis* (2nd ed., pp. 377–396). New York: Russell Sage.

Becker, B. J., & Schram, C. M. (1994). Examining explanatory models through research synthesis. In H. Cooper & L. V. Hedges (Eds.), *The handbook of research synthesis* (pp. 357–382). New York: Russell Sage.

Bedeian, A. G., Taylor, S. G., & Miller, A. N. (2010). Management science on the credibility bubble: Cardinal sins and various misdemeanors. *Academy of Management Learning & Education, 9,* 715–725.

Begg, C. B. (1994). Publication bias. In H. Cooper & L. V. Hedges (Eds.), *The handbook of research synthesis* (pp. 399–409). New York: Russell Sage.

Begg, C. B., & Mazumdar, M. (1994). Operating characteristics of a rank order correlation for publication bias. *Biometrics, 50,* 1088–1101.

Berlin, J. A., & Ghersi, D. (2005). Preventing publication bias: Registries and prospective meta-analyses. In H. R. Rothstein, A. J. Sutton, & M. Borenstein (Eds.), *Publication bias is meta-analysis: Prevention, assessment, and adjustments* (pp. 35–48). West Sussex, UK: Wiley.

Bettencourt, B. A., Talley, A., Benjamin, A. J., & Valentine, J. (2006). Personality and aggressive behavior under provoking and neutral conditions: A meta-analytic review. *Psychological Bulletin, 132,* 751–777.

Bijmolt, T. H. A., & Pieters, R. G. M. (2001). Meta-analysis in marketing when studies contain multiple measurements. *Marketing Letters, 12,* 157–169.

Billings, R., & Wroten, S. (1978). Use of path analysis in industrial/organizational psychology: Criticisms and suggestions. *Journal of Applied Psychology, 63,* 677–688.

Bloom, B. S. (1964). *Stability and change in human characteristics.* New York: John Wiley.

Bobko, P. (1983). An analysis of correlations corrected for attenuation and range restriction. *Journal of Applied Psychology, 68,* 584–589.

Bobko, P., & Reick, A. (1980). Large sample estimators for standard errors of functions of correlation coefficients. *Applied Psychological Measurement, 4,* 385–398.

Bobko, P., Roth, P. L., & Bobko, C. (2001). Correcting the effect size of *d* for range restriction and unreliability. *Organizational Research Methods, 4,* 46–61.

Bobko, P., & Stone-Romero, E. F. (1998). Meta-analysis may be another useful research tool but it is not a panacea. In G. R. Ferris (Ed.), *Research in personnel and human resources management* (Vol. 16, pp. 359–397). Greenwich, CT: JAI Press.

Bonett, D. G. (2007). Transforming odds ratios into correlations for meta-analytic research. *American Psychologist, 62,* 254–255.

Bonett, D. G. (2008). Meta-analytic interval estimation for bivariate correlations. *Psychological Methods, 13,* 173–189.

Bonett, D. G. (2009). Meta-analytic interval estimation for standardized and unstandardized mean differences. *Psychological Methods, 14,* 225–238.

Bono, J. E., & Judge T. A. (2004). Personality and transformational and transactional leadership: A meta-analysis. *Journal of Applied Psychology, 89*(5), 901–910.

Borenstein, M. (1994). The case for confidence intervals in controlled clinical trials. *Controlled Clinical Trials, 15,* 411–428.

Borenstein, M. (2005). Software for publication bias. In H. R. Rothstein, A. J. Sutton, & M. Borenstein (Eds.), *Publication bias in meta-analysis: Prevention, assessment, and adjustments* (pp. 193–220). West Sussex, UK: Wiley.

Borenstein, M., Hedges, L. V., Higgins, J. T., & Rothstein, H. R. (2009). *Introduction to meta-analysis.* London: Wiley.

Borman, G. D., & Grigg, J. A. (2009). Visual and narrative interpretation. In H. Cooper, L. V. Hedges, & J. C. Valentine (Eds.), *Handbook of research synthesis and meta-analysis* (pp. 497–520). New York: Russell Sage.

Bozarth, J. D., & Roberts, R. R. (1972). Signifying significant significance. *American Psychologist, 27,* 774–775.

Brannick, M. T. (2006, August). *Comparison of sample size and inverse variance weights for the effect size* r. Paper presented at the first annual meeting of the Society for Research Synthesis Methodology, Cambridge, UK.

Brannick, M. T., Yang, L.-Q., & Cafri, G. (2011). Comparison of weights for meta-analysis of *r* and *d* under realistic conditions. *Organizational Research Methods, 14,* 587–607.

Brennan, R. L. (1983). *Elements of generalizability theory.* Iowa City, IA: ACT Publications.

Brogden, H. E. (1968). *Restriction in range.* Unpublished manuscript, Department of Psychology, Purdue University, Lafayette, IN.

Brown, S. H. (1981). Validity generalization and situational moderation in the life insurance industry. *Journal of Applied Psychology, 66,* 664–670.

Brozek, J., & Tiede, K. (1952). Reliable and questionable significance in a series of statistical tests. *Psychological Bulletin, 49,* 339–344.

Bryant, N. D., & Gokhale, S. (1972). Correcting correlations for restrictions in range due to selection on an unmeasured variable. *Educational and Psychological Measurement, 32,* 305–310.

Burke, M. J., & Day, R. (1986). A cumulative study of the effectiveness of management training. *Journal of Applied Psychology, 71*(2), 232–245.

Burke, M. J., & Landis, R. S. (2003). Methodological and conceptual challenges in conducting and interpreting meta-analyses. In K. Murphy (Ed.), *Validity generalization: A critical review* (pp. 287–310). Mahwah, NJ: Lawrence Erlbaum.

Bushman, B. J., & Wang, M. D. (2009). Vote counting procedures in meta-analysis. In H. Cooper, L. V. Hedges, & J. C. Valentine (Eds.), *Handbook of research synthesis and meta-analysis* (pp. 207–220). New York: Russell Sage.

Callender, J. C. (1983, March). *Conducting validity generalization research based on correlations, regression slopes, and covariances.* Paper presented at the I/O and OB Graduate Student Convention, Chicago.

Callender, J. C., & Osburn, H. G. (1980). Development and test of a new model for validity generalization. *Journal of Applied Psychology, 65,* 543–558.

Callender, J. C., & Osburn, H. G. (1981). Testing the constancy of validity with computer generated sampling distributions of the multiplicative model variance estimate: Results for petroleum industry validation research. *Journal of Applied Psychology, 66,* 274–281.

Callender, J. C., & Osburn, H. G. (1988). Unbiased estimation of the sampling variance of correlations. *Journal of Applied Psychology, 73,* 312–315.

Campbell, D. T., & Stanley, J. C. (1963). *Experimental and quasi-experimental designs for research.* Chicago: Rand McNally.

Campbell, J. P. (1990). The role of theory in industrial and organizational psychology. In M. D. Dunnette & L. M. Hough (Eds.), *Handbook of industrial and organizational psychology* (2nd ed., Vol. 1, pp. 39–73). Palo Alto, CA: Consulting Psychologists Press.

Carey, B. (2011, November 2). Fraud case seen as red flag for psychology research. *New York Times.*

Carlson, K. D., & Ji, F. X. (2011). Citing and building on meta-analytic findings: A review and recommendations. *Organizational Research Methods, 14,* 696–717.

Carlson, K. D., & Schmidt, F. L. (1999). Impact of experimental design on effect size: Findings from the research literature on training. *Journal of Applied Psychology, 84,* 851–862.

Carlson, K. D., Scullen, S. E., Schmidt, F. L., Rothstein, H. R., & Erwin, F. W. (1999). Generalizable biographical data validity: Is multi-organizational development and keying necessary? *Personnel Psychology, 52,* 731–756.

Carver, R. P. (1978). The case against statistical significance testing. *Harvard Educational Review, 48,* 378–399.

Cattin, P. (1980). The estimation of the predictive power of a regression model. *Journal of Applied Psychology, 65,* 407–414.

Chan, A. W., & Altman, D. G. (2005). Outcome reporting bias in randomized trials on PubMed: Review of publications and survey of authors. *British Medical Journal, 330,* 753.

Chan, A. W., Hrobjartsson, A., Haahr, M. T., Gotzsche, P. C., & Altman, D. G. (2004). Empirical evidence for selective reporting of outcomes in randomized trials: Comparison of protocols to published articles. *Journal of the American Medical Association, 291,* 2457–2465.

Chan, M. E., & Arvey, R. D. (2012). Meta-analysis and the development of knowledge. *Perspectives on Psychological Science, 7,* 79–92.

Chase, L. J., & Chase, R. B. (1976). Statistical power analysis of applied psychological research. *Journal of Applied Psychology, 61,* 234–237.

Chelimsky, E. (1994, October). *Use of meta-analysis in the General Accounting Office.* Paper presented at the Science and Public Policy Seminars, Federation of Behavioral, Psychological and Cognitive Sciences, Washington, DC.

Cheung, M. W. L. (2008). A model for integrating fixed-, random-, and mixed-effects meta-analyses into structural equation modeling. *Psychological Methods, 13,* 182–202.

Cheung, M. W. L. (2009). Constructing approximate confidence intervals for parameters with structural equation models. *Structural Equation Modeling, 16,* 267–294.

Cheung, M. W. L. (2010). Fixed-effects meta-analyses as multiple-group structural equation models. *Structural Equation Modeling, 17,* 481–509.

Cheung, M. W. L. (2012a). *MetaSEM: An R package for meta-analysis using structural equation modeling.* Manuscript under review.

Cheung, M. W. L. (2012b). *Three-level meta-analyses as structural equation models.* Manuscript under review.

Cheung, M. W. L. (in press). Multivariate meta-analysis as structural equation modeling. *Structural Equation Modeling.*

Cheung, M. W. L., & Chan, W. (2005). Meta-analytic structural equation modeling: a two-stage approach. *Psychological Methods, 10,* 40–64.

Cheung, S. F., & Change, D. K. (2004). Dependent effects sizes in meta-analysis: Incorporating the degree of interdependence. *Journal of Applied Psychology, 89,* 780–791.

Chinn, S. (2000). A simple method for converting an odds ratio to effect size for use in meta-analysis. *Statistics in Medicine, 19,* 3127–3131.

Clarke, M. (2009). Reporting format. In H. Cooper, L. V. Hedges, & J. C. Valentine (Eds.), *Handbook of research synthesis and meta-analysis* (pp. 521–534). New York: Russell Sage.

Coffman, D. L., & MacCallum, R. C. (2005). Using parcels to convert path analysis models into latent variable models. *Multivariate Behavioral Research, 40,* 235–259.

Coggin, T. D., & Hunter, J. E. (1987). A meta-analysis of pricing of "risk" factors in APT. *Journal of Portfolio Management, 14,* 35–38.

Cohen, J. (1962). The statistical power of abnormal-social psychological research: A review. *Journal of Abnormal and Social Psychology, 65,* 145–153.

Cohen, J. (1977). *Statistical power analysis for the behavior sciences* (Rev. ed.). New York: Academic Press.

Cohen, J. (1983). The cost of dichotomization. *Applied Psychological Measurement, 7,* 249–253.

Cohen, J. (1988). *Statistical power analysis for the behavioral sciences* (2nd ed.). Hillsdale, NJ: Lawrence Erlbaum.

Cohen, J. (1990). Things I learned (so far). *American Psychologist, 45,* 1304–1312.

Cohen, J. (1992). Statistical power analysis. *Current Directions in Psychological Science, 1,* 98–101.

Cohen, J. (1994). The earth is round (P < .05). *American Psychologist, 49,* 997–1003.

Cohen, J., Cohen, P., West, S. G., & Aiken, L. S. (2003). *Applied multiple regression/correlation analysis for the behavioral sciences* (3rd ed.). Mahwah, NJ: Lawrence Erlbaum.

Coleman, J. S. (1966). *Equality of educational opportunity.* Washington, DC: Government Printing Office.

Collins, D. B., & Holton, E. F. (2004). The effectiveness of managerial leadership development programs: a meta-analysis of studies from 1982 to 2001. *Human Resource Development Quarterly, 15,* (2), 217-248.

Collins, J. M., Schmidt, F. L., Sanchez-Ku, M., Thomas, L., McDaniel, M. A., & Le, H. (2003). Can individual differences shed light on the construct meaning of assessment centers? *International Journal of Selection and Assessment, 11,* 17–29.

Colquitt, J. A., LePine, J. A., & Noe, R. A. (2000). Toward an integrative theory of training motivation: A meta-analytic path analysis of 20 years of research. *Journal of Applied Psychology, 85,* 678–707.

Cook, T., & Campbell, D. T. (1976). The design and conduct of quasi-experiments and true experiments in field settings. In M. Dunnette (Ed.), *Handbook of industrial and organizational psychology* (pp. 223–236). Chicago: Rand McNally.

Cook, T., & Campbell, D. T. (1979). *Quasi-experiments and true experimentation: Design and analysis for field settings.* Chicago: Rand McNally.

Cook, T. D., Cooper, H., Cordray, D. S., Hartmann, H., Hedges, L. V., Light, R. J., et al. (1992). *Meta-analysis for explanation: A casebook.* New York: Russell Sage.

Cooper, H. (1997). Some finer points in meta-analysis. In M. Hunt (Ed.), *How science takes stock: The story of meta-analysis* (pp. 169–181). New York: Russell Sage.

Cooper, H. (1998). *Synthesizing research: A guide for literature reviews.* Thousand Oaks, CA: Sage.

Cooper, H. (2003). Editorial. *Psychological Bulletin, 129,* 3–9.

Cooper, H. (2010). *Research synthesis and meta-analysis: A step-by-step approach* (4th ed.). Los Angeles: Sage.

Cooper, H., & Koenka, A. C. (2012). The overviews of overviews: Unique challenges and opportunities when research syntheses are the principal elements of new integrative scholarship. *American Psychologist, 67,* 446–462.

Cooper, H. M., & Rosenthal, R. (1980). Statistical versus traditional procedures for summarizing research findings. *Psychological Bulletin, 87,* 442–449.

Copas, J. B. (1999). What works? Selectivity models and meta-analysis. *Journal of the Royal Statistical Society, Series A, 162,* 95–109.

Copas, J. B., & Shi, J. Q. (2001). A sensitivity analysis for publication bias in systematic reviews. *Statistical Methods in Medical Research, 10,* 251–265.

Cordray, D. S., & Morphy, P. (2009). Research synthesis and public policy. In H. Cooper, L. V. Hedges, & J. C. Valentine (Eds.), *Handbook of research synthesis and meta-analysis* (pp. 473–494). New York: Russell Sage.

Coursol, A., & Wagner, E. E. (1986). Effect of positive findings on submission and acceptance rates: A note on meta-analysis bias. *Professional Psychology, 17,* 136–137.

Coward, W. M., & Sackett, P. R. (1990). Linearity of ability-performance relationships: A reconfirmation. *Journal of Applied Psychology, 75,* 297–300.

Cronbach, L. J. (1947). Test "reliability": Its meaning and determination. *Psychometrika, 12,* 1–16.

Cronbach, L. J. (1975). Beyond the two disciplines of scientific psychology revisited. *American Psychologist, 30,* 116–127.

Cronbach, L. J., Gleser, G. C., Nanda, H., & Rajaratnam, N. (1972). *The dependability of behavioral measurements: Theory of generalizability for scores and profiles.* New York: John Wiley.

Cumming, G. (2012). *Understanding the new statistics: Effect sizes, confidence intervals, and meta-analysis.* New York: Routledge.

Cureton, E. E. (1936). On certain estimated correlation functions and their standard errors. *Journal of Experimental Education, 4,* 252–264.

Cuts raise new social science query: Does anyone appreciate social science? (1981, March 27). *Wall Street Journal,* p. 54.

Dalton, D. R., Aguinis, H., Dalton, C. M., Bosco, F. A., & Pierce, C. A. (2012). Revisiting the file drawer problem in meta-analysis: An assessment of published and nonpublished correlation matrices. *Personnel Psychology, 65,* 221–249.

Dean, M. A., Roth, P. L., & Bobko, P. (2008). Ethic and gender subgroup differences in assessment center ratings: a meta-analysis. *Journal of Applied Psychology, 93*(3), 685–691.

DeGeest, D. S., & Schmidt, F. L. (2011). The impact of research synthesis methods on industrial-organizational psychology: The road from pessimism to optimism about cumulative knowledge. *Research Synthesis Methods, 1,* 185–197.

Dickersin, K. (1994). Research registers. In H. Cooper & L. V. Hedges (Eds.), *The handbook of research synthesis* (pp. 71–84). New York: Russell Sage.

Dickersin, K. (2005). Publication bias: Recognizing the problem, understanding its origins and scope, and preventing harm. In H. Rothstein, A. J. Sutton, & M. Borenstein (Eds.), *Publication bias in meta-analysis: Prevention, assessment, and adjustments* (pp. 11–34). Chichester, UK: Wiley.

Dickersin, K., Min, Y., & Meinert, C. (1992). Factors influencing the publication of research results: Follow-up of applications submitted to two institutional review boards. *Journal of the American Medical Association, 267,* 374–378.

Dieckmann, N. F., Malle, B. F., & Bodner, T. E. (2009). An empirical assessment of meta-analytic practice. *Review of General Psychology, 13,* 101–115.

Doucouliagos, C., & Stanley, T. D. (2009). Publication selection bias in minimum-wage research? A meta-regression analysis. *British Journal of Industrial Relations, 47,* 406–428.

Doucouliagos, C., & Stanley, T. D. (2011). Are all economic facts greatly exaggerated? Theory competition and selectivity. *Journal of Economic Surveys, 10,* 1–29.

Dunlap, W. P., Cortina, J. M., Vaslow, J. B., & Burke, M. J. (1996). Meta-analysis of experiments with matched groups or repeated measures designs. *Psychological Methods, 1,* 170–177.

Dunnette, M. D., Houston, J. S., Hough, L. M., Touquam, J., Lamnstein, S., King, K., et al. (1982). *Development and validation of an industry-wide electric power plant operator selection system.* Minneapolis, MN: Personnel Decisions Research Institute.

Duval, S. (2005). The trim and fill method. In H. R. Rothstein, A. J. Sutton, & M. Borenstein (Eds.), *Publication bias in meta-analysis: Prevention, assessment, and adjustments* (pp. 127–144). New York: John Wiley.

Duval, S., & Tweedie, R. (2000). Trim and fill: A simple funnel plot based method of testing and adjusting for publication bias in meta-analysis. *Biometrics, 56,* 276–284.

Dye, D. (1982). *Validity generalization analysis for data from 16 studies participating in a consortium study.* Unpublished manuscript, Department of Psychology, George Washington University, Washington, DC.

Dye, D., Reck, M., & Murphy, M. A. (1993). The validity of job knowledge measures. *International Journal of Selection and Assessment, 1,* 153–157.

Eagly, A. H. (1978). Sex differences in influenceability. *Psychological Bulletin, 85,* 86–116.

Eagly, A. H., Johannsen-Schmidt, M. C., & van Engen, M. L. (2003). Transformational, transactional, and laissez-faire leadership styles: A meta-analysis comparing women and men. *Psychological Bulletin, 129,* 569–591.

Eagly, A. H., Karau, S. J., & Makhijani, M. G. (1995). Gender and the effectiveness of leaders: A meta-analysis. *Psychological Bulletin, 117,* 125–145.

Easterbrook, P. J., Berlin, J. A., Gopalan, R., & Matthews, D. R. (1991). Publication bias in clinical research. *Lancet, 337,* 867–872.

Egger, M., Smith, G., Schneider, M., & Minder, C. (1997). Bias in meta-analysis detected by a simple, graphical test. *British Medical Journal, 315,* 629–634.

Emerson, G. B., Warme, W. J., Wolf, F. M., Heckman, J. D., Brand, R. A., & Leopold, S. S. (2010). Testing for the presence of positive-outcome bias in peer review: A randomized controlled trial. *Archives of Internal Medicine, 170,* 1934–1939.

Erlenmeyer-Kimling, L., & Jarvik, L. F. (1963). Genetics and intelligence: A review. *Science, 142,* 1477–1479.

Fanelli, D. (2009). How many scientists fabricate and falsify research? A systematic review and meta-analysis of survey data. *PLoS ONE, 4,* 1–11.

Fiedler, K. (2011). Voodoo correlations are everywhere—not just in neuroscience. *Perspectives on Psychological Science, 6,* 163–171.

Field, A. P. (2001). Meta-analysis of correlation coefficients: A Monte Carlo comparison of fixed- and random-effects methods. *Psychological Methods, 6,* 161–180.

Field, A. P. (2005). Is the meta-analysis of correlations accurate when population correlations vary. *Psychological Methods, 10,* 444–467.

Fisher, R. A. (1932). *Statistical methods for research workers* (4th ed.). London: Oliver & Boyd.

Fisher, R. A. (1935). *The design of experiments.* London: Oliver & Boyd.

Fisher, R. A. (1938). *Statistical methods for research workers* (7th ed.). London: Oliver & Boyd.

Forsyth, R. A., & Feldt, L. S. (1969). An investigation of empirical sampling distributions of correlation coefficients corrected for attenuation. *Educational and Psychological Measurement, 29,* 61–71.

Fountoulakis, K. N., Conda, X., Vieta, E., & Schmidt, F. L. (2009). Treatment of psychotic symptoms in bipolar disorder with aripiprazole monotherapy. *Annuals of General Psychiatry, 8,* 27. Available at www.annals-general-psychiatry.com/contents/8/1/27

Francis, G. (2012a). The psychology of replication and replication in psychology. *Perspectives on Psychological Science, 7,* 585–594.

Francis, G. (2012b). Too good to be true: Publication bias in two prominent studies from experimental psychology. *Psychonomic Bulletin & Review, 19,* 151–156.

Francis, G. (2013). Publication bias in "Red, Rank, and Romance in Women Viewing Men" by Elliot et al. (2010). *Journal of Experimental Psychology: General, 142,* 292–296.

Freund, P. A., & Kasten, N. (2012). How smart do you think you are? A meta-analysis on the validity of self-estimates of cognitive ability. *Psychological Bulletin, 138,* 96–321.

Gardner, S., Frantz, R. A., & Schmidt, F. L. (1999). The effect of electrical stimulation on chronic wound healing: A meta-analysis. *Nursing Research, 7,* 495–403.

Gaugler, B. B., Rosenthal, D. B., Thornton, G. C., & Bentson, C. (1987). Meta-analysis of assessment center validity. *Journal of Applied Psychology, 72,* 493–511.

Gendreau, P., & Smith, P. (2007). Influencing the people who count: Some perspectives on reporting of meta-analysis results for prediction and treatment of outcomes with offenders. *Criminal Justice and Behavior, 34,* 1536–1559.

Gergen, K. J. (1982). *Toward transformation in social knowledge.* New York: Springer-Verlag.

Geyskens, I., Krishnan, R., Steenkamp, J. E. M., & Cunha, P. V. (2009). A review and evaluation of meta-analysis practices in management research. *Journal of Management, 35,* 393–419.

Ghiselli, E. E. (1949). The validity of commonly employed occupational tests. *University of California Publications in Psychology, 5,* 253–288.

Ghiselli, E. E. (1955). The measurement of occupational aptitude. *University of California Publications in Psychology, 8,* 101–216.

Ghiselli, E. E. (1966). *The validity of occupational aptitude tests.* New York: John Wiley.

Ghiselli, E. E. (1973). The validity of aptitude tests in personnel selection. *Personnel Psychology, 26,* 461–477.

Gigerenzer, G. (2007). Helping physicians understand screening tests will improve health care. *Association for Psychological Science Observer, 20,* 37–38.

Gigerenzer, G., Gaissmaier, W., Kurz-Milcke, E., Schwartz, L. M., & Woloshin, S. (2007). Helping doctors and patients make sense of health statistics. *Psychological Science in the Public Interest, 8,* 53–96.

Glass, G. V. (1972). The wisdom of scientific inquiry on education. *Journal of Research in Science Teaching, 9,* 3–18.

Glass, G. V. (1976). Primary, secondary and meta-analysis of research. *Educational Researcher, 5,* 3–8.

Glass, G. V. (1977). Integrating findings: The meta-analysis of research. *Review of Research in Education, 5,* 351–379.

Glass, G. V., McGaw, B., & Smith, M. L. (1981). *Meta-analysis in social research.* Beverly Hills, CA: Sage.

Glass, G. V., Peckham, P. D., & Sanders, J. R. (1972). Consequences of failure to meet assumptions underlying fixed effects analysis of variance and covariance. *Review of Educational Research, 42,* 237–288.

Gleser, L. J., & Olkin, O. (2009). Stochastically dependent effect sizes. In H. Cooper, L. V. Hedges, & J. C. Valentine (Eds.), *Handbook of research synthesis and meta-analysis* (pp. 357–376). New York: Russell Sage.

Gottfredson, L. S. (1985). Education as a valid but fallible signal of worker quality. *Research in Sociology of Education and Socialization, 5,* 123–169.

Green, B. F., & Hall, J. A. (1984). Quantitative methods for literature reviews. *Annual Review of Psychology, 35,* 37–53.

Greenhouse, J. B., & Iyengar, S. (1994). Sensitivity analysis and diagnostics. In L. V. Hedges & H. Cooper (Eds.), *Handbook of research synthesis* (pp. 383–398). New York: Russell Sage Foundation.

Greenwald, A. G. (1975). Consequences of prejudice against the null hypothesis. *Psychological Bulletin, 82,* 1–20.

Grissom, R. J., & Kim, J. J. (2012). *Effect sizes for research* (2nd ed.). New York: Routledge.

Gross, A. L., & McGanney, M. L. (1987). The range restriction problem and non-ignorable selection processes. *Journal of Applied Psychology, 72,* 604–610.

Grubbs, F. E. (1969). Procedures for detecting outliers. *Technometrics, 11,* 1–21.

Gulliksen, H. (1986). The increasing importance of mathematics in psychological research (Part 3). *The Score, 9,* 1–5.

Guttman, L. (1985). The illogic of statistical inference for cumulative science. *Applied Stochastic Models and Data Analysis, 1,* 3–10.

Guzzo, R. A., Jackson, S. E., & Katzell, R. A. (1986). Meta-analysis analysis. In L. L. Cummings & B. M. Staw (Eds.), *Research in organizational behavior* (Vol. 9). Greenwich, CT: JAI Press.

Hackman, J. R., & Oldham, G. R. (1975). Development of the Job Diagnostic Survey. *Journal of Applied Psychology, 60,* 159–170.

Haddock, C., Rindskopf, D., & Shadish, W. (1998). Using odds ratios as effect sizes for meta-analysis of dichotomous data: A primer on methods and issues. *Psychological Methods, 3,* 339–353.

Hafdahl, A. R. (2009). Improved Fisher's *z* estimators for univariate random-effects meta-analysis of Correlations. *British Journal of Mathematical and Statistical Psychology, 62,* 233–261.

Hafdahl, A. R. (2010). Random-effects meta-analysis of correlations: Evaluation of mean estimates. *British Journal of Mathematical and Statistical Psychology, 63,* 227–254.

Hafdahl, A. R. (2012). Article alerts: Items from 2011. *Research Synthesis Methods, 3,* 325–331.

Hafdahl, A. R., & Williams, M. A. (2009). Meta-analysis of correlations revisited: Attempted replication and extension of Field's (2001) simulation studies. *Psychological Methods, 14,* 24–42.

Hall, S. M., & Brannick, M. T. (2002). Comparison of two random effects methods of meta-analysis. *Journal of Applied Psychology, 87,* 377–389.

Halvorsen, K. T. (1994). The reporting format. In H. Cooper & L. V. Hedges (Eds.), *Handbook of research synthesis* (pp. 425–438). New York: Russell Sage.

Hamilton, M. A., & Hunter, J. E. (1987, August). *Two accounts of language intensity effects.* Paper presented at the International Communication Association Convention, New Orleans, LA.

Harmon, C., Oosterbeek, H., & Walker, I. (2000). *The returns to education: A review of evidence, issues and deficiencies in the literature* (Discussion Paper No. 5). London: Center for the Economics of Educations (CEE), London School of Economics.

Harter, J. K., Schmidt, F. L., Asplund, J., & Killham, E. A. (2010). Casual impact of employee work perceptions on the bottom line of organizations. *Perspectives on Psychological Science, 5,* 378–389.

Harter, J. K., Schmidt, F. L., & Hayes, T. L. (2002). Business unit level relationships between employee satisfaction/engagement and business outcomes: A meta-analysis. *Journal of Applied Psychology, 87,* 268–279.

Hartigan, J. A., & Wigdor, A. K. (Eds.). (1989). *Fairness in employment testing: Validity generalization, minority issues, and the General Aptitude Test Battery.* Washington, DC: National Academies Press.

Hedges, L. V. (1981). Distribution theory for Glass's estimator of effect size and related estimators. *Journal of Educational Statistics, 6,* 107–128.

Hedges, L. V. (1982a). Estimation of effect size from a series of independent experiments. *Psychological Bulletin, 92,* 490–499.

Hedges, L. V. (1982b). Fitting categorical models to effect sizes from a series of experiments. *Journal of Educational Statistics, 7,* 119–137.

Hedges, L. V. (1982c). Fitting continuous models to effect size data. *Journal of Educational Statistics, 7,* 245–270.

Hedges, L. V. (1983a). Combining independent estimators in research synthesis. *British Journal of Mathematical and Statistical Psychology, 36*(1), 123–131.

Hedges, L. V. (1983b). A random effects model for effect sizes. *Psychological Bulletin, 93,* 388–395.

Hedges, L. V. (1984). Estimation of effect size under non-random sampling: The effects of censoring studies yielding statistically mean differences. *Journal of Educational Statistics, 9,* 61–85.

Hedges, L. V. (1987). How hard is hard science, how soft is soft science: The empirical cumulativeness of research. *American Psychologist, 42,* 443–455.

Hedges, L. V. (1989). An unbiased correction for sampling error in validity generalization studies. *Journal of Applied Psychology, 74,* 469–477.

Hedges, L. V. (1992b). Modeling publication selection effects in meta-analysis. *Statistical Science, 7,* 246–255.

Hedges, L. V. (1995, February 14). Letter to Professor Herman Aguinis explaining sampling error variance of corrected correlations.

Hedges, L. V. (2009a). Effect sizes in nested designs. In H. Cooper, L. V. Hedges, & J. C. Valentine (Eds.), *Handbook of research synthesis and meta-analysis* (2nd ed., pp. 337–356). New York: Russell Sage.

Hedges, L. V. (2009b). Statistical considerations. In H. Cooper, L. V. Hedges, & J. C. Valentine (Eds.), *Handbook of research synthesis and meta-analysis* (2nd ed., pp. 37–48). New York: Russell Sage.

Hedges, L. V., & Olkin, I. (1980). Vote counting methods in research synthesis. *Psychological Bulletin, 88,* 359–369.

Hedges, L. V., & Olkin, I. (1985). *Statistical methods for meta-analysis.* Orlando, FL: Academic Press.

Hedges, L. V., & Pigott, T. D. (2001). The power of statistical tests in meta-analysis. *Psychological Methods, 6,* 203–217.

Hedges, L. V., & Pigott, T. D. (2004). The power of statistical tests for moderators in meta-analysis. *Psychological Methods, 9,* 426–425.

Hedges, L. V., & Stock, W. (1983). The effects of class size: An examination of rival hypotheses. *American Educational Research Journal, 20,* 63–85.

Hedges, L. V., Tipton, E., & Johnson, M. C. (2010a). Erratum: Robust variance estimation in meta-regression with dependent effect size estimates. *Research Synthesis Methods, 1,* 164–165.

Hedges, L. V., Tipton, E., & Johnson, M. C. (2010b). Robust variance estimation in meta-regression with dependent effect size estimates. *Research Synthesis Methods, 1,* 39–65.

Hedges, L. V., & Vevea, J. L. (1998). Fixed- and random-effects models in meta-analysis. *Psychological Methods, 3,* 486–504.

Hedges, L. V., & Vevea, J. (2005). Selection method approaches. In H. R. Rothstein, A. J. Sutton, & M. Borenstein (Eds.), *Publication bias in meta-analysis: Prevention, assessment, and adjustments.* Chichester, UK: John Wiley.

Heinsman, D. T., & Shadish, W. R. (1996). Assignment methods in experimentation: When do nonrandomized experiments approximate the answers from randomized experiments? *Psychological Methods, 1,* 154–169.

Higgins, J. P. T., & Thompson, S. G. (2001, October). *Presenting random effects meta-analyses: Where are we going wrong?* Paper presented at the 9th International Cochrane Colloquium, Lyon, France.

Higgins, J. P. T., Thompson, S. G., Deeks, J. J., & Altman, D. G. (2003). Measuring inconsistency in meta-analysis. *British Medical Journal, 327,* 557–560.

Higgins, J. P. T., Thompson, S. G., & Spiegelhalter, D. J. (2009). A re-evaluation of random-effects meta-analysis. *Journal of the Royal Statistical Society, 172*(Pt. 1), 137–159.

Hill, T. E. (1980, September). Development of a clerical program in Sears. In V. J. Benz (Chair), *Methodological implications of large scale validity studies of clerical occupations.* Symposium conducted at the meeting of the American Psychological Association, Montreal, Canada.

Hirsh, H. R., Northrop, L. C., & Schmidt, F. L. (1986). Validity generalization results for law enforcement occupations. *Personnel Psychology, 39,* 399–420.

Hoffert, S. P. (1997). Meta-analysis is gaining status in science and policymaking. *The Scientist, 11*(18), 1–6.

Hofstede, G. (1980). *Culture's consequences: International differences in work-related values.* Beverly Hills: Sage.

Hotelling, H. (1953). New light on the correlation coefficient and its transforms. *Journal of the Royal Statistical Society, B, 15,* 193–225.

Hoyt, W. T. (2000). Rater bias in psychological research: When it is a problem and what we can do about it? *Psychological Methods, 5,* 64–86.

Huber, P. J. (1980). *Robust statistics.* New York: John Wiley.

Huffcutt, A. I., & Arthur, W. A. (1995). Development of a new outlier statistic for meta-analytic data. *Journal of Applied Psychology, 80,* 327–334.

Huffcutt, A. I., Arthur, W. A., & Bennett, W. (1993). Conducting meta-analysis using the Proc Means procedure in SAS. *Educational and Psychological Measurement, 53,* 119–131.

Hunt, M. (1997). *How science takes stock.* New York: Russell Sage.

Hunter, J. E. (1980). Factor analysis. In P. Monge (Ed.), *Multivariate techniques in human communication research.* New York: Academic Press.

Hunter, J. E. (1983a). A causal analysis of cognitive ability, job knowledge, job performance, and supervisory ratings. In F. Landy, S. Zedeck, & J. Cleveland (Eds.), *Performance measurement and theory* (pp. 257–266). Hillsdale, NJ: Lawrence Erlbaum.

Hunter, J. E. (1983b). *Test validation for 12,000 jobs: An application of job classification and validity generalization analysis to the general aptitude test battery (GATB)* (Test Research Rep. No. 45). Washington, DC: U.S. Department of Labor, U.S. Employment Service.

Hunter, J. E. (1986, November). *Multiple dependent variables in experimental design.* Monograph presented at a workshop at the University of Iowa, Iowa City.

Hunter, J. E. (1987). Multiple dependent variables in program evaluation. In M. M. Mark & R. L. Shotland (Eds.), *Multiple methods in program evaluation.* San Francisco: Jossey-Bass.

Hunter, J. E. (1988). *A path analytic approach to analysis of covariance.* Unpublished manuscript, Department of Psychology, Michigan State University, East Lansing.

Hunter, J. E. (1995). PACKAGE: Software for data analysis in the social sciences. Unpublished suite of computer programs. (Available from Frank Schmidt, University of Iowa.)

Hunter, J. E. (1997). Needed: A ban on the significance test. *Psychological Science, 8,* 3–7.

Hunter, J. E., & Gerbing, D. W. (1982). Unidimensional measurement, second order factor analysis and causal models. In B. M. Staw & L. L. Cummings (Eds.), *Research in organizational behavior* (Vol. 4). Greenwich, CT: JAI Press.

Hunter, J. E., & Hirsh, H. R. (1987). Applications of meta-analysis. In C. L. Cooper & I. T. Robertson (Eds.), *International review of industrial and organizational psychology 1987.* London: Wiley.

Hunter, J. E., & Hunter, R. F. (1984). Validity and utility of alternate predictors of job performance. *Psychological Bulletin, 96,* 72–98.

Hunter, J. E., & Schmidt, F. L. (1977). A critical analysis of the statistical and ethical implications of various definitions of test fairness. *Psychological Bulletin, 83,* 1053–1071.

Hunter, J. E., & Schmidt, F. L. (1987a). *Error in the meta-analysis of correlations: The mean correlation.* Unpublished manuscript, Department of Psychology, Michigan State University, East Lansing.

Hunter, J. E., & Schmidt, F. L. (1987b). *Error in the meta-analysis of correlations: The standard deviation.* Unpublished manuscript, Department of Psychology, Michigan State University, East Lansing.

Hunter, J. E., & Schmidt, F. L. (1990a). Dichotomizing continuous variables: The implications for meta-analysis. *Journal of Applied Psychology, 75,* 334–349.

Hunter, J. E., & Schmidt, F. L. (1990b). *Methods of meta-analysis: Correcting error and bias in research findings.* Newbury Park, CA: Sage.

Hunter, J. E., & Schmidt, F. L. (1994). The estimation of sampling error variance in meta-analysis of correlations: The homogeneous case. *Journal of Applied Psychology, 79,* 171–177.

Hunter, J. E., & Schmidt, F. L. (1996). Cumulative research knowledge and social policy formulation: The critical role of meta-analysis. *Psychology, Public Policy, and Law, 2,* 324–347.

Hunter, J. E., & Schmidt, F. L. (2000). Fixed effects vs. random effects meta-analysis models: Implications for cumulative knowledge in psychology. *International Journal of Selection and Assessment, 8,* 275–292.

Hunter, J. E., & Schmidt, F. L. (2004). *Methods of meta-analysis: Correcting error and bias in research findings* (2nd ed.). Thousand Oaks, CA: Sage.

Hunter, J. E., Schmidt, F. L., & Coggin, T. D. (1996). *Meta-analysis of correlations: Bias in the correlation coefficient and the Fisher z transformation.* Unpublished manuscript, University of Iowa, Iowa City.

Hunter, J. E., Schmidt, F. L., & Hunter, R. (1979). Differential validity of employment tests by race: A comprehensive review and analysis. *Psychological Bulletin, 31,* 215–232.

Hunter, J. E., Schmidt, F. L., & Jackson, G. B. (1982). *Meta-analysis: Cumulating research findings across studies.* Beverly Hills, CA: Sage.

Hunter, J. E., Schmidt, F. L., & Le, H. (2006). Implications of direct and indirect range restriction for meta-analysis methods and findings. *Journal of Applied Psychology, 91,* 594–612.

Ioannidis, J. P. (2005a). Contradicted and initially stronger effects in highly cited clinical research. *Journal of the American Medical Association, 294,* 218–226.

Ioannidis, J. P. (2005b). Why most published research findings are false. *PLoS Medicine, 2*(8), 696–701.

Ioannidis, J. P., & Doucouliagos, C. (3013). What's to know about the credibility of empirical economics? *Journal of Economic Surveys, 13,* 1–8.

Ioannidis J. P., & Trikalinos, T. A. (2007). An exploratory test for an excess of significant findings. *Clinical Trials, 4,* 245–253.

Iyengar, S., & Greenhouse, J. (1988). Selection models and the file drawer problem. *Statistical Science, 3,* 109–135.

James, L. R., Demaree, R. G., & Mulaik, S. A. (1986). A note on validity generalization procedures. *Journal of Applied Psychology, 71,* 440–450.

Jensen, A. R. (1980). *Bias in mental testing.* New York: Free Press.

John, L. K., Loewenstein, G., & Prelec, D. (2012). Measuring the prevalence of questionable research practices with incentives for truth telling. *Psychological Science, 23,* 524–532.

Johnson, B. T. (1989). *D-Stat: Software for the meta-analytic review of research literatures.* Hillsdale, NJ: Lawrence Erlbaum.

Judge, T. A., & Bono, J. E. (2001). Relationship of core self-evaluations traits—self-esteem, generalized self-efficacy, locus of control, and emotional stability—with job satisfaction and job performance: A meta-analysis. *Journal of Applied Psychology, 86,* 80–92.

Judge, T. A., Bono, J. E., Ilies, R., & Gerhardt, M. W. (2002). Personality and leadership: A qualitative and quantitative review. *Journal of Applied Psychology, 87*(4), 765–780.

Judge, T. A., Colbert, A.E., & Ilies, R. (2004). Intelligence and leadership: a quantitative review and test of theoretical propositions. *Journal of Applied Psychology, 89*(3), 542–552.

Judge, T. A., Piccolo, R. F., & Kosalka, T. (2009). The bright and dark sides of leader traits: A review theoretical extension of the leader trait paradigm. *Leadership Quarterly, 20*(6), 855–875.

Judge, T. A., Thorensen, C. J., Bono, J. E., & Patton, G. K. (2001). The job satisfaction–job performance relationship: A qualitative and quantitative review. *Psychological Bulletin, 127,* 376–401.

Kelly, T. L. (1947). *Fundamentals of statistics.* Cambridge, MA: Harvard University Press.

Kemery, E. R., Dunlap, W. P., & Griffeth, R. W. (1988). Correction for unequal proportions in point biserial correlations. *Journal of Applied Psychology, 73,* 688–691.

Kemery, E. R., Mossholder, K. W., & Roth, L. (1987). The power of the Schmidt and Hunter additive model of validity generalization. *Journal of Applied Psychology, 72,* 30–37.

Kepes, S., Banks, G. C., & Oh, I.-S. (in press). Avoiding bias in publication bias research: The value of "null" findings. *Journal of Business and Psychology.*

Kepes, S., Banks, G. C., McDaniel, M. A., & Whetzel, D. L. (2012). Publication bias in the organizational sciences. *Organizational Research Methods, 15,* 624–662.

Kepes, S., & McDaniel, M. A. (2013). How trustworthy is the scientific literature in I-O psychology? *Industrial and Organizational Psychology: Perspectives on Science and Practice, 6*(3), 252–268.

Killeen, P. R. (2005a). An alternative to null hypothesis significance tests. *Psychological Science, 16,* 345–353.

Killeen, P. R. (2005b). Replicability, confidence, and priors. *Psychological Science, 16,* 1009–2012.

King, L. M., Hunter, J. E., & Schmidt, F. L. (1980). Halo in multidimensional forced choice performance evaluation scale. *Journal of Applied Psychology, 65,* 507–516.

Kirk, R. E. (1995). *Experimental design: Procedures for the behavioral sciences.* New York: Brooks/Cole.

Kirk, R. E. (2001). Promoting good statistical practices: Some suggestions. *Educational and Psychological Measurement, 61,* 213–218.

Kirkpatrick, D. L. (2000). Evaluating training programs: the four levels. In G. M. Piskurich, P. Beckschi, & B. Hall (Eds.), *The ASTD handbook of training design and delivery* (pp. 133–146). New York: McGraw-Hill.

Kisamore, J. L. (2003). *Validity generalization and transportability: An investigation of distributional assumptions of random-effects meta-analytic methods.* Unpublished doctoral dissertation, Department of Psychology, University of South Florida, Tampa.

Kisamore, J. L., & Brannick, M. T. (2008). An illustration of the consequences of meta-analysis model choice. *Organizational Research Methods, 11,* 35–53.

Kline, R. B. (2004). *Beyond significant testing: Reforming data analysis methods in behavioral research.* Washington, DC: American Psychology Association.

Kotov, R., Gamez, W., Schmidt, F. L., & Watson, D. (2010). Linking "Big" personality traits to anxiety, depressive, and substance use disorders: A meta-analysis. *Psychological Bulletin, 136,* 768–821.

Krakovsky, M. (2004). Register or perish. *Scientific American, 291,* 18–20.

Kulik, J. A., & Bangert-Drowns, R. L. (1983–1984). Effectiveness of technology in precollege mathematics and science teaching. *Journal of Educational Technology Systems, 12,* 137–158.

Kulinskaya, E., Morgenthaler, S., & Staudte, R. G. (2010). Combining the evidence using stable weights. *Research Synthesis Methods, 1,* 284–296.

Laczo, R. M., Sackett, P. R., Bobko, P., & Cortina, J. M. (2005). A comment on sampling error in d with unequal Ns: Avoiding potential errors in meta-analytic and primary research. *Journal of Applied Psychology, 90,* 758–764.

Landis, R. S. (2013). Successfully combining meta-analysis and structural equation modeling: Recommendations and strategies. *Journal of Business and Psychology, 28,* 251–261.

Landman, J. T., & Dawes, R. M. (1982). Psychotherapy outcome: Smith and Glass' conclusions stand up under scrutiny. *American Psychologist, 37,* 504–516.

Law, K. S. (1995). The use of Fisher's *Z* in Schmidt-Hunter type meta-analysis. *Journal of Educational and Behavioral Statistics, 20,* 287–306.

Law, K. S., Schmidt, F. L., & Hunter, J. E. (1994a). Nonlinearity of range corrections in meta-analysis: A test of an improved procedure. *Journal of Applied Psychology, 79,* 425–438.

Law, K. S., Schmidt, F. L., & Hunter, J. E. (1994b). A test of two refinements in meta-analysis procedures. *Journal of Applied Psychology, 79,* 978–986.

Lawshe, C. H. (1948). *Principles of personnel selection.* New York: McGraw-Hill.

Le, H. (2003). *Correcting for indirect range restriction in meta-analysis: Testing a new meta-analysis method.* Unpublished doctoral dissertation, University of Iowa, Iowa City.

Le, H., & Schmidt, F. L. (2006). Correcting for indirect range restriction in meta-analysis: Testing a new meta-analysis procedure. *Psychological Methods, 11,* 416–438.

Le, H., Schmidt, F. L., Harter, J. K., & Lauver, K. (2010). The problem of empirical redundancy of constructs in organizational research: An empirical investigation. *Organizational Behavior and Human Decision Processes, 112,* 112–123.

Le, H., Schmidt, F. L., & Oh, I.-S. (2013). *Correction for range restriction in meta-analysis revisited: Improvements and implications for organizational research.* Manuscript under review.

Le, H., Schmidt, F. L., & Putka, D. J. (2009). The multi-faceted nature of measurement error and its implications for measurement error corrections. *Organizational Research Methods, 12,* 165–200.

Lehrer, J. (2011, December 13). The truth wears off: Is there something wrong with the scientific method? *New Yorker Magazine,* pp. 52–56.

Lent, R. H., Auerbach, H. A., & Levin, L. S. (1971a). Predictors, criteria and significant results. *Personnel Psychology, 24,* 519–533.

Lent, R. H., Auerbach, H. A., & Levin, L. S. (1971b). Research design and validity assessment. *Personnel Psychology, 24,* 247–274.

Leone, F. C., & Nelson, L. S. (1966). Sampling distributions of variance components: I. Empirical studies of balanced nested designs. *Technometrics, 8,* 457–468.

LePine, J. A., Piccolo, R. F., Jackson, C. L., Mathieu, J. E., & Saul, J. R. (2008). A meta-analysis of teamwork processes: Tests of a multidimensional model and relationships with team effectiveness criteria. *Personnel Psychology, 61*(2), 273–307.

Levine, J. M., Kramer, G. G., & Levine, E. N. (1975). Effects of alcohol on human performance: An integration of research findings based on an abilities classification. *Journal of Applied Psychology, 60,* 285–293.

Levine, J. M., Romashko, T., & Fleishman, E. A. (1973). Evaluation of an abilities classification system for integration and generalizing human performance research findings: An application to vigilance tasks. *Journal of Applied Psychology, 58,* 149–157.

Li, J. C., Chan, W., & Cui, Y. (2010) Bootstrap standard error and confidence intervals for correlations corrected for indirect range restriction. *British Journal of Mathematical and Statistical Psychology, 64,* 367–387.

Light, R. J., & Pillemer, D. B. (1984). *Summing up: The science of reviewing research.* Cambridge, MA: Harvard University Press.

Light, R. J., Singer, J. D., & Willett, J. B. (1994). The visual presentation and interpretation of meta-analyses. In H. Cooper & L. V. Hedges (Eds.), *The handbook of research synthesis* (pp. 439–453). New York: Russell Sage.

Light, R. J., & Smith, P. V. (1971). Accumulating evidence: Procedures for resolving contradictions among different research studies. *Harvard Educational Review, 41,* 429–471.

Linn, R. L., Harnisch, D. L., & Dunbar, S. B. (1981a). Corrections for range restriction: An empirical investigation of conditions resulting in conservative corrections. *Journal of Applied Psychology, 66,* 655–663.

Linn, R. L., Harnisch, D. L., & Dunbar, S. B. (1981b). Validity generalization and situational specificity: An analysis of the prediction of first year grades in law school. *Applied Psychological Measurement, 5,* 281–289.

Lipsey, M. W., & Wilson, D. B. (1993). The efficacy of psychological, educational, and behavioral treatment: Confirmation from meta-analysis. *American Psychologist, 48,* 1181–1209.

Lipsey, M. W., & Wilson, D. B. (2001). *Practical meta-analysis.* Thousand Oaks, CA: Sage.

Lockhart, R. S. (1998). *Statistics and data analysis for the behavioral sciences.* New York: W. H. Freeman.

Lord, F., & Novick, M. (1968). *Statistical theories of mental test scores.* New York: Knopf.

Lumley, T. (2009). Rmeta meta-analysis. R package version 2.16. http://CRAN.R-project .org/package=rmeta

Mabe, P. A., III, & West, S. G. (1982). Validity of self evaluations of ability: A review and meta-analysis. *Journal of Applied Psychology, 67,* 280–296.

MacCallum, R. C., Zhang, S., Preacher, K. J., & Rucker, D. D. (2002). On the practice of dichotomization of quantitative variables. *Psychological Methods, 7,* 19–40.

MacMahon, S., Peto, R., Cutler, J., Collins, R., Sorlie, P., Neaton, J., et al. (1990). Blood pressure, stroke, and coronary heart disease: Part 1: Prolonged differences in blood pressure: Prospective observational studies corrected for the regression dilution bias. *Lancet, 335,* 763–774.

Magnusson, D. (1966). *Test theory.* New York: Addison-Wesley.

Maloley et al. v. Department of National Revenue, Canadian Civil Service Appeals Board, Ottawa (1986, February).

Mann, C. (1990, August 3). Meta-analysis in the breech. *Science, 249,* 476–480.

Mansfield, R. S., & Busse, T. V. (1977). Meta-analysis of research: A rejoinder to Glass. *Educational Researcher, 6,* 3.

Marin-Martinez, F., & Sanchez-Meca, J. (2010). Weighting by inverse variance or by sample size in random effects meta-analysis. *Educational and Psychological Measurement, 70,* 56–73.

Martinussen, M., & Bjornstad, J. F. (1999). Meta-analysis calculations based on independent and nonindependent cases. *Educationa and Psychological Measurement, 59,* 928–950.

Matt, G. E., & Cook, T. D. (2009). Threats to the validity of generalized inferences. In H. Cooper, L. V. Hedges, & J. C. Valentine (Eds.), *Handbook of research synthesis and meta-analysis* (2nd ed., pp. 537–560). New York: Russell Sage.

Maxwell, S. E. (2004). The persistence of underpowered studies in psychological research: Causes, consequences, and remedies. *Psychological Methods, 9,* 147–163.

McDaniel, M. A. (1986a). Computer programs for calculating meta-analysis statistics. *Educational and Psychological Measurement, 64,* 175–177.

McDaniel, M. A. (1986b). *MAME: Meta-analysis made easy. Computer program and manual. Ver. 2.1.* Bethesda, MD: Author.

McDaniel, M. A. (1990, April 14). *Cumulative meta-analysis as a publication bias method.* Paper presented at the annual meeting of the Society for Industrial and Organizational Psychology, New Orleans, LA.

McDaniel, M. A., & Nguyen, N. T. (2002, December 5). *A meta-analysis of the relationship between in vivo brain volume and intelligence.* Paper presented at the Third Annual Conference of the International Society for Intelligence Research, Nashville, TN.

McDaniel, M. A., Rothstein, H. R., & Whetzel, D. I. (2006). Publication bias: A case study of four test vendors. *Personnel Psychology, 59,* 927–953.

McDaniel, M. A., Schmidt, F. L., & Hunter, J. E. (1988a). Job experience correlates of job performance. *Journal of Applied Psychology, 73,* 327–330.

McDaniel, M. A., Schmidt, F. L., & Hunter, J. E. (1988b). A meta-analysis of the validity of training and experience ratings in personnel selection. *Personnel Psychology, 41,* 283–314.

McDaniel, M. A., Whetzel, D. L., Schmidt, F. L., & Maurer, S. D. (1994). The validity of employment interviews: A comprehensive review and meta-analysis. *Journal of Applied Psychology, 79,* 599–616.

McNatt, D. B. (2000). Ancient Pygmalion joins contemporary management: A meta-analysis of the result. *Journal of Applied Psychology, 85,* 314–322.

McNemar, Q. (1960). At random: Sense and nonsense. *American Psychologist, 15,* 295–300.

Meehl, P. E. (1978). Theoretical risks and tabular asterisks: Sir Karl, Sir Ronald and the slow progress of soft psychology. *Journal of Consulting and Clinical Psychology, 46,* 806–834.

Mendoza, J. L., & Mumford, M. (1987). Correction for attenuation and range restriction on the predictor. *Journal of Educational Statistics, 12,* 282–293.

Mendoza, J. L., & Reinhardt, R. N. (1991). Validity generalization procedures using sample-based estimates: A comparison of six procedures. *Psychological Bulletin, 110,* 596–610.

Mendoza, J. L., Stafford, K. L., & Stauffer, J. M. (2000). Large sample confidence intervals for validity and reliability coefficients. *Psychological Methods, 5,* 356–369.

Miller, N., Lee, S., & Carlson, M. (1991). The validity of inferential judgments when used in theory-testing meta-analysis. *Personality and Social Psychology Bulletin, 17,* 335–343.

Millsap, R. (1988). Sampling variance in attenuated correlation coefficients: A Monte Carlo study. *Journal of Applied Psychology, 73,* 316–319.

Millsap, R. (1989). The sampling variance in the correlation under range restriction: A Monte Carlo study. *Journal of Applied Psychology, 74,* 456–461.

Moher, D., & Olkin, I. (1995). Meta-analysis of randomized controlled trials: A concern for standards. *Journal of the American Medical Association, 274,* 1962–1964.

Morris, S. B. (2007). [Review of the book *Methods of meta-analysis: Correcting error and bias in research findings* (2nd ed.).] *Organizational Research Methods, 11,* 184–187.

Morris, S. B. (2008). Estimating effect sizes from pretest-posttest-control group designs. *Organizational Research Methods, 11,* 364–386.

Morris, S. B., & DeShon, R. P. (1997). Correcting effect sizes computed from factorial analysis of variance for use in meta-analysis. *Psychological Methods, 2,* 192–199.

Morris, S. B., & DeShon, R. P. (2002). Combining effect size estimates in meta-analysis with repeated measures and independent groups designs. *Psychological Methods, 7,* 105–125.

Mosier, C. I. (1943). On the reliability of a weighted composite. *Psychometrika, 8,* 161–168.

Mosteller, F., & Bush, R. R. (1954). Selected quantitative techniques. In G. Lindzey (Ed.), *Handbook of social psychology: Vol. I. Theory and method.* Cambridge, MA: Addison-Wesley.

Mosteller, F., & Colditz, G. A. (1996). Understanding research synthesis (meta-analysis). *Annual Review of Public Health, 17,* 1–17.

Mosteller, F., & Moynihan, D. (1972). *On equality of educational opportunity.* New York: Vintage.

Mount, M. K., & Barrick, M. R. (1995). The Big Five personality dimensions: Implications for research and practice in human resources management. In G. R. Ferris (Ed.), *Research in personnel and human resources management* (Vol. 13, pp. 153–200). Greenwich, CT: JAI Press.

Mullen, B. (1989). *Advanced BASIC meta-analysis.* Hillsdale, NJ: Lawrence Erlbaum.

Mullen, B., & Rosenthal, R. (1985). *BASIC meta-analysis: Procedures and programs.* Hillsdale, NJ: Lawrence Erlbaum.

Murphy, K. R. (1997). Meta-analysis and validity generalization. In N. Anderson & P. Herriott (Eds.), *International handbook of selection and assessment* (pp. 323–342). Chichester, UK: Wiley.

Murphy, K. R. (Ed.). (2003). *Validity generalization: A critical review.* Mahwah, NJ: Lawrence Erlbaum.

Murphy, K. R., & DeShon, R. (2000). Interrater correlations do not estimate the reliability of job performance ratings. *Personnel Psychology, 53,* 873–900.

Myers, D. G. (1991). Union is strength: A consumer's view of meta-analysis. *Personality and Social Psychology Bulletin, 17,* 265–266.

Nancy-Universite. (2008, October). International workshop on meta-analysis in economics and business, Nancy, France.

Nathan, B. R., & Alexander, R. A. (1988). A comparison of criteria for test validation: A meta-analytic investigation. *Personnel Psychology, 41,* 517–535.

National Research Council. (1992). *Combining information: Statistical issues and opportunities for research.* Washington, DC: National Academy of Sciences Press.

Nicol, T. S., & Hunter, J. E. (1973, August). *Mathematical models of the reliability of the semantic differential.* Paper presented at the Psychometric Society, Chicago.

Nouri, H., & Greenberg, R. H. (1995). Meta-analytic procedures for estimation of effect sizes in experiments using complex analysis of variance. *Journal of Management, 21,* 801–812.

Nunnally, J. (1978). *Psychometric theory.* New York: McGraw-Hill.

Nunnally, J. C., & Bernstein, I. H. (1994). *Psychometric theory* (3rd ed.). New York: McGraw-Hill.

Nye, C. D., Su, R., Rounds, J., & Drasgow, F. (2012). Vocational interests and performance: A quantitative summary of over 60 years of research. *Perspectives on Psychological Science, 7,* 384–403.

Oakes, M. (1986). *Statistical inference: A commentary for the social and behavioral sciences.* New York: John Wiley.

Oh, I. S. (2007). In search of ideal methods of research synthesis over 30 years (1977–2006): Comparison of Hunter-Schmidt meta-analysis methods with other methods and recent improvements. *International Journal of Testing, 7,* 89–93.

Oh, I. S. (2009). *The Five-Factor Model of personality and job performance in East Asia: a cross-cultural validity generalization study.* Unpublished doctoral dissertation, University of Iowa, Iowa City.

Oh, I. S., Postlethwaite, B. E., & Schmidt, F. L. (2013). Rethinking the validity of interviews for employment decision making: Implications of recent developments in meta-analysis. In D. J. Svyantek & K. Mahoney (Eds.), *Received wisdom, kernels of truth, and boundary conditions in organizational studies* (pp. 297–329). New York: Information Age Publishing.

Olson, C. M., Rennie, D., Cook, D., Dickersin, K., Flanagin, A., Hogan, J. W., et al. (2002). Publication bias in editorial decision making. *Journal of the American Medical Association, 287,* 2825–2828.

Ones, D. S., & Viswesvaran, C. (2003). Job-specific applicant pools and national norms for personality scales: Implications for range restriction corrections in validation research. *Journal of Applied Psychology, 88,* 570–577.

Ones, D. S., Viswesvaran, C., & Schmidt, F. L. (1993). Comprehensive meta-analysis of integrity test validities: Findings and implications for personnel selection and theories of job performance. *Journal of Applied Psychology Monograph, 78,* 679–703.

Ones, D. S., Viswesvaran, C., & Schmidt, F. L. (2012). Integrity tests predict counterproductive work behaviors and job performance well: Comment on Van Iddekinge, Roth, Raymark, and Odle-Dusseau (2012). *Journal of Applied Psychology, 97,* 537–542.

Orlitzky, M. (2011). How can significance tests be deinstitutionalized? *Organizational Research Methods, 20,* 1–30.

Orwin, R. G. (1983). A fail-safe N for effect size. *Journal of Educational Statistics, 8,* 147–159.

Orwin, R. G., & Cordray, D. S. (1985). Effects of deficient reporting on meta-analysis: A conceptual framework and reanalysis. *Psychological Bulletin, 97,* 134–147.

Orwin, R. G., & Vevea, J. L. (2009). Evaluating coding decisions. In H. Cooper, L. V. Hedges, & J. C. Valentine (Eds.), *Handbook of research synthesis and meta-analysis* (pp. 177–206). New York: Russell Sage.

Osburn, H. G. (1978). Optimal sampling strategies for validation studies. *Journal of Applied Psychology, 63,* 602–608.

Osburn, H. G., & Callender, J. C. (1990). Accuracy of the validity generalization sampling variance estimate: A reply to Hoben Thomas. *Journal of Applied Psychology, 75,* 328–333.

Osburn, H. G., & Callender, J. (1992). A note on the sampling variance of the mean uncorrected correlation in meta-analysis and validity generalization. *Journal of Applied Psychology, 77,* 115–122.

Osburn, H. G., Callender, J. C., Greener, J. M., & Ashworth, S. (1983). Statistical power of tests of the situational specificity hypothesis in validity generalization studies: A cautionary note. *Journal of Applied Psychology, 68,* 115–122.

Overton, R. C. (1998). A comparison of fixed effects and mixed (random effects) models for meta-analysis tests of moderator variable effects. *Psychological Methods, 3,* 354–379.

Ozer, D. J. (1985). Correlation and the coefficient of determination. *Psychological Bulletin, 97,* 307–315.

Palmer, T. M., Peters, J. L., Sutton, A. J., & Moreno, S. G. (2008). Contour-enhanced funnel plots for meta-analysis. *The Stata Journal, 8,* 242–254.

Payne, S. C., Youngcourt, S. S., & Beaubien, J. M. (2007). A meta-analytic examination of the goal orientation nomological net. *Journal of Applied Psychology, 92*(1), 128–150.

Pearlman, K. (1982). *The Bayesian approach to validity generalization: A systematic examination of the robustness of procedures and conclusions.* Unpublished doctoral dissertation, Department of Psychology, George Washington University, Washington, DC.

Pearlman, K., Schmidt, F. L., & Hunter, J. E. (1980). Validity generalization results for tests used to predict job proficiency and training success in clerical occupations. *Journal of Applied Psychology, 65,* 373–406.

Pearson, E. S. (1938). The probability integral transformation for testing goodness of fit and combining tests of significance. *Biometrika, 30,* 134–148.

Peters, J. L., Sutton, A. J., Jones, D. R., & Abrams, K. R. (2010). Assessing publication bias in meta-analysis in the presence of between-study heterogeneity. *Journal of the Royal Statistical Society, 173*(Pt. 3), 575–591.

Peters, L. H., Harthe, D., & Pohlman, J. (1985). Fiedler's contingency theory of leadership: An application of the meta-analysis procedures of Schmidt and Hunter. *Psychological Bulletin, 97,* 274–285.

Peterson, N. G. (1982, October). *Investigation of validity generalization in clerical and technical/professional occupations in the insurance industry.* Paper presented at the Conference on Validity Generalization, Personnel Testing Council of Southern California, Newport Beach.

Peto, R. (1987). Why do we need systematic overviews of randomized trials? *Statistics in Medicine, 6,* 233–240.

Pinello, D. R. (1999). Linking party to judicial ideology in American courts: A meta-analysis. *The Justice System Journal, 20,* 219–254.

Powell, K. S., & Yalcin, S. (2010). Managerial training effectiveness: a meta-analysis 1952-2002. *Personnel Review, 39*(2), 227–241.

Premack, S., & Wanous, J. P. (1985). Meta-analysis of realistic job preview experiments. *Journal of Applied Psychology, 70,* 706–719.

Pritchard, R. D., Harrell, M. M., DiazGranadaos, D., & Guzman, M. J. (2008). The productivity measurement and enhancement system: a meta-analysis. *Journal of Applied Psychology, 93*(3), 540–567.

Raju, N. S., Anselmi, T. V., Goodman, J. S., & Thomas, A. (1998). The effects of correlated artifacts and true validity on the accuracy of parameter estimation in validity generalization. *Personnel Psychology, 51,* 453–465.

Raju, N. S., & Brand, P. A. (2003). Determining the significance of correlations corrected for unreliability and range restriction. *Applied Psychological Measurement, 27,* 52–72.

Raju, N. S., & Burke, M. J. (1983). Two new procedures for studying validity generalization. *Journal of Applied Psychology, 68,* 382–395.

Raju, N. S., Burke, M. J., & Normand, J. (1983). *The asymptotic sampling distribution of correlations corrected for attenuation and range restriction.* Unpublished manuscript, Department of Psychology, Illinois Institute of Technology, Chicago.

Raju, N. S., Burke, M. J., Normand, J., & Langlois, G. M. (1991). A new meta-analysis approach. *Journal of Applied Psychology, 76,* 432–446.

Raju, N. S., & Drasgow, F. (2003). Maximum likelihood estimation in validity generalization. In K. R. Murphy (Ed.), *Validity generalization: A critical review.* Hillsdale, NJ: Lawrence Erlbaum.

Raju, N. S., & Fleer, P. G. (1997). *MAIN: A computer program for meta-analysis.* Chicago: Illinois Institute of Technology.

Raju, N. S., Fralicx, R., & Steinhaus, S. D. (1986). Covariance and regression slope models for studying validity generalization. *Applied Psychological Measurement, 10,* 195–211.

Raudenbush, S. W. (1994). Random effects models. In H. Cooper & L. V. Hedges (Eds.), *The handbook of research synthesis* (pp. 301–322). New York: Russell Sage.

Raudenbush, S. W. (2009). Analyzing effect sizes: Random effects models. In H. Cooper, L. V. Hedges, & J. C. Valentine (Eds.), *Handbook of research synthesis and meta-analysis* (pp. 295–315). New York: Russell Sage.

Raudenbush, S. W., & Bryk, A. S. (2002). *Hierarchical linear models: Application and data analysis methods.* Thousand Oaks, CA: Sage.

R Development Core Team. (2010). *R: A language and environment for statistical computing.* Vienna, Austria: R Foundation for Statistical Computing. http://www.R-project.org/

Reed, J. G., & Baxter, P. M. (2009). Using reference databases. In H. Cooper, L. V. Hedges, & J. C. Valentine (Eds.), *Handbook of research synthesis and meta-analysis* (pp. 73–102). New York: Russell Sage.

Renkewitz, F., Fuchs, H. M., & Fiedler, S. (2011). Is there evidence of publication bias in JDM research? *Judgment and Decision Making, 6,* 870–881.

Richard, F. D., Bond, C. F., Jr., & Stokes-Zoota, J. J. (2003). One hundred years of social psychology quantitatively described. *Review of General Psychology, 7,* 331–363.

Riketta, M. (2008). The causal relation between job attitudes and job performance: A meta-analysis of panel studies. *Journal of Applied Psychology, 93*(2), 472–481.

Rodgers, R. C., & Hunter, J. E. (1986). *The impact of management by objectives on organizational productivity.* Unpublished manuscript, Management Department, University of Texas at Austin.

Rosenberg, M. S., Adams, D. C., & Gurevitch, J. (1997). *MetaWin: Statistical software for meta-analysis with resampling tests.* Sunderland, MA: Sinauer Associates.

Rosenthal, R. (1961, September). On the social psychology of the psychological experiment: With particular reference to experimenter bias. In H. W. Riecken (Chair), *On the social psychology of the psychological experiment.* Symposium conducted at the meeting of the American Psychological Association, New York.

Rosenthal, R. (1963). On the social psychology of the psychological experiment: The experimenter's hypothesis as unintended determinant of experimental results. *American Scientist, 51,* 268–283.

Rosenthal, R. (1978). Combining results of independent studies. *Psychological Bulletin, 85,* 185–193.

Rosenthal, R. (1979). The "file drawer problem" and tolerance for null results. *Psychological Bulletin, 86,* 638–641.

Rosenthal, R. (1983). Assessing the statistical and social importance of the effects of psychotherapy. *Journal of Consulting and Clinical Psychology, 51,* 4–13.

Rosenthal, R. (1984). *Meta-analysis procedures for social research.* Beverly Hills, CA: Sage.

Rosenthal, R. (1991). *Meta-analytic procedures for social research* (2nd ed.). Newbury Park, CA: Sage.

Rosenthal, R., & Rubin, D. B. (1978). Interpersonal expectancy effects: The first 345 studies. *The Behavioral and Brain Sciences, 3,* 377–386.

Rosenthal, R., & Rubin, D. B. (1979a). Comparing significance levels of independent studies. *Psychological Bulletin, 86,* 1165–1168.

Rosenthal, R., & Rubin, D. B. (1979b). A note on percent variance explained as a measure of the importance of effects. *Journal of Applied Psychology, 64,* 395–396.

Rosenthal, R., & Rubin, D. B. (1982a). Comparing effect sizes of independent studies. *Psychological Bulletin, 92,* 500–504.

Rosenthal, R., & Rubin, D. B. (1982b). Further meta-analytic procedures for assessing cognitive gender differences. *Journal of Educational Psychology, 74,* 708–712.

Rosenthal, R., & Rubin, D. B. (1982c). A simple, general purpose display of magnitude of experiment effect. *Journal of Educational Psychology, 74,* 166–169.

Rosenthal, R., & Rubin, D. B. (1983). Ensemble-adjusted *p* values. *Psychological Bulletin, 94,* 540–541.

Roth, P. L. (2008). Software review: Hunter-Schmidt Meta-Analysis Programs 1.1. *Organizational Research Methods, 11,* 192–196.

Roth, P. L., BeVier, C. A., Bobko, P., Switzer, F. S., III, & Tyler, P. (2001). Ethnic group differences in cognitive ability in employment and educational settings: A meta-analysis. *Personnel Psychology, 54,* 297–330.

Roth, P. L., BeVier, C. A., Switzer, F. S., & Shippmann, J. S. (1996). Meta-analyzing the relationship between grades and job performance. *Journal of Applied Psychology, 81,* 548–556.

Roth, P. L., Bobko, P., Switzer, F. S., & Dean, M. A. (2001). Prior selection causes biased estimates of standardized ethnic group differences: Simulation and analysis. *Personnel Psychology, 54,* 297–330.

Rothstein, H. R. (1990). Interrater reliability of job performance ratings: Growth to asymptote level with increasing opportunity to observe. *Journal of Applied Psychology, 75,* 322–327.

Rothstein, H. R. (2003). Progress is our most important product: Contributions of validity generalization and meta-analysis to the development and communication of knowledge in I/O psychology. In K. R. Murphy (Ed.), *Validity generalization: A critical review* (pp. 115–154). Mahwah, NJ: Lawrence Erlbaum.

Rothstein, H. R. (2008). Publication bias is a threat to the validity of meta-analytic results. *Journal of Experimental Criminology, 4,* 61–81.

Rothstein, H. R. (2012). Accessing relevant literature. In H. Cooper (Ed.), *APA Research Methods in Psychology: Vol. 1. Foundations, planning, measures, and psychometrics.* Washington, DC: American Psychological Association.

Rothstein, H. R., & Hopewell, S. (2009). Grey literature. In H. Cooper, L. V. Hedges, & J. C. Valentine (Eds.), *Handbook of research synthesis and meta-analysis* (pp. 103–126). New York: Russell Sage.

Rothstein, H. R., McDaniel, M. A., & Borenstein, M. (2001). Meta-analysis: A review of quantitative cumulation methods. In N. Schmitt & F. Drasgow (Eds.), *Advances in measurement and data analysis.* San Francisco: Jossey-Bass.

Rothstein, H. R., Schmidt, F. L., Erwin, F. W., Owens, W. A., & Sparks, C. P. (1990). Biographical data in employment selection: Can validities be made generalizable? *Journal of Applied Psychology, 75,* 175–184.

Rothstein, H. R., Sutton, A., & Borenstein, M. (Eds.). (2005). *Publication bias in meta-analysis: Prevention, assessment, and adjustments.* London: Wiley.

Rubin, D. B. (1990). A new perspective on meta-analysis. In K. W. Wachter & M. L. Straf (Eds.), *The future of meta-analysis*. New York: Russell Sage.

Rubin, D. B. (1992). Meta-analysis: Literature synthesis or effect size surface estimation? *Journal of Educational Statistics, 17,* 363–374.

Sackett, P. R., Harris, M. M., & Orr, J. M. (1986). On seeking moderator variables in the meta-analysis of correlational data: A Monte Carlo investigation of statistical power and resistance to Type I error. *Journal of Applied Psychology, 71,* 302–310.

Sackett, P. R., Laczo, R. M., & Arvey, R. D. (2002). The effects of range restriction on estimates of criterion interrater reliability: Implications for validation research. *Personnel Psychology, 55,* 807–825.

Sanchez-Meca, J., Lopez-Lopez, J. A., & Lopez-Pina, J. A. (in press). Some recommended statistical analytic practices when reliability generalization studies are conducted. *British Journal of Mathematical and Statistical Psychology.*

Sanchez-Meca, J., & Marin-Martinez, F. (1998). Weighting by inverse variance or by sample size in meta-analysis: A simulation study. *Educational and Psychological Measurement, 58,* 211–220.

SAS Institute, Inc. (2003). SAS/STAT software, Version 9.1. Cary, NC: Author. http://www.sas.com/

Schimmack, U. (2012). The ironic effect of significant results on the credibility of multiple study articles. *Psychological Methods, 17,* 551–566.

Schmidt, F. L. (1971). The relative efficiency of regression and simple unit predictor weights in applied differential psychology. *Educational and Psychological Measurement, 31,* 699–714.

Schmidt, F. L. (1972). The reliability of differences between linear regression weights in applied differential psychology. *Educational and Psychological Measurement, 32,* 879–886.

Schmidt, F. L. (1988). Validity generalization and the future of criterion-related validity. In H. Wainer & H. Braun (Eds.), *Test validity* (pp. 173–189). Hillsdale, NJ: Lawrence Erlbaum.

Schmidt, F. L. (1992). What do data really mean? Research findings, meta-analysis, and cumulative knowledge in psychology. *American Psychologist, 47,* 1173–1181.

Schmidt, F. L. (1996). Statistical significance testing and cumulative knowledge in psychology: Implications for the training of researchers. *Psychological Methods, 1,* 115–129.

Schmidt, F. L. (2002). The role of general cognitive ability in job performance: Why there cannot be a debate. *Human Performance, 15,* 187–210.

Schmidt, F. L. (2003). John E. Hunter, 1939–2002. *American Psychologist, 58,* 238.

Schmidt, F. L. (2008). Meta-analysis: A constantly evolving research tool. *Organizational Research Methods, 11,* 96–113.

Schmidt, F. L. (2010). Detecting and correcting the lies that data tell. *Perspectives on Psychological Science, 5,* 233–242.

Schmidt, F. L. (in press). History of the development of the Schmidt-Hunter meta-analysis methods. *Research Synthesis Methods.*

Schmidt, F. L., Gast-Rosenberg, I., & Hunter, J. E. (1980). Validity generalization results for computer programmers. *Journal of Applied Psychology, 65,* 643–661.

Schmidt, F. L., & Hunter, J. E. (1977). Development of a general solution to the problem of validity generalization. *Journal of Applied Psychology, 62,* 529–540.

Schmidt, F. L., & Hunter, J. E. (1978). Moderator research and the law of small numbers. *Personnel Psychology, 31,* 215–232.

Schmidt, F. L., & Hunter, J. E. (1981). Employment testing: Old theories and new research findings. *American Psychologist, 36,* 1128–1137.

Schmidt, F. L., & Hunter, J. E. (1984). A within setting test of the situational specificity hypothesis in personnel selection. *Personnel Psychology, 37,* 317–326.

Schmidt, F. L., & Hunter, J. E. (1992). Development of causal models of job performance. *Current Directions in Psychological Science, 1,* 89–92.

Schmidt, F. L., & Hunter, J. E. (1996). Measurement error in psychological research: Lessons from 26 research scenarios. *Psychological Methods, 1,* 199–223.

Schmidt, F. L., & Hunter, J. E. (1997). Eight common but false objections to the discontinuation of significance testing in the analysis of research data. In L. Harlow, S. Muliak, & J. Steiger (Eds.), *What if there were no significance tests?* (pp. 37–64). Mahwah, NJ: Lawrence Erlbaum.

Schmidt, F. L., & Hunter, J. E. (1998). The validity and utility of selection methods in personnel psychology: Practical and theoretical implications of 85 years of research findings. *Psychological Bulletin, 124,* 262–274.

Schmidt, F. L., & Hunter, J. E. (1999a). Comparison of three meta-analysis methods revisited: An analysis of Johnson, Mullen, and Salas (1995). *Journal of Applied Psychology, 84,* 114–148.

Schmidt, F. L., & Hunter, J. E. (1999b). Theory testing and measurement error. *Intelligence, 27,* 183–198.

Schmidt, F. L., & Hunter, J. E. (2003). History, development, evolution, and impact of validity generalization and meta-analysis methods, 1975–2001. In K. R. Murphy (Ed.), *Validity generalization: A critical review* (pp. 31–66). Mahwah, NJ: Lawrence Erlbaum.

Schmidt, F. L., Hunter, J. E., & Caplan, J. R. (1981a). *Selection procedure validity generalization (transportability) results for three job groups in the petroleum industry.* Washington, DC: American Petroleum Institute.

Schmidt, F. L., Hunter, J. E., & Caplan, J. R. (1981b). Validity generalization results for two job groups in the petroleum industry. *Journal of Applied Psychology, 66,* 261–273.

Schmidt, F. L., Hunter, J. E., McKenzie, R. C., & Muldrow, T. W. (1979). The impact of valid selection procedures on work-force productivity. *Journal of Applied Psychology, 64,* 609–626.

Schmidt, F. L., Hunter, J. E., & Outerbridge, A. N. (1986). Impact of job experience and ability on job knowledge, work sample performance, and supervisory ratings of job performance. *Journal of Applied Psychology, 71,* 432–439.

Schmidt, F. L., Hunter, J. E., Outerbridge, A. N., & Goff, S. (1988). Joint relation of experience and ability with job performance: Test of three hypotheses. *Journal of Applied Psychology, 73,* 46–57.

Schmidt, F. L., Hunter, J. E., Outerbridge, A. M., & Trattner, M. H. (1986). The economic impact of job selection methods on the size, productivity, and payroll costs of the federal workforce: An empirical demonstration. *Personnel Psychology, 39,* 1–29.

Schmidt, F. L., Hunter, J. E., & Pearlman, K. (1981). Task differences and validity of aptitude tests in selection: A red herring. *Journal of Applied Psychology, 66,* 166–185.

Schmidt, F. L., Hunter, J. E., & Pearlman, K. (1982). Progress in validity generalization: Comments on Callender and Osburn and further developments. *Journal of Applied Psychology, 67,* 835–845.

Schmidt, F. L., Hunter, J. E., Pearlman, K., & Caplan, J. R. (1981). *Validity generalization results for three occupations in Sears, Roebuck and Company.* Chicago: Sears, Roebuck and Company.

Schmidt, F. L., Hunter, J. E., Pearlman, K., & Hirsh, H. R. (1985). Forty questions about validity generalization and meta-analysis. *Personnel Psychology, 38,* 697–798.

Schmidt, F. L., Hunter, J. E., Pearlman, K., & Shane, G. S. (1979). Further tests of the Schmidt-Hunter Bayesian validity generalization procedure. *Personnel Psychology, 32,* 257–381.

Schmidt, F. L., Hunter, J. E., & Raju, N. S. (1988). Validity generalization and situational specificity: A second look at the 75% rule and the Fisher's *z* transformation. *Journal of Applied Psychology, 73,* 665–672.

Schmidt, F. L., Hunter, J. E., & Urry, V. E. (1976). Statistical power in criterion-related validation studies. *Journal of Applied Psychology, 61,* 473–485.

Schmidt, F. L., & Kaplan, L. B. (1971). Composite vs. multiple criteria: A review and resolution of the controversy. *Personnel Psychology, 24,* 419–434.

Schmidt, F. L., Law, K. S., Hunter, J. E., Rothstein, H. R., Pearlman, K., & McDaniel, M. (1989). *Refinements in validity generalization methods (including outlier analysis).* Unpublished paper, Department of Management and Organization, University of Iowa, Iowa City.

Schmidt, F. L., Law, K. S., Hunter, J. E., Rothstein, H. R., Pearlman, K., & McDaniel, M. (1993). Refinements in validity generalization methods: Implications for the situational specificity hypothesis. *Journal of Applied Psychology, 78,* 3–13.

Schmidt, F. L., & Le, H. (2004). Software for the Hunter-Schmidt meta-analysis methods (versions 1.0 and 1.1). Iowa City: University of Iowa, Department of Management & Organizations.

Schmidt, F. L., & Le, H. (2014). Software for the Hunter-Schmidt meta-analysis methods (version 1.2). Iowa City: University of Iowa Department of Management & Organizations.

Schmidt, F. L., Le, H., & Ilies, R. (2003). Beyond Alpha: An empirical examination of the effects of different sources of measurement error on reliability estimates for measures of individual differences constructs. *Psychological Methods, 8,* 206–234.

Schmidt, F. L., Le, H., & Oh, I.-S. (2009). Correcting for the distorting effects of study artifacts in meta-analysis. In H. Cooper, L. V. Hedges, & J. C. Valentine (Eds.), *Handbook of research synthesis and meta-analysis* (pp. 317–334). New York: Russell Sage.

Schmidt, F. L., Le, H., & Oh, I.-S. (in press). Are true scores and construct scores the same? A critical examination of their substitutability and the implications for research results. *International Journal of Selection and Assessment.*

Schmidt, F. L., Ocasio, B. P., Hillery, J. M., & Hunter, J. E. (1985). Further within-setting empirical tests of the situational specificity hypothesis in personnel selection. *Personnel Psychology, 38,* 509–524.

Schmidt, F. L., & Oh, I.-S. (2013). Methods for second order meta-analysis and illustrative applications. *Organizational Behavior and Human Decision Making, 121,* 204–218.

Schmidt, F. L., Oh, I.-S., & Hayes, T. L. (2009). Fixed vs. random models in meta-analysis: Model properties and comparison of differences in results. *British Journal of Mathematical and Statistical Psychology, 62,* 97–128.

Schmidt, F. L., Oh, I.-S., & Le, H. (2006). Increasing the accuracy of corrections for range restriction: Implications for selection procedure validities and other research results. *Personnel Psychology, 59,* 281–305.

Schmidt, F. L., Pearlman, K., & Hunter, J. E. (1980). The validity and fairness of employment and educational tests for Hispanic Americans: A review and analysis. *Personnel Psychology, 33,* 705–724.

Schmidt, F. L., & Raju, N. S. (2007). Updating meta-analysis research findings: Bayesian approaches versus the medical model. *Journal of Applied Psychology, 92,* 297–308.

Schmidt, F. L., & Rothstein, H. R. (1994). Application of validity generalization methods of meta-analysis to biographical data scores in employment selection. In G. S. Stokes, M. D. Mumford, & W. A. Owens (Eds.), *The biodata handbook: Theory, research, and applications* (pp. 237–260). Chicago: Consulting Psychologists Press.

Schmidt, F. L., Shaffer, J. A., & Oh, I.-S. (2008). Increased accuracy for range restriction corrections: Implications for the role of personality and general mental ability in job and training performance. *Personnel Psychology, 61,* 827–868.

Schmidt, F. L., Viswesvaran, C., & Ones, D. S. (2000). Reliability is not validity and validity is not reliability. *Personnel Psychology, 53,* 901–912.

Schmidt, F. L., & Zimmerman, R. (2004). A counter-intuitive hypothesis about interview validity and some supporting evidence. *Journal of Applied Psychology, 89,* 553–561.

Schmitt, N., Gooding, R. Z., Noe, R. A., & Kirsch, M. (1984). Meta-analysis of validity studies published between 1964 and 1982 and the investigation of study characteristics. *Personnel Psychology, 37,* 407–422.

Schulze, R. (2004). *Meta-analysis: A comparison of approaches.* Cambridge, MA: Hogrefe and Huber.

Schulze, R. (2007). Current methods for meta-analysis: Approaches, issues, and developments. *Journal of Psychology, 215,* 90–103.

Schwab, D. P., Olian-Gottlieb, J. D., & Heneman, H. G., III. (1979). Between subject's expectancy theory research: A statistical review of studies predicting effort and performance. *Psychological Bulletin, 86,* 139–147.

Schwarzer, G. (2010). Meta: Meta-analysis with R (R package version 1.6-0). http://CRAN.R-project.org/package=meta

Schwarzer, G., Carpenter, J., & Rucker, G. (2010). Empirical evaluation suggests Copas selection model is preferable to trim-and-fill method for selection bias in meta-analysis. *Journal of Clinical Epidemiology, 63,* 282–288.

Sedlmeier, P., & Gigerenzer, G. (1989). Do studies of statistical power have an effect on the power of studies? *Psychological Bulletin, 105,* 309–316.

Shadish, W. R. (1996). Meta-analysis and the exploration of causal mediating processes: A primer of examples, methods, and issues. *Psychological Methods, 1,* 47–65.

Shadish, W. R., Cook, T. D., & Campbell, D. T. (2002). *Experimental and quasi-experimental designs for generalized causal inference.* Boston: Houghton Mifflin.

Shadish, W. R., Matt, G. E., Navarro, A. M., & Phillips, G. (2000). The effects of psychological therapies under clinically representative conditions: A meta-analysis. *Psychological Bulletin, 126,* 512–529.

Shadish, W. R., & Ragsdale, K. (1996). Random versus nonrandom assignment in psychotherapy experiments: Do you get the same answer? *Journal of Consulting and Clinical Psychology, 64*, 1290–1305.

Shadish, W. R., Robinson, L., & Lu, C. (1999). *ES: A computer program and manual for effect size calculation.* St. Paul, MN: Assessment Systems Corporation.

Shah, B. V., Barnwell, B. G., & Bieler, G. S. (1995). *SUDAAN user's manual: Software for analysis of correlated data.* Research Triangle Park, NC: Research Triangle Institute.

Sharf, J. (1987). Validity generalization: Round two. *The Industrial-Organizational Psychologist, 25*, 49–52.

Simmons, J. P., Nelson, L. D., & Simonsohn, U. (2011). False-positive psychology: Undisclosed flexibility in data collection and analysis allows presenting anything as significant. *Psychological Science, 22*, 1359–1366.

Simonsohn, U., Nelson, L. D., & Simmons, J. P. (in press). *P*-curve: A key to the file drawer. *Journal of Experimental Psychology: General.*

Sitzmann, T., Brown, K. G., Casper, W. J., Ely, K., & Zimmerman, R. D. (2008). A review and meta-analysis of the nomological network of trainee reactions. *Journal of Applied Psychology, 93*(2), 280–295.

Slavin, R. E. (1986). Best-evidence synthesis: An alternative to meta-analytic and traditional reviews. *The Educational Researcher, 15*, 5–11.

Smith, M., & Glass, G. (1980). Meta-analysis of research on class size and its relationship to attitudes and instruction. *American Educational Research Journal, 17*, 419–433.

Smith, M. L. (1980). Sex bias in counseling and psychotherapy. *Psychological Bulletin, 87*, 392–407.

Smith, M. L., & Glass, G. V. (1977). Meta-analysis of psychotherapy outcome studies. *American Psychologist, 32*, 752–760.

Smithson, M. (2000). *Statistics with confidence.* London: Sage.

Smithson, M. (2001). Correct confidence intervals for various regression effect sizes and parameters: The importance of noncentral distributions in computing intervals. *Educational and Psychological Measurement, 61*, 605–632.

Snedecor, G. W. (1946). *Statistical methods* (4th ed.). Ames: Iowa State College Press.

Society for Industrial and Organizational Psychology. (2003). *Principles for the validation and use of personnel selection procedures* (4th ed.). Bowling Green, OH: Author.

Spector, P. E., & Levine, E. L. (1987). Meta-analysis for integrating study outcomes: A Monte Carlo study of its susceptibility to Type I and Type II errors. *Journal of Applied Psychology, 72*, 3–9.

SPSS, Inc. (2006). SPSS for Windows, Release 15. Chicago: Author. http://www.spss.com

Stanley, J. C. (1971). Reliability. In R. L. Thorndike (Ed.), *Educational measurement* (2nd ed., pp. 356–442). Washington, DC: American Council on Education.

Stanley, T. D. (1998). New wine in old bottles: A meta-analysis of Ricardian equivalence. *Southern Economic Journal, 64*, 713–727.

Stanley, T. D. (2001). Wheat from chaff: Meta-analysis as quantitative literature review. *Journal of Economic Perspectives, 15*, 131–150.

Stanley, T. D., & Jarrell, S. B. (1989). Meta-regression analysis: A quantitative method of literature surveys. *Journal of Economic Surveys, 3*, 161–169.

Stanley, T. D., & Jarrell, S. D. (1998). Gender wage discrimination bias? A meta-regression analysis. *Journal of Human Resources, 33,* 947–973.

Stanley, T. D., Jarrell, S. D., & Doucouliagos, H. (2010). Could it be better to discard 90% of the data? A statistical paradox. *American Statistician, 64,* 70–77.

StataCorp. (2007). *Stada statistical software: Release 9.2.* College Station, TX: Author. http://www.stata.com

Steel, P. D., & Kammeyer-Mueller, J. D. (2002). Comparing meta-analytic moderator estimation techniques under realistic conditions. *Journal of Applied Psychology, 87,* 96–111.

Sterling, T. C. (1959). Publication decisions and their possible effects on inferences drawn from tests of significance or vice versa. *Journal of the American Statistical Association, 54,* 30–34.

Sterling, T. C., Rosenbaum, W., & Weinkam, J. (1995). Publication decisions revisited: The effect of the outcome of statistical tests on the decision to publish and vice versa. *American Statistician, 49,* 108–112.

Sterne, J. A. C. (Ed.). (2009). *Meta-analysis in Stata: An updated collection from the Stata Journal.* College Station, TX: Stata Press.

Sterne, J. A. C., & Egger, M. (2005). Regression methods to detect publication and other bias in meta-analysis. In H. R. Rothstein, A. J. Sutton, & M. Borenstein (Eds.), *Publication bias in meta-analysis: Prevention, assessment and adjustments* (pp. 99–110). New York: John Wiley.

Stevens, J. P. (1984). Outliner and influential data points in regression analysis. *Psychological Bulletin, 95,* 334–344.

Stouffer, S. A., Suchman, E. A., DeVinney, L. C., Star, S. A., & Williams, R. M., Jr. (1949). *The American soldier: Adjustment during Army life* (Vol. 1). Princeton, NJ: Princeton University Press.

Stroebe, W., Postmes, T., & Spears, R. (2012). Scientific misconduct and the myth of self-correction in science. *Perspectives on Psychological Science, 7,* 670–688.

Strube, M. J. (1988). Averaging correlation coefficients: Influence of heterogeneity and set size. *Journal of Applied Psychology, 73,* 559–568.

Sutton, A. J. (2005). Evidence concerning the consequences of publication and related biases. In H. R. Rothstein, A. J. Sutton, & M. Borenstein (Eds.), *Publication bias in meta-analysis: Prevention, assessment, and adjustments* (pp. 175–192). West Sussex, UK: Wiley.

Sutton, A. J. (2009). Publication bias. In H. Cooper, L. V. Hedges, & J. C Valentine (Eds.), *Handbook of research synthesis and meta-analysis* (2nd ed., pp. 435–452). New York: Russell Sage.

Tamrakar, C. (2012). *Relationship of satisfaction and loyalty across industry and geographical regions: A meta-analysis.* Unpublished paper, Marketing Department, University of Iowa, Iowa City.

Taras, V., Kirkman, B. L., & Steel, P. (2010). Examining the impact of *Culture's Consequences:* A three-decade, multilevel, meta-analytic review of Hofstedes's cultural value dimensions. *Journal of Applied Psychology, 95*(3), 405–439.

Taveggia, T. (1974). Resolving research controversy through empirical cumulation. *Sociological Methods and Research, 2,* 395–407.

Taylor, P. J., Russ-Eft, D. F., & Taylor, H. (2009). Transfer of management training from alternative perspectives. *Journal of Applied Psychology, 94*(1), 104–121.

Terborg, J. R., & Lee, T. W. (1982). Extension of the Schmidt-Hunter validity generalization procedure to the prediction of absenteeism behavior from knowledge of job satisfaction and organizational commitment. *Journal of Applied Psychology, 67,* 280–296.

Terrin, N., Schmid, C. H., Lau, J., & Olkin, I. (2002, May 10). *Adjusting for publication bias in the presence of heterogeneity.* Paper presented at the Meta-Analysis Symposium, Mathematical Research Institute, University of California, Berkeley.

Thomas, H. (1988). What is the interpretation of the validity generalization estimate $S_p^2 = S_r^2 - S_c^2$? *Journal of Applied Psychology, 73,* 679–682.

Thomas, K. (2013, June 29). Breaking the seal on drug research. *New York Times.*

Thompson, B. (2002, April). What future quantitative social science research could look like: Confidence intervals for effect sizes. *Educational Researcher,* pp. 25–32.

Thompson, W. A. (1962). The problem of negative estimates of variance components. *Annals of Mathematical Statistics, 33,* 273–289.

Thorndike, R. L. (1933). The effect of the interval between test and retest on the constancy of the IQ. *Journal of Educational Psychology, 25,* 543–549.

Thorndike, R. L. (1949). *Personnel selection.* New York: John Wiley.

Thorndike, R. L. (1951). Reliability. In E. F. Lindquist (Ed.), *Educational measurement* (pp. 560–620). Washington, DC: American Council on Education.

Tracz, S. M., Elmore, P. B., & Pohlmann, J. T. (1992). Correlational meta-analysis: Independent and nonindependent cases. *Educational and Psychological Measurement, 52,* 879–888.

Trafimow, D., MacDonald, J. A., Rice, S., & Clason, D. L. (2010). How often is *p-rep* close to the true replication probability? *Psychological Methods, 15,* 300–307.

Trikalinos, T. A., & Ioannidis, J. P. (2005). Assessing the evolution of effect sizes over time. In H. R. Rothstein, J. A. Sutton, & M. Borenstein (Eds.), *Publication bias in meta-analysis: Prevention, assessment, and adjustments* (pp. 241–260). New York: John Wiley.

Tukey, J. W. (1960). A survey of sampling from contaminated distributions. In I. Olkin, J. G. Ghurye, W. Hoeffding, W. G. Madoo, & H. Mann (Eds.), *Contributions to probability and statistics.* Stanford, CA: Stanford University Press.

Turner, R. M., Spiegelhalter, D. J., Smithe, G. C. S., & Thompson, S. G. (2009). Bias modeling in evidence synthesis. *Journal of the Royal Statistical Society, 172*(Pt. 1), 21–47.

United States v. City of Torrance, 163F.R.D. 590 (C.D. Cal., 1995).

Vacha-Haase, T., & Thompson, B. (2011). Score reliability: A retrospective look back at 12 years of reliability generalization studies. *Measurement and Evaluation in Counseling and Development, 44,* 159–168.

Valentine, J. C. (2009). Judging the quality of primary research. In H. Cooper, L. V. Hedges, & J. C. Valentine (Eds.), *Handbook of research synthesis and meta-analysis* (pp. 129–146). New York: Russell Sage.

Van Iddekinge, C. H., Roth, P. L., Putka, D. J., & Lanivich, S. E. (2011). Are you interested? A meta-analysis of relations between vocational interests and employee performance and turnover. *Journal of Applied Psychology, 96,* 1167–1194.

Vevea, J. L., & Citkowicz, M. (2008, July). *Inference and estimation using conditionally random models: A Monte Carlo.* Paper presented at the third annual conference of the Society for Research Synthesis Methods, Corfu, Greece.

Vevea, J. L., Clements, N. C., & Hedges, L. V. (1993). Assessing the effects of selection bias on validity data for the General Aptitude Test Battery. *Journal of Applied Psychology, 78,* 981–987.

Vevea, J. L., & Hedges, L. V. (1995). A general linear model for estimating effect size in the presence of publication bias. *Psychometrika, 60,* 419–435.

Vevea, J. L., & Woods, C. M. (2005). Publication bias in research synthesis: Sensitivity analysis using a priori weight functions. *Psychological Methods, 10,* 428–443.

Viechtbauer, W. (2010). Conducting meta-analysis in R with the metafor package. *Journal of Statistical Software, 36,* 1–42.

Viswesvaran, C., & Ones, D. S. (1995). Theory testing: Combining psychometric meta-analysis and structural equation modeling. *Personnel Psychology, 48,* 865–885.

Viswesvaran, C., Ones, D. S., & Schmidt, F. L. (1996). Comparative analysis of the reliability of job performance ratings. *Journal of Applied Psychology, 81,* 557–560.

Viswesvaran, C., Schmidt, F. L., & Ones, D. S. (2002). The moderating influence of job performance dimensions on convergence of supervisory and peer ratings of job performance. *Journal of Applied Psychology, 87,* 345–354.

Viswesvaran, C., Schmidt, F. L., & Ones, D. S. (2005). Is there a general factor in job performance ratings? A meta-analytic framework for disentangling substantive and error influences. *Journal of Applied Psychology, 90,* 108–131.

Vul, E., Harris, C., Winkielman, P., & Pashler, H. (2009). Puzzlingly high correlations in fMRI studies of emotion, personality, and social cognition. *Perspectives on Psychological Science, 4,* 274–290.

Wachter, K. W., & Straf, M. L. (Eds.). (1990). *The future of meta-analysis.* New York: Russell Sage.

Whetzel, D. L., & McDaniel, M. A. (1988). Reliability of validity generalization data bases. *Psychological Reports, 63,* 131–134.

White, H. D. (2009). Scientific communication and literature retrieval. In H. Cooper, L. V. Hedges, & J. C. Valentine (Eds.), *Handbook of research synthesis and meta-analysis* (pp. 51–74). New York: Russell Sage.

Whitener, E. M. (1990). Confusion of confidence intervals and credibility intervals in meta-analysis. *Journal of Applied Psychology, 75,* 315–321.

Whitman, D. S., Van Rooy, D. L., & Viswesvaran, C. (2010). Satisfaction, citizenship behaviors, and performance in work units: A meta-analysis of collective construct relations. *Personnel Psychology, 63,* 41–81.

Wilkinson, L., & The APA Task Force on Statistical Inference. (1999). Statistical methods in psychology journals: Guidelines and explanations. *American Psychologist, 54,* 594–604. (Reprint available through the APA home page: http://www.apa.org/journals/amp/amp548594.html)

Wilson, D. B. (2009). Systematic coding. In H. Cooper, L. V. Hedges, & J. C. Valentine (Eds.), *Handbook of research synthesis and meta-analysis* (pp. 159–176). New York: Russell Sage.

Wolins, L. (1962). Responsibility for raw data. *American Psychologist, 17,* 657–658.

Wortman, P. M. (1983). Evaluation research: A methodological perspective. *Annotated Review of Psychology, 34,* 223–260.

Wortman, P. M. (1994). Judging research quality. In H. Cooper & L. V. Hedges (Eds.), *Handbook of research synthesis* (pp. 97–110). New York: Russell Sage.

Wortman, P. M., & Bryant, F. B. (1985). School desegregation and black achievement: An integrative review. *Sociological Methods and Research, 13,* 289–324.

Yong, E. (2012, July 12). Uncertainty shrouds psychologist's resignation: Lawrence Sanna departed University of Michigan amid questions over his work from 'data detective' Uri Simonsohn. *Nature/News,* pp. 2–4.

Zimmer, C. (2012a, October 1). Misconduct widespread in retracted science papers, study finds. *New York Times.*

Zimmer, C. (2012b, April 16). A sharp rise in retractions prompts calls for reform. *New York Times.*

Zimmerman, R.D. (2008). Understanding the impact of personality traits on individuals' turnover decisions: a meta-analytic path model. *Personnel Psychology, 61*(2), 309–348.

Author Index

Subject Index

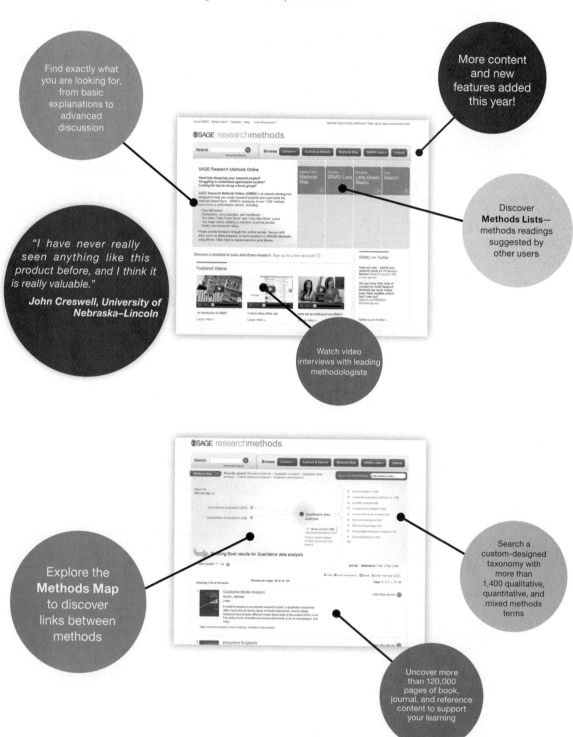

ⓈSAGE research**methods**

The essential online tool for researchers from the world's leading methods publisher

Find exactly what you are looking for, from basic explanations to advanced discussion

More content and new features added this year!

"*I have never really seen anything like this product before, and I think it is really valuable.*"
John Creswell, University of Nebraska–Lincoln

Discover **Methods Lists**— methods readings suggested by other users

Watch video interviews with leading methodologists

Explore the **Methods Map** to discover links between methods

Search a custom-designed taxonomy with more than 1,400 qualitative, quantitative, and mixed methods terms

Uncover more than 120,000 pages of book, journal, and reference content to support your learning

Find out more at
www.sageresearchmethods.com